PROPHET
OF
DEATH

Also by Pete Earley

Family of Spies

PROPHET
OF
DEATH

THE MORMON
BLOOD-ATONEMENT KILLINGS

PETE EARLEY

WILLIAM MORROW AND COMPANY, INC.
NEW YORK

It is the policy of William Morrow and Company, Inc., and its imprints and affiliates, recognizing the importance of preserving what has been written, to print the books we publish on acid-free paper, and we exert our best efforts to that end.

Library of Congress Cataloging-in-Publication Data

Earley, Pete.
    Prophet of death : the Mormon blood-atonement killings / by Pete
Earley
      p.   cm.
    ISBN 0-688-10584-X
    1. Murder—Ohio—Kirtland—Case studies. 2. Cults—Ohio—
Kirtland—Case studies. 3. Mormons—Ohio—Kirtland—Case studies.
4. Lundgren, Jeffrey. 5. Avery, Dennis. 6. Avery, Cheryl.
I. Title.
HV6533.O5E37   1991
364.1'523'09.771334—dc20   91-25557
                                                    CIP

Printed in the United States of America

2 3 4 5 6 7 8 9 10

BOOK DESIGN BY M & M DESIGN

*In Memory of Alice Lee Earley
and Belle Patterson*

CONTENTS

The easiest thing of all is to deceive one's self; for what a man wishes he generally believes to be true.
Demosthenes, Olynthiaca

PROLOGUE

J UST before dawn on a cool April day in 1989, a lone man climbed a hill a few miles outside Kirtland, Ohio, a village of six thousand, located directly east of Cleveland. As the morning sunshine began to filter through the branches of the apple and maple trees that towered over him, the man dropped to one knee and began to pray.

"What is thy will?" Jeffrey Don Lundgren asked out loud. "Give me a sign. Tell me what to do."

Lundgren stared upward into the morning light. He didn't move, didn't speak. For several minutes he waited, and then he nodded his head.

"I understand," he said, addressing a vision that only he could see. "Thy will be done."

It was misty on the night of April 17. There was no moon. The only light outside the farmhouse that Lundgren rented came from the neglected barn out back. It was a New England–style barn, painted red. It smelled inside of hay, rabbits, chickens, oil dripping from an abandoned car. An extension cord snaked across the floor leading into a little room at the rear of the barn. The cord had been tacked up the wall of the room and stretched out into the center of the ceiling. A single, naked bulb dangled down, illuminating a hole in the room's dirt floor. The hole had been carefully dug and was precisely six and a half feet wide and seven feet seven inches long. It was four feet deep. Underground water had seeped into it, turning the bottom into two-inch-deep mud. The water gave the brown clay walls of the pit a sheen that glistened in the overhead light.

Just before 7:30 P.M., two men could be heard talking as they walked from the Lundgren farmhouse toward the barn. One of them cried out as soon as they stepped through a door into the barn.

"Ouch! What are you doing? This isn't necessary. Goddamn it!"

The fifty-thousand-volt electric charge emitted by the hand-held stun gun was supposed to immobilize a man for several seconds, possibly even knock him unconscious. But when it was jabbed into Dennis Avery's side by the man walking beside him, it neither immobilized Avery nor knocked him down. It only stung and made him mad.

"Goddamn it!" Avery yelled when the gun was jabbed once again to his neck. "This isn't necessary!"

Four men had been hiding in the barn and when it became apparent that the stun gun wasn't working, they jumped out and grabbed Avery, forcing him down onto the floor. Avery didn't fight. He was in poor physical shape, with a watermelon belly. Even his friends regarded the forty-nine-year-old Avery as weak. His attackers, mostly men in their late twenties, were all in excellent physical condition. Within seconds, Avery's mouth, feet, and hands had been bound with gray two-inch-wide duct tape. His eyes, however, had not been covered. Jeffrey Lundgren had given specific instructions about Avery's eyes. "I want him to see who is administering justice," Lundgren had explained to his followers. "I want to look him eye to eye when I break his heart."

As he was carried from the front of the barn back into the lighted room, Avery's eyes flashed with anger. It was as if he were trying to communicate: "As soon as I'm loose, you are going to pay for doing this to me!" But the two men carrying him weren't afraid. They gently slid Avery down into the pit in the floor. He fell clumsily onto his side in the mud. Without speaking, the two men dashed toward the door.

The lone light bulb served as a spotlight over the pit, casting shadows into the room's corners. As Avery's eyes adjusted to the brightness, Jeffrey Lundgren stepped forward out of the darkness. He held a .45-caliber, stainless-steel, semiautomatic pistol in his right hand.

Avery managed to pull himself up so that he was sitting on his knees now. Lundgren raised his pistol. He would later recall with complete clarity void of all emotions what his thoughts were at that moment as he looked down on the bound man who had considered him to be his "very best friend." Lundgren was thinking about verses from the Old Testament book of Isaiah, chapter 30.

> Woe to the rebellious children, saith the Lord, that take counsel, but not of me. . . . You are a rebellious people, you lying children, you children who will not hear the law of the Lord. *

Lundgren's right hand tightened on the .45. "I had told Dennis Avery what would happen if he continued to sin, continued to deny the truth, continued to reject my teachings, but he continued to choose darkness rather than light and he had no one to blame but himself for leading himself and his family into this pit of damnation."

He slowly squeezed the trigger.

The first hollow-pointed slug smacked Avery's torso and knocked him sideways; the second round hit so quickly that it almost went in the same hole even though his body was recoiling. Avery's taped face hit the muddy bottom of the pit with a loud *smack*.

> Iniquity shall be to you as a branch ready to fall, and you shall break it—you shall not spare the wicked.

It was another verse from Isaiah.

"All right, everybody, come look at this, come see what death is," Jeffrey called to the others. The five men who had subdued Avery came into the room and gathered around the hole. Lundgren had warned them earlier that God would someday demand each of them to "slay the wicked." They would be forced to kill dozens, possibly more.

---

*All biblical passages are from The Holy Scriptures, inspired version as translated by Joseph Smith, Jr.

Lundgren examined the face of each man. He was still holding his .45 pistol. The men seemed terrified, yet mesmerized by the body in the pit. He knew that most of them had doubted him, doubted that he would actually go through with it.

"Okay, bring in the next one," he said. He had tasted death and was eager to continue.

Lundgren's plan was simple. Dennis Avery's wife, Cheryl, forty-two, would be the next to be put into the pit and executed. While Dennis was being murdered, Cheryl and her three daughters were sitting in the Lundgren farmhouse less than fifty yards away, visiting with the wives of the men in the barn. She would be lured from the farmhouse by one of Lundgren's accomplices, who would tell her that Dennis needed help in the barn sorting through some personal belongings stored there. Once inside the barn, she would be over-powered by Lundgren's followers and bound with duct tape. Her husband had no idea that he had been sentenced to death by Lundgren, nor would Cheryl. After Lundgren executed her, the Averys' daughters—Trina, fifteen, Rebecca, thirteen, and Karen, six—would be brought into the barn and put into the pit one at a time, the oldest first. Not only would their hands, feet, and mouths be bound, but their eyes would be covered with duct tape. The scriptures, Lundgren had explained, only required that the man of the family be allowed to see his executioner.

As Jeffrey waited for his followers to bring Cheryl into the barn, he glanced down into the pit. Blood was soaking into the back of Avery's plaid wool shirt. There was no sign of life. Killing him had been easy. The pistol in Jeffrey's hand felt good. Jeffrey decided that he had been smart to choose the .45 automatic. He had considered using a shotgun, but had rejected the idea because of the noise. Someone driving past the farm might have heard the blast and been curious. The cracking sound of a handgun was more crisp. He had considered using a .357 Magnum or a .9 millimeter, but was afraid that neither was powerful enough. Lundgren had read stories about police officers who had shot criminals three or more times with rounds from a .357 and still not killed them. There was no reason to prolong the Averys' pain. Of course, the .45 had certain disadvantages. Little Karen Avery only weighed thirty-six pounds and shooting her with the big handgun seemed a bit extreme. Only a few nights earlier, Lundgren had gone to the Averys' house for dinner and had bounced Karen on his knee. While she giggled at the excitement of being tossed up and down, he had wondered if he should use a smaller caliber pistol to kill her. But Lundgren had eventually settled on the .45 on the assumption that it would be better to use too much rather than too little firepower.

Lundgren could hear voices from outside the barn now. Cheryl Avery was being brought into the trap. Another scripture came to him: Revelation, chapter 6, the opening of the seven mystical seals that signal the second coming of Jesus Christ, Judgment Day, the beginning of the Millennium, the end of the world. He thought about verses 2 through 8, passages that describe the Four Horsemen of the Apocalypse.

> And when he had opened the second seal, I heard the second beast say, Come and see . . .

Cheryl was in the barn now. Lundgren could hear the sound of duct tape being ripped from its spool. It was only seconds before she would be brought to him. He stepped back into the shadows with his .45 automatic.

> . . . and there went out another horse that was red; and power was given to him that sat thereon to take peace from the earth, that they should kill one another . . .

PART ONE: CON MAN

If there arise among you a prophet, or a dreamer of dreams . . .

Deuteronomy 13:1

CHAPTER ONE

ALICE Elizabeth Keehler was eighteen when she met Jeffrey Don
Lundgren. She was a senior in high school. He was a freshman at
Central Missouri State University in Warrensburg, Missouri, about
forty miles southeast of Independence. Alice had caught a ride to
the campus with the youth minister from her church in Odessa, a
farming town north of the school. Usually her parents, Ralph and
Donna, didn't let Alice go out of town without a chaperon, but they
figured she was safe with the pastor, and Alice was intent on using
the college library. She was writing her senior English term paper
about the origins of the Book of Mormon and the public library in
Odessa had only a few books on the Mormon religion and its
founder, Joseph Smith, Jr. Alice was a member of the Reorganized
Church of Jesus Christ of Latter Day Saints, a branch of Mormonism, and she wanted to make certain that her paper was thoroughly
documented. Most of the "Gentiles" in her English class would scoff
at her beliefs. She considered Joseph Smith, Jr., a prophet, was convinced that God had spoken directly to him, and believed, as all
good Mormons did, that the Book of Mormon was as important as,
if not more important than, the Old and New Testaments in the
Bible. That was why Alice had to use the college library. If her paper

swayed just one of her classmates, then all the ridicule would be worth it. Alice loved her God and she was confident that He loved her.

On this particular Friday night in the spring of 1969, Alice finished at the library earlier than expected so she walked across campus to a former two-story house that had been converted by the RLDS Church into a student union. Alice immediately spotted an older girl from Odessa who offered to introduce her to the other students. The only boy Alice would later remember was Jeffrey. "He was dressed in a neatly pressed white short-sleeve shirt with tiny thin blue-and-yellow pinstripes," she gushed to her best friend later back in Odessa. "His shirt matched his blue corduroy slacks. He was also wearing brown penny loafers and *no* socks! Can you believe it. He wasn't wearing any socks!"

Although they had talked for only a few minutes, Alice was smitten. "Jeffrey was like no other man I had ever met," she said. Neither of them made any effort to keep in touch after that chance meeting. Alice returned home, graduated, and spent a week at a church-run summer camp. But she didn't forget Jeffrey. One of the other girls there had just finished her freshman year at CMSU and she had gone out on a date with Jeffrey. Alice quizzed her about him. "He tried to get me drunk and take advantage of me," the girl confided. Alice was horrified. She couldn't believe that the friendly boy she had met would be so pushy.

During evening vespers at the camp, Alice decided to ask God whom she would eventually marry. Alice had been taught that a woman's role was to serve her husband and raise a family. What would her husband be like? she asked, as she prayed silently with the other campers perched on a split-log bench around a bonfire. After several minutes of silence, one of the adult counselors stood up and began to prophesy. One by one, the counselor called out each camper's name. He was being moved "by the spirit" to give them a message from God. This was a common practice in the RLDS Church and Alice believed that whatever the counselor said was from the Lord.

"Unto my sister Alice," the man proclaimed, "thus saith the spirit. I have seen your tears and I have heard your prayers and I will never leave you comfortless. I will direct your path and I will hold your life in the palm of my hand for there I have engraven you."

While others might have thought the prophecy obscure, Alice

understood. She felt God was telling her not to worry about her future husband. "God was going to direct me to him!"

On the final day of camp, the group held a Sunday morning testimonial service. Because it was raining, they met in the dining hall and one of the RLDS's most revered patriarchs spoke. "We were told that the fellowship we had enjoyed that week had been acceptable in God's sight and that it was pleasing unto Him," Alice said. "The patriarch said that our generation was the one that would see the establishment of God's kingdom here on earth and that many of us would be instruments in His hands in the bringing forth of His kingdom in these latter days."

And then the speaker had looked directly at Alice, picking her out of the group for no apparent reason. He called her by name and said that God had given him a message for her.

"And unto you, my daughter Alice," he said, "thus saith the Lord. You shall have the answer to your prayers. You shall marry a companion whom I have prepared to bring forth my kingdom and he shall be great in the eyes of these people and shall do much good unto the children of men, for I have prepared him to bring forth a marvelous work and wonder."

Alice hadn't told anyone about her prayers. Yet the patriarch had known exactly what she had asked God. She began to cry. "God had chosen me," she said, "lowly me, to help bring about His kingdom on earth."

A few weeks after summer camp ended, Alice was asleep in her bedroom at night when she felt something pressing down on her. She was being crushed by what she would later describe as "an evil presence." Alice couldn't raise her arms, lift her legs, or roll off the bed. She was paralyzed, and as she lay there terrified, the weight of the evil presence began to increase until she felt as if she were about to be crushed by Satan himself. In a panic, Alice began to pray and when she called out Christ's name, the evil spirit was jerked off her as if a hand had reached down and grabbed Satan by the neck and pulled him away.

No one doubted Alice when she described her experience the next Sunday at the RLDS church in Odessa. Many in the congregation had shared similar supernatural experiences during testimonials at church. If anything, Alice's story was a comforting confirmation that Jesus Christ protected those who called for His help. After the church service, Alice was congratulated by members for giving such an inspirational and moving testimonial. She was clearly someone special and destined to do great things in the church.

When Alice enrolled at Central Missouri State University that fall as a freshman, one of the first boys she bumped into was Jeffrey. He was playing cards with his best friend, Keith Johnson, at the RLDS student union. Alice knew Keith from various church events and when he saw her, Keith waved her over and began introducing her to everyone.

"We've already met," Alice beamed when Jeffrey was introduced.

Years later, after Jeffrey had formed his cult in Kirtland, he would often reminisce about the first time he met Alice. "From the instant that I first saw her," he would say, "I *knew* she was my wife." It was as if he had always known her, as if they had been together before, he would say, as if they had always been together since the beginning of time. It was an enchanting story. It was also a lie.

When Alice looked up at Jeffrey on that fall day in 1969, she realized that he didn't remember anything about their first meeting a few months earlier.

"We met last spring," she said. "You weren't wearing any socks."

Jeffrey glanced down. He wasn't wearing any now either. They laughed. Keith invited Alice to play cards. He and Jeffrey let her win every hand. Afterward, they asked Alice if she wanted to go with them to a nearby ice cream parlor.

En route, Keith said: "Jeffrey wants to ask you out but he's too shy."

Jeffrey turned bright red. Alice laughed. Keith explained that he was having a picnic at his parents' farm that weekend. He already had a date, but Jeffrey didn't.

"Would you like to go?" Jeffrey finally asked.

"How many other couples are going?" she replied, recalling what she had heard during the summer about Jeffrey's bold conduct on dates.

"Eight or nine," Keith volunteered.

"Okay," Alice replied. "I'll go if there's a group."

As it turned out, all of the other couples except for Keith and his date dropped out. But Alice went anyway and she had a wonderful time with Jeffrey. At dusk, Keith and Jeffrey built a fire in a dry creek bed and spread out blankets to sit on. After a few moments, Keith and his date went for a walk. Jeffrey moved closer to Alice.

Nervous, she began talking fast. What tumbled out was a jumbled version of her life story. When she finished, Alice pelted Jeffrey with questions about his past. He was more guarded, but Alice was so persistent that he ended up telling her much more than he intended. He liked her.

As the fire crackled, Alice and Jeffrey discovered that they had come from much different backgrounds. Alice's family was poor. Jeffrey's was well off. Alice had low self-esteem. Jeffrey was arrogant. Yet psychologists would later testify that they had one common bond. They were desperately searching for someone who would love them.

Born in Independence on January 21, 1951, Alice was the oldest of four children. Her parents had both moved to Independence because of the RLDS Church's belief that it is where Jesus Christ will return and build Zion, a perfect city of peace and beauty. Ralph Keehler had met Donna at an RLDS church service shortly after World War II. They married in 1947 and he went to work as a welder. She stayed at home and raised four children.

For the first thirteen years of her life, what Alice wanted she generally got. New dresses, shoes, spending money—it wasn't that Ralph earned a huge salary. He didn't. But both parents put their children's desires first. If there wasn't enough money, Ralph and Donna would scrimp to get it. "Alice was very, very, very spoiled as a youngster," Donna recalled later. "All my kids were. I wanted them that way really. You see, I wanted them to have all the things that I never had, so if they wanted something, we generally did whatever we could to get it for them." Donna had been the youngest of eight children. Ralph was number eight in a line of nine.

One day in 1964, Ralph felt a pain in his right leg. By nighttime, he had lost all feeling in it. The next day, doctors diagnosed him as having multiple sclerosis. It was difficult for him to walk. He was put on disability. Donna, who had never finished high school, was forced to go to work. She was hired as a cook at an all-night café and worked from seven P.M. until seven A.M., leaving Alice to run the home. "It was very difficult for Alice to understand," her mother said. "When she wanted a new dress, I'd tell her, 'I'm sorry, honey, but we can't do that anymore. We can't afford it.' And that made her angry. I think she felt cheated."

Alice's role as a surrogate parent often put her at odds with her sisters, Susan and Terri, ages eleven and seven, and brother, Charles, age two. She was the nag who demanded that her sisters pick up their clothes, make their beds, do their homework. Susan and Terri were best friends and rough-and-tough tomboys. Alice was, in the words of her younger siblings, picky and prissy. Her escape from the family was the church. "I think the thing that I loved most about church was that they truly welcomed me there," she later told a psychologist. "I was loved and accepted and I didn't always feel loved and accepted at home. I felt alone and insecure."

Alice had officially become a "latter day saint" at age five in Independence when she was baptized by Carlos Kroesen who, in the close-knit world of the Mormon church, happened to be Jeffrey Lundgren's uncle. But it was as a teenager that Alice really became engulfed in religion. She rarely missed a service, participated in every youth activity, and developed a chilling certainty to her beliefs. While others might doubt Joseph Smith, Jr.'s unconventional claims and teachings, Alice didn't.

"Alice always wanted to be the center of attention," her sister Susan Keehler Yates said later. "She loved being in the spotlight, and at church, she was on center stage." Alice was particularly revered after she told the congregation about her experiences at summer camp and her bedroom bout with the devil. But at home, her sisters and brother viewed Alice's claims with skepticism. "Alice lives in her own little fantasy world and always has," brother Charles Keehler said later. "When we were growing up, she had her own room and she would go in there and fantasize about this and that." Alice was always looking for some knight in shining armor to come carry her away, he said. Alice's sister Susan agreed. "I'm not certain Alice knows sometimes the difference between the truth and lies. Alice has always been able to convince herself that whatever she wants to believe is the truth and nothing else matters. She was that way about religion and that way about her life."

Jeffrey had grown up in the RLDS Church just like Alice, but no one had ever prophesied over him and he had always questioned claims about visions and prophecy. "I would sit there on Sundays and people would be in tears talking about the Lord's presence and His love and all these strange events that they claimed had happened to them," Jeffrey recalled, "and I would think that something was wrong with me because I felt absolutely nothing and nothing had happened to me like what they were describing. I was stone cold to all this emotional drivel."

Jeffrey went to church because it got him out of the house.

The older of two sons born to Donald and Lois Lundgren, Jeffrey came from a well-pedigreed RLDS family. Lois's parents, Alva and Maude Gadberry, had helped found two RLDS congregations in Independence. Alva was a pastor at both. Maude ran the Sunday-school programs. On the Lundgren side, it was Donald's mother, Mabel, who was the religious stalwart. She had converted from the Lutheran faith as a young mother and had seen to it that her children rarely missed a service. Mabel later taught Sunday school for thirty years at the Slover Park RLDS congregation in Independence, one of the more prestigious in town. Everyone there called her "Grandma Lundy." Don and Lois had met at church. They married in 1948. Don rose to the rank of elder, a high-ranking post in an RLDS congregation. On most Sundays, he and Lois could be found sitting and holding hands in the sanctuary.

While Don and Lois were well known at Slover Park, they were not always well liked. Don was considered too opinionated by some, while Lois was viewed as being flashy. "In every church you have your show people who see if they can dress better than anyone else," a church member later explained. "You know the type—if someone shows up in a fur coat one week, they have to have one the next week. That was Lois Lundgren. Appearances were everything to her."

Don had spent his early years in rural South Dakota, where he had learned to hunt and fish, and, according to his younger sister, Mary Bennett, had earned a reputation for being a "terror" and "bully." By the time he had grown into adulthood, Don was no longer a hellion, but he was still seen as "a tough guy," his brother-in-law George Gadberry said later. Don was a man's man who spoke his mind, stood his ground, and was prepared to back up what he believed. There were two things, he often told other church members, about which he was fanatical. Don had served in the navy and was an unabashed flag-waving patriot. He also detested slackers. No one had ever given him anything, he was fond of saying. He had earned his own way, had never welshed on a debt, and couldn't abide those who did.

Unlike the Keehlers, Don and Lois were well off financially. Don had started as a construction worker but had been put in charge of a work crew that installed microwave towers for the telephone company. He was a handsome man, well built, self-assured, the leathery sort that cigarette companies liked to feature in advertisements. By the early 1960s, Don was earning $100 per day when the average salary in the nation was $100 per week. When George

Gadberry got into financial trouble operating a formal-wear rental shop in Independence, it was Donald who put up the $5,000 in cash to keep the store open. Eventually, he bought out his brother-in-law, put Jeffrey to work there after school and on weekends, and soon had it operating in the black. No one was surprised when Don sold it for a tidy profit.

Jeffrey would later joke that the reason his father had to earn a good income was because of his mother's unabashed spending. Lois liked to collect things, and her home was filled with so many knick-knacks that it often reminded visitors of a museum. During the first years of their marriage, Lois bought old furniture in secondhand shops and refinished it with painstaking care. Later, when she could afford it, Lois searched area antique stores and brought home their finest pieces. Each room of the house looked as if it had been arranged to be photographed for display in a magazine. As children, Jeffrey and his brother, Corry, who was nearly six years younger, were permitted to sit on the living room sofa only when guests visited. At all other times, they sat on a rug dropped in front of the television.

As a young woman, Lois had chestnut hair, ivory skin, and a figure that other girls envied. Even when she was a grandmother, she bleached her hair blond, dressed immaculately, and had a youthful sparkle.

Jeffrey would later insist, however, that his mother was cold toward him. "My parents were madly in love with each other, so much so that I don't think they had any love left over for me and my brother. I always had to fight for affection and my parents' love was always conditional," he charged. "It was always used as a reward and taken away as punishment when I was inadequate. I loved playing sports, but there was also a lot of pressure. I was always onstage. When the game ended, my parents would want to know how well had I done? How many hits did I get? Had I embarrassed the family? They were completely success orientated and worried constantly about how the Lundgrens looked in the community."

When Jeffrey played his first basketball game in sixth grade, he scored seven of the team's eleven points. After the game, his mother harangued him because of the "plopping" noise that his feet had made when he ran up and down the wooden floor. "She was so embarrassed that she made me practice running on my toes in the kitchen while she watched so I'd learn how to run quietly."

Jeffrey had only one close friend when he was young. Sarah

Stotts lived just down the street from the Lundgrens. They first met as toddlers in the church nursery at Slover Park. By the time they were in high school, they had become close friends. "We would talk on the phone a couple hours each day after school about what was happening," Sarah remembered. "It wasn't a boyfriend-girlfriend relationship. He just happened to be a boy and I happened to be a girl. But for me, talking to Jeffrey was just like talking to one of my girlfriends. He seemed to really understand me and he listened."

Both felt awkward around others. "Jeff wasn't popular and neither was I. We were very quiet, but we both wanted to be part of the group at church so we'd encourage each other. I'd say, 'Okay, I'll play volleyball if you'll play it,' and he'd say, 'I'll try this if you will try this.'"

Sarah didn't have a happy homelife and she didn't think he did either. "Jeff never felt that he was good enough for his father. He didn't think he could please him."

Jeffrey would later reiterate that same feeling of inadequacy to a psychologist. "No matter what I did, I never felt I was man enough for him. I always wanted an 'I love you' but what I got was male-on-male competition. We would play burnout. I'd throw a hardball as hard as I could for him to catch and he'd throw it back to me. I used to endure the pain when I was seven or eight just because I wanted to be with him. I can still remember one of the best moments in my life was when I was a freshman in high school and I had become strong enough to hurt him when I threw the ball back."

At William Chrisman High School in Independence, Jeffrey excelled as shortstop on the baseball team. He lifted weights every day, and by his senior year, he could throw a pitch close to one hundred miles per hour. But other students considered him a geek. "Here was this guy who wanted to be liked and was shy and afraid to participate, yet when he opened his mouth, he was a know-it-all," recalled a classmate. "You felt sorry for him until you started talking to him and then you realized that he was arrogant. No one really liked him."

Jeffrey didn't have a date to the senior prom so he asked Sarah to go with him. When she suggested that he invite someone he was interested in romantically, Jeffrey appeared hurt. "I don't like anyone but you," he told her.

Jeffrey's graduation picture in the 1968 high school yearbook stuck out. Others boys in the class were shown wearing long hair, a few brandished peace symbols, most were smiling, clearly eager to get on with their lives. And then there was Jeffrey, his hair cut in a 1950s buzz, dressed in a crisp white shirt, narrow tie, and jacket, completely out of step with his classmates. But it was the expression on his face that caught the eye. His uncle George Gadberry would later remember how one day when he was cleaning out a desk drawer, he had come across several school pictures of Jeffrey that had been taken as the boy moved up through the various grades. "Jeff was never smiling. He never seemed very happy as a boy." The photographs chronicled a boy who seemed to be angry and bitter inside.

During their picnic at Keith Johnson's farm, Jeffrey told Alice how he had played shortstop in high school and briefly mentioned his parents. But the only comment that she would later recall as odd was something Jeffrey said jokingly, or at least it sounded as if he were kidding. "My mother is not going to like your name," he told Alice. "She'll think it is much too plain." Alice didn't respond. She was having too good a time. Despite what she had heard about him, Jeffrey was a perfect gentleman. He didn't even try to kiss her. After Keith and his date returned, the four of them drove back to campus and Jeffrey escorted Alice to the front stoop of the women's dormitory. He politely asked if he could kiss her good night. Alice nodded.

A few minutes later, Alice was upstairs in her room when she heard the telephone ring in the hall outside her door. There was only one telephone on the entire floor and Alice's room was the closest to it. She hurried out to answer it, figuring she would page whoever it was for. It was Jeffrey. He wanted to thank her for spending the afternoon with him and he wanted to know what time she was getting up in the morning.

"Why?" she asked, giggling.

"Because I want to be waiting outside to carry your books," he replied.

"Oh, Jeffrey, you don't have to do that," she said.

"I plan to walk you to every one of your classes tomorrow," he said firmly.

They chatted for a few minutes and then Alice went to bed. The next morning when Alice stepped outside the dormitory, Jeffrey was waiting.

At the time, she thought it was simply wonderful.

CHAPTER TWO

T HE Mormon religion that Jeffrey and Alice learned as children was peculiarly American and unlike any other sect. Its founder, Joseph Smith, Jr., claimed he had a vision in 1820 at the age of fifteen while living with his parents on a farm near Palmyra, New York, about thirty miles east of Rochester. At the time, western New York was on the verge of what later became known as the Second Great Awakening—a religious revival marked by impassioned conversions and sensational Elmer Gantry-style tent meetings. So many Methodist circuit riders, itinerant Baptist preachers, and self-proclaimed evangelists swarmed into western New York State that it was soon nicknamed the "burned over" district because of the hellfire and brimstone preached there. Amid this fervor, young Joseph was trying to decide, as he wrote later, "Who of all these parties are right? Or, are they all wrong together?"

Smith's questions were answered one day while he was praying alone in the woods. A "pillar of light" fell down around him, he later said, and God and Jesus Christ appeared. It was Christ who told him that the existing churches "were all wrong" and "their creeds were an abomination in his sight." Christ ordered Smith not to join any denomination but to continue to pray for guidance.

Three years later, while Smith was saying his nightly prayers in his bedroom, an angel named Moroni appeared. The angel said that fourteen hundred years earlier, when he was still a mortal man, he had hidden a book made of golden plates in a stone box about three miles from the Smith farm. The plates contained the history of a band of ancient Hebrews who had traveled from Jerusalem to the New World before the birth of Christ. These Hebrews had settled in the Americas and were the forefathers of the Indians. Their history was nothing less than a volume of holy scriptures that God now wanted brought forth so that "the fullness of the everlasting Gospel" could be known.

Smith found the plates exactly where the angel had told him to look, but Moroni wouldn't let him take them from their hiding place. During the next three years, Moroni steadfastly refused to surrender the plates, but on September 22, 1827, the angel relented. Along with the plates, Smith was given two magical stones called the Urim and Thummim that were needed to translate the ancient writings into English.

Smith wanted to translate the plates immediately, but he was broke, and by this time he had a family to support. He contacted a wealthy farmer, Martin Harris, and asked him for help. Harris was intrigued by Smith's story about Moroni, but when the farmer mentioned it to his wife, she suspected a scam and demanded proof that the plates were genuine. Harris asked Smith to show him the plates. Smith politely refused. Moroni had instructed him not to show them to anyone, he explained, but he gave Harris a sheet of paper that contained strange markings which Smith said he had copied directly from the golden plates. Harris gave Smith fifty dollars and rushed the paper to Charles Anthon, a Columbia College classics scholar familiar with ancient writing. Anthon studied the markings and pronounced them fake. A dejected Harris returned home, where Smith was waiting with a ready explanation. Engraving the golden plates had been such a tedious process that the ancient Hebrew prophet and historian who had compiled the records had developed his own form of shorthand to save time and space. Smith identified the author as Mormon, who happened to be Moroni's father. He said that Mormon had transcribed the golden plates in "Reformed Egyptian," a dialect that only Smith could read.

Harris agreed to help bankroll Smith's venture and also offered to aid in translating the plates. Exactly how this was done is unclear. One historical account says that Smith placed the Urim and Thummim into his hat, buried his face in the hat, and then, covered with a blanket, dictated to a scribe what he saw. Other stories say that Smith wore the Urim and Thummim like eyeglasses, held the plates in his lap and read them aloud to Harris from behind a screen. Regardless, by 1830 the translation was finished. Smith called it the Book of Mormon, and on March 26 a local Palmyra printer, Egbert Grandin, published five thousand copies of it. The $3,000 printing bill was paid by Harris, who had become such an ardent supporter of Smith that he mortgaged his farm to raise the necessary cash. While Smith's "Gold Bible" caused an immediate stir, it didn't sell well and Harris lost his farm.

From the moment it was published, the Book of Mormon came under attack. Scholars pointed out that it described animals and plants in the New World that didn't exist in North and Central America until after Spanish and English explorers arrived. Prophets, who lived decades before Jesus Christ was born, were quoted talking about Christ's death on the cross as if it had already happened. The fact that Smith couldn't produce the golden plates didn't help his credibility. The angel Moroni had reappeared, Smith said, and had taken them back.

Smith's local reputation also raised suspicions. Four years earlier, he had been convicted in Chenango County, New York, of accepting money from a farmer in return for finding buried treasure with a "peepstone," a native crystal much like those used by fortune-tellers. The court had declared Smith "disorderly and an imposter."

Not everyone, however, was skeptical. Written much like the Bible, the Book of Mormon was filled with inspirational stories about religious heroes. It contained detailed descriptions of military battles and a slew of commandments that seemed to clarify statements by Jesus and others in the Bible. Most of all, it promised those who believed in it a chance to reign over the earth with Jesus Christ.

Smith taught that Christ was on the verge of returning to earth where he would judge every man, woman, and child. Christ would then rule the earth with a selected few for a period of one thousand years known as the Millennium. Those who joined Smith's church during these "last days" on earth were "the saints of the latter days," he said, and they would be the ones whom Christ would choose to rule with Him over everyone else.

On April 6, 1830, Smith and six other men officially incorporated a new religion which they called the Church of Christ. At the time, Smith was only twenty-four years old. He boldly declared that his new church was the "only true church" in the world. A short time later, Smith renamed his church to emphasize his teachings about the "latter days." He called it the *Church of Jesus Christ of Latter-Day Saints*. Anyone who didn't accept the Book of Mormon was a Gentile and was automatically doomed.

Besides offering his followers a new testament, Smith also taught that God played an active role in the lives of his "saints." Smith's God hadn't changed much from the one described in the Old Testament. He still sent prophets to direct his people through revelations and His spirit. Smith claimed that God had chosen him to be His church's first "prophet, seer, and revelator."

Despite such grandiose claims, Smith's church got off to a sluggish start in New York. Few joined. But shortly after the Book of Mormon was published, one of Smith's converts delivered a copy to Sidney Rigdon, one of the most influential preachers of the time. Rigdon would eventually fall from favor in Mormon circles and be relegated to a footnote in the church's archives, but he was far more charismatic than Smith. The bushy-haired, bearded, barrel-chested Rigdon could keep a congregation entranced for hours with his oratory. Even hardened men had been known to burst into tears at his services. Rigdon had already been a minister in two other denominations when he began reading Smith's new testament. Overnight, Rigdon was converted. Like Smith, Rigdon believed that the Millennium was imminent. He also believed that only a prophet who had been selected by God could have brought forth the Book of Mormon.

Rigdon lived in Kirtland, Ohio, and during his first thirty days as a Mormon convert, he baptized one hundred twenty-seven people into the new religion. Back in New York, Smith had attracted a following of less than half that number. In December 1830, Rigdon rode his horse to New York to meet the self-proclaimed prophet and tell him of the budding Mormon movement in Kirtland. Smith was so thrilled by Rigdon's success that he invited him to spend the night in his home. The next morning, Smith said that God had spoken to him during the night. Just as John the Baptist had prepared the way for Christ, God wanted Rigdon to prepare the way for Smith. He announced that he and his family were moving to Kirtland and he commanded all faithful Mormons to follow him there.

At the time, Kirtland boasted a population of 1,020, mostly former New Englanders. It had a rooming house, two churches, and a mill. The richest citizen was Newel K. Whitney, owner of the·

general store and one of Rigdon's recent Mormon converts. Smith immediately moved into the Whitneys' home and lived there until his followers built his family their own house. Once Smith was settled, he said that God had commanded him to rewrite the Holy Bible. Over time, it had been filled with errors because of sloppy translators and wicked church leaders, he explained. God had told him to publish an "inspired" version for the saints to use.

During the coming months, Rigdon and Smith recruited more and more converts, eventually developing a following of five hundred in the Kirtland area. Smith also began having almost daily revelations. Some dealt with minor events. When Smith and Rigdon tipped over in a canoe and almost drowned in a river, God revealed that He no longer wanted His prophet and Rigdon to travel on water, unless it was on a man-made canal. Other revelations contained sweeping theological announcements. One of the most important dealt with Zion. Smith said that God wanted the Mormons to "gather" together and establish Zion, a perfect community of love and trust where they would wait for Christ's return. Even though Kirtland had become the church's stronghold, the prophet said that God had designated Independence, Missouri, as the site of His "new Jerusalem." That was where Christ would eventually return.

On August 3, 1831, Smith, Rigdon, and other Mormon leaders held a dedication service in Independence at the "center spot" where Zion was to be built. Most of the land in Independence, however, was owned by Gentiles who didn't want anything to do with Smith or his religion. When Mormons began moving to Missouri, the Gentiles there turned hostile. One night, a mob tarred and feathered the Mormon bishop and forced other saints to flee at gunpoint. Faced with growing hatred in Missouri, Smith decided that the saints could remain in Kirtland a short while longer. He announced that God wanted His saints to build a temple in Kirtland as a demonstration of their love and faith.

Construction of the "House of the Lord" began June 5, 1833, and it was Rigdon who became the driving force behind it. Church historians would later write that Rigdon had "wet the walls with his tears" by coming to the construction site daily and offering emotional prayers there. Although the fledgling church had little money, the Mormons managed to construct what then was the tallest temple in Ohio. As a show of devotion, women donated their finest china to the church. It was crushed and mixed with the exterior plaster so that the walls would sparkle when hit by sunlight. At the dedication in 1836, Rigdon gave a two-hour sermon. Smith spoke too, blessing the building. Some of the saints at the service later claimed that an angel had appeared standing next to Smith when he spoke. One week later, Smith announced that while he was praying in the temple, Christ appeared, followed by Moses and Elijah.

Although the Mormons were prospering in Kirtland, they still were having trouble in Independence. On February 24, 1834, a mob attacked Mormon settlers. When word reached Kirtland, Smith made an angry declaration. God, he said, had promised to one day send a prophet to lead the saints against their enemies and redeem Zion.

"I will raise up unto my people a man, who shall lead them like as Moses led the children of Israel. . . ." Smith quoted God as saying.

There are conflicting stories about what happened next in Kirtland. The official church version says that the cost of constructing the temple put the Mormons heavily in debt. The completion of the temple also frightened Gentiles who feared the Mormons were becoming too strong. Anti-Mormons called for a boycott of the saints' stores and Gentile bankers stopped making loans to Mormon families. Smith responded by opening his own bank for Mormons, called the Kirtland Safety Society Bank. The saints were told that God expected them to exchange gold and silver for paper notes printed by the bank. Unfortunately, the Mormon bank went belly up during a national bank panic in 1837 and Smith and Rigdon were forced to leave Kirtland when angry Gentiles threatened legal action.

A less flattering account is told in the records at the Lake County deeds office and in old county-court documents. According to these records, Smith began buying large tracts of land, apparently in the hope that a railroad would run a line over his property and make him rich. When Smith ran out of places to borrow money, he opened the Mormon bank and used its deposits as if they were his own. To ease any qualms that Mormons might have about exchanging gold and silver for bank notes, Smith put several strongboxes filled with silver coins on display in the bank lobby. It wasn't until later, court records reveal, that Mormon depositors learned the strongboxes had been filled with sand and only the top layer had been made up of shiny fifty-cent pieces. When the bank went bust, Smith and Rigdon fled town at night to avoid furious creditors.

Whatever version is true, Smith moved his church first to a

Missouri settlement that he called Far West, located just north of Independence, and then later to Hancock County, Illinois, where he established his own town, which he named Nauvoo. Once Smith and Rigdon left Ohio, Rigdon's standing began to slip. When Rigdon's daughter accused Smith of locking her in a room and demanding that she have sex with him because God had ordered it, Rigdon's relationship with Smith was ruptured even more.

Seven years after the two men fled Kirtland, Joseph Smith, Jr., and his brother, Hyrum, were murdered by a mob in Carthage, Illinois. Their deaths left the Mormon Church without a leader. Rigdon argued that he should be in charge, but he no longer had enough clout to declare himself the new prophet. He was excommunicated and returned to his native Pennsylvania, where he died penniless.

The saint who stepped into Smith's shoes was Brigham Young, a charismatic and determined man who led the biggest bloc of Mormons on a difficult trek westward to Salt Lake City, Utah. Not everyone followed Young, however. A small faction of saints stayed behind in Independence, where they chose Smith's eldest son, Joseph Smith III, to head their church. Because he was only eleven at the time, his mother, Emma, took control.

Over time, the Mormons in Utah grew into a worldwide church of seven million members with tremendous wealth, power, and prestige. The saints who stayed behind in Independence renamed themselves the *Reorganized* Church of Jesus Christ of Latter Day Saints [RLDS]. Unlike their better-known Utah counterparts, the RLDS never attracted more than 250,000 members and its members were so poor that until recently they couldn't afford to build a temple of their own in Independence.

Besides wealth and membership, the two Mormon sects differed in their religious teachings. One point of contention was Smith's 1834 declaration that God would someday raise up a leader like Moses who would redeem Zion. Many Utah saints felt that Brigham Young had fulfilled that prophecy. Young, they argued, had successfully led the saints "out of bondage" in Missouri into the "new promised land" of Utah where he had "redeemed Zion." But such talk was heresy to the saints in Missouri. They considered Young a false prophet. Zion was supposed to be built in Independence—not Salt Lake City—they argued.

For many in the RLDS, the 1834 promise had never been fulfilled. They were still waiting for God to send them a prophet. Alice was among those RLDS members eagerly awaiting this new Moses,

and in the fall of 1969, she was more confident than ever that
Smith's 1834 revelation was about to come true. After all, one of
the church's patriarchs had told her and the others during summer
camp that their generation would establish Zion and that could mean
only one thing. God was planning to raise up a prophet in her life-
time. The patriarch had also revealed that Alice's husband was going
to help prepare the way for Christ's return. She had carefully memorized the patriarch's words:

> "You shall marry a companion whom I have prepared to
> bring forth my kingdom and he shall be great in the eyes of these
> people and shall do much good unto the children of men, for I
> have prepared him to bring forth a marvelous work and wonder."

After her first date with Jeffrey, Alice began to wonder: Could
he be the man whom God had chosen to be her husband? Was Jeffrey the one who would help bring forth God's kingdom?

The very thought made her tingle.

CHAPTER THREE

A long-stemmed rose arrived every day during the first week. Jeffrey was waiting outside the women's dormitory each morning to carry Alice's books. He was there after every class. If Alice needed to go to the library, the school cafeteria, the gymnasium, Jeffrey would escort her. Everything that he did revolved around Alice. Even after Alice had gone into the dormitory at night, he telephoned.

"What are you going to wear tomorrow?" he'd ask.

"I don't know yet," Alice would reply. "Haven't decided."

"I think you should wear that blue outfit," he'd volunteer. "You look beautiful in it."

"Okay," she'd say.

They'd talk for a while and then he'd tell her, "Say, you'd better get to sleep. Go right to bed now."

Alice would hang up the telephone, get her blue outfit ready to wear, and go to bed. The next morning, he would be waiting outside and would compliment her.

There was only one time that he upset her. He had suggested that she wear a white blouse and black skirt the next morning, but she forgot and chose something else. He didn't speak to her when they walked together to her first class.

"What's wrong?" she asked later.

"I'm just disappointed," he said. "I asked you to wear the blouse and skirt. I thought you agreed."

Once Alice was sitting in her freshman chemistry class when she felt as if someone were staring at her. She glanced over at the door and spotted Jeffrey watching her through a tiny window. Ten minutes later, she looked over again and he was still there, just staring at her.

Alice loved the attention.

"He's fascinating. He's handsome. He's athletic," she confided to a schoolmate. "He is everything that I have ever thought the perfect man should be and he is crazy about me."

One week after their first date, Jeffrey and Alice went on a hayride sponsored by the RLDS-run student union. During the ride, Alice looked at Jeffrey and he began to say something, but stopped.

"What'ya gonna do," she asked teasingly, "ask me to marry ya?"

He continued to stare at her.

"Yes," he replied solemnly. "I want you to be my wife."

Alice smirked and then she realized that he was serious.

"If you promise to fall in love with me, I will," she replied solemnly.

"I already am in love with you, Alice," he said.

In 1969, women could get married at age eighteen without parental consent in Missouri but men had to be twenty-one. Jeffrey was nineteen and he knew his parents would not approve. They wanted him to finish college. He was worried that Don and Lois were not going to like Alice. She was poor and had no status within the church.

"We'll have to figure out some way to get my parents' permission," he told her.

Alice would later tell psychologists that as soon as she and Jeff agreed that they were going to get married, he began to pressure her for sex. Despite her religious training, she didn't resist. Did it really matter? After all, they planned to get married. "It was as if I had opened the floodgates," Alice later confided to a friend. "All Jeff ever wanted to do was have sex, sex, sex. It was so contrary to my upbringing that I felt very ashamed. I felt dirty. But to him it was a sign that I loved him. 'If you love me, you'll do this,' he said. And I wanted him to love me."

When the Thanksgiving school break arrived, Jeffrey asked Alice to come to Independence to meet his family. Alice was terrified. Jeffrey's descriptions of Don and Lois didn't put her at ease.

"Don't be surprised if my father makes faces at you during the meal," Jeffrey said as they pulled into the driveway at his parents' home on Thanksgiving Day.

"What?" Alice replied.

"He's been practicing making faces at you so he can do it during the meal."

She thought he was joking.

"Alice, they don't think you are good enough for me," he said coldly. "They think you want to marry me because of their money."

Alice was about to cry. All during the meal, she stared at her plate. She was afraid to look at Don because she thought he might make a face at her. She was afraid to compliment Lois on her decorating skills because she might think all Alice cared about was possessions. Don and Lois were both gracious during the meal. They were friendly to her. But she was too scared to speak. Afterward, she and Jeffrey went to see the movie *Romeo and Juliet.* Alice spent most of the time in the ladies' room throwing up.

Jeffrey got called into the Dean of Students' office when college resumed. He had spent so much time escorting Alice around campus that he had missed most of his own classes. If he didn't stop cutting class, he would be put on academic suspension.

"You'd better tell Jeffrey to study for the final," a friend told Alice. "You know he's never even been to class."

Alice was shocked. She'd never asked him about his grades. When she confronted him the next day, Jeffrey lied.

"I'm going to class," he said. "It's just that no one sees me." He told Alice that after he walked her to her classes, he would dash across campus and slip into a seat in the back of his class. He'd leave a few minutes early so he could meet Alice. "The reason no one sees me is because I slip in and out so quietly.

"Besides," Jeffrey added, "I'm majoring in Alice. It doesn't matter if I go to class."

Jeffrey's grades weren't the only ones that had dropped. Alice's began slipping. There just wasn't enough time during the day for her to study. Jeffrey loved to play table tennis and he wanted Alice to watch him. He'd taught her how to play too, and together they had won the school's doubles championship, although Alice joked that her major contribution was jumping out of Jeff's way when he charged for the Ping-Pong ball. She'd never met anyone as competitive as Jeffrey, nor anyone who hated to lose as much as he did.

The semester passed quickly and it was soon time for the Christmas holidays. Jeffrey failed every one of his classes. He was told that he couldn't come back for the spring semester. Alice panicked. She knew that Jeffrey was going to lose his draft deferment. Even if he didn't get called up right away, he would still have to move back to Independence and live with his parents.

Alice telephoned her mother. "We've got to get married," she said. "We can't wait."

"If you truly love each other, then you'll still love each other in a few years after you finish college," Donna insisted.

Alice wasn't so certain. What she didn't and couldn't tell her mother was that sex had become such a big part of her relationship with Jeffrey that she was afraid he might break off their relationship if they spent time apart. "Sometimes I think the only reason Jeff wants to be with me is because of sex," she told a friend. "I don't know what he'd do if I ever told him no." Alice returned to Odessa at Christmas afraid that she might lose Jeffrey for good.

In Independence, Jeffrey telephoned Sarah Stotts over the holidays. She was home from Graceland College, a small school in Lamoni, Iowa, sponsored by the RLDS Church. When Jeffrey dropped by Sarah's house to visit, he was surprised. "I had decided to change my image when I went away to Graceland," Sarah said. "No one there knew that I was shy and scared to death so I jumped right in and decided to overcome my fears and it worked." Sarah had turned into an outgoing, self-confident woman.

After telling Jeffrey about Graceland, Sarah asked him what was happening in his life. Jeffrey was quiet and then he told her that he wanted to ask her an important question.

"I need to know if there is any chance at all of us getting together, you know, romantically," he asked.

"What?" Sarah replied.

"Is there a chance that we might end up getting together someday?" he said. "You know, getting married."

"I don't think so," said Sarah.

"Well, how about if you kiss me one time?" Jeffrey continued.

Sarah agreed, but when Jeffrey leaned over to kiss her, she burst out laughing.

"I guess it wouldn't work," he said. "The reason I had to know was because if I can't have you, I guess I will marry someone else who is as close to you as possible."

Sarah stopped laughing. She hadn't realized that he felt as strongly as he did about her. More than two decades later, Sarah would still remember what Jeffrey said that night.

"Jeff told me that Alice was pressuring him to get pregnant because she had a bad homelife and she wanted to get out of the house, you know, to get married. I told Jeff that he really needed to be careful or he was going to get into something that he didn't need to get into and he said it didn't matter."

"What do you mean, it won't matter?" she asked.

"If I can't have you, I'll marry Alice. But if you and Alice and I were all three in a boat that was sinking and I could only save one of you, I would save you first and if I had a chance, I'd go back and save Alice because I do love Alice, but if it came down to choosing between you and Alice, I'd save you first."

"Jeff," Sarah said, "if you really feel that way, you shouldn't be even talking about getting married. You shouldn't be rushing into this."

Sarah would later recall that conversation with confusion and sorrow. "I remember thinking that I had gone away to college and had changed. I had overcome my insecurity. But I don't think Jeff had ever gotten to the point where he really believed in himself. I think he was looking for someone to love him and tell him that he was worth loving."

Jeffrey invited Alice to his house on Christmas Day, but she felt self-conscious when she got there. She had brought gifts for the Lundgrens, but no one had bought her anything. When she and Jeffrey had a chance to talk in private, she asked if he had told his mom and dad that they wanted to get married. He avoided answering her.

A few weeks after the spring semester started at CMSU, Jeffrey and Alice drove to Odessa to talk to her parents. They had thought of a way to force Don and Lois to give their consent. This is how Donna Keehler remembers what happened. "We were sitting around the kitchen table when Alice and Jeffrey asked us if we would tell Jeff's parents that Alice was pregnant. I immediately asked her if she was and Alice said no, but they wanted us to lie to Don and Lois so they would have to agree to the marriage."

"I'm not going to lie for you," Donna told Jeffrey and Alice. "That's no way to start a marriage."

A month later, Jeffrey and Alice returned to talk to Donna and Ralph. This time, Alice said, no one was going to have to lie. Jeffrey called his parents from the Keehlers' kitchen and broke the news. Don and Lois were furious. Jeffrey asked Donna and Ralph if they'd go with him and Alice to face his parents.

Don led everyone into the family room where he had lined up six chairs. He and Lois had never met Ralph and Donna before.

"I have something to say," he announced, and for the next several minutes, he blistered Jeffrey. "My dad said I had embarrassed the entire family. That I had ruined the Lundgren name. That he and mom were so embarrassed by what I had done that they couldn't show their faces at the Slover Park congregation. Then he turned and looked at me and said, 'It is a great sorrow to me that my first grandchild has to be born a bastard.'"

During the next few minutes, Lois and Donna argued. Lois claimed Alice had trapped Jeffrey. "Lois called Alice a whore," Donna recalled. Alice began to cry. Donna fired back. This was no way for the Lundgrens to treat their future daughter-in-law. Don jumped into the fray. Jeffrey didn't have to marry Alice just because she was pregnant. Jeffrey stomped out of the room. He packed a few things and left with Alice and her parents.

The next day was Sunday and everyone cooled off. On Monday morning, Jeffrey, Alice, and Donna drove to the Independence courthouse to get a wedding license. Don and Lois had agreed to give their consent as long as Jeffrey and Alice promised not to have a big church wedding.

Lois was waiting at the courthouse but she told Jeffrey that she wanted to talk to him privately before they went inside. She led him to her car where his grandparents, Alva and Maude Gadberry, were waiting. For several minutes, Lois and the Gadberrys explained to Jeffrey all of the reasons why he didn't need to marry Alice. Jeffrey would later tell Alice that his mother had upped the ante. "She offered to pay me off if I would denounce you and walk away."

On May 5, 1970, Jeffrey and Alice were married at her RLDS church in Odessa. Jeffrey didn't tell his parents the time, date, or location because he was afraid they might disrupt the ceremony. Just to make certain that none of the Lundgrens showed up, Jeffrey had two of Alice's relatives stand guard at the front door. The church pews on the left side of the sanctuary, traditionally reserved for the friends and relatives of the bride, were packed with guests. The pews on the groom's side were completely empty except for one person.

Jeffrey's college pal, Keith Johnson, came to wish him well.

Jeffrey didn't have enough money to rent a tuxedo. Donna and Ralph paid for it and slipped him another six hundred dollars from their savings to pay for a honeymoon. Jeffrey borrowed the Keehlers' car and drove his new bride to Arlington, Texas, where they checked into a hotel near the Six Flags Over Texas amusement park. He had been there before with his parents and he figured Alice would enjoy the rides. He had booked a room in the same hotel that he had stayed in with his mom and dad. The morning after their wedding, Jeffrey and Alice arrived at the park early. Jeffrey wanted to spend as much time as possible on the rides. But when they got to the park, Alice's stomach was upset. It was morning sickness. Jeffrey took Alice back to their hotel, but he soon became jittery. He had already paid for two all-day passes. There wasn't much point in their both being stuck in the hotel. He kissed her on the forehead and left for the park. He would be back when it closed.

As soon as he shut the door to the room, Alice began to cry. She couldn't believe that Jeffrey had left her alone on their honeymoon. What had happened to the obsessed college boy who had sent her a long-stemmed rose each day for a week?

CHAPTER FOUR

MARRIAGE had seemed so simple when Jeffrey and Alice first fell in love. But that was before Jeffrey flunked out of school and before Don and Lois stopped paying for his room and board. When the newlyweds returned from their honeymoon in May 1970, they had no car, no money, no jobs, and no place to live. Donna Keehler came to the rescue. Jeffrey and Alice could live with her and Ralph rent-free in Odessa until they could afford a place of their own.

Jeffrey knew he was going to be drafted. It was a terrible time to be inducted into the army. By January 1970, some forty thousand Americans had already been killed in Vietnam. Ten thousand of them had died during 1969 alone. And even though Henry Kissinger had secretly begun negotiating an end to the war, some of the most intense fighting still lay ahead. Jeffrey decided to enlist in the navy under a delayed-entry program that didn't require him to report until late 1970.

Donna had always said that no household was big enough for two families, and between May and November, her axiom proved painfully accurate. What bothered Donna was Jeffrey's selfishness. He was fairly good at pitching in with household chores, but he refused to share. Whenever Jeffrey earned a few dollars doing odd jobs, he'd immediately spend it on himself without offering to chip in for groceries, gasoline, or other costs at the Keehler house. Some nights, Jeffrey would bring home a large pizza, but rather than sharing it, he would scurry into his bedroom with Alice and shut the door so that they could eat in private. Jeffrey's between-meal snacking also irked the Keehlers. Three or four times a week, he would buy a liter of Pepsi and frozen chocolate-chip cookie dough. After taking a few sips of the Pepsi, he would cut off the top of the plastic bottle and fill the container with ice, making it into a giant cup. He would drink the entire liter as he ate the raw dough.

There were other problems too. Jeffrey would borrow Donna's car at night so he could take Alice on rides. Donna understood how the young couple might want to get away. But when Donna got up early the next morning to leave for work, she would always find her gas gauge registering empty. Jeffrey never thought to fill the tank. He didn't seem to care about anyone but himself.

When Jeffrey left on November 8 for navy training at San Diego, California, only Alice was sorry to see him go. Their baby was due any day and she wanted Jeffrey at the hospital with her. Three weeks after he left, Alice gave birth to Damon Paul Lundgren. She called Jeffrey and told him they had a son. The arrival of a baby at the Keehler household caused new friction between Alice and her two sisters. "Alice always claimed that she was too tired to get up at night, so Sue and I got out of bed and took care of Damon, got him a bottle or whatever," Terri remembered later. "My mom was working nights so she wasn't home and didn't know we were doing all the work at night. We were gone to school by the time she got home. We all found out later that Alice was telling our mother that she had been the one who was up all night. She'd say she was exhausted, and our mother would end up taking care of Damon all day long. That was typical of Alice. She liked to get other people to do her work."

Jeffrey wasn't permitted to come home over the Christmas holidays. When he finally got back to Odessa on February 13, 1971, he told Alice that he had two big surprises for her. Alice had bought Jeffrey a mushy Valentine card and she immediately suspected that he had bought her something special to celebrate their first Valentine's Day as a married couple.

"Okay!" she said, excitedly. "Tell me, tell me!"

"I've been studying the scriptures," he announced. "Go ahead, say a verse; I bet I can tell you where it's located."

Alice didn't know what to say.

"C'mon, Alice," he pushed. "Test me. Just name one."

All Alice could think of was a well-known verse from the Book of Mormon. Jeffrey beamed when he named its location.

"I wanted to impress her," Jeffrey remembered years later. "The scriptures were very precious to Alice and I wanted to show her how much I had learned. At that time, she knew the scriptures much better than I did and she was always harping about them, so I had decided to study them for her."

Still expecting a Valentine present, Alice urged Jeffrey to tell her his second surprise.

"My father has agreed to bless Damon. It's all arranged."

While in San Diego, Jeffrey had written to Don and Lois and asked his father if he would perform a blessing, a major event in the Mormon Church. Jeffrey hadn't bothered to consult Alice or her parents. Instead, he and his parents had chosen a time, date, and place for the ceremony.

"Is there anything else?" she asked. Jeffrey didn't know what she meant. Without uttering another word, she handed Jeffrey the Valentine card. He opened it and blushed.

"Alice," he stammered. "I was so busy, I didn't have a chance to buy you one."

The next weekend, Jeffrey and Alice took Damon to Independence to meet his grandparents. Don scooped up Damon in his arms. Lois wasn't as friendly. Neither of them acknowledged Alice. The afternoon went well as far as Jeffrey was concerned, and Don and Lois asked them to stay for dinner. By the time it was over, Jeffrey was telling his father all about the navy while Lois rocked Damon.

"I was a non-person," Alice complained on the ride back to Odessa. "I was invisible, like I wasn't even there. I never want to go back to their house again."

Damon's blessing was scheduled for the following Sunday at the Slover Park congregation. The Keehlers drove to Independence with Jeffrey, Alice, and Damon. It was a beautiful ceremony. Damon was carried to the front of the sanctuary during the regular church service. Don held him and said a blessing. He had spent hours preparing it and after he finished, some in the congregation were wiping tears from their eyes.

Don and Lois invited friends to their house after church. Ralph and Donna were noticeably absent. Alice reluctantly tagged along. When she arrived, her mother-in-law was waiting. Lois threw her arms around Alice and gave her a hug. All of the anger and hatred she had felt toward Alice had "melted away" during Don's blessing of Damon, she explained. Alice was no longer a ghost, she was family. Lois began introducing Alice to her friends as her new "daughter." Jeffrey had to return to San Diego a few days later. Alice and Damon moved to California with him.

Jeffrey was assigned to work as an electrical repairman on the USS *Sperry*, a supply delivery and repair ship that serviced submarines. But it wasn't scheduled to leave San Diego harbor for several months so he was temporarily assigned to work as a lifeguard at a base swimming pool. Nearly every day, Alice and Damon would go to the pool with him. He and Alice would play badminton, sunbathe, and gossip about how the wives of other sailors flirted with men at the pool. "We both felt out of place in San Diego," Jeffrey later said. "It was just too wild for us. We weren't ready for the California life-style." A fellow crew member invited them to a party one night, but when they got there, everyone was smoking marijuana. Jeffrey was afraid the police would arrive at any second so he and Alice quickly excused themselves and hurried home.

Alice would later describe that summer as one of the happiest periods in her marriage. Yet there were problems. Jeffrey earned less than $200 per month and the monthly rent for their off-base apartment was $105. They could have lived in military housing for less, but Jeffrey didn't like having his co-workers as neighbors. Even if they had spent their money frugally, they would have had a tough time. But neither tried to budget or save. Jeffrey continued to snack on Pepsi and cookie dough. Alice hated to cook, preferring to eat out. They both called their parents at various times and asked for cash. Nearly every month, they ran out of food. When that happened, Jeffrey would go over to the ship and raid its galley. He'd smuggle some bread and sandwich fixings out to Alice, who waited in the car.

Besides money, sex was becoming a problem. "Alice wasn't warm sexually after we got married," Jeffrey later complained. "She felt guilty because she had gotten pregnant before we were married. She started getting these migraine headaches. I was very frustrated and I told her that she simply wasn't satisfying me." Alice later blamed Jeffrey for their sexual problems. "Jeffrey was fixated on sex. Sex, sex, sex. That was all he thought about, all he wanted to do. He'd do it several times a day if I let him, and when we did it, he just wanted to satisfy himself. He didn't care about me and my feelings."

In the spring of 1972, Jeffrey was transferred to the USS *Shelton*, a battle-tested Korean War destroyer with a crew of 275 men and two twin five-inch guns. On May 30, Jeffrey was told that the ship was going to Vietnam. He wrote his parents and asked if Alice and Damon could live in Independence with them while he was gone. They agreed. On June 13, Jeffrey kissed Alice and Damon good-bye. Twenty-seven days later, the USS *Shelton* arrived off the coast of Vietnam.

On board the ship, Jeffrey spent all of his free time reading the Book of Mormon. Like the Bible, it was divided into books, rather than chapters, and he studied all fifteen. He still wanted to know the scriptures better than Alice. One verse that Jeffrey read while studying bothered him. Verse 65 in the Second Book of Nephi said: "For the Spirit is the same, yesterday, today, and forever." Jeffrey was confident that he knew what it meant. God hadn't changed since the time of Moses. God was God. But if that was true and God hadn't changed, then why didn't He still do all of the wonderful things that He had done in biblical days? Specifically, why hadn't He intervened in Jeffrey's life? Alice had told him about her experiences at the summer camp and how an evil presence had tried to crush her in her bedroom. Jeffrey had never experienced any supernatural event. He had prayed for some sort of sign, but there was none.

While Jeffrey wrestled with the spiritual, back in Independence, Alice was learning about the secular. Lois was keeping her promise of accepting Alice as a member of the Lundgren family. Like Professor Henry Higgins, she was supervising a transformation. She taught Alice how to style her hair. She got Alice to stop biting her fingernails, and when she did, Lois rewarded her with a manicure. They went shopping together and Lois taught Alice how to select outfits that complimented her figure, how to mix and match blouses and skirts so they didn't clash. Lois taught Alice about antiques and showed her how to refinish furniture. She instructed her on etiquette, simple things really, such as how to correctly set a table and host a party. In the kitchen, Lois showed Alice how to cook meals that were more exotic than the meat and potatoes that she had grown up eating.

While Lois kept busy with Alice, Don focused on Damon. They became buddies. Each morning, the twenty-two-month-old would

fuss unless he got to eat his rice crispy cereal with his "paw-paw."
Jeffrey had told Alice that his father was a cold and harsh taskmas-
ter. But she saw none of that in the way Don treated his grandson.
If anything, he spoiled him.

On the clear and sunny Sunday morning of October 15, 1972,
Jeffrey's scripture studies were interrupted by a loud boom. The USS
Shelton was under attack. Naval Intelligence had assured the destroyer's captain that the island of Hon Co, called Tiger Island by
U.S. troops, was free of enemy artillery, but the reports had been
wrong. The first round fired by enemy artillery dropped short. The
second overshot the ship. Obviously, the North Vietnamese were
sighting in their weapon for the kill. But when the third round was
fired, it dropped short too. And then the firing ended. The ship's
captain described the brief attack in the ship's log as an "extremely
close call."

Four days later the destroyer was in the Gulf of Tonkin when
enemy artillery again began shooting. This time, the battle was
much more fierce. For thirty minutes, enemy guns exchanged fire
with the USS Shelton and a nearby cruiser, the USS Providence. The
two U.S. ships fired more than 120 rounds at the enemy. The North
Vietnamese fired just as many back. Yet neither U.S. ship was hit.
While the destroyer's crew joked about the enemy's poor marksman-
ship, Jeffrey began developing a different theory.

In mid-December, the destroyer again came under attack. The
captain of the USS Shelton would later report that more than 190
shots were fired at his ship. None hit. Two days later, the destroyer
was engaged in the biggest battle of its history. More than seven
hundred shots were fired at the USS Shelton by a battery of shore
guns. As Lundgren and other crew members manned their battle
stations, rounds peppered the water causing geyserlike eruptions. Despite the repeated firing, not a single round hit the destroyer. "Many
splashes within fifty yards were observed," the captain wrote in the
ship's log, "with one missing the port bow by only twenty feet." It
was, the captain noted, a "miracle" that the USS Shelton escaped
the onslaught of enemy rounds.

That was exactly how Jeffrey felt. "The enemy had us. They
fired shells over us. They fired shells short. They had us locked on
with radar. There was no way they could miss. But they fired and
fired and fired and they couldn't hit us. There was no reason for
them to miss except for one reason. God made it impossible for them
to hit the ship."

As the USS *Shelton* sailed out of the Gulf of Tonkin on December 22 and made its way home, the crew celebrated its good luck. Jeffrey watched with a knowing grin. None of his shipmates realized that the only reason they were alive was because of him, he explained later. He had been the only saint aboard the ship. A scripture popped into his mind. "For the Spirit is the same, yesterday, today, and forever."

"God had showed me a sign," Jeffrey said. "He had protected the ship because he didn't want me to die in Vietnam."

For the first time in his life, Jeffrey looked upon religion as something useful. He also remembered what Alice had told him about the patriarch's prediction. Alice's husband was going to do great things for the church. All the way home, Jeffrey studied his scriptures.

CHAPTER FIVE

W HEN the USS *Shelton* returned to San Diego on January 13, 1973, Jeffrey and the other crew members were awarded a slew of military decorations. Jeffrey received three from the navy: the National Defense Service Medal, Vietnam Service Medal with one Bronze Star, and the Combat Action Ribbon. The South Vietnamese government issued him its Republic of Vietnam Campaign Medal and he received a special letter of commendation for the outstanding job that he had done keeping electronic equipment aboard the ship in good working order. His evaluations by his superiors showed Jeffrey was an above-average sailor, skilled at his job and eager to please.

"I had an excellent time aboard that ship and if it weren't for Alice, I would have made the navy my career," Jeffrey complained later. "I liked the life-style, but the first thing that Alice said when I stepped off the ship and met her was 'Promise me that you'll never leave me again.' Those were her exact first words. She was so insecure."

Alice hadn't had time to find an apartment in San Diego before Jeffrey returned from Vietnam. They needed a place to stay while they looked. A friend mentioned that Louise Stone lived in San

Diego with her husband, Muril, whom everyone called Sonny. He was a chief petty officer assigned to the United States Marine Corps Recruit Depot just up the bay from the naval station where Jeffrey was stationed. Louise had grown up attending the Slover Park congregation. Her father, Damon Binger, had been the pastor. Because Louise was two years older than Jeffrey, she had been friends with a different crowd at church, but she recognized his voice when he called her.

"I was wondering if we could stay with you for a while?" Jeffrey asked. Even though Louise hadn't seen him in nine years, she agreed. It was common for saints to open up their homes to other church members in need. Sonny didn't care either. "Sailors help out sailors," he remarked.

During the week that Jeffrey, Alice, and Damon spent with Louise and Sonny, the two women became lifelong friends. "There was a chemistry between us," Louise said later. "I think I know her better than any other person on earth."

Sonny and Jeffrey got along too, but they were not close. There was something about Jeffrey that Sonny didn't like, although he couldn't pinpoint what it was that made him uneasy. After the Lundgrens found an apartment, they still got together nearly every weekend with the Stones. Once or twice a week, Alice and Louise would chat on the telephone, sometimes for hours.

Two months after the USS *Shelton* returned to port, the navy decommissioned it and the destroyer was sold to the Taiwan government. Jeffrey was put in charge of planning the farewell party for the crew. He asked Alice to help and she got to show off everything that she had learned from Lois. Jeffrey and Alice didn't drink alcohol, but there was plenty of liquor at the party and several crew members got drunk. At one point, an officer stopped at the table where Jeffrey and Alice were sitting with several couples. Throwing one arm around Alice's shoulders, the officer broadcast in a slightly slurred, booming voice: "Little lady, I want you to know that your husband was the *only* man who was faithful to his wife during our cruise." Alice's face blushed as she whispered a quick "Thank you." The other women sitting at the table were not as bashful. "What?" one shrieked. The officer repeated himself: "That's what I said. Good old Jeffrey was the only man who kept his pants zipped." Tempers flared as wives demanded explanations and husbands denied their accusations. Jeffrey and Alice slipped out of the room.

"Weren't you even tempted?" asked Alice.

"You are the only woman in the world that I will ever want," he replied.

Alice couldn't wait to tell Louise. Most of the time, Jeffrey was always criticizing Alice, calling her stupid, but sometimes he could say just what she wanted to hear.

"Sonny and I both thought that Jeffrey was tremendously rude to Alice," Louise said later. "Jeff would make decisions without consulting her or even telling her about them. He had complete control in all decision making, and he just expected Alice to accept that."

One night Louise got a telephone call from Alice after Jeffrey had gone to sleep. Alice had crept out of the bedroom to call her. She told Louise that Jeffrey had gotten angry because she had asked him how much money was in their checking account.

"I am not allowed to even touch the checkbook or to even know how much is in it," explained Alice. She was worried because Jeffrey hadn't been paying all the bills.

"Well, why don't you just ask him about it?" Louise asked.

"I can't," said Alice. "He'll explode."

"That's ridiculous," Louise replied.

That weekend when the two couples got together, Jeffrey was cold toward Louise. She learned later that he was irritated because he had heard about her conversation with Alice. "He thought I had too much influence over Alice."

Louise knew that many conservative RLDS members believed that God had created a strict hierarchy in every marriage. Much of this attitude was based on the New Testament writings of Paul in his first letter to Timothy, chapter 2, verses 11 through 15:

> Let the women learn in silence with all subjection. For I suffer not a woman to teach, nor to usurp authority over the man, but to be in silence. For Adam was first formed, then Eve. And Adam was not deceived, but the woman being deceived was in the transgression. Notwithstanding they shall be saved in childbearing, if they continue in faith and charity and holiness with sobriety.

What surprised Louise was how readily Alice accepted Jeffrey's dominance. "Jeffrey says it's a man's job to love and obey and to serve his God," Alice explained to Louise one afternoon. "God is the man's master. That means the man must submit his will to God. The woman's job is to love and obey and serve her husband. He is her master."

Such talk exasperated Louise. "I felt Jeffrey was in the process of making Alice into exactly what he wanted her to be. He wanted to control every part of her life and she gave him that control in return for his love. She tried to be exactly what he wanted—the perfect little housewife. She cleaned, she cooked, she canned, she changed diapers, washed clothes, and took care of Jeffrey, and she did it without complaining because she had total faith that he would take care of her and he would love her."

Jeffrey's next assignment was aboard the USS *Schofield*, a guided-missile frigate, which had a well-deserved reputation for being a lemon. He abhorred the ship and was unhappy. Alice had tired of navy life too and she hated the idea of Jeffrey's going away on another eight-month cruise. During 1973, Alice began complaining about migraine headaches that were so painful she was hospitalized for treatment. When Jeffrey learned that his ship was scheduled to leave on an extended cruise that fall, Alice became depressed. She was so distraught that Jeffrey suggested that she see a psychiatrist. If Alice could get a doctor to say that her mental anguish was caused by Jeffrey's going away on cruises, maybe the navy would grant him an early discharge. Alice underwent a psychiatric exam and blamed her problems on Jeffrey's career, but the navy didn't buy it. "My commanding officer told me, 'Lundgren, if we had wanted you to have a wife, we'd have packed one in your seabag.' There was no way the navy was going to let me go early."

Sonny Stone was a "lifer," and when he heard how Jeffrey had tried to use Alice's migraines as an excuse to get a discharge, he got angry. Other rifts began developing between the Lundgrens and Stones. Louise had decided that Jeffrey was fixated with sex. She and Sonny had bought a house with a swimming pool, and on warm nights, they would often skinny-dip together. "It became a joke. People would say, 'Hey, wonder if Sonny and Louise are in the pool tonight,'" Louise said. One morning, Alice and Jeffrey dropped in unannounced and spotted some of Sonny's clothing tossed beside the pool. Obviously, he and Louise had gone for a romantic swim the night before.

"We all joked about it at first," Louise recalled, "but Jeffrey just wouldn't let go of it. Every time we got together after that, he would bug us about having sex in the pool. 'Hey, did you use the pool last night?' he'd say. Or 'Hey, when are you and Sonny going to let us use your pool?' He put a lot of pressure on Alice to ask us to invite them to baby-sit our kids when we went out so that he and Alice could have sex in our pool. He just went on and on and on about it until it wasn't funny at all."

By the time that October arrived, the couples weren't meeting regularly although Alice and Louise remained close friends.

On November 23, Jeffrey's ship left San Diego for Pearl Harbor, the first stop on an eight-month trip that would take it to the Indian Ocean. Alice and Damon returned to Missouri, only this time they moved in with Alice's parents. She had just learned that she was pregnant again. Jeffrey promised to write every day. Alice said that she would too. She also told Louise that she would call her whenever she could afford it.

As he had done when he went to Vietnam, Jeffrey carried his copy of the Book of Mormon with him on the ship. Kevin Currie worked for Jeffrey in the electronics repair shop and was assigned to a bunk next to his. But Kevin didn't have much in common with his supervisor. Jeffrey was somber, humorless, a by-the-regulation boss. Although Kevin was only one year younger, the thin New York native didn't take life seriously. He had a tattoo on his leg that said "Just Passing Through," and that expressed his philosophy. Whenever his ship dropped anchor, Kevin was one of the first to race to the waterfront whorehouses and bars. Religion meant nothing to him. He had been raised in the Episcopalian Church, but had stopped going as a youngster.

Kevin didn't like Jeffrey at first. "Jeffrey always gave people the impression that he was looking down on them, that he was somehow better," Kevin said. But after they had spent a few months at sea, Kevin's opinion changed and he became intrigued. Jeffrey was always studying his scriptures. He didn't cuss, shunned coffee, wouldn't smoke, and he wrote letters to his wife every day, sometimes two or three times each day. Yet Jeffrey didn't browbeat anyone about the Bible or try to evangelize. If anything, he seemed to like keeping whatever he was reading a secret. It was as if he had made some important discovery that he wasn't that eager to share.

It turned out that Jeffrey was just as interested in Kevin. "Jeffrey was curious about my carefree attitude," Kevin said. "I did whatever I wanted and I think, to a certain degree, Jeffrey was envious."

Still neither made any effort to get to know the other until the USS *Schofield* stopped to refuel at the Anzuk Naval Base in Singapore. The crew received eight days of liberty and, by chance, Kevin and Jeffrey found themselves crammed into the same taxicab one morning with four other sailors going into the city. Jeffrey asked if any of the men wanted to go sightseeing with him. They laughed. They were headed to a whorehouse. But Jeffrey made the cultural sites on the island that he was going to see sound so interesting that the men finally agreed to join him. They hired pedal-carts, two-seat carriages powered by a man on a bicycle, to take them on their tour. Kevin and Jeffrey sat together. By nightfall, all of the men except Jeffrey had had enough culture. They stopped at a nightclub. Jeffrey waited outside while the others paid to see two women engage in lesbian sex acts. After the show, all the men but Kevin came outside. When he eventually appeared, he was carrying a cucumber.

"Why do you have that?" Jeffrey asked.

Kevin smirked.

"It's ah, uh, souvenir," he announced, as the other sailors guffawed.

Jeffrey later learned that the two women had used the cucumber to have sexual intercourse with each other. Kevin had paid one of the women after the show to have sex with him and then had stolen the cucumber. When they got back to the ship that night, Jeffrey wrote a long letter to Alice describing that day's events. He mentioned Kevin and talked about how the women had used the cucumber on each other. Jeffrey went into such detail that Alice incorrectly suspected that he too had seen the act.

The frigate left Singapore on March 13, 1974, and eventually returned to San Diego on June 5. Alice was waiting with Damon. They had flown to California a few weeks earlier and found an apartment. She was nine months pregnant. A few days later, Kevin asked Jeffrey at work one day about the Book of Mormon. Jeffrey invited Kevin to come to his apartment for dinner. Alice was appalled. All she could think of was the cucumber story. But Jeffrey insisted. When Kevin arrived, Alice began to relax. He was nicely dressed, polite, rail thin, and spoke with a quiet voice. He was nothing like she had imagined. As Kevin walked into the Lundgren apartment that night, he suddenly felt a "warmth" and he decided to tell Jeffrey and Alice about his past. As a child, he had been shuffled between relatives. "I attended fourteen different schools before I graduated." At age five, he had also been sexually molested. He had joined the navy to start a new life, but had begun using drugs. Nothing in life seemed to matter, he explained. Jeffrey began telling Kevin about Mormonism. He explained that the Book of Mormon was the history of a group of ancient Hebrews who had crossed the Atlantic Ocean before Christ was born and had settled in the New World where they split into two groups, called the Lamanites and Nephites. The Lamanites were wicked and they eventually waged war and destroyed the good Nephites during a great battle at the Hill Cumorah. Mormon was a prophet and historian and he recorded the history of the two tribes on golden plates. His son, Moroni, finished the last portion of the record and hid the plates on the Hill Cumorah before he was killed. Centuries later Moroni returned to earth as an angel and directed Joseph Smith, Jr., to where the plates were hidden. The saints were different from other religions, Jeffrey said, because they believed that God intervened in their lives and still sent them prophets. God had also given the saints a purpose in their lives. They were to build Zion and prepare for the second coming of Christ.

Kevin was impressed. He began stopping by the Lundgrens' apartment every night. Some weekends, he would sleep on the couch after he and Jeffrey ended their marathon late-night debates about various scriptures.

One night Jeffrey told Kevin about an event that had happened aboard the USS *Schofield* when the frigate was in the Indian Ocean. Jeffrey had gone up onto the deck to lift weights and exercise. He was all by himself. "The sea was like glass and a brilliant full moon made it possible for me to see in the darkness," he said. "It was clear except for one peculiar cloud. Rather than being white, this cloud was inky black, darker even than the rest of the sky.

"As I began working out, I noticed this cloud seemed to be following the ship," Jeffrey explained. "We were moving along, probably at twenty knots, cruising speed, and the cloud seemed to be trailing us, following behind us as we moved across the water.

"I decided to investigate. So I walked over to the rail that ran along the deck. As I looked at the cloud, it suddenly zoomed down. It took the shape of a human hand and it came directly toward me and attacked me. It began pushing me back against the guide wire and railing. I grabbed onto it because the cloud was literally pushing me off the deck, but I couldn't hold on very long because the cloud kept pushing and it was stronger than me. It was pushing against my chest and I suddenly realized that I was going to be pushed overboard, that I was going to be pushed into the ocean and drowned by this cloud. So I cried out, 'My God, save me! Deliver me!' and as soon as those words left my lips, I was released and within seconds the cloud had disappeared, completely vanished, and I was safe."

Why had the cloud attacked him? Kevin asked. What did it mean?

"I believe the cloud was Satan and the forces of evil, and he was trying to kill me to keep me from doing something that God has chosen me to do."

What? Kevin asked.

"I don't know," Jeffrey replied. "But there is no other interpretation. There has to be a reason why God is saving me and why Satan wants me dead."

On June 24, Alice gave birth to another boy, whom she and Jeffrey named Jason. When she came home from the hospital, she jokingly said that the family had really gained two "new" children. Kevin was spending so much time with them that he was their other "son."

Jeffrey asked a group of elders at a local RLDS congregation to conduct "cottage meetings" for Kevin. During the sessions, the elders explained the official history of the church and its doctrines. Since Jeffrey wasn't a member of the RLDS priesthood, he couldn't officially conduct a "cottage meeting" although he knew his scriptures better than the elders who spoke to Kevin. In October, Kevin was baptized into the RLDS. On November 4, 1974, Jeffrey was discharged. He had decided to return to Missouri. Jeffrey wasn't the sort of man who hugged another man, but when he and Kevin shook hands and said good-bye, he thought that he saw tears in Kevin's eyes.

Although the elders had officially prepared Kevin for membership, Jeffrey knew that he was really responsible for bringing him into the church. Jeffrey felt good about that. He had never thought of himself as being terribly persuasive, but he was learning.

CHAPTER SIX

ONCE Jeffrey was discharged, he and his family returned to Missouri and moved in with Ralph and Donna. Jeffrey didn't know what he wanted to do, so he decided to enroll in classes at Central Missouri State University. The GI Bill would pay his tuition and give him a bit more for living expenses. James Postlethwait, the assistant dean for admissions and records, agreed to give Jeffrey another chance at college despite his terrible academic record. As soon as Jeffrey was accepted, he went to the RLDS student union. His old pal Keith Johnson was playing Ping-Pong in the recreation room. It was as if time had stopped while Jeffrey had been gone. Keith explained that he had graduated, married, divorced, and returned to school to earn an advanced degree. While the two men were talking, a younger student interrupted.

"We need some help, Keith," he said, nodding toward the next room. "It's the liberals."

"C'mon, Jeff," Keith said. "You'll enjoy this."

A crowd of students were arguing about scriptures. Without waiting to be asked, Jeffrey jumped into the fray. Keith was surprised. The Jeffrey he'd known hadn't been much of a Bible student. "I've been doing quit a bit of studying," Jeffrey beamed afterward.

Jeffrey and Alice found an apartment not far from the campus, and when the first semester ended in late spring of 1975, Jeffrey had earned straight As—much to the delight of Assistant Dean Postlethwait. One of Jeffrey's professors, Hal Sappington, offered him a lab-technician job. It paid only $120 per month, but he took it. "I really liked working in the lab. I liked the interaction with students and I enjoyed the way the professors treated me. I decided that I wanted to be part of that world." That summer, Jeffrey told Alice that he planned to become a college professor. Dr. Jeffrey Lundgren. He liked how it sounded.

Besides doing well academically, Jeffrey quickly became a spokesman for "fundamentalists" at the RLDS student union. They were conservative RLDS students who were unhappy with changes taking place in the church. The students who favored the changes were the "liberals." The daily arguments that took place between the two factions mirrored a bitter debate that was going on within the RLDS church. During the late 1950s, the church had started to modernize under the leadership of the church's new "prophet," W. Wallace Smith, a grandson of Joseph Smith, Jr. By 1975, most RLDS churches were split between members who favored the old ways and those pushing for change.

Jeffrey loved arguing about religion. He spent all of his free moments at the student union. The most heated arguments were about the role of women in the church. The liberals favored letting them become priests. Jeffrey and the other conservatives claimed that only men could be ordained. During one bitter argument, tempers flared, and someone said the student union wasn't big enough for the liberals and Jeffrey Lundgren. Jeffrey reacted by inviting all of the conservatives at the union to walk out and come to his apartment.

Assistant Dean Postlethwait, who was an RLDS Church member and helped run the student union, eventually soothed the hurt feelings. But not before Jeffrey held a few meetings of his own at his apartment. Dennis Patrick and Tonya McLaughlin were two fundamentalists who attended.

Dennis and Jeffrey had first become allies during debates at the student union. Jeffrey had a photographic memory and was excellent at spouting scripture. No one could match him when it came to reciting verses. But Jeffrey had a high-pitched, almost whiny voice, and he was a bully. Dennis, on the other hand, had a booming, well-trained voice, and a salesman's knack for swaying people.

Slim, athletic, and personable, Dennis was the son of a career air force officer who had moved his family from base to base when Dennis was growing up. Whenever anyone asked Dennis where he was from, he would say Oregon because that was where he had gone to high school, but his real home had always been the church. The RLDS had been the common thread that had given Dennis continuity and stability. "My father was a district RLDS president and a high priest in the church," Dennis told Jeffrey shortly after they first met. "I used to go with my dad on his calls and I fully intend to carry on as I have been raised and taught. The church to me is not just a way of life, it is my life."

Tonya McLaughlin's parents had not been as active as Dennis's family. But like many other saints, when Tonya was growing up all of her friends had been church members. As a teenager, Tonya had lived only a few blocks from Don and Lois Lundgren, but she hadn't known Jeffrey, although she knew his brother, Corry. Shy and chunky, Tonya had beautiful bright red hair and ivory skin. She had met Dennis at a summer party at the student union. He had fallen in love immediately. Tonya hadn't. But she liked his company. Three weeks after they met, Dennis proposed and Tonya agreed. She figured she'd learn to love him. They had just gotten engaged when they met Jeffrey and Alice.

After Jeffrey led his fundamentalist revolt, he and Dennis began spending more and more time together studying the scriptures. Tonya and Alice also became friends. Alice was older, married, the mother of two boys, now ages five and one, and eager to give Tonya advice. One night Dennis asked Jeffrey if he would like to take a break from studying scriptures to play tennis. Jeffrey agreed and Dennis thrashed him on the court. Jeffrey was furious and swore that he'd practice round the clock if necessary, until he finally could beat Dennis.

Dennis, who was just as competitive, gladly accepted the challenge. They began meeting at the tennis court every day. The games quickly became an obsession. Try as he might, Jeffrey couldn't defeat Dennis. And then, after more than one hundred matches, Jeffrey finally won.

Afterward, Dennis noticed that Jeffrey made it a point to bring up his victory whenever he was talking to other students. "Jeffrey would tell everyone about how he had worked and worked and worked and had finally defeated me," Dennis later recalled. "But what he never mentioned was that after we played that set, we played again and I won. In fact, I don't think he beat me after that one time. But he made it sound like he had absolutely defeated me and that I was so crushed that I was never able to beat him again. I remember thinking, 'This is really odd.' But it was important to Jeff to be seen as a champion. He wanted people to believe that he could do anything he wanted once he put his mind to it. He really wanted to be somebody important."

In the fall of 1975, Jeffrey set his mind to something else besides tennis. Dennis was in line to become a priesthood member and Keith Johnson already had been ordained. Jeffrey could recite scripture better than either of them. It was time, he decided, for him to join the priesthood and get on with God's work.

In the RLDS, priesthood members ran local congregations. Unlike most denominations, the RLDS didn't have salaried, professionally trained ministers. Sunday services were conducted by men from each congregation who had been "called" by God to serve as priests. These men, who worked during the week at non-church jobs, divvied up the chores each Sunday. They either took turns preaching or chose one of their own to serve as the regular pastor.

The first step to joining the priesthood was to "receive the call." At least two priests had to feel "moved by the spirit" to recommend a saint as a priesthood candidate. Once two priests recommended a candidate, the district or "stake" office conducted a discreet background check to make certain the candidate was worthy. After that was completed, the candidate was asked if he wanted to become a priest, and if he agreed, his name was put before all of the priests in his local congregation for a vote. When he was approved, he served an apprenticeship under other priests and was finally ordained.

On paper, the process looked tough. In reality, it wasn't. In most congregations any man who came to church regularly and expressed an interest could become a priest. Jeffrey began dropping hints at the local RLDS congregation that he attended and he soon found two priesthood members willing to submit his name. By late 1975, Jeffrey felt certain that he was on his way.

CHAPTER SEVEN

JEFFREY'S life seemed grand. His college professor, Hal Sappington, had decided to take a sabbatical at the start of 1976 and the university had asked Jeffrey to help fill in by teaching a basic electricity course to freshmen even though he was still an undergraduate. The Farmers Home Administration had loaned $22,500 to Jeffrey and Alice so that they could buy a new three-bedroom, ranch-style house in Knob Knoster, a town of 2,040 people about ten miles east of Warrensburg. The months rolled by quickly and, on the surface, happily.

So Louise Stone was surprised when she received a telephone call from a tearful Alice.

"I need to see you," Alice anxiously explained. "I got to get away from here."

"Well, come on out," Louise said, reassuringly. "Stay as long as you need to."

Louise no longer lived in San Diego. She and Sonny had moved to Norfolk, Virginia, home of the Atlantic naval fleet. Sonny had just left on a nine-month cruise, leaving Louise home with their three children.

Alice brought Damon and Jason with her to Norfolk. After the two women got all of the children settled into bed, they went down to the living room to talk and Alice burst into tears.

"It's Jeffrey," she sobbed. "He's lying to me. Hiding things from me. My life is a total wreck."

Jeffrey had unhooked the bell on the telephone, Alice said. He had gotten a post-office box and had stopped having mail delivered to the house. At first Alice couldn't figure out what he was trying to hide. But then a bill collector had come by the house while Jeffrey was in school. "We are thousands and thousands of dollars in debt," she said. "He hasn't paid anything. I had to get away from it all. It's so embarrassing."

All that week, Louise and Alice talked about Jeffrey. Sometimes they would stay up until dawn. Each night, Alice seemed to grow more irritated at him. "Alice was just miserable," Louise said later.

And then Jeffrey arrived.

He had driven to Norfolk in a brand-new Chevrolet Monte Carlo that he had just bought. When Alice saw him pull into the driveway, she rushed outside and clapped her hands in excitement as Jeffrey proudly showed off their new car, opening the doors, trunk, and hood as if he were a salesman hustling a buyer.

"I couldn't believe what I saw happen," said Louise. "Alice was completely thrilled over this brand-new car."

While Jeffrey was outside loading Alice's luggage, Louise pulled Alice aside in the house.

"What about all the things that he hid from you? What about the bills? How'd he afford a new car?" she asked.

Alice brushed off her questions with a shrug.

"He's here," she gushed. "That's all that matters."

"I remember watching them drive away," Louise recalled later, "and thinking that the bottom line was that Alice had terrible self-esteem. The fact that someone loved her enough to buy her a car and come and get her simply overshadowed everything else."

Jeffrey had financed the car through a credit union that was largely owned by RLDS church members. His father was on the board, which is why he got the loan despite his terrible credit rating. Within a few months, Jeffrey's name appeared on the list of delinquent borrowers. Don, who knew nothing about the car loan, was so embarrassed that he resigned from the board.

In later years, Jeffrey blamed Alice for their financial woes. "Alice became just like my mother. Getting possessions, accumulating things, became extremely important to her. My mistake was in not putting my foot down and just telling her no. But I had trouble doing that because Alice and I were having a difficult time in our personal relationship and she wanted physical manifestations from me that showed that I loved her."

Alice's continuing guilt over being pregnant before they were married had turned her into a frigid spouse, Jeffrey claimed. "Alice would say that if we made love once every three months that was a compromise on her part. And I would tell her, 'Alice, what you don't realize is that the eighty-nine days that we didn't make love was a compromise on my part.'"

Not surprisingly, Alice would tell psychologists later that Jeffrey was to blame for their financial and sexual problems. "The first five years of our marriage, I never had an orgasm. I didn't even know what one was until I read about them in a magazine. All he cared about was getting off. He didn't care about my feelings."

There were problems outside the bedroom as well, Jeffrey said. "Alice was angry because she wasn't getting all the attention that she wanted. I wasn't spending enough time with her, she'd say. She'd complain about how much I was studying and working. Those were more important than she was. I'd tell her, 'Well, I have to support you and the family,' but she wouldn't accept that. The truth was that she wanted to be the focal point of the world and so she started demanding things.

"She'd say, 'Oh, if we just could afford to move into our own house, I'd be happy.' So I went down and got a loan from the Farmers Home Administration and we bought a house and she would be happy for a while and then she would say, 'Oh, Jeffrey, if you would just buy me . . .' It never ended. She wanted me to prove that I loved her, over and over and over again.

"And then she started feeling the need to compete with my mother," he continued. "My mother had told Alice that we would never have as much as they did and this superiority complex of my parents, which was entirely my mother's doing, really got to Alice. When my mother got a one-point-one-karat diamond ring for her wedding anniversary, Alice fussed until I bought her a one-point-two karat diamond ring. It had to be bigger than my mother's."

Exactly who was to blame for the couple's runaway expenses is impossible to tell. But relatives and friends later suggested that Jeffrey and Alice were both irresponsible with money. Much of their cash went for frivolous expenses—eating meals in restaurants, Jeffrey's constant snacking. Both loved to go to movies, as many as three or four per weekend. By January 1977, Jeffrey and Alice had accumulated $22,000 in unpaid bills and that didn't include their $22,500 house mortgage.

One morning, they were served with an eviction notice. Alice telephoned her mother. Unless they came up with $300, they were going to be kicked out of their house. Donna wrote them a check and Alice and Jeffrey drove over to get it. Alice said they were going to take the check directly to the Farmers Home Administration office, but on the way home, Jeffrey and Alice stopped to get something to eat. They cashed the check and used some of it to pay for the meal. The money never made it to the FmHA. The mortgage went unpaid.

Without explanation, Jeffrey quit school even though he was only a few credits short of graduation. Hal Sappington, who had returned to campus, was dumbfounded. "It was like Jeffrey vanished. He was here one day and gone the next." Assistant Dean Postlethwait was just as shocked. "Something was wrong, but no one knew what."

Jeffrey would later tell his followers that he had been forced to quit because of Alice. "She told me that her father could get me a good-paying job in the ironworkers union. We needed the income so I quit school and went to the union hall," he explained. "But I only got one job before there was a strike and I was out of work."

Alice would later tell investigators that Jeffrey had been forced out. "Jeffrey got caught stealing money. He had collected some sort of student fee in the electrical lab and instead of turning the money in, he spent it."

The records office at CMSU does not keep disciplinary files from 1977. Those records were shredded years ago. But a school official recalled that Jeffrey had been involved in some sort of disciplinary dispute. "He didn't just leave," this official recalled. "There was a reason."

Although he was now out of work, broke, and still deeply in debt, Jeffrey remained optimistic about becoming a priesthood member. It was the one area of his life where he was still successful. In the Knob Knoster RLDS congregation, he was earning a reputation as a spokesman for the fundamentalists, just as he had done at the student union. One evening after dinner, however, the priest who had recommended Jeffrey stopped by to tell him that the district RLDS office had decided against recommending Jeffrey for ordination. The president of the RLDS stake didn't know Jeffrey that well, the priest explained, so he had telephoned Keith Johnson, who had grown up the area, and asked him about Jeffrey. "Keith told him that I wasn't mature enough spiritually to be ordained," Jeffrey recalled. He didn't take the news well. "I felt betrayed, totally betrayed."

Jeffrey was so angry that he decided to drop out of the RLDS. Joseph Smith, Jr., hadn't needed a church to teach him about God and neither did Jeffrey. "They're going to regret doing this to me," he told Alice.

A few days before he was supposed to be evicted, Jeffrey telephoned his parents and they, in turn, talked to Jeffrey's grandfather, Alva Gadberry. He knew a contractor who needed someone to help do some electrical wiring at the Andrew Drumm Institute, commonly called Drumm Farm, in Independence. Some strings were pulled and Jeffrey was hired at five dollars per hour. It wasn't enough to keep the government from foreclosing on his house, but it was enough to buy groceries. Jeffrey worked hard and made a good impression on the institute's director. He offered Jeffrey a full-time job as the farm manager and Jeffrey agreed. The job included use of a rent-free cottage. Jeffrey and Alice moved to the farm. A short time later their house in Knob Knoster was sold on the courthouse steps.

Jeffrey's job at Drumm Farm was to repair equipment and oversee the livestock. Founded in 1930 by cattleman Andrew Drumm as a home for "orphan and indigent" boys, the institute was designed to be a working farm. Between fifty and sixty boys, ages six through seventeen, milked cows, tended livestock, and raised crops on some 360 acres. Jeffrey liked the work, and when he learned that the institute needed a couple to work as houseparents and oversee ten boys, he telephoned Dennis and Tonya. They had just finished college, were married, and were looking for work.

Dennis and Tonya took the houseparents job and moved to Drumm Farm, where they quickly resumed their friendship with Jeffrey and Alice. Most nights, the Patricks would drop by the Lundgrens' cottage. Alice and Tonya would chat while Jeffrey and Dennis studied their scriptures or played chess. Occasionally, Dennis and Jeffrey would go hunting at night. "The place was overrun with skunks and Jeff was afraid that one of them might bite one of the boys," Dennis recalled. The two men would ride across the farm at night on a tractor searching for the animals, who would stop and stare when hit by the beams from the headlights. Dennis wore glasses and was a lousy shot. Jeffrey had perfect vision and rarely missed. "I think I can see almost as good as an eagle," he told Dennis.

The Patricks were not the only friends who spent time with the Lundgrens at Drumm Farm. Sonny and Louise Stone stopped by once while passing through town. Alice was thrilled, but Jeffrey was aloof. He spent most of the night ignoring them. Near the end of the visit, however, someone asked Jeffrey about the farm manager's job and he began telling the Stones about his plans to artificially breed cattle. For the next hour, Jeffrey described in unnecessary detail how cattle reproduced and were artificially inseminated. "It was the most bizarre conversation I have ever heard," Louise later remembered, "because it became clear during it that Jeffrey was absolutely and totally fascinated with the sex life of cows. It was weird."

Less than a year after he had started work at Drumm Farm, Jeffrey abruptly resigned. When the Patricks asked why, Jeffrey told them that he had quit because he was worried about his children. Andrew Drumm had stated in his will that the farm was only supposed to be used to help good boys who didn't have a home. But Jeffrey claimed that the school was starting to admit juvenile delinquents and he told the Patricks that he didn't want Damon, who was now nearly eight, and Jason, age four, to be influenced by them.

Once again, Alice would later tell authorities a much different story. "Jeffrey got caught stealing hay from the farm. He was selling it and keeping the cash."

Jeffrey and Alice were broke and didn't have anywhere to go. What's more, Alice was pregnant again. She turned to her relatives for help. Her father had a sister who worked at Drumm Farm as a cook and she agreed to loan them enough cash to rent an apartment. Within a week, Jeffrey announced that he had found a job at Trans World Airlines. He was part of a "preflight inspection crew" that checked airplanes when they were on the ground at night to make certain they were safe to fly. Jeffrey would leave for work just before 7:00 P.M., but he never came home at the same time. He told Alice that his hours varied because he could never be certain how much work any individual aircraft might take. If the airplane was in good shape, he'd come home early. Otherwise, he'd have to work late. It made sense to Alice, but she began to get suspicious after a few weeks when she noticed that things were disappearing from the house. A pair of candlesticks vanished. Jeffrey had also sold a rifle that he owned. Alice suspected that Jeffrey was either selling or pawning their valuables to get cash for groceries. She decided to ask him when TWA was going to give him a paycheck.

"I won't get a check until the end of the month," he replied.

Alice thought it was odd that TWA would make a new employee wait a full month before paying him, but she believed Jeffrey. When six weeks went by and there was still no sign of a paycheck, she once again confronted him. This time, Jeffrey told her that someone in the accounting department had made a mistake and had given his check to the wrong person. It was going to take several days to fix the error. Alice was angry, but not at Jeffrey. She blamed TWA.

"Well how do they expect you to feed your family?" she asked.

Jeffrey promised to press TWA for the money.

The next morning, Alice used her neighbor's telephone to call Donna. She explained that TWA still hadn't paid Jeffrey and she asked Donna to loan her $300. Donna sent Alice a check. When another week passed and Jeffrey still hadn't gotten paid, Alice decided to take matters into her own hands. After Jeffrey left for work, she jimmied the drawer to his desk. She was looking for some sort of employment papers from TWA that would tell her when Jeffrey was supposed to be paid. She suspected that he was hiding his paychecks from her. What Alice found instead was a stack of hard-core pornographic magazines and an angry letter from their landlord telling them that they were going to be evicted because their rent was overdue.

The next day when Jeffrey left the apartment to run an errand, Alice raced next door to use her neighbor's telephone. She called TWA's personnel office and demanded to know why her husband hadn't been paid for nearly two months.

"I'm sorry, lady," the TWA clerk replied, "but we have no record of a Jeffrey Lundgren working at TWA."

"That's impossible," Alice said. "He goes to work at the airport every night."

During the long pause that followed, Alice realized that Jeffrey had lied to her. She called Donna. "He's doing it again—lying to me," she sobbed. That night, she confronted Jeffrey.

"What have you been doing at night?" she demanded.

"Working at TWA," he said.

"You're a liar!" she screamed. Alice told him that she had called TWA's personnel office.

Jeffrey began to cry. "I've been out looking for jobs," he said.

"At midnight?" Alice demanded.

He changed his story. "I knew you'd worry if I told you I

couldn't find work," he said. He had been depressed. Most nights he went to a movie. Sometimes he sat in a nearby diner and ate a piece of pie. Alice didn't know whether or not to believe him.

The police arrived a few days later. In front of Alice and their two sons, Jeffrey was handcuffed and taken outside to a waiting squad car. "He had written a check for some gun that he wanted to buy and the check had bounced, but by then he had sold the gun for three hundred dollars and spent the money."

Alice was pregnant again. She had no money. No way to post bond. No telephone and no car. Jeffrey had wrecked the Monte Carlo a few weeks earlier. She put her two boys to bed and walked into the living room. She turned out all of the lights, sat down on the floor, and began to sob.

"I remember sitting in the corner crying and I kept saying to myself, 'What am I going to do? What am I going to do?,' and then Jeffrey came home and he picked me up and held me and he told me everything was going to be all right. I don't know how he got released and I never found out how he had gotten home. All I knew was that he had come home. I said, 'Jeffrey, what's happening to us?,' and he said, 'Don't worry, Alice, it is going to be okay. I will work it out.' And I believed him. I believed he would take care of me."

Jeffrey decided to ask his parents for money. "They can afford to help us," he said. Don and Lois had helped them out before, but this time, they refused. Don lectured Jeffrey. "I'm getting old. Who's going to take care of me if I spend all my savings on you?" he asked. Lois marched into the kitchen and returned with half a loaf of bread and a jar of peanut butter, which she handed to Alice. It was time, Don and Lois said, for Jeffrey to support his own family.

Alice decided to telephone Donna. "Mom, I don't have any money," she said. "The kids don't have any food to eat."

Donna was irritated. She and Ralph were just barely making it themselves. She was in her sixties but retirement was out of the question because of Ralph's medical bills. Still, Donna couldn't turn her back on Alice. She told Alice that she and Jeffrey could move in with them.

By this time, the Keehlers had moved from Odessa to Macks Creek, a town of fewer than one hundred residents in the rolling hills of southwestern Missouri. They lived in a modest prefabricated modular home on a gravel road. Jeffrey and Alice arrived late on a Friday, June 15, 1979. The next morning, Donna handed Jeffrey the local want ads. Incredibly, he found a job that seemed promising. A new ninety-bed hospital had just opened in Ozark Beach, a resort community about thirty miles east. It needed a biomedical technician, a fancy title for someone who repaired medical equipment. With his navy experience in electronics, Jeffrey felt he was qualified. On Monday morning, Jeffrey borrowed Donna's car and drove up state highway 54, to Ozark Beach. Bernie Wilson, the head of the hospital's maintenance department, spent less than thirty minutes talking with him before offering Jeffrey the job. Jeffrey rushed back to Macks Creek to tell Alice, but when he got there, she had news of her own. She was in labor. Jeffrey hustled Alice back to the Lake of the Ozarks Hospital where he had just been hired. Alice gave birth to a daughter, Kristen. Jeffrey was in the delivery room, and when he stepped outside, Bernie Wilson was waiting to congratulate him and hand him a stack of employment forms to sign. Eager to impress his new boss, Jeffrey volunteered to begin work that same day. Later in the afternoon, he stopped in Alice's room to see how she felt. Jeffrey had always wanted a daughter and he began to cry as he rocked "Krissy" in his arms. Alice began to cry too. "Everything's going to be okay, Jeffrey," she said. Surely, the worst was over.

CHAPTER EIGHT

BERNIE Wilson considered himself a good judge of character. He'd spent twenty-three years in the navy, rising to the rank of chief petty officer, and during that time he'd come across all kinds. He could tell Jeffrey was smart when he first interviewed him and he seemed enthusiastic. The hospital job paid six dollars per hour. It wasn't a big salary in 1979, but it was enough for a family to live comfortably on in rural Missouri if they stayed within a budget. One thing Wilson liked was that Jeffrey told him straight out that he was in bad financial shape and would be staying with his in-laws until he could save enough to pay rent.

Jeffrey did a good job at first. The hospital had just opened and there were plenty of maintenance chores. Jeffrey even volunteered to help Wilson with his paperwork. Because the hospital was new, the administrator wanted every department head to write out all the policies and regulations that they followed in their areas. Jeffrey ended up drafting most of Wilson's papers. "He did a darn fine job at writing," Wilson said later.

There was only one hitch during Jeffrey's first month. One morning when Wilson walked through a section of the hospital that still hadn't been opened, he found a room full of household furniture. Jeffrey said it was his. He needed a place to store some personal things that he'd moved down from Independence and he didn't think anyone would mind.

"You got to ask permission before you do something like that," Wilson said. Jeffrey turned red and apologized. He still didn't have enough money to rent a house and there was no room for his furniture at his in-laws.

"Look, I got a two-car garage," Wilson replied. "Why don't you store it there."

"Great!" said Jeffrey. But a week later, the furniture was still in the hospital. This time the problem was transportation. Jeffrey had been using his mother-in-law's car but now she needed it. Wilson again offered to help. He had just bought a new 1979 pickup truck, so he said Jeffrey could buy his older 1972 Chevrolet truck for $1,200. Jeffrey could pay him whenever he got the cash. It was a good deal. Wilson's "old" truck was dazzling. Its blue and white paint gleamed under thick coats of heavily applied wax, the eight-cylinder engine was tuned perfectly, the truck's cargo area looked unused. Jeffrey drove it home that night and moved his furniture into Wilson's garage that weekend.

Three months later, Wilson began to get irritated. Jeffrey's stuff was still in the garage. Wilson told him to come get it. When Jeffrey pulled up, Wilson was shocked. The 1972 truck that he had babied was a wreck. Its paint was scratched, the body was covered with mud, and the pinging noise coming from the engine reminded Wilson of the sound that after-dinner speakers at the hospital made when they tapped their spoons against their water glasses to get everyone's attention.

Jeffrey didn't seem to care that Wilson was upset. He'd found a place to rent, he announced. Wilson felt odd. Jeffrey hadn't paid him a cent for the truck. He clearly wasn't taking care of it. He had stored furniture in Wilson's garage all summer without ever bothering to say thank you. And yet when Wilson had started to complain, Jeffrey had a way of making *him* feel guilty.

Jeffrey moved the furniture into a house owned by Jacob Wilcox on eighty acres east of Macks Creek in a heavily wooded area. Wilcox and his family had restored much of the 1940s farmhouse by themselves. It had two bedrooms and a bath on the top floor, another bedroom and bath on the main level and an unfinished basement. The only reason Wilcox had decided to rent the place was because he and his family were going to be leaving town for about a year. He didn't want to sell it, but he couldn't afford to leave it sitting empty. A friend had told Donna that Wilcox might be willing to rent his home cheap to a family if they took good care of it. Donna had passed the message on to Jeffrey who had immediately telephoned Wilcox. The novice landlord had put Jeffrey off at first. "I wanted to check Jeff out," Wilcox later said. "This wasn't a rental property. It was my home. I planned to come back and live here." Wilcox called a friend who knew the Keehler family.

"Don't do it," the man warned. "That guy has been nothing but trouble."

Despite such advice, Wilcox decided to let Jeffrey move in. "The guy seemed so sincere," Wilcox recalled, "and to tell you the truth, I felt sorry for him." The rent was $100 per month, a figure well below the house's rental value. There was only one stipulation. Wilcox had moved all of his personal belongings into the garage and had put a padlock on the door. He told Jeffrey to stay out of there. Jeffrey agreed and wrote Wilcox a check for the first month's rent. That same day, Wilcox left Macks Creek. A few weeks later, Wilcox got a letter from his bank telling him that Jeffrey's check had bounced. Wilcox called Jeffrey, who quickly apologized and mailed him another check. It bounced too. Wilcox made another call and this time Jeffrey promised to mail him a check that was good. When it cleared, Wilcox figured the first two had been harmless errors. He would soon discover that he was wrong.

From the start, Alice didn't like the farm. It was too isolated. Every day when Jeffrey left for work, she was stuck alone with a new baby and two boys with no neighbors. The only adult she ever got to speak with was Jeffrey and their relationship was once again in trouble. Jeffrey claimed that Alice was a nag. She was always complaining and demanding attention, he said. Alice claimed that Jeffrey was cold and harsh. He didn't care about anyone's feelings but his own, she complained. Both agreed that sex was a problem.

Said Jeffrey: "Being happy sexually with Alice wasn't possible. She couldn't give me what I wanted. I would not be out of line to say that if we had sexual intercourse six times a year that was a great year. I used to say that you could tell how many times Alice and I had made love by counting our kids—it was supposed to be a joke, but it wasn't funny anymore."

Said Alice: "Jeffrey was impossible to satisfy when it came to sex. If Jeffrey didn't have seven or eight orgasms a day, he felt deprived."

One night, Jeffrey confronted Alice.

"Let's stop playing games," he said. "Let's deal with the issue. This is a marital relationship and I have certain sexual expectations and I expect you to meet those expectations."

Jeffrey later insisted that Alice got angry and refused to have sex with him. "She simply refused to meet my needs," he said, "and made it clear that she wasn't going to." Her refusal, he claimed, made him so frustrated that he began flirting at work with other women.

Alice later told a much different story about why she and Jeffrey were having sexual problems.

"Just before Thanksgiving, Jeffrey took me out to the farm we had rented. He left the kids at my mom's and he told me we were going out there to be alone and to make love. I went along with him because I wanted to make him happy but I wasn't prepared for what happened."

After they went into the farmhouse, Jeffrey told Alice to go upstairs and take a bath. While she was still in the tub, Jeffrey walked in naked. He told her to open the drain and let the water out, but he ordered her to stay in the tub. He then stepped into the tub so that he was facing her feet. According to Alice, Jeffrey bent down over her and defecated onto her breasts.

"I discovered that Jeffrey was fascinated with his own feces," Alice later told investigators and her psychologist. "He told me that he had been using it since he was thirteen. He would smear it on himself and masturbate with it."

After Jeffrey rubbed feces on Alice's breasts, they had intercourse and then bathed together, she said. "It wasn't that I was cold and uncaring," Alice explained. "I just didn't want to do all the things that he wanted me to do. I knew that my role as his wife was to satisfy him and I wanted to do that and make him happy, but after we moved to the farm, he not only wanted to smear his feces on me, he got so he liked holding me down and putting it on my face. . . . It was just too much . . . so I began telling him no and that is what made him angry and that is what caused all of the fights."

Jeffrey refused during interviews to discuss his sexual practices with Alice. He considered their sexual life to be private. All he would say was that he had never done anything with Alice that "she didn't want to do too." Later, when he was specifically asked if he had smeared his feces on Alice, Jeffrey became upset. "That's an

outright lie!" he said. "That is not part of my life-style." He accused
Alice of making up stories about their sex life in order to win sympathy for herself. He had never abused her or engaged in any unusual
sexual acts with her, he said.

Shortly after Thanksgiving, Jeffrey began coming home late
from work at night. He told Alice that he was taking a night class
at the hospital so that he could become an emergency medical technician. Alice didn't seem to mind until one Wednesday in December. Alice didn't have a washing machine or clothes dryer at the
rental house, so once a week, usually on Wednesday nights, Jeffrey
drove her into Macks Creek to a Laundromat. He'd drop her off and
go to his night class at the hospital and then return to take her
home. On this particular night, Alice finished the laundry and
waited for Jeffrey but he didn't show up on time. She waited another
hour and then called the hospital.

"Is the class still in session?" she asked.

The nurse, whom Alice knew, was confused. There were no
night classes being taught at the hospital, she replied.

Alice tried to hide her embarrassment. "Oh, I must have been
mistaken," she said. Alice didn't know what to do so she waited
another hour and then finally called Donna. They drove to the
rental house together. Jeffrey wasn't there. Donna took everyone
home with her.

The next day, Alice borrowed her mother's car and she and
Kristen drove to the farm. Jeffrey answered the door.

"What's going on?" Alice demanded. "Why didn't you pick me
up at the . . ."

Before she could finish, Jeffrey slammed the door. She beat on
it with one hand for several minutes until Kristen began to cry and
then she drove back to her parents' house. "I didn't know what was
going on," she later said. "I knew he was mad at me because of our
sex life, but he wouldn't tell me what was the matter."

Alice and the kids spent Thursday at the Keehlers'. On Friday
morning, Jeffrey called. He wanted to take Alice and the kids to
McDonald's for hamburgers that night after work, he said. He
wanted to talk to Alice about their marriage and whether she was
willing to become a "good, subservient wife." Alice dressed the boys
in their best outfits and put ribbons in Kristen's hair. All of them
waited in the living room. Five o'clock. Six o'clock. Around nine
o'clock, Alice put the children to bed and she and her sister Terri
went out to find Jeffrey. His truck was parked at the hospital, but

he was gone. The following morning, Alice again drove to the farm in her mother's car looking for Jeffrey but he hadn't been there. It looked as if he had spent the night somewhere else. She sat down in the kitchen and wrote him a long letter. In it, she apologized for being, in her own words, "such a bad wife." She was sorry that she had made his life so miserable, that she couldn't satisfy him sexually or be obedient as the scriptures demanded. She begged him for forgiveness and finished the letter by asking him not to hate—or leave—her. "I felt that I had caused this entire mess," she recalled. "Not only had I displeased Jeffrey, but I'd also disobeyed God because I had not been subservient to my husband."

On Monday morning, Jeffrey pulled into the Keehlers' driveway. He hadn't talked to Alice for three days. He'd simply disappeared. He told Alice that he needed to speak with her in private. They went for a walk.

"Where have you been?" she asked.

Jeffrey said he had spent the weekend in Springfield, about fifty miles south of Macks Creek, at a motel with a woman who also worked at the hospital. He said the woman wanted to marry him.

"You're having an affair?" Alice later remembered asking.

"No," Jeffrey said, "I was going to, but I didn't." Jeffrey explained that he and the woman had ended up staying in separate rooms. She had wanted to make love with him, but he had been physically incapable of having sex because "I'm still in love with you, Alice, and I couldn't break our marriage vows."

Alice was stunned. "I knew he was angry with me, but I didn't know he was seeing another woman. He told me that he had gone with her because he was so unhappy with me and because I wouldn't do what he wanted. He said she told him that he was masculine and macho and everything that a woman wanted in a man, and she had offered herself to him and that he felt good about that, because that is how a woman was supposed to act, but that he didn't love her. He loved me."

Years later, Jeffrey repeated much the same story in an interview. "I got involved with this woman at work because I was sexually frustrated. It wasn't love. She had her problems, I had mine. It was nothing but animal heat. But I felt so guilty that I just couldn't do anything and then I confessed everything to Alice."

Jeffrey told Alice that he wasn't going to answer any questions about the Springfield trip. He just wanted her to know what she had driven him to do. "He blamed me totally and considered himself a hero because he had turned down this woman," Alice said.

Incredibly, Alice thanked Jeffrey for not committing adultery and for not leaving her and the children. Jeffrey then drove all of them back to the rental house. When it was time for bed that night, Jeffrey told her that he wanted to make love. He pointed toward the bathroom.

"I'll draw your bath," Jeffrey told her.

Alice said later that she understood what he wanted. She followed him into the bathroom and disrobed without complaint.

The next day after Jeffrey went to work, Alice telephoned her parents and told them where Jeffrey had spent the weekend. Ralph Keehler was angry. Was Alice really so naïve that she believed Jeffrey had spent a weekend in a motel with another woman and never touched her sexually?

"Drop that son of a bitch," he told his daughter. "Divorce him."

Donna was more conciliatory. "You decided to marry him, not me, and I'm not going to make the decision on whether you should break up your marriage," she said. "That's up to you." Then she asked her daughter if she still loved Jeffrey.

"Yes," said Alice. Besides, she added, "Who else would take me? I have a baby, two boys, and I'm twenty-eight years old."

All that week, Alice and Jeffrey avoided talking about his tryst. But on Friday afternoon while Jeffrey was at work, his girlfriend called and boldly asked Alice to give Jeffrey a message.

"Tell him I can't go away with him this weekend," she said.

Alice slammed down the receiver. When Jeffrey got home, she screamed at him. Jeffrey got angry.

"I can't believe you believe her!" he snapped. "She is making all this stuff up because I wouldn't have sex with her. It's all a lie! She's trying to get even with me."

Alice was caught off guard.

"Do you think she would call you if she wasn't angry and jealous?" he continued.

Jeffrey's explanation seemed to make sense, at least to Alice. "I believed him. I honestly believed that they hadn't gone to bed together." On Monday, Alice decided it was time for her to turn the tables. As soon as Jeffrey left for work, she telephoned the hospital and asked to speak to the woman.

"Why are you bothering my husband?" she yelled. "Why are

you making this stuff up? Is it because Jeffrey ditched you? Because he didn't want to have sex with you?"

"Is that what he told you?" the woman replied, mockingly. With a steady voice, she then recited the names of the motels and the times and dates that she and Jeffrey had been together. And then she added something else.

"She told me that Jeffrey had taught her how to have oral sex," Alice recalled, "and the way she described it and the words that she used—she was using Jeff's vocabulary—I knew she was telling me the truth because they were the words that he had used to teach me about oral sex. She wasn't lying. I knew that he had been the one telling lies."

Alice hung up and grabbed a telephone book. She called each of the motels and asked the clerks if a "Jeffrey Lundgren" had been a guest on the dates that had been quoted to her. "Every one of them told me that he had checked in. He even had used his real name. He didn't even try to hide it. Everything she had told me was true."

Alice dialed the long-distance number of her friend Louise Stone and told her about Jeffrey's affair. "I drove him to it," she said between sobs. "I am not as sexually active as he wants me to be. If I'd only done what he had wanted and accepted it, then Jeffrey wouldn't have looked elsewhere."

At this point, Alice didn't mention Jeffrey's fascination with feces. She was too embarrassed. She simply told Louise that Jeffrey wasn't happy with her attitude toward sex.

"Alice told me that she had decided that to make Jeffrey happy she was going to become a very sexual partner," Louise Stone said later. "She said she didn't know whether she could do it or not, but she said that she was going to convince Jeffrey that whatever he wanted was okay even if she couldn't enjoy it. I felt that she was trying her best to become what Jeff wanted her to become sexually."

When Jeffrey got home, Alice told him that she thought it was best if they never mentioned his affair again. "She said that she forgave me and for two weeks, she reclaimed me and I reclaimed her, and we had a good sexual relationship," Jeffrey said. "She did what wives are supposed to do and submitted her will to her Lord—me."

But the second honeymoon didn't last long. One night in February, Jeffrey told Alice to put the children to bed early and come to bed. There was something new that he wanted to teach her, he said.

"Jeffrey came up with two glasses and a bottle of cherry vodka and I was shocked because we didn't drink, but he told me that he wanted me to drink some Coke and cherry vodka and we began drinking."

While they sat on the bed, Jeffrey asked Alice what it was like to be a woman during sex. He was curious about how it felt. What was it like for a woman to have an orgasm? How did it feel to have a penis thrust inside her?

"I was getting pretty drunk and he told me that he wanted to do something different. He told me that he wanted me to give him a bath and wash his hair, which I did, and then he had me comb it and set it in rollers. He had me clean and file his fingernails and toenails and then polish them. Then he asked me for one of my nightgowns and he put it on. He asked me to shave his legs and I did and he put on a pair of my panty hose and I was pretty drunk by this time and he decided to model for me so I put makeup, women's makeup, on his face and took out the hair rollers.

"All this time, he was telling me to drink this vodka and Coke and I was really getting drunk. I was sloppy drunk and then he pulled this package out from under the bed and he said that he wanted to show it to me and he opened it up and took out a dildo and a leather harness and I thought, 'My God, what is he going to do to me?' But he told me that the harness was for *me* to wear. He wanted me to put on the dildo and he wanted me to have sex with him! He wanted me to have anal intercourse with him and it was supposed to be a rape. I said, 'No.' I said, 'Jeffrey, this is too weird. I may be drunk, but I'm not going to do that.' He said, 'Oh yes you are,' and we started arguing and that is when I decided just to get out of the bedroom so I went into the hallway and he came after me and he said, 'You are going to do what I tell you to do,' and I said, 'Oh no I'm not,' and he said, 'Well then, I'll get someone who will.' I was drunk and furious and I yelled at him. I said, 'Oh, you going to get your hospital whore?,' and he said, 'Yeah, she'll do it for me.' I yelled, 'You son of a bitch,' and I went for his throat. I dug my fingernails into his neck. I wanted to hurt him, hurt him so bad, hurt him like he had hurt me. I was so angry. I mean, I had tried and tried and tried to get him to tell me that he was sorry about having an affair, but he always refused. He always said, 'I'm not going to grovel in the dirt for you, Alice. It's your fault that it happened.' I was so furious about everything—the lies, the affair, every-thing—so I grabbed him around the throat and tried to hurt him and he grabbed me and pulled me off and when he did, he threw me against the wall and my back hit the door, the doorknob, right in the middle of the back and I remember just going limp with the pain and sliding down the wall. I remember the pain was excruciat-ing. I crawled into the bathroom and I locked the door and I passed out. He was trying to take the hinges off and was yelling at me to unlock the door, but I wouldn't and I passed out."

Jeffrey later recalled the confrontation in the hallway differ-ently. He did not mention anything about a sexual encounter or dildo. "One night I went downstairs to get something to eat and when I came back upstairs, she was waiting for me at the door of our bedroom with a baseball bat. She was enraged about the affair, almost catatonic, and she went on an angry tirade. She swung at me with the baseball bat and missed. I caught her with my arms and picked her up. I didn't have any feelings of anger. She claims that I threw her against the doorknob, but that isn't true. She didn't hit anything when I tossed her back. A few days later, she slipped while she was walking down the stairs and fell and hit her back. That's how she got hurt."

No one except Alice and Jeffrey actually knows what happened, but the result is documented in medical records at the Lake of the Ozarks Hospital. Regardless of the cause, Alice's spleen was ruptured and began leaking blood. The injury went unnoticed for two weeks until Alice collapsed and lost consciousness one morning while vis-iting Jeffrey at the hospital. He carried her into the emergency room, where doctors discovered massive internal bleeding and operated to remove her spleen. Twice during surgery, Alice almost died.

Jeffrey's parents came down from Independence to the farm to take care of the children while Alice was in the hospital. By the end of March, Alice was released, but her medical problems were far from over. She developed a series of painful complications and re-mained bedfast. One night when she was lying in bed half asleep and under heavy medication for pain, Jeffrey had sexual intercourse with her. She was so groggy that she thought it was a dream at first. A few weeks later, she discovered that she was pregnant again. Al-ice, who was still taking large doses of painkillers, was terrified. She was afraid that the drugs that she was taking might harm her baby.

Jeffrey, meanwhile, was facing his own worries. He had written bad checks to several area merchants. Some of the checks had been written on accounts that had been closed months earlier; other checks were from accounts that contained no money. A merchant tipped off Donna. A local businessman was so angry that he was going to ask the county attorney to prosecute Jeffrey. "I went over and paid the checks," Donna recalled later. "I collected quite a few of them. We do quite a bit of business with people and we live here. Credit was extended to Jeffrey and Alice because of us and I felt morally responsible to not leave them hanging." Once merchants heard that Donna was paying Jeffrey's bad checks, they began calling her at home. The calls came every night. None of the checks that Jeffrey was writing was for more than thirty dollars. Most were for gasoline or milk or other groceries. But as quickly as Donna paid them, he wrote more. Within a month, she had depleted what little savings she and Ralph had. She decided to confront her son-in-law.

"Jeff, you got to stop doing this," she said. "This is the third time that I've gone around and gotten these checks for you and we can't afford to do it anymore."

He didn't respond.

"If you got many more floating around, you better make them good because the prosecutor comes down real hard on bad checks around here."

Jeffrey nodded, but didn't follow her advice. He wrote another bad check to his landlord. The Lundgrens had lived at the Wilcox farmhouse for nearly one year, yet had paid only two months' rent. Wilcox started eviction procedures. Once again, Jeffrey and Alice and their children were forced to move in with Ralph and Donna.

Wilcox had felt bad when he decided to evict the Lundgrens, but when he visited the farmhouse after they were gone, whatever sympathy he had for the family vanished. The first thing that he noticed was that Jeffrey had broken into the garage where Wilcox had stored his personal belongings. Jeffrey had taken several items and had been using them inside the house. As soon as Wilcox stepped through the back door of his house, Wilcox's heart sank. "The place was a wreck. It looked like a tornado had sucked up everything and thrown it around." He suddenly smelled a pungent odor coming from the basement. Wilcox walked downstairs and nearly gagged. For some reason, Jeffrey had used a saw to cut through the pipe that drained the toilet. "There was toilet paper, feces, urine, everything—dropped directly down onto the basement floor just like in an outhouse," Wilcox recalled. "There was a pile of human waste at least one foot deep and six feet in diameter." Covering

his mouth, Wilcox hurried back up to the kitchen. How could someone live with such filth in the basement? he wondered. And why
would Jeffrey have done such a thing? Why would someone want a
pile of feces in the basement?

Wilcox went through the entire house looking for damage.
There was plenty. Holes had been knocked in the walls, carpets were
stained and filthy. When he reached the master bedroom upstairs,
Wilcox found something else that he thought was curious. Inside
one of the closets were stacks of pornographic magazines that Wilcox
later described as sadomasochism and bondage publications. Something tossed in the corner of the closet also caught his eye. Wilcox
reached down and picked it up, but as soon as he realized what it
was, he dropped it.

"It was a plastic dildo that was still caked with feces," Wilcox
said. "I mean it was caked with it. They hadn't washed it. They'd
just tossed it in there."

As he left the house, Wilcox couldn't help but wonder at the
contradiction Jeffrey posed. "He was radical in his religious beliefs.
He was intensely conservative and in one room of the house he had
left about every book you could think of about the RLDS religion.
He had rows and rows of them." Yet upstairs Wilcox had found the
opposite sort of literature. It was almost as if there were two different
Jeffrey Lundgrens, both extremes. One holy, one evil. "He just
wasn't operating from the same perspective that most people operate
from. I have never met a person who wanted to be liked more than
Jeffrey. He wanted to be liked, he wanted to be admired, yet he
didn't want to do anything to earn you liking him. At the same
time, I also never knew anyone who thought so much of himself. It
wasn't arrogance; it was intense self-importance. He simply looked
upon himself as someone who was unique, you know, special, and
he felt people needed to treat him special."

On August 6, Jeffrey came home from work and announced that
he had quit his job at the hospital. He had not said anything that
morning about quitting. He didn't have another job lined up. Alice
was dumbfounded. She was six months pregnant, they hadn't found
another house to rent, Jeffrey still owed local merchants for bad
checks.

"Why did you do it?" she asked. "What's wrong?"

"I can make more money in Independence," Jeffrey replied.
"Besides, they don't appreciate me at the hospital."

Jeffrey would not say anything more.

Years later, Bernie Wilson would recall why Jeffrey had resigned. That morning, a hospital employee had walked into an office
and caught Jeffrey and his girlfriend embracing. "Jeffrey denied that
he was having an affair, but he had been caught fondling this
woman's breasts and there was little doubt in my mind what they
were up to," Wilson said. "I didn't give him much choice but to
quit."

Jeffrey left for Independence the morning after he resigned. He
moved into an apartment with his brother, Corry, and told Alice
that he would send money whenever he could. During the four-
month period that Jeffrey was gone, he mailed her a total of five
dollars, Alice later said. In December, Alice went into labor and
was taken to Lake of the Ozarks Hospital. Jeffrey drove down from
Independence but was clearly uncomfortable at the hospital. Alice
still didn't know the truth about why he had resigned. Jeffrey spent
the night sleeping in the car in the parking lot rather than in the
lobby. The next morning, Alice gave birth to a boy.

"I was so terrified that the drugs I'd taken after my spleen was
removed had harmed my baby, but the doctor said, 'Alice, he's got
all of his fingers and toes.' And I was so happy that I started crying.
You see, I had wondered why God had spared my life when my
spleen ruptured. I should have died. My life was so miserable but He
spared me so that I could give birth. I looked over at Jeffrey because
I wanted to tell him and share it with him and I reached for his
hand and he knocked it away. He was crying and I said, 'What's
wrong? The baby's okay! He's okay!,' and Jeffrey glared at me and
he said, 'HE!,' and I said, 'Yes, honey, it's a boy,' and Jeffrey said,
'Alice, I wanted a girl! Can't you do anything right?,' and he turned
around and he walked out. He left me there with my son and just
walked out."

Alice named the boy Caleb, after Caleb the son of Jephunneh,
mentioned in the Old Testament book of Numbers. "I named him
by myself. I chose the name Caleb because Caleb in the Bible hadn't
been scared off by adversity and run away from things. He had also
told the truth when everyone else lied."

The day after Caleb was born, Alice mentioned to the doctor
that she wanted to have a tubal ligation. She didn't want any more
children.

"I don't think we can do that," the doctor replied.

Alice asked why. She was certain that her insurance would
cover the cost.

"What insurance?" the doctor asked.

"I thought that our insurance had covered all of my medical bills," Alice later explained, "because Jeffrey had been covered by the hospital's employee policy and he had told me that we were still covered by it even though he had quit. What I found out was that Jeffrey had taken me and the kids off the policy months earlier and had been pocketing the extra cash that he saved. We owed the hospital thousands and thousands of dollars from my spleen surgery and they weren't going to do anything else for us until they were paid."

When Donna came to visit her daughter and new grandson later that day, she found Alice in tears.

"Mama," Alice blurted out. "I married Jeffrey for better or worse, but it just keeps getting worse and worse and worse."

CHAPTER NINE

Even though Jeffrey was spending his weekdays in Independence searching for work, he would come to the Keehlers' on weekends, and late at night, he and Alice would explore what Jeffrey liked to describe as their "secret world."

"My mother had a sunken bathtub in the bathroom that we used and that is where most of this stuff with feces and urine took place," Alice later said.

During one visit, Alice mentioned that her parents were going to be gone during the upcoming weekend. She and Jeffrey, along with their children, would have the Keehler house to themselves. Jeffrey arrived home earlier than usual the next Friday and was impatient with the kids. As soon as Alice got them to bed, he hurried her into the bedroom. "Jeffrey told me to strip and I did, and then he told me to lie down on the bed. He had bought some rope and he had already cut it into four pieces that he used to tie me onto the bed. He told me that he wanted to see what it was like, you know, bondage. I went along with it because it didn't seem like such a big thing."

They had sex, and when it was over, Alice asked Jeffrey to untie her. He refused. "I began to panic and I said, 'Jeffrey, untie me,' and he said, 'Then it wouldn't be any fun.'" Alice would later claim that during the night, Jeffrey had sexual intercourse with her numerous times. The entire time, she was tied in various positions on the bed. In the morning, she told him that she needed to use the bathroom. He untied her legs but tied her hands together after freeing them from the bed. He led her into the bathroom and then he climbed into the sunken bathtub. "He ordered me to urinate on him and I did," she said. "Then we went back into the bedroom and he tied me back up." Alice later told a friend that Jeffrey had kept her tied to the bed all day Saturday and most of Sunday. He only released her a few hours before her parents came home. "He told the kids that I was sick and couldn't be disturbed so they stayed out of the room."

Although she later said that she did not enjoy the experience, she candidly acknowledged that she had not complained to Jeffrey at the time. "I wanted to please him. I wanted to make him happy. I kept thinking, 'Well, at least we are spending time together. At least he is not with some other woman.'"

Jeffrey found work at a hospital in Kansas City and he moved Alice and the kids up to live with him. But he only kept the job for a few weeks before quitting without explanation. He and Alice were broke as usual. When their landlord knocked on the door in late February 1981 demanding rent, Alice begged for more time. With tears running down her cheeks, she showed him her baby and her three other children and explained how Jeffrey was doing odd jobs to earn enough to feed them. He felt sorry for her and agreed to wait. Jeffrey, meanwhile, began writing bad checks.

One afternoon Alice received a telephone call. It was Jeffrey. He had been arrested by police for passing bad checks. Alice telephoned Donna for help. Jeffrey needed $300 in cash for bail.

"Honey, we just don't got it," Donna replied. Ralph suggested that they leave Jeffrey in jail, but Donna disagreed. She offered to put up their house as collateral.

Alice paused. "No, Mama, I can't let you do it. I'm afraid Jeffrey won't pay it back."

Donna sent her son, Charles, in her car to Independence to pick up Alice. She also telephoned Ralph's sister—the same woman who had worked at Drumm Farm as a cook and had helped them before when they needed cash. The aunt gave Alice a $300 check.

"Don't make it out to Jeffrey," Alice warned. "If I take it to our bank to cash it, they'll simply confiscate the money to pay for other bad checks."

The woman made the check out to Ralph. Alice and Charles drove to Macks Creek to get Ralph's signature and cash it. En route, Alice began to pray. "I reached the bottom, the absolute bottom. I had been married to this man for eleven years and we had nothing to show for it, absolutely nothing. I had always dreamed about having a house with a white picket fence and a nice family. But now I was thrilled just to have enough money to buy milk for the children. What had gone wrong? I remember Charles had fallen asleep in the front seat while I was driving and it was raining and I just started talking to God. 'What am I supposed to do?' I said. 'I'm married to this man for life. He lies to me. He can't keep a job. He cheats on me. Why, God, are You doing this to me?'"

As she drove toward Macks Creek, Alice remembered the summer of 1969 when the patriarch had said that she would marry a companion who would do great things for the church. "I began to think that maybe God had a purpose for doing this, but I just didn't see it."

A few days after Jeffrey was bailed out of jail, he got a job at one of Independence's oldest hospitals, St. Mary's, a 365-bed institution operated by the Roman Catholic Church. He worked as a biomedical technician and was paid $32,000 per year, the most money he had ever earned. Under pressure from Donna, Jeffrey used most of his first paychecks to clear up the bad checks that he had written in Macks Creek. In return, the charges against him were suspended and later expunged from his record.

For the first time in their lives as a couple, Jeffrey and Alice had enough cash to pay the rent, buy groceries, and still have a few dollars left over. Jeffrey began buying rifles. "I want to have a better gun collection than my father," he told Alice. She began buying antiques. "I want to have a better collection than your mother's," she told Jeffrey.

In the fall of 1981, Alice found a beautiful two-story stone house to rent located directly across from the Independence Medical Center on East Twenty-third Street. The rent was $400 per month.

Now that they had the money, Jeffrey and Alice began entertaining. Alice telephoned Dennis and Tonya Patrick, whom they hadn't seen since all of them worked at Drumm Farm. Dennis was now a manager at Bendix Corporation and Tonya had given birth to a daughter, Molly. They had just bought a new house in Independence and were attending the Slover Park congregation. Dennis had risen to the rank of elder in the church, which meant that several nights each week he called on other saints. The Patricks and Lundgrens had a good time when they got together. But Tonya told Dennis later that she felt Jeffrey and Alice had changed. Jeffrey's sexual jokes had made her feel uncomfortable.

"Oh, that's just Jeff," Dennis replied. "He's always been that way, saying things."

"No, Dennis," Tonya said. "This time it was different." In the past, she explained, Jeffrey had always tried to be funny. But this time she felt his innuendos were serious. "I think if I would have shown an interest, he would have jumped at the chance."

One day in autumn of 1982, Alice was outside the rental house raking leaves when an elder from the Slover Park congregation pulled his car to the curb and stepped out to speak with her. He told Alice that an adult Sunday school class at the church was going to begin a new series about the Book of Mormon on Sunday and he invited her to attend. When Alice mentioned the invitation later that night to Jeffrey, he became irritated.

"Why'd you even talk to him?" he asked. "You're my wife. Men shouldn't be walking up and talking to you in the front yard like that."

Jeffrey told Alice to forget about going to church, but Sunday morning, he awoke early. "I sat upright in bed for no reason," he recalled, "and I woke Alice up and told her to get the kids ready for church. She was shocked and so was I, but for some reason I had decided to go—no—it was more than that, I felt *compelled* to go."

The Book of Mormon class was being taught by Raymond C. Treat, a tall, lean man in his early forties, who had dedicated his life to proving that the Book of Mormon was an accurate historical account of early life in the New World. Treat had grown up in Wisconsin, where his parents owned a profitable cranberry marsh. They were not Mormons and neither was he, but in 1959, an employee at the marsh gave Treat a copy of the Book of Mormon and he was mesmerized. He converted to the RLDS and in 1961 married Mary Lee, whom he had met at church. She was fascinated by anthropology and together they decided to pinpoint where the ancient Nephites and Lamanites mentioned in the book had actually lived. Their studies took them to Mexico, and after months of work and study, they decided that the early Hebrews had settled in Mesoamerica, an area extending from central Mexico to Honduras and Nicaragua in which diverse pre-Columbian civilizations once flourished. Treat eventually inherited his family's lucrative cranberry marsh, but he felt moved by God in 1975 to sell it. He used the proceeds to establish the Zarahemla Research Foundation, a nonprofit operation dedicated to investigating the archaeological aspects of the Book of Mormon. The Treats chose the name Zarahemla because that was what the Nephites and Lamanites called their homeland. The foundation operated out of a nondescript brick building in downtown Independence and had two employees—Ray and Mary Lee. They lived on a shoestring budget, made trips to archaeological sites in Mesoamerica, and published their findings in their own newsletter called *The Zarahemla Record*.

Jeffrey and Alice had found Treat's slide presentation about Maya ruins fascinating but it was a comment that Treat made about how the Book of Mormon had been written that made Jeffrey snap to attention. "Everything in this book," Treat said, lifting up his well-worn copy, "every word is there for a reason. God had some reason for including it."

"It was like Ray Treat had put a key into my heart and turned it on full speed," Lundgren recalled. "I began to ask myself, 'Why is this story here? Why is this word used here? Why did God use this particular phrase? What is He really trying to tell us?' I began to look at the scriptures in an entirely different way. Each one was a clue left by God. Memorizing a scripture wasn't enough. You needed to examine each individual word and discover its meaning. When you did that you could actually see God's thought process. From that point on, no one could keep me away from church. I had to know more."

Jeffrey decided to make another try at joining the priesthood. Only this time around, he decided to lay the necessary groundwork so he wouldn't be rejected. "I volunteered to play the piano on Wednesday nights before the evening service. Every Sunday, I made certain that my family was in Sunday School and church. Churches are always looking for someone to volunteer and I was that person. I did all the jobs nobody wanted." Jeffrey also clued in Alice and together they used Dennis and Tonya to make contacts at Slover Park.

"Jeff and Alice were anxious to get prestige," Tonya later recalled. "They didn't have it, they wanted it. . . . They were constantly pushing us to introduce them to important people and then they would either latch onto them or try to."

Jeffrey's plan worked. Two elders told him privately that they were going to recommend that he be "called" into the priesthood. "I was actually amazed at how easy it was really," said Jeffrey. "I discovered that it really doesn't take much effort to take charge in a church and what really was shocking was how easily people were led. Most people didn't even read the scriptures. They had no idea what was in them." Alice agreed. Jeffrey could have hidden a *Reader's Digest* in his Book of Mormon and read from it and most people at Slover Park wouldn't have known the difference, she said.

While things were going well at church, Jeffrey was in trouble again at work. He had been given access to a company car because he was frequently required to drive between the main hospital and a satellite hospital in an adjoining community. One weekend in December 1982, Jeffrey was seen driving the company car when he clearly wasn't at work. Jeffrey's boss, Henry Thomas, asked him if he had been using the car for personal trips. Jeffrey said that he hadn't, but a few days later Thomas found out otherwise. "I called Jeffrey into my office again and I told him straight to his face that he had lied to me," Thomas later said. "He got all red and huffy. I wrote a disciplinary report about the incident and I told him that the next time he took that car and used it on his personal business and then lied about it, I was going to fire him. I came down hard and I figured that threatening him with termination would make him straighten out." It didn't.

Two days later, Thomas caught Jeffrey using the car to run personal errands. He fired him. It was three weeks before Christmas and Jeffrey was out of work. Alice called Dennis and Tonya. What was she going to do? she asked. She and Jeffrey didn't have any money to buy their children presents. Dennis and Tonya offered to help. Tonya took Alice shopping and spent $400 which was charged to the Patricks' credit cards.

"I didn't mind helping at first," Dennis remembered, "but Jeffrey started stopping by all the time and he'd be broke and he'd need gas money and he'd just sort of sit there until I gave him ten or twenty dollars. It was like he just expected it."

Three months after Jeffrey was fired from St. Mary's Hospital, his former boss received a telephone call from the personnel director of a company in Independence that sold equipment to hospitals.

"I'm thinking about hiring Jeffrey Lundgren," he explained.

"Oh, my God!" Thomas recalled saying. "I sure as hell wouldn't do that if I were you."

The director asked why, but Thomas was prohibited by hospital privacy regulations from telling him.

"Well," the director said, "I've interviewed him and I think he could help us and I'd like to help him. He's got a wife and kids and he is really active in his church."

"Let me give you some advice if you do," Thomas replied. "Hide the company credit cards, don't let him have a company car, and watch his expense accounts or it will come back to haunt you."

Despite the warning, the director hired Jeffrey as a salesman in April 1983 and issued him a company credit card and automobile. Both were to be used only for business purposes. Within a few weeks, Jeffrey was asked to resign because of questions over the charge card and car expenses. It was the last paying job that Jeffrey ever held.

CHAPTER TEN

WITHIN the RLDS Church, Dr. James H. Robbins was held in reverent esteem. A gentle, soft-spoken man in his early forties, Jim Robbins had converted to Mormonism in 1965 and had moved to Independence a short time later to help build Zion. By 1978, he had developed a lucrative medical practice and was regarded as one of the city's most successful podiatrists. But just as he reached the peak of his profession, Jim began to feel guilty. "I felt that God was advising me to give it up," he later told his fellow saints. "Money and status should not be the most important goals in life." For six months, Jim prayed, and then one evening he was visited by two church elders. Jim asked them to anoint his head with oil and pray for him by a "laying on of hands"—touching him on the head with their hands. While they were praying, one of the men said that he felt led by the spirit to tell Jim that God was "opening a door" for him and that he should not be afraid to go through it. After they finished praying, one of the men turned to Jim. "Are you thinking about selling your practice?" the elder asked.

"I was taken back by that question," Jim recalled, "and I said, 'Why yes.' And he said, 'I thought so, that came to me while I was praying for you.'"

Jim considered that incident a divine revelation. He felt God was instructing him to sell his medical practice. So he did just that. He stopped performing lucrative foot surgery, opened an office in his house, and began providing medical care to the elderly and poor, frequently without charge.

In the spring of 1982, at about the same time that Jeffrey was starting to work at his short-lived job as a biomedical equipment salesman, Jim was about to join two other devout Mormon families in what the church calls a "living in common endeavor." It was a concept that dated back in the Mormon Church to Sidney Rigdon's early teachings at Kirtland. Rigdon believed that the first Christians mentioned in the New Testament had lived communally and he encouraged his followers to do the same. One group established a commune outside Kirtland in 1830, but within a year they began quarreling over possessions. "What belonged to one brother, belonged to any of the brethren; therefore we would take each other's clothes and property and use it without leave," a member wrote in his diary. When Joseph Smith, Jr., moved to Kirtland, he disbanded the commune. Over time, numerous other devout Mormons had organized similar communes but few lasted.

"I was interested in a 'sharing all things in common' living arrangement," Jim later explained, "because I felt that God wants every man, woman, and child to live for one another, not simply to accumulate as much as they can for themselves." In October 1982, Jim and his wife, Laura, and their children were about to move into a commune when Jim suddenly became ill. Doctors found that he had stomach cancer. He was forced to back out of the commune but the other two families went ahead and combined their assets. Jim, meanwhile, was readied for surgery. As he prayed one night, Jim felt a "calmness" come over him.

"The peace of God settled upon me to a degree that I had never experienced before in my life. If you try to use logic, it will not make sense, but it was real and I found myself carrying on a two-way conversation with the Lord. I didn't hear voices or anything like that. What happened was that whenever I thought of a question in my mind, the answer would suddenly come to me. What he told me was that He was prepared to heal me when I first got cancer but that the unbelief of the saints was so monumental that if I had stood up and announced in church that the Lord had cured me of cancer, no one would have believed me. So what He said was that He had decided to go ahead and let me be stricken with cancer. That way, everyone would know that

I had it. He then told me that I could go ahead and have surgery, but not anything else. 'I will take care of you,' He said. God didn't tell me how long I would live and He didn't tell me that He was curing me. He simply said that He would take care of me."

Jim underwent surgery and had a large section of his stomach removed, but his doctors were not able to remove all of the cancer before it spread into his lymphatic system. His surgeon told Jim that he would have to undergo immediate chemotherapy. Jim refused and, despite the doctor's protests, returned home without undergoing any additional treatment.

Two months after his surgery, Jim and Laura Robbins were randomly paired with Jeffrey and Alice at a weekend church retreat for married couples. The two couples were supposed to spend most of the weekend together as part of the program. Jeffrey recognized Jim. By that time, Jim had already shared his "personal testimony" about his cancer operation with several congregations and his moving story was becoming well known in Independence. Some saints suspected Jim would soon die from cancer, but others believed that God was using Jim and his faith to inspire other saints. Regardless, Jim Robbins was a genuine celebrity and Jeffrey and Alice were eager to get to know him and Laura.

At first, Jim didn't like Jeffrey. He thought he was arrogant and pushy. But he was impressed by Jeffrey's ability to recall scriptures. After the weekend retreat, the two couples began socializing. They would get together in each other's homes for what Jeffrey and Jim called "scripture shootouts." Jim would cite a scripture and Jeffrey would counter with a scripture that seemed to either say the same thing or contradict it. Then the two men would continue citing verses until one of them ran dry.

"Jeffrey didn't enjoy light conversation, but he was captivated by the Book of Mormon and digging for hidden or deeper meanings in the scriptures," Jim said. "I was in the priesthood and he wasn't yet ordained but it soon became apparent that he was far more brilliant than I when it came to knowing verses."

In February 1983, two months after meeting the Lundgrens, Jim and Laura told Jeffrey and Alice that they wanted to help support them. "We knew Jeffrey was out of work and they were hard up so we decided to give them two hundred dollars a week," Jim said. In a moment that he would later have difficulty explaining, Jim also announced that if the Lundgrens were interested, he and Laura

would like to combine their two families into an "all things in common relationship." Jeffrey and Alice quickly agreed.

"As soon as I brought up the subject, I knew in my heart that
I was making a mistake," Jim recalled years later. "In looking back
on it, my only explanation is that I think I felt guilty. You see, we
had originally planned to join with these two other couples before I
was diagnosed as having cancer. They had gone ahead and had disbanded after about a year. I think asking the Lundgrens to form an
'all things in common relationship' was sort of like marrying on the
rebound after a divorce."

The day after he first mentioned communal living to Jeffrey and
Alice, Jim returned to their house and added a caveat. He and Laura
would participate only if they didn't have to go into debt.

What Jim and Laura didn't know was that Jeffrey and Alice
were being supported by other church members as well. Along with
the $200 that the Robbinses were giving them each week, the Lund-
grens were receiving periodic donations from two other families, and
the church was paying their rent and utilities from a special fund set
aside for poor Mormons. Jeffrey and Alice were also calling on
Donna and Ralph when they needed cash and were still borrowing
small sums from Dennis and Tonya.

Sonny and Louise Stone, the Lundgrens' friends from their navy
days, moved to Independence at about this time and Louise was
shocked when she saw how Alice and Jeffrey were living. "I met
Alice one afternoon and we went shopping. She told me that Jeffrey
was unable to find a job and that she didn't know how they were
going to feed the kids that night. She literally didn't have any food
in the house. All the time that we were gone, she was fussing about
how they were broke. When we got back to her house, we walked
up the steps and their front porch was covered with groceries. I
mean, bags and bags of food."

"Help me carry these inside," Alice told Louise.

"Alice, where did all this come from? Who left it here?" Louise
asked.

"Oh, I don't know. Jeffrey told me that he was going to pray
about getting us enough to eat and he prayed last night about it."

"What?" Louise asked incredulously.

Alice became irritated. "Louise," she lectured, "I don't question
God and neither should you."

"I told Alice that it wasn't right for her and Jeffrey to live off
other people," Louise remembered. "I asked her why Jeffrey didn't

go get a job like everyone else. She told me that Jeff had things to do for God and therefore he wasn't required to work like everyone else. Other people were supposed to take care of him. That was their job. His was to serve God."

Once the Lundgrens became friends with the Robbinses, they no longer had as much time for Dennis and Tonya or Sonny and Louise. Jeffrey, in particular, didn't want to bother studying scriptures with Dennis. "He can't keep up with me," Jeffrey complained to Alice. "He's just not as sharp as Jim."

There was one passage of scriptures in particular that Jeffrey and Jim were trying to decipher. It was recorded in the Doctrine and Covenants, a Mormon book that contained all of Joseph Smith, Jr.'s revelations from God, as well as those given by God to Smith's successors. This particular revelation was identified as "Section 76." [The book listed revelations in numerical order but used the word "section" rather than "number" to identify them.] According to it, Joseph Smith, Jr., and Sidney Rigdon had been meditating on February 16, 1832, when they were shown a revelation and a vision. What the two men saw was eternity and it was quite different from the simple heaven and hell concept that most other religions described. There were actually three different levels in heaven, Smith later explained. These included the Celestial [highest], the Terrestrial [middle], and Telestial [lowest]. Only the most devout saints could make it to the Celestial where God himself dwelt. Section 76 described in detail what kind of person would be assigned to each level. In the final sentences of the passage, the revelation also said that God had permitted Smith and Rigdon to see other "great and marvelous . . . works." But He told them that they couldn't reveal what they had seen.

> "For they are only to be seen and understood by the power
> of the Holy Spirit, which God bestows on those who love him
> and purify themselves before him; to whom he grants this privilege of seeing and knowing for themselves."

Jeffrey and Jim wanted to know what "great and marvelous" mysteries the two men had seen but had been forbidden to describe? So they came up with a plan. If God had appeared to Smith and Rigdon in Kirtland, Ohio, then Jeffrey and Jim would drive to Kirtland and ask God to show them what He had shown Smith and Rigdon.

They made plans to leave with their wives in March. Jeffrey had never seen the Kirtland temple but he had read about its history. He knew that after Joseph Smith, Jr., and Rigdon had fled Kirtland because of the Mormon bank failure, the temple had been abandoned and had fallen into disrepair. At one point, a Gentile farmer had used it as a sheep shed. After Smith was murdered in 1844, the Mormons in Utah and those in Independence both claimed ownership of the church. But in February 1880, a county judge ruled that it belonged to the RLDS. Since then, the RLDS had restored the temple and opened it for tours.

The Robbinses and Lundgrens drove to Kirtland in an old station wagon that the Lundgrens had been given. They stayed in the home of a local church official who knew the Robbinses. Jeffrey and Jim had gotten permission to pray inside the temple after it was closed to tourists. About an hour before it was time for them to go inside, Jeffrey became fidgety.

"What's bothering you, Jeffrey?" Alice asked, but he didn't reply. Jim and Laura Robbins noticed that Jeffrey was acting strangely.

The two men had been told that they would have thirty minutes to pray in the temple before they would have to leave. They quickly hurried inside and sat on one of the wooden pews in the front. All of a sudden, Jim realized that he didn't have any idea what to do next.

"I guess we should pray," he finally said. Jeffrey nodded, so Jim knelt down and asked God if He would show them the hidden mysteries described in Section 76.

Nothing happened.

Jim returned to his seat, feeling rather foolish. "It was obvious to me that we were in no condition spiritually to have such a marvelous experience as Smith and Rigdon had had."

Jeffrey stood up and began to pray out loud, but rather than asking God to show him a vision, Jeffrey asked God to heal Jim of his stomach cancer. As Jim listened, Jeffrey became so emotional that he could hardly speak. He began to weep.

"I was touched by what he said, that he would ask God to cure me, and I was touched by his show of emotion because I had never seen that before in Jeffrey," Jim later recalled, "but I told Jeffrey as we were leaving the church that I didn't expect God to heal me. God had promised before my operation to take care of me and I trusted Him to do that. He never said that He'd cure me of cancer."

When Jeffrey later told his followers about his prayer and experience with Jim Robbins at the Kirtland temple in March 1983, he would claim that Jim collapsed as soon as he stepped outside the building. Jim would remember what happened a bit differently. According to Jim and Laura, the two couples rode to a nearby restaurant for dinner and while they were eating, Jim began to shake and became faint. He had recently had a bad viral infection and he thought that he was suffering a relapse. By the time Laura had paid the restaurant bill, Jim was shaking uncontrollably with chills. Jeffrey helped him crawl into the back of the station wagon and they left immediately for Independence.

"I think we should get him to a hospital," Alice said after they had ridden on the highway for about an hour. Jim entire body was shaking. Laura didn't know what to do, but Jeffrey was calm.

"He is going to be fine," he said. "He didn't get sick in a day and he's not going to be cured in a day."

Alice glanced over at Laura. Neither one of them knew what Jeffrey was talking about. They stopped for the night at a motel in Richmond, Indiana. The next morning, Jim still felt ill. When they reached Independence, Jeffrey helped Laura put Jim in bed. The next morning, Jim said he felt fine when Jeffrey came to see him. Jim was certain he had been suffering from a virus. Jeffrey wasn't.

"Jim, I want you to know what happened," Jeffrey said. "The reason that I was so nervous before we went into the temple was because God had spoken to me. He said that I had a choice. I could see the vision—the same one that Joseph Smith and Sidney Rigdon had seen—or I could choose to have you healed of your cancer." Jeffrey paused. "The reason why I was so upset was because I actually had to think about it before I told God to heal you. I felt terrible. That's when I realized that I had come to the temple for the wrong reasons. I had come because I was selfish. That's why I prayed in the temple for God to cure you."

Jim didn't know what to say.

"You see," Jeffrey continued, "that's why you were sick after we left the temple. God was healing you. He was healing you of cancer because I had made the right choice. I've come over here today to tell you that you are completely healed. The cancer is gone."

After a few moments, Jim spoke. He had chosen his words carefully. "Jeffrey, I appreciate what you are saying, but I don't have that same testimony. All I know is that God promised to take care of me. I don't know that I'm healed."

"Well, I'm telling you that you are healed," Jeffrey replied.

"You are healed because I chose that rather than to see the vision."

On Sunday when the Robbinses went to church, a woman hurried up to them. "Isn't it wonderful!" she exclaimed. Jim looked confused. "I'm talking about how Jeffrey Lundgren prayed for God to heal you and He did! Jeffrey told us all about it this morning. It's a miracle."

Jim Robbins wasn't so sure.

CHAPTER ELEVEN

T HE friendship between the Robbinses and Lundgrens became strained after their trip to Kirtland for reasons besides Jeffrey's claims that his prayers had healed Jim. Jeffrey and Alice had found a piece of land in Independence that they felt would be ideal for a "communal" duplex. They could live on one side and the Robbinses could live on the other. Jeffrey estimated that it would cost about $60,000 to buy the land and build a duplex. That sounded reasonable to Jeff and Alice, but Jim and Laura balked. Jeffrey was still unemployed and, Jim suspected, wasn't really looking for a job. If the Robbinses sold their home, they still would have to borrow at least $10,000 to cover all the construction costs. "I'm wondering if the hand of God isn't protecting us," Jim told Laura one afternoon. "Maybe He doesn't want us to move in with Jeffrey and Alice." Later that day, Jim reminded Jeffrey of the caveat in their deal. "I'm not going to do this if we have to go into debt," he said. Jeffrey scrapped the duplex plans.

It was income-tax time, and when Laura began going over her records, she discovered that she and Jim had given the Lundgrens more than $2,000. She also realized that they weren't going to be able to continue supporting the Lundgrens and keep up their financial pledge to the church.

"We can't keep doing both," she told Jim. "One of us has to tell Jeff and Alice, and soon."

That night when the Lundgrens came over to visit, Laura kept waiting for Jim to tell them, but the closest he came was asking Jeffrey if he'd had any luck finding work. He hadn't. The next Sunday, Laura cornered Alice at church.

"Is Jeff really looking for a job?" she asked.

"Why?" Alice replied, coldly.

"Because we just don't have the money to keep supporting you," Laura blurted out.

Badly embarrassed, Alice hurried to find Jeffrey. Laura thought she had better warn Jim, who had stayed home that morning. She got there too late. Jeffrey had beat her home. He had pounded on the Robbinses' door and had come right to the point when Jim answered.

"Your wife told my wife that you don't want to continue your relationship with us," Jeffrey huffed.

"What are you talking about, Jeffrey?" Jim asked.

"Your wife informed my wife that you can't help us any longer financially."

"That's right, Jeff," Jim said solemnly. "We just can't afford it. It's too much of a burden right now."

"What kind of an excuse is that?" Jeffrey demanded. "I expect you to keep your commitments to me."

Jim got mad. "Jeff, you are the most ungrateful person I've ever known. How can you stand there and carry on like this because now I'm telling you we can't afford it anymore? You act like we owe you this money."

Jeffrey spun around and walked away.

The next Sunday at church, the Lundgrens and Robbinses avoided each other.

In early October 1983, Jeffrey was ordained at Slover Park into the RLDS priesthood. He had been out of work for more than one year, but the elders in the church didn't hold that against him. Jeffrey asked his father to perform the ordination ceremony. Dennis Patrick, whom he had befriended again, assisted. Now that Jeffrey was in the priesthood, he could preach on Sundays. Years later, regular members would still recall his first sermon. He didn't speak from a prepared text. Instead, he read a series of scriptures. Every one of the verses was about God's wrath and how he would destroy the wicked.

Jim and Laura were in the congregation. Neither had ever heard such a scathing denunciation, but Jim wasn't surprised. "During our scriptural studies, Jeffrey always focused on scriptures that would enable him to mentally put people he didn't like into the lake of fire and brimstone. He would say, 'See this scripture? Why, God could be talking about so-and-so. He could be calling that person a Son of Perdition [evil].' And I'd say, 'Why, Jeff, you don't know what you are talking about. That person is not a Son of Perdition. It's like you are finding pleasure in condemning people. The Lord wants to save lives, not destroy them by casting them into the pit.' But he always argued with me. 'So-and-so fits all the criteria of that scripture,' he'd say. 'They should be destroyed.'"

So many members complained about Jeffrey's discourse that the church sent an elder to talk to Jeffrey. "Our God is a God of love, not damnation," he told Jeffrey.

"I reminded the pastor that all I had done was read scriptures," Jeffrey later recalled, "and I asked him if he was telling me that a member of the priesthood shouldn't be allowed to read scripture in church."

The pastor didn't argue. Jeffrey was not asked to preach again.

A few days later, on Halloween night, Damon Lundgren tripped while running across a parking lot after a youth group meeting at the church. By the time an adult reached the thirteen-year-old, he was holding his rib cage in obvious pain. They hurried him home.

"I think you should get Damon to the hospital," the church's youth group sponsor told Jeffrey.

"We don't have any insurance," Jeffrey replied. "He'll be okay." He yelled at Damon to get out of the car, but the sponsor interrupted.

"The church will pay for it. This kid is in pain."

"Well, I can't take him because I'm here alone with the other kids," Jeffrey replied. The sponsor offered to stay with them so that Jeffrey could take Damon across the street to the emergency room at the Independence Medical Center.

"I don't like leaving my children with strangers," Jeffrey replied.

Exasperated, the sponsor decided to admit Damon into the emergency room by himself. Jeffrey went along to sign the necessary hospital paperwork and then hurried back home and telephoned Alice, who was visiting Tonya. Alice asked Dennis if he would come to the hospital and pray for Damon. He anointed Damon's head with oil and asked God to comfort him. A short while later, doctors told Alice that Damon had broken a rib, which, in turn, had punctured his liver. They were going to operate to stop the internal bleeding. Dennis went across the street to fetch Jeffrey. Jeff had telephoned Don and Lois and once they arrived, he and Don went to the hospital, leaving Lois with the children. As soon as Damon saw his grandpa, he smiled. Damon had always been Don's favorite. When Damon was little, Don used to squeeze his leg and count. Damon would see how long he could take the pain before he yelled. They called it the "pain game."

"I think I made a ten on the pain scale, Grandpa," Damon said.

"I think you did too, honey," Don replied. Jeffrey noticed that there were tears in his father's eyes. He was surprised and jealous.

The surgery went well, and after it was completed, Jeffrey went home and Don and Lois left. Alice slept on a cot next to her son in the hospital. She had Jeffrey bring her clean clothes in the morning. She showered and ate there too. "I don't want to leave him," Alice told Jeffrey. "I know what it's like to be alone in a hospital after surgery." Alice's comment was a reference to when her spleen was removed following her confrontation with Jeffrey. He hadn't been there when she woke up after the operation.

Five days after Damon's surgery, Jeffrey told Alice that he wanted her to come home, if not to see him, then to spend some time with the other three children. She agreed, but when she walked across the street, she found that Jeffrey had already put the children to bed. He had grilled two steaks over charcoal and set the table for a romantic candlelight dinner. When they finished their vanilla ice cream dessert, Alice stood up to leave.

"I think I'll dash over to check on Damon," she said.

Jeffrey exploded. He grabbed her arm and pushed her against the dining-room wall.

"By God, woman, you belong in this house and this is where you are going to stay!" he yelled. "Now get in the bedroom."

Now it was Alice's turn to get angry.

"What's wrong, Jeff?" she asked mockingly. "Are you feeling neglected because you had to go five whole days without any sex?"

He threw her onto the floor. "He tore open my blouse and he raped me. He raped me on the floor and when he got done, he got up and took my bathrobe and threw it at me. I went into the bathroom and I sat on the floor and cried and cried and then I got into the tub and after about a half hour, he came in with a red rose that he had put into a vase and he put it next to me and he sat down next to the tub and he stroked my face and he told me that he loved me and he was glad that we were married. It was like we were two normal persons, like nothing had happened."

(When asked later about Alice's account, Jeffrey said that it was impossible for a husband to rape his wife since her purpose in life was to please him sexually.)

The next day, Alice telephoned Louise Stone. "Jeffrey raped me," she said. Alice decided to tell Louise everything, including how Jeffrey liked to smear his feces on her. "What am I going to do?" she asked.

Louise suggested a divorce and offered to help her find a lawyer. "I'll stand by you no matter what you want to do," she offered. Alice promised to think about it.

When Jeffrey got home later that day, he told Alice that he had to tell her something important. He began by reminding her of the summer in 1969 when the patriarch made his prophecy about Alice and her husband.

"Alice, on the night that Damon was taken to the hospital, I had a vision," he announced. Years later, he would repeat during an interview what he told Alice that night in October 1983. As he spoke, he became emotional and began to cry. It was, he explained, the most heartrending experience in his life.

"I had gone out onto the front porch of our house because I could see the emergency room from there and I was trying to see what was happening with Damon across the street. I began to pray but I didn't know what words to use. Suddenly words started coming into my mind and I began to pray for the son, but it wasn't Damon that these words were about, it was the son of God, Jesus Christ, and just as I started to say them, the hospital dissolved away and I was no longer in Independence. I was at Calvary and I was facing the cross. I was standing to the right of it. This was not like a movie. I was actually there. I was physically, totally, completely there, and I looked up at Christ and He was in total agony and I realized that there were plenty of people who could pray for my son, but no one had prayed for the son—Jesus Christ. All of the disciples had been upset about losing Him, but no one had prayed for Him. And I heard Him call out with a loud voice. He was calling for Elias and it was horrible. I could hear Him struggle and see His breath. He would struggle to raise Himself up to get a gasp of air and then His entire body would sag, and I wanted to take Him down and He looked at me and I could tell that He wanted me to take Him down, but I couldn't take Him down because I needed Him to die just as every other creature needed Him to die. We all helped crucify Him because we needed Him to die for our sins so I didn't help Him. I rejected Him. I had to say 'Crucify Him' just like everyone else because I needed that atonement. It was like I had put a nail in His hand. I looked at Him and I knew and He knew that I was rejecting Him. You see, I understand rejection. I understand what it is like to be rejected and He knew too. So I just walked up to the base of the cross and I began to weep and, I don't know how to explain this, but all of a sudden, all I can say is, I was looking out of Christ's eyes. I saw everything and I was aware that I was in His head and in His consciousness and I could see all things, all eternity, from the beginning of time to the present into the future. It was like a giant panorama, and then I felt His pure and total love and I understood that there was no anger in Him at all. Then I saw my own life and I realized that love was a foreign object to me, that I didn't understand love, especially love like Christ's. And then it was over. The scene dissolved back and I found myself staring at the hospital. I began to weep and the next thing that I knew, Dennis Patrick was walking up the steps to see if I was okay. He thought I was crying about Damon, but I was crying because I had been with Christ and felt His love and then been brought back to reality."

Alice told Jeffrey that she thought his vision was the most beautiful religious experience that she had ever heard anyone describe. "But what does it mean?" she asked.

"I'm not sure yet," he replied, "but God is preparing me for something. He is directing both of our lives."

Later that day, Louise telephoned Alice to learn whether or not she was going to divorce Jeffrey.

"I can't leave Jeffrey," Alice told her. "He told me about a vision that he had. He told me that he has work to do for God. He told me that if I left him, he wouldn't be able to do what God wanted."

"What are you talking about, Alice?" Louise asked.

"Louise, haven't you been listening to me? God told Jeff that He is preparing him for an important mission in the church. I can't leave him now. It's impossible."

CHAPTER TWELVE

THE pastor at Slover Park asked Dennis Patrick to teach an adult Sunday school class in the fall of 1983. Dennis asked Jeffrey to help. They were supposed to teach a course about Zion. Twenty adults attended the first session and Dennis was pleased. But the next Sunday he told Jeffrey that there was a problem. Dennis had been asked to coordinate a new training program for young church leaders. "I'm not going to have time to teach the class anymore," he told Jeffrey. "Would you mind taking over?"

Jeffrey was delighted. He saw God's hand at work. The next Sunday, he strolled into the classroom. "We are going to change this class into a study of the Book of Mormon," he announced. "I am going to be the teacher, you will be the students. I will teach, you will learn. If there is time for questions at the end, I will answer them. Otherwise, don't interrupt. I'm not here to debate." With that, Jeffrey opened his books and began his lecture.

His classes were immediately controversial. Nearly everything Jeffrey taught was based on fundamentalist RLDS doctrine, but those conservative beliefs were no longer in vogue. The fight between the liberals and the fundamentalists, which Jeffrey had first gotten involved in back in 1975 at the student union at CMSU was still going on, but the liberals were clearly winning. The reforms started in the late 1950s by RLDS president-prophet W. Wallace Smith had made it possible for his son and successor, Wallace B. Smith, to steer the RLDS even closer toward mainstream Protestantism. The idea that the RLDS was God's "only true church" was being deemphasized. Some liberals had even suggested that the Book of Mormon was a fictional "morality play," not holy scripture. Such talk infuriated fundamentalists, and in 1978, when Wallace B. Smith took charge, a group of conservative church members in Vancouver, Washington, voted to secede. They announced that their congregation was going to become a "restoration" RLDS church, which meant that its members were going to "restore" their church to the RLDS's original traditions. The new president-prophet responded by "silencing" the elders at Vancouver and by going to court to seize their church, a recreational building, and the congregation's $3,000 bank account. By the time Jeffrey began teaching the adult class at Slover Park, Wallace B. Smith had gone to court five times in Texas and Missouri to prevent fundamentalists from breaking away. Despite such efforts, the RLDS Church was clearly headed toward a split and most members expected the final break to occur when the church held its worldwide conference in April 1984 in Independence. That was when Wallace B. Smith was going to recommend that the church permit women to become priests.

Jeffrey's class soon became a refuge for fundamentalists, particularly those opposed to ordaining women. As far as Jeffrey was concerned, Wallace B. Smith was misguided and history was repeating itself. God had picked Joseph Smith, Jr., to restore the "only true church" on earth because the other denominations had been corrupted over time by men. Now Smith's church was heading down that same path. Such talk did not endear Jeffrey to the elders at Slover Park. But even though his views were in the minority, his class still drew about twenty loyal members so he was allowed to continue teaching. Georgia Milliren was an avid Jeffrey supporter. Like Jeffrey, Milliren had been raised in the Slover Park congregation, but she was six years older than he and didn't really know Jeffrey until she began attending his class. "Jeffrey was a dynamic teacher, a real challenger," she recalled. "He and Alice used to tell us that they wanted to stretch our thinking, and he really did."

Jeffrey peppered his lectures with dire predictions of God's coming wrath and destruction. He was so convincing that Milliren began tucking extra clothing into her children's backpacks just in case

Christ returned to earth while they were in school. The fact that Jeffrey was unemployed bothered Milliren. "But," she said, "you had to admire the fact that he spent so much time studying. No one knew scriptures like Jeffrey did. He knew them and he could interpret them and even if you didn't agree with him, you couldn't disprove him because everything he said, he backed up with scriptures."

Another fervent backer of Jeffrey's was Cheryl Avery. She and her husband, Dennis, were appalled with the liberalization of the church and privately suspected that Wallace B. Smith was being led astray by Satan. Cheryl thought Jeffrey was an extraordinary teacher, so much so that others in the class began to joke that Jeffrey had become Cheryl's "personal guru."

In April, the delegates at the RLDS worldwide conference did exactly what the fundamentalists feared and supported a "revelation" by Smith that allowed women to be ordained. Cheryl was devastated and Jeffrey became even more belligerent in his class toward Wallace B. Smith and the church hierarchy. That June, Jeffrey taught a lesson that simply pushed the Slover Park elders too far.

"God and Christ are the same entity," Jeffrey announced. "They are not separate and distinct personages as you have been taught by the church. If they were, then we have a very selfish God because that means He sent someone else to do His dirty work on earth and to die on the cross. It means that He let His own son die, rather than giving up His own life and saving His son's."

As several class members listened in horror, Jeffrey read scriptures from the Book of Mormon and Joseph Smith, Jr.'s inspired version of the Bible that suggested that God and Jesus Christ were the exact same being.

"God wasn't selfish," Jeffrey continued. "He didn't send His son to die on a cross. He came down Himself. He was on the cross. He was so loving that He created mankind knowing in advance that mankind would reject Him and later crucify Him."

Jeffrey's comments not only contradicted RLDS doctrine, they also raised questions about Joseph Smith, Jr.'s first vision. The saints had been taught that God and Jesus Christ had appeared as two separate individuals in front of Smith.

A woman in the class jumped to her feet. "Are you saying Joseph Smith was a liar? That he made up the story of his vision?" she asked.

Jeffrey tried to explain that he had discovered at least four different accounts in church archives of Smith's first vision and each was substantially different from the others. But the woman refused to listen.

"You're not preaching God's word," she yelled. "You're preaching the devil's."

Georgia Milliren would later recall the trouble that Jeffrey's lesson sparked. "I remember when he said that God and Jesus were one—it simply blew me away. . . . It was very troubling to me and others in the class." The elders in the church told Jeffrey that he was through teaching. His class was discontinued.

As he had done when in college, Jeffrey reacted by inviting Georgia, Dennis and Tonya Patrick, Dennis and Cheryl Avery, and about six other couples to his house on Sunday afternoons for scripture classes of his own. He was not going to let anyone tell him what to preach. About fifteen people showed up. Like the Averys, most were unhappy with the RLDS.

Shortly after Jeffrey's class was disbanded at the church, he had another vision. "I was in a room and there was a table in it that was filled with great riches and I was told to make a choice. I could take the riches and live a normal life or I could choose to go down a path and worship God. I told the Lord that I wanted to walk down that path and serve him. I rejected the world's riches.

"The wealth suddenly disappeared and I found myself walking on a path. Dennis Patrick was there and two other personages [angels]. The path led me beside a tiny stream and there was a highway nearby and a rowdy bar where sinners were drinking and there was evil all around, but the path was light and if you stepped off it, people could grab you, but you were safe as long as you remained on it.

"While we were walking, we came to a place where there was heavy fog and I was told to reach into the fog, and I did, and I was given a set of gold plates. These were not the golden plates that Joseph had been given and had already transcribed. These were other plates that God had not yet revealed to mankind.

"God told me that He wanted the plates translated so I began searching for someone who could transcribe the plates and I went to the world church headquarters in Independence because I was going to give the plates to Wallace B. Smith to translate, but when I went into the building, God asked me why I had brought the plates there and when I told him, He told me that Smith couldn't translate them. He told me that the church had been given the greatest truth that mankind had received but it had done the least with it and because of this, it had lost the truth.

"I continued my search but there was no one who could translate the plates. There was no one to give them to so I returned to the path and when I got there Dennis Patrick tried to wrestle the plates from me and we struggled and finally I got them loose from him."

Neither Alice nor Jeffrey spoke for several minutes after he finished describing his vision, and then Alice asked him: "What do you think this means?"

"I'm not certain," he replied, "but I think that it means that God wants me to bring forth some new revelation. I think it means that Wallace B. Smith is a fallen prophet and is leading the church to destruction. I think it means that Dennis Patrick will try to stop me from accomplishing my task because he will be more worried about winning the glory of the world than about winning the glory of God."

"Jeffrey, are you telling me the truth?" Alice asked, immediately realizing that her question had insulted him. Before he could answer, she said: "Oh, I know it's true. I'm sorry I doubted. I know it's true because it's exactly what I was told when I was growing up. Remember, I was told by the patriarch that I was going to marry a man whom God was going to 'prepare to bring forth a marvelous work and wonder.'"

The next day, Jeffrey told the Patricks about his vision, but he skipped over the part about how Dennis would try to wrestle the gold plates from him.

Jeffrey seemed sincere, they later recalled. "In our tradition, visions are not uncommon and the vision that Jeffrey described was not something that either Dennis or I would have questioned or thought odd," Tonya explained. "If you had gone to any Wednesday night prayer service that week, you probably would have seen someone stand up and talk about how God had inspired them to say something or shown them a vision. It just wasn't that unusual."

While the Patricks did not see Jeffrey's account as anything spectacular, he considered it momentous. "When I had that vision, I became convinced that I would walk on an actual path someday like the one that I had seen and would actually be given or shown some sort of mysterious records. I was going to be instrumental in bringing them forth. I did not see myself as a prophet at that point, but after I had that vision, I began studying what kind of man I needed to become to be acceptable to God so that I could do what He wanted. My entire attention was focused on the prophets and how I could be like one of them."

One afternoon in July, Jeffrey was mowing the grass and thinking about God. "I began asking God questions in my mind. I was trying to figure all of this out and I asked, 'What would you have me do?,' and God put a thought in my mind. 'The answer is already written,' He said."

Jeffrey shut off the lawn mower and ran inside where he grabbed his copy of the Doctrine and Covenants and began flipping pages. He stopped at Section 38.

"I got it!" he suddenly hollered. "I know what I am supposed to do!"

Jeffrey showed Alice paragraph 7b of Section 38, one of Joseph Smith, Jr.'s earliest revelations from God. In it God orders Smith to leave New York and go to Kirtland to be with Sidney Rigdon.

> For this cause I gave unto you the commandment, that you should *go to the Ohio* and there, I will give unto you my law and there *you shall be endowed with power from on high,* and from thence, whosoever I will, shall go forth among all nations, and it shall be told them what they shall do.

"We are moving to Ohio," Jeffrey proclaimed. "We must go to the Kirtland temple because that is where the scriptures are telling me to go if I want to be endowed with the power."

He shut the book, walked outside, and finished mowing the lawn, leaving Alice in the house dazzled. Later that night, Alice asked Jeffrey how he planned to finance the move. "God will show us," he told her.

A few days later, Alice noticed an advertisement in a church newsletter. The RLDS was seeking volunteers to work as tour guides at the Kirtland temple. Applicants had to be financially self-sufficient because they would not receive a regular salary, but the church would provide a house and pay for the utilities.

"God is showing us the path," Jeffrey explained. He answered the ad that same day. When asked about his finances, Jeffrey lied. He said that his parents had decided to give him his inheritance and that it was enough for his family to live on for one year without his earning a salary.

A short time later, the church offered him the job. That same day, Jeffrey received a job offer from an Independence company. He would later tell his followers that the company had offered to pay him $65,000 per year. "It was just like in my vision," he said. "I was being given a choice. I could have the riches of the world or I could choose to go down the path that God was showing me. I chose God."

Alice was just as certain as Jeffrey that God was leading them to Kirtland. "I told Jeffrey, 'Don't take that company job because if you do, it will be the only reward you will have in life.' The Lord wanted us in Kirtland."

Jeffrey decided they needed $1,500 to move. He began selling his gun collection and ordered Alice to sell her antiques. He borrowed $600 from various church members and asked his parents for a donation as well. "I wrote my parents a fifteen-page letter describing why I was going to Kirtland, citing all the scriptural references." Don and Jeffrey's grandfather, Alva Gadberry, responded by coming to Jeffrey's house. "Grandfather Gadberry told me that God was not calling me to Kirtland, Satan was. He warned me against going and told me that I would be following the devil if I did."

When Jeffrey broke the news to the group who met at his house each Sunday afternoon for class, Cheryl Avery and Georgia Milliren immediately suggested that they have a going-away picnic at a nearby park for Jeffrey and Alice. About ten couples came to say good-bye. They gave $120 to Jeffrey and Alice as a going-away present. Georgia wanted the group to get up early the next morning and surprise the Lundgrens by waiting at the outskirts of town and waving to them when they drove past. But she decided that the class might not spot them on the busy highway so she dropped the idea. Dennis Avery told Jeffrey that he admired his dedication. "This is so exciting," Cheryl said. "You've got to tell us what you find there." Alice was crying by the time the picnic ended. Dennis and Tonya followed them back to their house for a final good-bye.

Jeffrey told Dennis that he was still $50 short of the $1,500 that he needed to raise. As they were talking, someone knocked on the door. "We had an old washer and dryer sitting on the porch and this couple had seen them and our garage-sale sign and had come up to buy them," Jeffrey recalled. "They gave us fifty dollars."

Once again, Jeffrey saw God at work.

The next morning, Jeffrey, Alice, and their children climbed into their old station wagon. All of their possessions were in a U-Haul trailer that they were going to tow. Jeffrey would later recall how he felt that morning. "Everyone considered me a failure. My father, my mother, even Alice, because I had not accumulated a bunch of possessions or stayed at one job. But it suddenly dawned on me why. God had been trying to get my attention. He didn't want me to succeed at all those other jobs. He wanted me to fail so that I would eventually come to Him and do what He wanted me to do. In fact, I believe that He caused me to fail.

"I had been created for one purpose and it wasn't working in a hospital. I loved the scriptures and everyone told me that I knew them better that anyone. Why? Because it was all part of His plan."

As they left Independence, Jeffrey knew that he was not going to fail this time. He would prove to Don, to Lois, to his grandparents, and to Alice and everyone else who had ever doubted him that he was not a loser. He was special and important.

"The Lord had chosen me—me—for a great mission. He hadn't chosen them. He hadn't given my father this vision. He hadn't given it to Wallace B. Smith. He had chosen me. I truly believed that and I saw this as a new adventure, a new start. We were going down God's path and I wasn't going to let Him down.

"I was going to do whatever God commanded."

PART TWO: PROPHET

Thou shalt not hearken unto the words of that prophet, or that dreamer of dreams . . .

Deuteronomy 13:3

CHAPTER THIRTEEN

THE first white settler in Kirtland arrived in May 1811 from Berkshire County, Massachusetts, aboard an ox-drawn covered wagon. Legend has it that he built his log cabin along the Indian trail that he had followed through the dense woods and rocky inclines of northern Ohio. Those who came later also built their cabins next to this Indian trail and over time, a town emerged. It was not a carefully platted community with neat square blocks. Rather, it grew haphazard much like wild flowers sprouting next to a meandering stream. Wherever the ground was level enough for a house, one was built. Today, most homes and shops face this same trail that once Erie Indians walked. It is officially designated on maps as State Highway 306. But the five-mile section that runs through Kirtland is called Chillicothe Road by the locals. It's the town's de facto main street. Beginning in the north, the narrow two-way blacktop guides motorists past a dilapidated red brick combination city hall and police department, a smattering of shops, Kirtland's public schools, a well-tended football field, and a failed Dog & Suds restaurant now painted dark brown with boarded up windows. Farther south it passes the entrance of Chapin Forest, a large park and nature reserve, before it finally intersects with State Highway 6 near the end of the city limits. The Kirtland cemetery is located adjacent to this one-stoplight interchange; so is a feed store and Lupica's Country Corner which promises customers genuine Amish-made cheese and hand-packed fruit baskets.

There is no McDonald's in Kirtland, no local movie theater, no bowling alley, no Wall-Mart with discount prices. But the town does have churches—ten of them at last count, including six that broke off from either the Baptist or Mormon denominations. About halfway through town, a sign proclaims JESUS SAVES. It was not erected by any religious group. It was made by a Kirtland man who stuck it in his front yard much as a realtor puts up a For Sale sign. On the outskirts of Kirtland, the city council has erected welcome signs that describe Kirtland as a community of "faith and beauty."

On August 19, 1984, Jeffrey Lundgren and his family turned onto State Highway 306, the last leg of their move from Independence to Kirtland. They had been traveling on Interstate 90, a restless major east-west thoroughfare that runs parallel to the southern shoreline of Lake Erie and connects Cleveland with the myriad of bedroom communities to its east. Had Jeffrey turned left when he exited the bustling interstate, he would have driven into Mentor, a sister-city to Kirtland, and a much larger and more prosperous mecca of strip zoning. Mentor is everything that Kirtland has avoided: neon-lighted fast-food eateries, budget hotels, and sprawling shopping malls. But Jeffrey had turned right and bypassed Mentor. The Lundgrens' car had swooped down a steep hill and crossed the bridge that spans the eastern branch of the Chagrin River where Sidney Rigdon first baptized Mormon converts. As their station wagon sputtered up the incline on the southern bank, Jeffrey gazed through the windshield at a sight that brought tears to his eyes and caused Alice to whisper a quick "Praise God!"

The "House of the Lord" towered before them, its white walls glistening in the afternoon sun as light reflected off the slivers of broken china mixed in the exterior stucco. Joseph Smith, Jr., had chosen this location on the northern tip and highest hill in Kirtland because he wanted the Gentiles in Mentor, which even in the early 1830s was considered a much more worldly place than Kirtland, to see the kerosene lamps burning inside the temple at night. Like a lighthouse beacon, the church would pierce the darkness and silently witness to the world that

God's "only true church" was standing watch and eagerly awaiting Jesus Christ's imminent return.

A one-story clapboard building identified as the VISITORS' CEN- TER was located a few hundred feet from the temple's front doors. Directly across Chillicothe Road from the temple was the red-brick Kirtland RLDS Church and next to that building was a large house where Sidney Rigdon had once lived.

Eleanor Lord was the first to welcome the Lundgrens when Jef- frey stepped into the visitors' center, causing a bell dangling from the door to jingle. She and her husband, Bill, were in charge of the temple staff, although there really wasn't much of one to oversee. Besides the Lords, there was another retired couple who gave tours, and during summer months, three or four college students were paid by the church to help out.

An attractive, gracious woman in her mid-sixties, Eleanor ex- plained with a bit of embarrassment that Bill was running an errand and she didn't know where he had left the keys for the church- provided house where the Lundgrens would live. It was a two-story house, circa 1950, built right next to the visitors' center. Like all of the other temple property, it was painted white. Jeffrey didn't want to wait for Bill, so he jimmied open a window and Damon crawled through and unlocked the doors. Alice almost began to cry when she stepped inside. "We discovered the church was a slumlord," Jef- frey later recalled.

"Alice, you got to give me a couple of weeks," said Jeffrey opti- mistically. "We'll get it into shape. I promise."

By the time they had unloaded the trailer, Bill showed up and quickly invited them to a backyard cookout that he and Eleanor were hosting the next day in appreciation of the four college students who had spent their summer as temple tour guides. Jeffrey accepted the invitation and then asked: "When can I start work?"

The question surprised Bill, who had figured that the Lundgrens would need at least a week to get settled. But Jeffrey didn't want to waste time. "I'd like to learn how to give tours as quickly as I can." At Bill's urging, he agreed to wait for at least a day.

The next morning while Alice unpacked, Jeffrey took his chil- dren for a ride. Less than an hour later, he returned home and burst inside.

"I want you to go with me now!" he exclaimed. "You've got to see what I've found!"

They left Damon in charge of the others and drove to Chapin

Forest. "Look at that!" Jeffrey said excitedly after he parked the car. "Over there!"

Alice saw a pond shrouded by trees and a footpath.

"That's it!" Jeffrey said. "The path in my dream. The path that I walk down to get the plates. C'mon."

He hustled her to it and then suddenly stopped. "Do you feel something?" he asked. Without waiting for a reply, Jeffrey told Alice that most of the rock used in the foundation of the Kirtland temple had been cut here in Chapin Forest.

"This feels like hallowed ground," said Jeffrey.

"I was thinking the exact same thing," Alice replied.

"Remember how I said the path was by a little stream, and a highway, and how there was a bar nearby? Look, look, look!"

The path in the park was next to a brook that ran parallel to Chillicothe Road. Through the trees, Jeffrey could see a building, which he told Alice was a local bar and restaurant called PJ's Pub.

"Joseph left something for me here," he said. "I'm sure of it."

"Oh, Jeff, this is so exciting," Alice replied. "Do you really sense that?"

The comment irritated him. Why did she always doubt him? They walked down the path for several minutes, but they didn't find anything so they returned home for lunch.

Later that day, Jeffrey, Alice, and their children went to the cookout across the street at the Sidney Rigdon house where Bill and Eleanor Lord lived.

"I remember watching them as they came up the driveway," Eleanor later said. "I remember thinking how happy I was that they had come. It was so unusual for someone so young to be able to work as tour guides. I felt they would bring a youthful vitality to the temple."

Neither Jeffrey nor Alice mentioned their experience in Chapin Forest, nor did they volunteer much information about themselves. Instead, they quietly ate their hamburgers and potato salad and let Bill and Eleanor do the talking. They were a devout and kindhearted couple. Bill had worked for U.S. Steel and later as a maintenance supervisor at a college in Long Island, New York, before retiring in 1981. At age sixty-five, he was a small, thin-framed man with close-cropped hair, metal glasses, a quick laugh, and ready smile. His grandfather had been a fervent Methodist minister, but his parents hadn't seen much use in religion and neither had Bill as a teenager.

But when he was in his twenties, a friend gave him a copy of the Book of Mormon and he converted.

Eleanor had grown up in the RLDS and it was one of two great passions in her life. Her other love had been the stage. When she was twenty-two, Eleanor was living in New York and trying to decide whether she should be a music teacher or audition for roles on Broadway. During a prayer meeting, an elder told her that God had a message for her. God wanted Eleanor to use her talents in His service. Eleanor interpreted that to mean that she should forsake the stage and teach music. "From that point on, I offered my talent to the Lord and within six months all of that burning desire to be on-stage was gone," she recalled. "I felt a wonderful peace with God." She and Bill had met shortly after that and married in 1953. The church had been the focal point of their lives, and after Bill retired they decided to become temple tour guides to, as Bill put it, "give something back to the Lord." The Lords had studied their church's history and were familiar with the stories about Joseph Smith, Jr.'s treasure hunting and alleged attempts to seduce Sidney Rigdon's daughter. But such talk didn't shake their belief in the validity of the Book of Mormon. "There is just too much in it to be the creation of a boy's imagination," Eleanor explained. Besides, she asked, who were they to question why God had chosen Joseph Smith, Jr., as His prophet? Hadn't God blessed King David even after he committed adultery with Bathsheba and arranged for her husband, Uriah, to be killed?

As the two couples became better acquainted that night, Bill asked Jeffrey how he could afford to work as an unpaid tour guide at such a young age. Jeffrey said that his grandparents were giving him $800 per month as part of his inheritance, and then he quickly changed the subject by asking Bill questions about the temple, visitors' center, and tour-guide job. About 25,000 persons toured the temple each year, Bill said. No one was ever permitted to go inside unless a guide was with them. There was always a chance that some anti-Mormon visitor might deface the temple. Before each tour, visitors were shown a fifteen-minute slide show in the visitors' center that explained the highlights of Joseph Smith, Jr.'s life and how the temple was built. After that, a tour guide led the visitors into the temple.

The tours always began in the temple vestibule, a narrow room in the front of the building. It was there that guides would explain that the temple contained three floors. The bottom floor, called the lower court, was used as a sanctuary; the second floor, which was nearly identical to the lower court, had been built as a school for priests; the attic story with its dormer windows made up the third floor. It was divided into a series of rooms which could be used either as offices or for classes. There was also a steeple and belfry complete with a weather vane whose tip was one hundred twenty feet above ground. One of the first features of the temple that the guides would mention was how the three floors were connected. There were two winding staircases on each side of the vestibule and there were exactly thirty-three steps between each floor—"One step for each year of Christ's life," said Bill.

The temple was a jumble of architectural styles: Greek Revival, Georgian, Colonial, Federalist, and Gothic. The most curious designs inside were the intricate decorative carvings on the columns, doors, and moldings. Guides often speculated about what these hand-carved designs represented.

The tours always ended exactly where they had started—in the church's entryway, where visitors, if they felt so inclined, could make a cash donation to the temple.

When Jeffrey wasn't giving a tour, he would sit inside the visitors' center where souvenirs and religious books and pamphlets were for sale. The most expensive item was the Holy Scriptures, Joseph Smith Jr.'s rewritten version of the Bible, which sold for twenty-six dollars.

After the Lundgrens had gone home that night, Bill told Eleanor that he felt Jeffrey should be given some sort of responsibility besides being a tour guide because he was younger and eager to prove himself. "I think I'll put him in charge of the financial records," Bill said. The temple generated at least $20,000 per year in souvenir sales and offerings.

"Yes," Eleanor agreed. "That would be a good job for him."

The next morning, Bill gave Jeffrey a copy of the standardized speech that tour guides used, issued him a set of keys to the temple, and told him that besides his regular duties, he would be in charge of collecting the offerings left at the temple and keeping track of sales at the visitors' center.

A few nights later, when Bill and Eleanor went for a walk after dinner, they noticed that someone was inside the temple even though it was closed. Bill was about to telephone the police, when he thought of Jeffrey. He decided to investigate and found Jeffrey inside the temple.

"I didn't mean to worry you," Jeffrey said. "It's just that I want to investigate every nook and cranny in this place." Bill didn't complain. When he and Eleanor resumed their walk, Bill remarked that he had never seen anyone so enthusiastic when it came to learning about the House of the Lord. Eleanor agreed. "They are an answer to our prayers," she said.

CHAPTER FOURTEEN

FOUR days after the Lundgrens arrived in Kirtland, Cheryl Avery knocked on their front door. She and Dennis and their three daughters had come to visit. Jeffrey was not happy to see them, but Alice invited them in. The Averys were planning on staying the weekend. Cheryl was distressed. She and Dennis had gone to a Wednesday night prayer meeting at Slover Park and hadn't felt comfortable. She still couldn't get over the fact that the church had decided to ordain women. She and Dennis had talked about leaving the RLDS. But where could they go? No other denomination believed in the Book of Mormon except for the Utah Mormons and they were considered worse heretics than other Protestants.

Jeffrey took the Averys on a tour of the temple. Although he was only beginning to investigate the building, he said he'd already made two important discoveries. "God, Himself, was the architect of this temple," he explained solemnly. "It is the only temple in the world that we know was designed by Him." According to historical records, Joseph Smith, Jr., Sidney Rigdon, and church member Frederick G. Williams saw a vision of the temple while they were praying in the summer of 1833. The temple was constructed, under Smith's direction, based on that vision. The fact that God had shown Smith how to construct the temple was extremely significant, Jeffrey said. "By studying it, we can see how God thinks." It was the same logic that Jeffrey had applied to his studies of the Book of Mormon. Why had God decided to use a specific word in a parable? Why had God designed a temple with two separate front doors? "The entire building is a clue."

Jeffrey's second discovery was a carving in the temple. He had found it on a pulpit used by a priest. "This is the symbol of man," Jeffrey said. "Every book about symbols says that this design means man. I have searched and searched and there is no symbol on any of the pulpits for woman. None." To Jeffrey, the message was clear: "God never intended for women to be ordained as priests; otherwise he would have put the symbol for woman on a pulpit."

Dennis and Cheryl were astounded. It was just like the Old Testament story in Daniel, Cheryl said, where King Belshazzar blasphemed God by using the Hebrews' sacred vessels from their temple as wine goblets at a feast. The fingers of a man's hand had suddenly appeared and the hand had written a strange warning to the king on the palace wall. Only the prophet Daniel could interpret the strange writings. In Cheryl's mind the fact that God had once communicated with men by writing a message on King Belshazzar's wall was prima facie evidence that He might have included a few messages on the walls and pulpits of the Kirtland temple.

The Averys' reaction was so enthusiastic that Jeffrey decided to tell them about his dream and the path that he had found in Chapin Forest, but first he swore them to secrecy. When he finished, Dennis asked Jeffrey what the dream meant. "I'm not certain," Jeffrey said, "but clearly the RLDS is without a prophet and God is going to bring forth a new one to preach the truth."

Dennis and Cheryl asked Jeffrey to show them the path in Chapin Forest, so Jeffrey and Alice drove them to the park. But when they got there, Dennis began complaining about how cold it was outside and Cheryl slipped on a wet stone and fell, hurting her hip. Jeffrey grew impatient and the enthusiasm that the two couples had felt at the temple waned. They returned to the Lundgrens' for dinner. After everyone had gone to bed that night, Jeffrey told Alice that he didn't think Dennis's chill and Cheryl's fall were accidents. "God was keeping them from walking down the path," he said. "The Lord doesn't want them to know the truth."

The rest of that weekend, as far as Jeffrey was concerned, was unbearable. "All the Averys did was complain about life," said Jeffrey. "They were not people we would have sought out as friends."

The relationship between the Lundgrens and the Averys had always struck people who knew them as odd. Behind their backs, Jeffrey and Alice constantly belittled the Averys. And yet the Averys often described the Lundgrens as their best friends.

To most, Dennis and Cheryl seemed strange. Dennis was mousy. Cheryl was uncomfortable around strangers. Neither dressed fashionably or was good at small talk. Cheryl had grown up in Centralia, Washington, a town of about 10,000 south of Tacoma. She had never really known her own father, Hiram Clisby. He had been in the merchant marine during the 1940s when he met and married Donna, Cheryl's mother. At the time, Donna was working in Yakima, a town in central Washington, and living with her aunt. She had gone to college for one year, but was forced to drop out because she couldn't afford tuition. Donna met Hiram at an RLDS church meeting. They met, married, and then just as quickly, Hiram left for sea, leaving his bride behind at her aunt's house pregnant with their first child. Lance Clisby was born in 1945. Two years later, when Cheryl was born, Donna was still living with her aunt waiting for Hiram to finish another one of his Pacific voyages. In January 1948, Donna filed for divorce and moved with her two children to Centralia to live with her parents. Cheryl was seven months old. Two years later, Donna married Howard Bailey, a carpenter and general handyman. They moved into a house just across the railroad tracks from where her parents lived, only a block away from the RLDS church. Donna gave birth to another son, Donald, in 1951. By that time, Cheryl was four. "We never had much money," Donna recalled. "We were almost on welfare sometimes, particularly in the winter when my husband was off work. But Cheryl never seemed to mind."

As a youngster, Cheryl's closest friends were her two brothers. "Cheryl was very loyal to Lance, in particular," her mother said. "They'd walk to school together even when both of them were in high school. She helped out Donald too, even though he was younger. She was almost like a mother to both of the boys."

Cheryl didn't participate in many high school activities after school. She didn't date, didn't give a hoot about being popular, and really had only one close friend: Barbara Carter. "Cheryl wasn't ever a goofy person—even as a teenager," Carter recalled. "She didn't go crazy over the Beatles and didn't care a bit about boys, like most of us. She was uncomplicated, stubborn, modest, and serious." When

Carter had a slumber party for her sixteenth birthday, she invited Cheryl. It was the first sleep-over that Cheryl had ever attended. No one had ever invited her before.

Carter knew that Cheryl was deeply religious although she rarely mentioned it. She didn't drink alcohol, didn't smoke, never used profanity, and considered makeup, trips to the beauty parlor, and fancy clothes to be worldly vanities. "I remember when all the girls began wearing nylon stockings and flats in high school," Carter recalled. Cheryl continued to wear white bobby socks and saddle oxfords. "She simply wore what she wanted to wear, without being influenced by others' opinions," said Carter.

When Cheryl graduated in 1965, a teacher called her by the last name of Clisby, not Bailey. Carter was surprised. "Although I was her closest friend, she had never told me that Mr. Bailey was not her father. Even after this revelation, Cheryl supplied no details and was very angry that her real name had been divulged. She was a very, very private person."

After high school, Cheryl enrolled at a community college in Centralia, but didn't like it. She was even more out of sync in college than she had been in high school. It was the dawning of the Age of Aquarius, the antiwar movement was just getting started, feminists were burning their bras. By contrast, Cheryl's favorite movie star was John Wayne. Her favorite song was Tennessee Ernie Ford's "Sixteen Tons." She had never been out on a date. Cheryl stayed in school one semester and then transferred to Graceland, the RLDS's conservative college.

Located about four miles from the Iowa-Missouri state line in tiny Lamoni, Graceland had an enrollment of eight hundred, nearly all white students from middle-class homes. Cheryl arrived for the spring term in 1966 and was assigned to a room in "Kimball Manor," a fancy name for the third floor of the women's dormitory. At Graceland, each floor had its own name to give the dormitory a more homelike atmosphere. Ann Sherman, a shy freshman from Independence, lived down the hall, and the two women became friends. During spring break, Ann invited Cheryl home with her. Cheryl had never been to Independence. She loved it, and Ann's parents, Robert and Velma, adored Cheryl. Ann was an only child. "We liked to joke that we were the sister that neither of us ever had, but both wanted," Sherman later remembered. "We both felt the same way about most things."

The Shermans were not wealthy. Robert made his living by refinishing furniture. Velma was a secretary. But they were devout RLDS members, and when the spring semester ended and they learned that Cheryl might not be able to return to Graceland in the fall because of money problems, Robert and Velma decided to help. They invited Cheryl to spend the summer with them and Robert found her a job as a clerk at a Montgomery Ward store. Cheryl faithfully saved her earnings, but when it was time to enroll at Graceland, she still was short of cash. The Shermans wanted to help her, but they couldn't afford to pay for both girls to attend Graceland. Ann unselfishly suggested that she and Cheryl transfer to Central Missouri State University in Warrensburg, the same school that Jeffrey and Alice would later attend. Cheryl agreed and the Shermans had enough to pay for both women's tuition. Ann and Cheryl roomed together. "The school cafeteria didn't serve Sunday supper and neither of us had much money so we would buy a can of spaghetti and heat it up and for dessert we would have baby food—a little jar of pudding or peach cobbler," Ann Sherman remembered.

Although Cheryl would sometimes tag along with Ann and her boyfriend to a football game, Cheryl didn't go out on dates. She wasn't unattractive, but she was plain and she did little to enhance her appearance. She had a round face and black wavy hair that had first started showing streaks of gray in college. She wore it cut short and most mornings simply brushed it. "I let it do what it wants to do," she often joked, "because it will do that anyway." She was five feet three inches tall, weighed one hundred and thirteen pounds, and had a nice figure, but even when she was in her early twenties, Cheryl had a matron's air to her. Finding a husband wasn't as important as earning a college degree in elementary education. "Cheryl was a very determined person," said Ann. "If she wanted something done, she went out and did it and if you got in her way, tough luck."

During Labor Day weekend in September 1969, Ann and Cheryl attended a weekend church retreat for singles held at a campground in Excelsior Springs north of Independence. The men and women were paired off on Saturday night so that they could get to know each other. Cheryl was matched with Dennis Avery. Despite Ann's probing later that night, Cheryl didn't say much about Dennis. But that weekend, he called. They went to church together. She was twenty-two. It was her first date and it was his first date too. He was twenty-nine. Eight months later they were married. The wedding was held on May 29, 1970. They picked that date because Cheryl's birthday was May 27 and Dennis's birthday was May 28.

They figured it would be easy for them to remember their May 29 wedding anniversary.

Donna Bailey came to Independence for her daughter's wedding. "I was let down when I first saw Dennis. I had been introduced to Ann Sherman's boyfriend and I remember thinking, 'Why couldn't Cheryl get someone like him instead of someone like Dennis?,' but I changed my mind after I got to know him and realized what a kind person he was."

Dennis didn't make a good first impression. A neighbor of the Averys would later tell a reporter for the Cleveland *Plain Dealer* that Dennis was "the typical nerd, with his pocket protector and everything." He was a small-framed man, standing only five feet seven inches, weighing less than one hundred twenty-five pounds. Yet in photographs, he seemed to be overweight and to have a double chin. He slumped, wore thick glasses with self-darkening lenses, had a receding hairline, and seemed, according to several who knew him, to be rather slow-witted except when it came to quoting scriptures. Dennis pored over his Bible and the Book of Mormon. There wasn't a time in Dennis's life when the RLDS wasn't important to him.

The oldest of four children, Dennis grew up in Baldwin Park, a suburb of Los Angeles, where his father worked at a company that manufactured electrical medical equipment. His mother stayed at home until her children were grown. Then she became a librarian. She had been raised in the RLDS. His father was a convert. Their family life revolved around the church and Dennis never questioned his faith.

Like Cheryl, Dennis was always serious. As a child, he was chosen to appear on *The Art Linkletter Show*. Along with four other children, he was interviewed by Art during a segment called "Kids Say the Darndest Things." Dennis gave short, somber replies that didn't spark many laughs. Art quickly moved on.

At Baldwin Park High School, Dennis was later remembered as one of those students who passed through unnoticed. "He was not someone who stuck in your mind," said a classmate who graduated with Dennis in 1958. After graduation, Dennis worked as a clerk at a bank and then landed a job in the mail room at Edwards Air Force Base. "He never did go off, like some youth in the area, with those who were protesting back in the sixties," Lois Hartnet, an elder at the Covina RLDS congregation, later told reporters. "He was a dependable churchgoer who lived a good, puritanical life-style." Dennis lived with his parents for eleven years after high school. When he finally decided in 1969 to move out, he decided to "gather" to Independence. He rented a room from a family and a short time later met Cheryl.

Dennis couldn't afford a honeymoon. He didn't own a car. Money was a problem. It always would be. Dennis worked nights at the Centerre Bank in Kansas City, where he ran a machine that sorted canceled checks. He would eventually work there for seventeen years, and during that time, he would never be promoted to a better job nor earn more than $24,000 per year. "He was a pleasant fellow," said a fellow employee, "but he had absolutely no ambition. I think he was scared to try new things. I always thought he was rather simple-minded, but one day he began talking about religion and he really knew his scriptures."

Each year, Barbara Carter received a Christmas card from Cheryl. "She would talk about how poor they were. She wasn't complaining, it was just a fact. No matter how hard they tried, they always were broke."

Cheryl taught school after she got married. But she quit when their daughter, Trina Denise, was born on March 7, 1974. They had another daughter, Rebecca Lynn, on January 23, 1976. Shortly after that Dennis suffered from prostate and urinary problems and didn't think that he could father any more children. But on August 3, 1982, Karen Diane was born. Dennis and Cheryl called her their "miracle" baby.

No one was certain why Dennis and Cheryl decided to attend the Slover Park congregation because they clearly didn't fit in. Cheryl either made her family's clothing or bought it secondhand at a Salvation Army store. "I think one of the reasons why the Averys latched onto Jeffrey and Alice was because they were nicer to them than most people in the church," recalled Georgia Milliren. "The Averys were not particularly easy to like. They were wimpy, mousy people and a lot of members just simply avoided them."

When Cheryl first mentioned Jeffrey Lundgren in a letter to her mother, Donna was pleasantly surprised. She knew his mother. Lois had lived in Centralia with her parents, Alva and Maude Gadberry, for a short time. She and Donna had been in the same Sunday school class as children. It was one of those ironic twists of fate, Donna told Cheryl, that frequently happened in the close world of the RLDS saints.

Even though Jeffrey and Alice complained about the Averys, they did nothing to sever the friendship. When Cheryl had to go into the hospital for an appendectomy, it was Alice who volunteered to prepare a meal for Dennis and his girls. Later, she got Tonya Patrick to go with her to tidy up the Averys' house before Cheryl came home. The place was filthy and cluttered with junk. There were holes in the walls, the toilet was leaking water, the yard needed to be weeded and mowed. A storm had damaged the roof and the roofers had simply tossed the old shingles down on the grass when they made the repairs. Dennis hadn't bothered to pick them up. Nor did he volunteer to help the women clean. Instead, he sat in his easy chair as they worked around him. When it was lunchtime, he told his daughters to make him a sandwich and bring it to him. Tonya was exhausted and irritated when she got home later that night. She told her husband that Dennis Avery was the laziest man that she'd ever met.

At Slover Park, there were lots of other stories about the Averys. One church member recalled how he had stopped by the Averys' house on a particularly cold winter night and found their living room icy cold. "Dennis was sitting in his chair complaining about how cold it was, so I looked around and noticed that someone had closed the air vents in the room. There was no way for warm air to blow inside. I said, 'Well, Dennis, here's your problem—someone closed your vents. Just open them up.' What amazed me was that he knew the vents were closed! He said, 'Oh, I just haven't had time to get around to opening them.' That family spent the entire winter freezing in the living room because he was too lazy to open the vents!"

Another church member recalled how she had gotten a panicky telephone call from Cheryl one night. "What do you use to get orange juice off the floor?" she asked. The church member suggested a well-known cleaner. "Oh, that's wonderful," Cheryl replied. She explained that one of the girls had spilled the juice four days earlier. "Cheryl had been fretting the entire time about what to use to get it up. She couldn't make up her mind," the woman recalled. "I often wondered how either of them ever made it in this world."

Ann Sherman would recall Cheryl and Dennis much less critically. "Cheryl was definitely the strong one in the family, and sometimes she would complain about Dennis because he didn't help out much around the house. But he wasn't lazy. He went to work faithfully. The thing about Dennis was that he had an easygoing nature about him. He didn't get real concerned about most things and he didn't always follow through on things once he got started." Years later, Ann would also recall that Dennis seemed to withdraw even further after he befriended Jeffrey and Alice. "He sort of adopted an attitude that the Lord will provide. He felt the Lord was directing his life, almost to the point that he didn't have to do anything in terms of planning. It was like he was depending on God to figure out a way to make things happen. That was kind of his philosophy. God was in charge."

Donna Bailey also saw a change in her daughter once she and Dennis became friends with the Lundgrens. Cheryl and Dennis became "fanatical," she said. "Cheryl had always studied her scriptures, but she was reading them over and over and over again." When the RLDS held its controversial worldwide conference in April 1984, Cheryl asked Donna if she would come to Independence to baby-sit for her granddaughters. She and Dennis wanted to attend the debate at the conference about ordaining women into the priesthood. Neither Cheryl nor Dennis told Donna the entire reason why they wanted her there. Both of them felt that a vote in favor of letting women become priests would be a clear signal that Satan had successfully steered the RLDS away from God's truth. Dennis even speculated that God might respond by bringing the earth to an end. If that happened, Dennis and Cheryl wanted Donna to be with their daughters.

Donna agreed to make the trip, but before she left for Independence, she received a letter from her daughter that troubled her. "Cheryl told me that she and Dennis had decided that their girls couldn't watch television anymore and she said that they were against playing cards too." Donna and her husband both liked to watch television and play cards. Donna decided to telephone Cheryl.

"Won't you make an exception for Dad's sake?" Donna asked.

"No," said Cheryl. No television. No card playing. Donna agreed to baby-sit anyway. "Cheryl and Dennis were heartbroken when the church decided to ordain women," she recalled. "Cheryl told me that there was only one man at Slover Park who was brave enough to tell the truth and oppose women being ordained. That was Jeffrey, and she said that he had told her that he had gotten death threats because of what he preached."

Unlike the Lundgrens, Dennis and Cheryl enjoyed their weekend visit in Kirtland during August 1984. They returned to Independence electrified about what Jeffrey had showed them in the Kirtland temple. Cheryl was so excited that she wrote her mother a long letter. Because Jeffrey had sworn her to secrecy, she didn't mention

Jeffrey's dream, the path in Chapin Forest, or how God was going to choose a new prophet to replace Wallace B. Smith. But she did mention that she had, at last, found someone who could give her the "answers" that she had been seeking. There was something about Jeffrey Lundgren, she wrote, that was special.

CHAPTER FIFTEEN

J EFFREY'S discovery of a symbol for man, but not for woman, convinced him that he was on the right track. But the temple was filled
with other carvings and no one knew what they meant. During his
first two weeks on the job, Jeffrey went through all the historical
records in the temple archives. He'd even got Eleanor Lord to check
art books at the local libraries. But the meaning of most designs
remained a mystery. In October, Jeffrey learned that Raymond Treat
was lecturing for several nights at an RLDS church in Pittsburgh.
As always, Ray was talking about similarities that he had found between the Nephites and Lamanites in the Book of Mormon and the
Maya culture in Mesoamerica. Jeffrey figured that Ray might be able
to identify some of the symbols in the temple because he was a
trained archaeologist. So Jeffrey and Alice drove to Pennsylvania to
listen to Ray's speech. It wasn't too different from the one that Jeffrey had first heard at the Slover Park congregation in 1982, but as
Jeffrey watched the color slides of Maya ruins, he noticed that a few
of them contained symbols that looked to him like those in the Kirtland temple. After Ray completed his speech, Jeffrey introduced
himself and explained how it was Ray who had first gotten him excited about reading the Book of Mormon. Jeffrey then mentioned

that several of the designs in the Kirtland temple seemed similar to those in Ray's slides. Ray was intrigued.

Although there was some printed material available before 1830 about archaeological discoveries in Mesoamerica, Ray was confident that Joseph Smith, Jr., and other early Mormons in Kirtland would not have known about the Maya. If Maya symbols were in the temple, then Ray would be able to add another bit of proof to his theory that the Mormon religion and the Maya were somehow linked. He told Jeffrey that he would gladly drive to Kirtland the next morning to look at the symbols. Another man joined Ray and Jeffrey as they talked. Tom Miller had accompanied Ray from Independence to Pittsburgh. Tom was an elder in the church and was interested in seeing the temple too.

When the two men arrived in Kirtland the next day, Jeffrey hustled them into the temple and Ray carefully examined all of the symbols. He agreed that some seemed similar to those found in Mesoamerica, but he couldn't be certain until he had done more research. Tom was impressed by Jeffrey. "He clearly had a special understanding about the temple," he later recalled. "Jeffrey was seeing things there that others had missed." Both men found Jeffrey's discovery of the symbol for man interesting, especially Tom. He had been a delegate at the 1984 world conference and had personally felt that women shouldn't be ordained. Yet, when it came time for a vote, he had raised his hand in favor of permitting women to be priests simply because all those around him had raised their hands. Now he was certain that his decision had been a mistake.

After the tour, Jeffrey invited Ray and Tom to his house to meet Alice and talk more about the temple. Within an hour, Jeffrey and Tom were, as Alice later put it, "clicking like crazy." Tom was well versed in the scriptures and there was an authority to his voice when he spoke, partly because of his background. At age thirty-eight, Tom had worked as a police officer and as a game warden. But he had eventually quit both jobs, he explained, because of "politics." Tom prided himself on being a man who didn't "kiss up" to anyone. If he thought that his boss was doing something stupid, he told him so.

Tom and Ray had met at a church service in Independence and become friends. Ray had invited Tom to come with him to Pittsburgh because Tom was between jobs. His wife, Patti, worked at a medical lab in Independence.

Jeffrey decided to take Ray and Tom to Chapin Forest so they could see where the stones used in the foundation of the temple had been cut. He told them that he felt that the quarry area was hallowed ground, but he didn't tell either of them about his dream or the significance of the footpath. As they walked down the path, Tom spotted several holes that had been drilled into stones in the creek bed that ran adjacent to the path. Tom's college degree was in agronomy and he told Ray and Jeffrey that in the 1800s, stonemasons frequently cut stones in a quarry by drilling a line of holes in them. The holes would be four or five inches apart. The masons would then fill the holes with water and when it froze, the water would expand and cause the stone to crack along the line of holes. "These holes were probably made by the men who built the temple," he said.

Jeffrey, Tom, and Ray climbed down a small embankment to get a closer look at the holes in the creek bed. It was about a five-foot drop to the stream from the path. After the men examined the holes, they turned around and started to climb back up the embankment, but Tom suddenly stopped. "Hey! Look at this!" he hollered. Part of the embankment was made of stone—the same gray stone found in the creek bed and the temple foundation—and someone had drilled nearly a dozen holes into it. These holes, however, were different from the ones in the creek bed. They were nearly twice as large and they had been drilled at angles and in a circular pattern. Each hole looked as if it eventually met the others somewhere deep inside the rock.

"Why would someone drill there?" Jeffrey asked.

Tom put his mouth against one of the holes and blew into it. There was no resistance. "There's got to be a chamber in there," he announced. Tom Miller would later recall during an interview the excitement that he felt that afternoon in October 1984. "We broke off a branch and stuck it in one of the holes and we never hit the end," he said. "Man-oh-man, we were really having fun. The more we talked, the more convinced we all became that we had really found something. We speculated that these were air holes that led to some secret chamber. The next thing we knew, we were convincing ourselves that Joseph Smith, Jr., had hidden something in this chamber—gold plates probably. We were on a roll." Tom decided to ask God if there was a hidden chamber behind the stone. He left Jeffrey and Ray and walked down the path to pray alone. "I can't tell you now whether I wanted to see something so bad that I imagined it or whether I truly had a vision that day," Tom said later. "But I came back to Jeff and Ray and I said, 'My understanding is that there is a chamber hidden here and there are gold plates hidden in it.'"

Ray and Tom needed to get back to Pittsburgh for Ray's lecture that night, but they promised to return to Kirtland the next day. After they had gone, Jeffrey told Alice about Tom's statements in the park. It fit perfectly with his dream. They began speculating about what might be hidden there. The Book of Mormon contained plenty of stories about brass and gold plates that had never been found. There was another mystical artifact mentioned in the book that had vanished centuries ago. It was a magnificent gold-and-jeweled sword known as the Sword of Laban, and it played a role in one of the most important and controversial stories in the Book of Mormon. According to the Mormon scriptures, God told a Hebrew prophet named Lehi that He wanted him to leave Jerusalem and go to the New World. But Lehi didn't want to make the journey without several brass plates that contained the genealogy of his family. The plates were being held by a man named Laban, so Lehi sent his son, Nephi, to fetch them. Laban, however, refused to give up the plates and no matter what Lehi offered him, he wouldn't budge. One night Nephi decided to make a final attempt at getting the plates. He went to talk to Laban and found him drunk. Nephi also spotted Laban's magnificent gold sword.

According to the Mormon scriptures, God told Nephi to kill Laban, but Nephi hesitated because he knew that murder was wrong.

> And it came to pass that the Spirit said unto me again, "Slay him, for the Lord hath delivered him into thy hands. *Behold the Lord slayeth the wicked to bring forth his righteous purposes.*"

Nephi grabbed Laban by his hair and cut off his head with the golden sword. He then took the brass plates and the sword with him. Although the sword appeared in other passages in the Book of Mormon, it wasn't clear what finally happened to it, and over time it developed into a symbol of mystical power. In December 1836, for example, the sword was mentioned in a prophecy that Joseph Smith, Sr., the father of the Mormon prophet, said in the Kirtland temple on behalf of his grandson, Joseph Smith III. [It was Joseph Smith III who eventually became the leader of the RLDS Church.] The senior Smith prophesied that his grandson would someday "have power to wield the Sword of Laban." From that point on, the sword became synonymous with the leadership of the church. As with the mythical Excalibur that young Arthur pulled from the stone, proving that he was the rightful heir to the English throne, Jeffrey believed God would permit only His chosen prophet to wield the Sword of Laban. Obviously, if someone found the sword, he would automatically be declared the church's true prophet. At least that is what Jeffrey thought.

"Do you think it could really be hidden in the park?" Alice asked.

Jeffrey was sure of it. He showed Alice a map of New York and drew a line from the spot where Joseph Smith, Jr., said he found the golden plates to the Kirtland temple. The line went directly through Chapin Forest. "It's entirely possible that the angel Moroni hid the Sword of Laban and other golden plates in a secret chamber in Chapin Forest while he was alive and on his way to New York to hide the other golden plates," Jeffrey said.

"Do you think you can find it?" Alice asked.

Jeffrey wasn't sure, but he intended to try.

The next morning, Alice told Jeffrey that she had something important to share with him.

"I had a dream last night," she gushed. "You were standing in the temple and a tall thin man was on your right and a shorter, more muscular man was on your left. I was sitting in the temple in the back row and when I looked up, there was this beam of pure white light coming down on the three of you and it was so white and so intense that all I could see was the outline of you three and then a pure white personage appeared and talked to you and exchanged something with the three of you. I couldn't quite make out who it was until I saw his hands."

"Who was he?" Jeffrey asked.

"His hands had nail prints in them," Alice said, her eyes filling with tears. "It was Jesus, Jeffrey! Jesus appeared to you!"

She was certain, she added, that the two men in her dream with Jeffrey were Ray Treat and Tom Miller.

"Oh, Jeffrey," she continued. "This is just like the patriarch said it would be. God wants you to bring forth a great message. He wants you to prepare the way for Christ's return."

That night, Ray and Tom again drove to Kirtland from Pittsburgh. Alice didn't mention her dream and Jeffrey didn't mention his theory about the Sword of Laban. If it was there, he was going to find it by himself.

The three men ended up talking about the symbols in the temple just as they had the day before, and then Jeffrey suggested that the three of them spend the night at the temple praying. If they did, perhaps God would show them a sign. Ray and Tom agreed to stay over. Jeffrey was excited. He had successfully set the stage for Alice's dream to come true.

"All of them expected something to happen that night," said Alice. The three men prayed and meditated until three in the morning, but despite their efforts, nothing happened.

"So much for your dream," Jeffrey told Alice the next morning.

Ray and Tom returned to Pittsburgh and Ray taught his last class that night. The next afternoon, he and Tom left for Independence. They stopped in Kirtland around dinnertime to say good-bye to Jeffrey and Alice. Jeffrey invited them in and both men were shocked when they saw what the family was having for dinner. All the Lundgrens had to eat was a basket of biscuits. It looked as if there was only enough for one biscuit per person.

"We had asked Jeff earlier how he survived and he had told us that he depended on the Lord to feed his family," said Tom. "It was pretty clear that they were broke and the kids were hungry."

Even though Tom was unemployed and strapped for cash, he gave one hundred dollars to Jeffrey. Ray added another hundred. Jeffrey thanked both of them and they left. A few miles outside of Kirtland, Tom began to feel uneasy. He and Ray had told Jeffrey that they would be stopping by their house around dinnertime, and for a brief moment, he wondered if Jeffrey hadn't staged the dinner-table scene. There was something about how he and Ray had gotten there at exactly the same moment that Jeffrey and Alice were sitting down at the table. It all seemed too perfect. But then Tom pushed his suspicions out of his mind. It was his old police training, he decided.

Saints were supposed to trust each other.

CHAPTER SIXTEEN

ALICE would claim later that she never knew that Ray and Tom had given Jeffrey money. She never knew where any of Jeffrey's money came from, she said. She never asked. The $1,500 that she and Jeffrey had raised to finance their move to Kirtland was quickly spent. The church didn't pay Jeffrey. He didn't have any obvious financial support. Yet whenever Alice and Jeffrey went to the grocery store or to buy clothing, he would pull a five, ten, or twenty dollar bill from his pocket. "I just assumed that the Lord was providing," she later claimed.

Had she asked, Jeffrey was ready with a heart-tugging story. "We ran out of money almost immediately," he later recalled. "There wasn't any food in the house and everyone was hungry. It was just about dinnertime when two elderly ladies knocked on the door and I explained to them that the temple was closed. But they had driven a long distance, so I decided to break the rules and let them in. They were inside the temple for only about fifteen minutes, but when they came out, they were crying and one of them took my hand to shake it and when I took her hand, I felt paper. 'This is for you,' she said. 'God made me aware that you need this.' I didn't look at it until she had gone. It was a one-hundred-dollar bill and that is what we lived on that week. The rules said we were supposed to turn in all the money that we received. But she had told me that God wanted *me* to have it and that's how I operated. If people said it was for me, I kept it. God had directed me here. He wanted me to do His business, so I expected Him to take care of me and my family."

In October, a group of priesthood members from upstate New York held a weekend retreat at the temple. Most arrived Friday afternoon but it began to snow and some were delayed. Bill Lord gave the men a tour of the temple. Jeffrey stood inside the temple at the door waiting for stragglers. When he heard the sound of footsteps, he opened the door. As soon as he saw who was coming, he began to smile. Kevin Currie, his buddy from the navy, walked up the steps. They hadn't seen each other in ten years. Jeffrey quickly explained that he was a tour guide and pointed next door to the white house where he lived.

"Be sure to stop by later," he said. "There are some things that I've got to share with you."

Jeffrey hurried to tell Alice about Kevin. When he came over to their house, Alice gave him a big hug. Kevin told them that something significant had happened that night. Back in 1974 when Jeffrey first introduced him to the Book of Mormon, Kevin had seen a vision. "Just for an instant in my mind's eye, I saw a door and it had a brilliant white light coming from behind it," he said. Kevin didn't know what it meant so he hadn't paid much attention to it. "But tonight as I was walking up to the temple, I saw that very same door and it opened and there was a bright light shooting out from behind it," Kevin said. He paused and then continued: "Jeffrey, the door that I saw in my mind ten years ago was the door to the Kirtland temple. It was the door that you opened tonight."

Kevin didn't think their reunion was a coincidence. There had to be a reason why he had had his vision. "Why are you here?" he asked.

Jeffrey said that he had come to Ohio "to be endowed with the power—just like it says in the scriptures." He then told Kevin that he had recently made an astounding discovery. After swearing Kevin to secrecy, Jeffrey opened his copy of the Doctrine and Convenants and read out loud the first eight paragraphs of Section 83, a revelation that Joseph Smith, Jr., said God gave him on September 22 and 23 of 1832. The first three paragraphs were about Independence, but it was the fourth paragraph that Jeffrey wanted Kevin to hear:

Verily, this is the word of the Lord, that the city New Jerusalem shall be built by the gathering of the Saints, beginning at this place, even the place of the temple, which temple shall be reared in this generation.

"Kevin," Jeffrey said excitedly. "I'm going to prove to you that for all these years everyone has been waiting at the wrong place for Christ to return."

Kevin was intrigued.

"I'm going to prove to you," Jeffrey continued, "that the real site of Zion is Kirtland—not Independence."

During the next hour, Jeffrey read Kevin more than a dozen scriptures from the Bible and the Book of Mormon that were messages from God delivered by prophets. In each case, the prophet began by saying "This is the word of the Lord" or "Thus saith the Lord."

"A prophet has got to make it clear right up-front that he is delivering a message from God," Jeffrey explained. He then told Kevin to read the first three paragraphs of Section 83. Those paragraphs didn't have any such declaration. "The reason is because God never said those three paragraphs. Those were words written by men," Jeffrey said, his voice becoming a whisper now, as if he were afraid someone might overhear. "Those words were added after Joseph fled Kirtland to justify the saints moving to Independence."

Jeffrey told Kevin to read the fourth paragraph of the revelation. It began with the sentence: "Verily, this is the word of the Lord."

"This is where God's message really starts," Jeffrey explained, "and it says 'the city New Jerusalem shall be built' at the same spot as the temple—right here in Kirtland."

That night in the Lundgrens' kitchen, Kevin once again felt that God was speaking to him through Jeffrey. What Jeffrey was saying seemed to make sense. Other revelations in the Doctrine and Convenants began with a "Thus saith the Lord" preface. Why didn't Section 83?

"It became clear to me that Jeffrey was correct. The only commandment that God had ever given was that He wanted His people to go to the Ohio to be endowed with the power."

Kevin was hooked. Every weekend during the next two months, Kevin rode the bus to Cleveland on Friday nights. Jeffrey picked him up and they studied the scriptures together until Sunday afternoon when Kevin caught another bus back to his hometown of Buffalo,

New York. During their visits, Kevin confided in Jeffrey and Alice. He had gotten married after he left the navy, he said, but it didn't last and he ended up divorced and depressed. He'd stopped going to church, started drinking heavily, and had gotten involved in a homosexual relationship. Nothing in life seemed important. Eventually, Kevin had returned to Buffalo where his mother lived and gone to work at the Veterans Administration hospital. He had started attending church again, but he still was miserable—until he started studying again with Jeffrey.

"For the first time in years," Kevin told them, "I feel a purpose to my life."

This is how Jeffrey later recalled his feelings toward his navy pal. "Kevin was a leech really and a leech needs to be attached to a host. I became that host. You see, religion seemed to touch Kevin from time to time, and give him stability and a purpose in his life. He also wanted to be part of a family. He'd never had his own. In a way, Kevin wasn't that much different from all the others who eventually joined my group. They all were drawn to me because there was something lacking in their own personalities and lives. They wanted me to provide it for them. They were weak. I was strong. I was their host."

In January 1985, Kevin requested a transfer to a VA hospital outside Cleveland, and when it was approved, he moved in with Jeffrey and Alice. He slept on a bed that Jeffrey put in the room where Damon and Jason slept. In the beginning, Kevin gave Jeffrey money each week to help pay for groceries. But Jeffrey and Alice took Kevin aside in early March and suggested that he give them all of his paycheck each month. "They told me that in order for Jeffrey to maintain respect in his children's eyes as the breadwinner of the family, I needed to turn over my entire paycheck to them," Kevin said. "And that is basically what I did." Kevin earned about $1,600 per month. On paydays, Kevin would find Jeffrey waiting on the porch for him when he got home. Jeffrey said that he didn't want to get the money inside because the children might see it.

Kevin was happy to turn over his pay. "I was having a good time. Jeffrey and Alice were fun to be around and Jeffrey was revealing new things all the time in the scriptures. I was glad I lived with them."

Besides, Jeffrey was making more-and-more-dramatic discoveries and Kevin was eager to hear about them. One night, Jeffrey shook Kevin awake and motioned to him to follow. They walked into the kitchen where Alice was waiting. Jeffrey quickly explained that he had been praying in the temple when he saw a ghost.

"I saw a personage, totally white, moving up the stairs," he explained, "and I knew who it was—I immediately recognized him."

Jeffrey paused to catch his breath.

"I asked God, 'What do I need to do to repent before I meet this person? What would you have me do?,' and after a period of time, I felt that God was telling me that it was okay for me to go before this personage, to meet him, so I followed him up the stairs."

Alice and Kevin were clearly mesmerized.

"I could feel the power of his glory as I walked up the stairs. It was like when you get near to an electric power generator, you can feel the power. I went up to the third level and there he was and—"

Jeffrey stopped. He suddenly began crying. "When I came into his presence, I suddenly saw myself as I truly am. For the first time in my life, I saw myself as a dirty rag, the filthiest thing on the face of the earth. I didn't have a right to be in the same room with this figure. I was so unclean. I couldn't move. I couldn't touch him. I couldn't engage him in conversation because I was so unworthy. I had to shrink away because I was so filthy."

"Who was it?" Alice asked, excitedly.

"It was Joseph," he said. "I saw Joseph Smith, Junior, in the temple."

The next Sunday, Jeffrey stood up during the worship service at the RLDS Kirtland congregation and recalled what had happened, only rather than telling everyone that he had seen Joseph, he simply said that he had seen an "angel." He also added a moral.

"If I had been clean, who knows what I could have asked or what this angel could have shared with me. But I lost out because I am a sinner and unclean."

Afterward, some members of the church said it was the most dramatic personal witness that they had ever heard. As far as Kevin was concerned, it was completely believable.

"Among the more traditional RLDS church members, spiritual experiences were something sought after because having a spiritual experience is a sign that God is communicating with you. I figured that if God was going to talk to anyone, it would probably be Jeffrey because he was the most pious person I knew."

CHAPTER SEVENTEEN

T OM Miller kept in touch with Jeffrey after he returned to Independence, and by the spring of 1985, the two men chatted weekly on the telephone about their scriptural studies. A robust, powerfully built man with short blond hair, chiseled features, and a hearty laugh, Tom was having trouble with the liberal changes taking place in the RLDS. "Things have to be logical for me to accept them, and when they aren't, it's tough for me to believe in them," he told Jeffrey during one call. Lots of changes in the church, he added, weren't logical in his view. "I find nowhere in the scriptures where it says women should be priests."

Tom had always had problems with the church, dating back to when he had served a stint as pastor of a small RLDS congregation in Iowa. While he enjoyed preaching on Sundays, he felt uncomfortable when it came to recommending young men for the priesthood. What bothered Tom was the church's policy about having each candidate recommended by two priests who both felt that they had received a "call" from God. Pastors were supposed to recommend young men, but no matter how hard Tom prayed, he never felt that God was telling him to "call" anyone. So Tom didn't, and the men in his Iowa church who wanted to become priests began to complain.

"I got to thinking, 'Hey, is it me or are all these other guys who are claiming to have revelations from God about who to call just a bunch of liars?'" Tom decided to ask the pastor who had submitted his name as a priesthood candidate. What sort of revelation had he received about Tom? "I asked him: 'Why did you recommend me for the priesthood? What did God tell you about me?' And this man sort of hemmed and hawed, and he finally admitted that he really hadn't had any special experience. He just felt that it was the right thing to do, so he did it. I began to wonder if the whole process was all a farce."

Tom might have left the RLDS had it not been for the voice that he heard a short while later. He was asleep in the bedroom of his house when it woke him up. "I mean to tell you it *was* a voice! I thought it was my imagination at first, but then I heard it again and then it repeated itself one more time. The voice said: 'Arise, cleanse thyself and clothe thyself for I am coming.' My first thought was that I should take a shower and put on my suit because the Lord is coming tonight, but then I thought, 'Come on, is putting on a suit going to make me less of a sinner?'"

Tom got out of bed and walked outside onto the wooden deck behind his house. "It was the most beautiful night that I'd ever seen. The moon was full and the shadows cast by the oak and hickory trees were just fantastic. I was standing there, reveling in the beauty, just praising the Lord, when I looked over to the east and there were two bright stars and between them I saw a figure. It was Christ on the cross. I rubbed my eyes. I slapped myself on the head. I told myself that I was seeing something that wasn't there. But I looked and it was. It was there and it was not something that I was imagining. Believe me, I put it through every test that I could think of and everything I did convinced me that what I was seeing was real. Christ was hanging there."

When Tom moved to Independence, he and his wife, Patti, joined the Enoch Hill RLDS congregation, an ultraconservative group where prophecy was viewed as a vital part of every Sunday service. After several Sundays, Tom was asked to anoint a woman with oil and join other elders by putting his hands on her head and prophesying. Everyone waited for Tom to begin. "I didn't know nothing from nothing, but I got caught up in the emotion of it and I started prophesying and pretty soon I was spouting out all sorts of things about this woman and what she was going to do with her life. It was purely emotional and none of it ever came true. I was really going wild." Afterward, Tom felt guilty. "I knew that this woman believed everything I had said and I knew it was nonsense so I went to see her and I told her that I had been making stuff up, but she refused to believe me. She still thought what I had told her was from God. It seemed that there was no place in the church for intelligence. You either had to be caught up in the emotionalism of religion or you weren't seen as a true believer. Intelligence was viewed as a block to being religious."

Tom talked about his experiences with Jeffrey, who quickly agreed that most RLDS members were caught up in the emotionalism of religion, rather than intelligent study. Tom decided to read every verse in the Bible and the Book of Mormon that described contact between God and the Hebrew people. When he finished, he called Jeffrey. "Emotions are more a response to Satanic influence than the things of God," Tom announced, "because emotions cloud your vision and your understanding of the truth."

Jeffrey agreed, so Tom continued. "The truth is purely intellectual. In order to understand God, we must find out how He thinks and then attempt to become one with Him, make our thoughts into His thoughts, and share His intelligence and His truth. And that is an intellectual process, not an emotional one."

Tom and Jeffrey were both excited by what Tom was saying. They talked for nearly an hour on the telephone. The next Sunday, Jeffrey claimed credit in the adult RLDS Sunday school class in Kirtland for an important discovery. He announced that he had studied every scripture that described God's contact with the Hebrews and had found that "intelligence, not emotion" was the key to understanding God. Jeffrey repeated Tom's conclusions almost verbatim. There was only one slight change. Jeffrey made it sound as if everything he said was *his* idea, not Tom's.

No one in Kirtland said much about Jeffrey's "discovery," but in Independence, Tom's denouncement of emotional outbursts had irked most members of Enoch Hill. One night, however, a couple from the church stopped at Tom's house. "They told me that I had all the indications of being ready to receive a special truth. I listened and what they said was so astounding, I didn't know whether to continue listening or run through the door without bothering to open it."

The couple told Tom that there was a secret way to decipher God's truth by using intelligence, rather than emotion. It was called chiasmus. During the next two hours, the couple explained the process to Tom. Most Old Testament books, such as Psalms, Proverbs, Lamentations, Micah, Obadiah, Habakkuk, Nahum, and Zephaniah, were long Hebrew poems, they said. Prophetic books, such as Isaiah, Job, Joel, Amos, Hosea, and Jeremiah, also contain lengthy segments of poetry. Unlike English poetry, Hebrew poetry doesn't have rhyme or meter. Instead, Hebrew poems were written in a style called "parallelism." Put simply, Hebrew poets always repeated themselves. A poet would write a line and then repeat the same thought in the next line only in a slightly different way. This was called "rhyme of thought rather than sound." In Psalm 19, verse 1, the Hebrew poet wrote:

> The heavens declare the glory of God;
>   and the firmament showeth his handiwork.

Both lines say the same thing but in different ways. Over time biblical scholars found a variety of "parallel" poems. Some poets alternated lines that were synonymous. In Psalm 27, verse 1, the poet wrote:

> The Lord is my light and my salvation:
>   Whom shall I fear?
> The Lord is the stronghold of my life;
>   Of whom shall I be afraid?

Scholars were finding so many different types of parallel writing that they developed a way to diagram them. They marked the first line of a poem with the letter A and whenever they came to another verse that was synonymous, they marked it with an A too. This "alphabet code" made it possible for the scholars to see how the poem was structured.

> [A] The Lord is my light and my salvation:
>   [B] Whom shall I fear?
> [A] The Lord is the stronghold of my life;
>   [B] Of whom shall I be afraid?

Once biblical scholars began using this marking system, they discovered an entirely new form of poetry which they called chiasmus. A chiasm is much more difficult to see because it doesn't follow the traditional A-B-A-B repeating sequence. Instead, it reverses it.

When diagramed, a chiasm is structured like this: A-B-B-A. Some biblical scholars call this form of writing "mirror imaging." Verse 27 in chapter 2 of the New Testament book of Mark is a chiasm.

> The sabbath was made for man,
> and not man for the sabbath.

This is how the couple divided it for Tom:

> [A] The *sabbath*
> [B] was made for *man,*
> [B] and not *man*
> [A] for the *sabbath.*

A longer chiasm was found in Isaiah, chapter 6, verse 10:

> [A] Make the heart of this people fat,
> [B] and make their ears heavy,
> [C] and shut their eyes;
> [C] lest they see with their eyes,
> [B] and hear with their ears,
> [A] and understand with their hearts . . .

Once biblical scholars became proficient at identifying and diagraming chiasms, they made another startling discovery. Unlike other Hebrew poems, chiastic verses frequently had one line that was not repeated. This line was nearly always in the center of the poem. For example, Isaiah, chapter 55, verses 8 to 9, read:

> [A] For my thoughts are not your thoughts,
> [B] neither are your ways my ways . . .
> [C] For as the heavens are higher than the earth,
> [B] so are my ways higher than your ways,
> [A] and my thoughts than your thoughts.

The words "thoughts" and "ways" were clearly repeated in typical A-B-B-A fashion, the couple told Tom. But stuck in the middle of the chiasm was line [C] and it stood completely by itself. There was no parallel line that mirrored the verse: "For as the heavens are higher than the earth. . . ."

The couple who explained all of this to Tom told him that the center line of a chiasm was the poet's "secret" message. It was the most important verse in the poem, the one that the poet had really meant to emphasize. Readers who didn't know how to diagram a chiasm would read these verses in Isaiah and interpret them to mean that God's "thoughts" and His "ways" were far superior to the "thoughts" and "ways" of human beings, which was the most common interpretation. But what the Hebrew poet was actually saying was that ". . . the heavens are higher than the earth."

In other words, the poet's cryptic message was that heaven was an actual, physical place located directly above the earth. By locating chiastic poems and diagraming them, Tom could learn the "secret" truths of the Bible that were hidden from everyone but those intelligent enough to use chiasmus.

"What I was hearing was a totally new way to read the scriptures," Tom recalled. "It was one of those rare moments when you feel that a truth has been illuminated to you."

As soon as the couple left that night, Tom telephoned Jeffrey. It was late, but he didn't care. He had to tell Jeffrey that there was a way to separate God's truth from "the church's emotional garbage."

CHAPTER EIGHTEEN

KEVIN Currie started noticing several subtle changes in the Lundgren house in April 1985, once he began turning his paychecks over to Jeffrey. "When I first moved in, I was treated like an equal, an adult, and my opinions were respected. But once I began giving Jeffrey my paycheck, he and Alice started acting more like parents to me and exercising more and more control over my life."

Kevin was the only person in the house earning a salary, yet whenever he needed money, he had to ask and explain to Jeffrey why he wanted it. The few times that Kevin did ask for cash, Jeffrey made it clear that he was taking it away from the rest of the "family" for his own selfish needs.

A few weeks after he moved in with Jeffrey and Alice, Kevin noticed another change. He was doing more and more household chores. It started when he volunteered to wash the dishes one night. All of the sudden, that became his job. So did baby-sitting for the children when Jeffrey and Alice went out, and cleaning the house. Kevin was soon cooking most of the meals at night too. "I had become the maid," he said.

Jeffrey had spent quite a bit of time studying the scriptures with Kevin at night, but during the summer of 1985, four college-age interns arrived to help give tours through the temple and Jeffrey and Alice began focusing on them. Of the four, they liked Sharon Bluntschly and Daniel D. Kraft, Jr., the best.

"The interns didn't know anyone else in town and Bill and Eleanor Lord were so much older that it was natural for them to turn to Alice and me," said Jeffrey. "Sharon, in particular, was lonely so she started coming over to our house all the time."

One of five children, Sharon had grown up in Beaverton, a farming town of 1,100 in the middle of Michigan, where she had done well academically in high school but had always been somewhat of a wallflower. She had enrolled at Graceland College in 1977, but she couldn't make up her mind what she wanted to study so she eventually dropped out and went to work as a tour guide at the RLDS historical site in Nauvoo, Illinois. This was where Joseph Smith, Jr., had established a Mormon community after being driven out of Missouri by angry mobs in 1838. After that stint ended, Sharon had gone to Independence to work as a tour guide at the church's headquarters. The RLDS had only three historical sites, and since Sharon had worked at Nauvoo and Independence, Kirtland was the only one left, so she had arrived to complete the trio. Jeffrey considered Sharon "a complete loser."

"Sharon had never been on a date, never kissed a boy. She was short and weighed about two hundred and thirty pounds. It looked like she cut her own hair by putting a bowl over it. She acted like an old maid even though she was only twenty-seven. The only joy in her life was food. She had no self-esteem, no ambition. All she had ever done was float around the church as a tour guide."

A few days after Sharon arrived in Kirtland, Alice invited her over to the house. "I was sitting on the couch with Alice in her living room and she began talking to me about really strange things," Sharon later testified. Alice told Sharon that Joseph Smith, Jr., had appeared to Jeffrey in the temple. She mentioned that when she was in summer camp in 1969, a church patriarch had proclaimed that Alice would someday marry a man who would do great things for the church. "Alice continued telling me things and it was getting to the point where my mind couldn't handle a whole lot more when Jeff suddenly walked in," Sharon said. Jeff had been working in the visitors' center when, he said, he felt that someone was talking about him at home. Alice immediately confessed that she and Sharon had been doing just that.

"How did you know?" Alice bubbled. Jeffrey didn't reply. He just smiled.

Sharon was impressed. "How could he have known what we were talking about. . . . It was really amazing to me that he came in just at that time."

Years later, Sharon would be more skeptical. "To me now," she would testify, "it seems like it was a setup." But when it happened, Sharon thought Jeffrey had the power to "sense" things that others couldn't. Alice buttressed Sharon's thinking. "Jeffrey isn't like other men," Alice told her. "He has been chosen by God for a special purpose. Someday he will be famous."

That summer, Alice "adopted" Sharon. Alice taught Sharon how to fix her hair, how to buy clothing that complemented her figure, how to fix her nails. She was doing for Sharon what Lois Lundgren had once done for her. But Alice was adding a twist of her own to the transformation. She became Sharon's sexual adviser. "Alice wanted me to work on being carnal, sensual, and devilish," Sharon said later.

"Sharon knew nothing about sex," Alice recalled, "so I set out to educate her." Alice had Sharon watch a videotape of the sultry rock singer Tina Turner. "Tina may not be the most beautiful person in the world, but her body language makes her sexy," Alice said. She and Jeffrey also rented a variety of soft porn to show Sharon to help her loosen up. Finally, Alice asked Kevin to take Sharon on a date.

While Alice made Sharon her summer project, Jeffrey worked on Danny Kraft, Jr., a lovable nineteen-year-old wisenheimer. At age six, Danny had decided to become a musician. At age eleven, he decided to become an artist. By the time he graduated in 1982 from high school in Nauvoo, he had mastered nine musical instruments, won dozens of art awards, and maintained a straight-A average. He was skinny, energetic, impressionable, and eager to please. Jeffrey originally had opposed Danny's working as a guide. Although Danny regularly attended an RLDS church in Nauvoo, he had never been baptized. As soon as Danny arrived, Jeffrey began pushing him to join the church.

Just as they had done with Sharon, Jeffrey and Alice invited Danny into their home and quizzed him about his past. Jeffrey quickly decided that Danny's carefree attitude was a facade. Danny's parents had divorced in 1974. "He's covering up the pain," Jeffrey told Alice later. "Danny is looking for someone to love him—to take the place of his mom and dad and be his family."

A few days later when Danny dropped by the house, Alice told him that she was uncomfortable being addressed as "Mrs. Lundgren." It made her feel old, she joked. "Why not just call me 'Mom'" she told Danny. "You can call Jeffrey 'Dad.'"

Kevin had watched how Jeffrey and Alice manipulated Sharon and Danny, and he realized that neither of them realized it. "Jeffrey began using me to do reconnaissance that summer," Kevin said. "He would send me over to spy on the summer interns, and when I came back to the house, he'd grill me about what they were saying and doing. He especially wanted to know what they were saying about him and Alice. I noticed that he would use the information to his advantage. He was a master at telling one person one thing and then telling someone else another thing and keeping them both in the dark."

On Memorial Day weekend, a group of young people from Independence arrived at the temple for a tour. Shar Olson and Richard Brand were among them. They were best friends. Both of them had made a similar trip on Memorial Day in 1984 and had enjoyed it so much that they had organized this one. By this time, word about Jeffrey had filtered back to most RLDS churches in Independence. "We had heard about this man who worked at the temple and supposedly knew a lot about it so we decided to ask him to teach a special class about the temple for our group," Shar later recalled. Jeffrey quickly agreed to give the group a longer tour than usual. During it, he pointed out the symbol for man on the pulpit and mentioned there wasn't a symbol for woman. Shar and Richard had both strongly opposed the ordination of women as priests and Jeffrey's discovery intrigued them. After the tour, they stayed behind to ask Jeffrey additional questions. Before the group left, they collected a "love offering" and gave it to Jeffrey, who had mentioned several times during the tour that he didn't receive any salary from the church but instead relied on God to provide for him and his four children. The group gave him $400.

A few days after the group left, Bill Lord called Jeffrey into an office at the visitors' center.

"You can't ask for or accept money for giving tours," Bill said. One of the parents who had been chaperoning the Memorial Day tour group had complained. "You're going to have to turn that money over to the church."

Jeffrey quickly apologized and turned over the money. But he asked Bill if it would be okay if the church used the money to buy paint and carpet for the house where he and Alice lived. "Bill agreed," said Jeffrey, "so I got it anyway." He ended up getting even more. When Richard Brand heard what had happened, he became upset and mailed Jeffrey a check for $620. Jeffrey didn't tell anyone about it, but he did write down Richard's name and address. He was someone Jeff planned to remember.

By June, Sharon was spending every free moment at the Lundgrens'. She ate all her meals there too. Jeffrey mentioned this one afternoon when it was time to buy groceries, and Sharon volunteered to turn over her salary of $500 per month to the family. It was added to the $1,600 per month that Kevin gave the Lundgrens. Although Jeffrey had been warned not to solicit donations, he still did. Jeffrey bragged to Kevin about the biggest gifts—$500 from one church group and $300 from another—but no one, not even Jeffrey, kept tabs of the ones, fives, and tens pressed into his hands after he gave a tour.

Sharon decided to stay in Kirtland when summer ended. Jeffrey had convinced her that it, not Independence, was the true site of Zion. She got a job at Holzheimer's Grocery Store as a checkout clerk. The church agreed to let her continue to live in a tiny apartment near the temple that was normally reserved for student guides. But it began charging her rent. Sharon continued to turn over her paychecks to Jeffrey and Alice. In turn, Jeffrey promised to pay her bills and feed her. Danny, who had been baptized into the RLDS by Jeffrey in July, returned to art school but promised to come back to work as a guide the next summer.

After the four student interns had gone, Bill Lord told Jeffrey that it was time to audit the books for the temple and visitors' center. This was the first year that Jeffrey had been responsible for the records and when Bill examined them, he was disappointed. Donations to the temple were substantially less than what was expected. In previous years, sales of books and souvenirs and contributions at the temple had always increased. But not this year, and Bill couldn't figure out why. When he checked the visitors' log at the temple and discovered that a record number of tourists had visited the temple, Lord became suspicious. He called Jeffrey into his office.

"Something is wrong here," Lord said.

Jeffrey looked nervous.

"There is money missing," Lord continued.

Jeffrey suddenly blurted out an explanation. He said that he had been reluctant to mention it during the summer, but he suspected that one of the student interns had been stealing from the cash register. He put the blame on a student he had never liked.

"We didn't have any proof," Lord said later, "so there was nothing we could do." At the time, neither Bill nor Eleanor Lord suspected that the real thief was Jeffrey.

Shortly after that encounter, Kevin, Jeffrey, and Alice went to see the movie *Manhunter*, which is based on the Thomas Harris bestselling novel *Red Dragon*. Jeffrey and Alice both loved to watch movies and they were constantly seeing parallels between various films and their own lives. Jeffrey was mesmerized by *Manhunter*, which described a fictional FBI investigator's pursuit of a ruthless serial killer. The agent eventually caught the murderer by figuring out how he thought. In the movie, this was called developing the same "mindset." After the show, Jeffrey, Alice, and Kevin spent more than an hour discussing it in the kitchen of the house and then Jeffrey went to study his scriptures. Years later, Kevin would still recall what Alice said once they were alone.

"Jeffrey reminds me a lot of the agent in that movie," she told Kevin. "He figures out a person's mindset—what they want, how they think, what their weaknesses are—and then he uses that to get whatever he wants from them."

CHAPTER NINETEEN

IN the fall of 1985, the adult Sunday school teacher at the Kirtland RLDS congregation decided to take a break, so Jeffrey was asked to teach. He immediately began showing the twenty-five class members how to diagram chiastic poems. Most of them had heard about chiasmus because of an article printed by Ray Treat in *The Zarahemla Record*. It had pointed out that the Book of Mormon, like the Bible, contained chiastic poems. Treat claimed this was significant because, in his eyes, the fact that both books contained chiasms was proof that the Mormon scriptures had been written thousands of years ago by a band of Hebrews, not by an imaginative twenty-four-year-old New York boy in Palmyra.

Jeffrey told the adults that Treat had missed the point. By diagraming chiastic poems, he explained, a reader could discover the "secret" truths in the scriptures. Chiasmus reminded Jeffrey of "hidden picture" drawings that he had seen as a child. When you looked at such a drawing the first time, you would see a picture—the face of an old woman with a big nose, for instance. But if you stared at the drawing long enough, the old woman's face disappeared and you could see a completely different drawing—the outline of a young woman wearing a feathered hat.

"Jeffrey was just phenomenal when it came to finding these chiasms," Eleanor Lord recalled. "Everyone in the class was intrigued when he first diagramed them and explained how they worked."

While Eleanor liked Jeffrey and enjoyed his classes, she often was uncomfortable about some of his claims. "Jeffrey had a habit in class of making people believe that what he was teaching was some kind of personal discovery that he had made," she said. Most weeks, she and Jeffrey would talk at the visitors' center about the scriptures and various concepts. She was the first one, in fact, to show him Ray Treat's article about chiasmus. She also knew that Jeffrey got many of his ideas from Tom. "But when Jeffrey taught the class, he always . . . gave the impression that what he was saying was based on some great inspiration that he had received by himself."

In October 1985, Jeffrey learned that the Church was going to hire another tour guide, so Jeffrey telephoned Tom and urged him to apply. Tom's wife, Patti, didn't want to move. She had a good job in Independence and Tom was still unemployed. "But if we move to Kirtland," Tom argued, "I can sit and study and examine records all day long and I will finally be able to learn the truth." Patti reluctantly admitted that ever since Tom had been studying the scriptures via the telephone with Jeffrey, the two of them had made some remarkable discoveries. She agreed to move, and in November 1985, Tom reported to work at the visitors' center.

That same month, Jeffrey received a telephone call from Jim Robbins. Even though the two men had quarreled before the Lundgrens left Independence, Jeffrey and Jim had renewed their friendship. Jeffrey had initiated the peace process by writing to Jim about the symbols in the temple. Jim responded with a letter and the two men were soon writing regularly. Almost immediately, Jeffrey asked Jim in a letter for a personal loan and suggested that he and Laura once again consider supporting him and Alice. Jim had declined, but had continued to write. Jim had called because he and Laura wanted to spend Thanksgiving with the Lundgrens in Kirtland. Jeffrey was excited about the visit. "I have many new discoveries to share with you," he told Jim. The Robbinses planned to spend three full days in Kirtland, but the morning after they arrived, Jeffrey began lecturing Jim about the secret power of chiasmus and how Kirtland was the true location of Zion. Finally, Jim protested.

"Jeff, I just don't see it the same way as you do," he said. But Jeffrey continued to hammer away. The next morning, Jim and Laura announced that they were driving to Pennsylvania to visit a friend. They wouldn't be back until late that night. "We just had to get away from him," said Jim. When the Robbinses returned that night, Jeff was clearly peeved. "He let me know that he didn't like us coming up to see them and then going away for a full day. He wanted us there and the reason why was because he wanted to convince us to move to Kirtland." The next day was Thanksgiving, and after Jeffrey carved the turkey that Jim and Laura had brought with them, he launched into another lecture. By the next morning, Jim and Laura were eager to leave. While they were backing their car out of the Lundgrens' driveway, Jeffrey stepped up to the car window for one last-ditch attempt to persuade Jim that he needed to move.

"Jim, this is where the action is going to be—here in Kirtland, not Independence," he said. "I expect you back here soon."

"Jeffrey," Jim replied coldly, "you will never see me back in Kirtland unless the Lord Himself tells me to come back. There will be no more friendly visits here." With that, Jim rolled up his window and left.

That was the last time that Jim and Laura ever saw the Lundgrens. Years later, when Jim recalled that final exchange, he would remember how he felt while driving away. "As crazy as it sounds, even though I had rejected everything that Jeffrey had said, while we were traveling down the road, I turned to Laura and said, 'Maybe we ought to think about moving to Kirtland.' Jeff had this magnetism about him. He never expressed any doubts and when he said something, it was like the Lord Himself had said it. To a member of the RLDS, that is very appealing. You are trained to relate to that and I did. Only after we had driven further down the road did I realize that what he was preaching was simply nuts."

Not everyone thought so. Alice would later insist that at this point in her marriage to Jeffrey, she genuinely believed that he was fulfilling the patriarch's 1969 prophecy. "I felt God was directing our lives." She and Jeffrey still argued, particularly about sex. But both of them had eased up and were getting along better than they ever had. "The feces wasn't so common. Mostly, he would just bend my body in all sorts of uncomfortable positions. He was really getting into dominance and wanting to control me—in the bed and everywhere else. But I still loved him and I truly believed that Jeff could be someone important in the church."

Jeffrey was working hard to become such a person. Besides learning everything that he could about biblical prophets, Jeffrey was poring over the history of the church. In Kirtland, he found information in the archives that he had not been taught in Sunday school as a youngster. One such account was an embarrassing moment in Mormon history in 1843, when Joseph Smith, Jr., was given six metal plates that had been discovered next to human bones in an ancient Indian burial mound near Kinderhook, Illinois. The bell-shaped plates were marked with strange hieroglyphics and Smith was asked if he could decipher them. After studying the plates, the prophet declared that he could, indeed, read them, and he translated a sample paragraph. He noted the discovery in his private journal.

> Monday, May 1—I insert fac-similes of the six brass plates found near Kinderhook. . . . I have translated a portion of them, and find they contain the history of the person with which they were found. He is a descendant of Ham, through the loins of Pharaoh, king of Egypt. . . .

The discovery of the Kinderhook Plates sparked rumors of a sequel to the Book of Mormon and sent church members scurrying to their scriptures for clues that would help them identify the mysterious "descendant of Ham." Smith had always said that God showed him only a few of the records made by the ancient Hebrews.

Shortly after Smith publicly declared the plates genuine, three men from Kinderhook came forward with an announcement of their own. The entire thing was a hoax. The men had cut six pieces of copper from a strip and inscribed letters on each with acid. These "hieroglyphics" were actually characters copied from the lid of a Chinese tea box. The copper was "aged" by rust and hidden in the Indian mound. A gullible Mormon elder was later led to the site, where he unearthed the plates and was urged to rush them to Smith.

Despite the scam, Smith insisted that other plates made by the ancient Hebrews would someday be found. His claims were consistent with passages from the Book of Mormon that predicted that God would eventually reveal the history of the ancient Hebrews to a prophet [a.k.a. Joseph Smith, Jr.] but would keep part of the records "sealed" because they contained information that the world was not yet ready to receive. Among other things, the records supposedly contained "a revelation" that would explain all things "from the foundation of the world unto the end thereof."

Jeffrey had been to Chapin Forest several times trying to find an entrance to the "secret chamber" behind the strange holes that he had found along with Tom Miller and Ray Treat. But he hadn't had any luck. One morning, Jeffrey came across a passage in Section 101 of the Doctrine and Covenants that described a revelation purportedly given by God to Joseph Smith, Jr., on April 23, 1834. According to it, God ordered Smith to build a "treasury" for "all the sacred things" that God had given him. Jeffrey read the verse to Alice.

"Joseph was in Kirtland when he received this revelation," he explained, so it was only logical that the prophet would build a treasury in Ohio. "It's got to be in Chapin Forest."

Jeffrey told Alice that he was going out to the park for one final look. About an hour later, he returned and hurried Alice into the bedroom.

"I found it," he whispered. "I found the treasury!"

Jeffrey told Alice that there hadn't been anyone else at Chapin Forest when he arrived. He had walked down the path—the same one that he had seen in his dream—to where the strange holes were located. Jeffrey had knelt down and was praying when he heard footsteps.

"My first thoughts were 'Oh, gosh, some hiker is going to see me praying and think I am stupid,' but I continued to pray. When I looked up, there was a personage [angel] there and he explained that God had sent him. He was in charge of the treasury. He told me that he had never suffered death and that he had been a guardian of the treasury from when it was built."

The personage led Jeffrey to a secret opening, he said. "The guardian told me that the treasury could only be opened if God wishes it to be opened so even if other people go look, they won't be able to find it." While Jeffrey waited, the figure went into the treasury. "I looked inside and saw that it was a large chamber. The figure came out with one plate, a single plate, and I looked down and read part of what it said, and then he took it back into the treasury."

Alice drilled him with questions. Who was the personage? Was the plate that Jeffrey saw made of gold? What did the chamber look like? Had he seen the Sword of Laban? But the big question that she wanted answered was: "What was written on the plate?"

"I can't tell you everything that I read," Jeffrey replied solemnly, "because I am not supposed to reveal it yet."

But, he continued, with a flash of excitement, "I can tell who the writing was about."

"Who?" Alice asked.

"Alice," Jeffrey replied dramatically, "the writing on the plate was about *me and what God wants me to do.*"

Alice was excited. "Jeffrey had finally found a niche in life. He was really, really good at giving tours and really, really good at interpreting scripture. It was perfect for him, and we had Kevin and Sharon supporting us financially, so for the first time in our marriage, I didn't have to worry about where the next meal was coming from. We had stability and all these wonderful things were happening to Jeffrey. He was seeing things and things were happening to him that just didn't happen to anyone else."

God had used the scriptures to direct Jeffrey to Kirtland. God had created an opening at the temple so that Jeffrey could be a guide there. God had caused Jeffrey to have visions. And God had sent word to Alice through a patriarch at the 1969 summer camp warning her about her future husband. Like pieces of a puzzle, everything was beginning to come together. As she stood there, wondering exactly what it all meant, Jeffrey told her something else.

"Take off your clothes," he said. "We are going to have anal sex."

Alice stared at Jeffrey and then quietly disrobed.

All of her life, she had been taught that every religion required its members to make a so-called "leap of faith." Alice had decided that her marriage to Jeffrey required the same.

"I had reached a point where I had to choose: Was I going to believe what Jeffrey was telling me and support him or was I going to doubt and question him?"

As far as Alice was concerned, there was no choice. "I decided that he truly was my Lord and my master."

CHAPTER TWENTY

N OT many visitors came to the temple during the winter of 1985 and early 1986 so Jeffrey and Tom Miller had plenty of time to study their scriptures. Eleanor Lord would join them some days. All three had become proficient at finding chiastic verses. But Jeffrey was the champ. "Chiasmus was becoming an obsession with him," Eleanor noted.

One morning Jeffrey burst into the center and announced that he had made an astounding discovery. He had been reading the First Book of Nephi in the Book of Mormon, which is the equivalent of Genesis in the Bible, and he had found a new meaning for a phrase it contained. According to the book, the prophet Nephi explained that he had written the history of the Nephites *"in the language of my father, which consists of the learning of the Jews and the language of the Egyptians."* Most Mormons felt this was a reference to "Reformed Egyptian," the term that Joseph Smith, Jr., used to describe the writing on the mystical golden plates. But Jeffrey had a different explanation.

Before Jeffrey revealed one of his discoveries, he always laid the groundwork by quoting scripture and this time he began in chapter

41 of Genesis, which tells how God caused Pharaoh to dream *two* strange dreams. Jeffrey read part of verse 32 aloud:

"   . . . the dream was doubled unto Pharaoh twice; it is be-cause the thing is *established by God* . . ."

"Why did God cause Pharaoh to dream twice?" Jeffrey asked. Without waiting for a reply, he told Tom and Eleanor to turn to the Old Testament book of Job, verse 14 in chapter 33, which read: *"For God speaketh once, yea twice, yet man perceiveth it not."*

Jeffrey paused and then summarized his points. The Hebrews had written their poetry by repeating each line. God had caused Pharaoh to dream *two* dreams. And the writers of Job said that God "speaketh once, yea twice."

"What the scriptures are telling us," Jeffrey said, "is that God says everything twice—He speaks chiastically!" In Jeffrey's eyes, it made perfect sense. The reason the ancient Hebrews had used "par-allelism" in their poetry is because they wanted to praise God in His *own* language, he explained. So when the prophet Nephi used the phrase the "language of my father" and the "learning of the Jews," he was referring to chiasmus.

Tom thought Jeffrey was on to something, but Eleanor wasn't so certain. "I now realize that this was a turning point for Jeffrey," she said, "because in his mind, he had found a great truth. Jeffrey felt that he had found a foolproof way to separate God's words from man's words. If a scripture was chiastic in structure, then it was of God. Otherwise, it was from man, and didn't really count."

Jeffrey was so confident that he used a red marker to cross out the lines in the Bible and his Mormon scriptures that didn't pass the test.

A few days after Jeffrey made this discovery, Eleanor asked him if he planned to discard the Lord's Prayer and Christ's Sermon on the Mount since neither was a chiastic poem. Did Jeffrey really be-lieve that those scriptures didn't matter?

Jeffrey said he needed more time to figure it out, but he was sure enough of his theory to teach it the next Sunday to his adult Sunday school class. When the class ended, a woman took Jeffrey aside. "While you were teaching, I saw a vision of Moses standing next to you!" she told him. Another class member said that God had given him a revelation for Jeffrey. "Thus saith the

Lord, you are to continue on the path that you are on, teaching the truth."

Jeffrey sent letters about chiasmus to the Patricks and the Averys in Independence. Both couples wrote back asking for more information. At home, he explained his discovery to Kevin Currie, who still lived with him, and Sharon Bluntschly, who continued to spend most of her time at the Lundgrens' house.

But his biggest booster was Alice. "Maybe this is it!" she gushed. "Maybe this is the revelation you are supposed to bring forth—the one that was prophesied by the patriarch!"

There was one person who didn't think Jeffrey was anyone special. The Reverend Dale Luffman had become the RLDS stake president in the Kirtland area in January 1986. As such, he was supposed to make sure that the twelve congregations in his stake operated smoothly and adhered to church policy. Luffman was a full-time, salaried employee of the RLDS who answered to church officials in Independence. He was not warmly welcomed at the RLDS congregation in Kirtland. The church rolls listed 150 members, but a handful of elders really ran the brick church across the street from the Kirtland temple and they were fundamentalists who considered Luffman a "liberal" sent from church headquarters to bring them into line. In their eyes, the new stake president represented everything wrong in the RLDS. He had attended another denomination's seminary: Princeton University in New Jersey. [How, fundamentalists asked, could Luffman have learned anything by going to another religion's school, especially one that didn't believe in the Book of Mormon?] Worse, Luffman had received an undergraduate degree from an Oregon college run by the Roman Catholic Church. In the 1970s, he had helped organize a boycott of grapes on behalf of migrant farm workers and he had led student demonstrations against the Vietnam War. If that weren't enough, shortly after Luffman arrived in Kirtland, he described himself as an "ecumenicist." That meant that he didn't believe that the RLDS was God's only "true church." Within days after Luffman arrived, a rumor swept through the congregation in Kirtland. Luffman had befriended a minister from another church and was thinking about joining the local ministerial alliance. To fundamentalists, such a move was blasphemy.

Luffman hardly looked a rebel. A lanky man in his early forties, he had a closely trimmed salt-and-pepper beard and thick glasses, and spoke with a stuffed-nose twang. He had grown up poor, was well read, and didn't seem too concerned about the pomp and circumstance of organized religion. If anything, the first impression that most people had was that Luffman was pretty ordinary.

Within two weeks of his arrival, Luffman and Jeffrey clashed. It happened after Luffman preached his first sermon in the Kirtland church. He talked about how Christ's death and His love had saved the world. After the worship service, Luffman planned to attend Jeffrey's class, but he got delayed by a telephone call. Seconds later, as he walked down the hall to the class, he heard his name being mentioned. He paused outside the classroom and listened.

"You all heard the stake president's sermon today," Jeffrey announced, "and before we start, I want to talk about it." During the next fifteen minutes, Jeffrey accused Luffman of preaching "lies." "Our God is a God of vengeance," Jeffrey said, "and He expects only one thing from us—repentance. Repent, repent, repent. Those who do not repent will perish."

Luffman stepped into the classroom and took a front-row seat. Without a hint of embarrassment, Jeffrey began that day's regular lesson. Afterward, Luffman called Jeffrey into the church office.

"Your action was completely unethical," Luffman declared. "Everyone has a right to a difference of opinion. That's one thing. But you're telling people that I lied and that only *you* know the truth! Who are you to speak for God? What right do you have to tell people what is the truth?"

Jeffrey didn't defend himself. He simply listened as Luffman berated him.

"I expect an apology," Luffman finally concluded.

"I apologize," Jeffrey said, without any visible sign of remorse.

Jeffrey had never been particularly well liked in any church. Alice was the one who always made friends quickly while Jeffrey was aloof and haughty. But the fundamentalist elders at Kirtland rallied around Jeffrey. "I think Jeffrey found in the Kirtland congregation a unique climate," Luffman said later. "The few elders running the show saw in Jeffrey a spokesman for their point of view and Jeffrey liked to feel important. I think the two groups fed on each other."

During the following weeks, each time that Luffman preached at the Kirtland congregation, Jeffrey rebutted the sermons line by line in the adult class. As always, he got away with it by using his amazing memory of scriptures. Rather than attack Luffman in person, Jeffrey simply recited verses that contradicted whatever Luffman had preached.

Even though Luffman was furious, there was little he could do. Jeffrey worked for Bill Lord, who reported to the office of historical sites in Independence. Luffman reported to an entirely different office. The stake president didn't have any say over who worked at the temple.

"He's untouchable," Luffman complained after church to his wife, Judy. "I can't fire him."

There was, however, one way in which Luffman could discipline Jeffrey. The elders in the church had recommended that Jeffrey be promoted within the RLDS priesthood to the rank of elder. As stake president, Luffman got first shot at that request. He rejected it. If anything, the rejection seemed to win Jeffrey even more status.

"Jeffrey became almost a folk hero in the eyes of many fundamentalists in the church and he was gaining a tremendous following," Alice said later. "All day, every day, we had people coming to our front door, asking to see Jeffrey. Even Mormons [LDS] invited him to speak to them about the temple. People would come and ask if they could have their picture taken with Jeffrey because of his growing reputation."

It was about this time that someone noticed that Jeffrey's profile resembled a photograph in the temple of a death mask that had been made of Joseph Smith, Jr., after his murder. "I had little girls who were Mormon missionaries coming to the door asking me what it was like to be married to someone who looked like the beloved Joseph Smith," Alice said. Jeffrey found the comparison flattering and began mentioning the similarities during tours. He would tell people jokingly that he was Smith reincarnated.

As Jeffrey's popularity increased, Luffman tried new ways to undercut him. He decided to start another adult Sunday school class in the Kirtland church in the hope that it would draw members from Jeffrey's. It didn't. Jeffrey turned the tables on Luffman. Fundamentalists would come to Jeffrey's class, but would boycott church whenever Luffman preached. One Sunday, so many elders avoided the worship service that Luffman didn't have the required number to serve communion. Luffman reacted by organizing a leadership recruitment drive, an attempt to get "new blood" onto the various church committees that ran the church. He was trying to push out the old fundamentalists. But that didn't work either. "The situation deteriorated—fast," Luffman recalled.

At home, Kevin noticed that Jeffrey was spending hours talking about how he would lead a revolt of RLDS fundamentalists. He'd oust Wallace B. Smith, fire Luffman, kick the women out of the priesthood, restore the "true" RLDS church, and declare himself the new president-prophet.

At work, Jeffrey became bolder. He acted as if the temple were his personal domain. When Jeffrey felt a group of elders from out of town weren't paying attention during a tour, he belittled them. "I preached for forty-five minutes about how this temple was sacred and they had no right to come into it unless they were spiritually prepared." Afterward, one of them agreed, but others complained.

"You've got a real ego problem," an elder told him.

One Saturday morning in late April, Jeffrey mentioned that he wanted to leave work early because he and Alice were going to an antiques show. There hadn't been many visitors that morning, so Tom volunteered to stay at the visitors' center until noon by himself and then lock up. Jeffrey told him not to worry about taking the money out of the cash register. "I'll come over later and do it."

Tom knew that Jeffrey was adamant about being the only person who counted the daily receipts at the visitors' center. But when it was time to lock up, Tom didn't want to leave money in the register. He was afraid that he'd be blamed if it got stolen or came up short. So Tom counted the money and compared the total to the cash-register tape. The receipts and cash didn't match. Sixty-seven dollars was missing. Tom checked his figures again, but he hadn't made a mistake. Someone had taken sixty-seven dollars. "The only logical explanation is that Jeffrey took the cash," he told his wife that afternoon. They agreed that Tom should give Jeffrey a chance to explain before telling Bill Lord.

On Monday morning, Tom confronted Jeffrey. "Hey, the receipts show sixty-seven dollars missing." Tom didn't mean it to sound like an accusation but his old police training had kicked in and that is exactly what it sounded like. "Did you take it?"

Jeffrey turned red. "We were a little short," he replied, "so I borrowed it. I'm going to pay it back."

"Hey, that's stealing, Jeffrey. That is contrary to everything we are all about here."

"No, it's not," Jeffrey retorted. He was going to put an IOU in the cash register, he said. He took the money because he needed to buy milk for his children. Tom didn't believe him. The way he remembered it was that Jeffrey had left early Saturday to go to an antiques show. Tom didn't believe Jeffrey was hard up for cash. Once Jeffrey had showed him a three-hundred-dollar hunting knife that he had bought at an antiques store. When Tom reminded him of that fact, Jeffrey said that Alice had actually taken the money. She was the thief.

"His story kept changing," Tom said, "and it kept getting worse and worse." Finally, Jeffrey broke into tears. "He began crying, really sobbing . . . he starts blubbering like a baby about how I couldn't turn him in because he didn't have anywhere else to go. He told me that I'd ruin his family and his life and his children's lives. It was quite a tirade and it pissed me off. I told Jeffrey, 'Hey, buddy, you made the bed, you lie in it. If this is what you are about, then I got no time for you.'"

When Tom said that he was going to tell Bill Lord about the money, Jeffrey raced out the visitors' center door. "A few minutes later, Alice shows up and she starts pleading and starts crying too," said Tom. "She says, 'Oh, this will ruin our kids, please think about them,' and I said, 'Hey, lady, you think about it, you did it, not me.' And then she starts telling me about how Jeffrey didn't mean to hurt anyone and how I was going to destroy him. I was outraged that Jeffrey would send his wife over to beg me."

Despite the pleas, Tom told Bill that Jeffrey had stolen the money. Jeffrey and Alice rushed in to speak privately with Bill as soon as Tom finished. Both were in tears. "Jeffrey told me that he had taken the money to buy bread and milk for his children," Bill said later. "Those were almost his exact words, and I felt sorry for him."

Bill asked Jeffrey why he was broke. "I thought you told me that you were receiving money each month as part of an inheritance," Bill said.

"They didn't get it to us soon enough this month, but as soon as they do, I'll pay it back," Jeffrey replied.

Bill needed time to think it over. He wanted to consult with his boss in Independence. Jeffrey and Alice left. "We had never had a tour guide who was as enthusiastic about the temple as Jeffrey was," said Bill, "and he was a young fellow and he had a family and I felt that he deserved another chance. I felt he was truly sorry and figured it was just a minor mistake." After lunch, Bill called Jeffrey into the office. "We've decided to let this go," he said. Jeffrey would have to refund the sixty-seven dollars, but that was it.

Tom was flabbergasted when he learned that Jeffrey had gotten off the hook. What was even more incredible was that Bill had left Jeffrey in charge of the books. Tom felt betrayed. Part of the reason he had moved to Kirtland was to study with Jeffrey. He had believed he was someone special and now he felt Jeffrey was nothing but a common thief. "We could have been best friends. . . . We had gotten so far in our studies . . . and yet it clearly didn't mean anything to Jeffrey. He knew how to say all the right words, but they didn't mean anything to him."

CHAPTER TWENTY-ONE

HAD the Reverend Dale Luffman known that Jeffrey had been caught stealing from the cash register, he would have used that information to get him fired. But no one told Luffman. Tom Miller didn't like him and Bill Lord didn't feel it was any of the stake president's business. As a result, Jeffrey's image as a pious fundamentalist spokesman continued untarnished. A short time after the theft episode, Jeffrey was invited to speak about the temple to an RLDS congregation in Richmond, Missouri. Since the church was only a few miles from Independence, Jeffrey wrote a short letter to Richard Brand and invited him to the lecture. Cheryl Avery happened to telephone and Alice invited her too. Jeffrey's lecture and slide show went well and afterward Jeffrey sought out Richard and thanked him for the $650 that he had given him the summer before. He also began recruiting Richard. After all, if Jeffrey planned to launch a fundamentalist revolt, he was going to need someone to lead. "God's calling you to the temple," Jeffrey told Richard. "When are you moving there?" Richard demurred.

Cheryl Avery and her daughters tracked down Jeffrey and Alice at the lecture. Each was carrying a cherry pie. Cheryl wasn't that good a cook, Alice later said, and as a joke, Jeffrey had once made a big fuss about one of her cherry pies. "He had eaten one of them all by himself. So here comes Cheryl and the girls with four pies for us." Jeffrey rolled his eyes at Alice when Cheryl wasn't looking. Cheryl just didn't understand.

When they returned to Kirtland, Jeffrey wrote a letter to Richard urging him to join them. Meanwhile, Jeffrey and Alice avoided Tom at the visitors' center. Instead, they spent their time welcoming the new batch of college-age students who had come to work as summer tour guides. As promised, Danny Kraft, Jr., had returned. He had walked into the Lundgrens' house and yelled, "Dad and Mom—I'm home!" With Danny's help, Jeffrey had started teaching nightly classes at his house for the summer students as well as Kevin and Sharon.

On Memorial Day, Richard and Shar Olson returned with another church group just as they had in 1984 and 1985. This time, they brought Richard's best friend, Greg Winship. Shar asked Jeffrey to give them a tour and teach a class, which he did. Only this time, Jeffrey openly declared that Kirtland was the real site of Zion.

"Are you listening, Richard?" Jeffrey asked in front of everyone.

Richard had just graduated from the University of Missouri and everyone assumed that he would find a job or attend graduate school, but a few days after he and the others returned to Independence, Richard announced that he was moving to Kirtland to study with Jeffrey.

"Richard had been brought up believing that religion was the most important part of your life," Jeffrey said later. "He felt that I could help him understand the truth." Kevin, Sharon, Danny came, in Jeffrey's opinion, " because they were losers or thrill seekers or because they thought they could get something from me. Richard came because he loved the truth."

The youngest of three children and the only son of Wilmer G. and Twylia Brand, Richard grew up in what authorities would later describe as a "quintessential all-American home." His father was an air-traffic controller, an ordained RLDS elder, and a good provider. Twylia stayed at home to look after her children. As a student at William Chrisman High School, the same Independence school that Jeffrey had attended, Brand did all the right things. He was a member of the National Honor Society, the baseball and basketball teams, and a writer on the school newspaper. He graduated in the top 2 percent of the 1981 class and was later remembered by his classmates as being an intelligent, deeply religious, handsome student who was popular with his peers and liked by his teachers. At college, he earned a bachelor of science degree in civil engineering with a grade-point average of nearly 3.5 and was later characterized by a professor as an "outstanding young man full of potential."

Richard arrived in a new Mitsubishi pickup truck that he had just bought. He'd gotten the money, he told Jeffrey, from the estate of his grandmother. She'd left him $17,000 in cash. He had spent $13,000 to buy the truck, brought $1,000 in cash with him, and had another $3,000 in a savings account back in Independence. It didn't stay there long.

Originally, Richard planned to rent an apartment, find a job, and study with Jeffrey part time. But Jeffrey suggested that Richard move in with him for a while first and "get up to speed" on his scriptural studies. Richard agreed and fixed up a classroom area in the Lundgrens' basement. Each morning, Richard would go downstairs to study. Jeffrey had taught him how to diagram chiastic verses and he was eager to discover the scriptures' "hidden" messages. But he didn't have much luck and he became depressed.

"I told Richard that the reason he wasn't getting anywhere was because he was worshiping a false god," Jeffrey recalled. "I told him that he worshiped his truck. I said, 'You spend more time bowing down before your truck, washing and polishing it, than you do bowing down before your God,' and after a few days, he agreed that possessions had always been too important in his life."

Jeffrey suggested a solution.

"Sell your truck," he said. "Get rid of your false god."

Richard offered to sell it to Jeffrey for one dollar.

"No, you will still be driving it and worshiping it, and although we could use a dependable vehicle, the issue is that you must get rid of it because it is coming between you and God."

The Mitsubishi truck had less than two thousand miles on it and was only five months old. Richard sold it for $5,500. He gave the money to Jeffrey as evidence that he no longer intended to let possessions rule his life. Jeffrey was pleased. He told Richard that he was welcome to move in permanently with him and Alice and he said that Richard didn't need to find a job. Jeffrey would take care of him, in return, for the rest of Richard's inheritance. Richard agreed.

"I told him that he was doing the right thing in the eyes of God," Jeffrey remembered, "and his depression went away and he started making real headway in his studies."

By the fall of 1986, Jeffrey had attracted a core group of "disciples." Kevin and Richard lived with him in the house. Danny and Sharon lived across the street in student apartments that they rented from the church. About twice a week, Jeffrey would teach special classes just for them at his house. Most focused on how the RLDS Church had fallen away from the scriptures by becoming too liberal. The group studied scriptures that talked about how God would some-day cause a new prophet to rise up and restore Zion.

It was during this period that Alice had a strange dream. It was dark in her dream and all she could hear at first was a whirling noise, like the sound of helicopter blades chopping the air as they began to turn. A light appeared—a spotlight illuminating a boxing ring. Alice was inside a huge auditorium, high up, away from the ring, in the cheap seats. Two men were wrestling, their muscular, well-tanned bodies dressed in skintight trunks. One of them lifted his opponent and slammed him on the mat. Everyone yelled, but Alice turned away. She knew someone was watching her. Someone was waiting for her. At that point, Alice woke up. She told Jeffrey about the dream the next morning.

"God is trying to show me something," she said. "But I don't understand."

A short time later, Kevin saw the movie *The Highlander*, and when he got home, he told Jeffrey and Alice that they had to see it. They went the next afternoon. The movie began in total dark-ness. Blood-red words suddenly appeared on the screen and the voice of Sean Connery vibrated through the theater.

> "From the dawn of time we came, moving silently down through the centuries, living many secret lives, struggling to reach the time of the gathering, when the few that remain will battle until the last. No one has ever known that we were among you—until now."

The screenplay, based on a story by Gregory Widen, followed the adventures of Conner Macleod, a Scot who should have died in 1536 when he was wounded in battle, but who miraculously survived and later discovered that he was a member of a rare race of immor-tals. These men could be killed only when they were beheaded with a sword. During the centuries that followed, Macleod and the other immortals lived like ordinary people until the time of the "gather-ing," when all of them met to fight. Only one could claim the ulti-mate prize—complete knowledge of everything in the world.

Within seconds after the move began, Alice grabbed Jeffrey's arm. "This is it!" she announced. "This is my dream."

The first scene in the movie was shot in an auditorium where a yelling crowd was watching a professional wrestling match. The camera panned the fans and then zeroed in on the hero, who was sitting near the top of the auditorium in the cheap seats scanning the mob for his adversary.

"It is exactly like my dream," Alice whispered. During the next 110 minutes of the movie, Alice repeatedly squeezed Jeffrey's arm. She didn't have to say anything to him. He knew what she meant. He saw dozens of similarities between the film and his life.

"It was like watching our own lives being played out on the screen," Jeffrey later explained. "The term 'the gathering' was straight from Joseph Smith, Jr. . . . The prize was also scriptural. One man gets the power . . . to know everything in the world. Holiness is defined in the Book of Mormon as knowing all things, becoming one with God."

After the movie, as Jeffrey and Alice were walking to their car, Alice suddenly stopped.

"Listen," she said.

Jeffrey looked around. He was quiet.

"It's the same whirling noise that we heard in the theater," said Alice.

She looked at Jeffrey and waited for him to look directly at her.

"Why is this happening to us?" she asked. "Jeffrey, why are you so different from other men?"

Jeffrey didn't say anything.

"I want to see it again," Alice said. "The movie."

They returned to the theater. That afternoon they watched the movie over and over and over again until the theater closed. The next day the two of them came back. They saw the show a total of seven times that weekend.

The following night, Jeffrey got out his scriptures and spread them and several other books out on the floor of the living room. He was looking for a specific story in the Book of Mormon about three Nephites whom God made immortal. These faithful saints, according to the Mormon scriptures, are still walking among ordinary humans, ministering to the faithful, unknown to everyone.

"I became convinced that God had moved the director and screenwriter of that movie," said Jeffrey. "God had moved them to make it solely because he wanted Alice and me to see it. He wanted me to know that I was truly different from other men."

Alice watched Jeffrey as he read his scriptures. "Jeffrey was totally oblivious to everything around him when he studied," she recalled. "He called it 'Becoming one with the word' and the house could be on fire and he wouldn't know it. I never knew anyone who loved to learn as much as him. It was second only to his love of sex."

Alice went out into the living room, sat beside him, put her arms around him and asked: "Jeffrey, who are you?"

"Who do you think I am?" he replied.

"I don't know, Jeffrey, but you are not like anyone I've ever known or seen."

"I think we need to find an answer to your question," he replied. "I think it is time to find out who I really am."

Self-proclaimed prophet Jeffrey Don Lundgren told jurors that he executed the five members of the Dennis Avery family because God ordered him to "destroy the wicked." The Averys' biggest sin: questioning whether Lundgren was really a prophet. CURT CHANDLER/CLEVELAND *PLAIN DEALER*

Jeffrey Lundgren is returned to Lake County in handcuffs from San Diego, California. Claiming that the prophets in the Old Testament had worn their hair long for religious reasons, Jeffrey refused to cut his before trial. DUNCAN SCOTT/*NEWS HERALD*

At her trial, Alice Lundgren claimed that she was a battered wife who had suffered years of psychological and sexual abuse. But Jeffrey's followers described Alice as Jeffrey's "cheerleader" and closest adviser. "If Jeffrey wants me to be his doormat, then I'll be happy the rest of my life cleaning his shoes," Alice was quoted as saying.
CURT CHANDLER/CLEVELAND *PLAIN DEALER*

Kirtland Police Officer Ron Andolsek examines the pit in the barn where the bodies of the Averys were found nine months after the murders. Jeffrey selected a corner that flooded from rainwater, explaining that the Averys had to be covered with water just like the Egyptians who drowned while pursuing Moses across the Red Sea.
LUCI WILLIAMS/CLEVELAND *PLAIN DEALER*

Dennis and Cheryl Avery were wooed to Kirtland, Ohio, by Jeffrey Lundgren's fundamentalist teachings. The Averys gave Jeffrey and Alice a car and $10,000 in cash. But when the Averys ran out of money, Jeffrey shunned them and eventually told his followers that God wanted the Averys murdered as a human sacrifice. Dennis, Trina, and Cheryl are pictured standing in back row. Rebecca, in overalls, and Karen are in front. MARLENE JENNINGS

When Alice was eighteen, a church patriarch prophesied that she would marry a "companion" who would "be great" and "bring forth a marvelous work and wonder." Although Alice was certain that Jeffrey was that man, his parents opposed their marriage until she became pregnant.
RECENT PHOTO OF ALICE IN THE OHIO REFORMATORY FOR WOMEN COURTESY OF ALICE LUNDGREN

A devout church member, Shar Olson believed Jeffrey was a prophet until she caught him lying. At the time Olson left the group, Jeffrey was planning to take over the Kirtland temple by force and behead the Reverend Dale Luffman. Olson tipped off Kirtland Police Officer Ron Andolsek to the threat. CURT CHANDLER/CLEVELAND *PLAIN DEALER*

Kirtland Police Chief Dennis Yarborough (left), one of the first to become suspicious of Jeffrey, confers with Lake County Prosecutor Steven C. LaTourette and Assistant Prosecutor Karen Kowall on the morning the Averys' bodies were unearthed. CURT CHANDLER/CLEVELAND *PLAIN DEALER*

Two paramedics remove a body from the barn on the farm that Jeffrey Lundgren and his followers rented outside Kirtland, Ohio. GEORGE HEINZ/CLEVELAND *PLAIN DEALER*

Follower Kathryn R. Johnson left her husband and four children after Jeffrey convinced her that she had been created from one of his ribs and was supposed to be his wife. She later gave birth to Jeffrey's child and at her court sentencing proclaimed that her only crime was "loving Jeffrey." CURT CHANDLER/CLEVELAND *PLAIN DEALER*

Dennis Avery's younger brother, Tim, and his wife, Lisa, suspected that Jeffrey Lundgren was a fraud but were unable to convince Dennis and Cheryl. After the murders, Tim and Lisa were escorted by Chief Yarborough through the barn where the bodies were found. CURT CHANDLER/CLEVELAND *PLAIN DEALER*

Kirtland Police Chief Dennis Yarborough kneels beside several holes drilled into a slab of rock at Chapin Forest. Jeffrey told his followers that the holes were air vents that led to a hidden treasury that contained golden tablets inscribed with holy scriptures and that the opening to the treasury was guarded by an angel.

CURT CHANDLER

Damon Lundgren begged for mercy at his trial and claimed his father forced him to participate in the murders. Testimony showed that Damon became physically ill when his father made him look at Dennis Avery's bloody body moments after he was executed. Jeffrey Lundgren reacted by giving Damon, then eighteen years old, a fatherly hug. CURT CHANDLER/ CLEVELAND *PLAIN DEALER*

Kirtland Police Officer Ron Andolsek stands in front of the barn where the Averys were buried. He became so engrossed in the case that he suffered fits of depression. CURT CHANDLER

CHAPTER TWENTY-TWO

J EFFREY went to the temple to pray. But he didn't know exactly what to ask. "Alice got real pushy after we saw *The Highlander*. She'd say, 'Are you the great last prophet that we're all looking for?' . . . The thought had hit me from time to time. I would wonder, 'Why am I the only one seeing these things?' The thought entering my mind was 'Who the heck am I even to think that I am this man?' but Alice kept pushing and I kept wondering, 'Could it be true? Could I really be this prophet, this seer? Is God choosing me?'"

The longer Jeffrey thought about it, the more logical it seemed. He had read about all of the prophets and he thought that he had the same qualities as they had. "The most important thing is your willingness to do what God asks. I have never cared what other people thought. I had always loved the scriptures. I began to realize that it could be true. I could be the last seer. Why not?"

There was only one real glitch in his mind. Prophets were supposed to proclaim a great revelation. Joseph Smith, Jr., had brought forth the Book of Mormon. What did Jeffrey have to reveal? "I said to God, 'Okay, if I'm supposed to be this great last servant, the one like Moses, then what am I supposed to reveal to the world? Tell me, God. Show me what you want me to reveal. And I began to pray."

Five. Ten. Fifteen minutes. Nothing happened. No voices. No beams of light. No personages. No signs of any kind came to Jeffrey. After an hour, his mind wandered. He thought about *The Highlander*, about being immortal. He decided to read his scriptures, and for no apparent reason, he turned to Genesis and read chapter 6. In the standard Bible, chapter 6 contains twenty-two verses that describe the descendants of Adam and the building of Noah's ark. But Jeffrey was reading the "inspired" Bible as translated by Joseph Smith, Jr., and when Smith rewrote chapter 6, he added forty-nine verses. Most described men who later showed up in the Book of Mormon. Their names were inserted in the genealogy of Adam to prove that they were his direct descendants and not fictional characters. Perhaps the most amazing addition that Smith made, however, was a series of verses in Genesis that described the eventual birth of Jesus Christ, the Millennium, and how the latter-day saints would be raised up to rule the earth. It was these verses that Jeffrey was reading, and when he came to verse 60, a specific line caught his eye.

. . . In the language of Adam, Man of Holiness is his name; and the name of his only Begotten is the Son of Man, even Jesus Christ, a righteous judge, who shall come in the meridian of time.

By this time, Jeffrey had fallen into the habit of diagraming every verse that he read to see if it was "God's words or man's."

[A] In the language of Adam
  [B] Man of Holiness
    [C] is his *name*
    [C] and the *name* of his only begotten
  [B] is the Son of Man
[A] even Jesus Christ

Lines [C] clearly mirrored each other because the word "name" was in each. Jeffrey decided that the [B] lines also were parallel because "Son of Man" was synonymous with "Man of Holiness." But the [A] lines clearly didn't match. The first one talked about the "language of Adam." The second line talked about "Jesus Christ."

Jeffrey closed his Bible. He was frustrated. He tried to pray, but he couldn't concentrate. "I felt that God was telling me that He had already shown me everything that I needed to know. All I had to do was open my eyes." Jeffrey glanced around the temple. "God had directed me to Kirtland. The scriptures said that if I went to the Ohio, I would be endowed with the power. The secret had to be in the temple. What was I missing?"

He decided to read every verse in the scriptures that described the building of temples. He began in Exodus, chapter 25, where he came across these lines:

> And let them make me a sanctuary; that I may dwell among them. According to all that I show thee after the pattern of the tabernacle, and the pattern of all the instruments thereof . . .

The word "pattern" had been repeated. Jeffrey continued on. In First Chronicles, chapter 28, he read several verses that quoted God telling David how his son Solomon was to build a temple. Verse 11 read:

> Then David gave to Solomon his son the *pattern* . . .

It was in verse 12 too:

> And the *pattern* of all that he had by the spirit . . .

Jeffrey found it again in verse 19:

> All this, said David, the Lord made me understand in writing by his hand upon me, even all the works of this *pattern* . . .

Jeffrey felt that he was on to something. Like a bird eating bread crumbs dropped in a line, he continued on. He turned to chapter 43 of Ezekiel. At this point in Jewish history, Solomon's temple had been destroyed and the Hebrews had been taken into captivity in Babylon. In verse 10, Jeffrey read about Ezekiel's vision of how the temple—the house—should be rebuilt and how the Jews—the House of Israel—should construct it.

> Thou son of man, show the house to the House of Israel,
> that they may be ashamed of their iniquities; and let them mea-
> sure the *pattern*. . . .

"Everywhere I looked, I found mention of this 'pattern' but I
still didn't know what it was, only that it came from God."

In the New Testament book of Hebrews, chapter 8, verses 5
and 6, Jeffrey found the word "pattern" once again.

> . . . See, saith he [God], that thou *make all things according
> to the pattern* . . .

"Was it coincidence," Jeffrey asked, "that every time there was
a mention of a temple, there was talk about this mysterious 'pattern'
from God?"

Jeffrey decided to see if the word "pattern" was mentioned in
his Mormon scriptures. In Section 52 of the Doctrine and Covenants, he found this verse:

> And again, I will give unto you a *pattern* in all things, that
> ye may not be deceived; for Satan is abroad in the land, and he
> goeth forth deceiving the nations. . . .

Jeffrey closed his scriptures. He knew that God had given Moses
a "pattern." He knew that God had given David a "pattern." He
knew that God had given Ezekiel a "pattern." According to Section
52, this "pattern" was in all things that God made and those verses
also told him that he could use this pattern to tell whether or not
he was being deceived by Satan.

But what was the "pattern"?

Jeffrey had an idea. God told Joseph Smith exactly how he
wanted the Kirtland temple to be built, so the pattern had to be in
the temple. What made the Kirtland temple different? Jeffrey looked
around. Other churches usually had only one or two pulpits and they
were always located at the front of the sanctuary. But the Kirtland
temple had pulpits at the front and rear of the chamber. This was
something that visitors frequently asked about. Why so many pulpits—more than twenty? Jeffrey knew that the pulpits were used by
various priesthood members.

"I had looked at these pulpits every day, but until that night,
I had not really seen them," Jeffrey said. "Suddenly my intelligence

clicked in and I saw the pattern. If you cut the temple exactly in half, you would have the exact same number of pulpits on each half. You would have the exact same number of columns, the exact same number of doors, the exact same number of windows. Both sides would mirror each other. The entire building was chiastic.

"I had finally found the pattern. I realized that everything that God does is according to this mirror imaging or chiastic pattern. Everything."

Jeffrey decided to check his theory. "What was the most important thing that God has created? Man. He created man in his own image. I thought about my own body. If you cut a man in half lengthwise, both sides would be equal."

There was only one problem. It was the same nagging one that Eleanor Lord had first mentioned. What about all of the scriptures that weren't written chiastically, such as the Lord's Prayer and Christ's Sermon on the Mount? If everything made by God was chiastic, then why not these verses?

Jeffrey thought for a moment and then had the answer. Just because the verses didn't appear to mirror each other in English didn't mean that they weren't synonymous in Hebrew. "Maybe they were translated wrong." And then Jeffrey had an even more startling thought. "Why would God worry about English or Hebrew?" If God spoke chiastically, then the words were chiastic, and if they didn't seem synonymous to humans that was because "mankind really doesn't understand how to interpret God's words."

"Ordinary people wouldn't be able to interpret them because that was the job of a prophet," Jeffrey said. "Only a seer could see how the verses were chiastic."

Jeffrey opened up his Bible and looked again at verse 60 in Genesis.

> [A] In the language of Adam
>   [B] Man of Holiness
>   [C] is his *name*
>   [C] and the *name* of his only begotten
>   [B] is the Son of Man
> [A] even Jesus Christ

If Jeffrey was correct, lines [A] had to match. As he sat there studying them, Jeffrey suddenly received "the power" to see "the truth."

"The scales fell from my eyes." The line "in the language of Adam" was exactly the same as the line "even Jesus Christ," Jeffrey decided, because "Jesus Christ spoke in the language of Adam."

"It all fit."

Jeffrey began reading other scriptures. He discovered that every one of them held some new meaning that only *he* could reveal by way of the pattern. Jeffrey had found his great revelation. Now he could declare himself a prophet.

"I immediately began searching the scriptures to see what my role was." A few hours later, Jeffrey returned home and woke up Alice, who had gone to bed. He told her that he finally understood the vision that he had seen on Halloween night in 1983 when Damon ruptured his liver and had been rushed to the hospital for surgery. That was when Jeffrey suddenly had been at the foot of the cross watching Jesus die.

"I didn't imagine that," he explained. It really hadn't been a vision at all. It had been a *flashback.* "Alice," Jeffrey said, "the reason why I could see the crucifixion was because I was *actually* there when it happened."

In what sounded remarkably like the plot of *The Highlander,* Jeffrey explained that God had created eight great seers at "the beginning of time." These men had lived through the centuries without knowing that they were immortal until God needed them. At that point, God gave them the power to understand who they were.

"I have lived countless other lives before!"

"What?" Alice replied, startled.

"I had no recollection of my previous lives because my eyes were sealed by God. But now it is my time. I am the last seer. My eyes are being unsealed so that I can bring the pattern into the world and redeem Zion."

Jeffrey was so excited that he couldn't sleep. He decided to return to the temple and pray. When he walked into the lower court and looked up at the pulpits, he saw an angel. Years later, during an interview in the Lake County jail, Jeffrey would recall what he saw that night in the Kirtland temple. During the story, he would break down in tears and take several minutes to regain his composure.

"The angel was Joseph [Smith Jr.]. He didn't speak," Jeffrey said. "But I looked at him and he smiled. He smiled a big smile and all the fear that I had in my heart was pulled away and I felt the greatest joy and peace that I had ever felt. I sensed the purity of

Christ's love. . . . And I understood why he was smiling. He looked at me, and in a very simple sense, there was a change of command taking place. He had waited for me a long time and now his job was finished. I was finally at the point where it could happen, where he could turn the role of the prophet over to me so that the scriptures could be fulfilled."

CHAPTER TWENTY-THREE

NEITHER Jeffrey nor Alice felt it was "scriptural" for them to announce in the fall of 1986 that Jeffrey was the last seer. Christ had waited for his disciples to figure out for themselves that He was the "Son of the living God." Even so, Jeffrey and Alice decided it would be okay to drop a few hints. At the visitors' center, Alice asked Eleanor and Tom why Jeffrey had so many curious things happen to him.

"Why does he see revelations in the scriptures that no one else sees?"

Later, Tom would blame Alice for Jeffrey's belief that he was a prophet. "She pushed the idea, but she would never come out and say it. That was typical. Alice loved secrecy. She'd tell us, 'I know something you don't know about Jeffrey, but I've sworn that I can't tell anyone.'"

At home, Alice posed similar questions to Kevin Currie, Richard Brand, Danny Kraft, Jr., and Sharon Bluntschly during Jeffrey's classes. "Isn't it strange that God is revealing all these things to Jeffrey?" she'd say.

Jeffrey was more subtle. He would describe what a prophet did and then he would describe what he was doing.

Even Eleanor, who had come to look upon Jeffrey and Alice as if they were her own children, felt the two of them were acting strange. "Jeffrey became more and more arrogant," she said. "He would never come out and say to me, 'I am a prophet of God,' but I knew that was what he thought. At first, I wanted to take him aside and say, 'C'mon Jeffrey, get real!' But then I thought, 'Who am I to say whom the Lord might raise up to be a prophet?'"

Kevin Currie felt differently. He had known Jeffrey the longest of any group member, and when Jeffrey explained the pattern, Kevin was skeptical. "Jeffrey was basically developing his own language," Kevin said. "He would diagram a verse and then he would say that the words that he had placed opposite each other were synonymous. Oftentimes, they clearly weren't. Sometimes they were antonyms. But he didn't care. He would say, 'Well, these words might appear opposite to you, but in God's eyes they are exactly the same.' I just didn't see any point in it because he had basically come up with a way for him to say anything that he wanted to say, interpret scripture any way that he wanted to interpret it, and if you disagreed with him, he told you that you were wrong and didn't understand the pattern because you weren't the seer."

Jeffrey knew that Kevin didn't believe him. One Sunday afternoon, the men in the group played a game of touch football. Afterward, Kevin complained that his shoulders were sore. Richard began to rub them. They were sitting in the living room, and when Jeffrey and Alice walked in, Jeffrey quickly called Richard into the kitchen to talk. The rest of that night, Richard avoided Kevin. "Jeffrey and Alice told Richard that I was gay and that he should be careful around me," Kevin remembered. They had told Richard that Kevin was trying to seduce him. "That's when I first began to realize that they were splitting me away from the others." Kevin felt Jeffrey and Alice were playing different group members against each other, in his words, "creating an environment of fear so the only people you felt that you could trust was them." Kevin decided to move back to Buffalo.

Jeffrey didn't try to stop him. "Jeffrey told me that it was good that I was going because I had a spirit contrary to the spirit of God and I had brought this evil spirit into the house." As soon as Kevin left, Jeffrey called Richard, Sharon, and Danny into the living room. "The real reason why Kevin left," he said. "is because he's fallen in love with another man."

At about the same time that Kevin left, Jeffrey received a letter from Dennis and Tonya Patrick. He had written to them about the pattern and his discoveries. "We're moving to Kirtland," Dennis announced in the letter. Dennis explained that he had used Jeffrey's pattern to make some exciting revelations of his own. Dennis also said that a voice had told him to move. "It was an audible voice," Dennis later recalled writing to Jeffrey. "The voice said, 'It is my will and my desire that you sell your house and move to Kirtland.' Then it told me how much I should sell my house for." Dennis had resigned from his job at Bendix Aerospace and would move as soon as he and Tonya sold their house, the letter said.

Jeffrey was outraged. "Who does Dennis think he is?" Jeffrey asked Alice. "There is only one person God speaks to and that is *His* prophet and I am that man, not Dennis Patrick." For more than two days, Jeffrey fumed. "God told me this would happen," he said. Jeffrey reminded Alice of his vision, the one where he was given gold plates to interpret. "Dennis tried to wrestle those plates away from me and that's exactly what he is trying to do now . . . seize all the glory for himself."

Jeffrey wrote the Patricks a scalding reply. "You are not welcome here. . . . You are not coming to Ohio for the right reasons."

The Patricks were devastated. Dennis telephoned their realtor and stopped the sale of their house. He called Bendix, but someone had already been hired to fill his old job. Dennis called Jeffrey, but that didn't help. "I'm not inviting you up here," Jeffrey scolded, "until you are ready to learn the truth."

Meanwhile, Jeffrey was pressing Greg Winship to join his group. He had come to Kirtland to visit his pal Richard Brand. Greg had first met Jeffrey during the Memorial Day trek that Richard, Shar Olson, and he had made earlier that year. Since then, Richard had written Greg letters about Jeffrey and his discovery of a "perfect way to find the truth."

"Greg was very sharp when it came to the scriptures," Jeffrey said. "I liked him." Greg also came from a wealthy family. During his weekend visit, Jeffrey and Alice pumped Greg for personal information. They learned that he was the middle son in a family with three boys. His father, Gerald, was a former Missouri state senator and owner of Winship Travel, a thriving travel agency, where Greg worked. His mother, Carol, had stayed at home and raised the boys. Greg had never been in any serious trouble. He had received good grades at Harry Truman High School where he had been the drum major for the marching band, a member of the school choir, and active in school plays. After graduation, he had attended Graceland College where he was co-captain of the cheerleading team and on the junior varsity volleyball squad. Greg was twenty-six years old, slender, and meticulous in his appearance and habits. Each night he faithfully recorded all of that day's activities in a diary.

Greg's life sounded idyllic. But the more Jeffrey probed, the more certain he was that Greg was unhappy. By Saturday night, Jeffrey knew what was wrong. While Greg was in college, his parents had divorced. The split had badly shaken Greg. "He thought they had a perfect marriage," Jeffrey later told Alice. Part of the reason why Greg was upset was because of his interpretation of Matthew, chapter 6, verses 35 and 36, which quoted Jesus Christ as criticizing divorce:

> . . . whosoever shall put away [divorce] his wife, saving for the cause of fornication, causeth her to commit adultery; and whosoever shall marry her that is divorced, committeth adultery.

Not only was Greg worried about his parents' divorce, he was worried about his own failing marriage. Greg had married Anna Marie Crownover in Independence after he returned from college, but the relationship was a disaster.

The next day, before Greg left, he asked Jeffrey for advice. "Greg was trying to decide whether or not he should get a divorce. What he wanted to know was . . . if he got divorced and then remarried, would he be committing adultery?"

Jeffrey told Greg that God had created Eve by taking a rib from Adam. "Flesh was taken from flesh to create flesh," he said. God had used Adam's rib to create a "perfect companion" for Adam. God had, in fact, created a perfect companion for every saint. "Greg, there is a woman in this world who is flesh of your flesh, bone of your bone," Jeffrey explained. "She was created specifically for you so it doesn't really matter if you are married or you are divorced. If the woman that you are living with right now isn't your true companion—the one that God made for you—then you are committing adultery and you will continue to commit adultery until you are paired with your perfect mate."

Was his wife this perfect companion? Greg asked.

"Greg, I can't tell you right now who your perfect companion is," Jeffrey said, "but I can tell you that the woman you are now with is not the one."

Shortly after Greg returned to Kirtland, he filed for divorce and made plans to move to Ohio to join Jeffrey's group.

Besides the Patricks and Greg, Jeffrey had notified three others about the pattern. Jeffrey had told his old college chum Keith Johnson and Dennis and Cheryl Avery. The Averys had visited Kirtland earlier in the summer, and during that visit, Jeffrey had found out something about Dennis that had made him friendlier toward him. Dennis had mentioned that his mother had died and left him several thousand dollars. Rather than spend the money on new furniture, a better car, or a vacation, Dennis had used it to pay off the mortgage on his house. Even then, Dennis still had a few hundred dollars left over, which he had used to buy a nine-year-old Toyota sedan as a second car.

"I don't owe a penny to anyone," he bragged to Jeffrey. "I consider that part of being a good steward."

Jeffrey thought Dennis was stupid. But he didn't say so. Instead, he massaged Dennis's ego and he gradually moved the conversation from the Averys' finances to his own. Jeffrey explained how he and Alice were completely dependent on the Lord to take care of them.

"We don't even have a car," he explained. The station wagon that the Lundgrens had driven to Ohio in 1984 had long ago been junked.

Dennis felt sorry for Jeffrey, and when he returned to Independence, he telephoned Jeffrey. "We want to give you the Toyota," Dennis announced. He and Cheryl had discussed it on the ride home.

Since that time, Jeffrey had gone out of his way to write letters to Dennis and Cheryl, even though he loathed them. "Jeff and Alice didn't have a phone so they would get calls at the visitors' center," recalled Tom Miller. "The Averys would call up and Jeffrey would be really nice to them, almost encourage them, and then after he had hung up, he would deride those people something terrible and make fun of them. He and Alice both would. I kept thinking, 'Well, if he really despises them, then why is he so friendly when they call?'"

Tom had met the Averys. They seemed pretty ordinary. He began to suspect that Jeffrey was scheming to get something from them. But he couldn't figure out what it was.

CHAPTER TWENTY-FOUR

J EFFREY would later claim that he had never encouraged Dennis
and Cheryl to move to Kirtland. But they certainly felt that he did.
In February 1987, an excited Dennis stopped at the home of his
younger brother, Tim, in Independence. Dennis and Cheryl were
returning home from a weekend visit with Jeffrey and Alice.

"I know you won't understand this," Dennis declared as soon
as he walked into Tim's house, "but we are moving to Kirtland."
Tim began to object, but Dennis cut him short. "We are firm on
this and we're going to leave as soon as possible."

Why now? Tim asked.

The answer was simple. Jeffrey had told them it was time.

Dennis had been taught by the church that he was to help build
Zion. Section 6 of the Doctrine and Covenants admonished the
saints to "seek to bring forth and establish the cause of Zion." Previous generations had succumbed to sin and failed. Now it was his
generation's turn. As they talked that night, Dennis explained how
Jeffrey had discovered the pattern, a revolutionary way to interpret
scripture. Based on what Jeffrey had shown him, Dennis was convinced that Jesus Christ was about to return and he was going to
appear at Kirtland.

At one point, Dennis took a piece of paper from his pocket and showed it to Tim. Jeffrey had given it to him. It was a chiastic diagram. Tim recognized a few of the lines. "Dennis tried to explain it to me." According to Jeffrey, the diagram proved Zion was in Kirtland. "Dennis said that he and Cheryl had to go to the Kirtland temple if they wanted to see Jesus." After his brother left that night, Tim got out his scriptures and looked up the verses that Jeffrey had diagramed. "Why, they didn't say anything at all like what Jeffrey said they meant. He was twisting the scripture all around."

Although Dennis was nine years older, Tim knew that he was gullible. He was afraid that he was being conned.

Dennis and Cheryl were so eager to move to Kirtland that they didn't bother listing their house for sale with a realtor. Instead, they sold it for $20,000 to some people that they knew.

"Your house is worth much more than that," Tim complained.

Dennis didn't care. "All that matters is that we get to Kirtland."

On February 19, Dennis gave notice at Centerre Bank. After seventeen years, he was resigning. In March, he and Cheryl drove to Kirtland to find a house. Realtor Margaret Mitchell took them around. Jeffrey tagged along to make certain, as he put it, "you don't get taken in." They rented a modest house just down the street from the Kirtland temple. As soon as they got back to Independence, they began packing. Dennis asked Tim if he'd help load the U-Haul truck that they had rented. Tim tried to talk his brother out of moving.

"I'm afraid you think Jeffrey is a prophet," Tim said. "I'm afraid you're making a big, big mistake."

"I'm trying to keep an open mind," Dennis snapped. "Maybe he is a prophet, maybe he isn't."

Tim knew he couldn't change his brother's mind. "He felt Jeffrey had discovered this great truth, this pattern."

It took only a few hours to load the Averys' meager furnishings. Tim waved good-bye when they drove away. In Kirtland, Jeffrey was waiting. "They came right to my house. I had all the guys in my group go to their house, help them unpack the U-Haul, and get everything into place," said Jeffrey. "Alice took them meals and helped Cheryl get their three girls enrolled at school. Dennis and Cheryl were both so helpless that if we hadn't led them by the noses they would have been lost."

During the Averys' first two weeks in Kirtland, Jeffrey and Alice stopped by to check on them every day. One afternoon when they came by, Cheryl was chatting with one of her neighbors. Cheryl introduced Jeffrey and Alice to her as "our best friends."

On May 4, Dennis opened a bank account at the National City Bank. Jeffrey had recommended it. Dennis deposited $20,532.55, which included his savings and the money that he was paid for his house.

The smiles that Jeffrey and Alice put on when they were with the Averys quickly disappeared whenever they weren't around. "Jeffrey went to great lengths at the visitors' center to say that he wished the Averys hadn't come," recalled Eleanor. "He and Alice both used to mock them something terrible behind their backs."

Inside the Lundgren house, the Averys became the butt of every joke. "The Averys were called lazy. . . . Jeff called Dennis a wimp," recalled Sharon. "Everything was backward. Cheryl was the one who made the decisions. She was the one that wore the pants."

But whenever the Averys came to see Jeffrey and Alice, everyone in the group was friendly, so much so that Cheryl invited the group over for dinner after she and Dennis got settled. Richard and Sharon refused to go, but Danny said he'd go with Jeffrey and Alice. When they arrived, Alice went into the kitchen to talk to Cheryl.

"I'm making a special pizza tonight!" Cheryl said.

"C'mon, Cheryl," Alice said, "what are you going to put on the pizza?"

Cheryl grinned and took a jar of dill pickles from the refrigerator. She diced a couple and spread them over the sauce and dough.

When Alice walked into the living room, she whispered to Jeffrey: "You aren't going to believe what's on this pizza."

Jeffrey thought it tasted terrible, but worse was yet to come. Cheryl had made rhubarb pie and she cut Danny a huge slice because she knew it was his favorite. He took a bite and nearly gagged. Alice almost burst out laughing. Danny fidgeted until Cheryl left the table to get something from the kitchen. When she returned, Danny's piece of pie was gone. Alice knew that he hadn't eaten it, but she didn't see where he could have hidden it. A short time later, Jeffrey, Alice, and Danny left. As soon as they were outside, Danny pulled off his boot.

"He had dumped the pie inside it," Jeffrey recalled. "He'd been walking with rhubarb pie in his boot since dinner." Everyone at the house thought the story was hilarious.

A few days later, Richard overheard Alice and Jeffrey talking.

"Why are the Averys here?" Alice asked.

"So I can have their money," Jeffrey replied.

CHAPTER TWENTY-FIVE

W ITHOUT explanation, Jeffrey invited Dennis and Tonya Patrick to move to Kirtland in January 1987. He didn't mention the
couple's aborted attempt some three months earlier. But he did suggest that Dennis and Tonya sell their house and bring the proceeds
with them. Two weeks after they listed their home for sale, they had
an offer. It was the exact price that the "voice" had told Dennis to
ask for. Dennis saw it as a sign. On February 28, they drove into
Kirtland in a rental truck filled with their belongings and stopped at
the Lundgrens' house. Dennis knocked on the front door. Tonya and
Molly, the Patricks' six-year-old daughter, stood beside him. Jeffrey
greeted them with an icy stare. "Jeff and Alice didn't want to have
anything to do with us," Tonya said later. "Jeffrey had ordered Alice
not to even talk to me."

"What's going on, Jeff?" asked Dennis.

"There are things you have to learn," Jeffrey replied. "Until you
do, you are not part of the family."

Dennis was dazed. Tonya was in tears. Molly was confused.
They got back into the truck and drove down the street to the Hill-
top Apartments. That Sunday, the Patricks sat by themselves in
church. The Reverend Dale Luffman was thrilled when he spotted

Dennis. He had known Dennis and had been good friends with his parents when they lived in Oregon.

"We've been praying for a priesthood member to come in and help us clean up this mess at the church here," Luffman earnestly confided to Dennis after the service.

"What's the problem?" asked Dennis.

"Real simply—a man named Jeff Lundgren."

"Jeffrey is why we're here," Dennis replied.

Luffman was disappointed. "I knew right then and there that I had lost them," he said. "They were part of this group of dissenters that Jeffrey was building around himself."

Besides the Patricks and the Averys, Greg Winship had moved to Kirtland to study with Jeffrey. He had gotten a job as a tour guide at the temple. Jeffrey had also started to recruit another couple, Ron and Susie Luff, who had gone on a tour of the temple with him. They lived in Springfield, Missouri, and Jeffrey was corresponding with them.

At least once each week, Jeffrey taught a scripture class to members of his group. They included Richard, Sharon, Danny, Greg, Dennis Patrick, Tonya, Dennis Avery, Cheryl, Alice, and, on most occasions, Damon Lundgren, who was now sixteen. Jeffrey told them that they had to "erase everything" from their minds about religion.

"This is not my rule," Jeffrey explained, "it is what God is commanding you to do!"

Jeffrey told the group to open their Mormon scriptures to Section 90 in the Doctrine and Covenants, a record of a revelation that Joseph Smith, Jr., purportedly received from God on May 6, 1833. Jeffrey read part of it to them:

> ". . . [the] wicked one cometh and taketh away light and truth, through disobedience, from the children of men, and because of the tradition of their fathers. But I have commanded you to bring up your children in light and truth."

He then diagramed the verse:

> [A] [the] wicked one cometh and taketh away *light and truth*
> [B] through disobedience from the *children* of men
> [C] and because of the tradition of their fathers.
> [B] But I have commanded you to bring up your *children*
> [A] in *light and truth*

Lines [A] were parallel because they both contained the words "light and truth," he said. Lines [B] mirrored each other because they had the word "children" in them. Line [C] stood alone. It was the "secret" chiastic line.

"God says light and truth are taken away because of the 'tradition of their fathers,'" Jeffrey explained. These traditions, he continued, were everything the RLDS had taught them. "You must get Satan's garbage out of your memory banks," he said. "I will teach you what to think, what to believe."

Dennis would later recall Jeffrey's presentations with a certain awe. "He was very calculated and extremely effective. Jeffrey never said anything without having scriptures to back it up and he would explain each verse and build on each verse, piece by piece, until he had constructed an elaborate foundation and proven his point. It was difficult to challenge him because when he got through, it didn't seem like *he* was telling you to do something—it seemed like *God* was telling you to do it based on the scriptures."

Dennis noticed something else about Jeffrey's classes. Everyone had to agree with Jeffrey. If they didn't, they were criticized. "He would use the pattern to tell us what a scripture actually said and then ask us if we could see it. If anyone didn't see it, he would go over it again and again and again, until everyone in the room finally agreed with what he said."

One night, Jeffrey marched into class and barked out an order. "Open your Bibles to Malachi." He read the first verse of chapter 3 aloud to the group:

> "Behold, I will send my messenger, and he shall prepare the way before me; and the Lord whom ye seek, shall suddenly come to his temple . . ."

That verse, Jeffrey lectured, contained an extraordinary secret. "It tells us that Christ 'shall suddenly come to his temple.'" Where, Jeffrey asked, is this temple? And then he quickly answered his own question. "The temple is in Kirtland." And who has God sent to the temple? Again, he answered his own question. "The messenger who is preparing the way." How, Jeffrey continued, would this messenger prepare the way? This time, Jeffrey paused before answering. The last messenger, Jeffrey said, was sent by God to reveal the pattern to the world. That was how members of the group could identify him. The messenger was the person teaching the pattern.

Dennis snapped. "Jeffrey was telling us that he was the last messenger."

After several weeks of classes, Dennis and Tonya finally began to feel that they were being accepted by the others in the group. On a late summer night, Jeffrey came to their apartment. He wanted them to join the "family." The Lundgrens called their own children the "naturals," he explained. Richard, Greg, Sharon, and Danny were the "unnaturals." Everyone in the "family" called Alice and Jeffrey "Mom and Dad." Before Dennis and Tonya could become one of the unnaturals, however, there was something they had to do. Jeffrey opened his Bible to the New Testament book of Acts and read them chapter 4, verse 32, which describes how the early Christians lived communally with "all things in common."

If the Patricks wanted to become part of the family, then Dennis was going to have to turn over to Jeffrey the paycheck that he got each week from working at a local health spa.

"I want you to submit a monthly budget to me," Jeffrey said. "I will decide how much money you need."

Jeffrey then asked Dennis what he had done with the cash that he'd received from selling his house in Independence. Most of it had gone to pay bills, Dennis replied.

"Jeffrey got angry and told me that I had wasted the money. He said I should have given it to him instead of paying off a bunch of Gentiles. He was the one who was going to build Zion. . . . Gentiles didn't matter. The only reason why God had put them on earth was so we could use them."

Dennis and Tonya agreed to give Jeffrey all of their cash and future earnings. "We felt we were going to build Zion and we wanted to do our part," said Dennis. "I was willing to do whatever it took to do this right and see Christ."

Before he left, Jeffrey read Dennis and Tonya another story from the Bible. This one was from chapter 5 in Acts, which describes how Ananias and Sapphira, an early Christian couple, held back some of their possessions from the communal pot. When the apostle Peter questioned them about it, both lied and were immediately struck dead by God. Dennis and Tonya got the point.

Now that the Patricks were part of the family, they were invited to the Lundgrens' house for scripture classes much more often than once a week. They were also privy to the private going-ons of the group. Both of them discovered that Jeffrey not only controlled the family's money, but also directed their personal lives as well.

Jeffrey claimed that all of his followers' names were hidden in the scriptures, just as his was, along with the names of their "true companions"—the spouses that God had created specifically for them. It was this claim that had helped convince Greg Winship that he should file for divorce and move to Kirtland to find the woman who, Jeffrey claimed, had been made from "flesh of his flesh." As soon as Greg had gotten settled, he had asked about the name of his future spouse.

"I'm still looking for yours," Jeffrey said, "but I have found the names of others."

Greg asked him who? But Jeffrey wouldn't say. Alice did. One afternoon, she took Sharon aside.

"Jeff and I were wondering if Richard isn't the one for you," she told her.

"Yeah," Sharon replied, "I was wondering the same thing."

Sharon was pleased to be matched with Richard, but he was not enthused when he heard what Alice had said. Although Sharon had gone on a diet and lost several pounds, she still was chunky. Richard was used to dating striking, slender, stylish women. Sharon was plain. As always, Jeffrey would later tell his followers that he really had nothing to do with matching Richard and Sharon. It was God who had ordered them to become married.

"I looked in the scriptures and they were clear about it," he said. "Sharon was flesh of Richard's flesh."

But the timing of the match happened to coincide with a conversation between Richard and Jeffrey that had irritated the "father" of the family. Richard had poked fun at Jeffrey one afternoon while the two men were lifting weights by pointing out how pudgy he was getting. "Richard had an aversion to fat," Jeffrey later said, "and my physical shape bothered him. Sometimes my weight would get up to two hundred and seventy pounds and I'd have a tummy on me. That was repulsive to Richard." As soon as the men finished lifting weights, Jeffrey hurried inside and grabbed his scriptures.

"God is fat," he declared. He showed Richard several verses that described God as being "heavy" and "stout." "Those words are synonymous with fat," Jeffrey insisted. "God has a stomach on him." Richard had laughed.

It was shortly after that exchange that Richard was matched to Sharon. While Jeffrey later denied that there was any connection between the two events, the irony of matching a "pretty boy" with

Sharon did cause him to smile. Perhaps God, he later quipped, had wanted to teach Richard a lesson.

Although Richard did not find Sharon attractive, Jeffrey ordered him to begin courting her, and Richard complied.

At about this same time, Jeffrey announced that Dennis and Cheryl Avery were going through their money much too quickly. Everyone in the family knew that the Averys were never going to be fully accepted. Like the Gentiles, they were being provided by God, Jeffrey said, for the group to use. Jeffrey decided that he was going to have a special class specifically designed to get the Averys' cash. He and Alice would do most of the talking. The unnaturals would do their part by agreeing with everything they said and pressuring Dennis and Cheryl to turn over the proceeds from the sale of their house. No one balked at the idea.

On the night of the special class, Jeffrey quoted the same scriptures that he had used on the Patricks. Others in the group explained how much they were contributing to the communal pot. On June 27, Dennis Avery came to see Jeffrey. He and Cheryl had decided to give Jeffrey a check. They wanted to be "of one heart and of one soul" with everyone else. In return, Jeffrey promised to pay their rent. Dennis took out his checkbook and began to write, but Jeffrey stopped him. "Make it out to cash, not to me," he said. He did not want the Internal Revenue Service asking about the income. Dennis wrote in an amount and showed it to Jeffrey for his approval. Jeffrey nodded and sent him to a nearby bank. When Dennis returned, he gave Jeffrey an envelope filled with bills. It was $10,000. Jeffrey thanked Dennis and sent him home.

CHAPTER TWENTY-SIX

WITHIN an hour after Dennis handed him $10,000 in cash, Jeffrey was at Veith Sports Supply buying a .45-caliber Interarms semi-automatic pistol. From there, he drove to Pistol Pete's, another Ohio sporting goods store, and bought a .243-caliber Ruger hunting rifle and another .45-caliber Colt semi-automatic pistol. He waited one week and then returned to Pistol Pete's and bought a Ruger .44-caliber magnum handgun. During the next few days, Jeffrey bought camouflage clothing, tents, camping supplies, canned food, and hundreds of rounds of ammunition. Jeffrey was stockpiling weapons and supplies for his "storehouse." Many saints believed in keeping a one-year supply of food and other goods needed for survival during the last days of tribulation. According the Book of Revelation, the world would be stricken with famine, disease, and wars shortly before Jesus Christ returned. Jeffrey was going to be prepared. By the end of June, Jeffrey had added another Mini-14 Ruger assault rifle to his cache. He now had enough guns to arm all the men in his family. Richard already owned his own guns. Danny, Greg, Dennis Patrick, and Damon were issued weapons that Jeffrey had bought.

During the summer of 1987, Jeffrey and his group came to focus during their scriptural classes on one of Joseph Smith, Jr.'s best-known revelations. It had to do with the persecution of saints and the "redemption" of Zion. In November 1833, an angry mob beat and tarred and feathered several Mormon elders in Independence. The mob then forced dozens of Mormon settlers at gunpoint to leave the county. The saints' homes were looted and their property was seized. When word of the attack reached Kirtland, Joseph Smith, Jr., was outraged. He announced that God had given him a revelation, which was later recorded as Section 98 in the Doctrine and Covenants. According to it, God had commanded his saints to "redeem Zion," which, Smith said, meant that they were supposed to launch an armed attack on the Gentiles in Independence. Smith used the revelation to whip up support, and in May 1834, he set off for Missouri with two hundred armed men. He called his army "Zion's Camp." Church historians would later claim that Smith hoped that this show of force would intimidate the Gentiles, but when his band arrived at the Jackson County line, it was met by a much larger group of armed Missourians. Rather than fight, Smith appealed to state officials to avoid bloodshed by compensating the Mormons for the land and property that had been stolen from them. The governor ignored Smith's request and the two armed camps faced off in a stalemate. When cholera swept through the ill-prepared Mormon troops, the prophet was forced to retreat to Kirtland with little to show for his effort.

Jeffrey told his followers that Section 98 had been misinterpreted by Smith and the RLDS Church. It actually had nothing to do with the 1833 attack on Mormons. Rather, the revelation contained secret instructions from God to Jeffrey and his followers. These instructions were concealed in a part of the revelation known as the "parable of the vineyard."

Joseph Smith, Jr., had claimed that God told him this parable. It was about a rich nobleman who was once given a choice spot of land to use as a vineyard. He sent his servants to plant olive trees on the property and he sent watchmen to build a lookout tower there and also construct a wall around the vineyard to protect it from attack. The watchmen built the tower, but they decided that there wasn't any need for them to put up a wall so they ignored the nobleman's orders. One night, an enemy attacked, plundered the vineyard, and destroyed the lookout tower. When the nobleman heard what had happened, he sent his warriors to reclaim the vineyard and take revenge.

Smith had said the parable was an example of what can happen when the saints didn't follow orders from God [the nobleman in the parable]. But Jeffrey put an entirely different spin on the story. He diagramed each sentence in the parable and then revealed the "secret" messages that they contained. According to Jeffrey, the vineyard in the parable was actually Kirtland, the lookout tower was the Kirtland temple, and God was ordering Jeffrey's followers to guard the temple.

"I am the last messenger that God has sent to the Kirtland temple to prepare the way for Christ's return," Jeffrey reiterated, "and the reason why He has called you here is because you are going to help me protect it."

Jeffrey told his followers that major earthquakes would erupt during the final days before Christ returned and a huge mountain would rise up underneath the Kirtland temple, lifting it into the sky. This was based on Jeffrey's interpretation of verses 2 and 3 in chapter 2 of Isaiah. Jeffrey read the crucial lines to his followers:

> "And it shall come to pass in the last days, when the mountain of the Lord's house shall be established . . . all nations shall flow unto it. And many people shall go and say, Come ye, and let us go up to the mountain of the Lord . . ."

Once the temple was raised on this mountain, Satan's armies would swarm to Ohio in a final attempt to destroy the temple, kill the "last messenger" and thereby prevent Christ from returning to earth, he said. Jeffrey and his band would be waiting on the mountain for the onslaught.

"We will not have electricity. We won't have houses. We will have to live off the land and we will have to protect the temple by whatever means possible until Christ shows up." That was why Jeffrey was buying tents, food, and military-style weapons.

"When the armies of Satan come against us," Jeffrey preached, "when they come to kill me and to kill you, we must be ready to fight and to die. We must be ready to shed blood.

"And," he added, "there will be lots of it spilled—lots and lots of it."

It sounded gallant and everyone agreed. If they were going to have to kill in order to protect the temple, then they would do just that.

CHAPTER TWENTY-SEVEN

IN the late spring of 1987 while Jeffrey was preparing his followers for Armageddon, Tom Miller was reaching some conclusions of his own about what the scriptures said and what the RLDS Church espoused. "Everything we have been taught and everything I understood is completely false," Tom announced one morning to Jeffrey while they both were at work in the visitors' center. "I have come to the understanding that the RLDS is a church of men. There is a church of God, but to my knowledge it doesn't exist on earth as I perceive it to be defined in the scriptures."

Jeffrey agreed with him.

"Then why don't we walk out together?" Miller suddenly suggested. "I'm going to resign right now. Why don't you go with me? We'll go over to Dale Luffman's office and both quit."

Jeffrey declined.

Miller pressed him. "Why stay on if you don't believe any of this? Why preach lies?"

"I'm not preaching lies," Jeffrey replied, "because I'm not teaching what the RLDS is putting out. I'm teaching the truth." Jeffrey still planned to someday lead a fundamentalist revolt. He would restore the truth to God's "only true church."

"Sure," Miller retorted. Later when he recalled their conversation, Miller said: "I knew enough about what Jeff was teaching to know that it was erratic and illogical and not consistent with the scriptures. The reason Jeffrey didn't want to resign was because he was all puffed up about teaching his Sunday school class and he had these followers. He liked feeling important."

Miller marched across the street and tossed his priesthood card on Luffman's desk. "I told him that I had no time for him, no time for the church. . . ." Luffman was not sorry to see Tom Miller go. He had been part of the group of troublemakers. By June 1987, Luffman had been the stake president for eighteen months, but he still hadn't been able to get rid of Jeffrey nor quiet the growing feud that was splitting the congregation. If anything, Luffman was losing. The adult Sunday school class that Jeffrey taught had become an ironclad stronghold for dissidents. Not everyone in the class felt comfortable with Jeffrey's constant harping about chiasmus. But the presence of Jeffrey's group—Richard, Greg, Danny, Sharon, the Patricks, and the Averys—each Sunday stifled all debate. Even Bill and Eleanor Lord were beginning to feel intimidated.

In July, Luffman felt the conflict had become, in his words, "almost demonic." He decided to confront his critics head-on. On Sunday morning, he walked into Jeffrey's class and made a fifteen-minute plea for peace. "I want to appeal to you to join the body of Christ," he said. He talked about the need for the congregation to come together and said that it was wrong for one clique to believe it had "higher or more important knowledge" than anyone else. He complained about members who boycotted the worship service and he berated those closest to Jeffrey who had not made any effort to participate in church functions. When he finished, Luffman expected a rebuttal from Jeffrey or someone in the class. But no one said anything.

"I stood there in dead silence for what seemed like an eternity, and then after a while, Jeffrey stood up and said, 'It is time for our lesson,' and everyone opened their books. I realized that I had reached absolutely no one."

When the class ended, Luffman marched up to Jeffrey. "This is the last time you are teaching in this church. Your class is finished."

Luffman was personally disbanding Jeffrey's class. Jeffrey was usurping the power of the local church to choose its own teachers. As stake president, Luffman was recognized under Ohio law as the legal representative for the Kirtland church and if he was forced to physi-

cally bar Jeffrey from teaching by calling in the police, he was prepared to do so. Luffman had had enough.

Jeffrey didn't show up the next Sunday. Neither did members
of his group. Luffman felt good. He had finally won a battle with
Jeffrey. At least that is what he thought. "The next week, I noticed
a whole lot of folks on Sunday morning going down the street into
the home of a fundamentalist member," Luffman recalled. "After a
couple weeks of this, I spotted Jeffrey walking over there too."

Jeffrey was still teaching. He'd simply moved his class into the
living room of one of his supporters.

Now it was Jeffrey's turn to fight back. He ordered the members
of his group to begin withdrawing their memberships from the RLDS
church. "Every time Luffman baptized someone and added a name
to the church rolls," he recalled, "I had one of my people resign.
That way, Luffman could never get ahead." Richard, Danny,
Sharon, Greg, the Patricks, and the Averys all played along. Luffman seethed.

In early August, Kevin Currie knocked on Jeffrey's front door.
He was homesick, he told Jeffrey, and wanted to move back in with
them. Jeffrey said it was okay, but as punishment, he made Kevin
sleep for one week in the basement. Later, he joked, "I'm gaining
more followers than Luffman."

If anything, Jeffrey's confrontations with Luffman made him
more cocky, and less cautious. One afternoon in late August, Jeffrey
was giving a youth group a tour. As usual, he mentioned the pattern
and how it could be found in anything that God made or said. One
of the adult leaders asked if Jeffrey had found it in the Doctrine and
Covenants. Without thinking, Jeffrey replied that he had found it
in all of Joseph Smith, Jr.'s revelations, but not in some of the more
recent ones. Which ones? the visitor asked. Jeffrey said that Section
156, the 1984 declaration that allowed women to join the priesthood, was not chiastic and, therefore, was "man's word, not God's."

Eleanor Lord was helping Jeffrey give the tour and when she
heard what he said, she knew he had made a big mistake. In effect,
Jeffrey had just called the church's President-Prophet Wallace B.
Smith a fraud.

"You really blew it, Jeff," she said after the tour. "Instead of
hedging your bets and telling that man to determine for himself
whether or not the pattern was in the Doctrine and Covenants, you
had to give them your answer."

Eleanor explained that the adult sponsor who had questioned

Jeffrey was a high priest in the church, one of the loftiest positions, and an obvious supporter of Wallace B. Smith.

"Jeffrey was stunned and afraid," Eleanor recalled later. "He hadn't realized until then exactly what he had done."

At the very minute that Eleanor was criticizing Jeffrey, the high priest was storming across the street to see Dale Luffman.

"Who is this Jeffrey Lundgren?" the high priest asked.

"Confidentially, he's a guy I've got a lot of problems with and I'd like to hang his butt and get him out of here," Luffman replied.

The priest told Luffman what Jeffrey had said during the tour. Luffman got excited. "Would you do me and the church a big favor?" he asked. "Write down word for word exactly what happened and give me a copy." Luffman said he would make certain that reports of the incident would be sent to Jeffrey's boss and also Wallace B. Smith.

"You bet I will," the high priest replied.

A few days later, Bill Lord received a letter from church officials in Independence. It said there were too many full-time guides at the visitors' center and that Jeffrey should be fired. The letter made Bill Lord angry. "I didn't hire Jeffrey," he told Eleanor. The director of historic sites had hired Jeffrey. Bill sent word back to Independence. If the church wanted Jeffrey fired, then the director who hired him was going to have to get rid of him. No one in Independence did anything.

Luffman became frustrated. "No matter what I tried, I couldn't get rid of this guy."

And then Luffman's luck changed. A church official, who was completely unaware of the dispute over Jeffrey, happened to notice that contributions to the Kirtland temple and sales at the visitors' center had plummeted to an all-time low. The church ordered an audit. "Over the period of time that Jeff Lundgren had been assigned the task of taking care of the financial records [two and a half years], the church calculated that he had extracted out of the till between seventeen and twenty-one thousand dollars," Luffman later said.

Although the church was certain Jeffrey had stolen the money, it didn't have any evidence. A church official was sent to Kirtland to confront Jeffrey. The two men made a deal. Jeffrey would resign as a temple guide. In return, the church would permit him to continue working one more month and would let him stay in his church-provided house rent-free until he found somewhere to move. The church also promised to keep quiet about the missing money.

Because the accusations against Jeffrey were dealt with in such a hush-hush fashion, Bill Lord wasn't told the real reason why Jeffrey was being forced to resign. He incorrectly believed that Jeffrey was being ousted because of his controversial teachings. Consequently, Lord left Jeffrey in charge of collecting donations to the temple and tallying the cash register receipts at the visitors' center, a move that even Jeffrey found to be incredible.

Jeffrey moved quickly to protect his reputation. He called everyone in his group together and explained that the church was kicking him out because, as he put it, "I am preaching the truth.

"Whenever a prophet begins to prophesy," Jeffrey explained, "the people turn against him. The scriptures say that prophets are 'cast out.' That is happening now. I am being 'cast out' of the temple. I have been told to resign."

It didn't take Jeffrey long to come up with a new scheme. Jeffrey wanted to form a commune. He and his group would create their own Zion. Jeffrey began calling realtors. A few days later, Stanley Skrbis called. Skrbis owned a five-bedroom farmhouse on a 15.07-acre tract on the southern edge of Kirtland. At one time, it had been a beautiful apple orchard with a comfortable two-story farmhouse and picturesque red barn. But the trees had been neglected and the house and barn were in bad need of repair. Skrbis was willing to rent it cheap—the entire acreage for $650 per month—if Jeffrey would fix up the property.

"This is just what I want," Jeffrey announced. Later that night, he called everyone together and explained what he had in mind. They would pool their money and rent the Skrbis property. They would repair the house and barn and work to make the apple orchard productive. Over time, they would open the barn as a combination crafts and antiques store. Jeffrey and Alice would buy and sell the antiques. Group members would provide homemade crafts. They would sell quilts, handicrafts, even homemade apple cider and apple pies. Eventually, they would buy the farm and become so prosperous that none of them would have to work anywhere else. They would wait on the farm for Christ to return.

The longer Jeffrey talked about the commune, the grander the expectations became. He even had a name picked out for the antiques business: Kristen's Kupboard, after his daughter and favorite child. By the time the class ended around midnight, everyone was enthused. "This is going to be just wonderful," Alice declared.

In mid-September, Shar Olson arrived in Kirtland to visit Richard and Greg. During the weekend visit, Jeffrey fussed over Shar. He told her about the pattern and how the group was moving to the farm. "I felt that I was being called to go," she said. Privately, Jeffrey also assured her that he could find the name of her "true companion" in the scriptures. Shar hurried back to Independence, quit her job, and moved to Kirtland. She moved in with Sharon.

Jeffrey also contacted Ron and Susie Luff and invited them to move to Kirtland. Ron had been writing Jeffrey letters since May when the Luffs first met him during a temple tour, and the Luffs were convinced that Jeffrey was someone special. Ron quit his job at the James River Power Station in Springfield, Missouri, listing his reason for leaving as: "desired relocation and church work." He and Susie, along with their two small children, Matthew and Amy, arrived in Kirtland during September. Jeffrey sent them to stay in Greg's apartment.

As soon as Jeffrey paid the first month's rent on the Skrbis farmhouse, he and his followers went to work. They hauled away trash, gutted the interior, hung Sheetrock, painted, papered, cleaned, and polished. Within two weeks the rickety farmhouse was a showplace. By late September, it was ready. Jeffrey announced that Kevin, Richard, Shar, Danny, and Sharon would live with his family in the farmhouse. The Patricks, Averys, and Luffs would live in their own apartments but would still be required to financially support the commune. Greg had been invited to live at the farm, but had decided to keep his apartment.

Bill Lord would later recall that Jeffrey's last day at work as a temple tour guide fell on a Saturday. Even though he was being forced to resign, Jeffrey gave several tours that morning and seemed as enthused as ever when he talked about the temple. When it was time to close the visitors' center, Jeffrey emptied the cash register, tallied that week's receipts—some $1,600—and put the money into a bank bag for the last time. He told Bill that he would deposit it, as usual, that afternoon.

"Jeffrey was upset about being fired," recalled Eleanor. "He and Alice both were. They felt abused and picked on, but in their hearts, I think they knew better." It was a tearful time for the Lords. Despite the problems, they both adored Alice and genuinely liked Jeffrey.

The next Monday, Bill went over early to open the visitors' center. Within minutes after he had unlocked the front door, Jeffrey burst in. He had bad news. On Saturday, he had stopped at the post office before taking the temple's $1,600 to the bank. "I left the money bag on the front seat of my car when I went inside and must have accidentally left the doors unlocked," he told Bill. "When I came back, someone had taken it."

"Did you report it to the police?" asked Bill.

"I didn't think it would do any good," Jeffrey replied. "I'm sure the thief is long gone."

Bill simply nodded his head.

CHAPTER TWENTY-EIGHT

LIFE on the farm seemed wonderful—at least to Shar Olson. "I felt a real sense of belonging," she later remembered. "It began when we fixed up the house." For two weeks everyone worked side by side. "We'd get off work, meet at the farm, and begin knocking down walls. We'd work until we dropped. Jeff would go buy us a bucket of chicken and we'd sit on the floor covered with plaster and eat and laugh and talk about how we were going to make this all work and how we were going to bring about Zion. I really felt like we were becoming a family."

That was something Shar craved in the fall of 1987. By her own account, she felt lonely. Born less than a mile from RLDS headquarters in Independence, Shar was the youngest of three children and an only daughter. "I was a daddy's girl and I loved it," she said. "I thought we had a perfect family." When Shar was eleven, her parents divorced. "I remember lying in bed at night listening to them argue." After her parents separated, Shar and her mom became best friends, and the church became central to their lives. "I went through all the girls' groups. I started in Skylarks, the RLDS version of Brownies, and moved up through the various programs." She spent six weeks each summer in church camps, rarely missed a Sunday service, prayer meeting, youth group. She grew up inside an RLDS cocoon, thinking everyone believed in the Book of Mormon. She found out otherwise when she went to a Baptist-affiliated college for one year. "Everyone kept asking me if I was saved." She stuck out, felt out of place.

Her father had remarried so Shar went to live with him for a few months in New Orleans. She felt just as awkward in that sultry city as she had at college. Shar returned to the center spot. She was a beautiful girl with straight blond hair that dangled to her waist, an attractive figure, an effervescent personality. Worlds of Fun amusement park hired her to work as a character escort. She guided a fellow employee dressed in an animal costume through the amusement park where they posed for photographs with children. Shar became reacquainted with Greg Winship at an RLDS meeting of young adults. He introduced her to Richard. A short time later, Shar's mother married Greg's uncle. "The church had always been the one part of my life that was rock solid," she later recalled. In 1984 that changed. Shar was in the RLDS auditorium when delegates approved the ordination of women into the priesthood. She burst into tears. "It seemed like all the foundations that I had grown up with were crumbling." Shar's mother moved to Texas. Richard and Greg went to Ohio. Following her pals to Kirtland seemed natural.

At the farm, Shar began calling Jeffrey and Alice "Dad" and "Mom." It fit. "Alice was motherly." Each night, Alice would rub lotion on Shar's feet because she had dry skin.

"Shar liked to get attention," recalled Jeffrey. "I would be sitting on the couch with my daughter Krissy curled up next to me and Shar would come over and curl up on my other side. It wasn't sexual. She just wanted someone to love her."

Late one night after the group moved to the farm, Shar knocked on the door of the Lundgrens' bedroom. Jeffrey and Alice were watching television. She sat on the edge of their bed.

"Mom and Dad, I need to know something," she said. She and Danny had been spending a lot of time together. Shar wanted to know if that was okay. "I don't want to get involved if he's not my true companion."

Alice began to giggle. "I was hoping you two would hit it off!" she exclaimed.

"It's okay for you two to spend time together," added Jeffrey.

The next morning, Shar asked Alice if Danny was the one.

"I can't say," Alice replied. "Only a prophet can answer that."

"So, like do we know any prophets?" Shar replied innocently.

Alice looked directly at Shar. "Do you?" Alice asked.

"Do I?" Shar replied, confused.

"I guess you will have to figure that out for yourself," Alice replied.

"That is when I first realized that Alice thought Jeff was a prophet," Shar said later. "She was really pushing that idea. She wanted to be a prophet's wife."

That night during scripture class, Jeffrey told Danny and Shar to sit next to each other. Although Shar didn't know it, Jeffrey had told Danny before she arrived in Kirtland that the next woman to join the group was his companion. Danny was pleased. He had quickly fallen in love with Shar.

Ron and Susie were also happy about their move to Kirtland. Like Shar, they had become disenchanted with the liberalization of the RLDS. Both of them considered themselves spiritually gifted. Ron, who was twenty-seven, had written a book of inspirational poetry. Susie felt she had the gift of prophecy. Jeffrey hadn't liked either of them when they met. "When they first started writing me, they would tell me all this spiritual nonsense," he said, "so I would write back these horrible letters and really chastise them. I thought I'd never hear from them again, but they would always write back and tell me that what I had written had been right. It was like they were saying 'Hit me! Oh, hit me more! I deserved that.'"

Ron had grown up in Independence, where he had been a weight lifter and football star at Harry Truman High School. After graduating in 1978, he had joined the navy. He had started dating Susan Edson, who was a year older and had also grown up in Independence, during a trip home. They were married February 7, 1981, by Ron's father, an RLDS priesthood member. Like Jeffrey, Ron had a weight-lifter's build with broad shoulders and thick arms. Susie was slender and a nonstop talker.

"Like most of the others," Jeffrey said, "Ron and Susie came because they wanted me to give them something. They felt I could take them to see Christ."

At the farm, Jeffrey held scripture classes every night. Everyone but the Averys was required to attend. "The classes were basically to reestablish and reaffirm very strongly in our minds that there was such a thing as the pattern and that the pattern was true," Ron later told federal investigators. "The basic precept was that if you used the pattern you could not err, you absolutely could not flaw." Once the group accepted that precept, Jeffrey moved to the next step. "Ultimately, anyone who believed in the pattern also came to believe in the seer who brought it forth," recalled Ron. "And since the pattern could not err, they came to believe that the seer could not err either."

In short, Jeffrey was infallible.

Most classes lasted two or three hours, unless someone made a mistake. "Then there would be a 'session' time," said Ron, and "sometimes those would get to be real loud discussions and they would lead to the early hours of the morning, sometimes three or four o'clock."

The word "session" was a reference that Jeffrey originally had used when disciplining his children. Damon was rather meek, but Jason, then thirteen, was stubborn. "It would take ten or fifteen licks before he finally gave in. I called them a session because they took so long."

Dennis Patrick, Susie Luff, and Dennis and Cheryl Avery received the most "sessions" from Jeffrey—and Alice. "The slightest little mistake would evolve into a whole big example of sin," said Ron. "This was continuous and basically what that evolved into was that people were taught that they couldn't do anything right." Jeffrey would tell someone to do a task and then chastise them for not doing it the way that he would have.

"But you didn't tell us how to do it," a group member would respond.

"You should have known without asking," Jeffrey would reply.

There was only one correct answer to any question, Ron said. "You had to become one heart and one mind with Jeffrey."

One night everyone was eating dinner at the farm and talking about the Old Testament prophet Isaiah, when Susie announced: "I'd like to meet a prophet face-to-face." For several seconds everyone was quiet. Susie was sitting across from Jeffrey.

"Susie," Alice replied, "you wouldn't know a prophet if he was sitting across the table from you." Everyone laughed. Susie didn't understand. But Ron did.

"It took some time and it took the classes to do it," he later told investigators, "but I came to believe . . . that Jeff was the seer of the last days, the one that Malachi speaks of . . . he was the prophet of the last days who had come to prepare the way for Christ's return."

Everyone worked at the farm except for Jeffrey and Alice. Prophets were forbidden by God to have regular jobs because that would require them to submit to another human being, Alice told the group. "Prophets only answer to God."

"Alice didn't have to work either," said Shar, "because she was the wife of the prophet."

Richard had gotten a $22,400-per-year job as a civil engineer in a nearby town. Kevin collected about $18,000 annually as a clerk at a Veterans Administration hospital near Cleveland. Sharon earned minimum wage as a cashier at a convenience store. Shar got a job as a clerk at the Makro Department Store. Danny framed pictures at Gallup's Fine Art store. Dennis Patrick worked first at Scandinavian Health Spa and later at Chemical Financial Corporation, earning $20,850 annually. Greg earned $20,275 yearly as an accountant at Astro Travel Service. Ron operated a forklift at Cleveland Electric Illuminating Company, earning $17,630 per year. Investigators would later estimate that Jeffrey and Alice were collecting between $1,500 to $2,000 per week from their followers. Jeffrey was supposed to use the income to pay everyone's bills, but he didn't. No one but Jeffrey knew how the money was being spent. The Averys were the only ones not making weekly contributions. That was because Dennis had already given Jeffrey $10,000 and because Dennis and Cheryl were now broke. Dennis had held a slew of low-paying jobs since moving to Kirtland, but none paid more than minimum wage and the family was forced to apply for food stamps.

Whenever anyone wanted money, they had to ask Jeffrey, and Shar discovered that he was tightfisted when it came to everyone's needs except his and Alice's. The Patricks were told that there was no money for such frivolous expenses as buying a pizza on Friday night. Yet, at least once a week, Jeffrey would announce that he and Alice needed some time alone and they would go out to dinner and to a movie. If Alice didn't like what was being fixed for supper, she would send Jeffrey for a shrimp party platter from the local Red Lobster and the two of them would gorge themselves in their bedroom.

Everyone who lived in the farmhouse, except Alice, had chores. Shar was supposed to dust the hardwood floors downstairs once a week, do everyone's laundry, clean the refrigerator and stove. Sharon cleaned the upstairs and was responsible for picking up the four Lundgren children's clothing, making their beds, and tidying their rooms. Richard took care of the trash, Danny cleaned the bath-

rooms, Kevin helped cook. Even Tonya and Susie, who didn't live
at the farmhouse, were expected to come every Saturday and help
clean. "Alice mostly slept," Shar recalled. Jeffrey began referring to
the women at the farm as "Alice's handmaidens."

Despite the inequalities, no one complained. All of them believed in the pattern. All of them believed in Jeffrey. All of them
thought that he was a prophet.

At first Jeffrey seemed content at the farm, but his mood soon
changed. He began complaining to Alice about how the RLDS had
treated him, how unfair it was that a "fool" like Dale Luffman was
recognized as a minister while God's "last messenger" remained
anonymous, how he was once again forced to resign from a job.
"Jeffrey missed giving tours," said Alice. "He was used to having
fundamentalists seek him out for advice." At the farm, no one came
to the door to take his picture, no one slipped hundred-dollar bills
into his hand, no one remarked about how much he resembled Joseph Smith, Jr. Jeffrey had once talked about overthrowing Wallace
B. Smith. Now he spent his mornings building hutches for the rabbits that the group had decided to raise.

Less than two weeks after moving to the farm, Jeffrey announced that he had found a startling message in the scriptures. He
had been studying the "parable of the vineyard" when he had come
across this line:

. . . the lord of the vineyard said unto one of his servants . . .

Jeffrey reminded the class that the "lord of the vineyard" was
God. He then pointed out that he—Jeffrey—was "one of his [God's]
servants." Obviously, he said, the parable contained a hidden message "to me from God."

To learn what this secret instruction was, Jeffrey had used the
pattern to divide the parable. He had done this by putting the words
that came directly *before* "the lord of the vineyard" at the top of his
diagram and those that came directly *after* that phrase at the bottom.
This is what he wrote.

[A] saved my vineyard from
   [B] the hands of *the destroyer*
      [C] and the lord of the vineyard
   [B] said unto one of his *servants*
[A] Go, and gather together the residue of my servants

When he did this, Jeffrey discovered that the word "servant" was synonymous with the words "the destroyer" because they were both on [B] lines and mirrored each other.

"God is giving me a new name and a new job," Jeffrey declared. "Besides being the last messenger, I am now to be called 'the destroyer.' People will die at my hands."

Whom did God want him to destroy? Jeffrey asked rhetorically.

The answer was in the [A] lines. Jeffrey explained that God wanted him to gather "the residue of my servants"—a symbolic reference to Jeffrey's followers—and with them, he was to cleanse the vineyard until it was "saved."

"The enemies that I am to destroy are the persons now in control of the vineyard," Jeffrey said. He then quickly reminded his followers that the vineyard was symbolic of the Kirtland temple.

"Dale Luffman and the RLDS Church are the enemy," he said. "They are the wicked who have seized control of the vineyard."

Jeffrey opened his scriptures and read several lines of the parable aloud to the class. He was visibly excited and his voice rose as he spoke: "Go ye straightway unto the land of my vineyard. And redeem my vineyard, for it is mine . . . avenge me of mine enemies."

Jeffrey slapped shut his book. "Ladies and gentlemen, God is commanding us to take over the Kirtland temple. I am the destroyer. We must destroy the wicked who are now in control of the temple if we want Christ to return.

"And that is exactly what I intend to do."

Jeffrey had not only found a way to take revenge on Dale Luffman but he had come up with an idea that was bound to make him famous once again.

CHAPTER TWENTY-NINE

J EFFREY wanted to prepare his followers for the takeover of the Kirtland temple. He began by bringing home war movies. *First Blood*, the story of John Rambo, a Vietnam veteran who took on an entire town's police force single-handedly and won, was one of the first that he rented. Next came *Apocalypse Now*. Jeffrey canceled class so that everyone could watch it. When it ended, Jeffrey rewound the videotape and started it over. He watched it four times in a row. The next night he canceled class again. This time, he shared his experiences in Vietnam with the group. He said he had participated in covert missions in enemy territory. He'd killed untold numbers of Vietcong both with his rifle and in hand-to-hand combat. He'd cut off the ears of some as souvenirs. He was so deadly that his peers nicknamed him "killer."

"Jeffrey convinced us that if a policeman was holding one of us as a shield, all we had to do was stand perfectly still and Jeffrey could shoot him between the eyes," recalled Shar. "'It might make you deaf for a while,' he told us, 'but otherwise you'll be okay.'"

When Jeffrey resumed teaching his nightly classes, he fed his followers a steady fare of violence from the Book of Mormon and the Bible. He talked about how Jael, in chapter 4 of the Old Testa-

ment book of Judges, had pounded a tent stake through the head of
Sisera as he was sleeping. He recalled how Moses had murdered an
Egyptian, how Nephi had slain Laban, and then Jeffrey read everyone the story of the prophet Jacob in the Book of Mormon. Jacob
was preaching when his enemy, Sherem, demanded proof that Christ
had risen from the dead. Jacob said there was only one way to convince a skeptic such as Sherem and that was by asking God to strike
him dead. And that, according to the Mormon scriptures, is what
God did.

"God was not afraid to kill," Jeffrey pointed out.

He then reminded everyone how God had ordered him in Section 38 to "go to the Ohio . . . and there you shall be endowed
with *power* from on high."

"How am I supposed to receive this power?" Jeffrey asked. Before anyone could answer, Jeffrey referred to the murder of Sherem.
"When God wanted to show that He had power, God killed the
wicked. If I want to show that I have God's power, if I want to be
endowed with that power, then I must kill the wicked."

"I had always believed in the scriptures," said Dennis Patrick.
"They couldn't be wrong and everything Jeffrey showed us came directly out of the scriptures."

Just before Christmas, Jeffrey began revealing in class specifics
about how he would take over the Kirtland temple. As he did with
everything, Jeffrey tied the temple takeover to the return of Jesus
Christ. He said that Christ could only return if there was no wickedness in or near the temple. That meant every man, woman, and
child who lived within a one-block radius of the temple, some twenty-five people, would have to be executed. This would include Bill
and Eleanor Lord. The only family who would not be murdered during the first step of the takeover was Dale Luffman's. Luffman, his
wife, Judy, and their three children, ages thirteen, ten, and five,
would be bound and gagged and brought into the temple where they
would be taken before Jeffrey. After reading several scriptures, Jeffrey
would offer the Luffman family to God as a human sacrifice. He
would then behead all five of them, beginning with Luffman and
moving down the line. In Moses' day, the Jews made sacrifices to
God to atone for their sins. Because Christ had not yet returned,
Jeffrey claimed that he and his followers were still living under the
same laws as Moses. Therefore, the Luffmans would serve as the
blood-atonement offering from Jeffrey. They represented the wicked

who had seized "the vineyard." Their blood would be spilled to "cleanse it."

Cutting off their heads was also scriptural, Jeffrey taught. Nephi had beheaded Laban, and Conner Macleod, the hero in *The Highlander*, had used his sword to behead his opponents. Obviously, the scriptures didn't actually mention Conner Macleod, but Jeffrey claimed that God had inspired the makers of the movie and that was good enough. After all, the Mormon scriptures said that the glory of God was intelligence. "What better way to cut off a man from God than to sever his head from his body," Jeffrey asked, "making it impossible for him to use his intelligence?"

Once the Luffmans were sacrificed, Jeffrey would chant a secret prayer that would cause "the mountain of the Lord," as described in Isaiah, to rise up. A great earthquake would then erupt and everyone living in Kirtland would be killed. Only the people inside the temple would be spared. Christ would appear and the Millennium would begin. Jeffrey and his followers would be Christ's new disciples.

Alice was the first to hear Jeffrey's entire plan. She would testify later that she didn't believe he was serious. She became even more suspicious when she surprised Jeffrey one morning while everyone else who lived at the farm was at work. Jeffrey was reading military manuals. After he read a page, he would rip it out and burn it in the fireplace, she said. "I couldn't figure out why he was destroying the book until later that night at class. He taught the military stuff like it was all his idea."

Jeffrey also changed the way that he taught. He had always encouraged his followers to read along with him when he quoted scripture. But now he ordered them to close their books. "Jeffrey kept his open," said Alice. "I was sitting right next to him and could see what he was doing. He acted like he was reading a verse from *one* book, but I could see that he was taking a verse from one book and a verse from another book of scripture and combining them. He was making up his own scriptures."

Alice confronted Jeffrey when they were alone in their bedroom that night. "I said, 'Since when do we start taking things out of context, Jeffrey?,' and he said, 'What'ya mean?,' and I said, 'Now, Jeffrey, this is Alice you're talking to and I saw what you did. You were mixing and matching those verses.'"

Jeffrey exploded in a rage, she said. "He said, 'You shut up about this. You shut up.' He started to shake me. . . . I think that's when I first began to see that Jeffrey was a con man. I believed that he was giving everyone a line of baloney and I decided the temple takeover stuff was bullshit."

If Alice felt that Jeffrey was, as she said, a "con man," she kept quiet about it. "There was never any expression of unbelief on Alice's part," Kevin later said. If anything, Alice became Jeffrey's cheerleader. The two of them reminded Kevin of a tag team in professional wrestling. Jeffrey would declare the "word of the Lord" in a class and then Alice would "rush in and convince everyone that what Jeffrey was saying was the truth."

One night when Shar and Alice were alone, Shar asked her if Jeffrey was serious about killing the Luffmans and taking over the temple. "Alice looked right at me," Shar recalled. "She said, 'Jeffrey is dead serious. If he says he's going to do it, he's going to do it.'" And then Alice added another statement that stuck in Shar's mind. "You've got to understand," Alice said. "I'm not only putting my life on the line here, but I've put my children's life on the line for this. Jeffrey is a prophet. He is who he says he is. You've got to believe it and so do I. I've got to."

Jeffrey assigned everyone tasks. Richard was told to get copies of city maps that showed where gas and other power lines were located. Danny built a replica of the temple and the houses around it and put numbers on the ones where people were to be executed. Since Dennis Patrick lived less than one block from the police station, he was told to watch it and record when the officers changed shifts. Sharon compiled a list of area gasoline stations. Jeffrey said that he might blow one up to create a diversion. The women in the group were shown different bullets and told that they would have to learn to identify them by touch in case they needed to load the men's weapons at night. Shar and Tonya practiced in a room with all the lights off. Jeffrey gave every man a code name. He called himself Eagle-One because, as he put it, "I am in charge and my eyesight is as good as an eagle's." His son Damon, now age seventeen, was Eagle-Two. Danny was Eagle-Eye; Richard, Talon-One; Dennis Patrick, Talon-Two; Ron, Falcon-One; Greg, Falcon-Two. The family farmhouse was dubbed "Eagle's Nest." The red barn was "Red Eagle." The temple was "Eagle's Mound."

No one would later remember what Dennis Avery was called. It simply didn't matter. Dennis and Cheryl still came to classes, but only about once a week. Dennis was working as a night watchman for Wackenhut Security and it was difficult for him to attend at night. Cheryl didn't feel comfortable leaving her three daughters home alone, even though the oldest was thirteen. "The Averys are so stupid," Jeffrey told the class one night, "that the first they will know about the temple takeover is when they see us on television inside the temple."

In February 1988, Jeffrey revealed that he had found the secret prayer that he was required to say in order to make the "mountain of the Lord" rise. God had hidden it in Isaiah, chapter 57, verses 13 and 14. Everyone scrambled to their Bibles. Jeffrey said the key words were "cast ye up, cast ye up."

"Why are those words repeated?" he asked. "Because that is how God talks."

A few days later, Jeffrey made another exciting announcement. God had given him a specific date to attack the temple. "He told me it was posted somewhere in the temple," he explained, "so I went to find it. I looked everywhere and then God's wisdom came to me. If you go to see a doctor, how do you know when he will be in his office? You know by looking at the front door because that is where a doctor posts his office hours." Jeffrey grinned. "God has done the exact same thing. He posted the date that His temple will be redeemed right on the front doors."

The temple doors were decorated with five circles: two large ones and three small ones. The two big circles were symbolic of the second month in the Jewish calendar, Jeffrey said. The three small ones represented days. "God is telling us that He wants us to take over the temple on May third."

Jeffrey asked if anyone knew why that date was significant. Only Alice did.

"May third is Jeffrey's birthday," she volunteered. That was another sign, Jeffrey solemnly declared, that proved he was God's last messenger.

It soon seemed that Jeffrey was having almost daily revelations from God about the takeover. Everyone in the group was getting excited. One night, Jeffrey announced that God wanted them to actually take over the temple on May 1, and then hold the police at bay until May 3 when Christ would appear. "We are going to have a shootout with the police," he said. The next day, Jeffrey showed the group six gas masks that he had bought to use if the police fired tear gas into the temple. But none of Jeffrey's revelations caused as much panic as when he announced that only twelve members of his group were going to survive the shootout and actually be there when Christ appeared. There could be only twelve, Jeffrey said, because Christ had had only twelve disciples when He was alive. Jeffrey, Alice, and Damon were guaranteed safe passage. But only nine of the remaining adults would make it. That meant four of them were going to be killed.

"No one knew if they were on the list," recalled Shar. "It became very divisive and competitive."

Shar asked Jeffrey one day in private if she would make it. "You and Danny are two of the twelve," Jeffrey assured her. Shar asked about Greg and Richard. Jeffrey wasn't certain about Richard, but Greg was safe. Jeffrey then volunteered the names of three group members who were "expendable."

"Kevin is definitely going to die," Shar later quoted Jeffrey as saying. "Even if Kevin survived the takeover, Jeffrey was supposed to shoot him with a shotgun because Kevin was unclean and couldn't be there when Christ returned." Dennis and Tonya were also going to be killed by Jeffrey. "Jeffrey was going to tell the police that we had hostages," Shar said. "He was going to kill Dennis and Tonya and Molly and throw their bodies off the roof of the temple to show the police that we were serious."

Although Shar didn't know it at the time, everyone who asked Jeffrey if they were among the lucky twelve were privately assured that they were safe. They were also told the name of someone who wasn't going to survive. Jeffrey told Kevin that the Patricks were going to die. He told the Patricks that Kevin was going to die.

Shar and Kevin commuted to their jobs in Cleveland each morning together. Most days, Shar slept while Kevin drove. But she was too nervous to sleep during February 1988. "I wanted to warn him, to tell him that he was going to be killed," she explained. "But I was afraid too because if Jeff was who he said he was, then Jeffrey was only doing what God wanted him to do. I figured that God must want Kevin dead."

Shar didn't need to warn Kevin. He had figured it out on his own. "I had picked up several signals." Still Kevin didn't get really scared until he saw how Jeffrey reacted one day when he developed a kidney stone. Jeffrey was in tremendous pain, yet when it was time for the men to lift weights, he performed his normal workout. "Jeffrey always tried to claim that he was sort of a super human, that he was immortal," Kevin said. "The fact that he had a kidney stone showed that he was no different from any other man." But there was something else that bothered Kevin. Jeffrey had been in agony, yet it was so important for him to show off that he had endured the excruciating pain. "I realized just how important all this was to him—how important being a prophet had become. I also realized that he was drawing off our energies. Each time someone new came into the group, Jeffrey gained more confidence in himself. He figured that he was right, that he was a prophet. We were feeding off his fantasy and he was feeding off our fantasy and together we were creating an even bigger and bigger fantasy that was beginning to take on a life of its own."

A few days after Jeffrey recovered from the kidney stone, he and Kevin bumped into each other in the kitchen. For a brief second, their eyes met. "It was strange, but at that very instant, we both knew," said Kevin. "He knew that I no longer believed in him and I knew that he would not, could not, allow me to doubt him. He had too much to lose."

On February 16, the group had a chocolate sheet cake for dessert after dinner.

"Whose birthday is it?" chirped Kristen Lundgren, then age nine.

Jeffrey looked at Kevin. "It's Kevin's going-away cake," he said. Everyone laughed. Kevin had run off before and come back, so everyone assumed that Jeff was kidding him.

Kevin interpreted Jeffrey's comment differently. "He was going to kill me." The next morning, Kevin left for work as usual, but when he got there, he turned in his resignation and hurried to the bus station. Kevin had driven to work by himself that morning. Shar had taken a different job and no longer rode with him into Cleveland. Everyone at the farm wondered where Kevin was that night when he didn't come home. Just before dinner, the phone rang. As always, Jeffrey answered it. A woman was on the line. She refused to give her name, but said that she was a friend of Kevin's.

"The car is parked at the Cleveland bus station," she said.

Jeffrey slammed down the receiver.

"That son of a bitch has run off," Jeffrey swore and then, in front of Alice and Shar, he declared: "Kevin's as good as dead. I'm going to track him down and kill him."

CHAPTER THIRTY

FOR three days, Jeffrey stormed around the farmhouse, openly discussing how he was going to kill Kevin. "He's in Buffalo hiding. I could get up there and do him and be back overnight." He telephoned Kevin's mother but Kevin had already warned her not to tell Jeffrey where he was hiding. He telephoned the Veterans Administration hospital where Kevin had worked in Cleveland and the one in Buffalo too, but Kevin had not left a forwarding address. Jeffrey finally gave up. "Whether he dies at my hand or whether he dies because I say the prayer that raises the mountain and causes the earthquake really doesn't matter," Jeffrey told the group. "Kevin is dead to God."

In March, Jeffrey learned that Bill and Eleanor Lord had resigned as tour guides and were moving out of the Sidney Rigdon house. He and Alice insisted on helping them move. Jeffrey's group moved everything in one day. Bill was impressed. "It was swell." It reminded the Lords of an old-fashioned barn raising where everyone got together to work hard and build a barn in one day. Jeffrey and Alice refused to accept any cash so Bill took everyone out to dinner. Jeffrey was happy. The Lords had moved far enough from the temple that he wouldn't have to kill them.

By the first of April, the takeover permeated every conversation at the farm. Frequently, it was Alice who brought it up. As the "mother" of the family, Jeffrey had assigned her the job of taking care of the minor children during the temple takeover. Besides Jason, Kristen, and Caleb, she would have to watch the Luffs' two children, and Molly Patrick. She was in charge of buying food for the takeover too. The family would need food between May 1, when they seized the temple, and May 3 when Christ appeared.

"What do you like to eat when you are under stress?" Alice asked Shar one afternoon.

"I don't know," Shar replied. "Why?"

"Oh, I was thinking about the takeover. Isn't this weird? I mean, what we're talking about is the insurrection of a national historical monument!" During the next few minutes, Alice speculated about how long it would take the television cameras to arrive and whether the group would be on the national news. Would 60 *Minutes* do a segment on the family? Alice's sister, Terri, had moved to Saudi Arabia with her husband. Alice wondered if the television stations in the Middle East would broadcast the story. "Everyone was getting geared up," said Shar.

One night in mid-April, Jeffrey announced that he was not going to teach his regular class nor drill the group on various military procedures. Instead, he read a passage from the Book of Mormon. It was verses 1 through 47 in the Third Book of Nephi, chapter 5, which told how Jesus Christ had appeared to the ancient Hebrews in the New World after he had been crucified by the Jews.

> . . . They cast their eyes up again towards heaven; and behold, they saw a man descending out of heaven. And he was clothed in a white robe, and he came down and stood in the midst of them . . . And it came to pass that he stretched forth his hand, and spake unto the people, saying, Behold I am Jesus Christ, of whom the prophets testified should come into the world . . .

By the time Jeffrey finished reading the verses, there were tears in his eyes. He had always lectured them against becoming emotional but Jeffrey couldn't control himself—or so it seemed.

"This is what we can accomplish if we follow God's words," Jeffrey concluded, his voice cracking. "We can actually see Jesus Christ." He paused and then said, "I am going to see Him. No one is going to keep me from it."

That night, many of Jeffrey's followers couldn't sleep. A few went down to the kitchen and talked about what Jeffrey had said. The idea that they were going to meet Jesus Christ and become one of his chosen disciples, just like Matthew, John, and Peter, was so fantastic that it was difficult to grasp.

The group got a new member in April. It was Jeffrey's cousin, Debbie Olivarez. Because she was from Jeffrey's "bloodline," she didn't need to undergo an orientation period as the Patricks had. "Understanding the pattern will be natural for her," Jeffrey said. Debbie's mother was Lois Lundgren's sister, and as children, Debbie and Jeffrey had frequently played together. Debbie had always been her grandmother Gadberry's favorite grandchild, a fact that had irked Jeffrey. But Debbie had fallen out of favor with the Gadberrys and the Lundgrens when she married John Olivarez in 1969 while still in high school. Debbie had thought that she was pregnant at the time. "I really didn't love John when we got married," Debbie later confided to Jeffrey. "But I felt so guilty about the sexual relationship that I was afraid no one else would want me. I felt like used merchandise."

During the next eighteen years, Debbie and John appeared to be a perfect RLDS family. They were youth leaders in their local RLDS congregation, and John held a series of important church financial jobs. Together they had four children and Debbie became a registered nurse. The two of them eventually opened a family-run Mexican restaurant in Independence. But privately, Debbie was becoming disenchanted. She never had really fallen in love with John and she didn't think that he loved her. When she confided in an RLDS marriage counselor, he told her that she was to blame. "I was the woman. If I would just do whatever my husband told me to do, then our marriage would be fine." After Debbie left the counseling session, the priest called her husband and told him everything Debbie had said in confidence.

In November 1986, Debbie filed for divorce. When the divorce became final in March 1987, Debbie became despondent. She wrenched her back at work and was put on disability. She began going on shopping sprees to boost her spirits. By the fall of 1987, she was heavily in debt and suicidal. To help cheer her up, her grandparents asked Debbie to drive them to Kirtland to visit Jeffrey and Alice. "They had just moved to the farm and it was wonderful. I felt really at peace." Debbie returned to Independence, but Jeffrey invited her back at Christmas and mailed her an airplane ticket.

"Deep down I had always been looking for a knight in shining armor to carry me away and Jeffrey convinced me that he could deliver that person to me," Debbie recalled. "He had told me that he knew who my 'true companion' was. . . . He said, 'You will never have a normal relationship unless I help you. You will never find the man that you want. I am the only one who can do that for you.' I believed him and I wanted someone desperately to love and someone to desperately love me."

Debbie returned to Independence, put her house up for sale, and told her parents that she was joining Jeffrey's commune. Jeffrey helped Debbie find a job at a Cleveland hospital. Eleven days after she moved to the farm, she was working as a nurse and stealing medical supplies for use during the temple takeover. "It didn't seem wrong. Everything Jeffrey said fit into place with the scriptures that he cited."

Jeffrey told Debbie that Greg Winship was her true companion. They began dating. "I was happy," Debbie said.

On April 22, Jeffrey went over the final details of the takeover. Everyone would arrive at the farmhouse on May 1. The men would dress in full camouflage military outfits, their faces painted black. They would hike through the apple orchard behind the farm and then follow a right-of-way owned by the electric power company to the back of the RLDS church property. They would split into two groups. Ron, Dennis, and Greg would break into the temple. Danny, Richard, Damon, and Jeffrey would go from house to house killing the occupants. They would capture the Luffman family and bring them to the temple. By that time, the women and children would be safely inside with the other men. Jeffrey would behead the Luffmans. He had already bought a machete and had practiced swinging it in front of the group. Jeffrey would say the secret prayer and the men would get ready for the inevitable shootout with the police. On May 3, the mountain of the Lord would rise up and Christ would appear and bless the twelve adults who had survived.

There was only one problem. Jeffrey wasn't certain what year God wanted the temple taken over. The front doors listed only the month and day. Jeffrey told his followers that he would get up early in the morning and go to a hill where he would ask God to appear and tell him if this was the year. Everyone was nervous and tense.

When the Patricks left the farmhouse that night after attending Jeffrey's class, Jeffrey called everyone back together. That included Ron and Susie, Greg, Debbie, Richard, Sharon, Danny, Damon,

Shar, and Alice. "It was always understood that the Patricks would not make it," Shar later testified. "Jeff always said that Dennis was jealous of Jeff, that he wanted to be in Jeff's position, and that he was a doubter in Jeff's power."

On this particular night, Jeffrey added a new twist. He would kill Dennis once everyone was in the temple, he said, but God wanted someone else to murder Tonya and Molly. "Alice will do it," Jeffrey said. She was required to kill to prove that she believed in Jeffrey. He had bought Alice a 9-millimeter pistol and taught her how to shoot it, he said.

"I looked at Alice," Shar recalled later in court testimony, "because it kind of took me aback and she kind of sat back on the chair and rubbed her hand on the edge of the table and she said, 'We all have to do what we have to do.'"

CHAPTER THIRTY-ONE

KEVIN spent February and March in Buffalo hiding from Jeffrey. He stayed mostly with friends. Only his mother knew where he was and sometimes Kevin didn't tell her. He'd simply call her for messages. When she told him that Jeffrey had telephoned, Kevin panicked. "Jeffrey was so much a part of my psyche," Kevin later recalled, "that I was afraid he could anticipate my moves."

Kevin hadn't taken any of his belongings when he fled Cleveland. He hadn't wanted to arouse suspicion at the farm by packing a suitcase. On the day that he escaped, he had telephoned a woman in Buffalo and asked her to buy him a bus ticket. By noon, Kevin was on his way out of town. He had less than five dollars in his pocket.

He was terrified at first. He couldn't sleep. He started smoking, a habit he'd kicked. Whenever he went outside, he would scan the license plates of approaching cars. If the plate said Ohio, he panicked. Even after several uneventful weeks, Kevin remained scared. Finally, he decided to tell the Federal Bureau of Investigation about the temple takeover. He looked up the address in the telephone book and had a friend drop him off there.

"I didn't even make it past the front lobby. An agent came out to interview me and I could tell from the questions he asked that he figured I was a nut case."

Kevin couldn't blame him. The agent didn't know anything about Joseph Smith, Jr., the RLDS, or the Kirtland temple. Talk about beheadings, the Sword of Laban, and "redeeming the vineyard" sounded fantastic. After listening to Kevin's story, the agent said that the takeover sounded like a "problem for the local authorities." He then asked permission to take Kevin's photograph. "He was more interested in investigating me than Jeffrey."

Kevin hurried out of the FBI field office. He felt foolish. He decided to forget about tipping off the police. But he couldn't shake the image of Jeffrey lifting weights even though he had a kidney stone. "I knew he was going to kill someone." Kevin dialed information and scribbled down the number for the Kirtland Police Department. Maybe there he could find someone willing to take him seriously.

April 28, 1988, was a mundane day for Kirtland Police Chief Dennis T. Yarborough and that was exactly how the forty-three-year-old, slightly balding, tobacco-chewing chief liked them. "Cops generally start working in a small city police department and then go up the ladder until they land some high-paying, big federal-agency job," Yarborough later explained. His twenty-three-year career had taken the opposite track. Yarborough started at the top—as a plainclothes army security officer stationed at the White House in 1965. Four years later, he moved to Pennsylvania as a state-highway trooper. Next came a six-year stint with the Cuyahoga County Sheriff's Department, whose jurisdiction included the Cleveland area. Finally in 1979, Yarborough was named chief of the six-officer Kirtland Police Department. From national, to state, to county, to city: to Yarborough, being police chief of a tiny town was the best possible job. There were two types of law. Hands-on-the-hood, spread-your-legs, I'm-bustin'-your-ass big-city law, where a cop made a name for himself by racking up "collars," and what Yarborough liked to describe as down-home "heartbeat" law, as in "You get so close to your people that you can hear their hearts beating." That was the sort of law that Dennis Yarborough practiced.

There had been only one murder in Kirtland since 1979. In 1987, a total of 91 serious crimes were reported. That was an average of 7.5 crimes per month, about one serious crime every four days. Most of them were not major by big-city standards. Sixty-three of the crimes were thefts, such as stolen bicycles and missing tools from construction sites. Not a single armed robbery. Not a single bank robbery. Not a single arrest related to illegal drugs. There were only five, count 'em, five, burglaries in the entire city during the entire year.

Still, Yarborough and his officers kept busy. Much of what Yarborough did as chief didn't fit into a statistical breakdown. It wasn't unusual for a drunk to rap on Yarborough's bedroom window at 3:00 A.M. looking for a ride home or for frantic parents to call and demand that Yarborough find their wayward teenager who was still carousing on the streets.

There were two reasons why Yarborough had applied for the chief's job. The first was his wife, Gail. Her family could trace itself back to the founders of Kirtland and she had never wanted to live nor been happy living anywhere else. She and Yarborough had met in sixth grade, had fallen in love in seventh, and had never been interested in dating anyone else. In high school, she was the band's majorette. He was the scrappy quarterback of the Kirtland Fighting Hornets football team, good enough to get four scholarship offers from small colleges. Yarborough chose Kent State University instead, but eventually dropped out and joined the army. He and Gail married when they were both twenty. Gail came back sixteen times that first year to visit her folks in Kirtland. It was the first time she had been away from home and she hated living in suburban Washington, D.C. It was Gail who eventually got him to apply to be police chief. Gail worked as a secretary at the high school. She knew everyone in town. On most Sundays, her parents came for supper.

Gail's folks considered Yarborough a "newcomer" even though his family had moved to Kirtland in the 1950s after his stepfather, a welder by trade, was hired at a nearby General Motors auto plant. Yarborough had grown up poor—a family of five all living in a twenty-seven-foot-long trailer. He never minded.

The other reason why Yarborough was police chief, besides Gail, was because he genuinely, some would even say naïvely at times, wanted to help other people. The way that Yarborough treated "old Edna" was typical. By everyone's standards, she was mean and nasty. Only her cats seemed to like her. She had about a dozen. The chief got stuck with handling her chronic complaints. One hot afternoon, Yarborough spent an hour listening to Edna blab about some insignificant gripe. Finally, he interrupted and asked Edna the names of her cats. It turned out that each of her cats was

named for a character from Shakespeare. Pretty soon, Edna was gab-
bing about the famous English playwright. When it was time to go,
Edna berated Yarborough, but begrudgingly added that he was better
than the last chief. It was Yarborough who later found Edna dead,
lying naked on the floor of her bathroom. She had suffered a stroke.
Before Yarborough called the morgue, he took a housecoat out of
the closet and put it on the corpse. Several neighbors had gathered
outside. "I just didn't want anyone to see her like that," he said.
"She would have been embarrassed."

Yarborough recognized the name Jeffrey Lundgren, when Kevin
called. Although he was a backslider, Yarborough was raised RLDS.
He'd heard all about Jeffrey's ongoing feud with Dale Luffman. Gail
and her parents were fundamentalists. Yarborough's mother, who
lived with him and Gail, supported Luffman. The chief had gotten
an earful from both about the church's problems.

Yarborough had always thought Jeffrey was odd. Shortly after
Jeffrey moved to town in 1984, he stormed into Yarborough's office.
People were peeking through the windows of his house at night, he
claimed. Yarborough waved off the charge. It was probably young-
sters, curious about their new neighbors, or tourists who had mistakenly thought the house was part of the temple. Jeffrey didn't think
it was funny. A few days later, Yarborough noticed that Jeffrey had
painted the glass on all the basement windows green to prevent anyone from seeing inside. All the shades in the house were kept down
all day too. "I wondered what he was trying to hide."

A few months later, Yarborough had spotted Jeffrey driving a
1952 green Chevrolet. Yarborough had owned one like it as a teenager. He ran a check on the license plate and discovered it belonged
to Danny Kraft, Jr. Curious, Yarborough asked a few questions and
discovered that Jeffrey had attracted several young followers.

He hadn't heard much recently about Jeffrey, although his relatives had mentioned that Jeffrey had resigned as a tour guide and
started a commune at the old apple orchard. And now Kevin Currie
was on the phone, telling Yarborough that Jeffrey was going to lead
an armed takeover of the temple and behead Dale Luffman.

By the time Kevin finished talking, Yarborough was "ninety percent" certain that it was true. But it was so bizarre that Yarborough
decided to get a second opinion. He telephoned the FBI office in
nearby Painesville and asked to speak to Special Agent Robert Alvord. Yarborough considered Alvord a personal friend. A tall, lanky
man in his early forties, Alvord had been with the bureau eighteen

years and was an ex-F4 Phantom-jet pilot who had served two tours in Vietnam.

"This is Yarborough," he announced when Alvord came on the line. "Do I have something that is going to ring your bell!" He quickly highlighted Kevin's story. "I think he's telling the truth, Bob," Yarborough concluded. "How can you guys help me?"

Alvord wasn't sure he could, particularly since the FBI office in Buffalo had already interviewed Kevin in person and decided he was unreliable. Unless Yarborough came up with some sort of evidence to collaborate Kevin's story, Yarborough was on his own.

The chief felt trapped. If Kevin was lying, Yarborough would look like a rube for believing him, especially since the FBI hadn't. But if Kevin's story was true and Yarborough didn't respond—just the thought made Yarborough shudder. The chief sorted through the stacks of papers on his desk and eventually fished out a calendar. He had three days until May 1. "I was trying to figure out how I could possibly corroborate Kevin's story. I didn't have a clue."

Yarborough decided to quiz his six officers. Had any of them noticed anything suspicious about Jeffrey and his group? One had. Ron Andolsek, a chain-smoking, skinny thirty-five-year-old patrolman, had butted heads with Jeffrey only a few days earlier. A neighbor had complained because geese from Jeffrey's farm were running loose. Andolsek had told Jeffrey to keep the geese penned. When Andolsek told the neighbor that the geese were being rounded up, she had told him that Jeffrey and his followers were weird. Caleb Lundgren had told her daughter that on May 3 the "earth was going to open up and all of the devils and demons were going to come up." Andolsek had figured the story was the result of an overactive imagination, but now he wondered: Had Caleb overheard his father talking about the temple takeover? Kevin Currie had mentioned that there was going to be a great earthquake on May 3. That seemed to fit with Caleb's story.

Buoyed by Andolsek's remarks, Yarborough briefed Kirtland Mayor Mario Marcopoli and asked for permission to pay his officers overtime so that he could stake out the Lundgren farmhouse. The story struck Marcopoli as unbelievable, but he authorized the extra pay.

Later that night, Yarborough drove his unmarked brown station wagon to a spot near the farm where he could see the house and the route that Jeffrey was supposedly going to use in three days to reach the temple. It had been less than twelve hours since Kevin had

called. Kevin said the takeover was scheduled to happen between
9:00 P.M. and 1:00 A.M. Yarborough wanted to make certain that
Jeffrey hadn't moved up the date. He stayed at his post watching the
house through binoculars until 1:00 A.M. and then he went home.
Yarborough hoped Kevin *was* a nut.

During the next three days, Yarborough quietly talked with
church officials and learned that Jeffrey had been fired for stealing
church funds. He was told that Jeffrey despised Dale Luffman. With
time running out, Yarborough decided to confront Jeffrey. "I didn't
want to tell him that we knew about the takeover because then he
would have figured out that Kevin had called us. But I wanted Jeffrey
to know that he was being watched." Kevin had mentioned that
Jeffrey and his group had conducted military training drills in the
orchard. Yarborough telephoned the farm and asked Jeffrey to stop
by the station.

"We've had some complaints about paramilitary groups being
spotted in your orchard," Yarborough said. "Have you seen them?"

"No," Jeffrey replied.

"Probably guys playing war games with paint guns," Yarborough
continued, trying to sound nonchalant. "We'd appreciate you keeping an eye out for them."

"Sure," Jeffrey volunteered.

"Of course, we'll be watching for them too," the chief added.

Jeffrey seemed nervous. Yarborough asked him if he owned any
guns. Only a couple of rifles for hunting and some black-powder guns
that he collected, Jeffrey said, lying.

Jeffrey had what the chief later called "dancing eyes." "He kept
glancing around. He was like a frightened rabbit."

After Jeffrey left, Yarborough spoke to one of his officers. "How
can anyone follow that guy?" Yarborough asked. "He's a real dud."

Later that day, Yarborough made a private telephone call to a
friend from his days in the army. "I need a favor," he said. A few
hours later, the chief picked up a .45-caliber Ingram Mac-10 machine gun capable of firing 1,200 rounds per minute.

On the night of May 1, Yarborough and three of his men staked
out the temple and church. Nothing happened. They were there the
next night too. Again, nothing happened. Yarborough hoped his
talk had scared Jeffrey away. But he couldn't be certain.

On the afternoon of May 3, Yarborough briefed his officers. "If
it's gonna happen, then tonight's the night." One of them asked if
they had sufficient "probable cause" to begin shooting if they spotted

Jeffrey and his squad coming toward the temple. There were seven of them and Kevin had said that they would be carrying semi-automatic weapons. Did Yarborough really plan on yelling "Stop! Police!" before opening fire?

"If we see them in military gear with weapons," Yarborough replied quietly, "that's all the probable cause we need."

At about 8:30 P.M., Yarborough drove behind the RLDS church. He positioned himself so that he would be the first to see Jeffrey, the first to confront the group, the first to begin shooting. He also would be the group's most likely target. Yarborough placed the Mac-10 machine gun in his lap. He was angry. Things like this weren't supposed to happen in Kirtland.

"I had resolved myself," he said later. "If Jeffrey came up behind the church with his followers, they were never going to make it to the temple alive."

CHAPTER THIRTY-TWO

SHAR Olson got out of bed early on the morning that Jeffrey was scheduled to ask God when He wanted the Kirtland temple taken over. She walked downstairs in the farmhouse and found Jeffrey eating breakfast in the kitchen.

"Why are you up?" Jeffrey asked.

Shar had a ready explanation. "I figured if you were going to go see God, then I should get up and support you."

Jeffrey smiled and praised her for being such a devoted daughter. A few minutes later he left. Shar watched through a large picture window in the farmhouse as Jeffrey walked toward a hill that he claimed was the largest mountain in Ohio. [It wasn't but no one in the group had ever checked.]

Shar had lied. She had gotten up because she wanted to make certain that Jeffrey really did go to the "mountain." Shar had started to doubt that Jeffrey was a prophet and his comments that morning had made her even more suspicious. A real prophet would have known why she had gotten up early.

Shar sat at the window for more than an hour. Jeffrey had told his group that God always appeared in a brilliant beam of light. She didn't see any beams of light, but she noticed two clouds in the sky almost directly over where Jeffrey had gone. When Jeffrey returned to the farmhouse, he again thanked Shar for getting up with him.

That night Jeffrey told the group during scripture class that God had indeed appeared to him that morning in a beam of light that had shone down through a completely clear blue sky. Shar knew immediately that Jeffrey was not telling the truth. She had seen two clouds in the sky. But she kept quiet and continued to listen to Jeffrey's story.

God had been angry when he appeared, Jeffrey said. He was disappointed in Jeffrey's followers. Despite Jeffrey's teachings, his followers still needed to repent. "Thus saith the Lord, this is not the year for Christ to return to His temple," Jeffrey said. "You are unclean."

"The reason why it did not happen," Ron later told investigators, "was because . . . our sin would not allow us to come into the presence of God." Christ could only return to the temple if it had been cleansed. "There was too much sin in Jeffrey's household," Ron said.

That night, Jeffrey went one by one through the group and described each person's sin. Only one person was pure enough to meet Jesus. That was Jeffrey. Alice's sin was disobedience because she still did not submit her will to Jeffrey. Dennis Patrick's sin was pride and arrogance because he still attempted to interpret scripture by himself rather than blindly accepting what Jeffrey said. But Jeffrey's harshest criticism was aimed at Richard. It was his refusal to marry Sharon that was the primary reason why the temple takeover had been called off. At one point during the class, Jeffrey took out a .45-caliber pistol and placed it next to his scriptures. Looking directly at Richard, Jeffrey said: "I will get you to meet God—one way or another."

After that class, the mood at the farm changed, Shar said. Richard blamed himself for letting the group down. Everyone else felt guilty. People began to bicker. Alice and Jeffrey fought too. Shar had gotten a job as a waitress at night, which meant that she didn't have to go to work until late in the afternoon. She was generally the only group member home in the mornings with Jeffrey and Alice. One morning, Shar was awakened by the sound of Alice and Jeffrey arguing.

"When are you going to submit your will?" she heard Jeffrey holler. "When are you going to obey your Lord and master and do what I command?"

A few minutes later, Alice stormed out of the bedroom and left the farmhouse. She got as far as the gravel drive before she stopped, began to cry, and returned to the house.

"She spent three days in bed after that," Shar said. "Alice didn't come out of her bedroom and Jeffrey catered to her." He made her milkshakes, brought her shrimp platters, bought her presents. When she finally emerged from the bedroom, Alice said there was something she wanted to tell the group. "She apologized to the family and said it wouldn't happen again," said Shar. "It was pretty typical of Alice. After all of these outbursts of hers, she would calm down and she'd say that she was a broken woman now and that she was perfect and she was the submissive wife, but it wouldn't be too long before they'd be back into it again."

In May, Shar got a telephone call at work from a creditor who complained that she was several months behind on her car payments. Jeffrey had assured her that he was paying her bills. Like everyone else, she turned over all of her cash to him. That night at dinner, Shar mentioned the call. Jeffrey ordered everyone to leave the room but the two of them.

"I don't owe those Gentiles anything," Jeffrey said. "God doesn't need credit and neither should you." He then criticized her for being "rebellious."

A few days later, Jeffrey and Shar clashed again. This time it was over a Mother's Day telephone call. Jeffrey didn't allow anyone to use the telephone without his permission and he caught Shar talking to her mother. That night at class, Jeffrey said Alice was sick in bed because of Shar's disobedience. "I was told that Alice was my mother . . . and I had greatly hurt her because of my sins."

The next day when Shar went to apologize, she found Alice lying in bed with the curtains drawn.

"I'm really sorry," Shar said. "I didn't mean to hurt your feelings."

"As a mother," Alice replied slowly, "it's just a burden I'm going to have to bear."

Alice stayed in bed three days before she felt well enough to rejoin the group.

Shar decided that it was time for her to quit the family. But she wasn't going to sneak away like Kevin Currie. She wasn't going to leave all the clothing and the furniture that she had brought from Independence. She went to see Jeffrey one night while he was in an office that he had made in the barn.

"I want out," she said.

"You wait here," he replied sternly. Jeffrey rushed over to the farmhouse and when he returned, he had Alice and Danny with him. For the next two hours, Alice and Danny pleaded with Shar to stay. Alice cried. "You can't do this!" she said. Alice reminded Shar that she was supposed to marry Danny. Their names were written in the scriptures. When Alice and Danny failed to sway Shar, Jeffrey weighed in, only he was nasty.

"You will never amount to anything if you leave," he said. "God will curse you."

Shar started to cry. "I was sitting on an old ammo box and they had formed a semicircle around me with their chairs and they just kept going on and on and on and then finally Danny said, 'Hey, wait a minute.' He looked over at Jeffrey and he said, 'You said that Shar was one of the twelve who was going to make it, going to survive the temple takeover. You said her name was written in the book.' Jeffrey turned red and then he said, 'No, if she leaves, she dies.' And then he looked at me and put his finger in my face and said, 'I'll see to it that your flesh will rot if you leave.'"

Shar became hysterical. "I'll stay, I'll stay," she mumbled.

And then something strange happened. Alice became irritated and accused Shar of staging the entire evening. She claimed that the real reason Shar wanted to leave the group was because, in Alice's words, "you're just horny." No one was allowed to have sex at the farm unless they were married. "The bottom line is that you want out because you want to go get screwed."

Shar was crushed. "Sex had nothing to do with it, but for some reason, Alice fixated on it."

For two weeks, Shar stuck it out, and then one night, Alice came prancing into her bedroom wearing a sexy pair of pink silk pajamas.

"Jeffrey bought them for me," she gushed. "What do you think?"

That very morning Shar had asked Jeffrey for ten dollars to buy a new pair of tennis shoes because her only pair had a hole in them. "We don't have enough money right now," he'd told her.

"Mom," Shar told Alice, "I want out. I don't want to live here anymore."

Jeffrey was waiting the next morning when Shar came downstairs.

"Get your shit and get out," he said.

As Shar started to leave, Jeffrey came after her. He reminded her that when she had moved to the farm, he had paid to put some of her belongings in storage. He was keeping two expensive quilts that Shar had inherited to pay that bill, he said. Shar didn't care.

There was no way for Shar to move everything that morning but she didn't want to spend another night at the farmhouse. A waitress at work said she could live with her until she found her own apartment. Shar drove to the farm the next day in a small U-Haul truck to collect her belongings. Jeffrey and Danny carried Shar's furniture from the farmhouse. Neither spoke to her. When the U-Haul was packed, Jeffrey stepped up to Shar.

"You know what your problem is, Shar?" he said. "You have a real problem being submissive to men."

"Show me a man," Shar shot back, "worth being submissive to."

As Shar drove away, Jeffrey decided that Alice had been right.

"What Shar needed," he said later, "was a man to give her a good fuck."

CHAPTER THIRTY-THREE

SHAR'S departure threatened Jeffrey. He knew it. So did Alice. Shar hadn't fled in fear like Kevin. She'd simply walked out and Jeffrey hadn't been able to stop her. Worse, Jeffrey had prophesied that Shar and Danny were going to be married and that Shar was going to be one of Christ's twelve disciples during the Millennium. If that was true, why had she gone?

No one in the group had said anything, of course, but Alice figured it would only be a matter of time before others began doubting Jeffrey. There were plenty of warning signs about what was ahead. Despite Jeffrey's nightly harangues, Richard still hadn't married Sharon, Greg hadn't moved to the farm as Jeffrey had demanded nor had he married Debbie, and Dennis Patrick was still questioning Jeffrey's scripture interpretations in classes. Privately, Alice suspected that one reason Jeffrey had started bringing his .45 pistol to class with him every night was because, without it, he was afraid that no one was going to take him seriously.

During the summer of 1988, Alice began drinking heavily. She would stay up until two or three in the morning watching videotapes and then sleep until one or two in the afternoon. She'd drink a beer before dinner and take a few Excedrin P.M. to quiet her nerves.

Some nights she wouldn't come to class. Instead, she'd have Jeffrey buy her a six-pack or a bottle of wine and she would drink in her room and pop painkillers while watching television. Alice's drinking got to be a joke in the class because of comments that Jeffrey had made.

"Everyone knew when the beer started following Alice into the bedroom that Jeffrey had told her he wanted to have anal sex," Debbie later remembered.

Jeffrey had talked openly about it. He had decided that Alice's vagina had stretched after childbirth, making it difficult for him to achieve orgasm. As a result, he had turned almost exclusively to anal intercourse. Alice hadn't protested, at least not to anyone in the group. The beers and pills supposedly helped Alice deal with the pain of anal sex.

While that might have been one reason for Alice's drinking, pill popping, and depression, there was another. When Alice was, as she later put it, "gut level honest" with herself, she didn't really believe that Jeffrey was a prophet. Worse, after Shar left, Alice began to suspect that Jeffrey knew that his wife suspected he was a fraud. "I was expected to believe in him, that he was a prophet. If I didn't believe him, I think he felt no one would."

Alice's doubts and Jeffrey's insistence on anal sex were linked, she later claimed. "Jeffrey was always dreaming up ways for me to prove that I really loved him. I decided it was because of his childhood. The only way that he had received attention and love was by proving that he deserved it, so Jeffrey was always demanding that I do things to prove to him that I loved him. He would say, 'I'm testing you, Alice. I want to see how much you love me.' And I would say, 'Why do I have to be tested?,' and he would say, 'The Lord constantly tests the faith of his servants.' Whenever he began to suspect that I doubted him, he would become more dominant in the bedroom. He had to control me. It became an obsession with him."

"At first," Alice continued, "he used a lubricant when we had anal intercourse, but later he decided my own blood was the best lubricant."

One night in July, while Alice was lying in bed sipping a beer, she listened to Jeffrey teaching the group outside her bedroom. The four Excedrin that she had taken started to make her feel lightheaded. She knew that Jeffrey was going to cut this class short because he had already told her that he wanted to have anal sex after class. She took two more Excedrin and another swig of beer. She began to feel sorry for herself. "I thought, 'Alice, all you've ever wanted in life was a decent house and a nice family. Is that so much to ask for?'"

As she lay in bed, she thought back to the summer of 1969 when the patriarch had prophesied about her future. She had been so certain, so filled with dreams. Jeffrey hadn't lived up to any of them. The only time in their marriage when they weren't poor was when the group members supported them. How long would that last? How long before Jeffrey blew it again?

Alice wasn't certain how late it was when Jeffrey slipped into their bedroom, but by the time he got under the covers and began to kiss her, she was wallowing in self-pity and was drunk. As Jeffrey started to roll her over and pull off her pajama bottoms, Alice let loose with a string of profanity. During the next few minutes, she blistered Jeffrey in a voice that was slurred and often incoherent. She would later not be able to recall precisely what she had said that night nor was she really certain that she had actually said all of the words that she had been thinking. But the next morning, there was one word that seemed etched in her mind: LOSER.

A short time after that encounter, Jeffrey told Alice that he wanted her to come to class. Instead of opening his scriptures, Jeffrey read a passage from Sun Tzu's *The Art of War*. It was a short story that described how the King of Wu decided to test Sun Tzu's leadership skills one day. The king asked Sun Tzu if he could take any group of people and turn them into a well-disciplined fighting force. When Sun Tzu replied that he could, the king sent him 180 women from the royal harem. Sun Tzu divided the women into two groups on the military parade ground and commanded them to "Face right!" The women burst into laughter. Some faced right, some left, others didn't move. Sun Tzu repeated his instructions, and this time when the women giggled and turned the wrong way, he ordered two of the king's favorite concubines to step forward. While everyone watched, Sun Tzu beheaded the women. He then gave the order "Face right!" and every woman did exactly that. Sun Tzu told the king that his new troops were ready to do whatever they were ordered.

Jeffrey didn't say much after he read the story and none of his followers was certain why it was important. They were to learn soon enough.

CHAPTER THIRTY-FOUR

DENNIS Avery had always had a terrible sense of timing and he proved it by showing up at the farmhouse to complain shortly after Shar left the group. Dennis had discovered that the $575 monthly rent for his three-bedroom house in Kirtland hadn't being paid for nearly a year. Jeffrey had promised to make the payments but he hadn't and Avery's landlord was threatening eviction. Jeffrey didn't have time to waste on Dennis Avery. "Dennis represented everything that I hated in a person," Jeffrey later recalled. "He was a physical and spiritual weakling who couldn't keep his house in order." Jeffrey's anger flashed. There was sufficient income coming into the commune to pay the Averys' back rent, Jeffrey said, but he was not going to do it. Why should he help a Gentile get rich? he asked.

Jeffrey told Dennis that he was going to have to move. If he left during the night and didn't leave a forwarding address, his landlord probably wouldn't be able to find him, and even if he did, so what? Dennis and Cheryl were broke. Taking them to court would be a waste of time.

Dennis had always been proud that he didn't have any debts, his brother Tim later recalled. In this case, Dennis didn't have much choice. Dennis went home and told Cheryl to begin packing. On

July 15, 1988, the Averys moved into a three-bedroom house that rented for $450 per month in Madison, twenty-four miles east of the farmhouse. Dennis didn't leave a forwarding address nor tip off his landlord that he was going.

Investigators would later wonder why the Averys remained loyal to the Lundgrens. This is how Jeffrey explained his hold on Dennis and Cheryl: "All of their lives the Averys had been losers. They'd never fit in, never really been accepted by anyone. They were odd-balls and they knew it and deep down they hated it because they believed that they were just as good as anyone else; in fact, Dennis thought that he was better. What I offered them was a chance to be exactly that. They believed that Jesus Christ wanted them to be His disciples. Can you imagine—them as His disciples? But they believed it was true because they wanted to believe it was true and as long as they believed that I could take them to meet God, then they were going to follow me."

For whatever reason, when Cheryl enrolled Trina, Becky, and Karen in the Madison school district on August 15, she identified Alice Lundgren as the person the school should notify if it couldn't find either parent and there was an emergency. And when Dennis filled out job applications, the first name that he always listed as a reference was Jeffrey's.

Trina Avery hadn't wanted to move. She was just getting settled in the Kirtland schools. Being in ninth grade was difficult enough without being the new kid, especially when you were a heavyset, awkward, self-conscious girl much more at ease with a book than with other teenagers. Most people thought Trina looked like her mother. She had shoulder-length dark curly hair and a round face. But she had inherited both of her parents' shyness. Trina hadn't wanted to leave Independence and shortly after they arrived in Kirtland, she bought a bulky hot-pink sweatshirt and had the words WHY ME? printed on the front of it in big black letters. "I put 'why me?' on everything because I hate Ohio and I put it on my sweatshirt to get other kids' reactions," she told her grandmother. "Most kids think it's crazy." The question "Why Me?" became Trina's trademark at school, where she stayed close to her younger sister Becky. Trina wrote "Why Me?" on her notebooks and included it in letters sent to a classmate back in Independence. Cheryl figured Trina would get over it. She and Dennis looked on Trina as their "brainy" child. She got good grades and often acted more like an adult than a youngster. Still, at age fourteen in 1988, Trina slept with a night-light in her room and hadn't yet gotten rid of her stuffed animals and dolls. The night-light was a gift from her mother and was a white unicorn with a bulb inside. In her sparse bedroom, Trina had tacked up a poster. It was not a photograph of a teenage heartthrob or rock-and-roll star, but a picture of three Care Bear cartoon figures hugging each other. She had gotten it during an RLDS summer camp. "Good friends are worth holding on to," it said.

The Averys' middle daughter, Becky—only her father called her Rebecca—was twelve when the family moved to Madison and was so different from Trina that strangers never would have guessed they were related. She was such a picky eater that Cheryl worried that Becky might be anorectic. A school counselor dismissed her fears, suggesting instead that Becky's poor eating habits were simply a way for her to show her independence. Becky was stubborn, always on the go, and a tomboy ready to take on any dare. Shortly after the family moved to Ohio, Becky decided to try her mother's curling iron without telling anyone. Within ten minutes, she had gotten her long stringy hair so tangled up that it took Cheryl two hours to free it. Becky's most prized possessions were her pet goldfish, which she named "Happiness," a twenty-eight-inch-tall [she had measured him twice] stuffed dog named "Big Carl," and a special white pillowcase that she had made in Independence while in Orioles, an RLDS girls' group. It was divided into six squares and each contained the outline of a human hand that had been first drawn on and then stitched with thread. Besides the outline of Becky's own hand, the prints on the pillowcase belonged to the four other girls in her Orioles group and her leader. Becky always showed her pillowcase to visitors and quickly confided that she had liked Carey, who was "really, really nice," but not another girl whose hand was on the case because she had been "creepy." Such comments would embarrass Cheryl, but Becky didn't care. She said what she thought.

Karen, who had just turned six when the family moved to Madison, was the baby. She was, in Becky's words, "a giggle-box," who was always smiling, always laughing. If Karen wasn't playing with her favorite doll—"Linda"—she was sprawled on the floor with her pick-up sticks. Once the family got to Madison, Karen went to first grade at the Red Bird Elementary School. She had enjoyed herself until a boy made fun of how she talked. Words such as "okay" and "see" came out sounding like "oway" and "thee." Trina told Karen to ignore the boy. Becky suggested that Karen kick him in the leg.

Cheryl had taught all three girls to sew and Trina and Becky were both making quilts. They worked on them after school on special racks kept in the living room. The racks weren't in the way. There wasn't much other furniture in the house. The family room contained a well-worn sofa and a folding lawn chair. The walls were decorated with drawings by the children, posters from magazines, and cross-stitch pictures that Cheryl and the girls had sewn. Karen had just finished making a bunny rabbit on a cross-stitch pattern for her father.

Jeffrey would later accuse the Avery girls of being ill-mannered and disobedient, but no one else in his group would remember them that way. Even if they had been, they were not as troublesome as the Lundgrens' own four children. Damon, who was about to turn eighteen in the fall of 1988, was a slender, rather docile boy whose goal in life seemed to be trying to please his father. Jeffrey had decided to make Damon his successor and was molding him into being a leader. In Jeffrey's mind, that meant making Damon tougher. It was a difficult job, according to Damon's grandmother, Donna Keehler, because Jeffrey had spent most of Damon's life beating the spunk out of him. "You get whipped so many times for being disobedient, and you don't be disobedient," she explained. Still, Damon tried to live up to his father's arrogant ways. When his father put him in charge of cleaning the weapons and leading the men in exercises, he strutted around the farm. "One time Damon came in the room where Richard and I were," Sharon later testified. "Damon told Richard he had to stand at attention when he [Damon] entered. Another time, he told Richard to kiss his feet or something like that." Debbie had known Damon all his life and she noticed a change. "Jeffrey made him a two-star general. He answered only to Jeffrey."

Ironically, Damon's younger brother, Jason, couldn't care less about doing what his father wanted. Yet when it came to a family pecking order, Jason was Jeffrey's favorite son. Although Jason was only fourteen, he was built like his father and could overpower Damon and give most of the men in the group a good fight if he wished. Jeffrey said Jason was too young to study with the adults and that suited him fine. "I thought all that stuff he was teaching was boring," he later said. No one at the farmhouse except for Jeffrey could tell Jason what to do, and even Jeffrey frequently had to back up his orders with physical threats to make Jason comply.

Daughter Kristen, who was nine years old, was an active, beautiful girl, but even by Alice's account she was "completely spoiled by her father." Behind her back, group members called her "prissy" rather than "Krissy." Whatever she wanted, Jeffrey made certain that she got. The Lundgrens' youngest child, Caleb, age seven, was mostly ignored by his parents. He was a sweet child, but Jeffrey had always thought him dense and he treated him with disdain.

During late July and early August, Jeffrey moved to reinstate his authority over the group. One night when Greg Winship wasn't in class, Jeffrey told everyone that they were going to have a special class designed to pressure Greg into moving into the farmhouse. Greg was an avid volleyball player, and after the temple takeover was called off, he had started to drift away from the group. Jeffrey's special class worked. On Labor Day, Greg moved in and was rewarded by Jeffrey with an expensive antique bedroom set. Other group members got rewards too. Jeffrey had just received a surge of cash. Debbie's house in Independence had sold and she had also settled the workman's compensation claim that she had filed after she hurt her back working in an Independence hospital. Combined, those two checks totaled $32,492.32, all of which Debbie dutifully turned over to Jeffrey.

Jeffrey bought clothes for Alice and together they went antiques shopping. He bought himself a .54-caliber black-powder rifle for his gun collection and he purchased a 1986 Nissan pickup truck. He took everyone to a nearby amusement park for a day, and he and the other adults went out to dinner several times. Jeffrey encouraged Richard and Sharon to go out on dates and sent Greg and Debbie dancing at the Brown Derby, a popular Kirtland restaurant-bar. Jeffrey concentrated on cementing his relationship with Ron Luff too. He bought toys for the Luff children and went out of his way to spend more time with Ron. Both of them enjoyed weight lifting, and when they worked out together, Jeffrey began sharing with Ron what seemed to be confidential information about the group and scriptures. "Basically what he told me was that I was to be the spokesman for the seer in the last days," Ron later told investigators. "That became a second-in-command type situation for me." As Jeffrey's new lieutenant, Ron was expected to help keep the group in line. Whenever Jeffrey decided to "session" someone in class, Ron would jump in.

There was only one family that didn't benefit from Debbie's cash. Jeffrey didn't do anything special for Dennis and Tonya Patrick or their daughter, Molly. "They don't deserve it," he told Alice.

In September, Jeffrey announced that he had used the pattern to discover a new revelation that had made the taking of the Kirtland temple no longer necessary. Jeffrey had discovered a way for his followers to meet God face-to-face. In fact, if the group followed Jeffrey's instructions, every one of them would not only be able to see God, but also to *touch* God. According to the Book of Mormon, an ancient Hebrew identified as the "Brother of Jared" was so righteous that God appeared before him. Jeff was fascinated by the story and claimed that he had discovered a way for the group to compel God to appear to them in the same way.

It took Jeffrey several weeks to explain how this process would work and, as always, he first laid an intricate foundation by citing dozens of scriptures and using the pattern to reveal hundreds of hidden messages. But in the end, his plan was actually quite simple. In order to take his followers before God, Jeffrey would first have to become "endowed with the power." The way for him to obtain this power was by killing the "wicked" and offering them as a human blood-atonement sacrifice to God. Jeffrey wasn't certain how many people he was supposed to kill or who they were. But once he offered God this blood sacrifice, then he would received the "power" to take his followers to meet God.

There was only one catch. Everyone in the group had to go before God at the same time, and if any of them had any "sin" at all, God would destroy the entire group. This was because, as Ron Luff later told federal investigators, "nothing unclean can come before God."

Jeffrey told his followers that he had come up with a way for them to purge themselves of all sin. After Jeffrey made the human sacrifice, the group would isolate itself from the evils of society by going into the "wilderness." In this case, the "wilderness" would be somewhere remote where the group could camp without being disturbed and focus on becoming "of one heart and mind" with God. "I don't know where the wilderness is," Jeffrey said. "But God will lead us there."

A short time after Jeffrey explained his revelation, he called his followers together and told them to open their Mormon scriptures to Section 105 of the Doctrine and Covenants, a revelation that Joseph Smith, Jr., said he received from God on July 23, 1837. Jeffrey read them the key lines:

> "Behold, vengeance cometh speedily upon the inhabitants of the earth. . . . And upon my house shall it begin. . . . First among those among you . . . who have professed to know my name and have not known me. . . ."

Jeffrey told the group that God was telling him through these verses that he was to select someone to sacrifice from within his own "house," someone who had claimed to worship God but who really did not know Him.

Jeffrey didn't say anything else. The message was clear. The only question was "Who would it be?"

CHAPTER THIRTY-FIVE

WHEN Jeffrey Lundgren and his men didn't come charging up the embankment behind the RLDS church during the night of May 3, Chief Yarborough was relieved. Still, he didn't want to take any chances so he had his ambush set up on the night of May 4 just in case Jeffrey came late. He didn't. Yarborough was back to square one. Had Kevin Currie bamboozled him or had Jeffrey simply postponed the takeover because he knew that the police were watching?

Yarborough went to see Kenneth Fisher, an RLDS bishop who lived near the Kirtland temple and was one of the people on Jeffrey's hit list. Fisher gave the chief a list of fifteen people who were members of Jeffrey's group. Yarborough didn't recognize any of the names. All of them were "outsiders," not from Kirtland. He turned the list over to Ron Andolsek, who immediately began checking with federal, state, county, and city law-enforcement agencies. It didn't take Andolsek long to discover that none of Jeffrey's followers had a criminal record.

"On paper they were perfect, law-abiding citizens," the chief recalled. "It just didn't fit. How could they be involved in a plot to behead a preacher and his family?"

Yarborough checked out several library books on religious cults and mind control. He found his copy of the Book of Mormon. "I'm going to figure out what makes this guy tick," he told Andolsek. "I don't want to spend every May third wondering if this is the year he's going to attack." Andolsek had a few ideas of his own. He began parking his squad car on the blacktop near the Lundgren farmhouse. He acted as if he were using his radar to check for speeders, but he was actually spying on the commune. By the end of August, both men had collected a large file on Lundgren. They had found out where Jeffrey did his banking, where his followers worked, what model of cars the group used, and had even obtained a list of the videotapes that Jeffrey had recently rented. But neither the chief nor Andolsek had found a single piece of damaging evidence that would corroborate Kevin's story. Late one hot Friday night in August, the two men went over everything in their file, piece by piece. When they finished, Yarborough shook his head in disgust. The only crime that Jeffrey had committed was a zoning violation.

"We could arrest him for having too many people in one house," the chief said. "But that would make it harder for us to do surveillance."

Andolsek agreed.

It looked as if they'd hit a dead end.

What neither of them realized was that only a few miles down the road from the Kirtland police station, the one person who could provide them with the help that they needed was busy working as a waitress at Chi Chi's Restaurant, serving platters of chicken tacos and bean burritos. Shar Olson was not on the list of cult members that Bishop Fisher had given Yarborough. Shar had arrived after Jeffrey had been fired by the church. Fisher didn't know her. During his stakeouts, Andolsek had spotted Shar's 1986 Nova at the farmhouse but she had quit the group in June, and since she never showed up at the farmhouse again, he had assumed that she had just been passing through. Shar didn't plan on contacting the police. She didn't want to get Greg, Richard, or herself into trouble. She just wanted to be left alone.

In August, a fellow waitress told Shar that her father was in the lobby waiting to speak with her.

"My dad?" she replied. And then Shar realized that it was Jeffrey.

"What do you want?" she demanded.

Jeffrey told her that Richard had received a letter from his parents, Wilmer and Twylia Brand, who were trying to get him to quit the group. Richard's parents had been suspicious of Jeffrey from the start, particularly when they learned that Richard had sold his prized truck shortly after moving to Kirtland and given Jeffrey all of the money that his grandmother had left him. In the letter, the Brands mentioned the sexual affair that Jeffrey had engaged in while at the Lake of the Ozarks Hospital. How could Jeffrey be a prophet, the Brands had asked, if he was guilty of adultery? Richard had shown the letter to Jeffrey and he had immediately known that Shar was the source. Alice had once told Shar about the affair.

"Why'd you tell Richard's parents?" he asked, "and what *else* did you say?"

"I didn't tell Richard's parents anything," Shar replied innocently. Technically, she was telling the truth. "Jeffrey had always played word games with us," she later explained. "I was turning the tables on him because I hadn't told Richard's parents, I'd told Richard's sister and she had told them."

Jeffrey seemed unconvinced. "Well, someone told them," he replied.

"Listen," Shar snapped, doing her best to sound assertive, "let's not play games. I'm not out to get you in trouble. All I wanted was out of the group. I'm not going to say anything about your teachings and plans."

Jeffrey changed tactics. "Danny loves you," he said. "Sharon and Debbie are going to pick out engagement rings. You could do that too."

"Just leave me alone," Shar repeated. She turned and walked away.

The Brands telephoned Shar a short time later and pressed her for more details about the group. Why had she quit? Shar avoided answering but they were persistent. Finally, she blurted out: "Jeffrey's threatened me. He told me my flesh will rot. I can't say anymore."

Jeffrey returned to Chi Chi's several weeks later to see Shar. The Brands had written their son another letter. This time they were threatening to report Jeffrey to the Internal Revenue Service for tax evasion since he hadn't paid any income taxes on the money he received from his followers.

"Jeffrey was furious and he accused me of telling them things," Shar recalled, "so I said, 'That's right, Jeff. I'm tired of your stupid games. I did tell them and if anything happens to me, there won't be any questions about where it came from.' He stormed out of the restaurant."

A week later, Danny's stepmother called Shar. Obviously, the Brands were spreading the word to other parents that Shar had left Jeffrey's group. On September 20, Shar got yet another call, but this time it was Dale Luffman on the phone. He was conducting his own probe, he explained, because he wanted to get Jeffrey thrown out of the RLDS. The squabble between fundamentalists and liberal factions had finally reached the breaking point in the Kirtland congregation. The church was splitting. A group of fundamentalists was starting its own "restoration RLDS" congregation. Luffman felt Jeffrey was partly to blame and wanted to bring him up on charges within the church of encouraging members to quit the RLDS. After some prodding, Shar agreed to meet Luffman at a Bob Evans restaurant in a neighboring town. After swearing Luffman to secrecy, Shar unloaded her story. He was horrified. Chief Yarborough hadn't told Luffman about the temple takeover plot nor had anyone told the minister that Jeffrey had been planning to behead him and his family. As soon as they finished talking, Luffman raced to the Kirtland Police Department. Ron Andolsek happened to be on duty.

"Jeffrey Lundgren is running a cult," Luffman announced, "and is planning on killing me and my family."

Ten minutes later, Andolsek telephoned the chief. "I got something you need to hear," he said. "We got another informant."

Shar was angry when Andolsek telephoned her early the next morning. She had told Luffman not to tell anyone about the plot. But she finally agreed to meet Andolsek a day later, on September 23, at 11:30 P.M. at Maxx Doogans Tavern, a popular college hangout about fifteen miles west of Kirtland.

Shar was nervous during the meeting, but she told Andolsek everything that she knew about the plot, and then Shar pulled out a spiral notebook. She had kept detailed notes during Jeffrey's classes.

"When he started talking about killing people," she told Andolsek. "I paid real close attention."

Andolsek flipped through the pages. Written in flawless script were descriptions of various types of bullets, instructions for how to use gas masks, lists of military terms. Instructions for dismantling an AR-15 semi-automatic rifle were followed by scriptural notations about ancient Hebrew warfare.

The next morning, Andolsek typed a nine-page single-spaced account of his interview with Shar and gave it to Yarborough. As soon as he finished reading it, the chief dialed Special Agent Robert

Alvord's number. This time, the chief was certain that he could get him to listen.

Across the street at the RLDS church, the Reverend Dale Luff- man was putting the finishing touches on his own report about Jef- frey. He had already telephoned various church officials in Independence and briefed them. He'd also warned them—if Jeffrey did something crazy, it was going to reflect badly on the entire RLDS denomination.

"We've got to get this guy out of the church," Luffman had said. "Fast."

In his letter, Luffman had asked the church to take the extraor- dinary step of excommunicating Jeffrey. On October 10, Luffman received a package of documents from the church. According to the church's bylaws, Jeffrey was entitled to a formal hearing, similar to a court trial, before he could be excommunicated. If he wished, he could argue his case in person before a church council. Jeffrey would have three days to reply to the charges that Luffman had filed.

Luffman had been careful not to mention the temple-takeover plot in his formal charges against Jeffrey. Yarborough had asked him to keep that hush-hush until the police could get more evidence. Jeffrey was being accused of teaching doctrines contrary to the church's beliefs and of encouraging members to quit the church.

Luffman telephoned an elder in the Kirtland congregation and asked if he would ride with him to the farmhouse. Luffman needed a witness from the church to prove that Jeffrey had been served the excommunication papers. Luffman also figured it would be safer if someone went with him to the farm when he confronted Jeffrey.

When Luffman turned his sedan into the farm's driveway, he spotted Jeffrey working outside in the yard. Neither man wasted time with social niceties. Luffman walked up to Jeffrey and stuck out the excommunication papers.

"Do us both a favor, Jeff," Luffman said. "Don't bother fighting this."

"I'll think about it," Jeffrey replied coldly.

Luffman turned around and left.

At about six o'clock that same day, a thunderstorm rolled through the Kirtland area. It left a beautiful rainbow behind. Jeffrey noticed that it was really two rainbows side by side, and he began yelling to everyone in the farmhouse to "come and see—come and see." There was a reason why he used those particular words. After everyone saw the double rainbow, they hurried back inside and grabbed their scriptures. They wanted to discover what significance the rainbow had since it had appeared on the same day that Jeffrey was served with excommunication papers. Jeffrey sat at the kitchen table watching Greg, Richard, and Danny searching their scriptures. He already knew what they were going to find and if they didn't, he would nudge them toward it. He had known from the moment that he spotted the rainbow exactly what the scriptural importance of it was—or at least, what he would tell them it was. That night in class he would announce that God had sent them a sign. It was time for them to make preparations to go into the wilderness. It was time for them to make a human sacrifice. Jeffrey was certain of it and he knew exactly who he was going to kill.

CHAPTER THIRTY-SIX

MARTIN Luther, the German theologian and leader of the Protestant Reformation, didn't believe the Book of Revelation belonged in the Bible because of its graphic accounts of how God would someday torture and kill the wicked. The book was written at a time when the Roman Emperor Nero was setting Christians on fire in his garden to provide light for his evening meals, and Luther claimed that its message of retribution was aimed more at building up morale among the suffering Christians than establishing some long-lasting Church doctrine. The angry bloodletting in Revelation certainly didn't fit with Christ's turn-the-other-cheek teachings.

It was Jeffrey's favorite New Testament book.

No one would later remember who was the first to turn to the Book of Revelation shortly after the double rainbow appeared. But someone mentioned chapter 6 of the book and within minutes everyone in the kitchen was reading the story of the Four Horsemen of the Apocalypse and the seven mystical seals that were to be opened just before Christ returned to rule the earth for one thousand years. Verse one read:

And I saw when the Lamb opened one of the seals, one of the
four beasts, and I heard, as it were, the noise of thunder, saying,
Come and see.

Everyone in the group saw the similarities:

• The verse contained the words "the noise of thunder." Just
after Jeffrey received his excommunication papers, a thunderstorm
had rolled across Kirtland.

• The verse contained the words "Come and see." That is what
Jeffrey had called out.

"Is it possible," one of the men said, "that God opened the first
seal today?"

Jeffrey was enjoying himself. "Read the second verse," he told
them.

And I saw, and behold a white horse; and he that sat on him
had a bow; and a crown was given unto him; and he went forth
conquering; and to conquer.

• The verse said the man on the horse had a "bow." A rainbow
had appeared after the storm.

Jeffrey was quick to tell the group that the word "bow" also had
a secret meaning. It could be used to describe a pair of eyeglasses,
he explained, because the piece that connects the two lenses and
holds the glasses on a person's nose is shaped "like a bow." That was
significant, Jeffrey continued, because eyeglasses were invented to
help people see. "Helping people see is also the job of the seer or
prophet," Jeffrey said. Accordingly, the word "bow" could also mean
"seer or prophet."

"What this verse is telling us is that God has given the rider of
the white horse a bow or the ability to prophesy."

That night at class, Jeffrey told his followers that the similarities
between what had happened that day and chapter 6 in Revelation
were not a coincidence. He told them that God had opened the first
seal and that now it was up to the riders on the four horses to begin
opening the other seals that would eventually bring about the earth's
destruction. Jeffrey then announced that he was going to reveal to
them, by using the pattern, the identity of the riders.

During the next few nights, Jeffrey led his followers on an incredible, intricate trip through the Bible, Book of Mormon, and

Doctrine and Covenants that was designed to ultimately lead them to one inescapable conclusion: God had chosen Jeffrey to be the rider not only of the white horse but of the next three as well.

"I am God's prophet. I am the last messenger. I am the destroyer. I am the rider of the white horse. God has chosen me to open the seals."

Now that Jeffrey had made that declaration, he told his followers to continue reading the story of the opening of the seven seals. The next verse read:

> And when he had opened the second seal, I heard the second beast say, Come and see.
> And there went out another horse that was red; and power was given to him that sat thereon to take peace from the earth, and that they should kill one another; and there was given unto him a great sword.

Jeffrey told his group that God had opened the first seal by causing the rainbow to appear. Now it was up to Jeffrey to open the remaining ones.

"The rider of the red horse is required by God to show blood," he declared. "His job is to kill."

Jeffrey continued. "This verse in Revelation is another sign from God that my job is to destroy the wicked."

As far as Jeffrey was concerned, everything that he had learned by using the pattern to interpret scripture was beginning to fit together and it all pointed to one event.

God had told him in the "parable of the vineyard" to kill.

God had told him that if he wanted to be endowed with power, he had to kill.

God was now telling him to kill if he wanted to open the seven seals.

"I checked and checked the scriptures over and over and they all kept coming back to the same thing," Jeffrey said. "There was absolutely no doubt whatsoever about what God was commanding me to do."

CHAPTER THIRTY-SEVEN

ONCE the first seal was opened, the clock was running. Richard Brand would later tell federal investigators that Jeffrey was required to perform the human sacrifice within six months. The rainbow had appeared in October 1988. That meant Jeffrey had until April 1989 to, as he liked to put it, "show blood." The remaining seals would have to be opened during the six months that followed the human sacrifice if Jeffrey wanted to successfully bring the world to an end.

This one-year deadline for opening the seals was based on scriptures. Jeffrey had taught that a Hebrew named Enoch had taken one year to accomplish a task that God had given him. Jeffrey was expected to do the same. While Enoch was not a major character in most Protestant Bibles, in the RLDS inspired version, Enoch was a monumental figure. Most of his exploits were described in sixty-one verses that Joseph Smith, Jr., added to chapter 7 of the Old Testament book of Genesis. Although Enoch lived in the days described in Genesis, God had allowed him to see the crucifixion of Christ and the Millennium. Jeffrey told his followers that God had shown him Jesus dying on the cross and the earth's final days, too. No one in the group had missed the similarities between Enoch's life and Jeffrey's claims, but rather than suspect that Jeffrey was imitating

Enoch, they assumed God was treating Jeffrey in the same way.

Picking someone to kill had been easy for Jeffrey. He had always detested the Averys and he felt that he could prove to the group that Dennis, Cheryl, Trina, Becky, and Karen Avery were "wicked." The Averys had stopped attending Jeffrey's classes shortly after they moved to Madison. Because of this, they didn't have any idea that Jeffrey was going to offer God a human sacrifice. Jeffrey made certain that they didn't find out. He instructed everyone in the group not to tell the Averys what was going on. At the same time, he began wooing them back to class. When the Averys did attend, Jeffrey taught token classes. He told them that the group was going into the wilderness to see God and he assured them that he wanted them to go too, but Jeffrey never mentioned that he planned to sacrifice them or anyone else.

By March, *everyone* in the group knew for certain that the Averys were to be killed, Richard later told investigators. Talk of a human sacrifice preoccupied the group whenever the Averys weren't around. "We constantly talked about shedding of blood," Debbie later testified. "That it had to be done, that we were going to the wilderness, we were going to see God there."

Later, in interviews, Jeffrey would repeat much of what he told his group about Dennis and Cheryl and why God wanted them killed. He cited verse 17, in chapter 9 of the Book of Alma in the Book of Mormon to prove that the family was wicked.

"And therefore he that will not harden his heart, to him is given the greater portion of the word, until it is given unto him to know the mysteries of God, until they know them in full.

"And they that will harden their hearts, to them is given the lesser portion of the word, until they know nothing concerning his mysteries.

"And then they are taken captive by the devil, and led by his will down to destruction."

"By not attending my classes, the Averys have 'hardened their hearts,' to the word," Jeffrey told his followers. "They are not interested in learning the 'greater portion of the word.' Instead, they have chosen to receive 'the lesser portion.'" Accordingly, the Averys had been "'taken captive by the devil and led by his will down to destruction.'"

"I told my people that they should thank God for the Averys.

You see, God had provided the Averys to us to be used as sacrifices."

The only question in Jeffrey's mind by mid-March was how he would kill them. Debbie would later recall a conversation that she had one morning in March while sitting in the kitchen with Alice. Jeffrey had come in with his scriptures and announced that he had discovered how to kill the Averys. Wicked men were supposed to be beheaded, according to the Old Testament. Women were supposed to be stripped naked and then split open so that their internal organs could be pulled out. Children, meanwhile, were supposed to be picked up by their feet and swung against a wall until their heads were smashed. Jeffrey was perplexed because he wasn't certain whether Becky, who had just turned thirteen, was a woman or a child, Debbie testified later. It was Alice who came up with a solution.

"Alice said that it would depend on whether or not Becky had started her period," Debbie recalled.

Jeffrey quickly agreed and asked if either of them knew if Becky had started menstruation. Neither did. Jeffrey put it on his list of things to find out.

As April approached, Jeffrey started assigning his followers different roles in the murders. He sent Debbie and Greg to a local library to find out how hot a fire had to be in order to cremate a body. At the time, Jeffrey was thinking about killing the Averys in their home in Madison and then setting their house on fire. Debbie told him that a house fire wouldn't be hot enough to destroy incriminating evidence. Jeffrey rejected the plan. Damon, meanwhile, was told to familiarize himself with explosives. Danny was asked to forge birth certificates in case the group decided to change their identities.

While the murders were being planned, Jeffrey was also getting his group ready for the wilderness trek. He told his followers that each of them would be expected to learn a special survival skill. "Sharon liked to study plants so her assignment was to figure out what we could eat if we lived off the land," Jeffrey said. "I would provide the meat by hunting, Sharon would provide the foliage." One night during their scriptural class, Sharon served the group deep-fried dandelions. "They were delicious," Jeffrey said.

Besides such duties, every man was to be a soldier in Jeffrey's "Army of Israel." Jeffrey declared himself the four-star general. Alice made him a flag. It was purple with a white star and a red eagle. By mid-March, Jeffrey had amassed more than four thousand rounds of ammunition and had added to his arsenal a forty-eight-pound, hand-made .50-caliber rifle that cost $2,700. He bought it because he wanted a gun capable of shooting down a helicopter.

On March 16, Jeffrey's buddy from his college days, Keith Johnson, and his wife, Kathy, arrived in Kirtland. Jeffrey had been busy recruiting Keith for months. He'd even paid during February to fly Keith from Missouri to Kirtland for a three-day visit. Jeffrey had told Keith then about the opening of the first seal and had urged him to join the group when it went into the wilderness. Jeffrey needed Keith, he later said, because the scriptures required the rider of the four horses in Revelation to have seven servants. At the time, Jeffrey had only six—Danny, Richard, Greg, Dennis Patrick, Ron, and Damon. Keith and his family moved into the apartment rented by the Patricks. There was no sense in getting a place of their own since the group was scheduled to go into the wilderness during the week of April 17.

Jeffrey announced that everyone would be allowed to take six sets of warm clothing and six sets for summer weather with them. The rest was to be sold at flea markets. Jeffrey also ordered everyone to apply for as many credit cards as they could. Ron and Susie got the most—four. Running up large bills on credit was a way for the group, in Jeffrey's words, to "spoil Babylon" by sticking the Gentiles with unpaid bills.

As March came to a close, everything seemed to be on schedule. And then Jeffrey made another discovery. It happened while he was teaching a scripture class. He was in the midst of diagraming a verse from the Book of Mormon when he came across a passage that told how a great Mormon general had lost ten of his men in combat. They had died fighting to protect the mysterious golden plates that Joseph Smith, Jr., would later find. Jeffrey didn't say anything to his followers, but later that night, he reviewed the scriptures and interpreted them to mean that he was supposed to kill ten persons—not just five. Jeffrey mentally ranked each group member according to their "sins." He decided that he would sacrifice Dennis and Tonya Patrick and their daughter, Molly, and Richard and Sharon as well as the Averys.

During the next few days, word that Jeffrey had decided to kill ten, not just five, leaked out to everyone but those who were slated to be murdered. The Averys had never been liked, but the Patricks and Richard and Sharon were. Debbie Olivarez would later recall a conversation that she had with Alice while the two of them were driving to a local grocery store.

Why, Debbie asked, were Richard and Sharon to be killed? "I said, 'None of us is perfect and I don't understand what makes their sin different than my sin.' And Alice said that they were ripened in iniquity and they couldn't change. They were so sinful there was no help, no hope that they would change and repent."

During the first week of April, Jeffrey began pressuring Greg to marry Debbie, and Richard to marry Sharon. He had told them earlier that they had to be married before the group left for the wilderness. On April 4, Greg and Debbie were married by Jeffrey. The next day, Richard married Sharon. The only difference in the ceremonies came when Jeffrey asked Richard why he was marrying Sharon.

"Because you want me to," Richard said.

On April 10, Jeffrey took Ron Luff and Keith Johnson out into the barn at the farm. He had decided that it wasn't practical to kill ten people by beheading the men and splitting open the women. Instead, he had found a verse in his Mormon scriptures that said: "I will make thy horn *iron*, and I will make thy hoofs *brass*." Jeffrey interpreted the verse to mean that he could shoot his victims with bullets because a .45-caliber cartridge had a *brass* shell and an *iron* slug. He planned to shoot all ten after they were put into a pit. Jeffrey showed Ron and Keith where to dig and told them how big to make the hole. Damon volunteered to help. The location of the pit was also scriptural, Jeffrey claimed. Moses had freed the Jews from captivity by leading them from Egypt across the Red Sea into the wilderness. Jeffrey was going to lead his people into the wilderness after murdering ten of his followers. "The barn was red," Ron Luff later explained, ". . . and the barn has an area that floods every spring when it rains . . . so the area within the barn that floods was to be where the people were to be buried so they would be covered over within the Red Sea."

Alice would later claim during testimony that she really didn't believe Jeffrey was serious. She had simply been playing along. "I didn't think he would kill anybody," she testified, "because he would come up with these wild-haired plans all the time and he didn't carry through with them. I thought this was just another one of his insane ideas. Like the Kirtland temple takeover, or like the obtaining of the golden plates, or obtaining the Sword of Laban, saying words and making an earthquake happen."

Jeffrey knew that Alice doubted him. He suspected that others in the group did too. "I made it clear that I was serious about this and I was not joking, but I could tell that some of them didn't take it serious. No matter how many times I warned them about God's wrath and fury, they just didn't get it. Even Alice didn't understand that this was not a joke. That I was going to do exactly what I said."

CHAPTER THIRTY-EIGHT

CHIEF Yarborough was two steps behind Jeffrey. During the fall of 1988, while Jeffrey was busy deciphering the mysteries of the Four Horsemen of the Apocalypse, Yarborough was still investigating Jeffrey's plans to take over the Kirtland temple.

Yarborough had telephoned FBI Special Agent Alvord in September when Shar Olson had come forward. The chief had told him that there were now two informants willing to testify that Jeffrey had planned an assault on the temple. The fact that Shar Olson corroborated Kevin Currie's story interested Alvord, but he still felt the case was a local matter. The chief was investigating Jeffrey on charges of "conspiracy to commit murder," and that was a state crime, not necessarily a federal one. There was another reason why Alvord was reluctant. Both informants had told Yarborough about Jeffrey's plans to overthrow the temple on May 3, 1988. That was nearly four months ago. More important, Jeffrey hadn't done it. If the chief wanted to make an arrest, he was going to have to come up with new evidence that showed Jeffrey was still planning an attack. Alvord wasn't certain Yarborough could do that.

Still, Alvord wanted to help. He trusted Yarborough's judgment, and if the chief felt that Jeffrey was dangerous, then Alvord wanted to get him locked up. But Yarborough was going to have to come up with some hook that would justify the FBI's entering the investigation. Otherwise, Alvord knew his bosses wouldn't go for it.

In October, Yarborough called Alvord with an idea. Instead of investigating Jeffrey on charges of "conspiracy to commit murder," Yarborough suggested that the FBI go after him for possible violations of "domestic security" statutes and alleged violations of his followers' "civil rights." Both of those were federal crimes that fell under the purview of the FBI. Alvord liked it.

On October 13, Alvord telephoned Yarborough—the FBI was officially entering the investigation. Alvord had convinced his bosses that Jeffrey was a potential domestic terrorist.

Now that Alvord was authorized to investigate the cult, he told Yarborough that he wanted to talk to Shar as soon as possible. Ron Andolsek, who had befriended Shar, set up the meeting. Alvord was impressed with Shar. She was smart and articulate. She'd make a good witness. She was also cooperative.

During the interview, Shar mentioned that she still spoke regularly with Greg Winship. In fact, Shar and Andolsek had talked about the possibility of her wearing a concealed microphone to lunch one day with Greg. She felt that Greg would tell her if Jeffrey was still planning on taking over the temple in May. Andolsek was in the process of trying to borrow a "wire" for Shar to wear. The Kirtland Police Department didn't own one. It had never needed such a device.

Alvord quickly nixed the idea. If anyone in the group thought that Shar was helping the FBI, she might be harmed. Instead, Alvord suggested that Shar give the FBI permission to monitor her telephone calls. She agreed, and on October 27, Shar telephoned Greg. At this point, Jeffrey had not completely discarded his plan to take over the temple, so Greg talked about it as if the group still might launch an attack.

At one point, Shar asked Greg if he really was willing to kill someone.

"If God can tell Nephi to go slay Laban, then He can tell me to go kill whomever," Greg replied. He said, however, that he wanted to make certain that it was God giving the directions. "We're talking ten years to life and I'm not ready to do that. I'm not ready to run out and kill somebody, but I'm definitely thinking about it, whereas I wouldn't have even thought about it before."

Did Greg know when Jeffrey might take over the temple? Shar asked.

"This May, who knows?" Greg replied.

Alvord had heard enough. He sent a reconnaissance team to fly over Jeffrey's farm and take photographs of the route that Jeffrey and his group were supposed to use when they made their way through the apple orchard to the RLDS church. He dispatched a surveillance team to take pictures of Jeffrey and members of his cult. Alvord also contacted the FBI field office in Buffalo and asked that an agent there be sent to interview Kevin Currie. This time, the agent was to take whatever Kevin said seriously. Alvord then arranged to meet with Dale Luffman.

Within a matter of weeks, Alvord had become as engrossed in the case as Chief Yarborough and Andolsek. One night, he found himself driving by the farmhouse. He just wanted to see it. Like Yarborough, Alvord was trying to figure out how Jeffrey thought. He wasn't having much luck.

Just before Christmas, the FBI set up another telephone call between Shar and Greg. But this time, Greg was guarded on the phone and refused to discuss the takeover. Jeffrey had told everyone that he had seen a strange van parked outside the farmhouse for long periods. He figured Yarborough was watching him.

On February 24, 1989, Alvord wrote a confidential report for his superiors. He concluded that Jeffrey was dangerous and was mostly likely planning to attack the temple on May 3, 1989. But, Alvord said, there was not sufficient evidence to file charges against him. The statements by Kevin and Shar were too old and they were about an event that hadn't happened.

The FBI generally gives an agent sixty days to complete an investigation. After that, there has to be a good reason to continue spending an agent's time and the government's money. Alvord's sixty days would end on March 3. He asked for an extension into April and got it. But Alvord was told that unless he came up with something concrete, he'd be ordered to close the case.

Alvord drove to Kirtland and conferred with Yarborough. They decided to ask the U.S. attorney in Cleveland for permission to search Jeffrey's farmhouse. Maybe they'd get lucky and find something that would provide them with enough "probable cause" to arrest Jeffrey. Both men felt that if Jeffrey was taken out of the group, his followers would most likely scatter.

Alvord typed up a detailed memo and submitted it to the U.S.

attorney. He also sent a copy to the FBI's legal-review department. Both offices told Alvord that there was insufficient evidence to justify getting a search warrant.

Once again, Alvord drove to Kirtland to talk to Yarborough. "We both knew the guy was dangerous, but we couldn't touch him," the chief recalled. "It was frustrating as hell."

The two investigators decided to take a risky step. They would confront Jeffrey at the farm without a search warrant. They would flood the area with officers: sixteen from the FBI and all six members of Kirtland's police force. They had been told that they didn't have enough probable cause to get a search warrant, but Jeffrey didn't know that. There was always the chance that he might *assume* that they could get a warrant and simply give them permission to search in order to avoid a hassle. "To be truthful about it," Yarborough later admitted, "we were going way, way beyond our authority." Even so, both men wanted to do something.

If nothing else, Alvord and Yarborough agreed that their plan would show Jeffrey that he was being watched. He'd been scared off before. Maybe he'd be scared off again.

"So when do we do it?" asked Yarborough.

Alvord wanted to wait until the last possible moment. "April eighteenth," he said. It was a Tuesday. That would be good because he and the chief could brief their men on Monday.

Yarborough agreed.

Neither knew that Alvord had picked a date that was exactly one day too late.

CHAPTER THIRTY-NINE

DIGGING the pit in the barn was much harder than Jeffrey had expected. Although the floor in the room frequently flooded, the ground had been packed down after years of use. When Ron and Keith took a break to eat lunch on April 10, a Monday, they told Jeffrey that it would take them at least five days to dig the pit. That was okay with Jeffrey. He had plenty of other tasks to complete.

"It was time for me to inquire of the Lord to see if He had changed His mind," Jeffrey recalled. He went to the mountain near the farm and knelt down.

"I said to God, 'What is thy will? Give me a sign. Tell me what to do.' And then I opened my scriptures and began looking. I quickly realized that all I was getting were 'go' statements."

On Tuesday, April 11, Keith took a break from digging the pit and went with his wife, Kathy, to buy two horses. Jeffrey said he needed to take horses into the wilderness because he was, after all, the rider of the four horses in Revelation. He bought an ATV [all-terrain vehicle] too because, as he put it, "the scriptures told me that I was to have a chariot in the wilderness."

On Wednesday, April 12, Jeffrey bought a .44-caliber Smith &

Wesson revolver. There wasn't any particular verse that told him to buy the gun. He simply wanted another one.

Later that night, he and Alice went to the Averys' to eat dinner. After the meal, Alice helped Cheryl sort through the family's possessions and decide what could go to the wilderness and what was being left behind. Jeffrey played with Karen. As she giggled, he bounced her up and down on his leg. When they got home, Alice told the group that the Averys had a microwave and some Corelle dishes that they could take with them.

On Thursday, April 13, Jeffrey told officials at Kirtland Elementary School that he was taking Kristen and Caleb out of their classes for one week because the family was going to Disneyland.

By Friday, April 14, all of the group members had quit their jobs, and Ron and Susie and their two children had moved from their apartment into the laundry room at the farmhouse. Jeffrey wanted his second in command at the farm to help plan the executions. That same day, Richard and Dennis Patrick drove to the Averys' house and started moving the family's belongings into the barn at the farm, where they were quickly picked over by group members. At one point, Cheryl showed up and asked Jeffrey why she and Dennis and their girls hadn't been invited to stay at the farm like the Luffs. "I told her we didn't have room," Jeffrey said, "but the truth was I didn't want them in my house because they were evil." Instead, Jeffrey issued the Averys five sleeping bags and told them to stay in their now-empty house until he sent someone for them.

On Saturday, April 15, the pit was nearly ready, but Jeffrey wasn't. "My intelligence told me that what I was doing was right," he later said, "but my flesh was weak. I was still struggling with the thought of killing ten people. These were not strangers. I wanted to wait at least one more day to make certain that I was absolutely right in what I was doing."

That morning, Dennis Patrick came to the farm to see if he could help pack supplies. Jeffrey sent him to the barn to help Ron and Keith. Dennis didn't know that he was digging his own grave.

Later that night, Dennis Avery called Jeffrey. He had forgotten to mention it earlier, but he had been issued a credit card with a $1,500 limit that hadn't been used. Jeffrey told Dennis that they would go shopping the next day.

On Sunday, April 16, Jeffrey decided to check his scriptures one last time. "I was looking to see if there was some way to extend mercy to any of the ten," he later said, "and as I looked, I suddenly said, 'Ah-ha! I can extend mercy.'"

The verse that Jeffrey found was in the New Testament book of First Corinthians, chapter 7, verse 14, which read: "For the unbelieving husband is sanctified by the wife . . ."

"Tonya and Sharon were doing the best they could and God was telling me that because of the women, their husbands had been ransomed from the pit."

Jeffrey looked for a scripture that would save the Averys. Instead, he found the opposite in Isaiah, chapter 30, verse 17. The crucial part read: "at the rebuke of five, shall ye flee."

"God was telling me to get on with it," he said. "The verse clearly said that I was to rebuke [kill] the Averys and go into the wilderness."

After Jeffrey finished his studies, he picked up Dennis Avery and drove to Chagrin International Arms Company where they used Dennis's MasterCard to buy a .30-caliber M-1 carbine, another .45-caliber automatic pistol, and a .380-caliber Colt pistol for a total of $1,349.

While Jeffrey was buying guns, Alice was driving Greg to a local auto-repair shop to retrieve his car. "Alice asked me how I felt about people such as the Averys having to die for my sin. My response was that I would that no one would have to die for my sin: I would that all men would repent and come unto Christ."

Later that night while several of the men at the farm were playing basketball, Jeffrey turned to Richard and said, "Tomorrow is D day."

On Monday, April 17, Jeffrey was confident that he was supposed to execute the Avery family, but he claimed that he once again asked God if they could be spared.

"I said 'Lord, show me, show me, speak to me in your word. Don't let me be blind. Let me see.'"

Prosecutors would later argue that Jeffrey really didn't have much of a choice on April 17. If he didn't kill the Averys, his followers would stop believing in him. He had ordered them to quit their jobs. He had told them that the Averys had to be sacrificed. He had already lost face because he had backed down from taking over the Kirtland temple. That was the pragmatic view.

Jeffrey later offered a different one. "I was being asked to cross a line. . . . I could lose everything precious to me in this world: my wife, my children, my life. But if what I was teaching was real, if the pattern existed and if there was a God and there was a Bible and there were golden tablets, then I was being offered something no other man on earth was being offered.

"I was going to set into action events that would make the world as we know it come to an end—events that would bring about the return of Jesus Christ.

"What it all came down to was, did I *really* believe I was teaching the truth or was I going to shrink away? . . . Either I was teaching a lie and I was a false prophet and none of it was true or I was teaching the truth, in which case, my path was clear. Those were the two choices. God was saying, 'Okay, Jeffrey, do you really believe? Are you willing to step across the line?' And at that instant, I understood. I knew what I had to do."

On the morning of April 17, Jeffrey told Alice that the Patricks and Richard and Sharon had been spared. Jeff and Alice drove into Kirtland to the Patricks' apartment. Dennis was gone. Because Keith and Kathy Johnson were still living there, Jeffrey and Alice hurried Tonya to an upstairs bedroom to talk in private.

"Jeff told me that Dennis was not getting his act together," Tonya later recalled. "That he was sinful but that I was doing all right and he had no problems with me and because of that, Dennis wasn't going to be killed. He told me that he had planned to kill Dennis, Molly, and me that night but not now. I was in shock."

Once Jeffrey finished talking, Alice jumped in. "Alice told me how worried she'd been about it and how happy she was that I was saved," Tonya said. Jeffrey told Tonya not to tell Dennis about their talk. He would tell him personally that night.

Meanwhile, back at the farm, Greg was making a reservation at the Red Roof Inn in Kirtland for the Averys. If the police, for some reason, ever went looking for them, Jeffrey wanted the Averys' last known address to be a motel, not the farmhouse.

After Greg made the motel reservation, he drove into Cleveland and bought a stun gun for $59.99.

At 11:30 A.M., the Averys were picked up at their house and brought to the farm for lunch. Jeffrey and Alice, as well as Debbie and Ron and Susie, ate sandwiches and leftovers with them and then Ron drove the Averys to the motel.

There are conflicting stories about what happened next. Sharon Bluntschly later testified under oath that she and Alice went on an errand to a nearby bank, and while en route, Alice told her that she and Richard were not going to be sacrificed that night because of

Sharon's efforts and subservience. When they returned to the farm, Alice told Jeffrey what she had done and he got angry because she had upstaged him. Alice claimed that Jeffrey had told Sharon that she and Richard had been saved. Regardless, by late afternoon on Monday word had spread through the farmhouse that only the Averys were to be killed.

At 3:00 P.M., Jeffrey left the farm by himself and drove to Tom Miller's house. The police would later speculate that Jeffrey went to recruit Tom. That was wrong. Jeffrey wanted to tell Tom that God had chosen him—not Tom—to be the rider of the horses in Revelation. The two men had once talked about leading a revolt of fundamentalists in the RLDS. That was nothing compared to what Jeffrey was about to do.

"Jeffrey was totally unkempt when he arrived," Tom Miller said later. "His hair was dirty and he was very rushed and he said, 'I didn't come here to convince you to follow me,' and I interrupted and said, 'Jeff, that's great 'cause I wouldn't follow you anywhere.'"

Jeffrey stopped speaking. "His face went blank and his mouth fell open and he just sat there for the longest time," Miller said.

"I decided that there was no point in trying to share the truth with him," Jeffrey later recalled. "He'd made it clear that he was not interested in knowing who I was."

Jeffrey got up to leave.

"Jeff, are you running from something?" Miller asked. "Are you running drugs or in trouble? Maybe I can help you."

Jeffrey hurried out to his truck and drove away. He was angry. Who did Tom Miller think he was to offer to help him?

When Jeffrey returned to the farm, he went into his bedroom and got one of his .45-caliber pistols. He chose the stainless-steel Combat Elite semi-automatic and took enough bullets for twenty-seven shots. He could smell dinner being cooked. He quickly loaded the gun.

Jeffrey had told Debbie that he wanted roast beef, mashed potatoes with gravy, corn, and a salad with bread for dinner. A few minutes after six o'clock, Richard arrived with the Averys. He had driven past the front door of the Kirtland Police Department en route to the Red Roof Inn.

As soon as Karen Avery came into the room, she ran toward Alice and gave her a big hug. The little girl said that she had drawn Alice a picture, but had forgotten and left it at the motel.

"That's okay, honey," Alice said reassuringly. "We'll get it later."

Karen was wearing a shirt with a rainbow and ponies on it. Alice recognized it. She had given it to Karen.

Dinner was served at exactly 6:30 P.M., but Debbie didn't eat. She was too upset. "I couldn't eat with them, knowing they were going to die." She went upstairs. The Patricks and the Johnsons were the only ones not at the farm. Jeffrey didn't want them there. He didn't believe Keith and Dennis had enough guts to kill anyone. During the meal, Danny, Richard, Sharon, and Greg tried to avoid the Averys. Jeffrey, Alice, and their children, and Ron and Susie Luff and their children, were friendly.

While everyone was eating, Dennis Avery noticed that Karen hadn't tried everything on her plate. He told her to eat some corn.

"Daddy, I don't want to," she replied.

Jeffrey would later cite that exchange as a sign from God. "She was a rebellious and wicked child," he said.

Ron Luff was amazed, not because of what Karen had said but because the Averys clearly had no idea what was going to happen. He would later tell federal investigators that he had tried to warn the Averys several times during scripture classes. "I would say, look, this is what the wicked do—but that's exactly what you are doing. And this is what happens to the wicked." It was clear to Ron, as he watched the Averys eating their "last supper" that they simply didn't realize how serious Jeffrey was about destroying the "wicked." They really were like sacrificial lambs. "I believe we could have come out . . . and told them exactly what was going to happen and they still wouldn't have known."

As soon as Alice finished eating, she popped up from the table and announced that it was time for her and Jason, Kristen, and Caleb to leave. Jeffrey had told her that she was to go buy some picnic tables after dinner for the group to use in the wilderness.

"Call before you come back," Jeffrey told her.

Alice was about to walk out the front door when Jeffrey stopped her. He needed some paper and envelopes. Jeffrey had told all of his followers that they were supposed to write letters to their parents telling them that they had left Kirtland. Everyone was supposed to give their parents a fictitious forwarding address. He had just learned that Cheryl hadn't written a letter to her mother, Donna Bailey. Jeffrey handed Cheryl a sheet of paper and dictated the letter.

Dear Mom and Dad—Just a hurried note to let you know

that things have happened very fast and Dennis has accepted work in Wyoming and we needed to get there fast. We will let you know address and details when we get settled. . . . Thanks. Love Cheryl.

After Cheryl finished, Jeffrey took the letter and went into his bedroom. All of the men except for Dennis Avery, who was still eating, followed him there. He shut the door and picked up his .45 pistol. "Everyone had done their part," he said later. "Now I wanted them to know that I was going to do mine."

Jeffrey looked at each of them, including his eighteen-year-old son, Damon, who was still a senior in high school.

"Are you in or are you out?" he asked solemnly. One by one, Ron Luff, Greg Winship, Richard Brand, Danny Kraft, Jr., and Damon nodded.

"Okay," Jeffrey said, "let's do it."

CHAPTER FORTY

DENNIS Avery had always been a slow eater. Behind his back, the others had cruelly joked that he was so lazy that even chewing was a chore. But now that he was finished eating, Dennis noticed that he was the only man still in the farmhouse. All the other men had followed Jeffrey outside. None of them had said anything to Dennis.

Dennis was about to ask where the men had gone when Ron came into the kitchen from the back door. Jeffrey was in the barn, Ron explained, and he wanted Dennis to come show him what he and Cheryl wished to take with them into the wilderness. Dennis started toward the door but stopped. He couldn't decide whether or not he should wear his glasses because it was misty and he hated to get water spots on the lenses. He took them off, then put them on, and then asked Cheryl what she thought he should do as Ron waited patiently, the 50,000-volt stun gun hidden in his pocket. Cheryl suggested that Dennis take them off, which he did. It was just before 7:30 P.M.

"When Dennis walked through the door of the barn," Ron later recalled, "I lifted his shirt and tried to use the stun gun a couple of different places." Jeffrey had told Ron that the gun would work only if it hit certain nerves on the hip, neck, and chest, so Ron tried all three.

"What are you doing?" Dennis screamed as Ron zapped him. "Goddamn it. This isn't necessary!"

"All the stun gun was doing," Ron later said, "was causing a lot of pain."

Greg, Richard, Danny, and Damon knocked Dennis onto the ground. They quickly taped his hands, feet, and mouth with two-inch-wide gray duct tape. "We were not supposed to apply tape to his eyes," Richard later testified, "because he was supposed to see Jeff when Jeff shot him."

Although Jeffrey was waiting in a room in the back corner of the barn where the pit had been dug, he could hear what was happening and he had heard Dennis yelling.

"Dennis had cursed God," Jeffrey said later. "He was clearly under Satan's power."

Once Dennis was bound, Richard lifted him by the shoulders and Danny raised his feet. They carried him through the barn into the room at the back of the barn and slid him into the muddy pit. Jeffrey would later tell his followers that Dennis had managed to climb onto his knees in the pit. He had looked up from the hole at Jeffrey, who was standing over him with the .45.

"I looked him in the eyes," Jeffrey said later, "because I wanted him to know who was sending him before God for his wickedness." The scriptures required him, Jeffrey explained, to look Dennis face-to-face and then "pierce his heart."

Greg was supposed to run a chain saw outside the barn during the shootings to cover up the sounds, but for some reason he hadn't started and Jeffrey decided not to wait. As Richard and Danny bolted toward the exit, Jeffrey fired his first shot. Ron, who was standing guard outside the room, slammed the door closed just as Richard and Danny reached it.

"Got to keep this door shut," he yelled.

He was worried that the noise might be heard by neighbors. Trapped inside, Richard turned his head just in time to see Jeffrey standing at the edge of the pit firing his second round. The noise reverberated inside the barn.

"I fired two shots directly into his heart," Jeffrey told everyone later.

Ron opened the door. "Is it done?" he asked.

"All right, everybody, come look at this," Jeffrey said. "Come see what death is."

Ron, Richard, Greg, Danny, and Damon walked over to the lip of the pit together, as if each were afraid to go by himself. "When I looked in," Damon later recalled during testimony, "Dennis was laying there on the ground . . . you could see blood all over his shirt. I started crying—I couldn't believe it. I'd never seen anything like that before. It was my own father that had just did that."

Everyone was quiet for several seconds and then Jeffrey realized that he hadn't gotten the key to the Red Roof motel room from Dennis before he was shot. Jeffrey planned to clean out the motel room to make it look as if the Averys had left town.

"Damon, get the key out of his pocket," Jeffrey ordered.

Damon didn't move. He was crying.

"I can't do it," he said. "I can't believe he is dead. I can't believe he is dead."

Jeffrey walked over to his son and put his arms around him. He still had the .45 in his hand.

"It's okay," he said, "you're growing up at a young age."

Jeffrey glanced around. It was dark except for the lone light bulb that Damon had hung earlier. He still needed the motel key.

"If nobody else will do it," said Ron, "I will."

He jumped down into the pit and grabbed Dennis by his belt. When he lifted up the body, there was a loud "sigh" as air escaped from the corpse. Everyone flinched.

"That was his last breath of life," Jeffrey said.

Ron fumbled through Dennis's pockets with his free hand, but he couldn't find the key, only a driver's license and library card. He dropped Dennis back in the mud.

"We've got to have that key," Jeffrey said.

No one moved. Jeffrey walked out of the room, leaving the others alone with the body. As soon as Jeffrey was gone, they hurried out.

Jeffrey went inside the farmhouse and asked Cheryl for the key. She gave it to him. Jeffrey silently chided himself. He should have known that Dennis would have given his wife the hotel key. That was the sort of guy he was. Jeffrey returned to the barn and removed the .45 from its hiding place under his shirt. Damon was crying so Jeffrey told him to climb into the loft and stand by the window. He could be a lookout.

"Okay, Ron, bring out the next one," Jeffrey said. He had not said "Bring out Cheryl." He had not wanted to say her name.

Ron walked to the farmhouse. Cheryl was inside with Debbie, Susie, and Sharon.

"Ron told Cheryl that Dennis needed her help in the barn," Debbie later testified, "so she left with him."

Greg, Richard, and Danny surrounded Cheryl as soon as she stepped into the barn.

"Be calm," Ron said, "don't struggle—just give it up."

Confused and frightened, Cheryl stood perfectly still as the men wrapped tape around her hands, ankles, mouth, and eyes. Jeffrey didn't want Cheryl's eyes uncovered.

In the farmhouse, Debbie paced across the kitchen floor. She heard Greg start the chain saw.

"You can't have that," someone said. Debbie spun around. Trina and Becky were arguing in front of the refrigerator. They were looking for dessert. Debbie told them to take whatever they wanted and then snapped: "Close the door!" As soon as she said it, she felt bad. She hadn't meant to be sharp. Susie walked over to her.

"Do you think it's happening?" Susie whispered.

"I hear the chain saw," said Debbie. "I think so."

Dennis had been almost too heavy for Danny to carry, so once Cheryl was taped and lying on the barn floor, Richard asked Ron if he would help carry her into the pit. They lifted up Cheryl and lugged her across the barn into the back room where Jeffrey was waiting. Ron and Richard gently eased Cheryl into the pit. The mud quickly soaked through her baggy sweatpants. Ron stayed inside the room this time to make certain that no one opened or closed the door. Richard stepped out into the main portion of the barn.

Jeffrey got up and moved to the pit. He raised his gun and started pulling the trigger. Cheryl's body smacked into the side of the pit when hit by the slugs. The autopsy would later show that Cheryl was struck twice in the right breast and once in the abdomen. All three bullets were later recovered, and unlike the soft-pointed hollow-points that were fired into Dennis, these were full-metal-jacketed rounds designed to penetrate, not mushroom. Jeffrey had switched shells intentionally. He was experimenting.

"According to the scriptures, I was going to kill again. I wanted to learn as much as I could from this experience."

Jeffrey would later recall that at one point he had talked to

Ron about going into the pit after the murders to stab the corpses: "Just to see what it would feel like." But Jeffrey had decided against it.

No one came to look at Cheryl's body. After she was shot, Jeffrey and Ron left the room and went outside into the night air. The autopsy would later show that despite the wounds, Cheryl hadn't died instantly. A coroner would estimate that she had been alive in the pit for up to five minutes after being shot.

Jeffrey had waited this time for Greg to run the chain saw, and when Jeffrey and Ron stepped out of the barn, he was squeezing the trigger hard so the engine would rev and then slowly releasing it. He was trying to mimic the sound of a saw cutting wood. Jeffrey and Ron walked around the barn, checking the highway and the lights at neighbors' houses to see if anyone had become suspicious. Lee and Lois Myers, who lived east of the barn, were coming in from their patio when Lois heard the chain saw and what sounded like a gunshot. Dorothy Green, who lived across the street from the barn, heard the chain saw and at least one gunshot. But neither woman thought it was odd. It wasn't uncommon for people to hunt in the area even at night.

"Bring out the next one," said Jeffrey.

Trina Avery was in the living room reading a magazine when Ron told her that her mother needed her in the barn. The fifteen-year-old sighed and obediently followed him outside.

"Here she comes!" yelled Damon.

The men swarmed around her as soon as Trina stepped inside. Ron told Trina that they were going to play a game. Most of the children had played hide-and-seek in the barn at one time or another. The previous Halloween, the kids had used the barn for skits and a spook house. Trina didn't ask any questions. Ron told her to relax. It was going to be fun. The men taped her feet and hands, and wrapped the tape around her face.

"It's just like the three monkeys—see no evil, hear no evil, say no evil," one of them said.

No one could tell if Trina was smiling. Her head was wrapped like a mummy. Ron and Richard lifted her up and started to carry her through the barn, but as they were walking, Richard accidentally tripped on the extension cord that led to the light over the pit. The bulb fell and broke, leaving Jeffrey in the dark.

"Get a new bulb!" Jeffrey yelled.

Ron and Richard put Trina down on a mound of dirt and trash.

Ron stayed with her and told her not to worry, while Richard hurried to another part of the barn to get a bulb. Within a few minutes, the light was restrung and the two men picked up Trina and carried her into the room. They lowered her into the pit next to her parents. Jeffrey stepped up and took aim. Since he had shot her parents in the upper body, Jeffrey decided to shoot Trina in the skull to see, as he later put it, which caused death more quickly—a "head shot or by shooting them in the heart." Just as he squeezed the trigger, however, Trina turned.

"Ouch!" the teenager shrieked, even though her mouth was taped.

Thinking he'd missed her head or just grazed it, Jeffrey quickly lowered the barrel and fired two shots into Trina's back. She slumped forward. He looked down at her. She wasn't moving so he decided that he didn't need to shoot her again.

Just as they had done before, Jeffrey and Ron walked around the barn to see if any of the neighbors were watching. It didn't look like it.

There were only two children left now. Becky and Karen. Ron found them playing video games in the house.

"Who wants to see the horses in the barn?" he asked cheerfully.

Both girls dropped the video-game controls, jumped up, and rushed toward the back door.

"I can only take you one at a time," he announced.

Karen, the smallest, returned to the video game. She was used to being the last in line. Ron told her that he'd be right back.

"Oway," she replied.

After Becky left, Karen noticed that her mom and dad and sister Trina were missing.

"Where's my mama?" she asked.

"It's okay," Susie answered automatically, "she'll be right back."

As Susie watched Karen return to her video game, she suddenly realized what she had said. She turned away from the child. She couldn't stand to look at her.

By this time, each man had found his own specialty. Damon was the lookout, Ron escorted the victims, Richard and Danny handled the taping, Greg ran the chain saw, Jeffrey did the killing.

Unlike her obedient sister, when Becky got to the barn and saw the duct tape, she asked: "What's going on?"

"We told her that we were just playing a game and that she was going for a ride," Richard recalled later.

Within seconds, Ron and Richard had carried her into the room and put her in the pit. Jeffrey shot her, but he didn't think that his first shot killed the feisty thirteen-year-old. She was still breathing. The impact of the bullet had knocked her over and she had hit her mother's corpse.

"I fired again," Jeffrey later said, "and when this shot hit her, her hands, which had been in her lap, went forward as if she was reaching to touch her mother's body—as if she instinctively knew that her mother was there beside her."

Ron went to fetch Karen while Jeffrey reloaded. As soon as Ron stepped inside the farmhouse, Karen was on her feet, eager to see the horses. Ron scooted down and the six-year-old rushed over to him and climbed onto his back. He had given piggyback rides before. His son, Matthew, was the same age as Karen; his daughter, Amy, was four. Karen put her arms around his neck and laughed as Ron bounced her on his back and walked outside.

Like her sisters, Karen didn't resist when the men wrapped her with duct tape, although she was clearly frightened when they put it around her eyes and mouth. She only weighed thirty-six pounds, so Ron picked her up by himself and carried her into the room and pit.

Jeffrey had already fired hollow-points, full-metal-jackets, and silver-tipped 184-grain bullets. He had shot his victims in the back, breasts, skull, and legs. Because Karen was so tiny, he didn't want to risk missing her. He also wanted to try a different angle of penetration. This time, Jeffrey chambered a .225-grain hollow-point slug that he had loaded himself. He stood directly over Karen, who was sitting in the mud. Since her eyes were taped, she had no idea that her parents and sisters were sprawled dead around her.

"I fired straight down into her skull," Jeffrey recalled. "I was less than two feet away and I pulled the trigger, bang, bang."

He was trying to put both shots into the same hole. Karen's body jumped when hit and then slumped over.

It was now almost 11:00 P.M.. Jeffrey told Richard and Ron to dump bags of lime on the bodies. He thought that the lime would help them decompose. Richard carried a bag to the pit and slit it open. He tried to pour it on the bodies without looking at them.

"It didn't seem real," Ron said later. He would later not be able to recall Becky and Karen's names when he eventually described their murders to police. "I'm kind of foggy on this business," he'd say.

Once the lime was spread, they began to cover the bodies with rocks. They would then refill the hole and fill the room with trash.

Jeffrey took his pistol and left the other men to do the work.

"Before I went into the farmhouse," Jeffrey later recalled, "I walked into the apple orchard and looked up at the heavens and said a prayer. 'God,' I said, 'I have been thy sword of judgment this day. May my offering be acceptable. May all I've done be acceptable to you this day.' Then I went inside and cleaned up."

CHAPTER FORTY-ONE

A LICE had driven directly to the Patricks' apartment when she and three of her children left the farmhouse after dinner. She dropped Kristen and Caleb there to play with Molly Patrick and drove to Makro, a large discount department store in a nearby town, where she bought two picnic tables. Jason tagged along to help load them into the truck. A clerk had to get the tables out of a storeroom, and by the time Alice had paid and bought two one-pound bags of chocolate candy for her kids and a bag of cashews for herself, it was 10:30 P.M.

Alice returned to Kirtland and hurried inside the Patricks' apartment without knocking. She went directly to the telephone and called the farmhouse. Debbie answered.

"Can I come home now?" Alice asked.

It had been about five minutes since Karen Avery had been taken into the barn.

"You'd better wait for about fifteen minutes," said Debbie.

After Alice hung up the receiver, she went into the living room and sat on the sofa. Keith and Dennis sat on each side of her. They could tell she was upset. Dennis took her hand. Keith would later testify that Alice had a strange look on her face.

"The fog is bloodred over the barn tonight," Keith quoted Alice as saying.

Shortly after eleven o'clock, Alice returned to the farm with her children. She went into the bedroom to talk to Jeffrey. Kristen, Caleb, and Jason were supposed to go upstairs to bed, but Jason came down a few minutes later.

"I asked Sharon where the men were," Jason recalled. He was fond of Richard and wanted to see what he was doing. Sharon told Jason that all of the men were in the barn and Jason started toward the back door. Sharon rushed into the bedroom.

"Jason—Jason is heading out to the barn," Sharon stammered.

"Stupid!" Alice screamed, "How could you let him do such a thing?"

She raced out and yelled at Jason to get back into the house. Once Alice made certain that he and the other two children were in bed, she rejoined Jeffrey.

Jeffrey told Alice and Damon that he wanted them to come with him to the Red Roof Inn. He took along two green trash bags. When they got there, all three of them hurried upstairs to the Averys' room. Once inside, Jeffrey handed Alice and Damon trash bags and told them to start collecting the Averys' possessions. Purses, toothbrushes, the girls' dolls, Becky's pillowcase from Orioles with the outline of hands on it—everything was thrown into the bags as the three carefully swept through the room. Suddenly, Alice gasped. On the counter in front of her was the picture that Karen had drawn of the rainbow.

It said: "To Alice—I Love You—Karen."

Alice picked it up and slipped it in the trash bag.

Before they left the room, Jeffrey had Damon mess up the double beds and the rollaway to make it look as if they had been slept in. The room had been paid for in advance with cash so the Averys weren't expected to check out. Jeffrey tossed the motel key on the television and pulled the door shut so that it locked automatically. They hurried down to the truck and drove home.

By the time they reached the farmhouse, the men had finished filling in the pit in the barn. Keith and Kathy Johnson and Dennis and Tonya Patrick had arrived at the farm for scripture class. Jeffrey had telephoned them before leaving for the motel and told them to come out. One by one, the adults filed into the living room and waited as Jeffrey took the trash bags from the truck into his bedroom.

"It was stone cold silent," Alice recalled.

When Jeffrey returned, he opened the Book of Mormon and began to read:

"Behold the Lord slayeth the wicked to bring forth his righteous purposes."

It was the verse from First Nephi that described how God had ordered Nephi to behead Laban.

Jeffrey shut his scriptures and looked up at the group. Everyone in the room, except for him, appeared to be in tears.

"Ron," Jeffrey said, "did my servant Richard serve me well tonight?"

Ron replied; "Yes, your servant Richard served you well."

Jeffrey went through the entire list of names and Ron's answer was the same until he reached Damon. When Jeffrey asked about his son, Ron replied; "Your servant Damon served you the best that he could."

Jeffrey told everyone that he was proud of how Damon had performed.

"Damon is a man now," he said. "He served me well."

Jeffrey turned and stared at Dennis and then at Richard. "We were told that we were lucky to be alive," Richard later said, "that Sharon and Tonya, because of their obedience to Alice, had pulled our cookies out of the sand."

Jeffrey berated both men for several minutes for being rebellious and he warned them that they could still end up like the Averys. Dennis was shaking. Richard lowered his head and bent down in his chair, his hands dangling lifeless between his legs.

There was no doubt whatsoever that Dennis Avery was under Satan's power, Jeffrey announced. "Even his last words were rebellious." Jeffrey explained that just before his mouth was taped shut, Dennis Avery had said, "This isn't necessary."

"He was still trying to tell me what to do," said Jeffrey. "He was trying to be the seer, the prophet."

Dennis Patrick felt physically ill. He looked around the room. "Knowing how close we had come to being in the pit with the Averys, I couldn't believe what he was saying. This was not the Jeffrey that I had known in Independence. This was someone else."

Tonya couldn't stop sobbing.

"I kept thinking about Karen," she said. "The last time I'd seen her, Jeffrey had been holding her on his lap. He had been playing with her and now he had just killed her."

Tonya would later quote Jeffrey as asking the group: *"Is this real enough for you?"*

Jeffrey wanted to know how everyone felt. He asked Richard first. "Nobody should have to die like that," Richard said. "That's just no way to go."

When it was Keith's turn to respond, he simply said, "Shit, shit, shit."

"There is no going back now," Kathy Johnson said.

This is what Alice remembered telling everyone. "Our lives are over. Life as we know it is gone. We are wanderers and strangers in a strange land."

Debbie Olivarez would later quote Alice's remarks differently. "Alice told us, 'You need to be thankful for this man.' She was talking about Jeff. She said, 'He is going to take you to see God. He did this for you. He killed these people so you could see God.' She was playing the role of cheerleader just as she always did for him."

Jeffrey told the women that they should "comfort" their men that night. "This is just the beginning," he reminded them. "The scriptures say we will have to kill many, many more."

For several minutes it was completely quiet except for the sound of crying.

"Now that the sin is gone," Jeffrey concluded, "we can go into the wilderness and see God."

Class was dismissed.

It was after 1:00 A.M. when everyone went to bed. Jeffrey started a fire in the bedroom fireplace and carried the trash bags with the Averys' belongings over in front of it. He began going through them, taking whatever he wanted, burning whatever he didn't. When he got to the drawing of the rainbow that Karen had made for Alice, he tossed it into the flame.

Neither of them could sleep when they first went to bed.

"At one point during the night," Alice later recalled, "Jeffrey asked me if I were asleep and I said, 'No,' and then I said, 'Oh, Jeff, why did you have to do it?,' and he was quiet and then he said, 'It was the will of God.'"

Alice didn't reply.

"Jeffrey truly believed. He thought he was becoming divine.

There was never any show of doubt. He genuinely believed that he was exactly who he said he was based on his reading of the scriptures."

Alice lay next to him in the morning darkness with her eyes wide open and then she reached over and took his hand into her hand and held it. He gently squeezed it and fell asleep.

CHAPTER FORTY-TWO

AT precisely 9:00 A.M. on April 18, FBI Agent Robert Alvord and Chief Dennis Yarborough began briefing the sixteen special agents and six police officers who were going to descend on Jeffrey and his followers. Alvord explained that the FBI would handle the interviews, the police officers would secure the area. The agents were shown photographs that had been secretly taken of Jeffrey, Sharon, Danny, Ronald, Greg, and Damon. Agents also were given profiles of Jeffrey and some key group members that were done by the FBI Behavioral Science Unit. Alvord and Yarborough had identified eight people to interview. They were: Jeffrey, Alice, Greg, Richard, Ron, Danny, Sharon, and Debbie. Of course, anyone else at the farmhouse would be questioned, but Alvord and Yarborough felt the list covered the most important group members.

There were three families not mentioned. They were the Johnsons, the Patricks, and the Averys. No one knew anything about Keith and Kathy Johnson. Ron Andolsek had spotted their yellow Chevrolet Sierra station wagon parked at the Lundgren farmhouse on April 3 and had gotten their names by tracing their Missouri license plates, but nothing else was known about them. Shar and Kevin had talked about Dennis and Tonya Patrick. Both said that the Patricks were disliked and were considered by Jeffrey to be untrustworthy. The Avery family was on the bottom of the suspect list. When Alvord wrote a synopsis of the case on February 24 for his supervisors, he mentioned the Averys in only two sentences.

> Dennis Avery, wife Cheryl, are members of the group, however, the Averys do not participate in the paramilitary activities of the group. Avery is also considered expendable by Lundgren in as much as both of them are considered to be "doubters."

Andolsek had tried to find out more about the Avery family, but he hadn't been successful. Seven months earlier, Andolsek had gone to the house that they rented in Kirtland but it was empty, and when he checked with the post office, he found that the Averys hadn't left a forwarding address. No one was even certain that they were still in the area.

Near the end of the briefing, Alvord reminded the agents that Jeffrey had a large number of weapons, including assault rifles. If Jeffrey or any members of his group began shooting, the agents were to pull back and wait for help from the Cleveland FBI office. By 10:00 A.M., everyone was ready to go.

There was no one in sight at the farmhouse when Alvord and Yarborough arrived. As soon as the men stepped from their cars, Yarborough put his right hand inside his jacket. He had a snub-nosed .38 pistol there. He planned to keep it pointed at Jeffrey through his coat the entire time that he was being interviewed.

When Alvord knocked on the door, Alice answered in her bathrobe.

"We need to talk to Jeffrey," Yarborough said.

"He's in the barn," she replied. "I'll get him."

She shut the door in their faces and ran through the house to the back door. Yarborough and Alvord raced around the side of the house. They turned the back corner just as Alice was hollering from the doorstep for Jeffrey. The two men looked away from the house toward the barn.

"I saw the fifty-caliber rifle, the huge gun, sitting out next to the window," Alice later recalled. "So I grabbed it and carried it into our bedroom and put it under the bedcovers and made the bed real fast so you couldn't tell it was hidden there."

Jeffrey, Alvord, and Yarborough came into the house. Other agents, who had been told to stay away from the farm until Alvord and Yarborough had found Jeffrey, now swarmed onto the property. Richard, Danny, Damon, Dennis Patrick, and Keith Johnson were herded into the front yard and ordered to sit on the porch. "Don't talk to each other," an agent barked.

Sharon and Susie were in the house. Greg had left the farm earlier that morning to dispose of several trash bags that contained property from the barn that belonged to the Averys. He was dropping the bags at random in Dumpsters around suburban Cleveland. Ron and Debbie had left the farm earlier to do some last-minute grocery shopping. Kathy and Tonya, meanwhile, were at the Patricks' apartment.

An agent hurried Alice outside and put her in a car. While she was waiting, Andolsek slid into the front seat. He had a list of questions on a clipboard. He began by telling Alice that she and Jeffrey were under suspicion for a crime that could end up with both of them receiving the death penalty.

"I froze," Alice later said. "I thought, 'How did they find out about the Averys!'"

Andolsek said that the FBI knew "everything."

Alice felt faint. "I kept thinking, 'How did they find out!'"

And then Andolsek said, "Alice, what does 'Redeeming the vineyard' mean?"

Alice suddenly relaxed. "I realized that he didn't know anything about the murders the night before. He was talking about the temple takeover. I about laughed."

Inside, Jeffrey was drawing that same conclusion based on the questions that Alvord and FBI Agent Lloyd N. Buck were asking him. "It was clear that Shar had talked to them," he said. "I knew they didn't have a clue about the Averys being in the barn."

The agents asked if Jeffrey would show them his guns. Jeffrey paused. "They didn't have a search warrant, otherwise they would have shown it to me, so I knew I could refuse to show them my guns. But I figured they'd just go get one and I had planned on leaving for the wilderness that day. I wanted them out of the house as quickly as possible."

Jeffrey took the men into his bedroom and got out the bag with the pistols in it. They checked the weapons and then told Jeffrey that they wanted to see his rifles, including the ones that he had hidden on the second floor behind a false wall in a bedroom. Now Jeffrey was certain that Shar was the informant because she had known about that hidden chamber. Jeffrey led Alvord upstairs and opened the false wall in the closet. He took out the rifles and the agents checked to see if he had altered any of them so that they would fire automatically, a violation of federal gun laws. He hadn't.

While the agents questioned Jeffrey, other group members were being quizzed outside. Once the group members realized that no one except them knew about the murders, the mood turned almost light-hearted.

"Yes, we have firearms," Damon said. He volunteered that his father also had a lot of rabbits. "We are not violent people. We kill our rabbits when they are sick . . . but wrestling in the backyard is the most violent thing we've ever done."

FBI agents later quoted Danny saying that he "could never kill anything, including animals." The movie *The Highlander*, he added, didn't have anything to do with Jeffrey's teachings.

Richard told agents that he believed Jeffrey was "very knowl-edgeable" about the church, but said that he could never be consid-ered a prophet because a prophet had to be able to perform great acts or miracles and Jeffrey hadn't done anything like that.

Susie said that she and Ron were leaving Ohio to look for work elsewhere.

Alice also played dumb. The only guns in the house, she said, were black-powder rifles. When Andolsek asked her if Jeffrey had ever seen Christ in a vision while the couple was visiting Niagara Falls—a tidbit that Kevin had told the FBI—Alice laughed. "That's a new one," she said. Andolsek realized that he was wasting his time and left Alice in the car with a woman officer. Alvord had specifi-cally assigned an FBI agent who was a member of the LDS church to interview Alice, and he took over, but he didn't get anything useful from her either.

Shortly after the agents began questioning the group, Greg drove by the farm and spotted the police cars. His first instinct was to keep driving, but he didn't want to look suspicious, so he parked his car and walked to the farm. Before he reached the house, he realized that he had Dennis Avery's credit cards in his back pocket. He had thought Jeffrey might want to keep them. It was too late for him to dispose of them now. He hoped no one searched him.

Alice glanced out the window of the car and saw Greg coming. She looked over to where the FBI had lined up the men. "Dennis Patrick and Keith Johnson were in la-la land," she recalled. "They were in total shock and scared to death. But when I looked at Richard, he gave me the thumbs up. He and Damon and Danny were acting like really cool dudes."

Alice announced that she wanted a glass of water and a woman agent escorted her from the car into the kitchen. The agent opened the cupboard and gave Alice a glass. Greg came in to get a drink too. "Greg opened the refrigerator and said, 'Gee, Mom, we're almost out of milk. Don't you think I should go get some for lunch?' I didn't catch on at first, but then I said, 'Yes, you'd better go.' They let Greg leave and he immediately went looking for Debbie and Ron to warn them not to come home."

Greg flagged them down a few miles from the farm and warned them. "Ron and I just started driving around," Debbie recalled. Greg, meanwhile, dropped Dennis Avery's credit cards into a trash bin behind a convenience store.

Alvord wasn't learning anything useful from Jeffrey. Nor had he or Yarborough seen any maps, drawings, or anything else that might give them probable cause to arrest him. They had found the stun gun, but had no way of knowing that it had been used the night before on Dennis Avery. They had also found camouflage uniforms and gas masks. But there was nothing illegal about either. At 11:51 A.M., Alvord conferred with Yarborough and both agreed that it was time to call it quits. Alvord would later file a written report about his conversation with Jeffrey.

> Lundgren advised that he believes that a judgment day is at hand, but it is at the hand of the Lord and not his, and Lundgren finds no justification in the scriptures for violently taking the temple or killing other individuals.
>
> He advised that he does not consider himself a prophet, but does consider himself a teacher.
>
> Lundgren advised that the camouflage uniforms were for hunting and the stun gun was purchased for his wife for her own personal protection. The gas masks are used for spray painting and refinishing.
>
> Lundgren advised that he does a great deal of hunting and his father was a collector of guns and he has just continued the tradition.

When the officers returned to the Kirtland Police Department, Yarborough told Alvord that they had "blown it."

"Bob, we didn't do what we were attempting to do out there today," Yarborough said. "We wanted to break them up and put the fear of—" he suddenly stopped because he didn't want to say the word God. He continued—"the fear of law enforcement in them. I'm afraid we actually tightened the cohesiveness of the group." If anything, Yarborough continued, Jeffrey probably now thought that he was invincible.

Alvord debriefed his agents. All of the suspects had denied that Lundgren was a prophet, except for one. Keith Johnson had been clearly nervous and had told FBI Agent John Powers and Kirtland Police Lieutenant Edward A. Dodaro a bizarre story. Keith said that the group was about to go to the "wilderness" because God was going to appear to Jeffrey on May 3, 1989, and bestow tremendous powers on him. Lundgren would be able to call fire down on his enemies, as well as lightning, and be able to cause earthquakes that would shake the earth and destroy most civilizations. After this was done, the Russians would take over the world and on May 4, 1990, Lundgren would lead an armed assault on the RLDS church in Kirtland, which he would rescue from the Russians. Lundgren would have the "Sword of Laban" when he did this. Keith told the officers that he believed Lundgren could do these things, but if God did not appear to Jeffrey on May 3, 1989, he would leave the group.

Keith's story was as strange as the ones that Shar and Kevin had told, and because of that both Alvord and Yarborough suspected that some of it was true. But Keith hadn't said anything that would justify the FBI's continuing to keep its investigation of Jeffrey going. Alvord knew that he had run out of time.

When Alvord left the police station that afternoon, he told Yarborough that he still wanted to help. Although the FBI's probe would be officially closed in a few days, he would personally be willing to check out any leads that the chief might develop. Yarborough thanked him.

Back at the farmhouse, everyone gathered in the living room as soon as the agents left. Jeffrey quizzed each person: "What did they ask you? What did you say?" Keith listened to what the others said and quickly realized that he had said too much. When Jeffrey asked him, Keith claimed that he hadn't told the officers anything. Greg didn't want to talk out loud. He grabbed a pad and pencil and wrote messages. The FBI, he scribbled on his pad, had bugged the room. Jeffrey doubted it.

Jeffrey turned to Alice. "Now do you have any doubt that I am who I say I am?" he asked.

"Jeffrey considered the fact that the FBI didn't know about the

Averys a direct confirmation of the fact that he could do anything he wanted," Alice later said, "and do it right under their noses."

"God has promised me that he will protect my back," Jeffrey said. "We don't have to worry. The Lord is with us."

Just the same, Jeffrey decided that he wanted to leave the farm as soon as he could. But first, he wanted everything in the house that had anything to do with the temple takeover destroyed. The city maps that Richard had stolen were burned in the fireplace. The replica of the temple that Danny had made was smashed and burned too. At one point, Jeffrey had talked about disguising Damon and Danny as paramedics during the temple raid. He had bought them white outfits and Debbie had stolen some paramedic patches from the hospital where she worked. The outfits and patches were tossed into the fire. Jeffrey had bought several old police badges at gun shows and those were dropped into the septic tank. Sharon, meanwhile, stood in the bathroom burning notes that she and others had taken during Jeffrey's classes. She flushed the ashes down the stool. The group burned so many items that they had to stop and clean out the fireplace. Jeffrey sent Damon into the apple orchard with ashes. "Break them up and spread them out," he ordered.

By 2:30 P.M., all the evidence about the takeover had been destroyed. The group got back to packing. At 3:00 P.M., Keith went to Tom's Sunoco Station, which is located next to the police department, to pick up his Sierra, which was having its clutch repaired. Andolsek had seen the distinctive school-bus-yellow truck parked there earlier, and when he spotted Johnson at the station, he called to Yarborough and the two of them hustled over to speak with Keith. They hoped he would feel free to talk now that he was away from the farmhouse. But Keith wouldn't comment. He was still going to the wilderness, he said. But if he ever left the group, he would contact the police. Back in the station, Yarborough and Andolsek agreed that Keith was the "weak link." Over time, both felt that he could be turned into an informer. The only question was whether the officers would get another chance to turn him.

Counting the children, there were twenty-four people making the trip to the wilderness. Debbie had bought over $2,000 worth of food that was spread all over the kitchen floor. There were still things in the barn that had to be sorted. Jeffrey decided that everyone was taking too long. He announced that he and his family, and Susie and her children, were going to leave. The others would load the U-Haul truck and leave as soon as they could. Jeffrey put the bag of pistols and all of the rifles into the Nissan truck that he was driving. He told his children and Alice to get in. Susie would drive the Luffs' 1978 Plymouth sedan. The others would ride in the U-Haul, Greg's Honda, and the Johnsons' Sierra that was going to be used to pull a horse trailer. Jeffrey appointed Greg to be in charge.

"I had no idea where I was going," Jeffrey said later. "The scriptures just said to drive in a southbound east direction." He and Greg looked at a map. Jeffrey pointed toward West Virginia. They chose a highway. Jeffrey said that he would stop at a motel at around eleven o'clock. He would stay in one that could be seen from the road. Greg's group should keep driving until they spotted Jeffrey's truck. In case they missed each other, Greg and Jeffrey agreed on a place to meet farther down the highway the next morning. Whoever got there first would wait for the others.

At dusk, Jeffrey and his family, and Susie and her children, left the farmhouse. Alice looked back as they drove away. She would later recall that only one FBI agent had asked about the Averys and he had asked only one question about them before switching the subject. The agents had no idea that the bodies of Dennis, Cheryl, Trina, Becky, and Karen had been buried less than twelve hours earlier.

Fifteen minutes after Jeffrey left the farm, he signaled Susie, who was following his truck, to turn in to a Burger King restaurant. The kids were hungry and so was he, but Alice couldn't eat.

It was nearly midnight by the time the others at the farm finished getting everything packed. A heavy fog had come over the farm. It was so thick that it was difficult to make out objects that were more than five feet away. The group decided that God had created the fog to make it difficult for the police or FBI to see them loading the truck. God was helping them escape. Debbie was excited when the caravan finally left the farmhouse.

"I was a bit nervous about who was on our tail at first," she said later, "but once we got out of Ohio, I began to relax."

Jeffrey had told Debbie that she and Greg were going to have a baby, even though Debbie had undergone a partial hysterectomy. He had told her that she would be healed and when she was packing for the trip, Tonya had given her some of Molly's old baby clothes to take. She wanted to have Greg's child. She loved him. She also believed in Jeffrey.

"He was going to take us to see God face-to-face. And I was really looking forward to that moment."

PART THREE : KILLER

*And that prophet, or that dreamer of dreams, shall
be put to death; because he hath spoken to turn
you away from the Lord your God . . .*

Deuteronomy 13:5

CHAPTER FORTY-THREE

And the Lord spake unto Moses, saying, Send thou men,
that they may search the land of Canaan, which I give unto the
children of Israel . . . (Numbers 13:1–2)

LIKE Moses, Jeffrey was leading his followers into the wilderness,
so it seemed fitting that after two days of traveling southeast on various state highways, they arrived in the Canaan Valley of West Virginia. When Jeffrey pulled into Davis, a town of 950, and spied a
motel called The Highlander, he declared that he had arrived at the
spot where God wanted them. While the family relaxed at a motel,
Jeffrey left early each morning to search for a suitable campsite.

His choice of the Canaan Valley almost did seem divinely inspired. Tucked in the Appalachian Mountains, Davis is located on
a jagged sliver of West Virginia caught between the states of Maryland and Virginia like a finger slammed in a car door. Settlers were
drawn to the valley in the 1880s because of its abundant timber,
clear streams, and coal. Today it is the Canaan Valley Ski Resort
and the Smoke Hole Caverns, both south of Davis, that attract
crowds. Neither interested Jeffrey, but two miles east of town, he
found exactly what he was looking for—a huge undeveloped and

isolated tract known locally as Yellow Creek Hollow. Officially, the miles of pine forests were owned by the Monongahela Power Company, but the hollow was a virtual no-man's land, open year-round without charge to the public for camping, fishing, and hunting. Best of all, Jeffrey learned, there was little supervision.

By April 23, Jeffrey had moved the group to a campsite in the hollow, but after some fishermen wandered through, he decided to go deeper into the forest. He settled near a stream and organized his camp "chiastically," with a group of tents on one side of the water and another group on the other. The sites were supposed to mirror each other "just like verses in the scriptures." Danny Kraft, Jr., designed a fifteen-foot bridge, which the men made out of logs, to connect the sites.

Jeffrey wanted his camp to be as comfortable as possible. A kerosene-powered generator supplied sufficient electricity to operate a deep freeze, a microwave oven taken from the Avery household, an electric fence used to pen the two horses, and a pair of televisions and videotape players. One television and VCR was kept on a picnic table for the group. The other was in Jeffrey's tent for his private use. There were more than two dozen movies including The Highlander.

Jeffrey and Alice lived in the largest tent. It was divided into three sections. One was used as a living room, the other two as bedrooms. Jason, Kristen, and Caleb had mattresses in one; Jeffrey and Alice slept in the other. Damon lived in a separate tent with Danny. Each family had its own tent. There was also a tent for supplies and one filled with toys for the children. A tarp strung over picnic tables served as an outdoor dining area and there was another tent for use as a kitchen.

Because Debbie Olivarez had worked as a cook at summer church camps, she made all the meals. Kathy Johnson tended the horses. Tonya Patrick oversaw the laundry, which was washed in water from the stream and rinsed in big plastic trash cans. Susie Luff and Sharon Bluntschly took care of the supply tent, watched the children, and cleaned the Lundgrens' tent. As was the case at the farm, Alice didn't have specific chores.

Jeffrey assigned each man a job. Richard Brand emptied the toilets—trash cans lined with plastic bags—and built a shower using a lawn sprinkler as a shower head. Greg Winship and Damon Lundgren helped care for the horses. Dennis Patrick was in charge of the firepit where trash was burned. Keith Johnson, Ron Luff, and Danny Kraft collected firewood and did the countless other chores that arose during the day. Jeffrey's job was hunting game in the mornings and teaching at night. Each of the men, except Jeffrey, also took turns standing guard. When they were on sentry duty, they were armed with a semi-automatic assault rifle. Most days, Jeffrey wore a .45-caliber pistol on his belt. By this time, he had promoted himself to the rank of five-star general in the Army of Israel. His army's ammunition and most of the guns were stored in a locker at the foot of Jeffrey's bed. The trunk had belonged to Cheryl Avery, who had saved her babysitting money as a teenager to buy it for her trip to college.

On May 3, Jeffrey arose early and announced that he was going to the top of a nearby mountain to meet God. It was Jeffrey's birthday, and now that he had sacrificed the Averys, it was time for him to be "endowed with power." He returned at midmorning, riding into camp on the ATV. Everyone swarmed around him.

"Jesus Christ appeared to me," Jeffrey proclaimed. Christ had descended from heaven in a beam of light and had told him that He was pleased with the blood atonement of the Averys and the group's trek into West Virginia. Because of Jeffrey's faithfulness, Christ had bestowed a new title on him. Jeffrey told everyone to open their Bibles to verse 5 of chapter 54 of Isaiah:

> For thy Maker is thine husband; the Lord of hosts is his name; and thy Redeemer the Holy One of Israel; the God of the whole earth shall he be called.

"I have taken on Christ's name," Jeffrey announced. "I am not Jesus Christ, but because I have taken on the task that He has commanded me to do, I can be like Jesus Christ and He has given me the title of 'God of the whole Earth.'"

Christ had made him immortal, Jeffrey said. He could no longer be "pierced" by bullets, knives, or any other objects. Christ had also made him divine. "I am the law," said Jeffrey. "There is no other law." No one in the camp was to question any command that he gave. "Would you question Jesus Christ?" Jeffrey asked them. "Then do not try to tell the God of the whole earth what to do." Anything less than total subservience was a "sin" and a sign of "rebellion" that would block the group from being able to stand before God.

During the next few weeks, a routine developed at camp. The women worked in the mornings while the men either hunted or studied their scriptures. Afternoons were reserved for family time when parents were supposed to teach their children the pattern and how to use it. Jeffrey taught a scripture class each night. There were two new concepts that Jeffrey promoted after he declared himself the "God of the whole earth." He called them "peradventuring" and "delusion."

Peradventuring was a word that Jeffrey had derived from the story of Sodom and Gomorrah, found in chapter 18 of Genesis. God had decided to destroy the town of Sodom because it was wicked, but Abraham bargained with Him and got God to promise to spare Sodom if "peradventure there may be fifty righteous within the city." Abraham couldn't find 50, so he asked God to make the number 45, then 40, 30, and 10. God finally ended up destroying the city, just as He had planned. Jeffrey said that Abraham's bargaining with God was "peradventuring." Abraham was trying to second-guess the Lord. Whenever anyone in Jeffrey's group made a suggestion or even used the phrase "Well, I just thought . . ." Jeffrey and Alice would accuse them of "peradventuring." The only person in the group who was supposed to think was Jeffrey. Everyone else was to "submit" their will to his.

The second concept that Jeffrey taught was called "delusion." According to the New Testament book of Second Thessalonians, chapter 2, verses 10 to 13, people who rejected God's truth were given "a strong delusion" by God so that "they should believe a lie." Jeffrey interpreted that verse to mean that he could lie whenever he wished. "If someone is wicked, then he is your enemy, he is under Satan's authority and you do not tell your enemy what you are doing," Jeffrey explained. "There is nothing wrong with deceiving your enemy—military generals do it all the time." Jeffrey said that if he told anyone in the group an obvious lie, he wasn't really at fault—he was giving them a delusion because *they* didn't want to hear the truth. They were to blame.

Greg Winship and others took notes during Jeffrey's classes. The police later confiscated some of these records and discovered that Alice acted as Jeffrey's cheerleader after most classes. She would jump up and lecture or chastise the class. Here is a sample of what the police found:

> Alice on July 9 [Explaining how women are to be sexually subservient to their husbands]: "Ladies, give till they can't take any more!"

Alice on July 22: "It's my observation you get into trouble
when you start using your own thoughts. Always ask what would
Dad [Jeffrey] do? What has Dad said to do? Every situation you're
in is an open-book test and you forget to use the books."

Alice on August 5: "If the rest of us think we will skirt by
without judgment—we're wrong. If Jeff says there is rebellion and
the thought comes 'I have no rebellion,' that's rebellion."

From the moment the group arrived in West Virginia, Dennis
Patrick was a problem. "I fell into a total depression after the Averys'
murders," he said later. "I didn't talk to anyone. I didn't eat. I
couldn't sleep. I was just numb." Tonya became frustrated. "I needed
Dennis and he wasn't there for me," she said. "Dennis was a complete zombie."

Dennis's depression irked Jeffrey. "I told Dennis to get his act
together. Everyone understood that God had ordered me to destroy
the wicked. Why then would Dennis mourn their destruction? Why
would he be upset that the wicked had been destroyed unless he too
was under Satan's influence?"

Despite Jeffrey's repeated warnings, Dennis couldn't shake his
depression. He was appalled by the murders. Jeffrey decided to have
a special class specifically about the executions to "shake up" Dennis.
Jeffrey wanted to remind him that he too would be sacrificed if he
didn't do what the "God of the whole Earth" demanded. "I related
to the class that I saw Cheryl and Trina being killed," Richard Brand
said later. "I told Dennis Patrick that was no way for anyone to die.
It was not even an option to consider—to be executed like that."

The most exhausting account of what happened in the barn on
April 17 was provided by Jeffrey, who described in incredible detail,
without any hint of emotion, exactly how he had killed each member of the Avery family. After class, he told Dennis that he was
going to meet a similar fate if he continued to show remorse over
the "destruction of the wicked."

Terrified, Dennis managed to put on a happier face, but he soon
found himself in trouble. It began when he and Tonya drove into
Davis to wash the group's clothing at a Laundromat because it had
been raining for a week, making it impossible to wash and dry the
clothes outdoors. Although wives were supposed to be subservient to
their husbands, Jeffrey had put Tonya in charge of the laundry. Den-

nis was merely sent along to help. Yet when they reached the Laundromat, Tonya found that she had only enough cash to wash and dry half the laundry. Jeffrey hadn't given her enough money. She decided to wash and dry half the load so that the group would have some clean clothing to wear, but Dennis told her that it would be better to wash all of the clothing and then take it back to camp wet where it could be put out to dry. After a brief but hot argument, Tonya relented. When they returned to camp, Jeffrey asked Tonya why none of the laundry was dry and she explained what had happened.

Jeffrey accused Dennis of peradventuring. Jeffrey had put Tonya in charge. By upsurping her power, Dennis had tried to second-guess Jeffrey's will.

Everyone in the group began chastising Dennis. "It may sound like a minor thing," Kathy Johnson said later, "but if Dennis couldn't obey a simple command, how could anyone count on him to obey a big one? The goal of the group was to become one heart and one mind with Jeffrey so we could see God. Dennis was keeping us from that."

That night at class, Jeffrey turned to Debbie. "How long would it take for Dennis to die," he asked, "if I strapped him to a tree and shot him in the balls?"

Dennis's face lost its color. The group became silent. Without waiting for Debbie to reply, Jeffrey slowly removed his .45 pistol from his belt. Dennis thought he was going to be killed.

"Jeffrey said that I wasn't being a man because I wasn't taking responsibility for keeping the commandments of God," Dennis Patrick recalled, "so if I were to have seed, that seed would be bad seed. He said he was going to destroy my seed by shooting off my balls, and then he was going to let me die a slow and agonizing death."

Jeffrey pointed his pistol at Dennis's crotch and for several tense seconds, everyone watched, fully expecting Jeffrey to pull the trigger. "I was going to shoot him," Jeffrey said later. "I had thought that my people had learned their lesson but Dennis still didn't get it. I was not joking around. God had ordered me to destroy the wicked and Dennis was clearly one of them."

Dennis begged for another chance "to get it right." He groveled.

"Okay," said Jeffrey. He lowered his pistol.

Dennis would get a final chance, but as punishment, Tonya and Molly were going to be taken out of Dennis's tent. He needed to be alone so that he could concentrate on his sin. Tonya and Molly were told to move in with Jeffrey and Alice. Dennis was forbidden to speak to his wife and daughter without permission from Jeffrey. The other men in the group were told to take away Dennis's weapons and instructed to stand guard at night over Dennis's tent to make certain that he didn't try to escape. "Every second after that," Dennis remembered, "I was being watched and my every move, my every comment was reported directly to Jeffrey."

During the next few days, Jeffrey talked openly about killing Dennis. At one point, Jeffrey said he was going to order the men to dig a pit for Dennis "just like the one that was dug for the Averys." Another time Jeffrey told Dennis that he would be killed while he was sleeping. "Jeffrey said he was going to have all the men surround my tent at night and simply open fire."

Alice encouraged Dennis's fears. "Jeff's got the same look in his eyes as he did on the day that he killed the Averys," Tonya later quoted Alice as saying.

"I lay awake for hours at night in the quiet and every time I heard a twig break or a leaf rustle," said Dennis, "I'd wonder if they were coming to kill me." He thought about getting a gun and shooting Jeffrey, but decided that he couldn't. "I'm not capable of killing someone." He thought about trying to escape, but rejected that thought too. "I didn't want to leave Tonya and Molly behind. Besides, if I went to the police and told them what kind of weapons Jeffrey had, there was going to be an armed attack and I didn't want Tonya and Molly killed." He thought about suicide, but didn't want to do that either. "Deep down, I still believed Jeffrey was a prophet and I really wanted to do everything right. I believed that Jeffrey could lead me to the Lord."

Dennis decided to keep his mouth shut. He didn't argue, didn't make suggestions, he simply did what he was told.

Jeffrey had always taught that if a man was so wicked that he had to be destroyed, then the rest of his family also had to be murdered. While Tonya was worried about Dennis's fate, she was also angry because she felt that he had put her and Molly into a precarious position.

"One night Tonya asked me if she and Molly were in danger," Jeffrey said, "and I told her that she was completely safe." That was not all Jeffrey told Tonya. Three days after she moved into his tent in early May, Jeffrey said that he was in love with her.

"He was very tender at first," Tonya said later, "very caring and kind." Jeffrey told Tonya that he had always felt a special "tenderness" toward her even during their college days before she had married Dennis, when all of them used to hang out at the RLDS student center in Warrensburg. Because of his warm feelings toward her, Jeffrey had asked God what role Tonya was to play in his life. The answer, he said, had dumbfounded him. Tonya was to be his second wife. "You are flesh of my flesh, bone of my bone," she later quoted him as saying. Jeffrey had come up with a new scriptural interpretation. He had already told everyone that God had created a "true companion" for every man. This companion was made by God out of the man's rib—just as Eve was made from Adam's rib. Jeffrey was now telling Tonya that God actually created two "true companions" for every man. "The rib cage is chiastic. There is a rib on each side, so God really takes both of them, not just one." Jeffrey told Tonya that she was his Bathsheba, that she was his "missing" second rib.

Tonya believed Jeffrey. She was also frightened of him. Within a week, the two of them were having sex. Tonya was worried that Alice would find out. Jeffrey assured her that Alice wouldn't know and if she did, he'd come up with an explanation to satisfy her.

Despite Jeffrey's assurances about Alice, she began suspecting within a month. "Tonya was a very prim and proper person when she first moved into our tent," Alice recalled. "She always wore a bathrobe, and then all of the sudden, she wasn't wearing one and wasn't being careful at all around Jeff."

In early June, Alice had one of her recurring migraine headaches. She didn't attend that night's scripture class but at one point, she walked outside the tent to use the bathroom. On her trip back, Alice spotted Jeffrey and Tonya walking hand in hand across the camp. "They stopped and kissed."

Alice fretted for more than a week and then she finally confronted Jeffrey. He denied everything, and with each denial, Alice became more convinced. "You're lying," she yelled. "You're nothing but a liar."

Jeffrey refused to change his story. Instead, he fell back on his scriptures. "Jeffrey had a habit of doing something and then looking for scriptures to justify his actions," Alice said later. "And that was exactly what he did when I confronted him."

By early July, Jeffrey had figured out a scheme. He told Tonya that it was time for him to announce that she was his second wife, but he cautioned her not to tell anyone that they had already been sexually active for two months. "He told me that he'd found a way to deal with Alice."

One morning, Jeffrey took Alice for a walk and when they stopped to rest, he told her that God was angry at her because of her rebellion. Opening his Bible, Jeffrey turned to chapter 54 in Isaiah. He read the first two verses to her. The key phrase was:

> . . . for more are the children of the desolate than the children of the married wife, saith the Lord. Enlarge the place of thy tent . . .

Jeffrey diagramed the passage and told Alice that it contained a secret message to him from God. This is what he wrote:

> [A] the married wife
> [B] saith the Lord
> [A] enlarge the place of thy tent

"The Lord is ordering me to 'enlarge my tent' by taking a 'married wife,'" Jeffrey said. "Who is 'the married wife'? Obviously, it is Tonya."

"No!" Alice shrieked. "You can't do this, Jeffrey!"

"It is your fault," he replied. Jeffrey explained that God had grown tired of Alice's constant quibbling and had decided to show her that it was not easy being the "God of the whole earth."

"You are always trying to second-guess me and be like God," Jeffrey said, "so God has decided to let you make a life-or-death decision."

God had ordered Jeffrey to "pierce" Tonya. He could do it with his penis by taking her as his wife and having sexual intercourse with her, he explained. Or he could shoot her with his .45 pistol. It was up to Alice to choose which it would be.

"Jeffrey said it didn't really matter to him which I chose," Alice said later, "and I believed that he was ready to shoot Tonya and Molly."

Falling to her knees, Alice begged him not to make her choose. "Jeff just stood there with his arms crossed across his chest. I cried and cried and cried."

"Choose ye this day," Jeffrey proclaimed. "You have to pay the price for your disobedience."

Alice stood up. "I guess you have another wife," she said, amid sobs.

When it was time for scripture class that night, Jeffrey told Tonya to stay in the tent. After his followers were seated, he opened his Bible and read the verses from Isaiah about the "married wife." He then took out his .45 pistol and held up a bullet so that the group could see it. He loaded and cocked the handgun.

"I'm only going to say this once," Jeffrey said solemnly, "so everyone listen. When I'm finished, I don't want any objections."

Jeffrey explained how God had become angry at Alice and had made her choose how Tonya would be "pierced." As Jeffrey spoke, Alice sat next to him staring at the ground.

"Rather than taking Tonya's life, Alice has agreed to my taking Tonya as a wife," Jeffrey announced. He raised the .45 pistol and pointed it directly at Dennis's forehead.

"Do you have any problems with this, Dennis?" he asked.

"I knew what my response was supposed to be," Dennis said later. "I answered, 'No, sir.'"

That night, Alice began crying when it was time for bed. Tonya was soon in tears too. The two women sat on the bed sobbing. "Tonya said to me, 'Alice, please don't hate me,' and I said to her, 'I could never hate you, Tonya.' And then Jeff came in and told me that he was going to go help Tonya take a shower and I said, 'Oh, Jeff, do you have to do it now?,' and he sat down and said, 'Okay, I won't do it tonight.'" Jeffrey told Tonya to sleep in the children's room that night with Molly.

The next morning, Jeffrey told Alice that he wanted her to go for a ride with him on the ATV. They rode several miles away from camp until they came to a stream. Jeffrey stopped the ATV and told Alice that there were two parts to her punishment. God had required her to make a life-or-death decision, which she had done. But since Jeffrey was Alice's personal "lord and master," he too had a right to punish her for her rebellion. Alice was going to have to prove to Jeffrey that she would obey his every command. She told him that she would.

Jeffrey told Alice to strip, and when she was standing naked in the woods, he ordered her to remove his clothing. "I thought we were going to make love," said Alice, "but instead, Jeffrey had a bowel movement and he instructed me to cover him with his own feces, leaving just enough for him to use to masturbate with. I did as he commanded and then he told me to tell him how beautiful he was, how wonderful he looked with all of this feces on him. I did this while he masturbated."

Jeffrey couldn't achieve ejaculation, Alice later said, so he commanded her to help stimulate him. "He took some of the feces and put it in his own mouth," Alice said later, "but he didn't swallow it. A lot of saliva come out and . . . he pulled me up and made me kiss him on the lips and then he . . . told me to perform oral sex on him without washing any of the feces off."

Alice did what he asked, but after several minutes, she became physically ill and began to gag. "He grabbed me and pushed his penis into my mouth and told me not to stop again for any reason. He told me to swallow everything—told me that I couldn't spit. I went on with it until he had obtained orgasm."

Afterward, Jeffrey led Alice to the creek. "I was told to give him a bath and he told me that I had been obedient and that I was forgiven and he thanked me for being a pure wife and I said, 'Okay.' And then he told me that he loved me."

They got dressed and returned to camp.

A few days later, Jeffrey announced that it was time for God's commandment to be carried out. He ordered Alice to "prepare the bed" in the tent for Tonya. He intended to "pierce" her. While Alice did what she was told, Jeffrey raced over to the camp's makeshift bathroom and surprised Tonya, who was inside. Grinning, he watched her for several seconds as she sat on the toilet and then announced that he wanted her back in the tent immediately.

When Tonya got there, Jeffrey ordered Alice to leave. She closed the tent flap behind her and hurried over to the kitchen where Debbie and Kathy were baking bread. "Alice was talking a mile a minute about funny things that her children had done," Kathy said later. "It suddenly dawned on me what was happening." All the other adults also figured out what was going on and they began gathering around Alice to give her moral support.

Jeffrey and Tonya were in the tent for only a few minutes when Jeffrey came scurrying outside. He rushed over to Alice.

"I couldn't do it," he announced in a voice that everyone could easily hear. Jeffrey explained that he had been unable to have sex with Tonya because she was not, as he put it, "flesh of my flesh.

"I was undressed and Tonya was undressed. I saw her and she saw me. I touched her and tried to find something to focus on that was arousing. I'm not trying to belittle her, but she is not my flesh and . . . I couldn't obtain an erection so I got dressed and said, 'I'm sorry, but if you want any satisfaction, you're going to have to do it by yourself.'"

That story is similar to the explanation that he first gave Alice when she discovered ten years earlier that he had spent the weekend in a motel with a fellow employee from Lake of the Ozarks Hospital. Despite the similarities, Alice appeared overjoyed.

"Oh, Jeffrey," she squealed, throwing her arms around him. "I knew you couldn't betray me."

The rest of the day, Jeffrey strolled through camp making jokes about his own inability to have sex with Tonya. He told everyone that he had been forced to "pierce" Tonya with his finger because he found her so unattractive that he simply couldn't obtain an erection. Kathy Johnson would later recall that Jeffrey had told her and Keith that Tonya had given a new meaning to the biblical phrase "withering away."

Tonya, who had been told to stay inside the tent all day, could hear what Jeffrey was saying and she was confused and hurt. She knew that he was lying. Why, she wondered, was he belittling her? That night, a completely different Jeffrey from the "loving" one who had wooed her, came into the tent. He briskly told Tonya that she was filled with sin. He had been studying the scriptures, he announced, to see what he was supposed to do with her. "Jeffrey had been telling me for weeks that I was pure and free of sin and now he was telling me I was wicked—just like that. All I could think was that he was setting the stage to get rid of me. He was tired of me and wanted someone else." Jeffrey told Tonya that she could remain in his tent, but he wasn't going to sleep with her and he warned her against telling anyone about their sexual encounters.

At scripture class a few nights later, Alice once again jumped to her feet and lectured the women about how they should do whatever their husbands demanded. Debbie would later recall Alice's comments. "She said, 'If Jeffrey wants me to be his doormat, then I'll be happy the rest of my life cleaning his shoes. He is my master and I live only to serve his desires.'"

Shortly after Alice made that declaration in late July 1989, Jeffrey told her that God had caused him to dream a strange dream.

"Jeffrey told me that God had shown him a woman's vagina in this dream," Alice later said. "He said that God had ordered him to find this vagina."

Kathryn Johnson was arrested by police in California shortly after Jeffrey and his family were caught. She had been living in a motel close to where Jeffrey and Alice were staying. Jeffrey had kept her presence a secret because he was afraid Alice would leave him if she knew his "second wife" was nearby. AP/WIDE WORLD PHOTOS

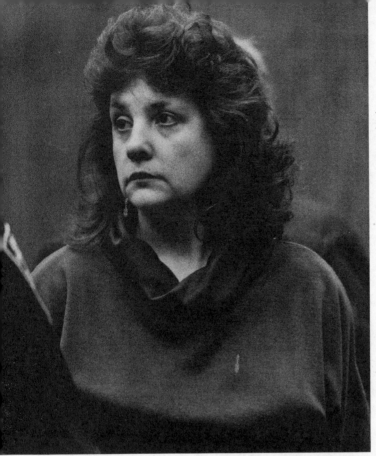

Troubled by a painful recurring back injury, near bankruptcy and newly divorced, Debbie Olivarez proved easy prey when her cousin, Jeffrey Lundgren, invited her to join his commune. He promised her a safe harbor. Instead, Olivarez ended up cooking the Averys their "last supper" and watching as the family members were led one by one from the farmhouse to the barn where they were executed. CURT CHANDLER/ CLEVELAND *PLAIN DEALER*

Keith Johnson told federal agents that five bodies were buried in a Kirtland barn after Jeffrey claimed Kathy Johnson as his second wife. Jealous and angry, Johnson wanted agents to find where Kathy was hiding and punish Jeffrey for the killings. CURT CHANDLER/CLEVELAND *PLAIN DEALER*

Dennis and Tonya Patrick were
college pals of Jeffrey's and early
followers, but he eventually turned
against both. Jeffrey threatened to
tie Dennis to a tree and shoot him
in the testicles. Later, he
announced that he was taking
Tonya as his new wife. After
several intimate weeks, Jeffrey
tired of Tonya and sent her back to
her husband. SCOTT SHAW/
CLEVELAND PLAIN DEALER

Bashful and homely, Sharon J.
Bluntschly had worked as a tour
guide at two other Mormon
historical sites before she moved to
Kirtland and met the Lundgrens.
Jeffrey and Alice decided
Bluntschly was too prudish so they
showed her soft-core pornographic
movies and told her that the Bible
required women to become
"carnal, sensual, and devilish."
CURT CHANDLER/CLEVELAND
PLAIN DEALER

"I cannot apologize for my assisting the prophet of God," follower Daniel D. Kraft, Jr., declared during a two-hour speech at his sentencing. Unrepentant, Kraft showed jurors drawings he had made of the Kirtland temple, which, he said, proved Jeffrey was "not a false prophet." A psychologist testified that Kraft had been "brainwashed" by Lundgren. CURT CHANDLER/CLEVELAND *PLAIN DEALER*

Gregory S. Winship ran a chain saw outside the barn during the Avery murders to cover up the sound of gunfire. He was later praised by Jeffrey Lundgren for his cleverness in squeezing and gently releasing the chain saw's trigger so that it mimicked the noise of a saw cutting through wood. CURT CHANDLER/CLEVELAND *PLAIN DEALER*

Richard Brand helped carry the Avery family members into the pit after they were bound and gagged so that Jeffrey Lundgren could kill them. Brand later became the state's chief witness but not without some trepidation. He told prosecutors that he was afraid Jeffrey Lundgren would simply laugh and stand up unharmed after an executioner threw the switch turning on Ohio's electric chair. CURT CHANDLER/CLEVELAND *PLAIN DEALER*

Another shot of Damon Lundgren; this one shows a scab on his lip that was the result of a jailhouse altercation. He was cold-cocked by another prisoner while walking out of his cell in the Lake County jail. CURT CHANDLER/CLEVELAND *PLAIN DEALER*

Follower Susie Luff was considered simple-minded by others in the Lundgren group, but when Alice Lundgren told her and three other women in private that God wanted them to perform a striptease for Jeffrey while he masturbated, Susie was the first to question why God would make such a peculiar request. CURT CHANDLER/CLEVELAND *PLAIN DEALER*

A former high school football player and navy veteran, Ronald B. Luff was Jeffrey's number-two man because he knew how to carry out orders. When Lundgren told Luff to come up with a way to lure the Averys out of the farmhouse and into the barn without arousing suspicion, Luff came through. He gave the last victim, six-year-old Karen Avery, a piggyback ride to her death on the pretense that they were going to see the horses in the barn. CURT CHANDLER/ CLEVELAND *PLAIN DEALER*

The Reverend Dale Luffman clashed with Jeffrey Lundgren during their first meeting and later succeeded in getting Lundgren booted out of the Reorganized Church of Jesus Christ of Latter Day Saints. Lundgren responded by plotting to kidnap Luffman and his family and behead them during an armed takeover of the Kirtland temple. The attack was nixed after Shar Olson tipped off the police. C. H. PETE COPELAND/ CLEVELAND *PLAIN DEALER*

A former navy pal of Lundgren's, Kevin Currie fled the communal farmhouse at Kirtland when he discovered that Jeffrey planned to kill him. Currie warned the FBI that Jeffrey was dangerous, but agents didn't believe him. CURT CHANDLER/ CLEVELAND *PLAIN DEALER*

Kirtland Police Officer Ron Andolsek seals off the Lundgren communal farmhouse on the morning that the grave was first uncovered. The house is to the left and the barn where the pit was located is in the upper right corner of the photograph.
LUCI WILLIAMS/CLEVELAND *PLAIN DEALER*

CHAPTER FORTY-FOUR

T HE day after FBI agents and the entire Kirtland police force descended on Jeffrey's farmhouse outside Kirtland, Patrolman Ron Andolsek telephoned a Cleveland-area psychologist for advice. The therapist confirmed Andolsek's fears. Now that Jeffrey had been confronted by police and had avoided arrest, he would probably claim that he was being protected by God, the therapist said. He might even tell his followers that he had become divine.

Andolsek drove by the farmhouse later that day and noticed that it seemed deserted. A short time later, a neighbor complained about rabbits, chickens, and other animals running loose at the farm. When Andolsek drove up to the house and peeked in the windows, he could tell that Jeffrey and his followers had fled.

"Damn!" Chief Yarborough said when he learned that Jeffrey was gone. "At least when he was at the farm we could watch him. Now we got to find him."

For four days, both men worked the telephones. They called Jeffrey's bank, the post office, the different places where group members worked. When that failed, they began calling various relatives of group members. No one knew where Jeffrey had gone. Shar and Kevin had both mentioned that Jeffrey was friendly with Tom Miller so Andolsek telephoned him. At first, Miller was reluctant to talk. He thought the RLDS was behind the probe. But when Andolsek explained that Jeffrey was suspected of conspiring to take over the temple, Miller cooperated. He recalled how Jeffrey had come to see him on April 17 and had acted weird. "He's gone off the deep end," Miller said. Like the others, however, Miller didn't have a clue where Jeffrey had gone.

On April 28, Andolsek got his first lead. He learned that Greg Winship had used his credit card to buy several items at a local store. Andolsek called Robert Alvord at the FBI office in Painesville and gave him the number of Winship's credit card. Alvord notified the bank that issued the card and officials there promised to send the FBI a list of Winship's recent purchases.

Meanwhile, Chief Yarborough urged Dale Luffman and RLDS Bishop Ken Fisher to leave town between May 1 and May 4. "We don't know when that idiot might come storming back with guns blazing." Both took Yarborough's advice.

There are few secrets in a small town, particularly after nearly two dozen FBI agents and police officers are seen swarming around a farm. By May 1, nearly everyone in Kirtland had heard about Jeffrey's plan to take over the temple on his birthday. People figured there was a fifty-fifty chance that he might show up.

Just before 9:00 P.M. on May 1, Yarborough and Andolsek drove to the same posts near the temple that they had manned one year earlier. But this time, they were not alone. Curious townsfolk cruised past the temple all night long looking for the chief. A few waved. Yarborough felt as if he was part of a circus sideshow.

On May 2, Andolsek got a call from the FBI. Special Agent Alvord said that Greg Winship had used his credit card on April 18 to rent a twenty-four-foot-long U-Haul truck. Greg had picked up the vehicle within hours after the FBI and police had finished questioning Jeffrey and left the farm. Andolsek telephoned the local U-Haul dealership, which had rented Greg the truck, and learned that Greg had dropped off the truck six days later at a U-Haul dealership in Falls Church, Virginia, a suburb of Washington, D.C. When Andolsek called the manager there, he was told that Greg had driven the truck a total of 603 miles and had returned it "full of red mud."

Andolsek got out a map of the eastern United States and drew a red line from Kirtland to Falls Church. He then began writing down the names of all the state and national parks along both sides of the line within a six-hundred-mile radius of Kirtland. After compiling the list, he telephoned the U.S. Park Service and asked if there were any parks in particular where red dirt was common. Most parks on his list, he was told, had spots where red soil could be found. Discouraged, Andolsek decided to try a different approach. After obtaining Chief Yarborough's permission, Andolsek asked the federal park service to send a Teletype to all of its rangers. He also sent the Teletype to state park officials and local sheriff's departments in a five-state area. The message described Jeffrey and his group.

> Lundgren contends to be a prophet and . . . advocates the use of deadly force . . . One member told FBI/Police that they were going to leave for the "wilderness" to find the "sword of Laban" which will be used to decapitate people. . . .

The Teletype contained the telephone number for the Kirtland Police Department and asked rangers to call immediately if they had any useful information. That night, Andolsek and Yarborough returned to their temple posts, but neither felt an attack by Jeffrey was likely.

"I figured Jeffrey had gone off somewhere trying to find the Sword of Laban," Yarborough said. "At first, I was relieved and then I thought, 'Oh, Lord, May third comes around every year.' Am I going to be sitting in the church parking lot every year waiting for that asshole?"

When May 3 passed without incident, Yarborough found that he was being criticized by some townspeople and had become the butt of several jokes. A few fundamentalists, who had attended Jeffrey's classes, claimed that Dale Luffman and the RLDS hierarchy had used Yarborough to unfairly persecute Jeffrey and drive him from town. Others claimed the chief had been taken in and had overacted to the insane ravings of a frustrated blowhard. Even Kirtland's mayor began to openly wonder if Yarborough hadn't become obsessed with Jeffrey, making him into a much bigger threat than he really was. Yarborough began to feel pangs of self-doubt. After all, there was still no proof that Jeffrey had broken the law. "Maybe I was wrong to spend so much time worrying about him since he and his group were gone—that's what I began to wonder."

Weeks passed without any word about Jeffrey's whereabouts. No one whom Andolsek had notified had seen the group. And then on June 5, Yarborough and Andolsek got lucky.

West Virginia Game Warden Harold "Rocky" Spencer had been on a routine patrol in Yellow Creek Hollow when he decided to check a remote area for turkey hunters. Turkey season had just opened and Spencer wanted to make certain that anyone hunting in the hollow had bought a valid license. Spencer had been going through the woods when he spotted Jeffrey's camp. As soon as he saw an armed guard standing watch, he became suspicious and ducked behind some bushes. The game warden crept close enough to copy down the license numbers on the cars parked in the camp. He then carefully retreated and contacted Sheriff Hank Thompson. At age twenty-nine, Thompson was serving his second year as sheriff of Tucker County, a 465-square-mile area that he patrolled with the help of only two deputies. A big man with boyish good looks, Thompson had grown up in Davis and had spent eleven years as a deputy before running for office. He was so well known in the county that he really hadn't needed to put his last name on his campaign posters. All it took was "Vote for Hank."

Thompson had seen a copy of the Teletype that Andolsek had sent to sheriff's offices and he rummaged through the pile of paper on his desk and retrieved it. He compared the license numbers that Spencer had given him with the ones on the flyer, and when they matched, he dialed Yarborough's number.

"So Jeffrey's in West Virginia," Yarborough said. "Well, I'm glad you have him and not me." The two lawmen spoke for nearly an hour. "My first concern," Thompson later said, "was keeping a lid on who they were. Ninety percent of the people in my county are coal miners and if they found out some religious cult was camping up there, the first thing they'd do is grab their guns and move them out. I'd have a massacre on my hands."

Since Jeffrey hadn't been accused of committing any crimes, there wasn't much Thompson could do except watch the group and keep Yarborough posted. He volunteered to do that. The next day, Yarborough called again. Yarborough called again the following day. The next day, Yarborough called again. Thompson, who had other problems to solve, began to wonder if Yarborough was investigating anyone besides Jeffrey Lundgren.

Thompson assured Yarborough that he was keeping an eye on Jeffrey, but the sheriff didn't feel that it made sense for him to go into the heavily armed camp and begin questioning group members without some legitimate reason. Jeffrey had started driving into Davis three or four times a week to buy kerosene for the camp's electric generator, and even though he was guarded in his comments, he seemed friendly enough when the sheriff spoke to him.

By the end of July, Yarborough was insisting that Thompson visit Jeffrey's camp. Yarborough had started receiving telephone calls from the worried relatives of various group members and he wanted to know for certain who was living in the camp. Even Alice's mother, Donna Keehler, had called and demanded to know where Jeffrey had gone.

In early August, Thompson decided to visit the camp on the pretense that school would be starting soon and West Virginia required all children to be enrolled. He decided, however, that before he hiked into the camp, he was going to buzz over it in a state-owned helicopter. That way he could see how Jeffrey and his band were going to react before landing. If the group started shooting, then Thompson could retreat and call in reinforcements.

Thompson telephoned Yarborough and explained his plan. The next day, Yarborough called Thompson. The chief had discovered that before Jeffrey left Kirtland, he had bought a .50-caliber rifle capable of shooting down a helicopter.

"I just wanted to warn you," said Yarborough.

"Oh, Christ," Thompson replied sarcastically. "That's just what I wanted to hear."

CHAPTER FORTY-FIVE

By the end of July, the group had been in the wilderness for nearly four months and everyone was becoming depressed. No matter what they did, Jeffrey claimed that there was still too much sin for his followers to go before God. Jeffrey was still meeting God on a regular basis. He would ride the ATV off to a nearby mountain and return several hours later with a new revelation or commandment. But he always told the others that they would be destroyed by fire if he took them along.

The biggest problem, Jeffrey said, was the women. They were "filled with pride." During the first week of August, all of them were hustled into the Lundgren tent for a private meeting with Alice. They were told that Jeffrey had decided that they had to be literally "stripped" of their pride. Kathy Johnson, Debbie Olivarez, Sharon Bluntschly, and Susie Luff were each going to have to humble themselves by performing a striptease in front of the "God of the whole earth." Because Tonya was Jeffrey's second wife, she did not have to perform. Neither would Alice.

Alice warned the women not to tell their husbands about the dances. No one was to know but them and Jeffrey. Alice would tell them when they were to come into his tent and perform.

Susie Luff was upset after the meeting. She was devoted to Ron and didn't understand how taking her clothes off in front of Jeffrey was going to free her from sin. Within an hour, she had told Ron everything that Alice had said.

Of all the men in the group, Ron was the strongest. He was also not afraid of Jeffrey. Ron found Jeffrey lifting weights and demanded to know what Alice was talking about. Jeffrey assured him that Susie had misunderstood Alice's instructions. He had no intention of asking the women to perform a strip show for him. He promised to explain everything that night at scripture class.

When the group got together later that evening, Jeffrey put a completely different spin on the story. He said God was disappointed with the group, so much so that He had even considered destroying everyone except for Jeffrey and starting over. But Jeffrey had come up with a way to appease God.

With his scriptures firmly in hand, Jeffrey explained that in Moses' day, a wife could "intercede" on her husband's behalf whenever he fell into disfavor with his lord and master. "The wife could beg the lord to spare her husband and family." That was still true today, Jeffrey said, and that was what God wanted the women in the camp to do. They were to "intercede" on their families' behalf with God's representative on earth—Jeffrey.

Jeffrey then moved on to the next part of his explanation. He told everyone to read verse 21 in chapter 28 of Isaiah, which said that the "Lord" would perform a "strange act." Jeffrey explained that he was the "Lord" mentioned in this verse and that God had ordered him to perform this "strange act."

Once again, Jeffrey referred everyone to the scriptures, this time chapter 32 of Isaiah, verse 11. It read:

> Tremble, ye women that are at ease; be troubled, ye careless ones; strip you, and make you bare, and gird sackcloth upon your loins.

Jeffrey said that this verse defined the "strange act." Each woman in the group was to come into Jeffrey's tent and strip. They were to dance in front of him completely naked for one hour. That was scriptural, Jeffrey said, because the word for "tremble" in verse 11 also meant "to dance" in ancient Hebrew, and the verse clearly stated that the women were to strip and be bare when they danced.

While the women were dancing, they would become humble

and their sins would be transferred onto Jeffrey because he was the "God of the whole earth."

"Christ took on the world's sin when he shed his blood for us on the cross," Jeffrey said. "I will do the same thing for you. I will take on your sins."

Jeffrey had already told everyone that he was immortal. "Obviously," he said, "I can't be crucified or shed my blood, but God has shown me a way that I can shed my blood symbolically and wash away your sins.

"In a rape case," Jeffrey continued, "a man's semen can be used to identify him, just as his blood type can be used to positively identify him."

In God's eyes, Jeffrey proclaimed, "blood and semen are the same."

While each woman was dancing naked in front of him, Jeffrey would masturbate and ejaculate his semen into each woman's panties, he said. "This will be the same as when Christ shed his blood."

After he had "soiled" each woman's panties with semen, he would hand them back and she would be required to wear them the rest of the day. This would fulfill verse 11, which said that the women were to "gird" their "loins" in "sackcloth."

Jeffrey said that he would be "loaded down" with the sins of the group after the dances. He would ride the ATV up to the mountaintop, where he would meet God and be purified by His presence. The group's sins would then be wiped clean.

There was only one catch, Jeffrey announced. If he did not ejaculate during a dance, then that woman's sins could not be cleansed and she and her family would have to be destroyed.

It took Jeffrey nearly two hours to explain his scheme. When he finished, no one objected. "Once everyone understood the scriptural basis for it," Jeffrey later recalled, "then no one had any trouble with it because they could see that it was not a sexual act at all and not some weird fantasy of Jeffrey's. Instead, it was a very loving and a highly spiritual undertaking."

Even so, Ron and Keith approached Jeffrey after class and told him that they were worried about sending their wives alone into his tent to strip while he masturbated. While neither wanted to come out and say it, Jeffrey knew why they were upset. They were afraid that Jeffrey was going to take their wives away from them just as he had taken Tonya away from Dennis. Jeffrey assured Ron and Keith that the scriptures said a man could have only two wives, no more.

To further calm their fears, Jeffrey announced that Alice would be beside him during the entire ritual and that he would keep a sheet in front of him so that the women wouldn't see his penis while he masturbated. Alice, he said, would be in charge of preparing the women. "I wanted them to know that this was all aboveboard," Jeffrey later explained, "so I put Alice in charge and they accepted that."

Alice was certain that Jeffrey had concocted the entire "intercession" scheme that afternoon after he had been questioned by Ron about having all of the women perform strip teases. "He was using the scriptures to get what he wanted," Alice said, "which was to see all of the women's vaginas so he could find the one in his dream."

Later, when she was asked why she hadn't debunked Jeffrey, Alice claimed that she was scared. "Jeff made it perfectly clear to me that if this was not successful . . . children were going to die," she testified.

Others in the group would recall Alice's demeanor somewhat differently. "Alice said that Jeff was afraid that we were going to mock him," Sharon later testified, "that we were going to make light of it, and Alice said, 'You're not going to do that to him.' She said, 'If I have to, I'll beat you to make you do this and I don't care if it takes hours and hours, you're going to get through it.'"

Debbie described Alice as an enthusiastic partner when Jeffrey first explained intercession. She quoted Alice as saying that women were "created with three holes in which they could be pierced by men—orally, vaginally, and anally." The women were to show Jeffrey each of these areas during their dance. Alice also suggested songs that were Jeffrey's favorites for the women to play while dancing.

On August 14, Tonya took all of the children out of camp so they would not know what was going on. Susie reported to Jeffrey's tent at 9:00 A.M. As instructed, Ron stayed in his own tent, reading scriptures and praying. Alice, who was wearing the sexy pink pajamas that Jeffrey had bought her, greeted Susie at the entrance and hugged her. She slipped Susie's hour-long tape into the stereo player, flipped it on, and then sat down beside Jeffrey. He was perched on the bed and was completely naked but was covered from the waist down by a sheet. Jeffrey nodded and Susie began to slowly undress. Alice had told the women that they were supposed to be cheerful and seductive. The striptease was supposed to be pleasing to Jeffrey and their panties were supposed to be the last piece of clothing to be removed. The women were also to be nude by the time the first song on their tape finished.

After Susie had removed her clothing, she handed Jeffrey her panties. He quickly wrapped them around his penis and began to masturbate while Susie went through the various moves that Alice had told her were required. Alice would later claim that each woman was also told to masturbate while she danced. This was a new twist that Jeffrey had added that morning.

"The night before the dances, when we were having sex, Jeffrey told me that he wanted to fantasize, and he asked me to tell him what Susie was going to do when she danced in front of him the next day," Alice said. "I said Susie was going to masturbate, and then the next day, he made me tell each woman when they came in that they were going to have to 'come unto the Lord' literally."

After Susie had danced for about forty-five minutes, Jeffrey ejaculated into her panties. He waited for several minutes and then slipped on his purple sweatpants and stood up.

"Are you stripped of pride, my daughter?" he asked.

As instructed, Susie replied: "Behold!" She then fell on the tent floor, facedown at Jeffrey's feet.

"Arise and come forth," Jeffrey declared.

Still naked, Susie stood and walked to Jeffrey, who was bare-chested. He opened his arms and while he embraced her, Alice darted behind Susie and held up a statement for Jeffrey to read. Alice had written it.

"Unto thee, I have shed my blood for thee," Jeffrey read. "I have bought you with a price. I have washed thee and sanctified thee. This day, thou has preserved thyself, and thy seed through my blood forever."

Susie had been told by Alice to reply by saying: "Yea, Lord, I know that thou speakest the truth."

Jeffrey then released Susie and handed her the panties. "Susie was told that she could get dressed," Alice recalled. "All of the women were to dress slowly in front of Jeff because you neither rushed into the presence of the Lord or rushed out of His presence." Before Susie left, Alice gave her a short statement that was nearly identical to the ones that she and Jeffrey had exchanged. Susie was told to go directly to her tent and read the first statement to Ron. He was then to come to the Lundgren tent, dressed in full military gear, and swear his allegiance to Jeffrey, which he did.

After Susie's dance, the adults had lunch. Later that afternoon, it was Sharon's turn. "When Sharon was completely undressed," Alice said later, "Jeffrey whispered to me: 'Richard's got nothing to complain about.' There was one song on the tape, I think it's called 'Only for You,' and Sharon sat down naked on the floor and spread her legs open wide and held her breasts in her hands and the singer was saying, 'Only for you, only for you,' and Sharon leaned back and began to masturbate but Jeffrey didn't find her stimulating so he signaled me to go under the sheet. I got under the cover and began licking and kissing him on the testicles while he masturbated."

Sharon later testified that she had watched Alice go under the sheet and that Jeffrey had ultimately ejaculated. After going through the same ritual that he had with Susie, Jeffrey sent Sharon back to her tent and Richard appeared in full military gear and swore his allegiance to Jeffrey.

Kathy danced the next morning at ten o'clock. From the moment that she entered the tent, Alice was jealous. Kathy rarely wore dresses, but had one on that morning. She had fixed her long brown hair so that it was on top of her head. As she danced, she undid her hair, letting it fall to her shoulders. Alice quietly started to smolder.

"This feeling washed over me as I watched Kathy dance," Alice later claimed, "and I looked at Jeff and he was totally enthralled by her dancing and when she got to the point where she was completely naked, she turned her back toward us and bent over at the waist and I heard Jeff say in the faintest whisper, 'There it is.' I knew he was talking about the vagina in his dream—the one that God had ordered him to find—and I said to myself, 'Take a good look, Alice, because this is your competition.'

"When it came time for him to masturbate," Alice continued, "Jeff obtained it rapidly and when he was all done, and she had fallen on her face on the tent floor, he told her to arise and come forth, and Kathy looked up from the floor and said, 'My Lord, may I kiss your feet?,' and he said, 'Yes,' and she kissed his feet and he took her in his arms and read her the message, and then she got dressed—but she stayed in the tent like they were old college buddies, just chatting away."

That day at lunch everyone in camp knew something had happened during Kathy's dance to irritate Alice. "Alice was pissed and I began to worry," recalled Debbie, "not about Jeffrey, but about what Alice would do if Jeffrey really liked my dance. I was more afraid of her than him at that point."

Debbie's turn to dance came that afternoon. She had dressed

in several layers of clothes and each was a completely different outfit, including one with suspenders. Even Alice later admitted that Debbie's dance was "really cute" but she remained irked after Debbie's performance. "I was still angry about Kathy," Alice recalled, "because I knew that Jeffrey was going to come up with some reason to bed her."

Jeffrey stayed in his tent for two days after the dances. Alice told everyone that he was physically ill because of the sins that he had taken on from the group. Only on the third day was he strong enough to come out of his tent and ride the ATV to the nearby mountain where he met God. When he returned to camp later that day, Jeffrey was chipper and in perfect health. God had cleansed all of the sins.

Shortly after he returned to camp, Jeffrey approached Keith in private. "He told me that Dennis had to die," Keith recalled. "I asked how much time Dennis had, and Jeffrey said, 'Not long.'" Jeffrey told Keith that Dennis was doomed because he didn't have anyone to dance on his behalf; therefore, he was still filled with sin. Tonya couldn't "intercede" for Dennis because she was now Jeffrey's wife. All of the other men in the group had been saved, he explained. Susie Luff had danced for Ron. Sharon had danced for Richard. Debbie had danced to save Greg. Kathy had danced on behalf of Keith. Jeffrey had told the group that his son, Damon, and Danny Kraft, Jr., were okay because Alice was their mother. [Although Danny was not part of the Lundgren family, he had never been married; therefore Alice was his true 'mother,' Jeffrey said.] That left Dennis Patrick.

Months later Keith would look back on his conversation with Jeffrey and realize that he was being set up, but at the time, he didn't sense what Jeffrey was pulling into play.

As soon as Jeffrey left him, Keith hurried to his tent and told Kathy that Dennis was going to be killed. "I didn't want Dennis to be destroyed," Kathy said later, so she told Keith that she was willing to dance naked again on Dennis's behalf if that would save him.

Keith and Kathy went to see Jeffrey. They found him exercising in the weight-lifting area. Alice was sitting next to Jeffrey reading scriptures out loud as he lifted weights.

"Kathy wants to know if she can intercede for Dennis," Keith said.

Jeffrey bolted upright from the weight bench. He appeared

angry. Dennis's fate was none of Keith's business, he said. "You are peradventuring!"

Alice was just as outraged. "Why are you asking questions about Dennis?" she demanded. "Don't you know that you can't just throw out a question like that? You know Jeffrey will have to act on it. He'll have to do something."

The penalty for trying to second-guess God was death, Jeffrey declared. Keith was going to have to be "pierced" either with a sword or bullet. Keith was dumbfounded. He immediately began apologizing.

"There is an alternative," said Jeffrey. Kathy could intervene on Keith's behalf once again. But this time, dancing naked in front of Jeffrey wasn't going to be enough. "Someone must be pierced. God demands it," Jeffrey said. Rather than shooting Keith, Jeffrey could use his penis to pierce Kathy.

"Alice was livid," Kathy said later. "She said, 'Didn't you realize what you were setting yourself up for?,' and I said, 'Well, no, I thought if anything it would be another dance experience.'"

"Well, now that you understand what you must do," Alice asked Kathy, "how do you feel?"

"Alice, if it saves a man's life, then I'll do it. I don't hold this flesh that precious," Kathy replied.

Alice stormed off to her tent. But Jeffrey stayed at the weight bench. He would give Keith one week to consider his options.

CHAPTER FORTY-SIX

W ORD spread quickly through camp about Jeffrey's ultimatum, and on August 25, Keith told Jeffrey that Kathy had agreed to have sexual intercourse with him in order to save Keith and Dennis. Jeffrey hurried over to talk to Kathy. "He wanted me to know that he wasn't going to hurt me," she said. "Jeff said that if I had any fears, or any questions, I should ask. . . . I told him that to be quite frank, my concerns were with Alice and Keith, I wasn't afraid of Jeffrey at all."

There weren't many things that Kathy Johnson was afraid of. At age thirty-six, Kathy had given birth to four sons, raised prize-winning goats, horses, and cattle, run a thirty-acre farm by herself, sold insurance, and done hard physical labor nearly every day of her life. Kathy was considered a "tomboy"—even as an adult. In a dress and nylons, she looked awkward. But in blue jeans, cowboy boots, and a wool shirt, Kathy was radiant. Of all the women in the group, she was the one most suited to the rugged outdoor life. She was strong, smart, and fiercely stubborn. She was also, the group discovered, extremely gullible. At times, Kathy herself would even joke about how she was a naïve "Iowa farm girl."

The oldest of five children, Kathy had grown up near Wood-bine, a town of 1,400 just north of Council Bluffs. When she was eleven, her parents decided to convert their four-hundred-acre farm into a dude ranch. Each summer, as many as seventy children would fill the ranch's bunkhouses. They came to learn how to ride horseback and it was Kathy's job to teach them. By the time she was in high school, she was an expert rider, experienced rodeo racer, and shrewd horse trader. She was an honor-roll student and an outstanding distance runner on the school track team. When she graduated in 1971, Kathy held school records in three track events.

Kathy had met Keith at Central Missouri State University where she planned to study nursing. She had enrolled at CMSU because her parents were both active RLDS members and they wanted her to attend a school near the center spot. Keith was a senior, she was a freshman, and when they were introduced at the RLDS student union, Kathy was instantly smitten.

Keith was handsome, with jet-black hair and engaging eyes. He was confident, funny, clever. They went out a few times and Kathy was soon deeply in love, but Keith decided to marry someone else. Heartbroken, Kathy left college after her freshman year, returned home, and eventually wed a boy who had worked for her parents at the dude ranch. Three years later, Kathy got a divorce, and Keith, who had got a divorce himself by then, began writing her. They were married on May 7, 1977.

It was Keith who had first introduced Kathy to Jeffrey and Alice. When they met, Kathy felt uncomfortable. She didn't like Jeffrey's sexual jokes and Alice seemed mousy. The newlyweds didn't really see much of the Lundgrens. The Johnsons were too busy. Kathy and Keith had bought a thirty-acre farm not far from Warrensburg. Keith worked as a machinist during the day. Kathy sold insurance and ran the farm. Their social life revolved around the church. After she got pregnant, Kathy quit the insurance business. She had three more sons in quick succession. When the first reached school age, Kathy founded Zion's Hope Country School. Later, she taught her boys at home rather than expose them to public schools. "Our goal was to seek the Lord," she recalled. "It was the center of everything that we did."

Keith worked hard in the church and moved up its ranks. At first glance, the Johnsons seemed to have everything—a good income, a nice home, a loving family, and status in their church and community.

But in 1983, Keith was laid off from his job and was unemployed for eighteen months. He and Kathy were forced to sell their farm and move into a house owned by Keith's relatives. They went into debt and their financial stress took a toll on their personal relationship, they both later said. Still, they stuck it out. It was during this same time that the RLDS decided to ordain women. At the RLDS worldwide conference in 1984 and later in 1986, Keith introduced numerous ill-fated motions aimed at preventing women from serving as priests. He soon found his fundamentalist viewpoint unwelcome among the church hierarchy.

Like most others in Jeffrey's group, Keith and Kathy had sought out Jeffrey and his teachings as an alternative to the liberalization of their church. It didn't take much prodding to convince both of them that the RLDS was being led by a fallen prophet. Their decision to join Jeffrey's group was supposed to be a rebirth for the Johnsons. They saw it as a chance to start over.

On the day that Kathy reported to Jeffrey's tent to be "pierced," Alice went for a walk away from camp. Keith read his scriptures. "I told Kathy to do whatever she had to do to keep us from being killed," Keith said later. Kathy found Jeffrey eagerly waiting in his tent.

"All it was supposed to be was intercession," Kathy said later, "but what actually transpired was something of a whole lot bigger magnitude. We both sensed that this was an incredible experience."

During intercourse, Jeffrey announced that he loved her.

Afterward, he told Kathy that he had always felt a "tenderness" toward her. He wasn't certain why, but he had felt it from the time that they first met. He was going to check the scriptures to see why she was different from other women.

Kathy had no way of knowing that Jeffrey was using exactly the same lines on her that he had used on Tonya four months earlier.

"I wasn't sure what was happening," Kathy recalled. The "God of the whole earth" had told her that she was special and she believed him. She had become convinced that Jeffrey was a prophet.

That night, Alice attempted to reclaim her turf. Greg, Sharon, and Debbie all had good voices and Alice asked them to sing several love songs to Jeffrey. "They were supposed to be from Alice to Jeffrey," Kathy recalled, "but I was sitting right across the picnic table from Jeff and he was staring at me and I knew he was thinking of me."

Worse, so did Alice.

The next morning, Jeffrey stopped by Kathy's tent while Keith was out hunting.

"I have a problem," he said.

"Oh," Kathy replied.

"You ruined me. I don't want anyone else sexually but you. All I can see and feel is you."

Kathy later recalled her feelings that morning. "Maybe I never lost the Iowa farm girl in me," she said, "but I was in love. I was totally in love with this man."

"How do we deal with all this?" Kathy asked Jeffrey.

"I'll look in the scriptures," he said. "I'll find a way."

That night, Alice once again tried to please Jeffrey. This time, she told the group that she was going to dance for him. "She had a dress on and heels and hose and she climbed up on one of the picnic tables and began to dance seductively," Debbie remembered. "She didn't strip and she didn't have any rhythm and Jeffrey ended up just getting really disgusted and pissed off because he didn't want his wife doing that in front of the other men. He said, 'What the hell are you doing this for?,' and that was the beginning of a world war because Alice had this big erotic thing planned and she had looked totally ridiculous."

Everyone in camp could hear Alice screaming that night at Jeffrey. The next morning, Alice stayed in her tent until noon and then she suddenly emerged and raced over to where the women were doing laundry.

"I hope all of you are happy," she said sarcastically. "Because of you and your stupid intercession, I haven't had a good fuck all week."

She then glared at Kathy and marched back into her tent.

Jeffrey had decided even before the intercession dances that he no longer wanted Tonya Patrick as his wife, and once he decided to seduce Kathy, he moved quickly to get rid of Tonya.

One morning shortly after the dances he abruptly announced that he was sending her back to Dennis. "He didn't want a sinful woman like me in his tent, he said." Jeffrey told Dennis that he was no longer in danger of being destroyed because he had reformed and because of Kathy's intercession. Tonya and Molly were moving back into his tent.

"Is she coming back as my wife?" Dennis asked, rather startled.

"Yes," Jeffrey said. "She is your wife, not mine."

That night at class, Jeffrey told the group that he had searched the scriptures and learned that Tonya was not really flesh of his flesh. Rather, she had been his "captive wife." Under the law of Moses, Jeffrey explained, a lord was allowed to take as many wives from his enemy as he wished. Tonya had been "captured" from Dennis in

May because Dennis had been sinful. But now that Dennis had re-formed, he was no longer an enemy and Tonya was being "restored" to him. Tonya felt foolish. "I thought to myself, 'What am I, the wife-of-the-month?'" But she didn't question Jeffrey and neither did anyone else. "All of us were playing roles by that point," Tonya later explained. "Jeffrey had become so crazy that we all just simply acted like we were supposed to. You couldn't tell who really believed in him and who was afraid."

Tonya had decided that Jeffrey was a "sham," but when she re-ported to Dennis's tent, she didn't share her feelings with him. She was afraid that he would report her to Jeffrey. Over time, the group had become so paranoid that they were all suspicious of the others.

Tonya's sudden return worried the other men. Most realized that Jeffrey could do the same thing to them that he had done to Dennis—simply accuse them of being sinful and claim their spouse as a "captive wife."

"After the dances, everything got real strange, real fast," Debbie recalled.

Jeffrey was beginning to make bolder and bolder statements about his divinity and powers and he seemed fixated on sex. One night after a scripture class, Jeffrey told Greg that they needed to talk in private. After swearing Greg to secrecy, Jeffrey explained that he had been studying First Samuel, chapter 18, which described how King Saul's son, Jonathan, had loved David. Jeffrey told Greg that when the chapter was divided by the pattern, the verses revealed that David and Jonathan were homosexual lovers. Although he wasn't certain, Jeffrey said the verses seemed to suggest that he and Greg were destined to become homosexual lovers as well.

Greg was so alarmed that he told Debbie that same night what Jeffrey had said. "Greg was not interested in Jeffrey at all," she re-called, "and he was worried about what Jeffrey might demand. It was like no one was safe from Jeffrey's sexual fantasies."

Debbie noticed that Jeffrey was making more pointed sexual re-marks around her too. She was worried that she was next on his "conquest list." She wasn't alone.

Ron began to pick up hints that Jeffrey was on the prowl. It seemed to him that Jeffrey was picking on Susie, criticizing her in an attempt to drive a wedge between them in a thinly veiled attempt to free Susie for his advances.

Richard also began to wonder about Jeffrey's sexual obsessions. Before the group left the farm in Kirtland, Richard had found hidden in the barn a dildo and a magazine that contained explicit photographs of homosexual acts. He was certain that both belonged to Jeffrey.

After the intercession dances, Jeffrey began talking about sex more openly in his scriptural classes at night. During one such session, Jeffrey announced that the Old Testament prophet Isaiah was a "cross dresser" who frequently wore women's clothing. Another night, Jeffrey claimed that the pattern had revealed to him that Jesus Christ had engaged in sex with various women and had even masturbated as a boy. But the strangest sexual interpretation came when Jeffrey interpreted verse 16 in Isaiah, chapter 3, which described the haughty "daughters of Zion." Jeffrey said that Isaiah had wanted to humble the "daughters of Zion" because they were filled with pride. Verses 17 through 24, Jeffrey said, told how Isaiah had examined the women's "secret parts" and made them "stink" instead of smelling "sweet." Because Jeffrey didn't go into detail, no one in the group was certain what he had meant, but Alice understood. Jeffrey was talking about smearing feces on women.

About ten days after Jeffrey and Kathy engaged in sex, Jeffrey announced that the two of them needed to go on a short trip together. During the summer, Jeffrey had sold the group's horse trailer to raise money for supplies. He had moved the horses from the camp, where they were having trouble living in the open, to a stable about thirty miles away. The stable owner was supposed to sell the animals, but instead he had been renting them to tourists for rides. Jeffrey had decided to retrieve the horses, and he said that Kathy was the only member of the group who was in good enough physical shape and smart enough about horses to help him walk the animals back to camp.

They began their trek through the mountains on September 5. Both later claimed that they got lost and had no choice but to spend the night together in the woods. It was during that night that Jeffrey told Kathy what he had found out about them in the scriptures. Just as he had done with Tonya, Jeffrey told her that she was his Bathsheba and that she was his missing "second rib."

"Does that mean that I am not flesh of Keith's flesh?" Kathy asked innocently.

"Yes, you are flesh of my flesh," he replied. "God made you from me exclusively for me."

"I didn't expect him to say that," Kathy later recalled.

Jeffrey told Kathy that he wanted her to move into his tent, but she said she needed time to think about it.

When Jeffrey and Kathy didn't return to camp that night, Alice became suspicious. The next morning, she sent Greg and Richard to look for them. They found Jeffrey and Kathy a few miles from camp. Jeffrey said one of the horses had become lame, but Greg and Richard didn't see anything wrong with it. Alice was furious.

The next day, Kathy signaled Jeffrey from the woods. She was willing to leave her husband and four children to become his wife, she said. "It really didn't make any sense for me to deny the truth," she later explained. "If I was flesh of Jeff's flesh, then I wasn't doing Keith any favors by living with him in sin."

Now that Kathy had made her commitment, she wanted to know when Jeffrey intended to tell Keith and Alice. Jeffrey wasn't certain, but he assured Kathy that he would find a way.

On September 15, Sheriff Hank Thompson swooped over the camp in a helicopter. Everyone ducked for cover. Thompson buzzed the camp again, but didn't land. He was checking to see how the group would react. As soon as the helicopter was gone, Jeffrey rushed over to Alice. Jeffrey announced that it was getting too dangerous for Alice and the children to stay in the camp. The police might arrive any minute and arrest everyone for the murder of the Averys. The group was also running low on cash and the weather was becoming frigid. Obviously, Jeffrey and his band were not going to be able to spend the winter camping in the hollow. Jeffrey told Alice that he wanted her to leave that very day for her mother's house in Macks Creek. He would join her later and they would find somewhere new for the group to live. He told her to take Jason, Kristen, and Caleb with her. Jeffrey also wanted Susie Luff and her two children to go. Alice agreed.

Jeffrey helped Alice pack the truck and then suggested that she take a nap so she wouldn't be tired when she made the thirteen-hour drive. After Alice retired into the tent, Jeffrey wandered over to Kathy's tent. It had been more than a week since she had agreed to be his wife and Kathy was irritated that Jeffrey hadn't told the group that she was flesh of the "God of the whole earth." Jeffrey knew that he'd be rid of Alice by nightfall, but he figured that he could slip into town with Kathy and be back before Alice woke up.

A few hours later, when Alice came out of her tent, she asked Ron where Jeffrey had gone. Ron said Jeffrey was in town cashing a check and making some telephone calls.

"Don't you think two and a half hours is a long time to make phone calls?" Alice asked. "Did anyone go with him?"

Ron tried to dodge the question, but Alice pressed him. "Kathy

Johnson went with him," Ron finally said. Alice turned around and stomped into her tent.

"I knew that Jeffrey had taken her into town to some motel so he could fuck her," she said later.

A few minutes later, Alice heard the ATV coming through the woods. Jeffrey slowed down and Kathy jumped off the back of the vehicle as soon as they got near the camp. Kathy ducked into her tent and Jeffrey continued into the compound. As soon as he stepped off the ATV, Alice attacked. She slapped Jeffrey across the face.

"You son of a bitch!" she screamed.

All the adults, except Kathy, watched as Alice slapped Jeffrey again and again.

"Here is your almighty God," she yelled. "You can have him!"

With that, Alice marched into her tent. Jeffrey ran after her. "Don't say anything to me, Jeffrey!" Alice hollered. "You've gone too far this time! You're a lying son of a bitch." Within seconds, Jeffrey came backing out of the tent. Alice was hitting him again.

"I came unglued," Alice later recalled. "I totally lost it. I hit him. I slapped him. I kicked him. I pulled his hair. I did everything I could do to hurt him."

When she finally stopped and returned to her tent, Jeffrey looked at the group. He was beaming. "It was a big thing to Jeffrey," Dennis said, "because he wanted everyone to see that she had attacked him and he had taken all of her blows without fighting back or hitting her."

Several minutes later, Alice emerged from the tent and yelled to her children that it was time to leave. They scrambled into the truck and Susie hustled her son and daughter into the vehicle too. Jeffrey walked up to the window. Alice was still fuming.

"When you move that whore into the tent tonight, have her bring her own pillow," Alice said. "I'm taking mine."

Jeffrey had tears in his eyes.

"You're wrong about Kathy and me," she later remembered Jeffrey telling her. "Alice, you're the only woman I will ever love."

As soon as Alice was gone, Jeffrey hurried over to talk to Kathy. He intended to announce that night in scripture class, he said, that she was his second wife.

CHAPTER FORTY-SEVEN

W HEN the operator asked if Donna Keehler would accept a collect telephone call from Jeffrey Lundgren, she immediately shouted, "Yes!" As soon as they were connected, Donna quizzed her son-in-law. "Where are you?"

"I'm not at liberty to say," he replied.

"What's happening?"

"I'm not at liberty to say," he repeated.

Donna tried several more questions and each was greeted by the same response. Finally she gave up. Jeffrey told her that Alice and the children were on their way to Macks Creek. They were bringing a friend and her two children with them. No problem, Donna said. She'd make room. Alice drove straight through. Donna was shocked when she saw her. "The Alice who came home to see me wasn't my Alice," Donna later said. "She was like a different person."

Alice had gotten fat—nearly one hundred pounds heavier than when her mother had last seen her one year earlier. Her face was marred by three open sores that she constantly picked. And she was foul-mouthed. Alice had also become a faithful beer drinker.

Donna had heard about the temple-takeover plot from Chief Yarborough whom she had telephoned earlier that summer. She'd also talked to Dennis Patrick's parents, who, in turn, had spoken with Dale Luffman in Kirtland. Donna began grilling her daughter.

"What in the world is going on?" she demanded. Alice lied to her about everything.

The next morning after Donna went to work, the telephone rang and Alice answered. It was Dennis Patrick's mother. She mistakenly assumed that she had reached Donna and she began talking. Alice played along. The sheriff in West Virginia had flown over Jeffrey's camp and was going to go in and question the group, Mrs. Patrick explained. She promised to call again when she had more details. After Alice replaced the telephone receiver, she began searching her mother's cupboards. Neither Ralph nor Donna was a drinker, but Alice's sister, Terri, had left several bottles of liquor behind when she and her husband moved to Saudi Arabia. Alice found some wine and rum. By midnight, she had drunk two bottles of wine and started on the rum.

Within an hour after Alice left West Virginia, Jeffrey began meeting individually with all of the men except for Keith. He explained that Kathy was his Bathsheba. Greg, Richard, Danny, Damon, and Dennis didn't seem surprised or that concerned. But Ron was troubled. He didn't believe in polygamy. Jeffrey had expected Ron to be distressed. That was why he had sent Susie along with Alice back to Macks Creek. He wanted Ron to know that Susie was safe. Jeffrey wasn't going to claim her as a wife.

Jeffrey had found more than a dozen scriptures that, when diagramed by the pattern, seemed to say a man could have two wives. He gave them to Ron to study, figuring that they would keep him busy for several days.

By 8:00 P.M., Jeffrey had finished his rounds and was ready for scripture class. Jeffrey had told the men that he wanted them to sit near Keith during class, in case he decided to challenge Jeffrey's decision to take Kathy as a wife. Meanwhile, Jeffrey tucked the .45 pistol that he had used to kill the Averys in his belt where everyone could see it. Jeffrey got right to the point.

"Kathy is now my wife," he proclaimed.

Keith thought Jeffrey was joking. He looked around the group. No one was smiling. Keith realized he was surrounded. He saw Jeffrey's .45. He glanced at Kathy. She was sitting next to Jeffrey where Alice usually sat. Jeffrey was serious.

"Do you have a problem with this?" Jeffrey asked Keith.

Keith tried to seem calm. He wanted to ask Jeffrey a question, he said. Keith reminded Jeffrey of the promise that he had made before the intercession dances. Jeffrey had said that he wouldn't take Kathy as his wife. Everyone in camp had heard him.

"How can any of us trust you if you lie?" Keith boldly asked.

"I didn't lie," Jeffrey snapped. "Kathy was never your wife."

Jeffrey said he had searched the scriptures and had discovered that Kathy was flesh of his flesh—not Keith's. "You were never married in God's eyes," he said. "If Kathy continues living with you, you will both be guilty of adultery."

Keith appeared unconvinced. He and Kathy had been married for twelve years. They had four sons. He wanted to speak to her in private.

"How do I know you won't hurt her?" Jeffrey asked. Keith agreed to speak to Kathy out in the open where Jeffrey could see them. Jeffrey said that would be okay. The estranged couple walked about thirty feet away from the group.

"Keith was stunned," Kathy recalled. "He had no idea about what had been going on right under his nose or how I felt about Jeffrey. I told him, 'This is what is right, Keith. . . .'"

Keith said that she was his wife. He didn't want her to go with Jeffrey.

"I want to be with Jeff," Kathy said. "I am flesh of his flesh."

She turned and returned to Jeffrey's side.

Now that everyone knew that Kathy belonged to Jeffrey, he had another announcement. He was going to split up the camp in case the helicopter returned. He and Kathy would move deeper into the woods. Ron, Damon, Greg, and Debbie would go with them. Dennis, Tonya, Keith, Danny, Richard, and Sharon would stay behind in the original camp. The reason Jeffrey wanted Ron, Damon, and Greg with him was because they were his "three witnesses." Joseph Smith, Jr., had produced "three witnesses" when people questioned him about the mysterious golden plates. Jeffrey had told the group that God would give him golden plates similar to the ones that He had given Smith. When that happened, Jeffrey wanted his three witnesses standing by to verify the event.

After class, everyone began moving tents. By midnight, the move was complete and Jeffrey and Kathy had the large Lundgren tent all to themselves. They spent the next three days on a "honeymoon."

Sheriff Thompson and Game Warden Spencer landed a few hundred feet from Jeffrey's original camp on the day after it had been split. As soon as they got out of their helicopter, Thompson noticed that several tents were missing. Dennis Patrick and Danny Kraft greeted the lawmen.

"The women just stood there and stared at us," said Thompson. The folksy sheriff asked Dennis why the group was camping in such an isolated area. "Our religious beliefs are different from most people's," Dennis replied. "We like the privacy." Thompson asked if the group planned to spend the winter in the hollow. Dennis didn't know, but he doubted it. He thought they might be moving to Missouri. At about that time, Sharon appeared with a tray of chocolate-chip cookies.

"Have one," she said. Thompson glanced at Spencer. Both were afraid that the cookies were poisoned.

"I don't think I need a cookie right now," Thompson said. "You want one?" he asked, looking at Spencer. The game warden shook his head.

Dennis Patrick picked one up and ate it. Thompson reminded Dennis that all of the children in camp had to be enrolled in school. Dennis nodded, but again explained that the group was probably going to move. A few minutes later, Thompson and Spencer got back in their helicopter and left. When Thompson returned to his office, he telephoned Yarborough. The first question that Yarborough asked was "Did you see Jeffrey?" They talked for several minutes. Neither of them brought up the Averys. Yarborough assumed that Dennis and Cheryl had gone with everyone else to West Virginia. Thompson figured that Yarborough already knew who was part of Jeffrey's group.

Keith Johnson decided to turn the tables on the prophet. Jeffrey had said that Kathy was his Bathsheba, so Keith went through the story of David and Bathsheba line by line. He then used the pattern to diagram several verses, and when he did, Keith made a shocking discovery. Two of David's sons had died, Keith told Dennis Patrick, so it seemed logical that if Jeffrey claimed to be David and Kathy was Bathsheba, then two of Jeffrey's sons would have to meet the same fate as David's sons. Dennis immediately raced over to Jeffrey and told him what Keith was preaching.

Jeffrey called all of the men together and had them bring Keith out into the woods. They formed a circle around him. Keith was unarmed. Jeffrey had taken away his guns. But Jeffrey had his .45 automatic.

"If you are threatening me, Keith," Jeffrey said, "then say so and let's deal with it right now."

Keith said that he wasn't threatening anyone. He had simply been studying the scriptures.

"It's not me," he explained, "it's the pattern."

Jeffrey looked at the scripture. "You've done this wrong," he declared. "It says that you should die and two of your sons will die too."

"There can be only one prophet," said Jeffrey, paraphrasing a line from the movie The Highlander. "I am that seer and the price for looking in the record for yourself is death."

Keith apologized and begged Jeffrey not to kill him. He talked about his four sons. Who would raise them if he was dead?

"I was prepared to execute Keith," Jeffrey later said. "The only reason why I didn't shoot him was because I had promised Kathy that I wouldn't harm him."

Just the same, Jeffrey ordered Keith to move his tent up to the new camp. Ron moved in with Keith to watch him.

After Sheriff Thompson visited the camp, Jeffrey decided it was time for the group to leave West Virginia. But he was broke. Reluctantly, Jeffrey drove to a flea market in Elkins, West Virginia, and began selling some of the group's rifles and pistols. He raised enough to buy a week's worth of groceries and enough gasoline for a round-trip to Missouri. Once there, Kathy would invite several fundamentalists to a special class on the pattern that Jeffrey would teach. Afterward, he would solicit money which he would use to move the rest of the group back to Missouri. Jeffrey, Kathy, and Damon left for Missouri the next day. Jeffrey left Ron in charge of the camp.

En route, Jeffrey stopped at a pay phone and told Alice that he was coming. When she asked about Kathy, Jeffrey used "delusion." He told Alice that Kathy was living with Keith back at the camp. He also told Alice that he had something exciting to show her. God had given him another revelation.

•   •   •

Alice was excited after Jeffrey called. She raced around the house like a schoolgirl getting ready for her senior prom. Alice fixed her hair, put on a dress, and eagerly waited. As soon as Jeffrey arrived, she darted out the door and threw her arms around him. Less than an hour before, Jeffrey had dropped Kathy at her mother's house outside Warrensburg. She was supposed to telephone her fundamentalist friends and relatives and arrange a place for Jeffrey to hold a class.

As soon as Jeffrey was alone with Alice, he told her about God's newest revelation. "Jeff said that he had gone up on the mountain in West Virginia and God had appeared and told him that He wanted Jeffrey to take a second wife. God had made a book appear and it had come down out of heaven and God had showed him the name of his second wife in this book."

Alice was furious.

"She hit me and threatened me. 'I'll turn you in right now. I'm going to call the sheriff on you. I'm going to tell about the Averys,' she said. Then she asked me if I knew who 'it' was, meaning my second wife, and I said, 'Yes,' and she said, 'Do you love her?,' and I said 'Yes,' and she said, 'I'll kill it! I swear I'll kill it. Who is she?' Alice was serious about her threat so I refused to tell her."

Alice already knew. "Who else could it have been but Kathy?" she later asked rhetorically. Then she added, sarcastically, "After all, it was her vagina that he had seen in his dream."

Jeffrey stayed in Macks Creek for two days, and then he told Alice that he had to hurry back to West Virginia. He left Damon behind with orders to watch Alice and make certain that she didn't tip off the police about the Averys. As soon as he left Alice, Jeffrey met Kathy and they went to Kingsville, a nearby town, where a friend of Kathy's had offered to let Jeffrey teach his class. Kathy had managed to get about a dozen friends to attend. One would later describe Jeffrey as a "wild man." His shoulder-length brown hair was dirty and matted. His face was badly sunburned, his shirt was dirty and half buttoned. For nearly an hour, Jeffrey rambled on about the pattern. He announced that he had personally seen Jesus Christ and had spoken to God. Michel Vick, a longtime friend of the Johnsons, later told a reporter for the *News Herald*, a Cleveland suburban newspaper, that she didn't believe anything Jeffrey said. If Jeffrey had been permitted to meet Christ and talk to God, Vick reasoned, then he would have been happy and exuberant. "One of the fruits of it would be joy," Vick explained. Instead, Jeffrey and Kathy looked like two fugitives on the run.

Jeffrey's spiel for money was a bust. No one was willing to help move Jeffrey's group from West Virginia back to Missouri. Jeffrey and Kathy returned to West Virginia with less money than they had left with.

Donna Keehler had grilled her son-in-law during his short visit, but he had not told her anything. As soon as he left, Donna began pressuring Alice to tell her the truth.

"Your father and I will protect you," she told Alice.

Alice would later testify that the reason she never told the police about the murders was because Jeffrey made certain that at least one of their children was with him at all times. "I never was allowed to have all of them with me at one time," Alice said. "I was afraid that he would hurt them if I called the police."

But that was simply not true. "There was a time when Alice had all of her children here," Donna said, "and Alice could have told us what was happening. I did my best to get her to tell us the truth. I pleaded with her. I told her that I would stand by her no matter what she and Jeffrey had gotten involved in. I promised her help, but Alice wouldn't tell me the truth."

Donna would later suggest that the reason Alice was reluctant to talk about the murders was not because she was scared of Jeffrey, but for another reason.

"Alice still loved Jeffrey. She was devoted to him."

Having failed to learn anything from Jeffrey and Alice, Donna began to pepper Susie Luff with questions. One morning when Alice was still in bed, Donna cornered Susie. The older woman stepped in front of the door to the utility room where Susie was doing laundry. "I blocked her way so she couldn't get past me."

"Look, Susie," Donna later recalled saying. "I want to know what is going on."

Susie began to cry. She looked as if she were going to tell Donna the truth, but then she caught herself.

"We are a deeply religious group," Donna later quoted Susie as saying. "Jeff is our teacher. We believe what he teaches us and we have done nothing wrong."

"Susie, if you're such a religious group," Donna asked, "then why do you use the filthy language that I've heard around here?

Why does my Alice drink? Why is Jeffrey smoking? This is not religion."

"Jeffrey is our teacher," Susie repeated, as if on automatic pilot. "We believe he is a prophet and we believe strongly in what he is teaching.'"

Donna looked directly at Susie. At least she had gotten her houseguest to admit that she thought Jeffrey was a prophet. "Susie," Donna said, "I'm Jeff's mother-in-law. I've known him longer than you. Now, I can't tell you what to believe, but if you think that Jeffrey Lundgren is a prophet, then you are a complete fool."

By October, life in West Virginia was miserable. The air became bitter cold. Jeffrey and Kathy had a portable heater in their tent, but the others went without. There was no money for food. Some days, Debbie would serve rice and cream gravy three times a day. "I wanted people to at least get some protein."

There were other problems as well. Richard had stopped talking to Sharon. Marrying her had been a big mistake, he had decided. Greg and Debbie were having marital problems too. Jeffrey had promised Danny that Shar Olson would eventually rejoin the group, but she hadn't and he was lonely. Ron missed Susie, who was still in Macks Creek. Keith was brooding over his loss of Kathy. Dennis and Tonya were still estranged.

In order to raise cash, Jeffrey ordered his followers to begin selling everything that they didn't need. He sent Dennis, Danny, Greg, and Richard to a nearby town in Maryland to look for work. As soon as they raised enough cash to rent a truck, they would move, he told them. But when the men were paid for a variety of minimum-wage jobs, Jeffrey collected their wages and drove into town with Kathy. He treated her to dinner. When they returned, Jeffrey announced that he was going back to Missouri to find a house where they could all live together. He left Kathy in charge and took Ron with him.

Months later, group members would recall with irony that life at the camp had started to deteriorate shortly after Alice left the group. Jeffrey had preached that women were "weaker vessels" than men and not as intelligent or strong, yet without Alice, Jeffrey didn't seem to know what to do.

Once again, Jeffrey spent only a few days at Macks Creek. He had brought Ron along, in part because he hoped that he could convince Alice that polygamy was not wrong. By this time, Ron had studied the scriptures that Jeffrey had showed him and become convinced that it was okay for Jeffrey to have two wives.

"Ron was always someone I could talk to," Alice said later, "and I told Ron that this was just not right. But he looked at me and said, 'Alice, we have to obey the will of the Lord.'"

Later, when Alice and Jeffrey were alone, she confronted him.

"Who is this person? Who is supposed to be your second wife? Or is it your third wife?" she asked. "How many more are you going to have?"

When Jeffrey refused to tell her, Alice slapped him. This time there was no one else watching, no one for Jeffrey to impress by absorbing Alice's blows. He smacked her and punched her in the stomach. She fell down and he reached over and slapped her face hard, rupturing her eardrum.

"We had a go at it," Jeffrey admitted later. "I told her that all I wanted to do was help her accept the truth, but she got angry and slapped me and that started it."

Jeffrey left for West Virginia the next morning. The day after he arrived at the camp, he went into town and called Alice. He wanted to apologize. She wasn't in the mood.

"You better get back here right now," she declared.

"Alice told me that she was turning me in for the murders if I didn't move back to Macks Creek immediately," said Jeffrey, "and stay with her."

The next morning, October 12, Jeffrey drove to a pawnshop in Elkins and sold both his .45-caliber pistols, including the one that he had used to kill the Averys. He had tried to switch the barrel on the murder weapon with another pistol that Damon owned. That would have made it difficult for police to link the handgun through ballistic tests with the Averys' deaths. But the two barrels were not interchangeable.

Selling his pistols gave Jeffrey enough cash to finance a return trip to Macks Creek. This time he took the Patricks with him and once again left Kathy behind. She was livid. He was running home to Alice and she was stuck dealing with Debbie, Greg, Richard, Sharon, Danny, and worst of all, Keith. The group was completely out of money and Kathy was on her own.

After Jeffrey was gone, Kathy rode on the ATV into Davis and began calling friends in Missouri. She finally found one who was willing to drive his semi-trailer truck to West Virginia and haul her and the others back to Kathy's mother's house. She returned to camp and told everyone to begin packing the tents.

On October 15, the group arrived at Kathy's mother's house in the back of a truck, like cattle. Everyone was crabby. Kathy had sent word to Jeffrey and he was waiting. He told Kathy that he and his children would continue living with Alice at the Keehlers' until the group could find a place to stay. Ron, Susie, Dennis, Tonya, and their children were sleeping in tents pitched in the Keehlers' backyard.

"Have you told Alice?" Kathy asked.

Jeffrey had told Alice that God wanted him to take Kathy as his second wife. But, he added, he'd given Alice the impression that he and Kathy hadn't started sleeping together.

Kathy, who was exhausted, was irritated. She had given up Keith and her four children to be with him. Now it was his turn to make a commitment, particularly since Kathy was now certain that she was pregnant. "We hadn't taken any precautions," Kathy explained later. "We both knew that there was a good chance it would happen." Kathy didn't intend to be kept hidden in the background.

"Alice is just going to have to face reality," Kathy said. "You are going to have to deal with her, Jeff."

He promised he would, but said he needed more time. He and Kathy would face Alice together once the group found a permanent place to live, he promised.

Once again, Kathy began telephoning her friends and relatives. She found one willing to let the group stay in an abandoned dairy barn on his farm near Chilhowee, a rural community south of Warrensburg. On October 21, the group moved into the abandoned and drafty barn. Ron, Susie, Dennis, Tonya, and their children rejoined the others. Everyone pitched their tents inside the barn. Kathy supervised setting up Jeffrey's tent and moved her belongings inside it. When Jeffrey arrived that afternoon, he assured everyone that he would soon find a house for them. "It will be just like it was in Kirtland," he promised. His followers would get jobs and support Jeffrey while he continued to search the scriptures. Meanwhile, he would divide his time between the dairy barn and Macks Creek.

Now that Kathy had found shelter for everyone, she once again confronted Jeffrey about her status as his wife, and he agreed to take her to Macks Creek with him. He had already told Alice that he would be bringing Kathy home with him. He wanted the three of them to live together. In fact, he was going to take Kathy back to Macks Creek that very night.

"I was nervous," Kathy recalled, "because I was going into *her* home. I also had to get over my own feelings. I didn't want to share him with Alice."

As they drove down the state highway toward Macks Creek, Kathy tried to reassure herself. "If God has truly ordained this," she said, "then I am certain that it will work out."

Jeffrey agreed. But he didn't sound nearly as confident as he had when the two of them had been sleeping together in the mountains of West Virginia and Alice was a thousand miles away in her mother's house.

CHAPTER FORTY-EIGHT

FROM the moment that Jeffrey and Kathy rode up the gravel drive-way at the Keehlers' house, Alice was annoyed. "Jeff walked around and opened her car door," Alice recalled. "He never opened a car door for me."

Jeffrey had told Donna and Ralph that Kathy needed someplace to stay. She and Keith were having marital problems, he said. Donna, who had no idea what was actually going on, said Kathy was welcome to stay in the guest bedroom across the hall from Alice's room. Donna and Ralph slept in the master bedroom at the opposite end of the house.

Alice hugged Jeffrey when he walked in and gave him a passion-ate kiss. Jeffrey motioned toward Kathy. With obvious disdain, Alice hugged her and grunted a welcome. Alice showed Kathy where her bedroom was.

It was nearly 11:00 P.M., and the Keehlers and the Lundgren children were all in bed. Jeffrey told Alice that he'd join her in her bedroom after he helped Kathy unpack. Alice slipped into her nightgown and perched herself seductively on the bed. After ten minutes of waiting, she crept into the hall and quietly opened the door to the guest room so that she could peek inside.

They were sitting on the bed kissing.

Alice hurried back into her bedroom and began to sob as loudly as she could.

"Are you all right?" Jeffrey asked a few minutes later when he came into the room.

"Oh, sure, Jeff, I'm fine," Alice replied bitterly. "This is my idea of a fun time!" He started to kiss her, but she pulled away.

"I could smell the residue of her kissing him," Alice later recalled. "I said, 'At least wash her off before getting in bed with me.' He got angry and accused me of being rebellious. He rolled me over on my stomach, pulled my gown up over my head, and began having anal intercourse with me."

The next morning, Jeffrey decided to take Alice, Kathy, and the children shopping. Alice had borrowed some money from her parents. All of the kids jumped into the back of the truck while Alice hurried outside and slipped into the center of the seat in the truck's cab. "Even when it came to something that little," Kathy recalled, "Alice wanted me to know that she was number one, that sitting next to him was her place."

As he drove down the highway, Jeffrey put his right arm on the back of the seat so that it touched both women. Alice noticed that he was playing with Kathy's hair.

It was almost lunchtime so Jeffrey stopped at a Taco Bell, and this time it was Kathy who hurried inside and scooted next to Jeffrey in a booth. Alice sat across from him and began handing out the food to her children.

"Jeffrey, you didn't get enough drinks," Alice announced. There were only six cups and there were seven people.

"Yes, he did!" Kathy retorted. "We *always* share *our* drink."

Alice left the table and hurried into the women's bathroom. "Jeffrey never, ever let me drink out of the same cup as he did," she said later. "It was humiliating." After about twenty minutes, Alice emerged to find everyone waiting for her in the truck.

When they got to the grocery store, Kathy started pushing the cart. Once again, Alice was angry. By the time the two women had reached the meat counter, Alice exploded.

"You whore!" she screamed at Kathy as other shoppers stared. "It was simply too easy for Kathy," Alice later said. "She was stepping into twenty years of marriage and it wasn't bothering her one little bit." Alice lunged at Kathy with her fingernails but Jeffrey grabbed her before she reached Kathy. Alice aimed her knee at his groin and Jeffrey pushed her back. She tried to kick him.

"I caught her leg," Jeffrey later said, "and swung her around and then I slapped her. I'm not proud of that, but I lost it. The scriptures say that it is better to slap someone than to have them perish for being unsubmissive so what I did wasn't wrong, particularly since Alice was asking for it. She always tries to look like she is poor and helpless, but she was going to hurt Kathy and I had to stop her."

Alice burst into tears and ran out of the store. As soon as she was gone, Kathy and Jeffrey finished shopping. Alice waited for them in the truck—in the center seat.

On the way home, Jeffrey decided to buy some shampoo at a Wal-Mart store. This time, he walked between the two women and pushed the cart.

"Since this is your first night together," Alice said cattily, "maybe you should buy something to make you feel feminine, Kathy." It was a thinly disguised slap at Kathy's tomboy manners.

"Don't worry about me," Kathy replied icily. "Jeffrey finds me feminine enough."

When they got back to Macks Creek, Kathy and Alice avoided each other. After Ralph, Donna, and the Lundgren children went to bed that night, Jeffrey ordered Alice to prepare his bath. Kathy went into the guest room and closed the door. "Jeffrey was my lord and master," Alice said, "so one of my jobs was giving him his nightly bath. I washed his body and his hair and dried him off. It was all scriptural. Christ was anointed by Mary so it was my job to anoint Jeff. I put his favorite perfume on him and he kissed me on the cheek and said, 'I'm going to spend some time with Kathy.' He said, 'Alice, I'm not on a timetable. I'll be back when I get back.' He then went into Kathy's room."

Jeffrey and Kathy would later claim that they did not have sex that night. They simply talked for a while, but Alice recalled that evening much differently.

"I went to bed, but I just laid there staring at the clock. At about fifteen till two, I went out into the hall and I could hear him snoring, then I heard him wake up and he and Kathy had sex. I went into my room. Finally, he came in and I acted like I was asleep and he shook my shoulder and said, 'Hey, you awake?' He told me that he and Kathy were really hungry and he wanted me to fix them hamburgers. I got up and cooked them hamburgers like he wanted and then I fixed him a big glass of Pepsi because I know Jeff likes to drink a big glass of Pepsi after he makes love. He usually kept one by the side of our bed just for that. I put the cup down and Kathy leaned over and she took a drink out of it. I don't know why but that was the ultimate insult. Here I was fixing that bitch hamburgers and she had just fucked my husband. I ran into the bedroom and started crying and Jeffrey came in and sat on the bed and then Kathy came in and I was in the fetal position and he was sitting at my knees with his hand rubbing my back and she was sitting on the floor stroking my hair and they were holding hands while they were doing this. Kathy says, 'It's okay to cry,' and then he moved me over on the bed and laid down and he put my head on one shoulder and Kathy laid her head on the other shoulder so that he had both of us in his arms. I wanted to die. I wasn't going to spend my life that way. The whole thing was so awful to me, I went into the bathroom and threw up. When I came out of the bathroom, she had gone to her bedroom and he had gone to sleep."

The next morning, Jeffrey announced that he needed to go to the dairy barn and get the ATV. Alice's brother, Charles, had offered to sell it and the electric generator. As they had the day before, both women hurried outside, both hoping to sit in the center of the cab next to Jeffrey. Alice won out, but before they reached the dairy barn, Kathy began to cry and Jeffrey pulled the truck to the side of the road.

"It's Kathy's turn to ride in the middle for a while," Jeffrey said. Alice traded places with Kathy.

When they got to the barn, Jeffrey left the two women alone in the cab.

"This isn't going to work," Alice said coldly.

"Of all the women in the world," Kathy replied, "I thought we could make this work out."

"Over my dead body," Alice replied.

The two women's eyes met. Both were furious.

That night after dinner, Jeffrey decided to take everyone to play miniature golf. Damon, Jason, Kristen, and Caleb piled into the back of the truck and Alice and Kathy argued about who was going to sit next to Jeffrey. Alice won and when they got to the course, Kathy decided to stay behind in the truck. She needed a break from Alice, she told Jeffrey.

The Lundgrens went on without her, but Alice had reached her limit too and she blistered Jeffrey with profanity while he and the children tried to play golf. Halfway through the course, Jeffrey quit and ordered everyone back to the truck. None of the children said a word. Kathy climbed into the back of the truck and rode with them. All the way home, Alice screamed at Jeffrey. She never mentioned Kathy by name. She simply called her "the bitch."

Alice went directly to her bedroom when they finally got home. Jeffrey suggested that Kathy go into the guest room while he tried to get Alice cooled down. He went into Alice's bedroom and told her that he was ready for his bath.

"There's the bathroom," she shrieked. "Do it yourself." Jeffrey walked across the hall to be with Kathy. Alice cried for several minutes and then went into the kitchen and retrieved a bottle of rum that she had hidden there. By 2:00 A.M., she was drunk.

"I could hear them horsing around next door," she recalled. "So I decided to join them." Alice swaggered across the hall and pushed open the door. She marched inside and pulled the sheets off Kathy.

"Get up!" she screamed. "Get out of here!"

"What the hell do you think you're doing?" Jeffrey yelled.

"The bitch is gone," said Alice. "The party is over, Jeffrey."

"Alice," he snapped. "Get control of yourself."

It was at this point that Alice would later claim that Jeffrey attacked her. Jeffrey would later insist that Alice attacked him. Kathy would claim that she had been asleep alone in the bedroom when Alice barged in and attacked her. Regardless, the noise woke the Keehlers and Donna hurried out of her bedroom. She found Damon and Jason, who had been asleep in the living room, fully dressed and standing near the back door of the house.

"What's wrong?" Donna asked.

"Mom's throwing us out," said Damon. "She told us to leave."

At that point, Jeffrey emerged from Alice's bedroom. "His face was bleeding and big pieces of hair had been torn out of his head," Donna recalled.

"My God!" Donna exclaimed.

"Alice is drunk," Jeffrey said. "She's throwing a fit. We're leaving."

"Wait a minute," said Donna. "Get those kids back in here. You can't leave in the middle of the night like this. It's cold out there."

Damon and Jason had already sent Kristen and Caleb outside to the truck. Jeffrey called them back into the house and told them to go back to bed. Kathy, meanwhile, came out of the guest room, carrying her suitcase. Jeffrey told Damon and Jason to drive her to the barn in Chilhowee. Kathy looked upset as Jeffrey escorted her outside.

Donna, meanwhile, hurried down the hallway to Alice's bedroom. She found her daughter sprawled on the bed.

"I told him to leave," Alice screamed. "I'm through, Mom! I've been cheated on and lied to and I'm not going to put up with it any longer."

Donna was mad. "What's he done this time?" she asked. "I'm going to talk to him."

Alice panicked. She shot up from the bed. "Don't interfere in this, Mama," she warned. "You don't know what he is capable of doing."

Donna went back to the kitchen to wait for Jeffrey. As soon as she left the room, Alice grabbed a bottle of extra-strength Excedrin. "I took all fifty pills," she later said. "I washed them down with rum. I wanted to kill myself."

Donna told Jeffrey that she wanted to talk to him, but he hurried past her, went into Alice's bedroom and shut the door. Donna decided to go back to bed.

"Jeffrey walked in and backhanded me," Alice claimed, "and then he saw the pill bottle."

"What have you done now?" he asked.

"I don't want to live anymore," Alice said. "I'm going to kill myself."

Jeffrey dragged her into the bathroom and forced her to vomit. He put her head under the shower and splashed her with cold water. Finally, he forced her to go outside into the chilly air and walk around.

"I remember him telling me, 'Live for me, Alice! Live for me! Don't die!'"

The next morning Alice felt sick and dizzy when she woke up. Her arms were bruised. Her head hurt and she was alone in bed. Jeffrey was loading the truck. He had decided to move into the dairy barn with Kathy and he was taking the children with him.

When Jeffrey came into the bedroom to tell Alice what he had decided, she began to weep.

"Don't take my children," she whimpered.

"You're an unfit mother," he replied. "You're a drunk."

"You can't leave me," she continued. "I can't live without you."

Jeffrey told Alice that he was tired of her rebellion and disobedience. She began to nod. "I'm sorry. I'm sorry. I'm so sorry," she said. "I know I've been bad, but I can change. I can stop being bad."

"Jeff told me that I needed to be punished," Alice later said. "He told me to go into the bathroom and take off my clothes. I did. He told me to lay down on the floor and when I did, Jeff squatted over me and had a bowel movement on my face. He rubbed it all over my face and then he turned me over and had anal intercourse with me. After he came, he lifted me up and put me in the tub and then he washed me very gently. He washed my hair and face and everything. He told me that I was purified now and I told him that I was no longer rebellious. He dressed me and put a coat on me to hide the bruises on my arms. He told me that he had decided to take me to the barn with him. I thanked him and he told me that he loved me."

Donna was waiting when Jeffrey and Alice came out of the bedroom.

"Alice, you don't have to go," she said, stepping between them and the back door.

"Yes, I do, Mother," Alice replied.

Donna put her hands on the sides of Alice's face. She made her daughter look directly into her eyes. "Alice looked so beat up, so sad," Donna later remembered. "It was breaking my heart."

"Alice, your father and I will do anything for you. You don't have to go with Jeffrey. You can stay here with us."

Jeffrey didn't say a word. Alice looked at her mother. "Yes, I do have to go, Mother," she said. "I want to go. I want to go with Jeff."

Donna stepped out of the way. As soon as Jeffrey and Alice drove down the driveway, Donna burst into tears.

When they got to the barn, Jeffrey told Alice to stay in the truck. He went inside and called everyone together. He told them that Alice had suffered a nervous breakdown and had tried to kill herself. Ron and Greg went outside to help bring Alice in. Everyone watched.

"Alice was shuffling her feet and she looked helpless," Debbie later recalled, "but I thought it was theatrics. Her eyes were bright and sharp. I asked Dennis what he thought because he had worked in a mental-health unit and we both decided that Alice was playing it for all she could. I really doubted whether she had even tried to kill herself."

When Alice got inside the tent, she noticed the bed was draped with a red-and-white quilt with lambs on it. It was Kathy's. "Get that rag off my bed!" she said. Ron grabbed it. Alice got undressed and crawled under the covers.

At dinnertime, Kathy made a cup of soup for her and went into the tent. Alice stared up at Kathy. She acted as if she didn't recognize her. Kathy couldn't tell whether Alice was playacting or had actually suffered a breakdown.

"Hello," Alice said. "These are from my husband." She was clutching a poem that Jeffrey had written her and other love notes from the past. "Do you know Jeffrey?"

Later that night, Kathy and Jeffrey put a pad on the floor in the section of the tent next to where Alice was sleeping. Although it was dark, Alice could see them through the slit in the partition that divided the tent into sections. They had turned on a portable heater and it cast a red glow on their bodies. Jeffrey and Kathy would later claim that they had simply gone to sleep that night. Alice insisted that they had sexual intercourse while she watched.

"They thought I was asleep, but I could see them," she said later. "They began making love. I turned away but I could hear the sound of his body going in and out of her body. I felt like I could feel the entire floor vibrating and I could hear everything that they were saying to each other. I felt sick so I decided to interrupt them and Jeffrey got angry. I kept calling to him every few minutes—'Jeffrey'—'Oh, Jeffrey'—'Jeffrey, I need you.' Kathy had an orgasm but he couldn't and he got off her and he began to cry because he couldn't do it because I was calling to him. She was saying, 'It's okay. I understand.' But he was crying because he wanted to come and he couldn't come and I was glad that he couldn't come. I was glad that I kept him from coming."

When it was morning, Jeffrey came into the portion of the tent where Alice was lying in bed. Jeffrey was angry about her antics during the night. He began to scold her and Alice immediately became submissive. "I said, 'What is my lord's bidding?'" Within a few minutes, she was performing oral sex on him. When she finished, Alice announced that she was going back to Macks Creek. He was welcome to come with her, but he had to choose between her and Kathy.

"Don't do this, Alice," he said. "I'm not leaving Kathy."

Jeffrey figured Alice was bluffing. He stepped out of the tent and told everyone that Alice was leaving. She got dressed. By the time she walked out of the tent, everyone was waiting to tell her good-bye. Jeffrey told Alice that Ron was going to drive her back to Macks Creek. He walked into another part of the barn to be with Kathy. Tonya and Susie both gave Alice a hug and said good-bye. Danny refused to speak to her. Greg told her that he loved her. Sharon came over and hugged her. "Mom," Sharon said, trying to cheer Alice up, "you look so pretty."

"It didn't keep my husband in my bed, did it?" Alice replied.

Everyone followed Alice out of the barn to the truck. When she got to it, she stopped and said she wanted to talk to Jeffrey. He and Kathy came out of the barn.

"You win, Kathy," Alice announced, and then she turned and looked directly at Jeffrey.

"I told him that I had always loved him and always would love him. I said I was sorry that I didn't make him happy and had disappointed him. And then I said, 'Some day, Jeff, when it's too late, you will realize that I am the only person who has ever truly loved you.'"

After Alice finished her speech, she got down on her knees in front of the group and kissed Jeffrey's feet. A few seconds later, she was gone.

CHAPTER FORTY-NINE

RICHARD and Greg wanted out. They had been plotting an escape for more than three weeks. Richard had first mentioned leaving back in West Virginia when Jeffrey had been on one of his trips to Macks Creek.

"I think it's time for me to get out of here," Richard had said offhandedly to Greg one morning when they were away from the others.

"Well, if you're leaving," Greg had replied with a chuckle, "take me with you."

Both men had intentionally made their comments sound like jokes because neither fully trusted the other. It was Richard who decided to risk telling the truth.

"You serious?" he asked Greg.

"Are you?" Greg had replied.

"Yes," Richard had said. "I want out."

Richard and Greg had been best friends most of their lives, but after they joined the group that had changed. Jeffrey had made certain of it. He had told Richard that he was going to eventually be asked by God to kill Greg with a shotgun. Jeffrey said he had seen Richard shoot Greg in a vision. Meanwhile, Jeffrey had told Greg that he shouldn't trust Richard because he was rebellious and most likely would end up being killed like the Averys.

On the day that Richard and Greg admitted that they both wanted to quit, they once again began to feel like friends.

On October 29, Greg's father drove to the dairy barn in Chilhowee and asked his son to leave with him. Greg refused. He figured he had a better chance of hiding from Jeffrey if he left on his own, rather than going directly to his father's house. The next day, Greg and Richard decided that they would escape on Halloween night. They weren't going to tell anyone, not even their "wives." Neither of them felt their marriages were legally binding. Not only were they rejecting Jeffrey as a prophet, they were divorcing themselves from Sharon and Debbie too.

Debbie was fixing chicken for dinner on October 31 when Greg and the other men returned to the dairy barn from work. The men had all found minimum-wage jobs as laborers at a nearby company that manufactured mail-order Christmas supplies. Greg had promised to help Debbie pluck and clean the chickens, and when he didn't come to the kitchen, she decided to look for him. When she went into their tent, Debbie noticed that Greg's suitcase was gone. Suspicious, she hurried to the barn's front door just as Greg and Richard ducked through it. She caught them as they were walking toward Greg's car.

"Where's your suitcase?" she demanded.

Greg told her that he was "airing it out."

Debbie looked over at Greg's car and saw the suitcase next to it. "I started screaming at him," said Debbie. "I knew he and Richard were going to sneak away."

Greg hustled Debbie into a field where they could talk without being overheard. "I love you," she said. Debbie reminded Greg that Jeffrey had promised them that they were going to have a baby. How could he leave her?

"I've just got to get away for a while," Greg said.

Debbie knew he was lying. Once he left, he would never come back. She started toward the barn to tell Jeffrey. Richard stepped in front of her. "I was going to hit Richard and I'm sure he would have hit me right back," Debbie said. "But Greg jumped in the way. He said, 'Debbie, get yourself under control. If you're going to hit someone, hit me.' So I decked him right in the jaw and he couldn't believe I had hit him and I couldn't believe it either."

Debbie ran between the two men.

"Richard and Greg are leaving," she yelled. "They're leaving. You've got to stop them!"

Richard and Greg didn't want Jeffrey running after them, so they walked back into the barn. "We told Jeff that we'd like some time alone away from the group to get our heads on straight," Richard recalled. Jeffrey asked them what they were going to do. They said they didn't know. Then Greg asked if it would be okay for them to leave.

"Richard," Jeffrey said, ignoring Greg, "there is nothing out there for you. I need you here with me."

"You don't need me," Richard said. "You can do this without me."

Jeffrey grabbed Richard by his shirt and pinned him against the barn wall. Jeffrey's face was bright red. He was angry.

"Don't you ever tell me what I need and don't need," Jeffrey yelled. "Do I make myself clear?"

"Yes, sir," Richard replied.

Jeffrey released him.

"I wanted Richard to know, I wanted all of them to know, that no one counsels their lord," Jeffrey later explained. "A prophet never tolerates people telling him what to do. Only God has that right."

"Get out of here," Jeffrey said.

Debbie couldn't believe he was going to let them leave. She grabbed Greg's arm. "Don't leave me," she shrieked. He jerked loose and hurried to his car. Debbie burst into tears. As soon as Richard was inside, Greg hit the accelerator. He checked the rearview mirror as the car sped away from the barn. He wanted to make certain Jeffrey wasn't going to shoot them or follow them.

As soon as they were gone, Sharon turned to Jeffrey. Did he think that they would tell the police about the Averys, she asked.

"If I thought they would," Jeffrey said, "I would have slit their throats."

Debbie had smoked in high school, but had stopped shortly after that. She bummed a cigarette from Ron and within an hour she had gone through an entire pack. "I was devastated."

Back in the barn, Jeffrey called everyone together and told them to open their Mormon scriptures to the Third Book of Nephi, chapter 13, verses 46 and 47.

And woe be unto him that will not hearken unto the words

of Jesus, and also to them whom he hath chosen and sent among them. For whoso receiveth not the words of Jesus, and the words of those whom he hath sent, receiveth not him; and therefore he will not receive them at the last day; and it would be better for them if they had not been born.

"Richard and Greg have rejected me and my teachings," Jeffrey said. "It would be better for them if they had not been born. They are damned just like the Averys."

Everyone understood. Leaving the group was the same as denying Jesus Christ. But Debbie didn't care. She felt abandoned. All she could think about that night was Greg and her children from her previous marriage. She had asked Jeffrey for permission to visit them in Independence and he'd promised to arrange it, but Jeffrey had been preoccupied with Kathy and Alice. As she lay in her tent that night, Debbie decided that she was going to see her children even if it meant being condemned by Jeffrey just as Richard and Greg had been.

Every Wednesday, Jeffrey drove to Macks Creek to visit Alice. Debbie knew he generally left the barn before 6:00 A.M.. The closest pay telephone was four miles away. Debbie had measured it one day on the truck's odometer when Jeffrey drove her into town to buy groceries. The back injury that she had suffered years ago while working at an Independence hospital still caused her considerable pain and made her limp. But she was determined to see her three children. Debbie began walking around the barn each night after dinner to build up her endurance. No one thought anything of it. By the second Wednesday in November, Debbie was ready. As soon as she heard Jeffrey leave the barn, she pinned a note on her pillow and quietly left the barn. She had already dressed and packed a few of her belongings. Debbie figured it would take her forty-five minutes to walk to the pay phone. Ron usually got up at 6:30 A.M. He would wonder why Debbie wasn't fixing them breakfast since that was her job. She was afraid that Ron would come after her once he realized she was gone. If he did, he'd intercept her before she made it to the telephone. Debbie quickened her pace and listened for the sound of a car engine.

Back at the barn, Ron had noticed that Debbie wasn't in the kitchen. He had told Susie to go into Debbie's tent and check on her. But Susie was scared. She was afraid that Debbie had killed herself. Ron finally decided to check for himself.

"Debbie," he hollered. "Debbie, are you all right?"

He pulled back the tent flap and spotted the note that she had left. Within minutes, everyone knew that Debbie had fled. "Are you going after her?" someone asked Ron, who was in charge whenever Jeffrey wasn't with the group. He paused.

"No," he said softly. "Let her go."

When Debbie reached the pay phone, she telephoned a friend. "Sure I'll come get you," the woman said, "but at seven in the morning? What's the rush!"

"Just come now!" Debbie said. "Right now!"

Alice was spending her days in Macks Creek drinking peppermint schnapps mixed with iced tea and feeling sorry for herself. She had chosen schnapps because she figured Donna wouldn't be suspicious of the smell of peppermint. Despite repeated pressure from her parents, Alice refused to tell them what was going on. Deep down, she figured that Jeffrey would come back. He had before. The first week after Alice left him, Jeffrey telephoned her every day. The second week, he had come down twice to see her, but he had refused to stay past 2:00 P.M. Even though she was willing to have sex with him, Jeffrey refused to spend the night. In mid-November, Jeffrey told Alice that she was "well" enough to be around her children. He brought Jason, Kristen, and Caleb for a visit. They went to a state park for a picnic even though it was cold. At one point, Jeffrey and Jason ran an errand and Alice grilled Caleb. The eight-year-old innocently mentioned that Kathy had gone with him and Daddy to Wal-Mart.

"So we're still playing house with Kathy, huh?" Alice asked when Jeffrey returned.

Jeffrey slapped her, she said later. He took her back to Macks Creek and drove with the kids back to the dairy barn.

On November 15, 1989, Sheriff Hank Thompson telephoned Yarborough. "They're gone!" Thompson announced. The sheriff had stopped by Jeffrey's camp in Yellow Creek Hollow and found the site deserted. The group had left behind one tent, a sewing machine, and a Bible that had Keith Johnson's name in it. Thompson had also found several garbage bags hidden near the camp. They were filled with animal bones. He figured the men had been killing deer illegally. Thompson told Yarborough that Dennis Patrick had mentioned something about returning to Missouri.

Nearly seven months had passed since Jeffrey had fled Kirtland. The FBI had closed its case. People had finally stopped kidding Yarborough about his obsession with Jeffrey. The chief was busy with other investigations. But Yarborough still was curious about Jeffrey. He decided to make a few phone calls. Within a few days, Yarborough had discovered that Alice was living in Macks Creek while Jeffrey and the others were camping in a dairy barn. He'd learned that Jeffrey had taken Kathy as his wife. It sounded as if the group was beginning to disintegrate. "There didn't seem to be much point in keeping tabs on Jeffrey," Yarborough recalled. Yet the chief just couldn't let go. He still wasn't certain who was in Jeffrey's group. He was particularly concerned about Keith Johnson. Why had Thompson found Keith's Bible in West Virginia? Had something happened to Keith?

Yarborough called Kevin Currie's mother in Buffalo and asked her to have Kevin call him. He was still hiding from Jeffrey. When Kevin called, Yarborough told him that the group was back in Missouri. Kevin would later remember asking Yarborough the names of the group members who had gone into the wilderness. The chief began reciting names but when he said Dennis and Cheryl Avery, Kevin stopped him.

"Are you sure the Averys went with him?" Kevin asked.

"Yeah," Yarborough said.

"I seriously doubt that, chief," said Kevin. "Jeffrey would never take the Averys with him. . . . There are certain things that Jeffrey just won't change. He might change scriptures and change his interpretations, but Jeffrey is convinced that the Averys are vile creatures and Jeffrey never changes his emotional judgments of people."

After talking to Kevin, Yarborough looked through his notes. No one had interviewed the Averys when the FBI questioned group members on April 18 at the farm. No one had seen the family since then either. Yarborough called Sheriff Thompson. Were Dennis and Cheryl Avery living at Jeffrey's camp? he asked. Thompson couldn't be certain. He knew that the Patricks had been there and that Danny Kraft had been in the group, but that was it.

"Damn!" Yarborough said, when he put down the telephone receiver.

The weather in Missouri turned so frigid just before Thanksgiving that Ron Luff contacted his brother, Rick, who owned a farm outside Warrensburg and asked him if the group could move onto his property. Rick had a loft in his house where the children could sleep at night. He had a barn that was just as big as the one in Chilhowee, but in better condition, and there was a small trailer on the property that Rick usually rented out. Rick said the group was welcome. Like Ron, he was deeply religious and he was curious about Jeffrey and his teachings.

No one missed the significance of the move. It had been Ron—not Jeffrey—who had made the decision. Ron had slowly taken over more and more control of the group. It was more by default than choice. Jeffrey simply wasn't around, and when he was, he didn't seem to care.

It took the group only one day to move. Jeffrey claimed the more comfortable trailer for himself, Kathy, and his children. Everyone else pitched their tents in the unheated barn. A rumor soon spread through the group: Jeffrey and Kathy were watching hard-core pornographic movies at night. Jeffrey was also using the group's money to take Alice shopping at Bannister Mall in Kansas City during the day. One of the Lundgren children had accidentally let slip that Jeffrey had bought his family all new clothes but had made them leave them in Macks Creek so no one in the group would know.

Jeffrey didn't care about the rumors. "I knew as soon as we left West Virginia that my people would turn against me," he said later. "The Lord was really telling me that it was time for me to start over. These people were too impatient and soft."

In mid-November, Jeffrey told Alice during one of his visits that he was making plans to shed his followers. The only one that he wanted to continue following him was Ron, he said. Jeffrey had decided to move to California once Alice was "well" enough to travel and he had collected enough money to finance the trip.

"What are you going to tell everyone?" Alice asked.

"I will tell my people that from time to time, prophets take a rest," Jeffrey said. "A prophet needs someplace to go where he doesn't have to deal with everyone's problems. I'll tell them that one reason why Christ had to leave his disciples was so they could bear witness to Him and now it is time for them to bear witness for me."

"How about Kathy?" Alice asked.

Jeffrey didn't answer so Alice pressed him. "I will not abandon what God has given me," Jeffrey replied. But, he said, God had shown him a vision about Kathy. "Jeffrey told me that God had told him that Kathy was going to die before the mountain of the Lord was raised," Alice recalled. "He told me that she wasn't going to make it. It was just going to be the two of us and our children."

Chief Yarborough wasn't the only person curious in late 1989 about the whereabouts of Dennis and Cheryl Avery. Dennis's brother, Tim, also wanted to know where they were. Tim had gotten married and he and his bride, Lisa, had sent Dennis and Cheryl a wedding invitation. Tim thought they'd come or at least send a card, but they had done neither. He thought it was strange that no one had heard from Dennis and Cheryl since April. Tim had called Cheryl's mother, Donna Bailey, and asked if she had heard from them. She hadn't. It was as if they had disappeared.

Through their contacts at church, Tim and Lisa had managed to piece together stories about Jeffrey. They knew that he'd declared himself a prophet and had taken his band to West Virginia. At first, Tim and Lisa didn't believe that Dennis and Cheryl had actually gone with Jeffrey. "They weren't the kind who would want to live in the wilderness," Lisa recalled. "Cheryl had a frog phobia." But Tim had pointed out that his brother and Cheryl weren't the sort who usually joined cults either. Anything seemed possible.

At one point, Tim and Lisa discussed driving to West Virginia to check on Dennis and Cheryl, but they decided against it after they learned that Danny Kraft's father had gone into Jeffrey's camp during the summer and had been unsuccessful at convincing Danny to leave. "We felt Dennis and Cheryl were old enough to run their own lives," Tim said. "What were we going to tell them? That they couldn't stay?"

Shortly before Thanksgiving, however, Lisa had a strange experience. "I was praying, asking God to protect them and the children," she recalled, "and I suddenly felt that God was telling me that it was okay, that Dennis and Cheryl and the children were okay, and I didn't need to be praying for them anymore."

That struck Lisa as odd. "I asked myself, 'Why wouldn't I need to be praying for Dennis's family? Why would God tell me that they were okay?,' and then it hit me. Maybe they're dead. Maybe that is why they are safe now—because they are with God."

Lisa didn't share her thoughts with Tim. She didn't want to alarm him. But she asked God in a prayer if Dennis and Cheryl and the children were with Him in paradise. Is that why she didn't need to worry about them anymore?

When Lisa Avery finished praying, she felt certain that God

had given her an answer. And she was even more disturbed than before about her in-laws.

Jeffrey had told all of his followers that they would never be able to make it on their own if they quit the group. About a week after Debbie left, she telephoned Jeffrey at Macks Creek.

"Can I come back?" she asked.

Debbie had visited with her children in Independence and also talked to a few friends. But she had spent most of her time searching for Greg. His parents wouldn't tell her where he was hiding. Now she was desperate. "I didn't have anyone else to turn to but the group," she said. "I didn't care if Jeffrey killed me. I just didn't want to be alone."

A friend drove her to Rick Luff's barn the day before Thanksgiving. Everyone was happy to see her, particularly Sharon. Debbie was still the group's nurse and Sharon had discovered that she was pregnant. She was going to have Richard's baby. Debbie had never seen a more forsaken lot. "All of us had staked our lives on Jeffrey. We had believed he was a prophet and now we were all beginning to realize that we had been deceived," she recalled. "It was a gloomy Thanksgiving."

Jeffrey had promised to spend Thanksgiving Day with Alice. Donna and Ralph were going to their son's house for dinner. Alice told Jeffrey to bring the kids around two o'clock. She got dressed and fixed a big dinner, but Jeffrey didn't arrive until nearly eight. He and Kathy had been quarreling, he said. Things at the barn were not going well.

"It's almost time for us to go to California," he told her.

Four days after Thanksgiving, Rick Luff and his father knocked on the door of the trailer where Jeffrey and Kathy were living. Rick had discovered that Jeffrey had two wives. He didn't believe in polygamy. He told Jeffrey to get off his property. The others in the barn were told that they were no longer welcome either if they were sticking with Jeffrey. Otherwise, they could stay until they found somewhere else to go.

Jeffrey and Kathy packed their belongings and then Jeffrey went to talk to his followers. He told them that they should each find somewhere to live during the winter. He was going away for a while, but he would contact them and tell them where to send him money. In the spring, they would get together. By then he would have new revelations and they would return to the wilderness and work on opening the third seal in Revelation.

With no show of emotion, Jeffrey got into the truck with Kathy and his children and drove away. He had decided to take Kathy to live with one of her girlfriends. He and the children would return to Macks Creek. As soon as Alice's brother sold the ATV, generator, and camping equipment, he would be ready to leave Missouri.

Debbie was astounded when Jeffrey left. She looked around. Dennis, Tonya, Keith, Ron, Susie, Sharon, and Danny were all standing in the chilly outdoors with absolutely no idea of what they should do next. Debbie had given up her career as a nurse, sold her house, and cut herself off from her children all because she had believed in Jeffrey. Sharon was pregnant and was now without a husband. Keith had lost his wife and his four sons no longer had their mother. Danny had given up a promising career in art. Dennis had almost been killed in the wilderness and there was no guarantee that his marriage to Tonya would survive. Tonya had been "claimed" by Jeffrey and then kicked out of Jeffrey's tent. Jeffrey had tried to drive a wedge between Susie and Ron in the wilderness. Greg and Richard were in hiding somewhere. All of the women had been humiliated by Jeffrey during his so-called "intercession" dances. Worst of all, he had killed Dennis, Cheryl, Trina, Becky, and Karen Avery and dragged the group into those murders. They had either participated or kept quiet about it afterward. And now Jeffrey was simply driving away.

"I realized at that moment that Jeffrey hadn't only killed five people," Debbie said later, "he had really destroyed all of us too. Our lives were ruined because of this man."

As Jeffrey's truck turned onto the road and left Rick Luff's property, Debbie quietly swore.

"Jeff," she whispered, "you can rot in hell."

CHAPTER FIFTY

WITHIN twenty-four hours, everyone but Ron and Susie moved away from the barn. Dennis and Tonya called Tonya's parents in Independence and went to live with them. Dennis also called a friend in Higginsville, a tiny town north of Warrensburg, who agreed to take in Danny. Debbie moved into a friend's apartment in Independence. She took Sharon along because she didn't have anywhere else to go. Keith Johnson and his four sons went to his parents' farm southwest of Warrensburg. Greg and Richard were still in hiding somewhere in Independence.

It took Rick Luff two days of nonstop counseling, but he finally convinced Ron that Jeffrey really wasn't a prophet. Ron still believed in the pattern, but he decided that Jeffrey had misused it for his own personal gain. Ron called Jeffrey at Macks Creek and told him that he was quitting the group. Jeffrey didn't argue. "The scriptures had told me that I would be betrayed," he said later.

As soon as Debbie learned that Ron and Susie had quit the group, she telephoned Dennis and Tonya.

"Ron and Susie are out," she announced. "Ron even told Jeff."

"And they're still alive?" Dennis asked.

"I'm quitting too," Debbie said.

Dennis telephoned Ron and asked if he'd really quit. They spoke for nearly an hour and when they finished, Dennis asked Tonya what she thought they should do. Tonya hadn't believed in Jeffrey for a long time. "Let's quit," she said. Dennis agreed. He telephoned Debbie. "We're out too," he said.

Debbie began working on Sharon and by nightfall had convinced her that Jeffrey was a fraud. Ron, meanwhile, telephoned Keith and told him that everyone was dropping out.

By December 6, a Wednesday, Kathy and Danny Kraft were the only two group members still loyal to Jeffrey. Everyone figured Kathy was a lost cause, but Ron and Dennis decided to visit Danny personally the following day.

That night, Keith telephoned Jeffrey and threatened to turn him in to the police for murdering the Averys unless he ended his relationship with Kathy by nine o'clock the next morning. "I told him to be a little rough on Kathy, to tell her that he never loved her and had only used her," said Keith, "because I wanted her back and I wanted her to know exactly what he was."

Jeffrey sounded nervous as they talked. "Now, Keith," he said, "there are other people to consider in this. Everyone has something to lose if you go to the police."

"Do as I say," Keith replied, "because I'm mad enough to do it."

Keith said he had written a letter about the murders and had given it to his attorney in a sealed envelope. If anything happened to him, the attorney was to open the letter and notify the police.

"Okay," said Jeffrey. "I'll tell her. I'll send Kathy back to you but I need another day."

"Just tell her," said Keith, "to come home."

As soon as they finished talking, Jeffrey telephoned Kathy in Odessa and told her about Keith's threat. The next morning, Jeffrey announced to Alice that he needed to run some errands. He drove to Odessa, picked up Kathy, and took her to a motel in a suburb of Kansas City where he was certain that Keith couldn't find her. They spent the day together and then Jeffrey drove to Higginsville to talk with Danny. He arrived shortly before Dennis and Ron were scheduled to meet him. Jeffrey realized that he was going to need someone to support him in California and Danny was the only wage earner they had left. "Danny's artistic skills were such that I knew he could find a job anywhere we went." As always, Jeffrey used his scriptures to convince Danny that God wanted him to go with the "God of the whole Earth" to a city by an ocean. Danny packed his bags and went with Jeffrey to Macks Creek. "We missed saving Danny by only a few hours," Dennis said later. "If we'd only got to him, I think we could have gotten him out."

The next morning, a Friday, Ralph and Donna Keehler left their house early for Independence where Ralph was scheduled for a routine checkup at a VA hospital. As soon as the Keehlers' car drove away from the house, Jeffrey and Alice packed up their belongings. Jeffrey no longer felt safe in Macks Creek. He figured that by this time, Keith would realize that Jeffrey was calling his bluff. Alice left her mother a note. "We may never see each other again," she wrote. "I'm sorry things turned out this way."

Jeffrey couldn't leave for California for at least one more day. Charles Keehler had found a buyer willing to pay $6,000 for the ATV and electric generator, but he wouldn't have the cash until sometime Saturday. Jeffrey drove to Osage Beach and checked his family and Danny into a motel there. Alice would later recall that it was one of the same motels that Jeffrey had stayed in ten years earlier when he had his first sexual affair with his fellow hospital worker.

On Saturday morning, Jeffrey met Charles and collected $5,400 of the $6,000. Charles kept $600 as a commission. Still worried that Keith might be hunting him, Jeffrey returned to Osage Beach and told everyone that they were moving to a different motel, this time in Springfield. On Sunday morning, December 10, Jeffrey informed Alice that he had to run a few more errands. He drove to Kansas City by himself, met with Kathy and gave her some of the cash. They agreed that she would stay behind in the Kansas City motel until Jeffrey sent for her. Somehow, he would force Alice to accept Kathy as a fellow wife.

Jeffrey was nervous when he returned to Springfield that night. "Whenever Jeffrey is under extreme pressure, he absolutely and totally engulfs himself in his sexual fantasies and shuts out the real world," said Alice. "It's how he copes." Jeffrey asked Alice to take him shopping. They bought a bra, panties, nylons, a dress, and low-heeled women's shoes, Alice said. Back at the motel, Alice gave Jeffrey his bath, shaved all of the hair off his body except for his head and put curlers in his shoulder-length hair. She spent nearly an hour applying makeup to his face. When she was finished, Jeffrey dressed in the women's clothing and they drove to a grocery store. "He had me walk with him up and down the aisle, but he was afraid to go through the checkout stand." Instead, Jeffrey hurried out to the truck and when Alice joined him, he hiked up his skirt and ordered her to perform oral sex, Alice said later.

On that same Sunday night, Jeffrey's ex-followers were meeting in the apartment where Debbie and Sharon were staying. By this time, Debbie had found Greg, and he and Richard were at the meeting. Greg had told Debbie that he cared about her as a friend, but he no longer considered them married. Richard had not been as cordial to Sharon.

During the meeting, everyone looked to Ron for guidance. He began by talking about how Jeffrey had duped them, but the conversation quickly turned to the murder of the Averys and their culpability. Everyone was optimistic at first. After all, it was Jeffrey who had done the actual shooting. None of the women had been in the barn. Tonya hadn't even been at the farm during the killing; neither had Dennis or Keith. The only thing that those two men had done was help dig the pit in the barn and they could claim that Jeffrey had told them it was a baptismal font. They could claim that they really didn't know what Jeffrey had planned. Greg, Richard, and Ron were going to have a tougher time since they had participated in the murders, the group decided. But all they had done was follow Jeffrey's orders. In fact, just before the men had gone into the barn, Jeffrey had called them into his bedroom at the farmhouse and shown them the .45-caliber pistol that he was going to use. He had asked them one by one if they were "in or out." That questioning could be interpreted as a death threat if the right spin was put on the story.

The longer the group talked about it, the better their rationalizations sounded. But when Keith suggested that they all march down to the police station and report Jeffrey, the room suddenly fell silent. Reality hit. Dennis, Cheryl, Trina, Becky, and Karen had been dumped into a pit and murdered. No one had stopped Jeffrey. No one had gone to the police before or afterward. Most of them had lied to the FBI on April 18 when questioned at the farm. Clearly, Jeffrey wasn't going to be the only person prosecuted. Some of them were going to be punished.

Why not lie? someone suggested. If they all stuck together, they could blame Jeffrey, Alice, Damon, and Danny. It would be their word against the others'. Dennis and Keith opposed that idea. Why should they commit perjury when they clearly weren't in as much trouble as everyone else? Self-preservation had kicked in.

About halfway through the meeting, Keith told everyone that

he had already given a letter to his lawyers that described the killings. "Everyone told Keith that he had to get that letter back," Debbie said later. What if Keith was killed in a car accident driving
home that night? The police would inadvertently find out about the
Averys.

"We have to do something," Keith said, "or else Jeffrey is just
going to go down the road and do this all over again."

Debbie finally made a plea. "I need some time with my children," she said. "I want a couple of months with my kids in case we
all go to jail." All of the others except for Keith openly agreed.
Keith didn't say another word. "It was clear that they didn't want
to go to the police, but I wasn't going to promise that," said Keith.
Not hearing any objection, Ron made it official. No one would go
to the police without first alerting the group, he said. That way,
they could get their stories straight, hire attorneys, and cut some sort
of deal so the blame would be put where it belonged—on Jeffrey and
Alice.

On Monday morning, Jeffrey, Alice, their children, and Danny
began their four-day drive to California in the Nissan truck. Jeffrey
had decided to go to San Diego because that is where he had been
stationed while in the navy and he was familiar with the city. As
they drove, Jeffrey asked Alice to read him the entire book of Isaiah.
He was looking for clues, he explained. He wanted to know what
God desired from the "God of the whole earth."

Jeffrey and the others arrived in San Diego on December 14,
according to the registration card at the Traveler Motel Suites, an
eighty-five-room motel located five miles from downtown San Diego.
Alice had used their actual names on the card. Their room contained a bedroom, kitchenette, and living room with foldout so-
fabed. During the ride west, Alice had asked Jeffrey where Kathy
was. He'd lied and told her that she had returned to Iowa. The
morning after Jeffrey and the others arrived at the motel, he urged
Alice, Damon, and Danny to take the children outside to play. He
needed to be alone to study his scriptures, he said. Alice suspected
that Jeffrey was trying to get rid of her so she waited outside the
motel room for five minutes and then flung open the door.

"Jeff was sitting naked on the bed masturbating while talking
on the phone. I knew it was her. He was talking to the bitch."

Jeffrey slammed down the receiver and accused Alice of being
rebellious. She started screaming. He pushed her into the bathroom
and slammed the door. He refused to let her out for three hours.

The next morning, Jeffrey drove Alice to the local welfare office, where she spent the day applying for financial aid. Once again,
she used Jeffrey's real name on all the forms. Twice, she called the
motel on a pay phone, but both times the operator told her that the
line to the room was busy. "I knew he was talking to Kathy again.
I knew he was figuring out a way to get that bitch out to California."
Alice collected some $300 in food stamps that day and another $938
through a program designed to help homeless families find housing
to rent. When she got back to the motel, Jeffrey ordered pizza for
everyone to celebrate her "looting" of the Gentiles. He and Alice
then went to a nearby Laundromat where they played video games
until 2:00 A.M. "Jeffrey got the highest score on the machine," Alice
gushed later. "He was just a tremendous player."

During the next few days, Jeffrey sent Danny to find a job. He
put Damon in charge of baby-sitting for the other Lundgren children. Alice slept during the day and watched television. Jeffrey,
meanwhile, spent his mornings and afternoons exercising in a nearby
gym and playing video games at the Laundromat. At night, Jeffrey
taught Damon, Danny, and Alice various new scriptural interpretations. At one point, Jeffrey talked about recruiting motorcycle-gang
members as followers. They would be tough enough to perform the
killing that God was about to order, he said. Jeffrey told Alice that
gang members frequented striptease bars in San Diego and he said
that God wanted him to begin visiting all of the nude nightclubs to
search for new disciples.

Jeffrey also announced that the third seal in Revelation had
been opened while the group was in West Virginia, although no one
except for him realized it. The third seal read:

> And when he had opened the third seal, I heard the third
> beast say, Come and see. And I beheld, and lo a black horse;
> and he that sat on him had a pair of balances in his hand . . .

The "pair of balances," Jeffrey explained, was a cryptic reference to Alice and Kathy. "The rider of the black horse is carrying
a pair of balances—in other words, he has two wives." That verse,
Jeffrey told Alice, was additional proof that God wanted him to be
married to both women.

Alice didn't believe him, but instead of challenging Jeffrey's interpretation, Alice asked him about the one-year deadline that he
had imposed for opening all of the seals. He had told everyone that

God expected all seven seals to be opened within twelve months once the Averys were murdered. It had been nine months since the sacrifice and Jeffrey was still on the third seal. Jeffrey had a ready explanation. Because he was divine, like God, he spoke chiastically. "In order for you to really understand what I am saying, you have to use the pattern to diagram my exact words," he said. Had anyone done that while the group was in the wilderness, they would have discovered that his words didn't always say what they seemed to say. They contained a hidden message and, in this case, that message was that there was no deadline for opening the seven seals.

Near the end of their first full week in San Diego, Jeffrey told Alice that God had instructed him to spend three nights on the beach. During one of those nights, the Mormon prophet Nephi would appear and tell him how to open the fourth seal. He announced that he was going out that very night to see if Nephi would appear. He took Damon with him to a nearby public beach. They stayed out until 3:00 A.M. and then returned to the motel to sleep. The next night, Jeffrey said that God wanted him to go alone. He didn't come back to the motel until nearly noon on the next day.

"Did Nephi appear?" Alice asked, when Jeffrey dragged in.

"No," Jeffrey replied. "I have to go out again tonight. It must be the night."

Alice hurried outside and looked in the back of the truck. "I found a mattress in the back and it was covered with sand."

Returning to the motel room, Alice asked: "Did you and Nephi roll around in the back of the truck?"

Jeffrey said that he had gotten tired and had taken the mattress along so that he could rest.

"Jeffrey," she replied, "you're lying again. It's Kathy. You brought her out here! You're hiding her somewhere. Now where is that bitch?"

Jeffrey denied that Kathy was in San Diego. "She's in Iowa," he insisted. But Alice wouldn't believe him. They argued until Jeffrey finally left the room. When he returned, he announced that God had spoken to him. God was so infuriated by Alice's constant rebellion that He had decided not to send Nephi to meet with Jeffrey. Instead, God wanted Jeffrey to humble Alice.

"You must sleep on the floor for the next three nights at the foot of your lord and master," Jeffrey announced. "This is what God demands."

That night, while Jeffrey slept on the motel bed, Alice lay on the floor, without a blanket or pillow.

"It was at that time that I became completely and totally, absolutely convinced that there was no validity to anything that Jeffrey said or taught," Alice said later. "Everything was a lie from the time we had met in college twenty years earlier."

The next morning, Alice challenged Jeffrey. "I told him point-blank that I didn't think he had ever had any revelatory experience, that I thought he'd made up everything in his mind and that the only god that he listened to was Jeff Lundgren.

"I began telling him what a lousy provider he had been for me and the kids, and all of a sudden, he became extremely kind and compassionate and he started crying. He said, 'Alice, I haven't treated you as I ought. I haven't provided for you as I ought.' And he began to beg me for forgiveness. He said, 'Please let me make love to you.' That was the first time since we had left West Virginia that he had asked to do anything for me. I said, 'No, Jeffrey, it's too late.' I got up and I walked out the motel door and he came running after me. He followed me the entire time that I was walking and he begged me not to leave him.

"He said, 'Alice, if you ever left me, I'd die. You've got to believe in me. You've got to believe I am who I say I am, otherwise I can't go on. I need you.'"

CHAPTER FIFTY-ONE

CHIEF Yarborough was at home helping Gail get ready for a New Year's Eve party when the telephone rang at 3:30 P.M. on December 31, 1989. Most of Gail's relatives were coming over later that afternoon to begin celebrating. But within seconds after Yarborough picked up the receiver, he forgot about the night's festivities. An agent for the federal Bureau of Alcohol, Tobacco, and Firearms was on the line calling from Kansas City with quite a story. Richard Van Haelst had just spent more than two hours interviewing a man who claimed that five murder victims were buried in a barn outside Kirtland.

Who, Yarborough asked, was Van Haelst's informant?

"Keith Johnson," the agent replied.

Who was supposedly buried in the barn?

A family named the Averys, Van Haelst said. Dennis, Cheryl, and their three daughters.

Yarborough didn't have to ask who the alleged murderer was, but Van Haelst volunteered the name. The triggerman, he said, was Jeffrey Lundgren.

"I felt sick," Yarborough later remembered. "I hoped like hell that Johnson was lying."

Van Haelst told Yarborough that a friend of Keith's had contacted another BATF agent, Larry Scott, that morning and had arranged for them to meet just before noon. Keith had told Van Haelst and Scott up-front that one of the main reasons why he had come forward was because he wanted the BATF to track down his wife and to arrest Jeffrey. There was a chance, the agent said, that Keith had concocted the entire murder story just to find Kathy and get Jeffrey into trouble. At least that was the theory of the Cleveland BATF field office. Before contacting Yarborough, Van Haelst had called an agent there who had quickly dismissed Keith's story as the rambling of a jilted spouse who was simply bored on New Year's Eve. Van Haelst had called Yarborough, in part, out of frustration. He was trying to find someone willing to go out to the barn and at least do some snooping around.

As soon as Yarborough finished talking to Van Haelst, he telephoned Ron Andolsek and asked him to contact the Averys' relatives. Before anyone scurried out to the barn, Yarborough wanted to make certain that Dennis and Cheryl were definitely missing.

"I really hoped Keith was lying," the chief said. "I hoped it was nothing but a hoax."

The next morning, New Year's Day, Andolsek told Yarborough that none of the Averys' relatives had heard from the family since April. No one was certain where they had gone, although Cheryl Avery's mother had gotten a note that mentioned Wyoming.

Yarborough's first impulse was to race out to the barn and begin digging. But he held himself back. He wanted to move cautiously. If there were five bodies buried in the barn, the Kirtland Police Department was going to be involved in the biggest investigation in its history and Yarborough didn't want to do anything spur of the moment that might result in Jeffrey or anyone else being found not guilty later because of a legal technicality. The chief told Andolsek that before either of them could search the barn, they had to get written permission from its owner, Stan Skrbis, Jeffrey's former landlord. That was going to take much of the day.

There was another reason why Yarborough wasn't in a rush. "I didn't want those bodies to be there. I blamed myself. I thought, 'Damn, Jeffrey turned on his own group. We stopped him from hitting the temple so he turned on his own people.' I kept thinking, 'What if I'd done this or done that?' We'd never really paid much attention to finding the Averys. They didn't seem like they were part of Jeffrey's plan."

By the time that Andolsek got all of the paperwork signed it was 10:30 P.M. He and Yarborough met outside the empty farmhouse. The last time that both of them had been at the farm together was April 18, the day after the alleged murders. That fact grated on the chief. *One day! One stinking day late!*

No one had rented the farm since Jeffrey had fled owing Skrbis several months' back rent. The front yard was overgrown with weeds. The apple trees needed tending. Yarborough and Andolsek flipped on their flashlights. The electricity in the barn had been turned off months earlier. The door creaked when they pulled it open. Their lights spotlighted a miscellany of junk abandoned inside the barn. Jeffrey and his followers had discarded everything they couldn't take with them to West Virginia, tossing it aside like litter carelessly dropped from a fast-moving car. Cardboard boxes over-flowing with books, green plastic trash bags bursting with clothing, letters, coats, toys, pieces of furniture—the scene reminded An-dolsek of a giant Goodwill box that hadn't been emptied for months.

Keith had told the federal agents that the Averys were buried on the east side of the barn. It took Yarborough and Andolsek sev-eral minutes to make their way through the debris and several more to clear a spot so they could see if there were any signs of digging. When they had at last removed enough trash to investigate the floor, Yarborough reached down and swept away a layer of straw.

"Hey, Ron," he announced, "this is concrete under here. He couldn't have buried anyone under this."

Yarborough felt a quick elation. Maybe Keith was lying. Maybe he had concocted the story. The two men shone their lights across the barn. Something moved. Yarborough flashed his light in the di-rection of the sound. A terrified chicken flew toward him. The chief jumped and then laughed.

Andolsek wondered: Could Keith had been confused? Or had Van Haelst given them the wrong directions? Maybe the bodies were buried in the west corner. The two men worked their way through the debris. Yarborough counted three abandoned cars piled with boxes. In the western portion of the barn, they found a room that was packed with so much junk that neither of them could squeeze inside to look around. The hope that Yarborough had felt dissipated. There was *too* much garbage piled inside. It looked as if someone was intentionally trying to hide something there.

They were going to need help clearing the room of debris. They'd have to wait for daylight, Yarborough said. "We'll come back tomorrow." As they walked back toward the door, Andolsek shone his flashlight on a box and spotted a formal-looking document. He picked it up. High School Diploma, it said. Cheryl Clisby. Class of 1965.

BATF agent Scott telephoned Yarborough the next morning to see if he'd found the bodies. The barn's floor was concrete, the chief explained. Scott offered to send a drawing that Keith had made of the barn. It showed exactly where the grave was located. Even if the bodies had been removed, there should still be some sign of digging.

"What's your fax number?" Scott asked.

Yarborough paused. The Kirtland Police Department didn't own a fax. The chief said he'd find someone else in Kirtland who could receive it.

Yarborough was waiting in his office for the diagram to be delivered when he looked up and saw Dennis Patrick walk into the police station.

"I just stopped by to let you know my wife and I aren't in Jeffrey's group anymore," Dennis volunteered. "Neither is Debbie Olivarez."

The three of them had quit, Dennis said, and had returned to Kirtland with a U-Haul truck because they wanted to retrieve some of their belongings from the barn. Would it be okay, he asked, if the three of them went onto the property to reclaim their things?

Yarborough could tell from Dennis's demeanor that he didn't know that Keith Johnson had tipped off the BATF to the murders.

"Why don't you come back later this afternoon?" the chief suggested. Yarborough said that he'd have an officer escort them onto the property so they wouldn't be accused of trespassing.

Dennis thanked him, offered the chief his hand, and walked out of the station without any clue about what was happening. The chief grabbed his telephone and called FBI Agent Robert Alvord. Once again, Yarborough was covering himself. He wanted Alvord to be there when Dennis returned later that day.

Alvord and the drawing from the BATF arrived at about the same time. Yarborough and Andolsek had been right. The grave was in the western half of the barn in the room strewn with trash.

At 3:00 P.M., Dennis returned to the station with Tonya and Debbie, who waited outside. The three of them had contacted Shar Olson and were planning on spending the night at her apartment. As soon as Dennis entered the police station, Yarborough and Alvord began questioning him about the Averys. Dennis panicked. He didn't want to appear uncooperative, but he didn't want to tell them the truth either. He was soon tripping over his own lies. Thirty minutes later, Tonya came looking for Dennis. When she saw him, she knew something was wrong. He looked terrified. Hurrying back outside, Tonya raced over to Debbie.

"They know!" she said.

"Oh, my God!" Debbie replied.

Dennis was shaking when he came out of the station. "We've got to find an attorney," he said. "We've got to talk to a lawyer." The trio rushed back to Shar's apartment, but they refused to tell her what was going on. Dennis telephoned a local attorney who belonged to the RLDS Church. The attorney told them to get back to Missouri as quickly as they could. They left immediately, leaving Shar completely bewildered. None of them had mentioned the murders to her. Once they were a few miles outside Kirtland, Dennis stopped at a pay phone and called Greg. "They know," he said. Someone had tipped off the police without warning everyone else.

"Keith!" Greg said. It had to be Keith.

Greg promised to alert the others. They'd meet at Minsky's, a pizza place just outside Independence. The Patricks and Debbie drove all night. They met Ron, Susie, Greg, and Richard at the restaurant. No one invited Keith. Sharon wasn't there either. By this time, she had returned to her parents' house in Michigan and had just given birth to a daughter. Greg had called her and told her that Keith had squealed. He'd promised to call after the meeting and tell her what everyone was going to do. Once again, the group discussed what might happen to them, and then Ron suggested that they each contact an attorney. No one spoke for several minutes. As they looked around the table, each of them realized that once they left the pizza parlor they were on their own. Keith had been the first to jump ship. Who would be next to cut a deal?

Back in Kirtland, Yarborough, Andolsek, and Alvord arrived at the barn at 9:00 A.M. on January 3 and began removing junk from the room where the grave was located. By four o'clock, they had removed enough for Andolsek to crawl inside. He made his way to one side of the room, where he spotted chunks of dried clay on several boxes.

"Someone's been digging here," he yelled.

All three men returned to the police station. Yarborough was now convinced that Keith's story was true. He telephoned the chief of Kirtland's Volunteer Fire Department and asked for his help. At seven o'clock that night, nearly a dozen firefighters assembled at the farm. They set up large floodlights to illuminate the barn and they began clearing debris from inside the room. Ron Andolsek had a firefighter videotape the entire operation. Within an hour, the room was clean. It was obvious where the grave was located. Everywhere else, the floor was hard clay, but the ground was soft where the bodies were buried. With Yarborough and Andolsek overseeing the exhumation, two firemen began digging. As soon as they overturned the first shovel of dirt, a stench rose from the ground. Within minutes, a putrid odor permeated the room. One of the men gasped for air, dropped his shovel, and rushed outside. Yarborough, Andolsek, and the others fought back the urge to vomit. The stench became so vile that the volunteer firemen began digging in shifts. Some could work only for a few minutes. Shortly after 9:00 P.M., one of the men unearthed a swatch of blue denim. He climbed into the hole and reached down with his hands to clear away the dirt. It was a hip turned sideways. The firefighter removed about twelve inches of dirt, revealing a man's belt and what looked like the bottom of a faded plaid shirt.

"That's enough," Yarborough said. There was no question now that Keith had told the truth. They had found one body. Yarborough ordered the firemen to stop digging. His small police department and the volunteer firefighters were unprepared for the job that Yarborough knew lay ahead. He told Andolsek to get everyone out of the barn and close off the area. Yarborough wanted an officer stationed at the barn round the clock. As soon as the chief was certain that no one would disturb the grave, he began calling various county officials. The Lake County Sheriff's Department had a lieutenant, Daniel Dunlap, who had received special schooling from the FBI on how to process a crime scene. Yarborough wanted his help. Lake County Prosecutor Steven C. LaTourette needed to be notified too. He would be in charge of filing charges against Jeffrey and the others. He'd also be the person responsible for making certain that they were convicted. Besides LaTourette, the county coroner needed to be contacted.

By midnight, all of the various officials who would play some role in the case had been notified. The county coroner drove to the barn to look at the grave. It was beginning to fill with water. While digging, the firefighters had accidentally cut through a drain. The coroner and Yarborough agreed that it would be better to resume the exhumation in the morning, after Dunlap arrived. That way there wouldn't be any more mishaps.

It was well after 2:00 A.M. when Yarborough walked over to his car. Before getting inside, he looked around. No one was watching him. He turned and vomited into the grass.

"I wanted to retire right then," he later said, "because I knew what we were going to find in the morning."

Lieutenant Dunlap and Rick Kent, a supervisor at the Lake County Regional Forensic Laboratory, took control of the site on January 4. Dunlap arrived just in time. Some of the volunteer firemen had returned to the barn with a hose that they wanted to use to drain the water from the grave. Dunlap ordered the men to bail out the hole with buckets. Each was then dumped through a sieve to check for evidence, such as bullets. Once the water was cleared, Dunlap and Kent began using hand trowels to remove the clay from around the hip of the partially uncovered corpse. Every scoop of clay was put into a bucket and carried outside to the sieve. The clay was so thick that the firemen had to use water to break it apart.

Because the body in the pit was badly decomposed, it was impossible to tell at first if it was Dennis Avery, although it seemed to be a man because of its size. As Dunlap and Kent continued to unearth it, they found another body at the feet of the first. It was Cheryl. When they started to unearth the head, both men grimaced. Gray duct tape was wrapped around the face, like a mummy.

As the two men continued digging, Steven LaTourette stood away from the grave next to the barn door where he leaned against an old washer and dryer. The thirty-five-year-old prosecutor had intentionally chosen to stand in a spot that prevented him from seeing directly into the grave. He felt that it was important for him to be present during the exhumation, but LaTourette had a daughter the same age as six-year-old Karen Avery and he was having trouble watching the grisly proceedings. An aide made trips back and forth from the grave to LaTourette, filling him in on what was happening.

"They found the first two bodies rather quickly and then there was quite a bit of time before they found the third," LaTourette said later. "You could feel the deflation in the room among the people working when the third one was found. All of us had hoped that the Avery girls weren't in the pit. That just the parents were buried there."

The third body was clearly a child, resting on her mother's corpse. It would later be identified as Becky. As they began uncovering it, they found a fourth body, smaller still, with its head touching the hips of Becky's corpse. It would later be determined through dental records that this fourth body was Karen Avery. Because of the location of Karen's body, Dunlap and Kent decided to remove the remains of the thirty-six-pound girl first. Her body was held together mostly by her blue jacket and jeans. Water had again seeped into the pit, turning the clay into a thick muck. It was bitter cold in the barn. A light rain was falling outside. The stench remained almost unbearable. Dunlap and Kent were becoming exhausted. As they gently began lifting the small corpse, the mud and air made a sucking noise and created a vacuum that pulled on the remains. From a distance, LaTourette and Yarborough watched as Kent and Dunlap finally freed Karen's tiny remains from the pit. As they lifted the body from the mud, the girl's left foot fell off.

"When I saw that little girl's foot fall off," LaTourette said later, "I began to feel nothing but pure, unadulterated hate for Jeffrey Lundgren."

To prevent the other bodies from breaking apart, Dunlap suggested that each one be wrapped in a sheet before it was lifted from the grave. He and Kent could then lift the sheets, rather than touching the delicate corpses. Becky's body and the remains of Cheryl and Dennis were removed in sheets and loaded into body bags.

Fatigued, Dunlap climbed out of the muck and turned his digging trowel over to Deputy Ronald Walters. A few minutes later, the fifth body was found, curled in a fetal position. This child, identified later as Trina, had been a few steps away from the others, facing her father's corpse. After Kent and Walters gingerly cleared away the mud from Trina, they gently lifted the corpse so that they could slip a sheet under it. As Walters raised Trina's head, the girl's scalp and braided hair came loose in his hand.

At a news conference held after all of the bodies had been taken away by ambulances, LaTourette became so emotional that he abandoned the traditional "they are innocent until proven guilty" role that legal protocol demanded. Instead, the prosecutor angrily denounced Jeffrey and his followers. "These people are . . . the cruelest, most inhumane people this county has ever seen," he said. "They're going to die in the electric chair for these crimes."

It was well after midnight when Chief Yarborough finally got home that night. Gail was already in bed asleep. Yarborough took a shower, tucked his clothes in the washing machine, and crawled in beside her. As he lay there, he could still smell the stench from the barn, and despite his best efforts to block it out of his mind, all he could visualize was Karen being lifted from the grave and seeing her foot fall off. Finally, exhaustion brought sleep, but he was jarred awake minutes later. His entire body had started shaking. "It was that damn smell," he said later. "I just couldn't stop smelling it." The image of Karen returned and within seconds, his mind's eye called up the sight of Walters holding a young girl's ponytail and scalp in his hand.

Yarborough felt ill. He got up and walked through his dark house into the living room, where he found a tin of Copenhagen. Tucking tobacco between his lip and front teeth, he stepped over to the front picture window in his home. It had gotten even colder outside and the drop in temperature had changed that day's gloomy drizzle into a light snow that difted down, reflected in the moonlight. As he peered outside at the pristine beauty, he shook his head. Things like this weren't supposed to happen in Kirtland.

Yarborough thought about Jeffrey. He was out there somewhere. Maybe he was awake, staring outside. Yarborough wondered: What sort of man can put three children into a pit and kill each one? What sort of man can then claim that God told him to do it? And what sort of people could follow such a cold-blooded killer? Only two days earlier, Yarborough had confronted Dennis Patrick. From all appearances, he seemed like a decent guy, not someone who would knowingly participate in such a crime. Why had he followed Jeffrey?

As he stood there alone in the darkness, Yarborough felt a sudden urge. There was something that he needed to do, a promise that needed to be uttered. It didn't matter that he was alone. Someone had to say it. Someone had to react to the insanity of that day, to Jeffrey's cruelty. Someone had to react to the stench of death. Someone had to care enough to not be able to sleep. God was a witness, maybe Karen was too, and maybe Yarborough was just talking to himself. Later, he wouldn't be certain why he had felt the need to speak. It didn't matter. He just did. Someone had to.

"He'll pay." Yarborough said. Jeffrey Lundgren was going to pay for what he had done.

CHAPTER FIFTY-TWO

"DAD! Mom!" Danny Kraft yelled, bursting into the motel bedroom that Jeffrey and Alice shared. "The barn is on television!"

Both of them scrambled out into the living room of their motel suite. On the screen, the bodies of the Avery family were shown being carried by ambulance attendants from the barn. An old photograph of Jeffrey appeared, followed by a film clip of LaTourette promising that Jeffrey and his followers were going to "fry." It was 11:30 P.M. in San Diego on January 4.

"Get the stuff packed!" Jeffrey told Danny. Turning to Alice, he announced, "Let's go!"

Alice and her children hurried out to the truck. Jeffrey told Danny that he'd come back for him later. With their four children in the back of the Nissan, Jeffrey pulled out of the motel parking lot as Alice looked up and down the street, half expecting a squad of police cars.

Jeffrey drove to National City, another suburb of San Diego, and cruised a strip of cheaper hotels. He was looking for one that wasn't part of a national chain. He was afraid that the police might have sent his photograph and description to the better-known motels.

"There's one," Alice said, as they approached the Santa Fe Motel. Fearing that he might be recognized, he sent Alice to register. "Use fake names," he warned.

Alice was nervous. She had chosen the name Anna for herself and planned to use James for Jeffrey. But as she filled out the registration, she couldn't think of an appropriate last name so she simply wrote: Anna James, and handed the clerk a fifty-dollar bill. He took the card without examining it and handed her the key to Room 29.

As soon as everyone was in the room, Jeffrey said he was going back to get Danny. "Don't wait for me," he told her. Alice suddenly felt angry. She suspected that Jeffrey was going to warn Kathy. She was certain that he had brought her to San Diego by bus and was hiding her somewhere. But as Jeffrey started toward the door, Alice called out and then ran up to him. She kissed him and they hugged. She was scared, really scared.

Jeffrey found Danny waiting in the room. Together, they drove to a nearby motel where Kathy was living. Jeffrey told Danny that he wanted him to stay with Kathy. He'd figure out some way for them to get out of town. It was after 2:30 A.M. when Jeffrey returned to the Santa Fe Motel. Alice didn't ask where Danny was. She didn't want to know. She was too preoccupied even to question Jeff about Kathy. Alice had been watching Cable News Network. "It's been on every hour," she told Jeffrey. "The prosecutor says we're all going to fry." Jeffrey tried to calm her, but Alice was too frightened.

"I want you to kill the children and me," she announced. She began to cry. "Do it now, while they are asleep, but kill me first."

Jeffrey looked at Alice. More than anyone, he knew that she had a habit of being melodramatic. But she was serious this time. "She really wanted to die and she wanted me to kill the children."

"Jeffrey was aghast," Alice said later. "He told me that he couldn't harm his own children. I said, 'Okay, let's call my mom, she'll come get them, but then I want you to kill me.' I just wanted to get it over with."

Jeffrey agreed that they needed to call Donna Keehler about the children. As far as killing Alice, that was something that he would have to consult God about, he said. The next day, Jeffrey and Damon walked to a pay phone. Damon dialed the number and asked for Donna. That had been Jeffrey's idea. He thought the police might recognize his voice, but not Damon's. As soon as Donna answered, Jeffrey got on the phone.

"Can you come get the kids?" he asked.

Donna was furious, but she didn't want Jeffrey to hang up.

"Of course I'll come," she said. "Where are you?"

"I can't say, just start driving west; call us at nine o'clock and we'll give you more directions," Jeffrey said. He gave her the number of a pay phone to call.

Donna was incredulous. How could she simply start driving west? she asked. But Jeffrey was afraid to stay on the line any longer. Even Donna was worried that it could be tapped.

As soon as she put down the phone, Donna grabbed a telephone directory. Jeffrey had given her a number with a 619 area code. According to the directory, 619 was in southern California. Donna knew Jeffrey was hiding in San Diego. It made sense that he would run to a city where he'd lived before. As she was closing the directory, the phone rang a second time. It was Jeffrey. He had given her the number of a pay phone that didn't accept incoming calls. He told her another number with a 619 prefix and reminded her to telephone him the next evening at nine o'clock based on Kansas City time.

Donna called her sister and brother-in-law. She didn't want to drive to California alone and she knew that Ralph couldn't make the trip. They agreed to go along. The next morning was a Saturday, January 6. As soon as Donna pulled out of her driveway, a car carrying BATF agents slipped in front of her, another car pulled up behind. The agents told Donna that they knew all about her conversation with Jeffrey. Worried about the fate of her grandchildren, Donna agreed to cooperate. She was, in fact, a bit relieved. "I wanted to get those kids out of there safely in case Jeffrey began shooting. They were what was most on my mind. Jeffrey had gone too far and I wasn't certain that Alice could be helped either."

The BATF had already traced both of the numbers that Jeffrey had given Donna. One was a pay phone outside a 7-Eleven store; the second was at a restaurant not far from the Santa Fe Motel. With her federal-agent escort, Donna drove southwest toward Springfield and then on to Tulsa, Oklahoma. Just before 9:00 P.M., she stopped in Oklahoma City at a restaurant and dialed the number that Jeffrey had given her. Damon answered and told his grandmother that she should keep driving west and call him on Sunday at noon Kansas City time for new instructions.

Agents from the San Diego BATF office had staked out the telephone and they watched as Damon completed the call. A plainclothes agent followed Damon as he walked back to the Santa Fe Motel, but the agent didn't see which room he went into. The stakeout was moved from the phone booth to the motel.

Inside Room 29, Alice was becoming more and more depressed. Caleb had started to cry. Kristen was sucking her thumb. Jason refused to speak to anyone. Damon was trying to comfort them but wasn't having much luck. Jeffrey had left the motel earlier that day and driven over to see Danny and Kathy. They were frightened too. Jeffrey had taken his family's laundry to Danny and told him to get it washed and dried. He had left Danny the Nissan truck so that he could bring the clean clothes back to the Santa Fe Motel when he finished. On his way to the Laundromat, Danny had taken Jeffrey back to his motel.

Damon told Jeffrey that Donna was in Oklahoma City and that everything was going as planned. Later that night, after Alice was certain that everyone was asleep, she asked Jeffrey if he had talked to God and learned whether it was okay for Jeffrey to kill her.

"The Lord says it's okay for you to die," he told her. But Jeffrey said that God expected Alice to take her own life and that He wanted her to wait until after the children were gone before she did it. Jeffrey figured the FBI would tail Donna to San Diego, but he told Alice that he had come up with a way to deliver the kids to her mother without being arrested. They would put them on a bus and then direct Donna to the next stop on the line. Once they said good-bye to their children, Jeffrey and Alice would come back to the motel and he would stay with her while she took an overdose of pills. Jeffrey had already sent Damon to buy two bottles of Excedrin P.M., two six-packs of beer and a bottle of Jack Daniel's whiskey. That would be sufficient to kill her, he said. Jeffrey still hadn't told Alice about Kathy. After he was freed of his children and Alice committed suicide, Jeffrey and Kathy would find somewhere to hide and he would start finding a new group of followers.

Alice decided to write a letter for her mother. "I told her not to question anything that she had done. I told her that I knew when I married Jeff that he was different from anyone I had ever met. I told her that I had already talked to Krissy about menstruation. I told her things about each of the children."

When Alice finished the letter, Jeffrey told her that he wanted to make love. Alice agreed. What began as a tender session soon turned violent, Alice later claimed. "I was on the bed with my head laying on the side and Jeffrey was thrusting himself into my mouth and he began doing it so hard that it began to hurt and I couldn't breathe," she said. "I began to gag and I began to vomit but he was so caught up in it that he refused to stop until he was finished.

"I went into the bathroom and threw up and I climbed in the

shower and Jeff came in and got into the shower and I said, 'Jeff, why do you have to do that? Why do you always have to hurt me? And he said, 'Because it felt so good.'

"He began to cry and he cried and cried and cried and begged me to forgive him. He told me that he loved me and there was no one in the world that he loved as much as me and he was sorry. I held him in my arms and told him that it was okay. When we went to bed, he curled up next to me and said, 'Mommy I'm afraid.' I said, 'It's okay. It's okay.' And we went to sleep."

A few minutes before ten o'clock, which would have been noon in Kansas City, Donna stopped outside Holbrook, Arizona, and called the pay phone in San Diego. She told Damon that she'd be in San Diego late that night. Damon told her to call that same number at midnight. Jeffrey had decided to send the children to her by putting them in a taxi, Damon said. Donna told him that everything was still okay.

BATF Agent Van Haelst watched Damon as he talked to his grandmother. Van Haelst had flown to California to supervise the arrest and he was sitting in an unmarked car across the street. Damon seemed nonchalant when he left the phone and started walking toward the motel. He didn't pay any attention to a woman who was jogging through the motel parking lot. She was an undercover agent, and when she saw Damon enter Room 29, she stepped into a telephone booth on the sidewalk directly in front of the motel and dialed a number that connected her with Van Haelst.

"He went into room twenty-nine," she said.

As she was speaking to Van Haelst, Jeffrey came out of the motel room and walked up to the pay phone next to the one that the undercover agent was using. He was calling Kathy.

Agent Van Haelst quickly asked the jogger if she could tell whether or not Jeffrey was armed.

"No!" she said, trying to hide her excitement.

Van Haelst decided to nab Jeffrey before he could get back into the motel and alert Damon and Alice. He ordered everyone to close in. Five agents raced up to the telephone booth and jerked Jeffrey outside. They shoved him onto the sidewalk where Van Haelst stuck his revolver next to Jeffrey's head and announced that he was under arrest.

Within seconds, another team of agents led by Agent Lanny Royer burst through the door of Room 29. "Mommy! Mommy!" Caleb yelled. Kristen screamed. An agent knocked Alice down on the bed and hurried past her to Damon, who was standing near the bathroom. He was shoved down on the floor. Another agent pointed his gun at Alice, "Move, bitch, and I'll blow your brains out!" They handcuffed Damon and dragged him onto the balcony. Alice was hustled out next. Inside, the agents found an AR-15 assault rifle, two .44 magnum revolvers that belonged to Damon and Jason, another pistol, and boxes of ammunition.

Just as Jeffrey was being put into the backseat of a car, he spotted Alice on the balcony.

"Good-bye, Alice!" he yelled.

Jeffrey, Alice, and Damon were taken to jail, strip-searched, fingerprinted, and issued white paper suits to wear. They were then taken to the BATF office where Van Haelst was waiting to question them.

At 6:50 P.M., Alice agreed to make a statement about the murders. She would later claim that Van Haelst had duped her into talking by threatening to send her children to a juvenile home if she didn't cooperate. He denied her accusation.

During the short videotaped confession, Alice told the agent that Jeffrey had killed the Averys. "The more Jeff learned," she said, "the more he felt he had authority to do things. The more knowledge he attained, the more he thought it made him"—Alice paused, searching for just the right word. Van Haelst offered her one.

"Divine?" he said.

Alice nodded.

Alice put all of the blame on Jeffrey. She said he honestly believed that he was doing what God had commanded him to do, and when Van Haelst asked her why she hadn't gone to the police, Alice said she was afraid that Jeffrey would kill her too.

After they finished, Van Haelst told Alice that Damon and Jeffrey wanted to speak to her. Damon came into the room first.

"It's going to be okay, Mom," he said. He kissed her cheek.

Jeffrey came in after Damon was gone. He bent down and looked at her. He told her that he loved her and that she should not lose faith in him. He was the last messenger. God would soon free him and he would free her. All she had to do was trust him, believe in him, not lose faith.

Jeffrey stood up to leave, and when he turned around, Alice noticed that the seam in the crotch of his jail-issued white paper overalls was torn. Jeffrey's naked buttock peeked through the tear. As she watched him walk away, Alice couldn't help herself. She suddenly began to laugh.

CHAPTER FIFTY-THREE

ON the morning of January 4, while the bodies of the Avery family were being extracted in Kirtland, Keith Johnson telephoned Greg and Ron and urged them to turn themselves in. Keith would later claim that he had been told by agent Larry Scott that anyone who surrendered voluntarily *before* the bodies were exhumed would be given immunity from prosecution. But after the Averys were removed from the pit, there would be no deals made.

Greg's father, Gerald Winship, had already hired a well-known Kansas City criminal attorney, John P. O'Connor, to represent his son, so Greg quickly disregarded Keith's advice. Besides, what Keith said didn't make sense to Greg. What difference would it make if someone confessed before the bodies were taken from the grave?

Ron was not nearly as skeptical. He and Susie had spoken to an attorney and had been warned repeatedly not to make any statements. But both of them trusted Keith. More important, they thought that turning themselves in was the right thing to do. Ron had been praying about it.

What they would not discover until much later was that Keith himself was worried about being prosecuted. Keith had assumed when he first came forward that the BATF would automatically grant him immunity in return for his help. Much to his horror, Keith discovered that Lake County Prosecutor Steven LaTourette was the only official who could make such a deal. The only thing that Scott and Van Haelst could do was to lobby LaTourette on Keith's behalf, and they were going to do that only if he continued cooperating.

Regardless of Keith's prodding, chances are Ron and Susie would have surrendered and confessed anyway. They thought of themselves as being righteous, godly people. Society and its laws were not as important as God's commandments, and now that both of them realized they had been duped by Jeffrey, they wanted to clear their consciences. As children they had been taught that confession was the first step to receiving forgiveness. Shortly after 12:00 noon, Ron and Susie arrived at the BATF office in Kansas City ready to repent.

As required, Van Haelst explained Ron's constitutional rights under the Miranda decision and asked him to sign a waiver of those protections. At 1:22 P.M. Ron did, and Van Haelst and Larry Scott immediately began grilling him. After two hours, Ron agreed to confess before a video camera in the BATF conference room. Van Haelst and Scott quickly set up their gear. At the beginning of the tape, Van Haelst *twice* warned Ron that anything he was about to say could be used against him in court.

"We've not made any promises and no threats have been made against you—is that correct?" Van Haelst asked.

"Yes . . . this is completely voluntary," Ron said.

Van Haelst wanted to make certain that jurors understood Ron was not being misled. The agent knew that once Ron was formally charged, his attorney would try to keep the tape from being introduced as evidence.

During the next two hours, Ron gave a detailed account of Jeffrey's teachings and how he had convinced the group that the Averys were wicked and needed to be sacrificed. In a nasal monotone, between puffs on cigarettes, Ron candidly recounted his actions on the night of the murders and those of the other group members. Only once did he show any emotion. When he recalled how he had jabbed Dennis Avery with the electric stun gun, first in the hip, then in the neck, and finally in the chest, Ron's voice cracked.

"He [Dennis] was in a lot of pain," Ron said, looking down at the floor, fighting back tears.

"Take your time," said Van Haelst sympathetically.

Agent Scott leaned forward with some tissues.

Ron sat upright, as if he were offended. "Well," he said, quickly regaining his composure, "that's fine." He pushed the tissues out of the way and continued in his southern Missouri twang.

As soon as Ron finished, the two agents interviewed Susie Luff, who proved just as candid and equally composed. Until the two of them confessed, neither Van Haelst nor Scott had known exactly what had happened inside the barn on the night of the murders. Keith had told them what he thought had happened based on comments that Jeffrey and other group members had made after the killings. But Keith hadn't been at the farm when the murders took place. More important, Keith hadn't given them a clearheaded narrative. "The message that came through from Kansas City," La-Tourette said later, "was that Keith Johnson was a knucklehead. . . . He couldn't tell the same story twice in the same way."

After interviewing the Luffs, Van Haelst telephoned LaTourette and told him that a copy of their video confessions would be delivered to his office by 10:00 A.M. the next day. In return, LaTourette sent Van Haelst warrants over a fax machine so that he could arrest Ron and Susie. That night, a SWAT team from Independence arrested Dennis and Tonya Patrick, and Debbie Olivarez. Hoping to avoid a similar spectacle, Sharon turned herself in to the police in Bay City, Michigan. By this time, Richard Brand's family had hired him an attorney, Charles Atwell. He and Greg's lawyer arranged for their clients to surrender the next day at the BATF office.

LaTourette slipped the Luff videotape into a player on January 5 when he received it and called in the top members of his staff to view it. What he saw sickened him. "What always bothered me about Luff and the others who eventually confessed and made videotapes was their total lack of emotion," LaTourette said later. "They would become real teary-eyed and boohoo when they talked about how Jeff had pimped them and led them down the path, but there was no show of emotion when they talked about killing these little kids."

A few hours later, LaTourette showed the Luffs' confessions to a grand jury meeting in the Lake County Courthouse located in Painesville, the county seat, about twelve miles east of Kirtland. The jury immediately issued indictments charging Jeffrey, Ron, Greg, Richard, Damon, and Danny with aggravated murder, punishable by death in Ohio's electric chair. Because Dennis Patrick hadn't taken part in the actual killings, he was charged with complicity to commit aggravated murder, the same charge levied against Alice, Susie,

Tonya, Debbie, Sharon, and Kathy. That charge carried a penalty of up to life in prison. LaTourette had planned on indicting Keith Johnson on a complicity charge, but Van Haelst urged him to grant Keith immunity because of his help. LaTourette resisted at first, but finally agreed. It was the first of several controversial decisions that the young prosecutor would make.

LaTourette had been the prosecutor in Lake County for only fourteen months when the bodies of the Averys were discovered. But he had already earned a reputation as a tough and shrewd courtroom fighter. Born and reared in Cleveland Heights, one of Cleveland's more posh neighborhoods, LaTourette had grown up in a rock-solid Republican family where politics dominated afterdinner conversations and being a member of the high school debate squad was more prized than being a star athlete. When LaTourette was just a toddler, his grandmother had taken him with her to deliver campaign literature for a Republican congressional candidate. He would later remember how he had walked up and down his neighborhood in 1960 pulling his red wagon filled with pamphlets for Richard Nixon's ill-fated race against John Kennedy. Politics came naturally. After high school graduation, LaTourette followed his girlfriend, much to his parents' dismay, to the University of Michigan. She was Jewish; he was Methodist. But the romance eventually faded, and after he graduated in 1976, LaTourette returned to Cleveland where he got a job as a shipping clerk and attended law school at night, earning his degree from Cleveland Marshall College of Law in 1979. LaTourette had worked briefly for a prestigious Cleveland firm, but he found civil law tedious, and in 1980, he joined the Lake County Public Defender's Office in Painesville at an annual salary of a mere $13,000 per year. He was hired by its chief attorney, R. Paul LaPlante, who quickly became LaTourette's mentor and close personal friend.

At the time, the office was a struggling, shoestring operation. Funded with just enough taxpayers' money to make do, the public defenders service got all of the cases that no one else wanted. "Our clients were the pains in the asses of the court system," LaTourette recalled: the four-time losers, the poor, and the rapists, child molesters, and murderers that private attorneys refused to represent. When his grandmother asked how LaTourette could represent such "scumballs," her grandson proudly declared that everyone was entitled to a fair trial. His stint as LaPlante's right-hand man was LaTourette's walk on the wild side. On Sunday mornings, he and the other underpaid public defenders would play softball and then pile into the 'blue eagle,' LaTourette's gigantic 1977 Chrysler Newport, and drive to Fitzpatrick's, a Cleveland bar, where they would thumb their noses at the establishment over mugs of cheap beer.

In 1982, LaTourette got married, resigned as a public defender, and took a job in a private firm in Painesville. Still, civil law bored him, so in 1984, he ran as a Republican in an overwhelmingly Democratic district for the job of Lake County prosecutor. LaTourette lost by 15,000 votes out of the 47,000 that were cast. The local newspapers characterized it as a dismal effort, but LaTourette was amazed that he had collected 16,000 votes, considering that he had campaigned with only a handful of volunteers and $5,000 of his own money. During the next four years, LaTourette unmercifully hammered the incumbent in letters to the editor and worked at building alliances with the county's few Republicans. When the prosecutor's office mistakenly let an accused murderer go free, LaTourette publicized the blunder on billboards that proclaimed criminals were "getting away with murder" in Lake County. Although he was still considered an underdog in the 1988 race, LaTourette waged a fierce campaign by attacking the prosecutor for plea-bargaining cases rather than taking them to trial. On weekends, LaTourette stuffed campaign brochures into mailboxes and went door to door soliciting votes. To everyone's surprise but his own, LaTourette won the $70,000-per-year prosecutor's post by a 4,400 vote margin.

From the moment the Averys' bodies were unearthed, LaTourette understood that his political future hinged on how well he prosecuted Jeffrey and his followers. LaTourette also knew that Jeffrey's case was so controversial that he would be represented by the Lake County Public Defender's Office, and that meant LaTourette would be facing his former boss, teacher, and friend, Paul LaPlante, in the courtroom.

At age forty-seven, Paul LaPlante was a bone-thin, white-bearded, scholarly man, who favored logic to courtroom hysterics. Born in rural Ontario, LaPlante had been rebellious as a teenager. "I didn't get along with authority figures," he recalled. Some said he still didn't. As a teenager, he dropped out of high school, married, and supported himself by working as a meter reader. LaPlante soon realized that he was in a dead-end job, so he earned his high school diploma and went on to college. By 1966, LaPlante was working as a salesman for a Cleveland-based wire and copper company. Without any real reason, he decided to attend law school at night at Cleve-

land Marshall, the same college that Steven LaTourette would eventually attend.

It was there that LaPlante first was introduced to the U.S. Con-
stitution and Bill of Rights, and he became fascinated by the delicate
balance between the state and each individual's civil liberties. Before
he could practice law in the United States, LaPlante was told that
he had to renounce his Canadian citizenship, a move that the thirty-
year-old thought unfair. "Once again, it made me look hard at what
rights an individual in our society should have." Despite his liberal
bent, LaPlante joined the Lake County Prosecutor's Office in 1973.
One of his first big trials was the prosecution of two men who had
murdered a gas-station attendant during a late-night robbery.
LaPlante asked for the death penalty and got it. That case was one
of the last successful death-penalty trials in Lake County.

Although he was an effective prosecutor, LaPlante felt uncomfortable in the role. When the county opened the Public Defender's
Office in 1979, he moved to the other side of the legal street by
becoming its leading defense attorney. "I quickly discovered that
most of my clients were guilty," said LaPlante, "but the question was
'Has the state done its job—can it prove that they are guilty?'" Over
the years, LaPlante had become convinced that the role of his office
was not to get criminals set free, but to protect the individual rights
of "the guilty *and* the innocent," so that no matter what they were
accused of, each defendant got a fair trial.

The morning after Jeffrey was arrested, LaPlante was on the
telephone conferring with a public defender in San Diego about Jeffrey's case.

Three days later, on January 10, San Diego Sheriff's Deputy
Jimmy Sims spotted Jeffrey's blue Nissan truck with Missouri license
tags speeding down state highway 79 about forty miles northeast of
San Diego. Sims motioned the truck over to the side of the road
and arrested its occupants: Kathy Johnson and Danny Kraft, Jr., who
each claimed to be someone else. They had been living in a tent in
the mountain community of Santa Ysabel. After Jeffrey's arrest, neither had known where to go. Kathy and Danny were taken to the
same San Diego County jail where Jeffrey, Damon, and Alice were
being housed.

A short time later, Paul LaPlante arrived at the San Diego jail
with his chief assistant, Charles R. Grieshammer. They had come
to meet their new client. "Jeffrey was clearly very intelligent and
very sincere in his religious convictions," LaPlante recalled. During

their first meeting that day, LaPlante didn't mention the murders. LaPlante was used to his clients' claiming they were innocent. He wanted Jeffrey to get to know him before they discussed the killings. He figured Jeffrey was more likely to tell the truth that way. The next morning, when LaPlante brought up the Averys, Jeffrey candidly admitted killing them. But he insisted that God had ordered him to do it. As they talked, LaPlante realized that if Jeffrey was asked in court about the murders, he would, as Jeffrey put it, "not deny what God had ordered me to do."

LaPlante and Grieshammer returned to Ohio convinced that their client was going to be found guilty. But that didn't mean that Jeffrey had to be sentenced to death. In Ohio, defendants facing the death penalty automatically received a two-stage trial. In the first, jurors decided whether or not the defendant was guilty. In the second, those same jurors decided whether the defendant deserved to be executed or, because of "mitigating" circumstances, should be granted mercy and receive a sentence of life in prison without parole. "We decided to focus all of our energies on the mitigating phase of the trial," said LaPlante. "There was no question Jeffrey would be found guilty of killing the Averys."

While LaPlante was returning from San Diego, his courtroom opponent, Steven LaTourette, was deciding how to prosecute the thirteen "cult cases." LaTourette concluded early on that he needed someone from Jeffrey's group to testify against the others. "I needed an eyewitness who had actually been in the barn during the killing." His first thought was Ron Luff. Obviously, Ron knew what had happened. But LaTourette was reluctant to negotiate a plea bargain with Ron for several reasons. In effect, Ron had already hanged himself with his videotaped confession. It would make more sense to offer some other follower a deal, especially one who might be difficult to convict otherwise. Ron also didn't have an attorney representing him and LaTourette didn't want to negotiate directly with a defendant. Finally, LaTourette had been genuinely repulsed by Ron's demeanor during his confession. The prosecutor couldn't get the image out of his mind of Karen Avery's foot falling when her corpse was lifted from the grave. Nor could he forget that it had been Ron Luff who had given Karen a piggyback ride to the barn on that night so that she could be murdered.

LaTourette's need for an eyewitness was quickly solved. Two days after their clients surrendered, attorneys representing Greg and Richard independently telephoned LaTourette and told him that their clients were willing to negotiate. "The first guy to the court-house door always does better with a plea bargain than anyone else," LaTourette recalled, "and these attorneys knew that." Both lawyers had been former prosecutors, LaTourette said, and they understood that their clients were not going to get off lightly. "They understood that their clients were going to have to plead guilty to substantial charges to avoid the death penalty."

LaTourette decided to interview both Greg and Richard person-ally before deciding which one would make the better witness. He flew to Kansas City and met Richard first. "He was clearly still under Jeffrey's spell. He was starting to come out of it, but he really thought that Jeffrey was capable of simply walking through the jail-house walls and coming after him." During their conversation, Rich-ard told LaTourette that even if Jeffrey was convicted, he still might seek revenge. "Richard said his biggest fear was that we would strap Jeffrey into the electric chair and throw the switch and nothing would happen. He was afraid Jeffrey would just stand up."

LaTourette met Greg Winship on January 19. He found Greg ill with a 104-degree temperature. "Greg was convinced that Jeffrey had caused the fever because he knew that we were talking that day."

During the next few days, LaTourette flipflopped over whether to use Richard or Greg. "Both said they would testify against each other, but they made it clear that they really would rather not, and I would not get their best testimony if they did."

LaTourette decided to cut deals with both. "Winship was emo-tional. He cried through the whole interview. Brand was matter-of-fact; he laid it all out. Together they made a strong team."

Richard Brand agreed to plead guilty to murder and Greg prom-ised to plead guilty to complicity to murder. Both charges carried prison terms of fifteen years to life. Of the two charges, Richard's was the more serious. This was because he had carried the Averys into the pit, while Greg had not directly been involved in the actual killing, but rather had been outside the barn operating the chain saw.

Now that LaTourette had two eyewitnesses, he felt confident that he had sufficient proof to convict all of the other men: Jeffrey, Damon, Danny, Ron, and Dennis. He now turned his attention to the women.

In February, LaTourette got a telephone call from one of the attorneys appointed to represent Alice. She was willing to plea-bargain. She was angry at Jeffrey.

After her arrest, Alice had refused extradition from California to Ohio. So had Jeffrey and Damon. Christ hadn't helped his accusers prosecute him and Jeffrey wasn't going to make things easy for LaTourette. But Alice had changed her mind and returned to Ohio on January 20, because of Kathy. Alice had suspected that Jeffrey had been hiding Kathy in San Diego, but until she was arrested, Alice hadn't been certain. She was enraged when Kathy was brought into her cellblock. "She kept coming to my cell trying to speak to me," Alice said later. "I would close the door and she would press her face up to the glass and say, 'I love you, Alice.' The bitch!"

An inmate approached Alice a few days after Kathy arrived. "Did you know she's pregnant? She's carrying your husband's baby?" the inmate asked.

Alice ran into her cell and began to cry. A few hours later, she told her attorney that she would waive extradition. She couldn't stand being in the same jail as Kathy.

"Alice wanted a deal in the worst way," LaTourette said, "But I wasn't sure that was a good idea." Based on his interviews with Richard and Greg, LaTourette had become convinced that Alice had played a crucial role in the murders even though she hadn't participated in the actual killing. "I came to believe that Jeffrey, all by himself, couldn't have gotten the others to commit the murders. Alice knew that he had never had a job, that he had committed adultery, that he was stealing from people, that he was lazy as dirt, basically. And for her to all of a sudden say, 'Hey, I've been married to this asshole for nineteen years and now he is a prophet of God'—for her to be his cheerleader and convince everybody that he was a prophet and to chastise them and so forth—was wrong."

Just the same, LaTourette knew that his case against Alice was flimsy. "She wasn't at the farm when the murders took place and I knew jurors might have a problem with that." LaTourette decided that it would be better to negotiate a deal with Alice that required her to serve time in prison than to bring her case to trial and lose.

After meetings with Alice's court-appointed attorneys, Mark A. Ziccarelli and Joseph Gibson, a deal was struck. In return for La-Tourette's reducing the charges against Alice, she would plead guilty to a charge that carried a maximum sentence of fifteen to fifty years, making her eligible for parole in as few as five years compared to a life sentence. Everyone involved seemed satisfied, except for the one court official who mattered most. All of the charges against Jeffrey and his followers had been filed in the Lake County Common Pleas Court, where they had been divided among three judges, each an elected official. Alice's case had been put on Judge Paul H. Mitrovich's docket. A no-nonsense, often blunt, and stern former prosecutor, Mitrovich was considered to be the harshest judge on the Lake County bench. Behind his back, he was referred to as "Maximum Mitrovich" because of his tendency to impose the maximum prison terms possible.

Cutting a deal with Alice was politically risky for LaTourette and Mitrovich. The 250,000 residents of Lake County had been deluged with sensational stories about Jeffrey and his cult, and if letters to the editor printed in local newspapers and the callers who jammed the switchboards of local radio talk shows were any indication, the 16,500 residents of Painesville were eager for blood.

After some deliberation, Judge Mitrovich nixed Alice's plea bargain. She was going to be held accountable in a public courtroom for her actions. The public demanded it.

Once Mitrovich rejected Alice's deal, LaTourette quickly turned his attention back to finding a woman in the group who could testify against the others. By chance, Sharon Bluntschly was the first group member scheduled for trial. Her case was scheduled to start in May. LaTourette knew that she was valuable and vulnerable. She had been the first woman to join Jeffrey's group. She was also still in love with Richard, even though he made it clear to prosecutors that he despised her. Only a few months earlier, Sharon had given birth to Richard's daughter. Obviously, Richard would be the state's main witness against her and that would be emotionally difficult for Sharon. As her trial date got closer, Sharon's attorney negotiated a plea bargain with LaTourette. In return for her cooperation, the prosecutor agreed to drop ten of the fifteen charges against her. She would plead guilty to five counts of conspiracy to murder, a charge that carried a sentence of five years.

Debbie Olivarez was in the Lake County jail when she heard about Sharon's plea-bargain deal. Debbie was irritated. She didn't think it was fair that Sharon was going to get special treatment. Debbie had her attorney contact LaTourette. She'd testify for the prosecution if he gave her a deal identical to Sharon's. LaTourette agreed. A short time later, Dennis and Tonya Patrick also agreed to cooperate in return for reduced charges.

By the end of spring, LaTourette had negotiated deals with six of the group members. The only ones left were Jeffrey, Alice, Damon, Danny, Kathy, and the Luffs. As far as the public was concerned, Jeffrey, Alice, and Damon were the most important cases.

"I wanted to bring Jeffrey to trial first," LaTourette said. "There was tremendous pressure being applied by the community that I was beginning to feel. There was a feeling of 'Okay, you made these plea-bargain deals, now let's see if they were worth it.' The public was demanding that someone pay for this horrible crime—that justice be done."

No crime in Lake County's history had sparked as much revulsion as the Averys' deaths. Unlike the bedroom communities that sprouted along the shores of Lake Erie east of Cleveland during the 1960s, Painesville was an established town with a strong sense of community pride. It was one of the first settlements in northern Ohio, dating back to 1800 when General Edward Paine and his sons bought one thousand acres and led sixty-six settlers from Connecticut into the area. By 1832, it was one of the few towns with its own newspaper, *The Painesville Telegraph,* founded by Eber Howe, a crusading editor who was later credited with coining the word *bogus* to describe the activities of a group of counterfeiters who operated there briefly before being caught and severely punished. When Joseph Smith, Jr., arrived in nearby Kirtland, Howe became his most vocal critic. In 1834, Howe wrote a book entitled *Mormanism Unvailed* [sic], considered by many to be the first exposé of the new religion, and when Smith was forced to flee, Howe cheered. Although Painesville had mellowed over the years, it remained a tough, largely blue-collar community where criminals were dealt with sternly.

Public Defender Paul LaPlante was well aware of the local feeling in the community and the building pressure to bring Jeffrey to trial. He also knew that his staff of seven employees was no match for LaTourette's office with its seventeen lawyers and twenty-four support personnel. Hoping to better the odds, LaPlante called in reinforcements from the Ohio Public Defender Commission, the better-financed state version of his county office. It immediately dispatched four investigators to help LaPlante. "I had decided that we needed to find out everything that we could about Jeffrey," said LaPlante. The investigators began searching for a sign of physical or mental abuse in Jeffrey's past that would win sympathy from jurors. Besides probing Jeffrey's past, LaPlante had two criminal psychologists evaluate him. Both told LaPlante what he already knew. While

Jeffrey suffered from a severe personality disorder, he was not insane, at least not by Ohio's criminal standards. There was no way that LaPlante could mount a "not guilty because of insanity" defense.

Under Ohio's speedy-trial act, all defendants must be tried within ninety days unless they request a delay. LaPlante assumed that Judge Martin O. Parks, who had been assigned the case, would automatically grant him a series of continuances. He was wrong. Parks had a full docket and he saw no need to drag out Jeffrey's trial. He scheduled it for June. LaPlante strenuously protested, so Parks agreed to delay it until July. But that was it. LaPlante was unhappy, but he felt he could meet the July deadline.

And then in May, LaTourette's office completely disrupted LaPlante's schedule. Karen Kowall, an assistant prosecutor, convinced LaTourette that he could undermine LaPlante's defense by demanding copies of all the investigative reports that LaPlante had received from the Ohio Public Defender Commission. Kowall shrewdly pointed out that the commission was financed by tax dollars and therefore fell under the state's "sunshine laws," which required public agencies to make their records available to the public on demand. In effect, Kowall's scheme would force the commission to release all of the background material on Jeffrey that its investigators had compiled for LaPlante. LaTourette demanded the documents, catching LaPlante completely off guard.

The move outraged LaPlante and the director of the state commission. Both claimed that the investigators' reports were protected by lawyer-client privilege. But LaTourette refused to back down and filed a writ before the Ohio Supreme Court demanding that the commission produce its confidential records.

As soon as LaTourette filed the writ, the four investigators working for LaPlante immediately stopped helping him. They were afraid that they might be forced to turn over their reports. "We were left with absolutely no one to help us," LaPlante complained later. "Everything we were doing came to a complete halt."

Three weeks before the trial, LaTourette dropped his request, but by then the damage had been done.

On July 12, LaPlante and LaTourette reported to Judge Parks's courtroom to review how jurors would be selected the next day for Jeffrey's trial. When the judge entered the chamber, LaPlante stood to be recognized. Once again, he asked Parks for a continuance. Once again, the judge denied it.

"Your Honor," LaPlante calmly replied, "I will not participate any further in this case. Regardless of how anyone may perceive Jeffrey Lundgren, he is entitled to be cared about, he is entitled to have the best defense possible, he is entitled to have the best preparation and vigorous presentation of the case. . . ."

In effect, LaPlante was backing Judge Parks into a corner. The defense attorney felt his client's rights were being trampled. He wasn't going to stand for it. The judge had to either grant the continuance or find a way to force LaPlante to do his job. Parks adjourned court. When he reconvened it later that afternoon, he found LaPlante guilty of contempt of court and sentenced him to ten days in jail. He then suspended all but eight hours of LaPlante's sentence and announced that Jeffrey's trial would be postponed until August 13 so that LaPlante could have more time to get ready.

While LaPlante's gutsy stand had won the defense more time, the continuance proved to be the worst possible move for Alice. Her trial was scheduled to begin one week after Jeffrey's. Now the spotlight shifted onto Alice. She would be the first group member to actually go to trial. With emotions running high inside and outside the courtroom, Alice's case gained a new prominence. LaTourette, who only a few weeks earlier had been criticized in the Cleveland *Plain Dealer* for the plea bargains that he had struck, was being forced to put his weakest case on first. The young prosecutor knew that he had to win Alice's case or his political career would be seriously weakened.

Alice's trial was to become the most sensational in Lake County history. What no one knew at the time was that it was also going to become one of the most vicious and melodramatic.

CHAPTER FIFTY-FOUR

JUSTICE in Lake County is dispensed in a red-brick and stone courthouse built in the 1840s directly across the street from the Painesville town square. There is a clock in the courthouse tower and on top of it is a large metal dome. A cupola rises from the dome and at its peak there is a statue of a gold-plated eagle with outstretched wings. Two quotations had been carved into the courthouse's front facade. THE RIGHT TO A FREE GOVERNMENT PRESUPPOSES THE DUTY OF EVERY CITIZEN TO OBEY THAT GOVERNMENT, says one. THAT REGARD BE HAD FOR THE PUBLIC WELFARE IS THE HIGHEST LAW, says the other.

On the morning of July 25, the first day of Alice's trial, dew still clung to the dark-green grass in the town square. The iron-and-wood park benches were damp to the touch. Two squirrels chased one another across an empty whitewashed gazebo before scampering up an ancient oak. In one corner of the park, a stone monument honored the militia, men who had volunteered to fight "the Rebs" in the Civil War. A brass plaque nearby explained that Abraham Lincoln had passed through the Painesville rail station twice. The first time the train carried him to his presidential inauguration; the second time it carried his body in a coffin back to Illinois. No one had ever been tried before in Lake County as an accomplice to mass murder.

Prosecutor LaTourette had decided early on that his main job would be prosecuting Jeffrey, so he had intentionally appointed two women to present the state's case against Alice. He had selected Karen Lawson and Sandra Dray, in part because he thought they could, in his words, "outbitch" her. Both women were tough-talking, hard-driving, bleached blondes who had specialized in prosecuting men accused of sexually abusing women and children. Weeks before the trial, Alice's attorneys, Mark Ziccarelli and Joe Gibson, announced that their client was a battered wife who had been emotionally and physically abused. In an ironic twist, Lawson and Dray, who usually championed the cause of abused women, now found themselves on the attack.

The first legal skirmish came when Ziccarelli and Gibson asked the judge in a pretrial motion for permission to use "battered women's syndrome" as part of Alice's defense. Only a few months earlier, the Ohio Supreme Court had ruled that women accused of killing their husbands could cite long-term physical abuse by their spouses as a legitimate defense. If a woman could prove that she had killed her husband during a moment of fear and in self-defense, then she could be found innocent of murder. Although Alice had not killed Jeffrey, her attorneys claimed that he had emotionally abused her for so many years that Alice had been incapable of stopping Jeffrey from murdering the Averys. They asked Judge Mitrovich for permission to bring in experts who could testify about the effects of long-term physical abuse. "There is sufficient evidence surrounding the circumstances of this case to indicate that the defendant believed herself to be in imminent danger of death or great bodily harm," Ziccarelli told reporters, "should she not submit to the demands of her overbearing, insistent, and often violent husband. . . . She was suffering from battered women's syndrome." Alice was a victim, the attorneys argued, just like the Averys.

The prosecutor's office objected to the request. In their court brief, Lawson and Dray argued that Ohio law permitted "battered women's syndrome" to be used by defense attorneys only when a woman was accused of murdering her husband, not when her husband was on trial for killing a third party.

Judge Mitrovich agreed. He denied Alice's request for expert witnesses, but told her attorneys that he would permit them to introduce a limited amount of testimony about how Jeffrey had treated Alice during their marriage.

From the start, Alice's trial was explosive. One of the first witnesses called by Lawson and Dray described the exhumation of the Averys' bodies in such horrendous detail that Alice's attorney jumped to his feet in objection. They accused the prosecution of trying to inflame the jury. Seconds after that exchange, Lawson and Dray introduced photographs taken during the autopsies. One photograph showed Cheryl Avery's face, which was amazingly well-preserved, in part because of the duct tape that had covered it. Her mouth was frozen in what seemed to be a scream. The photograph was so horrible that Mitrovich ruled that it was too grisly to be shown to the jury. The prosecution's next witness methodically showed jurors each article of clothing that had been removed from the corpses. As soon as the first plastic bag was opened and a garment was removed, a stench permeated the room. The odor was so repulsive that Lawson held a tissue filled with Vicks VapoRub against her nose.

In contrast to such graphic testimony, Dray and Lawson called a friend of Cheryl's, who described the Averys in loving terms. "We wanted to make certain," LaTourette later said, "that the jurors realized that five human beings had been destroyed. We wanted them to see them as people, not just faceless victims."

On the second day of Alice's trial, Lawson and Dray began introducing evidence about Alice and her role as "mother" of the group. Debbie Olivarez was that day's star witness. She recalled how Alice frequently chastised Jeffrey's followers, how she was his personal spy, how she constantly pushed the idea that Jeffrey was a prophet. "Alice was," Debbie testified, "Jeff's right-hand man in a lot of things. She was his confidante. . . . She would clarify things for Jeff. . . ." It would have been impossible for Alice not to have known about the murders, Debbie said. She recalled how Jeffrey had talked about the best way to kill the Averys and how Alice had suggested that they find out whether Becky had started menstruation so Jeffrey would know whether to rip her guts open or bash her head against a wall. Debbie recounted how Alice had hurriedly left the farm on April 17 after eating dinner with the Averys before the murders. She had taken Jason, Kristen, and Caleb with her to buy picnic tables, Debbie said, but had called the farm before coming home to ask if "the company was gone." Debbie had talked to Alice on the telephone that night and she said that Alice knew exactly what was happening in the barn.

"Who, if anyone," Lawson asked Debbie, "could have prevented the murders?"

"Alice," Debbie replied, looking directly at her, "could have."

Alice grabbed her mouth and announced that she was ill. Mitrovich recessed court.

On the third day of testimony, Sharon Bluntschly told jurors that Alice was lazy and expected to be "treated like a queen" by the group. On the day that the Averys were murdered, Alice was almost gleeful, she said. "Tonight's the night for the Averys," Sharon quoted Alice as saying.

The prosecution felt jurors had heard enough. Dray and Lawson rested their case.

The defense's main witness was Alice. Looking frail and weighing barely 100 pounds, some 120 pounds less than when she had been arrested only six months earlier, Alice testified for four hours. She told jurors that Jeffrey had lied to her repeatedly during their nineteen-year marriage. She talked about his sexual affair when he worked at the Lake of the Ozarks Hospital and told how he had pushed her so hard that her spleen had ruptured. "I was afraid of Jeff," she said, "because I knew he had the potential to be very violent. But I also was very much in love with him." But Alice did not go into great detail about her marriage and she mentioned nothing at all about her sexual experiences with Jeffrey. She had been too embarrassed to reveal the details of sex life with Jeffrey to her two male attorneys, she later said. She wasn't certain that anyone would believe her.

When Jeffrey first mentioned killing ten of his followers, Alice said she had confronted him.

> **Alice:** I went to him and I said, "Are you really saying that you're going to kill people?" And he said, "No, no, no, this is just a test of faith. I'm not going to do anything, don't worry about it." He said, "This is an Abraham and Isaac situation."
>
> **Question:** What do you mean by Abraham and Isaac situation?
>
> **Alice:** Abraham was a prophet who was commanded to sacrifice his only son. He took his son up on the altar and was going to sacrifice him, and at the last moment the Lord said, "You don't have to sacrifice him." That's what Jeff was telling

me. Nothing was going to happen. This was just a test of faith like Abraham's faith had been tested . . .

Question: And at that time did you believe that Jeffrey would kill ten people?

Alice: No, I didn't think he would kill anybody.

The fact that Jeffrey had decided to spare the lives of Dennis, Tonya, Molly, Richard, and Sharon further convinced her, Alice testified, that Jeffrey wasn't serious about killing the Averys.

When asked by her attorney to explain why she had left the farm on April 17 after eating dinner with the Averys, Alice insisted that she had simply gone to run an errand. She had called the farm later that night—not because she was afraid to come home until after the murders were done as Debbie implied—but because she wanted to see if Jeffrey needed her to bring him anything from town. She was completely unaware, she testified, that Jeffrey was actually going to murder the family. Alice's attorneys were happy with her testimony. They felt that she had made a good impression. As soon as they finished their gentle questioning, prosecutor Dray was on her feet. "Mrs. Lundgren," she declared, "you're a liar!"

If Alice had been terrified of Jeffrey, why hadn't she turned him in on April 18 when FBI agents and Chief Yarborough arrived at the farm to ask about the temple takeover? If Alice was a battered wife, as she claimed, then why did Sharon and Debbie testify that they had never seen Jeffrey physically abuse Alice, but they had seen Alice hit, scratch, kick, and punch him? Finally, Dray asked, how was it possible that Alice was the only adult at the farm on the night of April 17 who didn't know what was going to happen after the Avery family finished their "last supper"?

> **Dray:** Yes or no, nobody told you?
> **Alice:** No one told me.
> **Dray:** Nobody told the group's "mother" on April seven-teenth, "Holy schmoly, mom, do you know what dad's planning to do tonight?" Nobody told you that, right?
> **Alice:** No, nobody told me . . .
> **Dray:** Let me run through this again. Richard Brand, Sharon Bluntschly, Deborah Olivarez, Greg Winship, Susie and Ron Luff . . . Of the people who were there when the Averys came to eat dinner at your table, everybody knew it was going to be their last supper but you. Is that what you're telling us?
> **Alice:** (no response)

Dray: Yes or no?
Alice: Yes, everyone knew but me.

Mocking Alice, Dray began duck-walking toward the courtroom door, shouting her next question over her shoulder.

Dray: And so after dinner when you left to go to the Makro Department Store, you said, "I'm just going to Makro. I'm just going to buy picnic tables. I'll see you in a little while." Is that right?
Alice: Yes.

In his closing arguments to the jury, defense attorney Gibson reminded jurors that Alice hadn't been at the farm when the murders took place. He claimed that Alice had been mentally and emotionally abused by Jeffrey to the point where she was his pawn. "I didn't know Hitler, but I think Jeffrey was right up next to him," he said.

Prosecutor Lawson picked up on that theme when it was her turn to speak. If Jeffrey resembled Hitler, she told jurors, then Alice mirrored Josef Mengele, the notorious "angel of death" at the Nazi concentration camp of Auschwitz. "She was just as cold and calculating and wacko as her husband," Lawson charged.

The seven women and five men on the jury deliberated two days. Alice felt that was a good sign. She hoped that they were deadlocked. But on August 1, when the jury reached a verdict and filed into Judge Mitrovich's courtroom, Alice's hopes were quickly destroyed. The jurors found Alice guilty of all fifteen charges filed against her. Not only did the jury decide that Alice had "conspired" to commit aggravated murder, they also found her guilty of "complicity." Conspiracy meant that Alice had agreed with others to kill the Averys. Complicity meant that she had actively helped commit the murders even though she wasn't at the farm. The final five counts filed against Alice were for kidnapping. Alice's actions, the jury said, had deprived the Averys of their freedom to leave the farm on April 17 by use of deception. Dray and Lawson had won a complete victory. They hugged each other and cried when the verdict was read. Alice remained stone-faced.

In a last-ditch attempt to help their client, Alice's attorneys offered Judge Mitrovich a psychological evaluation of Alice before sentencing that said "Alice's involvement in criminal behavior was entirely secondary to her subservience to her husband." But Mitrovich was unmoved. On August 29, he sentenced Alice to the maximum prison term possible, a total of 150 years. She would not be eligible for parole until she served 115 years of the sentence.

"Good luck," he told her.

As Alice was being taken out of the courtroom, she suddenly stopped in the hallway and was quickly mobbed by reporters and television crews. During the next ten minutes, she read a statement that she had written the night before.

"My name is Alice Elizabeth Lundgren," she said. "I am not Josef Mengele and I am not the angel of death." Alice insisted that she was innocent and she lambasted Judge Mitrovich for not permitting her attorneys to call expert witnesses who could describe battered women's syndrome. "This whole process has not been so much about law or justice or truth," she said, "it has been about political fame and fortune. . . ." She accused LaTourette of cutting deals in order to get "the bigger fish—plea bargains that will allow for the women, who last had the opportunity to save the lives of Cheryl, Trina, Becky, and Karen, to serve very little prison time if any for saving themselves rather than the children." Alice's most heated criticism, however, was directed at Dray and Lawson. "The departure of accepted courtroom decorum displayed by the prosecutor as she screamed and shouted in my face: 'Holy schmoly, mom!' or 'Mrs. Lundgren, you are a liar' gave the jury a perfect example of a woman realizing that she had only exchanged batterers. . . . No matter how much pain or destruction or peril that has filled my life—no matter how tragic the deaths of Dennis, Cheryl, Trina, Becky, and Karen—that was not, nor ever could it be reason for me to accept the prosecutors's suggestion that 'Alice should have blown Jeff's brains out' as was offered in the closing remarks by the prosecutor. I find it ironic that the suggestion of aggravated murder was offered as an acceptable course of action to have prevented aggravated murder. That would have made me equal to Jeff Lundgren which can never be because I am not a cold-blooded murderer—*he is.*"

Alice broke down once while reading the statement when she mentioned Karen Avery. But she quickly regained her composure, and when she came to the end of her text, she smiled and said, "My life has taken on a whole new definition over the past several months. In a very real sense, I have known more freedom within the walls of the Lake County jail than I have known for years. . . . The correctional officers . . . have treated me with fairness and human dignity, which is a new and refreshing experience as compared to the dynamics of the group that I came out of."

As soon as she finished, deputies hurried her to jail.

During the next few days, reporters questioned jurors about their verdict and "Maximum" Mitrovich's sentence. They learned that the deciding factor in the jury verdict was not the judge's actions, the prosecutors' verbal attacks, or even the witnesses' descriptions. The jury had convicted Alice because of Alice's own words.

Alice had insisted that she hadn't known Jeffrey planned to kill the Averys on April 17. Yet after Alice was arrested in San Diego on January 7, she had made a statement to agent Van Haelst during her thirty-eight-minute videotaped conversation that had come back to haunt her. The complete video was shown during her trial, and it was Alice's own voice, her own words, reverberating inside the darkened courtroom that jurors later said convinced them that she was a liar.

"Did you know why the Averys were coming to the farm that night?" Van Haelst had asked.

"I suspected that it was the sacrifice," Alice had replied.

"Had he talked to you about that?"

"Not— Yes and no. It was like—not directly, but indirectly."

And then Alice had said the words that few in the courtroom would ever forget.

"You had to be stupid not to know what he was up to."

CHAPTER FIFTY-FIVE

STEVEN LaTourette had been halfway through Scott Turow's novel *Presumed Innocent* when the bodies of the Averys were discovered, and on August 23, LaTourette followed the advice of his fictional counterpart Rusty Sabich, who explained in the opening pages that all successful prosecutors looked a defendant directly in the eye when accusing them of a crime. During his opening statement to the jury in the case of *State of Ohio* v. *Jeffrey D. Lundgren,* LaTourette pointed his finger at Jeffrey's face and called him a con man and murderer. Jeffrey flinched, looked away, and avoided eye contact with LaTourette during the rest of the trial.

"The evidence in this case will reflect," LaTourette declared, "that during the spring of 1989, in or near Davis, West Virginia, Jeffrey Don Lundgren turned to a woman by the name of Deborah Sue Olivarez . . . and said, 'You know, death stinks, but I guess I will have to get used to it.'

"The evidence in this case, ladies and gentlemen," LaTourette continued, "will bring home the smell of death. . . . Unfortunately, it will bring it within the four walls of this courtroom."

For forty minutes, LaTourette dramatically explained how Jeffrey, "through a series of sideshow and medicine-show miracles and tortured scripture, set up schemes and manipulated good, God-fearing people in a way that would have made Jim and Tammy Faye Bakker swell with pride.

"Over time, he conned these people into supporting him and his family financially," LaTourette thundered, "into permitting him to act out his sexual fantasies, and ultimately in participating with him in the death of five people."

LaTourette's oratory, which his fellow attorneys and local reporters later described as the best that they had ever heard him deliver, was followed by a flat, three-minute response by assistant public defender Charles Grieshammer. Yet it was Grieshammer's brief comment that led the five o'clock newscasts that night.

"Jeffrey Lundgren did shoot and kill Dennis, Cheryl, Trina, Rebecca, and Karen Avery," Grieshammer said, declaring his client's guilt before the prosecution had called even a single witness. "We're not going to dispute that."

It had been Paul LaPlante who had decided to tell the jurors upfront that Jeffrey was a killer. "We weren't going to insult anyone's intelligence by pretending that Jeffrey wasn't guilty," he later said. LaPlante's plan was to hurry through the first stage of the murder trial. He had seen how Dray and Lawson had sensationalized the Averys' deaths in Alice's case, and he hoped to avoid the grisly details of the murders. Instead of focusing on the Averys, LaPlante wanted jurors to pay attention to Jeffrey. During the second phase of the trial, LaPlante hoped to convince the jury that Jeffrey had been emotionally abused as a child to the extent that he deserved the jurors' pity.

Just as in Alice's trial, the first day of testimony began with ghastly accounts of how the bodies were exhumed. At one point, jurors were taken in a bus to the farm and shown the pit where the Averys had been killed. Jeffrey did not go along on that trip. He stayed in his cell and read his scriptures.

On day two, the prosecution hauled Jeffrey's arsenal into court. Wooden boxes filled with ammunition, stacks of rifles, and numerous pistols were paraded before the jury. Photographs of the huge .50-caliber rifle that Jeffrey had bought appeared on the front page of the Cleveland *Plain Dealer* the next morning and were sent over the Associated Press wires. LaTourette was skillfully reconstructing the crime for the jury and the media.

LaPlante and Grieshammer didn't bother to question most of the prosecution's witnesses. They simply sat and listened to the testimony. Jeffrey spent the first two days of his trial reading passages from the Bible, Book of Mormon, and Doctrine and Covenants. Oftentimes, he didn't even bother looking at the parade of witnesses being called. Only once did he show any interest. When photographs of the Averys taken during the autopsies were introduced as evidence, Jeffrey pushed his scriptures aside and carefully examined each picture for several minutes after LaTourette handed them to LaPlante and Grieshammer to review. "When he studied those pictures I got really pissed," LaTourette said later. "I hated him more and more because it was clear that he was admiring his handiwork."

Judge Martin O. Parks's courtroom contained one large table which was used by both the prosecution and the defense. A podium in the center separated the two sides. LaTourette and LaPlante took the chairs closest to the lectern. Their assistants sat beside them and then, at the ends of the table, were the chairs that Chief Yarborough and Jeffrey used. Because of this arrangement, Yarborough and Jeffrey found themselves facing one another. Yarborough quickly made it his habit to stare directly at Jeffrey, hoping to make him nervous.

LaTourette's star witness, Richard Brand, testified on day three. Before he arrived, Yarborough and LaTourette took a roll of gray duct tape—the same kind used to bind and gag the Averys—and tore off four strips. They used the tape to make a rectangular outline on the courtroom floor. When it came time for Richard to describe the murders, LaTourette told him to step down from the witness stand and demonstrate for the jury exactly where he had put Dennis Avery when he and Danny had lowered him into the pit. Brand walked over to the taped outline, stepped inside, and dropped to his knees. He was only a few feet from Jeffrey. Holding the murder weapon in his hand, LaTourette left the podium and walked behind Richard. He dramatically raised the gun, pointing it directly at Richard's back.

Is this how Dennis Avery was murdered? he asked.

Yes, Richard had replied.

LaTourette wanted the jurors to visualize exactly what had happened. He had another reason for reenacting the scene. He wanted everyone in the courtroom, including Jeffrey, to see that the gun was pointed at Richard's back. Jeffrey had told his followers that he had looked Dennis in the eyes before shooting him. He had claimed that he had "pierced" Dennis Avery's heart. But LaTourette told the jury that Jeffrey had lied. "Dennis Avery was shot twice in the back," LaTourette proclaimed, "not in the chest, not in the heart."

Richard told jurors that Jeffrey never showed any emotion when he executed the Averys. Even little Karen failed to bring any sign of remorse to his face.

Later, Jeffrey stared at Sharon and Debbie when they testified against him, but neither broke down. "Frequently, Jeffrey would tease in sexual overtones," Debbie said. "He would come up behind me and say things like he was going to run his tongue up and down my body." Once, she testified, Jeffrey joked about his scriptural teachings. "If this doesn't work out, I guess I'll become a pornographic writer," he was quoted as saying.

After four days of testimony, LaTourette rested his case. He felt confident that he had proved that Jeffrey was a con man who had simply set out to steal the group's money and had murdered the Averys to keep his other followers in line.

In keeping with LaPlante's let's-get-this-over-with strategy, the defense announced that it would not call any witnesses to defend Jeffrey. As expected, the jury quickly found him guilty of five aggravated murders and five counts of kidnapping.

On September 17 the "mitigation phase" of Jeffrey's trial began. "It is now our show, our turn," LaPlante nervously explained before the proceedings began.

"In Jeffrey's first trial, we told you he killed this family," Grieshammer explained to jurors during his opening remarks. "In this second trial, we will hopefully prove why."

In chronological fashion, LaPlante and Grieshammer began to tell the "Jeffrey Lundgren story" from birth to the murders. Along the way, they gently suggested that Jeffrey alone wasn't to blame for what had happened, that he too was a victim. They offered jurors two culprits: Jeffrey's parents and the RLDS Church. Don and Lois Lundgren had refused to come to their son's trial. Privately, they told friends that Jeffrey had "lost his mind." Although Jeffrey was thirty-nine when he killed the Avery family, the defense suggested that Don and Lois had "emotionally abused" their son by being overly strict and demanding. The defense's first witness, Jeffrey's uncle George Harvey Gadberry, described Don as a "stern" father but admitted during cross-examination that he'd never seen any evidence that Jeffrey had been physically abused as a child. Mary Bennett, Jeffrey's aunt, claimed that Don Lundgren "had such a hard look of sternness it would make anyone melt in their shoes." But the worst example of punishment that she could cite happened when Jeffrey was three years old and popped a handful of salted peanuts in his mouth. Jeffrey hadn't liked the taste and had started to spit them out when Don became angry at the waste of food. He forced Jeffrey to keep the peanuts in his mouth for more than thirty minutes, Bennett said. The jury did not seem too impressed by the tale.

Jeffrey's high school friend, Sarah Stotts, said Jeffrey had felt inferior as a teenager because he could never live up to his parents' expectations. But under cross-examination, Sarah admitted that she had no proof that Jeffrey had been mistreated at home.

When LaPlante and Grieshammer began calling witnesses to talk about Jeffrey's religious bent, LaTourette felt relieved. The prosecutor was certain that the defense had failed to convince anyone that Jeffrey had come from an abusive home.

Jeffrey's religious side was first described by Georgia Milliren, who fondly recalled how Jeffrey had taught Sunday school at Slover Park RLDS Church, but had eventually become disillusioned with the church. She was convinced that he was sincere. Much to the prosecution's irritation, Keith Johnson testified for the defense and claimed that Jeffrey was not a con man. "Jeffrey came to the point where he believed his own lies," said Keith. Even Kevin Currie, who had been terrified that Jeffrey was going to kill him, testified for the defense, saying that Jeffrey had built his life around his scriptures and was sincere in his teachings.

LaPlante called two expert witnesses to pull his case together. The first was William D. Russell, a professor of religion at Graceland College, who said that the Mormon religion was much more vulnerable to self-proclaimed prophets, such as Jeffrey, than other sects because of its belief in "continuing revelation" and acceptance of Joseph Smith, Jr., as a prophet. "I really don't have any doubt that Jeffrey thinks he is a prophet," said Russell, who added that he knew of at least twelve other self-proclaimed prophets who had broken from the RLDS just as Jeffrey had done. "He seems sincere," Russell said.

The defense's final expert witness, Dr. Nancy Schmidtgoessling, a Cincinnati psychologist, hammered home the point that Jeffrey was not a con man. She said that Jeffrey was drawn to religion because he felt inferior. Based on the eighteen hours that she had spent talking to Jeffrey and administering various psychological tests, Schmidtgoessling said that "Jeffrey was emotionally abused and did not feel accepted by his peers."

As a child, "he did not fit in. The only way for him to relate to people was through religion. He found a niche in religion. He found a way to relate to people and his religion shaped and focused him." The deeper Jeffrey delved into the scriptures, the more out of touch with reality he became.

In order to overcome his feelings of inadequacy, Jeffrey developed the opposite feelings. He developed a "grandiose" personality to the point that he came to believe that he was superior to everyone around him. Schmidtgoessling said that Jeffrey had an IQ of 124, which is 24 points higher than average, and had a much higher ability than most at memorizing material. Yet he couldn't hold a job or support his family. He blamed everyone but himself for his failures. He became extremely narcissistic and retreated further and further into a world of his own making. As was typical of narcissistic personalities, Jeffrey found it difficult to appreciate the suffering of others and was preoccupied with his own power.

The reason why he hated the Averys was because Dennis Avery reminded Jeffrey of his own secret weaknesses, Schmidtgoessling theorized. Cheryl's independence threatened Jeffrey's masculinity. "In a sense, Lundgren was killing part of himself," the psychologist testified. "In killing Dennis Avery, he was killing the parts of himself he detested. Jeffrey felt overrun by women. Dennis Avery had some of those same characteristics. He had a wife who pushed him around."

Finally, Schmidtgoessling said that Jeffrey had "no insight at all" about his own personality. He had cocooned himself inside a religious fantasy world and, in doing so, had convinced himself that "God had commanded him to kill. He really believes it was right to kill those folks."

When it was LaTourette's turn to question Schmidtgoessling, the prosecutor was blunt.

"Is Jeffrey insane?" he asked.

"No," Schmidtgoessling replied. Jeffrey knew that he was breaking the law when he killed the Averys.

That was all LaTourette wanted to know.

"What we had to present in mitigation was very subtle," LaPlante said later. "We knew from the start that Jeffrey was not beaten as a child. There was no evidence that he had been raped or abused. There wasn't really anything you could hang your hat on—where you could say, 'Ah-ha, this is why Jeffrey turned out this way,' but we felt there was enough there in his past and in his religion to make jurors see that there are degrees of illness and Jeffrey was way off the scale when it comes to mental disorders."

It was now time for LaPlante to play his last card: Jeffrey. In

Ohio, a defendant facing the death penalty was allowed to make a final plea to jurors before he was sentenced. The law was designed to give a convicted murderer the opportunity to confess his sins, apologize, and beg for mercy. But Jeffrey had something else in mind. He wanted to teach a scripture class. LaTourette was furious when he learned what Jeffrey had planned, but he couldn't stop him. The prosecutor did, however, fuss over ground rules. "Lundgren wanted to use the lawyers' podium," LaTourette recalled. "I got mad. I was not going to dignify him by having him stand behind the podium. Paul [LaPlante] went nuts when I objected, but I didn't care. This statement of his was nothing but a cheap way for him to get in a lot of crap."

LaTourette and LaPlante, the onetime close friends, argued bitterly in Judge Parks's chambers until Parks sided with LaTourette. Jeffrey could speak, but not behind the podium.

Spectators began gathering outside the courthouse before dawn on September 19, to hear Jeffrey. It would be the first time that he had spoken publicly since his capture. The courtroom held only sixty-five persons and the media took up many of those seats. Jeffrey was scheduled to begin his statement shortly after 10:00 A.M.

The local *News Herald* had described Jeffrey before his trial in a one-inch-high headline as a SILVER-TONGUED DEVIL. A radio station had arranged to broadcast his speech "live" from the courthouse. A television camera in the courtroom stood ready to relay Jeffrey's speech to five trucks parked in the town square, which would beam them to Cleveland and Kansas City television stations for news bulletins.

As the spectators waited, they talked among themselves and to reporters about Jeffrey. "I'd like to throw the switch that kills him," said one bearded man, standing next to another who wore a white T-shirt with the words FRY JEFFREY written on it in black block letters.

"Why waste the electricity on him?" a third spectator volunteered. "Should take that son of a bitch and shoot 'im in the head just like he shot 'em three little Avery girls."

Jeffrey had been awake all night in his cell scribbling his thoughts on a yellow legal pad. LaPlante and Grieshammer had urged him to keep his comments simple and concise, but he had ignored them. By the time he was brought to the courthouse, everyone was ready. Bailiff Glenn W. Kanaga, Sr., had held a lottery to determine which onlookers got seats. Sheriff's deputies had paraded reporters and spectators through a metal detector to check for weapons. A local radio announcer was on the air, giving his listeners background material—much like a sports commentator during a pregame show. Judge Parks completed several routine courtroom chores and then told Jeffrey that he could begin. Jeffrey rose from his chair, glanced at his yellow legal pad one last time, cleared his throat, and faced the six men and six women who were to decide whether or not he should be put to death. He was wearing a light-brown jacket and brown polyester pants that Georgia Milliren had bought for him at a Salvation Army store. LaPlante's wife had washed and ironed Jeffrey's white shirt. His shoulder-length hair was pulled straight back and hung around his shoulders. In a calm, clear voice, Lundgren began.

"I am a prophet of God," he said. "I am even more than that—much, much more."

For five hours, Jeffrey spoke. He described his visions, quoted from the movie The Highlander, read numerous verses of scriptures, talked about chiasmus and the "pattern." He never apologized for killing the Averys. "Prophets have been asked by the Lord to go forth and kill since the beginning of time," he said. He ended his rambling discourse by quoting the Book of Mormon. "Repent ye, repent," he told the jurors. "For the Kingdom of God is close at hand. Prepare ye the way of the Lord."

The jury took less than two hours before recommending that Jeffrey be put to death. LaPlante and Grieshammer, both visibly upset, hurried from the courtroom without comment. LaTourette and Yarborough held a press conference.

Later that night, after Yarborough got home, he finally began to relax. Since the Averys' bodies were found, Yarborough had spent all of his time helping LaTourette prepare his case. The chief's dining-room table was covered with legal documents, newspaper clippings about religious cults, books about Mormonism.

"I feel good," he said, "because I think we were able to show that Jeffrey is not a prophet. He is a fat coward who is terrified unless he can hide behind his religious books. He is a baby killer."

Opening a box, Yarborough removed a well-worn, thick Bible. It had been Jeffrey's before it was confiscated, and Yarborough had spent hours studying it. Yarborough opened the book to chapter 6 of Revelation and the story of the Four Horsemen of the Apocalypse.

"Jeffrey made a mistake," the chief said, "when he read about the fourth rider." He read the verse aloud:

"And when he had opened the fourth seal, I heard the voice of the fourth beast say, Come and see. And I looked, and behold a pale horse; and his name that sat on him was Death, and Hell followed with him . . ."

Yarborough grinned.

"Jeffrey wasn't that rider," the chief explained. The justice system, the state of Ohio, the prosecution was on that horse. "We are death and we are going to see to it that Jeffrey goes to hell for what he has done."

That night, for the first time in months, Chief Yarborough got a good night's sleep.

CHAPTER FIFTY-SIX

O_N September 21, 1990, Judge Parks officially sentenced Jeffrey to die in Ohio's electric chair. Parks chose April 17, 1991, as the execution date because it was on April 17 that Jeffrey had murdered the Averys. The judge did not actually expect Jeffrey to be electrocuted that soon. Death penalty cases in Ohio are automatically appealed and it normally takes seventy-seven months for a case to work its way through the courts. LaTourette told reporters after the hearing that it would take ten years for Jeffrey to exhaust his legal appeals. Even then, there was a chance that his sentence might be commuted to life without parole. Ohio had not executed anyone since 1963.

Jeffrey was unruffled when Parks sentenced him. Later that afternoon, when LaPlante and Grieshammer went to speak with Jeffrey in the Lake County jail, they found him relaxed. The two attorneys weren't. Grieshammer liked Jeffrey and was depressed. LaPlante felt irritated at the legal process. From the start, he had argued that Jeffrey couldn't get a fair trial in Lake County because of the extraordinary publicity the murders had sparked. His suspicions were confirmed during voir dire, the jury-selection process, when many of the potential jurors admitted that they had already decided Jeffrey was guilty based on media accounts. Despite this, Judge Parks had refused to move the trial elsewhere. Instead, whenever prospective jurors said that they had already decided Jeffrey was guilty, Parks asked them if they could put aside their opinions and give Jeffrey a fair hearing. Nearly all had promised that they could. LaPlante wasn't certain they had.

Jeffrey ended up comforting his attorneys. "I told them that everything was okay."

What LaPlante and Grieshammer didn't realize, Jeffrey later explained, was that his death sentence was preordained. "This is all going according to God's game plan."

When Jeffrey was sentenced that morning, Judge Parks had made a point of saying that it was the "people of the state of Ohio" who had condemned Jeffrey to die. Parks was not personally doing it. Hadn't Pontius Pilate tried to wash his hands when he sentenced Jesus Christ to death? Jeffrey asked. "The scriptures say that a prophet must be rebuked by the people and that is what the judge said. 'The people of Ohio' have condemned me and now God is justified in destroying them.

"You see, God's tried all this before," Jeffrey explained. The inhabitants on earth had been destroyed eight times by God, he said. "The ground you walk on is made of bones." If people didn't "repent" after hearing Jeffrey's message, God would show Jeffrey how to continue opening the seven seals and the inhabitants of earth would be exterminated.

"God will simply start over."

Several events that happened during his trial were chronicled in the scriptures, he said. One of the biblical names that Jeffrey had given Richard Brand while the group was in West Virginia was "Bel" and in the Bible Bel was forced by God to bow down. During his testimony, Richard had been told by LaTourette to leave the witness chair and get down on his knees in the mock pit that had been outlined on the courtroom floor. At that point, "Bel was forced to bow before me, his lord and master," said Jeffrey.

Before Christ was crucified, he was mocked by his persecutors who lied about him. "LaTourette mocked and lied about me," Jeffrey said. "I am not a con man and I didn't shoot Dennis Avery in the back. I looked him in the eyes and shot him in his chest."

Jeffrey insisted that LaTourette and the county coroners had intentionally identified the *exit* wounds in Dennis's back as the *entrance* wounds in order to make Jeffrey look like a coward. "I shot

Mr. Avery in the chest. All you have to do is look at the wounds. The holes in the chest are smaller than the ones in his back, which proves I shot him in the chest."

But that was *not* what the wounds showed. The slugs that Jeffrey fired into Dennis were "hollow point" rounds designed to collapse and look like a "mushroom" on impact. Both had hit bones, which caused them to ricochet inside the body. During the autopsy, the bullets were recovered *inside* the corpse, according to Cuyahoga County Coroner Elizabeth K. Balraj and Lake County Coroner William C. Downing. There were no exit wounds. There were no bullet holes in Dennis Avery's chest. The only bullet holes were in his back. LaTourette hadn't lied. The proof was indisputable—to everyone but Jeffrey.

"They are lying. They will do anything to discredit me. I shot Dennis Avery in the chest."

Judge Parks had asked Jeffrey that morning during the sentencing hearing if he had anything that he wanted to say before the judge passed judgment. Jeffrey hadn't said anything. "But I thought about saying, 'Thank you, Judge, thank you, jury, and fuck you, Steve LaTourette.'"

Besides LaTourette, Jeffrey was irritated at Dr. Schmidtgoessling and her testimony that compared him to Dennis Avery. "I don't have any of the same characteristics as Dennis Avery. I would kill myself if I believed I did. . . . She said I have a profound hatred for women. That's stupid. I know more about womankind than most of the rest of the world because of what God has shown me. I have profound respect for women. . . ."

Now that the trial was over, God expected Jeffrey simply to wait, he said. "At some point, He will free me."

"I used to wonder," Jeffrey continued, "when this first began to happen—'Why me?' I think the simplest answer is that there was no one else to do it. It is what I was created for. I was created to put my life on the line. I was created to love the truth."

The convictions of Jeffrey and Alice left only one more major case. LaTourette had offered Damon Lundgren a plea bargain that would have required the nineteen-year-old to serve thirty years in prison, but Damon rejected the offer and instead insisted during his trial that he was innocent. Damon's lawyers claimed that Damon was dominated by his father and learned about the killings just hours before they were to occur. They said Damon did not participate directly in the shooting deaths. Prosecutors countered with testimony by Sharon, Debbie, Greg, and Richard. After deliberating for eight hours, a jury found Damon guilty of aggravated murder. During the mitigation stage, the defense called sixteen witnesses, including Bill Lord, Dale Luffman, and Donna Keehler. All three claimed Damon had been subjugated by his father. "He didn't have a chance," Bill Lord testified. "His father was over him all the time." In a fifteen-minute statement that caused many in the courtroom to weep, Damon begged the jury not to sentence him to death. "My whole life has been doing what my father told me to do. . . . I just want to tell you that I don't want to die. I have a whole lot of things I can contribute to society. . . . I'd like a chance to make up any way I can for some of the things my father did." The jury recommended that Damon be sentenced to life in prison.

Jeffrey's other followers, except for Ron Luff, agreed to plead guilty to reduced charges in order to avoid trials. Susan Luff pleaded guilty to five counts of conspiracy to murder, the same charges that Sharon and Debbie had accepted. Because Kathy Johnson was pregnant with Jeffrey's baby, her case was delayed during the summer. She was released on bond five months after her arrest. In June, Kathy gave birth to a daughter, whom she named Rasia, the Hebrew word for "rose." Kathy later pleaded guilty to obstructing justice. She had not been at the farm during the murders, but prosecutors said she was liable because she had not told anyone about the killings afterward. At her sentencing, Kathy was defiant. "I'm guilty of loving Jeff Lundgren," she said. "I'm not guilty of having assisted with anything he carried out." Kathy was sentenced to one year in prison.

Dennis and Tonya Patrick pleaded guilty to obstructing justice, the same charge as Kathy. But they were put on one-year probation and released. The difference between their sentences and Kathy's, Assistant Prosecutor Karen Kowall said, was that the Patricks "are very remorseful for what happened."

Danny Kraft, Jr., agreed to plead guilty to ten counts of aggravated murder and kidnapping after Jeffrey met with him privately in the Lake County jail and assured him that it was not necessary for him to stand trial. "Jeff is not a false prophet," Danny proclaimed during a two-hour speech that he delivered at his sentencing. "I understand how the killing of the Averys looks to people, but they are wrong. I cannot apologize for my assisting the prophet of God." Psychologist Paul R. Martin told Judge James W. Jackson that the twenty-six-year-old Kraft had been "brainwashed" by Jeffrey. In exchange for Danny's guilty plea, LaTourette recommended that Danny be sentenced to life in prison, rather than death. "He did fall under the spell of Jeffrey Lundgren," LaTourette said. "You're not going to get any argument from me that Jeffrey Lundgren is the most evil, vile, fat, smelly person ever to come into Lake County."

On December 5, Ron Luff's trial began in Toledo. Judge Parks had granted Luff a change of venue in October after Luff's attorney successfully argued that an unbiased jury could no longer be found in Lake County. Luff was found guilty of aggravated murder and kidnapping. However, the jury voted to spare his life and he was sentenced to 170 years in prison.

Before Alice and Jeffrey were sent to prison, they both asked Judge Parks to let them meet face-to-face in the Lake County jail one final time. Parks refused. Alice was sent to the Ohio Reformatory for Women in Marysville. Jeffrey was taken to death row at Ohio's maximum-security prison in Lucasville. Neither had regular access to a telephone, but they continued to correspond. Some days, Jeffrey would write as many as five letters to Alice. He was upset that she had described him as a "cold-blooded murderer" after her trial. She was irritated because he refused to "divorce" Kathy.

"Alice will not accept the fact that Kathy is my wife," he later explained. "She is angry. She is attacking me and rejecting the truth."

In order to placate Alice, Jeffrey told her in a letter that he was ending his relationship with "Mrs. Johnson." He was lying. He continued to correspond faithfully with Kathy. "If Alice repents, I will tell her the truth about Kathy, but if a lie is what will make her happy right now, then that's what I will give her. I will use delusion to tell her whatever she wants to hear. What is important is that she continues to believe. I love her and my job is to get her to the mountain [of the Lord] with Kathy and me."

Alice was skeptical when she got Jeffrey's letter. Not long afterward, she received a love letter from Jeffrey that contained vivid descriptions of various sexual acts that he wished they could engage in. In that letter, Jeffrey mistakenly referred to Alice at one point as Kathy. "He's writing that bitch the same love letters that he is sending me," Alice charged.

During Ron Luff's trial in December, Alice and Jeffrey were both called as potential witnesses and transferred from their respective prisons to the Lucas County jail in downtown Toledo. Both of them had access in the jail to telephones that were not routinely monitored by jail officials. They quickly arranged a conference call through an acquaintance outside the jail.

On the night before Jeffrey and Alice were scheduled to talk, Alice's opinion of her husband flipflopped by the minute. "Kathy is a bitch and Jeffrey is a liar," she said. "Everything he's ever told me is a lie. . . ."

Minutes later, she said, "You know, I'm still madly in love with that jerk. I always will be. There is nothing he could ever do to make me not love him."

Later, Alice was in tears. "Why doesn't Jeffrey ever tell me the truth? What am I, some kind of animal he keeps on a leash? I feel like a half-dead mouse that the cat keeps batting around. . . . I can't figure out why I still care. How can you continue to love a person who hurts you so much?"

On December 12, at 6:00 P.M., Alice and Jeffrey spoke for the first time since their arrest nearly one year earlier. They talked for nearly one hour, and afterward Alice felt triumphant. "I let him have it," she said gleefully. "I really grilled him about Kathy. I called him a liar."

Alice said that Jeffrey had assured her that he no longer cared about Kathy. In fact, he had agreed to write Kathy a "Dear John" letter and divorce her as his wife. Jeffrey had even offered to send the letter to Alice so that she could edit it and then mail it herself to Kathy.

"I really believe he is going to sever the tie this time," she said. The thought that Jeffrey might tip off Kathy beforehand about the letter apparently hadn't entered Alice's mind.

"Jeff told me that an angel had visited him in prison. It touched him and gave him a message from God," Alice explained. She had memorized what the angel had said: "Truly I say unto you, as a mongoose would rise against the cobra and consume it as its prey, so shall that which has come, rise against that which seems certain death. For I will turn your mornings into noonday . . . great shall be your joy . . . saith He that was and is and is to come. Lift up your voice in great joy for thou hast prayed mightily before my throne. Behold the measure is full, the hour of your deliverance by my hand draweth nigh."

On December 13, at 6:00 P.M., Alice and Jeffrey talked again, and during their conversation, Jeffrey assured Alice that he loved only her, not Kathy.

On December 16, Jeffrey and Alice talked once more. Afterward, Alice was ecstatic. Jeffrey had recited a love poem to her:

> "Do you think I'm horny?
> I think you make me wild,
> And when the Lord does free you,
> I will make you big with child."

God was going to release Jeffrey from prison within two years, Alice said. As soon as he was freed, he would come rescue her from Marysville and they would go see God together.

"He wants me to have another baby!" she gushed. "He is telling me the truth this time. I know it. I can feel it. He loves me. He loves me!"

On December 17, Alice and Jeffrey spoke for the final time. The next day, Alice was scheduled to be transferred back to Marysville prison. Jeffrey would leave shortly thereafter. They spoke for about an hour. All of the anger that Alice had felt earlier toward Jeffrey was gone. She apologized for calling him a "cold-blooded murderer." She had "gone to pieces," she explained, during her trial.

"I doubted you."

Alice told Jeffrey that she had gotten down on her knees in her cell after she had first arrived in Toledo and had prayed. "I was at the end of my rope. I told the Lord that I needed some proof, some evidence, that you were who you say you are. I said that I wanted to hear a voice." Alice was watching television later that same night in jail when she saw a news bulletin about Jeffrey. The reporter said that he was being brought to Toledo for Ron's trial. "I knew God was answering my prayer," she said. "Seeing something on television is just like having a visionary experience, isn't it?

"And now," Alice continued, "I have heard your voice on the telephone. You see, God answered my prayer. He gave me proof that you are who you say you are!

"I want you to know that I know you are right now, and I have never been so sure, and it feels so good."

"I understand," said Jeffrey.

The prophecy that the RLDS patriarch had made in 1969 about Alice had finally come true, she said.

You shall marry a companion whom I have prepared to bring forth my kingdom and he shall be great in the eyes of these people and shall do much good unto the children of men, for I have prepared him to bring forth a marvelous work and wonder.

"I am so ashamed of myself for doubting," Alice said.

Seconds later, she giggled. If she sent Jeffrey a pair of her panties would prison officials let him keep them? she asked.

No, Jeffrey replied, but he would have enjoyed receiving them. "Something like that would get me into a lot of shit."

"Well, we certainly both know what being in shit is like," Alice said.

They both laughed.

"Alice," he said. "I will come for you. I promise. You got to believe me. I am who I am. I am God's chosen one."

"I know you are," she said. "I do believe, Jeff. I really do."

"Hang in there, sweetheart," Jeffrey said.

"I will," Alice replied. "You don't have to worry about me anymore. . . . I'm not going to give up. I'm not going to quit. I'm not going to stop watching for you."

"Okay."

"And I'm not going to stop loving you."

"Thank you."

"I love you."

"Me too."

"I want you to know something."

"What?"

"I'd do it all again," Alice said. She was sobbing now.

"Thank you," he replied.

"Please take care of yourself."

"Hey, I can do it. You see, I'm unlike other people. I'm still just the same—big and strong. Okay? My faith never has wavered. . . ."

"I'm with you one hundred percent now," Alice said.

"Thank you."

"I'm very proud of you."

"Thank you," he said. "I'm very proud of you too."

"Oh, I'm so proud of you," she repeated. "I really am. . . . I love you."

"I love you too."

"I guess we should hang up now."

"Okay."

"Jeff," she said, her voice now a whisper. "I love you with all my heart."

She quickly got off the line.

"Alice?" Jeffrey replied. "Are you still there?"

He called her name once again.

"Alice?"

And then, after hearing no reply, Jeffrey began to cry and slowly hung up the phone.

EPILOGUE

JEFFREY D. Lundgren. Still on death row in Lucasville, Jeffrey continues to study his scriptures in search of a way to open the remaining seven seals in Revelation. Even though he is in prison, he continues to recruit new "disciples" by corresponding with people who have read about his case and expressed an interest in learning about the pattern. He has sent letters to some of his former followers warning them that when Christ returns to earth, He will free Jeffrey and encourage him to take revenge against those who have betrayed him. His case remains on appeal.

Alice Elizabeth Lundgren. When Alice returned to the women's prison in Marysville, she discovered that Jeffrey was still corresponding with Kathy Johnson. In March, Alice contacted the warden at Lucasville and had him add her name to a list of people whom Jeffrey is prohibited from contacting. She subsequently filed for a divorce. "I have a serious addiction problem," Alice said. "Jeffrey is as deadly to me as cocaine or heroin to some women. . . . I will never be completely free of what haunts me until I can stand over his grave—then it will be over, buried forever." Alice's case is currently under appeal. She continues to insist that she was powerless to stop Jeffrey because of years of emotional, sexual, physical abuse. Unless her conviction is overturned, she will not be eligible for parole until she serves 115 years.

Damon P. Lundgren. Currently serving a 120-year sentence, Damon will first be eligible for parole after 108 years. His tearful plea for mercy at his trial prompted an angry letter from Jeffrey, who told his son that he needed to worry more about what God thought of his actions than what jurors had to say.

Jason, Kristen, Caleb Lundgren. The minor children of the Lundgrens were placed under the care of Alice's parents, Ralph and Donna Keehler. Donna has forbidden her son-in-law to mention his religious beliefs in letters to his children.

Kathy Johnson. Kathy was scheduled for release from prison during the summer of 1991. For a short period, she was housed in the same women's prison as Alice in Marysville, but was later moved to a halfway house in Cleveland. The two women avoided each other while in prison. Kathy plans to move to Lucasville when she is freed so that she and Rasia can visit Jeffrey at the prison. She continues to insist that he is a prophet.

Keith Johnson. During Alice's trial, a BATF agent told the Lake County Prosecutor's Office that Keith was telling people that he was a prophet. The agent quoted Keith as saying, "If Jeff isn't the prophet, maybe I am." Keith later denied making such a claim. Keith lives with his parents and four sons in rural Missouri.

Richard Brand. As part of the deal that his attorney negotiated with prosecutors, Richard pleaded guilty to five counts of murder, but he was sentenced on only *one* of those counts. He received a prison term of fifteen years to life and will be eligible for parole after serving ten years.

Greg Winship. Greg also received a plea bargain, but it wasn't as good as Richard's even though Greg pleaded guilty to complicity to murder, a lesser charge. Richard's attorney had specified in his deal that his client could be sentenced on only one count. Greg's plea bargain did not contain any such limit. Because of this, Judge Mitrovich was free to sentence Greg to fifteen years to life in prison for *each* of the five counts levied against him. That came to a total of seventy-five years to life in prison. Greg will not be eligible for parole until he serves a minimum of twenty years.

Daniel D. Kraft, Jr. Currently serving a fifty-years-to-life prison term, Danny will not be eligible for parole until he serves thirty-seven years.

Debbie Olivarez, Sharon Bluntschly, Susie Luff. Because Debbie and Sharon cooperated fully with the prosecution and provided damaging testimony against Alice and Jeffrey, they expected to receive a lenient sentence from Judge Mitrovich. Instead, the judge sentenced them to the maximum prison term that he could: seven to twenty-five years in prison. Susie, who refused to cooperate with the prosecution, received the same sentence. All are housed in the same women's prison as Alice and will be eligible for parole in five years.

Ron Luff. Ron will not be eligible for parole until he serves 130 years.

Dennis and Tonya Patrick. The Patricks have returned to Independence, where they are trying to rebuild their lives.

Steven LaTourette. Although his willingness to grant plea bargains was criticized early on, LaTourette's handling of the Lundgren cases was widely praised. A political editor for a local newspaper predicted that LaTourette would be unbeatable in 1992 if he seeks reelection.

Dennis Yarborough and Ron Andolsek. Officer Andolsek prepared most of the evidence and testified at all three of the Lundgren trials. The stress of helping prosecute the cases caused him to suffer severe depression, he said, to the point that he felt suicidal. After the cases were resolved, Andolsek complained publicly about Judge Mitrovich's refusal to show leniency to Debbie Olivarez and Sharon Bluntschley. He also complained about the unequal treatment that Greg Winship received in comparison to Richard Brand. Andolsek has since returned to his regular duties on the Kirtland police force. In January, a local civic group honored Andolsek and Chief Yarborough with an award for distinguished public service. Yarborough remains Kirtland's police chief. He has declined offers from publishing houses and movie companies interested in telling his story. On May 3, 1991, he spent the night watching the Kirtland temple. He was afraid that pranksters or new followers of Jeffrey might attempt to deface it.

Reverend Dale Luffman. Shortly after Jeffrey's arrest, someone painted YOU'RE DEAD on the picture window of Luffman's home. Despite the threat, Luffman continues as RLDS stake president. When asked by a reporter from the Cleveland *Plain Dealer* if Jeffrey should be executed, Luffman said: "From a theological perspective our church believes life is sacred, but death is a part of life." In the case of Jeffrey, Luffman added, the death penalty was justified.

Donald and Lois Lundgren. Jeffrey's parents have refused to respond to letters that he has written them. Before Debbie Olivarez was arrested, she told Don and Lois that Jeffrey had considered killing his mother and recruiting his father into the group in order to get their money.

Shar Olson. Shar returned to Independence, where she remains friends with Dennis and Tonya Patrick. She continues to write regularly to Richard Brand, Greg Winship, and Debbie Olivarez.

Kevin Currie. "I understand the horror that took place," Kevin said at Jeffrey's trial, "but I still consider myself a friend of Jeffrey's." Even so, Kevin has an unlisted number and said that he still fears that Jeffrey might try to have him murdered. In the spring of 1991, Alice contacted Kevin and asked him to write her. "I'm still considering it," he said.

Dennis, Cheryl, Trina, Becky, and Karen Avery. The bodies of the Averys were returned to a suburb of Independence for burial. About 240 mourners attended the memorial service held at a "restoration" branch of the RLDS. The minister did not mention Jeffrey Lundgren, but in his eulogy, Elder Garth McCulloch warned mourners about following false prophets. "We must carefully lead," he said, "lest we are led astray."

AUTHOR'S NOTE

THIS book is the story of Jeffrey Don and Alice Elizabeth Lundgren, and the murder of the Dennis Avery family. To date, I am the only author to interview the Lundgrens. I first met Jeffrey in April 1990 at the Lake County jail in Painesville, Ohio, four months after his arrest. I conducted sixteen separate interviews with him, most of which lasted five hours and took place after his trial and sentencing in September 1990. My interviews with Alice were done in the Lucas County jail in Toledo in November 1990. I spoke with her over a five-day period, usually five hours per session. Besides tape-recorded interviews, I also conducted numerous telephone interviews with both Lundgrens, and have received nearly fifty letters from Alice since she has been in prison. All of Alice's immediate relatives agreed to speak with me, including her parents, Donna and Ralph Keehler, her two sisters, Terri Buller and Susan Yates, and brother, Charles Keehler. I also met with the Lundgrens' three minor children, Jason, Kristen, and Caleb, and two of Jeffrey's relatives who asked not to be named. It is safe to say that I have spent close to two hundred hours talking to immediate family members and many more hours with the other persons interviewed for this book.

Although Jeffrey and Alice cooperated with me, I did not pay them or any other person for their cooperation. Nor did I permit Jeffrey, Alice, or anyone else mentioned in this manuscript any editorial control over its contents. All of my conversations with Jeffrey and Alice were on the record and I made no deals as to how either of them would be portrayed. None of the persons mentioned in this book was permitted to read any of the manuscript before it was published.

In addition to the personal interviews I conducted, this book also relies on numerous trial transcripts, confidential police and FBI records, and other information that previously has not been made public. Perhaps the most important of these confidential sources was seven hours of confessions that were videotaped by the Bureau of Alcohol, Tobacco and Firearms. While bits and pieces of these tapes were made public at the trials of Ron Luff and Alice Lundgren, the bulk of them have never been shown and their contents have remained secret. The tapes include statements by Ron Luff, Susie Luff, Richard Brand, Alice Lundgren, Dennis Patrick, and Tonya Patrick. Not only did I find these confessions useful in reconstructing the murders of the Avery family, but they also enabled me to observe the demeanor of the defendants shortly before or after their arrests. This proved particularly helpful months later when I interviewed Alice Lundgren and Dennis and Tonya Patrick in person, and observed Richard Brand and Ron and Susie Luff during their court appearances.

Besides Jeffrey, Alice, and their relatives, I also personally interviewed the following persons: Ron Andolsek, Tim Avery, Lisa Avery, Donna Bailey, Kevin Currie, William C. Downing, Charles R. Grieshammer, Marlene Jennings, Kathy Johnson, Keith Johnson, R. Paul LaPlante, Steven LaTourette, Bill Lord, Eleanor Lord, Dale Luffman, Judy Luffman, Georgia Milliren, Debbie Olivarez, Shar Olson, Dennis Patrick, Tonya Patrick, James Postlethwait, James H. Robbins, Laura Robbins, Hal Sappington, Ann Sherman, Muril Stone, Louise Stone, Hank Thompson, Bernie Wilson, Dennis Yarborough, Gail Yarborough. I held brief conversations with some twenty other persons who were involved in this affair in some way.

Readers should note that Sarah Stotts, Jacob Wilcox, Henry Thomas, Barbara Carter, Tom Miller, and Patti Miller are pseudonyms used to protect the privacy of real persons. All quotes attributed to them are actual statements. All other persons in this book are identified by their correct names. Statements by Jeffrey's aunt

Mary Bennett and uncle George Gadberry were taken from their sworn testimony at Jeffrey's trial.

Fifteen other persons, including one of Jeffrey's followers, agreed to be interviewed, but asked that they not be identified. These included people who knew the Avery family in Independence and in Kirtland, as well as former classmates of Jeffrey's and church members who knew Alice as a teenager.

I attended all of Jeffrey's trial, and parts of the trials that were held for Alice and Damon. I had access to transcripts of those proceedings that I missed but felt were important.

During interviews, I found that people often recalled the same events quite differently. I have noted major disparities in the book, usually by giving more than one account, but in minor cases, I have chosen the version that seemed most likely to be true.

The most difficult information to verify dealt with the private life of Alice and Jeffrey. Oftentimes, only the two of them were present and they tell dissimilar accounts of what happened during these private moments. I found Alice to be amazingly forthcoming, particularly when describing her sexual practices with Jeffrey. I was able to verify most of what she told me by interviewing her relatives and longtime friends, such as Louise Stone, whom Alice had confided in long before the Avery family was murdered. In the few cases where I have been unable to substantiate what Alice said, I have used the words "Alice claimed" to warn the reader that her statements cannot be corroborated. While I felt that Jeffrey was frank during our talks, particularly when discussing his religious beliefs and the murders, when it came to talking about his sexual preferences and intimate relationships with Alice and Kathy, I found his stories inconsistent and often blatantly contrary to both women's versions. Once again, when I could not corroborate Jeffrey's statements, I used the words "Jeffrey claimed."

Whenever I described a character's feelings or thoughts in the book, I have based that information on that person's recollection of their feelings and thoughts at that moment. I have tried to verify this information when possible by questioning eyewitnesses.

Information about the ships that Jeffrey served on during his naval career was taken from each ship's log and sea records stored at the Naval Historical Center in Washington, D.C. I found these books and articles about the Mormon religion helpful: "Before Mormonism: Joseph Smith's Use of the Bible, 1820–1829," by Philip L. Barlow, *Journal of the American Academy of Religion*; *A Gathering of*

Saints: A True Story of Money, Murder and Deceit by Robert Lindsey; *The Mormons,* by Thomas F. O'Dea; *The Mormon Murders,* by Steven Naifeh and Gregory White Smith; *The Mormon Mirage,* by Latayne Colvett Scott; *Sidney Rigdon 1793–1876,* by F. Mark McKiernan; *Latter-Day Saint Beliefs: A Comparison Between the RLDS Church and the LDS Church,* by Steven L. Shields; *Defenders of the Faith: Varieties of RLDS Dissent,* by William Dean Russell; *An Illustrated History of the Kirtland Temple,* by Roger D. Launius; *No Man Knows My History: The Life of Joseph Smith,* by Fawn M. Brodie; *America's Saints: The Rise of Mormon Power,* by Robert Gottlieb and Peter Wiley; numerous pamphlets published by the Reorganized Church of Latter-Day Saints, and several articles published in *The Zarahemla Record.* Information about chiasmus was drawn from several sources including "Hebrew Poetry in the Book of Mormon," by Angela Crowell, *The Zarahemla Record; Kerygma,* by The Kerygma Study Program; "Chiasms in the Book of Mormon," by Raymond C. Treat, *The Zarahemla Record; Chiasmus in Antiquity,* by Wallace B. King. Information about Lake County was taken primarily from *Here Is Lake County, Ohio,* by the Lake County Historical Society.

These public officials provided me with help: Jamey Henderson, Department of Criminal Records, City Court, Independence, Missouri; Warden H. L. Morris, Ohio Reformatory for Women, Marysville, Ohio; Jack Bendolph, Southern Ohio Correctional Facility, Lucasville, Ohio; Sheriff James A. Telb, Richard D. Keller, and Sandi Guess, Lucas County jail; Jeffrey Farrone, Lake County jail. I also wish to thank Rob Whitehouse, staff writer, the *News Herald;* Maggi Martin, staff writer, and Curt Chandler, photographer, the Cleveland *Plain Dealer;* Bill McKay, reporter, and Belinda Prinz, producer, WJW TV-8, Cleveland.

As always, I am indebted to Patricia Hersch and Walter Harrington, two writers who gave me excellent editorial guidance, as well as, at William Morrow, my editor, Adrian Zackheim, and my copy editor, Joan Amico, and to Bob Mecoy at Avon Books. I am particularly grateful to my agent, Robert Gottlieb, and to Laura Shapiro and Irene Webb, all of the William Morris Agency. Special thanks to Yvonne M. Frament.

Others whose help I would like to acknowledge include the Reverend James C. Sprouse, the Reverend Richard G. Thayer, Toni Shaklee, Lynn and LouAnn Smith, Dr. C. T. Shades, Wayne and Donna Wolfersberger, and Carolyn Hunter. I wish to thank my parents, Elmer and Jean Earley, for reading this book in its earliest stages, and I am thankful for the support of my wife, Barbara, and children, Steve, Kev, and Kathy.

This book is dedicated to the memory of my sister, Alice Lee Earley, who died tragically at the age of sixteen, and my maternal grandmother, Belle Patterson, who inspired me with her poetry and artistic skills. I miss them both.

DEATH COMES TO THE NURSERY

CATHERINE LLOYD

KENSINGTON BOOKS
http://www.kensingtonbooks.com

KENSINGTON BOOKS are published by

Kensington Publishing Corp.
119 West 40th Street
New York, NY 10018

All Kensington titles, imprints, and distributed lines are available at special quantity discounts for bulk purchases for sales promotion, premiums, fund-raising, educational, or institutional use. Special book excerpts or customized printings can also be created to fit specific needs. For details, write or phone the office of the Kensington Special Sales Manager: Attn. Special Sales Department. Kensington Publishing Corp, 119 West 40th Street, New York, NY 10018. Phone: 1-800-221-2647.

Library of Congress Card Catalogue Number: 2019950864

Kensington and the K logo Reg. U.S. Pat. & TM Off.

ISBN-13: 978-1-4967-2322-2
ISBN-10: 1-4967-2322-8
First Kensington Hardcover Edition: February 2020

ISBN-13: 978-1-4967-2324-6 (ebook)
ISBN-10: 1-4967-2324-4 (ebook)

10 9 8 7 6 5 4 3 2 1

Printed in the United States of America

DEATH COMES TO THE NURSERY

Chapter 1

Kurland Hall,
Kurland St. Mary, England, 1825

Lucy, Lady Kurland, looked up dubiously at the smiling face of the beautiful young woman standing in front of her, and then back at the letter in her hand.

"You're Agnes's cousin, Polly?"

"Yes, my lady." Polly curtsied again. "Agnes wrote and said you were looking for a new nursery maid, and as I was wanting to be leaving London, she told me to apply for the position." She nodded at the letter Lucy held. "That's from you, isn't it? Offering me a job?"

A note of uncertainty crept into Polly's voice, and her smile faltered. "Don't tell me Agnes was making it up, and you don't want me. I've sold everything I have to buy my ticket here."

Lucy set the letter to one side and considered Polly anew. Yes, she looked nothing at all like her cousin Agnes, but just because she was pretty didn't mean she wouldn't be a hard worker. Agnes had spoken very highly of her, and Lucy had an excellent opinion of her son's nurse.

"I understand that you are experienced with dealing with young children?" Lucy asked.

"Yes, my lady. I have two younger brothers and a sister. I always had to help me mum out, especially after me dad scarpered."

"Have you been employed as a nursery maid before?"

"No, but I'm willing to learn. And with Agnes telling me what's what, I'm sure I'll pick it up in no time." Polly must have seen the indecision on Lucy's face because she carried on speaking. "*Please*, my lady. Just give me a chance. I promise I won't let you down."

Lucy sighed and picked up the letter again. "Let's start with a month's trial, shall we? If you settle in well and prove to be satisfactory, I will consider hiring you for a full year."

Polly clasped her hands together on her bosom, her blue eyes sparkling. "Oh, thank you, my lady!"

Lucy beckoned to Foley, who had accompanied Polly into the morning room. "Will you take Polly up to the nursery, Foley? Ask Agnes to take care of her cousin. I will come up to see Ned at suppertime as usual."

"Yes, my lady." Foley smiled fondly at Polly and held open the door. "Come along then, young 'un. I'll get James to bring up your bags."

Lucy tucked the letter into her pocket and made her way slowly through the house to the study of her husband, Robert. It was a bright late-summer morning in Kurland St. Mary, and sunlight flooded through the windows, patterning the wooden floors. Lucy knocked on the door and went in. Her husband was sitting at his desk dealing with the account books and didn't look particularly pleased to be interrupted.

"Robert . . ."

"What is it?"

"I just interviewed Polly Carter for the position of nurse-maid."

"And what does that have to do with me?" Robert asked. "Was Ned scared of her? Will she not suit?"

Lucy sat down in front of his desk. "I'm sure he'll love her. She's Agnes's cousin."

"As you are constantly telling me how wonderful Agnes is with our son, I'm wondering why you appear so doubtful about her cousin."

"She's . . . very pretty," Lucy confessed.

"So what?" Robert set his pen down. "Are you worried I'll run off with her?"

"Hardly." Lucy had to smile at that. "But I do wonder how the rest of the household will deal with her. Foley almost fell over himself being nice, and that isn't like him at all these days."

"He needs to retire," Robert said. "Have you reason to believe the girl will be incompetent?"

"None at all. Agnes recommended her," Lucy said. "I've offered her a month's trial before I make up my mind completely."

"Then perhaps you might give her the benefit of the doubt. It's not like you to be worried about a pretty face, my love." Robert came around his desk and sat on the edge directly in front of Lucy. "Why do we even need a new nursemaid? We have three women in that nursery already. I don't want Ned smothered in petticoats."

"He is hardly smothered," Lucy objected. "He spends much of his time with you, and he also enjoys going down to the stables and Home Farm with James."

"Still . . . ," Robert said. "Why add another maid?"

Lucy looked down at her hands, which were folded together in her lap. "I thought you might have realized why by now."

"Realized what?"

"That I'm increasing again."

"Good Lord!" Robert stuttered. "But you've been so . . . well."

"As opposed to my last experience when I was not well at all?" Lucy asked, and Robert nodded. "Grace says that every pregnancy is different, and that this time I may suffer no ill effects at all."

"I damn well hope so. But Grace is an excellent healer and I trust her judgment. I hated seeing you so indisposed," Robert commented. "When is the little blighter due?"

"Just before Christmas, I think."

Robert came over, lifted Lucy out of her seat, and sat down again with her in his lap. He kissed her cheek and wrapped an arm around her thickening waist.

"How wonderful to think that Ned might soon have a little brother."

"Or a sister," Lucy reminded him.

"Even better." He kissed her again. "In all seriousness, my love, what delightful news."

"I haven't told anyone else yet," Lucy confessed. "But now that you know, I'll probably speak to Dr. Fletcher and my family."

"If you are happy to do so, then go ahead."

She cupped his chin. "Are you really pleased?"

"Why would I not be?" He raised a dark eyebrow.

"Because Ned isn't even three yet."

"Which is why you have my full permission to employ as many people as you want in the nursery, so that you, my dear, don't wear yourself out." He smiled at her, his dark blue eyes full of amusement. "Polly can't be that pretty, now, can she?"

Polly wasn't pretty.

Robert let out his breath as the new nursemaid curtsied and sent him a very saucy smile. She was beautiful. Her hair was gold, her eyes were blue, and her skin was perfectly tinted, like a porcelain ornament. She also had the figure of a goddess.

"Good afternoon, Sir Robert. Right pleased to meet you." Polly smiled down at her small charge, who was building a brick tower on the rug in front of the nursery fire. "Young master Ned looks just like you."

"Welcome to Kurland Hall." Robert finally managed a reply. "I do hope you are settling in well?"

"Yes, indeed, sir. Everyone has been so kind to me." She sat down on the rug, presenting Robert with an excellent view of her bosom, and offered Ned another brick to add to his tower.

Robert took the chair beside the fire and reached forward to ruffle Ned's hair. "Good evening, old chap."

Ned gave him a ferocious glare that reminded Robert rather too forcibly of himself and returned to constructing his fortifications.

"He's a lovely little boy, sir." Polly commented. "So polite! Not like my little brothers, who can curse with the best of them."

"I don't think Lady Kurland would approve of that," Robert murmured. "Ned certainly does seem to have a pleasant disposition."

He glanced up as Agnes came into the nursery carrying a supper tray. Dark-haired, tall, and thin, she looked nothing like Polly.

"Good evening, Agnes. How lovely for you to have your young cousin working in the nursery with you now."

Agnes busied herself setting the tray down and did so with something of a thump. "I'm certainly glad to have another pair of hands, Sir Robert, what with Lady Kurland's news."

"Yes, another charge for you on the way," Robert agreed. "I am relying on you to keep an eye on Lady Kurland. She does tend to overexert herself."

"Don't you worry about that, Sir Robert. I know her ways."

Robert fought a smile. His wife did tend to be overly managing, even if she was often right about what needed to be managed.

The nursery door opened, and Lucy came in, her fond gaze immediately going to her son.

"Ned, are you ready for your supper?"

To Robert's relief, his son and heir ignored his mother just as completely as he had ignored his father and set another brick on top of the wavering tower.

Just as Robert was about to repeat Lucy's advice about his supper being ready, the tower crashed to the ground, and Ned's lower lip wobbled. Before Robert could react, Polly swooped the boy up and marched him over to the table.

"Never mind that, Ned. We'll build it even bigger next time. Now, come and eat your supper. Cook said she had something special for you tonight."

Robert caught Lucy's gaze and shrugged. Whatever else Polly Carter might be, she certainly had a way with children. Knowing his wife, that would more than justify her staying on at Kurland Hall.

He held out his hand to her as he rose from his seat. "Everything seems to be in order here, my dear. Perhaps we should leave Ned to enjoy his supper?"

"I . . ." For once, Lucy looked conflicted, her gaze straying to the table, where Ned was chatting away to Polly as she cut up his meat.

"We have your father, my aunt Rose, and all the Fletchers coming to dinner tonight. Perhaps it would be a good opportunity to share our news with them?" Robert suggested. "And are you quite certain Cook will provide us with sufficient victuals?"

"Of course she will." Lucy finally came toward him. "But I suppose it wouldn't hurt to check."

Robert hid a smile as he bid his son and the nursery staff good night, and escorted his wife down the stairs. Polly would either succeed in becoming a good nursemaid or she wouldn't. His wife was clever enough to decide the matter without referencing Polly's looks, and that was good enough for him.

He went into his dressing room and allowed his valet to offer him a new cravat to replace the wrinkled one around his neck. He tied it neatly, without help, and secured it with the jet pin Lucy had given him for his last birthday. His valet assisted him into his new winter coat, which was dark blue and cut in the severe military style he still favored.

Since his visit to Bath and the hot springs, he'd installed a large bath in the dressing room, which meant he could indulge in regular hot soakings. It didn't quite replicate the healing power of the waters in the Bath spa, but it was certainly a help for his wounded thigh. He barely needed to use his cane these days.

Lucy had already changed for dinner, so he met her down in the drawing room, where his father-in-law, the Honorable Ambrose Harrington, rector of Kurland St. Mary and its outlying parishes, was warming himself in front of the fire.

"Ah! There you are, Robert. I was just telling Lucy that it's time to put young Ned up on his first horse."

"He's two years old," Robert pointed out. "He's still mastering walking."

"Which is why it's the ideal time to do it." Mr. Harrington was a keen horseman who loved to hunt. He turned to his wife, Robert's aunt Rose. "Don't you think so, Rose?"

"I think it is up to Robert, my dear," Rose answered him, her warm smile reaching out to both of them. "I didn't set my children on a horse until they were four or five."

"But you lived in the city. Here in the countryside, being a good rider is essential." Mr. Harrington asserted. "Present company excepted, obviously."

Robert tried not to let the rector's comment bother him, but it was difficult. Before his horse had fallen on him at the battle of Waterloo and almost killed him, he, too, had thought like his father-in-law. Now he could barely manage to be around a horse without a thousand fears engulfing him.

"You don't have to do it yourself, Kurland," the rector

said encouragingly. "I'm sure one of your stable hands would be happy to help. Or even better, send the boy down to me, and I'll see that he's taught the proper way to do things."

"I know you would take great care of him, sir, but I'd rather wait a year or so until I am confident Ned will both understand and enjoy the process," Robert said firmly.

"And I agree with Robert." Lucy came up alongside him and linked her arm through his. "Ned loves visiting the stables with James, and that is quite enough for now."

"If you say so, my dear." Mr. Harrington sighed. "I'm only trying to make sure that my first grandchild is properly prepared for his responsibilities."

To everyone's surprise, the normally selfish and indolent Mr. Harrington had taken quite a liking to his fearless grandson. His interest in Ned's progress and desire to be involved with his life had come as quite a shock to everyone, especially his daughter.

"I do hope young Ned will be coming down to pay his respects to his grandparents this evening?" Mr. Harrington asked. "Mayhap we can ask him how *he* feels about learning to ride a horse by himself, eh?"

Lucy caught Robert's gaze, and he shrugged. He had no issue with Ned coming down for a few moments before he went off to bed, but he knew his wife was less inclined to encourage any unnecessary attention on him.

"I'll ask James to check if Ned is still awake." Lucy headed out toward the hall. While she attended to the matter, Robert welcomed his old friend Dr. Fletcher and his wife, Penelope, who had just entered the drawing room. His land agent, Dermot Fletcher, also joined them and made polite conversation until Lucy returned. Robert wasn't the kind of man who enjoyed large gatherings, but the people invited to dinner were all well known to him and therefore quite acceptable.

"Was our son and heir awake?" he murmured in Lucy's ear as she came to stand beside him.

"I believe he was. He'll be down in a moment. I told Agnes he should not stay above a quarter hour."

"In case his grandfather starts spoiling him?" Robert asked.

"In case Ned starts to think he can escape his proper bedtime every night," Lucy replied. "It is difficult enough to get him to go to sleep as it is without offering him too much excitement."

"Good Lord," Mr. Harrington murmured as he turned toward the door and raised his glass to his eye. "What have we here?"

Lucy sighed as a blushing Polly, who was holding Ned by the hand, curtsied to her father. "I assume Agnes was too busy to bring Ned down herself."

"One must assume so." Robert patted her shoulder. "Don't worry. I'll go over and make sure your father isn't saying anything too outrageous."

Robert cast a quick look around the room and noticed that both the Fletcher brothers were staring at the beauteous vision that had descended among them. Dermot cleared his throat as Robert went by him.

"Is that Agnes's cousin, sir?"

"Apparently."

"She looks nothing like her."

"She is rather fetching, isn't she?" Rose, who was standing beside his land agent, offered her own opinion of the nursery maid. She didn't appear concerned that her recently acquired second husband practically had his aquiline nose down Polly's rather excellent cleavage. "When did she arrive, Robert?"

"This morning."

"Ah, that explains why I didn't meet her," Dermot said. "I was out visiting the Home Farm."

"I'm sure you'll take the opportunity to introduce yourself to her fairly soon, Dermot," Robert said encouragingly. "You *are* the one who dispenses the wages and manages the household staff."

He went over to his father-in-law's side and rescued the blushing nursemaid from his attentions, directing them instead onto his grandson.

Polly curtsied to him. "Thank you, sir. I'll go and wait over there until Master Ned is ready to return to the nursery."

She retreated to the door. Robert returned to his wife, who was standing with Penelope Fletcher in the middle of what appeared to be an animated conversation.

"Well, if I were you, Lucy, I wouldn't allow that woman in my house."

"Why not?" Lucy asked mildly enough. "She appears to be an excellent nursemaid."

Lucy and Penelope had a somewhat fractious relationship. But Robert knew his wife would always champion her employee against her friend's objections.

"She is far too pretty!" Penelope rolled her eyes in Robert's direction. "You would not want to give your husband *ideas*, now, would you?"

"Ideas about what?" Robert joined the conversation.

"You know very well what I'm referring to." Penelope sniffed. "Men can be weak and easily mislead—especially when their wives are no longer in the first blush of youth."

Lucy raised her eyebrows. "As we are the same age, Penelope, are you suggesting that Dr. Fletcher will also stray?"

"Of course he won't." Penelope patted her hair. "I am still beautiful, whereas you, my dear Lucy, have never been much more than passable."

Robert hastened to intervene as his wife visibly drew herself up. "I can assure you that my wife has nothing to worry about. I am very content with my choice."

Penelope regarded him dubiously for a long moment and then nodded. "I will allow that, seeing as you turned down my beauty for her . . . average looks, maybe you aren't inclined to chase your nursemaid."

"Thank you, I think," Robert said. "But I believe you were the one to break our engagement, not me."

Penelope waved away his correction. "It hardly matters now, does it? We both ended up with the partners we deserved." She smiled fondly over at her husband, who was in deep discussion with his brother. "I, too, am well content with my lot."

Foley appeared at the door and loudly cleared his throat. "Dinner is served."

Ned disappeared back up the stairs with his new nursemaid without making a fuss, and Robert turned his attention to the prospect of his dinner.

As the gathering was informal, after making sure that Ned was on his way back to bed, Lucy accompanied Robert into the small dining room. Penelope's comments about her husband becoming enamored of a pretty face hadn't bothered her. She'd known as soon as Polly appeared and every man in the room stared at her that Penelope would say something. As Penelope was accustomed to being the most beautiful woman in the room, she probably hadn't enjoyed being outshone.

Lucy took her seat and waited as her father said grace before dismissing the servants so that they could serve themselves. Robert much preferred to eat his meals in comfort, and with her current guests being so familiar, she was more than willing to accommodate him.

He caught her attention as he sat down and raised his eyebrows as he picked up his wineglass. Lucy offered him a tiny nod in return, and he cleared his throat.

"My wife and I are happy to announce that we are expecting an addition to our family at Christmastime."

Everyone turned to smile at Lucy, who felt herself blush.

"How lovely!" Rose said. "A little brother or sister for Ned."

"Indeed." Robert gave one of his rare smiles. "We are delighted."

Dr. Fletcher winked at Lucy. "I'll assume that Grace is

caring for you, but don't hesitate to ask for my help if you need it, my lady."

"Gladly," Lucy replied. "In truth, I am feeling remarkably well this time."

"I'm pleased to hear it." Dr. Fletcher toasted her with his glass.

As everyone settled in to eat, Penelope leaned in close to Lucy.

"As you are expecting, I'll double my warning about allowing that young woman in your house. Even good men are known to stray when their wives are unable to accommodate their more physical needs."

"I have no concerns about that, Penelope." Lucy spoke as firmly as she could.

"Then let's just hope that your confidence in Sir Robert is justified," Penelope stated. "Because if *I* were in your shoes, Lucy Kurland, I wouldn't be *quite* so sanguine."

Chapter 2

"*I'll* accompany Master Ned to the stables."

"That's my job, Mr. Fletcher."

"And I'm telling you that I'm doing it today."

"You bloody well are not—"

Lucy hastened toward the two men, who were nose-to-nose at the bottom of the stairs in the main hall, glaring at each other.

"What on earth is going on?"

Dermot Fletcher swung around, his expression that of a small boy caught in mischief.

"Lady Kurland! I do apologize for disturbing you. I was just offering to walk young Ned down to the stables."

"Which is my job, as you well know, Lady Kurland." James, who was the most senior footman at the hall, jumped into the conversation. "I was just about to go upstairs to collect him and Miss Polly when Mr. Fletcher decided to interfere."

"I was not interfering, I simply—"

Lucy stared at both men until they fell silent. "I think I will walk with Ned today, so neither of you are needed."

Mr. Fletcher took a step back and bowed. "As you wish, my lady."

He stalked off into the house. Lucy distinctly heard his office door slam farther down the corridor.

"I'm sorry, my lady, but that Mr. Fletcher is being right annoying to Miss Polly," James said. "And she ain't for the likes of him, I can tell you that."

"I didn't ask for your opinion, James," Lucy said severely. "And I'm fairly certain that Polly would not appreciate you wrangling over her like two dogs with a bone. When she is with my son, she is doing her job and not to be distracted by either of you."

"Oh, she does her job, my lady. Don't you be thinking otherwise, and the young master likes her very much, and does as she tells him," James hastened to reassure her. "Now, I'd best be going upstairs, my lady. The young lad will be worrying as to where I am."

Lucy held up her hand. "I told you that I am going with Ned today. Please return to the kitchen and find something else to occupy your time."

James looked crestfallen as he bowed and went back toward the servants' stairs. Lucy raised her eyes heavenward and walked up the stairs to the nursery. Penelope had been wrong about Robert being interested in their new nursemaid, but in the past three weeks, every other male in the household, from Mr. Fletcher downward, had been acting like fools over the poor girl.

And to be fair to Polly, she was nothing but pleasant to everyone. She performed her job well and encouraged none of the men dancing around her for attention. It wasn't the first time Lucy had found the men of the household squabbling over Polly, and she suspected it wouldn't be the last.

When she reached the nursery, Ned came running toward her, his smile so like his father's that she couldn't help but smile back at him.

"Horses?" he asked hopefully.

"Yes, indeed." Lucy glanced over at Polly, who had her cloak and bonnet on and was ready to go. "It is a beautiful sunny day, and we will all enjoy the walk."

"Yes, my lady." Polly curtsied and turned to Agnes, who had just come in with a load of fresh linen. "We're off then, cousin."

"Hmmph," Agnes said. "Take your time. I've got to get this bed done."

Polly hesitated. "If you wait until I come back, I can help you."

"No need," Agnes nodded at Lucy. "It'll get done much faster without you and Ned helping."

Polly didn't seem to take Agnes's sharp words too seriously as she took Ned's hand. "Come on, then. Let's go."

Lucy held the door open to allow her son and his nursemaid to precede her. Polly hadn't seemed bothered by the lack of a male escort on her walk, which indicated to Lucy that, despite all the attention, she wasn't pining after any one man in particular.

They went out one of the many side doors of the old Elizabethan manor house, through the formal gardens at the back that led down to the stables and the Home Farm. Ned skipped ahead, his countenance cheerful, and Lucy simply enjoyed watching him. After two miscarriages, the birth of her son had changed her in so many ways. She was almost embarrassed by the depth of emotion she felt for him and tried hard to conceal it.

"He's a lovely lad, Lady Kurland." Polly fell into step beside Lucy. She was wearing a plain blue dress that did nothing to detract from her beautiful figure. "Such a sweet nature."

"One hopes he will keep it," Lucy agreed. "The advent of a baby brother or sister might cause some jealousy."

"Oh, aye." Polly chuckled. "I remember that with my family, but with all the attention Ned gets, I suspect he won't worry too much."

"That would be wonderful." Lucy walked on and then cast a glance at her companion. "How are you adjusting to living in the countryside, Polly?"

"I like it, my lady." Polly took a deep breath. "The air is clean, and there aren't too many people bothering me."

"If anyone is bothering you, I would like to hear about it," Lucy said firmly.

"Oh, you know men. They like to make cakes of themselves over a pretty face. I try not to encourage them, and eventually they stop pestering me."

Lucy had never thought about that aspect of being beautiful before.

"Or if they don't stop, my lady, I'm not averse to giving them a swift kick in the bollocks to set them straight."

Lucy struggled not to laugh. "Indeed."

"I grew up in the slums. I know how to take care of myself." Polly shaded her eyes to check on Ned, who had stopped to admire a patch of daisies. "Some old bloke tried to buy me from me mum when I was around five."

"Buy you? Whatever for?" Lucy asked.

"What do you think?" Polly's smile was touched with bitterness. "Some men like 'em young and pure."

"That's . . . horrible."

Polly shrugged. "It taught me to take care of myself, my lady. I'm not just a pretty face."

Lucy stopped by Ned and turned to Polly. "If you wish to stay on here, you are most welcome."

"Let's see how the next week goes, shall we?" Polly grinned at her. "You never know, maybe a handsome prince will turn up and sweep me off my feet."

Robert cast a distracted glance at his son and beckoned to his companion.

"James, will you keep an eye on Ned? I don't want him running out into the stable yard when a coach is coming in."

"I've got him, sir. Don't you worry." James nabbed the back of Ned's collar and hefted him up onto his shoulder. "Come here, youngster."

Robert had accompanied his son, James, and Polly down to the coaching inn in Kurland St. Mary, where

Lucy was expecting a parcel. He had also been instructed to pick up any correspondence for the house or the rectory. There had been no sign of the innkeeper, so Polly had gone inside to see if his wife was in the kitchens, leaving Robert to deal with his son.

It seemed that Ned had inherited his grandfather's love of horses, which was both a pleasure and a problem for Robert, who still struggled to go near them. No one would believe that he had once been in a cavalry regiment and had relied on his mount to see him through several engagements during the war. Since the end of his military career and almost his life at Waterloo, he'd lost his nerve, which wasn't a convenient thing at all for a county squire. The constant chaos of the arrival and departure of coaches, farmers' wagons, and people in the stable yard made him nervous.

Perhaps he might take up his father-in-law's offer to teach Ned to ride after all . . .

"I got the mail, sir." Polly came out with a pile of letters. "Mrs. Jarvis says she'll go and find her ladyship's parcel, and will be right out."

"Thank you." Robert took the mail and stowed it in the deep pocket of his coat. "Perhaps you might help James with Ned."

Polly looked over to where the mail coach was disgorging its passengers. James had Ned on his shoulder and was showing him the four horses harnessed to the vehicle. Polly went still, and an apprehensive expression dimmed her usual smile.

"If it's all the same to you, sir, can I wait until James stops talking to the ostler?"

"Why?"

Polly grimaced. "Because Bert Speers has taken to following me home every time I come to the village, and he won't leave me be."

Robert frowned over at the young ostler. "Is he, by Jove? I'll be speaking to his master about that."

"Don't you bother yourself, Sir Robert." Polly spoke fast, one eye still on the ostler and the coach passengers who were milling out into the yard. "It'll just make things worse if he thinks I'm complaining about him." She went on tiptoe and craned her neck to see around Robert's shoulder. "Oh dear, it looks as if James is giving him a piece of his mind again. I hope they aren't going to start fighting."

"Not with my son in the middle of it, they aren't," Robert said. "Polly, come with me, and get Ned out of the way."

Robert pushed his way through the crowded yard to where the two men were standing beside the mail coach. He grabbed hold of Ned and handed him over to Polly.

"Go and wait inside."

"Yes, sir." Polly took Ned's hand and ran with him toward the inn.

James didn't look away from the angry face of the ostler. "This blaggard is annoying Miss Polly, sir."

"Indeed." Robert turned his attention to the shorter man. His dark eyes, thick black hair, and ferocious scowl didn't inspire Robert to approve of him.

"If I find out you've been bothering a member of my staff, I will haul you up in front of the local magistrate—who happens to be me—and make sure you pay the price for your insolence," Robert snapped.

"You can't stop me asking a girl to walk out with me," Bert sneered.

"I can if the girl has repeatedly turned you down, and you still pursue her."

"Who says I'm doing that?" Bert glanced toward the inn, where Polly and Ned had retreated. "She's lying, sir. She lures us in and then laughs at us, and you expect us to do nothing? *Look* at her. She's a worthless whore who deserves everything she gets."

Robert shoved his finger in Bert's face. "If you say one more word, I will have you put into the county gaol."

"For what, sir?"

"For whatever I say you have done." Robert didn't like to use his privilege, but in this one instance, he was quite prepared to do so. "Who do you think they will believe? You stay well away from Polly Carter and keep off my land, and we'll say nothing more of this."

Bert finally stepped back and mumbled something that might have been an apology before disappearing into the stables. Robert let out an aggravated breath.

"Did you know about this, James?"

"I only found out yesterday when I was walking with Polly and Master Ned, sir, and Bert came after us." James shuffled his feet. "I was hoping to have a quiet word with him about it, but as you can see, he's not one to back down."

"Hopefully now he will," Robert suggested. "If he doesn't, I want to hear about it immediately."

"Yes, Sir Robert." James drew himself up to his full height, and Robert noticed the bruise on his cheek.

"Have you been *fighting*?"

"As I said, sir. Bert came after us yesterday. I sent Miss Polly and Master Ned on their way and waited for him to catch up." James rubbed a hand over his jaw. "We exchanged a few blows before he ran off, but nothing serious."

"This is not acceptable behavior where my son is concerned," Robert said severely. "What if you'd been knocked out and Bert had followed Polly home? What might have happened then?"

"I wouldn't have let that happen, sir. I'm twice the size of that little imp." James insisted. "I would give my life for the young master."

Robert shook his head and went back toward the inn, where Mrs. Jarvis was waving at him from the door. There was a lot he wanted to say to James, but he needed to gather his thoughts and speak to Lucy before he said something he didn't mean. His absolute fury at the thought of Ned being caught in such an ugly situation surprised him.

"There you are, Sir Robert!" Mrs. Jarvis smiled up at

him. "And how lovely to see your little boy! And I hear Lady Kurland is increasing again, so well done on that score." She winked and elbowed him in the side. "I have her parcel of fabric and lace from London right here, sir. Although she probably won't be needing any new gowns in her current condition, will she?"

"Probably not." Robert finally managed to get a word in edgeways. "Well, we must be on our way. It's way past time for Ned's nap."

"Always a pleasure to see you, sir. Mr. Jarvis will be sorry he missed you."

Robert lowered his voice and leaned in toward the innkeeper's wife "Your ostler. Bert Speers."

"What about him, sir?"

"Tell your husband that if I hear that Bert has been chasing after my nursery maid and my son again, I will be most displeased."

"Bert?" Mrs. Jarvis looked over toward the stables. "He's a quiet one. He hasn't been here above a month. He doesn't seem to have any friends and keeps to himself, except when he's had a few pints."

"He's been following Polly home."

"Well, she is rather beautiful. Who can blame him for trying?" Her smile faded as she registered Robert's expression. "You're serious, aren't you?"

"I most certainly am."

"Then I'll mention it to Mr. Jarvis the moment he gets back." She nodded. "It's not fair on Polly, who's a respectable girl and not one to lay out lures to the boys, despite her looks."

"Thank you." Robert nodded and stepped back into the stable yard, where James, Polly, and Ned awaited him. "Good day to you, Mrs. Jarvis."

Lucy looked up from her sewing as Robert came into her sitting room, shut the door, and proceeded to pace up and down the room, a frown on his face.

"Whatever is the matter?" she finally inquired.

"It's Polly." He turned to face her, his expression grim.

"Don't tell me that you have succumbed to her charms and are planning on running away with her after all," Lucy teased.

"No." He sighed and sat opposite her, his hands clasped together in front of him. "She is a pleasant enough girl, but everywhere she goes, she causes chaos."

"How so?" Lucy set her embroidery aside.

"I went to get your package from the inn this morning and found out that one of the ostlers has been following Polly home."

"That is hardly her fault," Lucy pointed out.

"I know." Robert paused to ponder his words, which was rather unusual for him. "James got into a fight with the man yesterday when he was escorting Polly and Ned home. If I hadn't intervened today, I suspect James would have started another fight, warning this Bert Speers to stay away."

"Oh, *dear*," Lucy sighed. "The other day I caught James and Mr. Fletcher arguing about who should be accompanying Polly and Ned on their walk down to the stables. And it isn't the first time I've seen such quarrels between the male staff."

"You see?" Robert flung up his hands. "Chaos wherever she goes. I don't like it, Lucy. I don't like my son being placed in such a vulnerable position."

Lucy considered his impassioned words. "I cannot help but agree with you about Ned, but I am loath to blame Polly for the lack of respect the men around her are showing. She is excellent with Ned, gets along well with Agnes, and performs her duties well. It seems unfair for her to lose her job over something she cannot control."

"I agree. But surely Ned's safety has to be our priority?"

"Of course it is." Lucy hesitated. "Perhaps you could speak to James and Mr. Fletcher privately, and ask them to leave Polly alone?"

"I can certainly do that, but I have no control over Bert Speers or any other man who fancies his chances with the new local beauty."

"Polly wants to stay on after her month's trial." Lucy said. "And I . . . I practically assured her that the job would be hers for the next year." To her astonishment, her voice wobbled. "I was hoping she would be here when the new baby was born."

"*Why?*"

"Because I *like* her, and—" Lucy swallowed hard and couldn't continue.

"Lucy." Robert reached for her hand. "Are you crying over a *nursemaid?*"

"*Yes.*" She searched frantically for her handkerchief. "I'm *sorry.*"

"It's all right." Robert considered her. "If Polly is truly important to your current state of well-being, then I'm loath to get rid of her."

"Thank you." Lucy dried her eyes. "Perhaps I could offer her a shorter term of employment—to next quarter day?"

"That's a good idea." Robert nodded. "In fact, let me speak to her so that she understands that it is my decision, and not yours."

Lucy stood and went over to put her hand on Robert's shoulder. "Thank you."

He looked up at her. "For what?"

"For being so understanding."

"Me?" His smile was pained. "Mayhap I'm mellowing with age."

She kissed his forehead. "One can only hope so, seeing as you will soon be worrying for two children instead of one."

"Understand me, though, Lucy." He met her gaze, his expression resolute. "If there is any hint of her bringing further trouble on Ned, or if he is caught up in any violence, she will be turned off."

Lucy nodded. "I wholeheartedly agree."

He reached up his hand to clasp hers. "Then let's just hope I can knock some sense into James, Dermot, and any other of my employees making sheep's eyes at Polly."

"I'm sorry, Sir Robert." Dermot Fletcher repeated as he faced his employer across his desk. "But I cannot agree with you on this matter."

"I *beg* your pardon?" Robert stared at the flushed face of his land agent. "You can't agree that it is improper of you to chase after my nursemaid?"

"Of course, that's not proper, sir, but it's not what I meant." Dermot rushed to speak again. "I respect Miss Polly!"

"Then you have a funny way of showing it," Robert shot back. "Arguing with other staff, following her around like a lost sheep, making excuses to visit the nursery at all times of day, sometimes when you should be doing your own work."

"She is surrounded by those who are far beneath her," Dermot insisted. "She is not what she seems, Sir Robert. She is very intelligent and well read."

Robert studied his land agent's face. "Are you trying to tell me you might come to care for her?"

"I *do* care for her," Dermot said earnestly. "I have already considered asking her to be my wife."

Robert sat behind his desk and gestured for Dermot to sit as well. It was not in his nature to be circumspect, yet he would try his best.

"With all due respect, Dermot, you have only known her for a few weeks, and she is hardly of your social class."

"What social class?" Dermot replied. "I'm an Irish Catholic who earns his living in the same house as she does."

"Has she given you any indication that she favors your suit?" Robert asked.

"Not yet, sir." Dermot frowned. "She is beset by many fools, and she tries to be pleasant to all of them."

"Then, perhaps you might allow her the chance to make

up her own mind when she is ready," Robert suggested. "From what I have observed, she treats all men the same."

Dermot met Robert's gaze. "You think I'm being a fool, don't you?"

"It is hardly my place to suggest anything of the sort, but—"

"You do think I'm a fool." Dermot sighed.

"I think that you are lonely, and that since Miss Anna Harrington became engaged to Captain Akers, you need to find a relationship for yourself."

Dermot winced. "Is it that obvious?"

"Only to those who know you well." Robert paused. "I just think it is too early for you to declare yourself to Polly Carter. She will be here for at least another quarter. Perhaps you should wait and see if she truly wishes to reciprocate your affections before you jump in and scare her off."

Dermot nodded. "I will think on what you have said, Sir Robert. Thank you for your counsel." He stood up and tried to smile. "I'd better get back to work. I probably have been neglecting things of late."

Robert asked him to send Foley in and waved Dermot away.

When Foley appeared, Robert gestured for him to sit down.

"I wanted to talk to you about James."

Foley raised his eyebrows. "Has he displeased you in some way?"

"Yes. Fighting with one of the ostlers from the Queen's Head, arguing with Mr. Fletcher, and pining over Polly Carter come to mind."

"Miss Polly is a pretty lass."

"Indeed, she is, but that doesn't mean my staff should stop doing their jobs. James is so busy defending her honor that he appears to have forgotten that his primary objectives are to serve this household and, more importantly, to safeguard my son from harm."

"He is a mite hotheaded about Polly," Foley admitted. "I've never seen him anything but kind and gentle before. These days, he threatens to fight anyone who as much as looks at her."

"So I've noticed." Robert shifted in his seat. "I want to speak to him personally. I'd also like you to address all the male household staff about their behavior around the female staff. Our nursery will be increasing in a few months, which will mean even more women in the servants' hall. I do not wish to hear of any problems."

"I understand, sir." Foley went to rise, which took him some time due to his rheumatism. "I was thinking James might make a fine butler after I retire."

"Until the last few days, I would've agreed with you. But I can't have someone brawling with potential visitors," Robert said. "Are you finally thinking about retiring then, Foley?"

"I think so, sir." His oldest retainer bowed his head. "You've settled down nicely now."

"I do believe I have." Robert offered Foley one of his rare smiles. "Lady Kurland has me well in hand."

"She does, sir. Thank God, and with another youngster on the way, your line is assured, and I can retire happy." Foley bowed.

Robert cleared his throat, aware that his butler was the last remaining member of his staff who had also served his parents. "You won't have to move far, you know. I'll find you a cottage on the estate, or in whichever of the villages around here you wish. Just say the word, and it will be yours."

"Thank you, sir." Foley straightened with some difficulty. "I'll think on the matter over the next few weeks. I'd planned to retire at Christmas, which gives you plenty of time to find my successor."

"Well then, let's hope young James minds his manners and redeems himself, and is ready to step into your shoes," Robert commented. "Send him to me now, Foley, and ask Agnes if she can spare Polly for a few minutes."

"Yes, sir."

While he waited for James to appear, Robert attended to the mail he'd picked up at the inn.

"You wished to see me, Sir Robert?"

"Yes, come in and close the door behind you."

He looked up as James entered and gestured for him to come forward. James's apprehensive stance reminded Robert of the young officers he had bullied and counseled into staying alive during the recent war. He decided young James could do with some brutal honesty and looked him right in the eye.

"I will not tolerate you fighting when you are in my employ, or tasked with guarding my son, or any member of my household. Do you understand me?"

James gulped at his arctic tone. "Yes, Sir Robert."

"If there are any problems with Polly and other men, I expect you to ensure the safety of my son and his nursemaid without resorting to violence."

"Polly doesn't encourage other men, sir," James protested.

Robert raised an eyebrow. "I didn't say that she did."

"She's a good girl, and one day, I hope she'll marry me."

"Has Polly suggested that she reciprocates your feelings?" Robert asked for the second time that morning.

"Recipro—what, sir?"

"Has Polly suggested she returns your affection?"

"No, sir, she hasn't, but that's because she's a respectable woman who wouldn't offer false hope, despite what Bert Speers says."

"If Polly is a respectable woman, she will not take kindly toward any man who gets into fights over her."

James nodded. "Yes, sir. She told me that herself." He shifted his weight from one foot to the other. "I promise I won't let you down again, sir."

Robert met his gaze. "You'd better not, or I can assure you that you won't be employed in this house for much longer."

"It's just that she doesn't ask for all the attention, sir, and I hate to see her being treated like she's a barmaid in a tavern, or something worse," James said earnestly. "There are people who mistake a kind word from her as something else entirely. Like Mr. Fletcher, sir, he—"

Robert held up his hand. "Mr. Fletcher is none of your concern."

"Yes, sir, but—"

"Rest assured that if the need arises, I will deal with Mr. Fletcher or any other man in this damn house who thinks he has a right to force himself on Polly's notice." Robert stared at James. "Are we quite clear?"

James nodded. "Yes, Sir Robert."

"Then go about your business." Robert waited until James had left before getting up from his desk and pouring himself a stiff brandy.

"Good, lord," he muttered. "I feel as if I've been thrown into a Drury Lane farce!"

There was another knock on the door, and Polly Carter came in. She wore a plain blue gown with an apron over it. Her blond curls were drawn away from her face under a cap. She curtsied low.

"You wished to see me, Sir Robert?"

"Yes, please come and sit down."

He resumed his seat behind the desk and waited for her to settle into her chair.

"I am concerned about the effect on my son of having you as his nursemaid."

Polly blinked her beautiful blue eyes at him. "How so, sir?"

Robert was done with diplomacy. "The men who hover around you and their tendency to fight."

"I don't know what you want me to say, sir." Polly pleated her apron with her fingers. "I do my best to be

pleasant to everyone who speaks to me, but I don't tolerate no rudeness, especially in front of your son."

"I'm not accusing you of anything, Polly. I'm just saying
that I don't want my son put in a position where he has to
run for his life when fists start flying." Robert studied Polly's
anxious face. "I am aware that Lady Kurland wished to
offer you the position of nursery maid for a full year. Due to
the current situation, I have decided to be more cautious,
and offer you employment only until next quarter day."

Polly stared at him for a long moment, a thoughtful expression on her face. "That's perfectly acceptable, sir, and
I quite understand your position on this matter."

Having braced himself for tears and maybe worse,
Robert found himself nodding with relief. "Good."

"Mayhap I should stay more in the grounds of the hall
and not venture into the villages?" Polly looked hopefully
at him. "At least for a short while until things have calmed
down."

"I suggest you discuss that with Lady Kurland and
Agnes," Robert suggested. "I would hate to restrict your
movements."

Polly rose, straightened her skirts, and offered him an
appraising smile. "You are a good man, Sir Robert. Most
employers would've turned me off without even bothering
to hear my side of the story."

Robert held her gaze. "And I will do so if my son comes
to any harm."

She curtsied. "I can promise you that he will not suffer
at my hands, sir." She turned and went toward the door,
her carriage erect and her head held high. She glanced at
the clock on the mantelpiece and then at him. "It's usually
my half day, sir. May I still take it?"

"Of course." Robert said. "As long as Agnes is aware of
your intentions."

Polly's lips curved into a mischievous smile. "Agnes
thought I was going to be dismissed, so she offered to pack

my belongings for me. I'll make sure she knows that isn't the case before I go out."

Robert had noticed some tension between the cousins but had accepted it as usual between family members. Did Agnes resent the fact the Ned obviously preferred Polly?

After Polly left, it occurred to Robert that the nurse-maid was rather adept at managing the men in her life— including him—and that he had better not forget it.

Chapter 3

"What is it, Agnes?" Lucy looked up from her letter writing to find her son's nurse hovering at her shoulder.

"I can't find Polly, my lady."

Lucy put down her pen. She was in her private sitting room at the rear of the house where she always started her day by interviewing the cook and her housekeeper, and then attending to the matters in her daybook.

"Is she unwell?"

"I don't know. She's just disappeared."

Lucy pushed back her chair and stood up, arching her back. "When did you last see her?"

"Yesterday around noon, just before she was asked to attend Sir Robert in his study." Agnes paused. "Is it possible that he dismissed her from her position?"

"He certainly didn't mention it, and I would've told you if the nursery were to be shorthanded. From what I understand of their conversation, Sir Robert merely warned Polly not to involve Ned in any of her romantic entanglements and offered her employment until quarter day."

"She didn't have the decency to tell me any of that." Agnes frowned. "But it doesn't surprise me."

Lucy headed for the back stairs, Agnes behind her, and ascended to the very top of the house where the servants had their bedchambers. The floor was deserted, as all the staff were already up and about. Lucy paused on the landing to catch her breath and waited for Agnes to join her.

"Which is Polly's room?"

"It's down here." Agnes turned left into the woman's section, walked down to the third door, and pushed it open. "Her bed doesn't look as though it has been slept in."

"No, it doesn't, but her possessions are all present." Lucy surveyed the gowns still on their hooks on the wall and the open chest full of petticoats, stockings, and undergarments. A tray of pins was scattered over the dressing table, along with a hairbrush and a discarded ribbon. Lucy also spied a half-filled bag.

"Yesterday was Polly's afternoon off," Agnes said. "When she returns, she usually pops her head into the nursery to say good night and to check on Master Ned, but last night she didn't come in at all."

"Mayhap she didn't return to the house," Lucy mused. "Is it possible that she spent the night somewhere with a friend and merely overslept?"

"She's only been here a month, my lady," Agnes pointed out. "She's hardly made any acquaintances except those in the house and on Kurland land."

Lucy turned a slow circle, trying to understand what had become of Polly, her thoughts flying in so many directions that she felt quite unwell. "I must speak to Sir Robert."

"Yes, my lady." Agnes hesitated. "Do you think she ran off?"

"I don't know," Lucy said. "She's your cousin. Do you think that is likely?"

"She seemed to like it here." Agnes grimaced. "Maybe it was too quiet for her, and she decided to go back to London."

"If that was the case, why would she not just pack up and go rather than agree to stay on for another three months?"

"I have no idea, my lady." Agnes headed for the door. "I need to get back to the nursery. Ned's upset enough as it is, what with Polly disappearing without a word . . ."

"Please go ahead."

Lucy paused to gather up a blue dress that Polly had thrown onto the floor and shook it out. There was a large mud stain on the hem of the skirt, which perhaps explained why she had discarded it rather than hanging it up. Her cloak was missing, as was her best bonnet and her stout boots—all things that she had probably been wearing as she left for her afternoon off.

But where had she gone?

Deep in thought, Lucy went down the stairs and found Robert in his study. He glanced up as she came in and immediately went still.

"What's wrong?"

"Polly's missing."

"As in has left entirely, or has not returned from wherever she went on her afternoon off?"

"Most of her possessions are still here, but she isn't." Lucy bit her lip. "Did she seem agitated when you spoke to her yesterday?"

"Not at all. In truth, she was remarkably understanding about the whole thing."

"Did you give her money?"

"No, of course not." Robert looked affronted. "We always pay our staff in arrears."

"Which means she was only paid last week for the first month of her service." Lucy frowned.

"An amount that I doubt would take her very far."

"I agree," Lucy said as she took a quick turn around the room. "Then I wonder where she is?"

"Perhaps she stayed overnight with someone and has forgotten the time?" Robert suggested.

"I had the same thought, but Agnes says Polly had not

made many acquaintances outside the hall." Lucy looked over her shoulder at her husband. "Did Polly indicate to you that she planned to meet someone yesterday?"

"No, after our discussion, she asked me if it was still all right to take her half day. I told her to carry on. That was the last I saw of her."

"That's the last anyone saw of her." Lucy sighed and resumed her pacing.

"Didn't she go back upstairs to tell Agnes she was leaving?" Robert asked.

"Not according to Agnes. And she didn't pop her head in and say good night to Ned when she returned, either."

Robert frowned. "I told Polly to make sure Agnes knew she was going out, and she promised she would do so." He paused. "I got the distinct impression that she and Agnes were not getting along. Perhaps Polly decided not to tell her cousin out of spite, because Agnes had assumed she was about to be dismissed and had offered to do her packing for her."

"Agnes didn't mention any of this, but I had wondered if all was well between them." Lucy frowned. "Ned is very taken with Polly, and I don't think Agnes particularly cares for it."

Robert rose to his feet. "Let's find Foley and begin a search of the house and grounds."

He strode ahead of Lucy and entered the door that led to the kitchens and the butler's pantry. By the time she caught up with him, he was already speaking to his butler and the cook. From what she could tell, everyone was surprised by his announcement and was shaking their head.

"Where's James?" Robert asked, his sharp blue gaze scanning the kitchen.

Foley scratched his head. "I haven't seen him this morning. Have you, Mrs. Bloomfield?"

The butler and the cook exchanged glances before she replied in the negative.

Michael, the second footman stepped forward. "Shall I go up and check his room? Maybe he's ill."

"Yes, please do that," Robert replied. "And come back here. I'll need you to go to the stables for me."

"Yes, Sir Robert."

Lucy leaned in and whispered, "I wonder if James is with Polly."

"I damn well hope not," Robert replied, equally quietly. "But the odds aren't looking good, are they?"

Dermot Fletcher came in through the back door, whistling, and then stopped dead as he saw his employers in the middle of the kitchen.

"Is something the matter?" he asked cautiously.

"Well, at least you are here," Robert said. "Polly is missing."

"Missing?" Dermot paled. "I saw her yesterday walking down the drive toward the village."

"At what time?"

"Just after midday. I heard the church clock chiming."

Michael came clattering down the back stairs and came over to Robert. "He's not in his room, sir, and his bed hasn't been slept in."

Lucy pressed her hand to her rounded stomach and briefly closed her eyes as the room swirled around her. Had James and Polly impulsively left together without a stitch of extra clothing and none of their possessions? Or had they simply gone off and would return when they felt like it? Either scenario annoyed her.

"Miss Polly wouldn't—" Mr. Fletcher started to speak, and Robert cut him off.

"Mr. Fletcher, I need you to go into the village, alert the rector, and make sure that James and Polly are not availing themselves of anyone's hospitality."

"James's parents have a farm about a mile away, sir," Michael said. "They could've gone there."

"Yes, of course." Robert nodded. "Go down to the stables, Michael, and alert Mr. Coleman as to what is going on. Ask him to send the grooms out to search the park-land. When you have done that, please come back here with a gig so that I can go to Mr. Green's farm and ascertain if James has turned up there."

"Yes, Sir Robert." Michael hurried out through the scullery.

While Robert issued his stream of orders and went off with Mr. Fletcher, Lucy sank down into a chair and helped herself to a cup of the strong, fortifying tea Cook kept ready in a teapot on the table. She knew that in her current condition, Robert would not allow her to rush out and search for Polly. Not that she felt like rushing anywhere when it was hard to breathe and she still felt nauseous.

"Are you all right, my lady?" Cook asked.

"Yes." Lucy summoned a smile. "I'm just worried about Polly and James."

"Do you think they've run off together? The boy did think the world of her."

"It certainly seems possible." Lucy sighed as Cook dropped a crushed lump of sugar in her tea. "Thank you."

As the kitchen returned to normal, she sipped her tea and contemplated what to do next. It was morning, and it was quite possible that Polly and James would come back to Kurland Hall. What they expected to happen next was hard to contemplate, as Robert would no longer wish to employ either of them. Perhaps they would simply collect their things and leave.

Was it possible that James had somehow found Polly in distress and saved her from Bert, the ostler? Perhaps, at that point, Polly had realized that she cared for James and had confessed her love. James might have taken her to his parents' farm to receive their blessing and they had stayed the night.

Even to Lucy, such a scenario sounded like it had been taken right out of a gothic novel, but then again, Polly did look like the perfect damsel in distress . . .

Lucy finished her tea and glanced over at the kitchen clock. There was little she could do at this time but speculate, and she refused to sit around worrying any longer. Agnes would be shorthanded in the nursery, and there was no one to take Ned out for his daily walk. She would change into her stout walking boots, find her cloak, and take her son to the park. Not only would she be getting some much-needed exercise, but she would also spend time with her son, who always required her full attention.

Robert put on his riding boots and thickest greatcoat and went out to the front of the house where Michael awaited him. He climbed up into the swaying gig.

"Do you know the way to the Greens' farm?" Robert asked as he settled onto the seat.

"Yes, sir." Michael gathered the reins and clicked to the single horse. "Just sit tight, and I'll get you there in no time."

"There's no need to rush," Robert stated. "I'd rather get there safely than not at all."

"Right, sir." Michael glanced over his shoulder as he carefully turned the gig around. It was fairly obvious to most of Robert's household that, unlike most country squires, their master was not comfortable around horses. Robert had long ago given up any pretense that he would ever be like the wild, horse-mad youth he'd once been.

He gripped the bench seat with one gloved hand and determinedly stared out over the flat fields that composed the bulk of his estate. Drainage was a major issue; it was a constant battle during the months when the Kurland River overflowed its banks and saturated his fields. Robert and Dermot had recently visited the estate of Coke of Holkham Hall in Norfolk to observe his methods of farming and gained some valuable insight into ditch digging and the power of water channels and windmills. They'd already started preparing the land closest to the river for new drainage.

The light dissipated as the overhead trees closed over the road like gnarly, interlocked fingers to form a green-tinged tunnel that darkened into an impenetrable gloom as they passed through the middle of a copse of oak trees.

"Not far now, sir," Michael said as they emerged once more into the light, leaving Robert blinking. "It's just past the Prentice farm."

"Thank you." Robert hadn't been out to visit the Green family for almost a year. They tended to come to see James at Kurland Hall and meet with Robert there, or to seek him out in Kurland St. Mary during market day.

There was no sign for the farm, but Michael seemed confident that the narrow track where he turned off was the correct one. Robert held onto his hat as the wind blew over the fields, making the growing wheat and corn rustle and sigh like a thousand whispers. The signs were that the harvest would be good, but one never knew what might happen with the weather. A week of rain could destroy the crops, and a week without it could have just as much of a devastating effect.

Such was the joy of farming . . . Robert was heartily glad that the main part of his income came from his family interests in the industrialized north, which continued to prosper even while his farming income waxed and waned.

He shaded his eyes as the farmhouse and outbuildings of the Greens' farm came into view. The stone-and-brick cottage had been re-thatched a year ago, and looked sturdy and well kept. Even as the gig drew to a stop among a cacophony of honking geese and barking farm dogs, the front door opened, and Mr. Green came out.

"Sir Robert!" He strode over to the horse and held its head while Robert stepped down to the ground. "I was just about to drive over to Kurland Hall."

"Why is that, Mr. Green?" Robert asked after a hearty handshake.

"Well, come in and see for yourself." Mr. Green walked

back to the front door and bellowed down the hallway. "Sir Robert's here himself, Gwen! No need for us to worry."

Robert followed him into the farmhouse and down the hall to the large, sunny kitchen at the rear of the building, where he discovered Mrs. Green tending to her son James, who lay on a settle covered with a blanket.

"Good morning, Sir Robert." Mrs. Green said. "Did you come seeking my son?"

"Indeed I did, Mrs. Green. Good morning to you," Robert removed his hat and sat down near James. "What happened?"

James sighed heavily and turned toward Robert. "Someone hit me, sir."

"Were you fighting again?" Robert asked quietly.

"*No*, sir. I was just walking to the village from the hall. Someone came up behind me and hit me hard enough to knock me off my feet."

"In broad daylight, Sir Robert!" Mrs. Green interjected. "What is the world coming to?"

"I have no idea, Mrs. Green," Robert said politely, and then returned his attention to James. "Then, how did you end up here, over a mile away from where you fell?"

"I don't know, sir." James groaned. "The next thing I remember was Nell, my dog, sniffing and pawing at me, and then I heard my father's voice."

Robert looked up at Mr. Green, who had sat on the trestle by the kitchen table, hands on his spread knees. "Where exactly did you find him?"

"Near the bottom of the track up to the farm, sir." Mr. Green patted one of the dogs that had gathered around him. "Not that I found him by myself. If it hadn't been for the dog, he could've lain there all day, seeing as I wasn't planning on going out." He nodded at his son. "I was up at five, milking the cows, when Nell practically dragged me out there by grabbing hold of my sleeve with her teeth."

"Clever dog," Robert said. "So none of you know how James came to be lying on your land after being attacked somewhere close to Kurland Hall?"

"I know it sounds odd, sir, but that's the truth of it," Mr. Green assured him. "We're just glad the boy is all right."

"Thanks be to God," Mrs. Green murmured.

Robert continued to study James, who was struggling to meet his gaze. "Would it be possible for me to speak to your son alone for a moment?"

Mr. and Mrs. Green exchanged puzzled glances. "If you wish, sir. We can go into the parlor."

"Thank you."

Robert waited until they left and then turned to James.

"I understand that you might not wish to reveal the truth of your actions in front of your parents, but I would ask for a full accounting now, please. Did you get into a fight with Bert Speers?"

"No, sir. I swear it."

"Did you see Polly yesterday?"

James's hand crushed the patchwork quilt in his fist. "I got off work just after she did, so I was . . . following her to Kurland St. Mary."

"Did you speak to her?"

"No, sir." James vigorously shook his head and then winced. "She was too far ahead. I tried to shout out to her, but I doubt she heard me."

"Or she chose to ignore you. Go on."

"Go on with what, sir?" James blinked at him. "I didn't catch up with her. Just before I reached the church, someone jumped me from behind, and that's the last thing I remember."

Robert contemplated his footman, who did look rather worse for wear and had a bloody wound on the side of his head.

"Did you see where Polly went when she entered the village?"

"No, sir. She was blocked from my view by the church."

"And you remember nothing since yesterday afternoon until your father found you early this morning?"

"That's correct, sir." James hesitated. "Did Polly say something different? Is that why you're asking me all these questions?"

It was an interesting thing for James to ask—almost as if he feared to be blamed for something. Robert considered his young footman and decided to be blunt.

"Polly has disappeared. I was rather hoping I'd find her here with you."

Lucy sat at her dressing table as Betty redid her hair. It was a windy day, and Lucy suspected that her loose curls would not fare well in the breeze when she ventured out on her walk. She'd instructed Betty to braid her hair tightly to her head so that she could fit it under her bonnet.

"That's much better." Lucy admired her reflection. "Thank you."

"You're welcome, my lady." Betty slid another pin into place. "Have you any news about Polly?"

"Not yet." Lucy sighed. "I can't believe she has just run off."

"Mr. Foley did say that James was missing, too." Betty paused hopefully. "Mayhap they are together. That will really put Agnes's nose out of joint. She's always been sweet on James."

"I didn't know that." Lucy turned in her seat so that she faced Betty. She wasn't normally one to gossip with the staff, but Betty had been with her since she'd lived in the rectory and was a trusted confidante. "Did you think Polly and Agnes got along well?"

"Not at all, my lady. Agnes is right jealous because Master Ned prefers Polly, and so does James." Betty set about tidying the pins. "Agnes wasn't pleased by that, and she let her cousin know it." She tutted. "The arguments those two had after Ned had gone to bed."

"They argued a lot?"

Betty nodded vigorously. "Yesterday morning, when I went up to the nursery to look for your missing book, my lady, I heard them through the wall. Agnes was insisting Polly was going to be dismissed, and that it was her just comeuppance. Polly would have none of it."

It occurred to Lucy that this must have been just before Polly went down to speak with Robert, never to be seen again.

"Agnes said that it would be a blessing if Polly left, and Polly accused her of being jealous." Betty straightened the bed coverings. "Polly didn't half slam the door on her way out down the stairs."

"Oh, my goodness," Lucy said. "Perhaps that is why Polly decided not to come back."

"I suppose it's possible, my lady, but why would she leave without her possessions?" Betty looked doubtful. "Do you remember when Mary went missing from the rectory? She took everything with her."

Despite the seriousness of that occasion, Lucy almost smiled. She would never forget that particular incident, which had drawn her into an uneasy alliance with a bedridden Robert and eventually ended up in their marriage.

Betty came over and patted her shoulder. "Now don't fret too much, my lady, especially in your condition. Sir Robert wouldn't like that at all."

"You're right," Lucy agreed. "But I do feel somewhat responsible. Polly is in my employ, and she seemed to want to stay on at least for the next quarter."

"Perhaps she's as flighty as she looks, and got a better offer, and decided to play us all for fools." Betty went toward the door. "That girl always struck me as a deep one, my lady."

Lucy considered Betty's opinion as she readied herself to go up to the nursery. It was all so confusing. Polly hadn't told her cousin that she was leaving for her half day;

Agnes hadn't mentioned that she and Polly had been arguing just before Polly left. But who was telling the truth?

Lucy decided not to say anything to Agnes until Robert returned from visiting the Green family. If Polly and James were found together, there would be plenty of opportunities to discuss the matter further.

Chapter 4

"I found James at his parents' farm." Robert came into Lucy's sitting room and shut the door behind him. "He has no idea where Polly is."

Lucy frowned. "Then where has he been? Foley told me that James only had a half day yesterday and did not have permission to stay the night at the farm."

"James claims that someone hit him on the head, and that he woke up the next morning in his father's hay cart with his dog next to him," Robert commented.

"You don't sound as if you believe him." Lucy studied her husband's face.

"Because it is quite fantastical! How can he not know how he ended up at his parents' farm?" Robert asked. "If he really was hit on the head, then why would his attacker pick him up and deposit him nearly a mile away where he was sure to be found?"

"I agree that it does sound somewhat strange," Lucy said slowly. "It makes one wonder why the person who supposedly attacked James knew him well enough to know where he lived."

"James lives here now, Lucy, and has done so for several years," Robert reminded her. "Why didn't his attacker drop him off at our front door?"

"Perhaps because he would've been found too quickly?" Lucy looked up at her husband. "If the person simply wished to get James out of the way, then the longer before he was discovered, the better."

"Mr. Green did say he wouldn't have found James so quickly if it hadn't been for his dog." Robert shoved a hand through his hair and sat down opposite Lucy. "And I'm still not convinced he was even attacked."

Lucy stilled. "Do you think he was fighting over Polly again?"

"Or fighting *with* Polly." Robert sighed. "He says he saw her walking ahead of him into the village, but that she was too far ahead to notice him."

"I suppose that is possible." Lucy bit her lip. "Robert, are you really suggesting that James is lying about everything?"

"I dealt with a lot of young men in my time in the cavalry, Lucy, and I'm fairly good at spotting the liars, the bullies, and the cowards." Robert hesitated. "I don't think James is telling me the truth, but I don't know why."

"Perhaps he argued with Polly, and she was the one to knock him out, and he's too embarrassed to admit it."

"It's possible, but how did he end up at his parents' farm?"

"He could've walked there," Lucy pointed out. "If he truly was dazed, he might have forgotten that."

"True." Robert was still frowning. "He did seem genuinely shocked when I told him that Polly was missing." He raised an eyebrow. "I assume she hasn't been found yet."

"Not yet. I was thinking I might go down to the Queen's Head and see if she bought a ticket on the mail coach." Lucy said.

"I'll go. I haven't had a chance to change yet, and the gig is still outside." Robert went to stand. "You stay here and rest."

"I'm not an invalid, Robert." Lucy sat up straight. "I'm not even tired."

"I am quite aware of your capabilities, my love, but I'd rather you coordinated our efforts to find Polly from *here*." Robert went toward the door. "If Polly is discovered before I return, send one of the grooms to find me."

With that, he was gone, leaving Lucy feeling mildly aggrieved at his display of high-handedness. In moments of stress, he had a tendency to order her around as if she were of inferior rank. Too restless to return to her book, Lucy went out into the hallway and toward the main entrance, which was in the oldest part of the house and led into the medieval hall.

She'd asked Foley and Mrs. Bloomfield to organize a search of the manor house, which, because of its construction, contained many unexpected nooks and crannies, staircases that went nowhere, and dark cellars. Polly wouldn't be the first member of her staff who had accidentally wandered off and gotten lost.

Mr. Fletcher had gone down to the rectory, and Aunt Rose had volunteered to check all the houses in the village. Lucy's father had ridden out to the outlying parishes of Kurland St. Anne and Lower Kurland to make sure Polly hadn't gotten lost on her walk and sought shelter somewhere.

On one of their shared walks with Ned, Polly had confided to Lucy that she found the countryside a confusing and somewhat frightening place—what with the open fields and lack of light. It was possible that she had just lost her way.

Lucy paused at the bottom of the stairs, for once unsure how to proceed. She could go up to the nursery and see Ned again, but she would be disrupting the routine she had very firmly put in place purely out of her own restlessness. Her certainty that Polly hadn't merely gotten lost and that something was truly wrong consumed her.

"Lucy?"

She blinked and turned to the now-open front door, where her sister Anna was smiling at her.

"Anna!" Lucy hurried toward her sister and embraced her. "How lovely! I was not expecting you back until next week!" She took her sister's hand. "Come and tell me all about your visit with the Akers family. How was Harry?"

Anna laughed and patted her shoulder. "Goodness me, Lucy. So many questions when all I want to do is run upstairs and see how my adorable nephew is!"

"You may go and see him later," Lucy said firmly as she gestured to Foley, who had come into the house behind her sister. "But, first, we will have some tea."

"As you wish." Anna untied the ribbons of her bonnet to expose her natural blond curls held in a loose bun on the top of her head. "I only just arrived back at the rectory, and no one was there except Cook. I decided to come up to the hall to see you first and tell you my news."

Anna pulled off her gloves and held out her left hand for Lucy to inspect. "I married Captain Akers."

Lucy gasped and pressed a hand to her chest. "You are *married*?"

"Yes." Anna blushed adorably. "I know you will wonder at such haste when we had decided to wait, but while I was staying at his home, he received new orders that will take him from our shores for almost a *year*."

Anna's bright smile dimmed. "Harry tried to pretend that everything was all right, but I knew that in his heart he was worried that another year of delay would make me forget him entirely." She shrugged. "Not that such a thing is possible, but you know how men are."

Lucy couldn't imagine Robert even thinking such a thing, but she nodded encouragingly.

"He asked me if I'd consider marrying him before he left, and I said yes," Anna continued somewhat breathlessly. "He managed to obtain a special license, and due to the necessity of speed, I was unable to invite my friends or family to join me. I do hope you will forgive me for that, Lucy."

"Of course!" Lucy agreed. She was disappointed not to have been present, but she was so surprised Anna had gone ahead with the marriage that her emotions were a mere nothing. Her sister had always been averse to marriage because of her fear of having a child.

Captain Harry Akers had not only gained Anna's love, but had convinced her that he was willing to do everything in his power to protect her from her own fertility. Lucy knew such intimate details only because she had inadvertently overheard a private conversation when she'd visited the Akerses and Anna had sought her advice.

"Where is Captain Akers now?" Lucy asked.

"He had to report to Southampton at the earliest opportunity." Anna looked as if she was trying not to cry. "His mother asked me to stay with her while he was gone, but I wanted to come home first and share my news with everyone."

Lucy took Anna's hand in hers. "I'm so happy for you, my dearest sister. Father will be delighted."

"He will certainly be surprised." Anna hesitated. "Do you think his feelings will be hurt that he was not able to officiate at the wedding?"

"I suspect his pleasure at your wedded state will easily outweigh his disappointment, Anna," Lucy said robustly. "When Captain Akers returns, perhaps Father can hold a ceremony blessing the marriage in Kurland St. Mary church."

"I'm sure he'd love to do that." Anna nodded. "And I'm quite certain Harry would not object at all."

Foley appeared with a tray of tea that he placed in front of Lucy.

"Apologies for the interruption, my lady, but I wished you to know that we have completed the search of the house and have found no trace of your missing maid."

"Thank you, Foley." Lucy busied herself pouring tea as

Anna unbuttoned her pelisse. "Did you walk up here, Anna?"

"Yes, because there was no one at home, which was most odd, because I sent a letter ahead announcing the time and day of my arrival." Anna took her cup. "Is something amiss?"

"My new nursemaid didn't come back after her afternoon off yesterday," Lucy said as she offered Anna a biscuit. "The whole village and hall are out looking for her."

"The poor girl!" Anna exclaimed. "That explains why Aunt Rose was not at home and Father's favorite horse was missing from the stables."

"They should be back soon enough," Lucy said. "I can send someone down to tell them that you are here at the hall if you wish."

"I told Cook. I'm fairly certain she will tell Aunt Rose when she returns, so there is no need to worry." Anna looked over at Lucy and smiled. "You look very well."

"Thank you." Lucy's hand came to rest on her rounded stomach. "I'm expecting another child in December."

'Oh!" Anna's smile dimmed. "Are you . . . happy about that?"

"I am." Lucy smiled to reassure her. "It's wonderful news."

"Yes, of course. How selfish of me not to immediately congratulate you." Anna reached for Lucy's hand. "You must think me such a shrew."

"Not at all." Lucy well understood her sister's fears. Losing their own mother in childbed had put its mark on both of them. "Robert is also pleased. He believed we would all spoil Ned rotten if he remained an only child."

"If you wish, I will stay with you until the birth, and then return to visit the Akers for the remainder of Harry's voyage," Anna offered eagerly.

"That would be lovely," Lucy said. "Otherwise, you will leave me with Penelope, who will tell me not to be

silly about the pain of childbirth after she sailed through it
with barely a squeak."

Anna rolled her eyes. "I would not wish ill on any woman
having a child, but Penelope has been rather obnoxious since
the birth of little Francis."

Lucy poured more tea, more grateful than she could've
imagined to have her sister back with her at Kurland Hall to
gossip with. "*And* she warned me that my new nursery maid
was too beautiful and would encourage Robert to stray."

Anna spluttered into her tea. "She did not."

Lucy nodded. "Unfortunately, it is that particular maid
who is missing. I'm rather surprised Penelope hasn't been
up here to inquire whether Robert is still in residence and
to remind me that she said that the girl would be trouble."

"I do hope she is found." Anna set her cup back on the
table. "Perhaps I should stay here at the hall for a few days
before I return to the rectory. I can help you manage the
nursery until she returns."

"I would appreciate that greatly." Lucy smiled at her
generous sister. "As long as Aunt Rose and Father won't
object."

"They will understand." Anna waved away Lucy's objections with a chuckle. "After I tell them about my unexpected wedding, they might kick me out altogether!"

Robert sent Michael around to the stable yard with the
gig and went directly into the Queen's Head, where he
found the proprietor, Mr. Jarvis, behind the bar.

"Afternoon, Sir Robert."

"Good afternoon." Robert nodded. "Do you have a
moment to speak to me privately?"

"Of course, sir." Mr. Jarvis beckoned Robert to follow
him into the back of the old inn and through to the kitchen.
"I'll get Mrs. Jarvis. She won't want to be left out."

Inwardly, Robert sighed, as Mrs. Jarvis tended to be
rather garrulous and was very fond of speaking her mind.

He waited in the small snug room to the right of the kitchen, with its low black beams and white wattle and daub walls, until they both joined him.

"Polly Carter didn't return from her afternoon off yesterday," Robert said. "Did she purchase a ticket for the mail coach here?"

The husband and wife looked at each other and then at Robert. "Not that I know of, sir," Mr. Jarvis answered for them both.

"Is it possible that she obtained a ride from another source without paying for it?"

"With her pretty face, I have no doubt that any number of men would've been willing to take her up," Mrs. Jarvis said. "But I can't say that I saw her here at all yesterday. Did you my love?"

"No, but I'll go and ask at the stable if you'll wait here for a moment, sir." Mr. Jarvis looked askance at Robert.

"I'd appreciate that."

Mrs. Jarvis decided to keep Robert company after her husband left. It didn't take her long to start talking again.

"If Polly had bought a ticket for the mail yesterday afternoon, she would've had to wait until this morning to leave, and she didn't stay here last night."

Robert grimaced. "I hadn't thought of that. Thank you."

"It's more likely that she smiled at some young farmer and he took her wherever she wanted to go. Where's she from?"

"London, I believe," Robert replied.

"Then the mail coach would have been the most sensible route." Mrs. Jarvis nodded. "If she could afford the ticket."

"She received her first month's wage last week."

"Was she not content up at the hall?"

"As far as I am aware, she was well settled."

"She was a nice girl, always happy to chat, and very respectful of her betters," Mrs. Jarvis commented. "Perhaps she got some upsetting news in that letter she picked up when you came in the other day."

"Perhaps she did." For once, Robert was glad that the landlady was willing to gossip and had noticed that Polly had received mail, which he certainly had not. "Her family is still in London."

"Then maybe that explains it." Mrs. Jarvis smoothed down her apron. "She waited for her money and left at the first opportunity. You'll probably get a letter as soon as she gets home."

"I would've preferred it if she'd just given her notice in the traditional manner," Robert commented. "Leaving without a word to anyone—even her cousin—is highly ir-regular."

"The young rarely think of these things, Sir Robert, do they?" Mrs. Jarvis heaved a sigh that almost dislodged her bounteous bosom from the low-cut bodice of her gown.

"Is Bert Speers still employed here?" Robert asked.

"I believe so," she said cautiously. "Mr. Jarvis had a word with him the other day about Polly, and he insisted that she was deliberately enticing him." Mrs. Jarvis chuck-led. "As if a girl like that would be interested in plain old Bert. I told him so as well."

Robert picked up his hat. "Perhaps I will make my way out to the stables and find Mr. Jarvis. I'm probably keep-ing you from your work."

"It's no trouble talking to you, sir." She winked as she opened the door. "Although we wouldn't want any gossip flying around the village about the two of us, would we?"

"No, we would not." Robert excused himself and hur-ried toward the door that led into the coach yard and sta-bles that sided onto the old inn. He'd already overcome one misunderstanding with his wife over the landlady of the Queen's Head, and he was reluctant to incite another incident.

Mr. Jarvis was already stepping out of the stables and came over to where Robert was standing.

"No one remembers seeing Polly Carter here yesterday, sir."

"Thank you." Robert paused. "What about Bert Speers?"

"He's not here today."

"Why not?"

"It's his day off, Sir Robert." Mr. Jarvis gestured at the half-empty yard. "We're never that busy on a Tuesday. I need them all here on market days and Saturday."

"Will you let me know when he returns?" Robert asked "You think Polly might be with him?"

Robert noted the incredulity in the landlord's voice, but he wasn't prepared to ignore any possibility, which stopped him worrying about much worse scenarios.

"One never knows the way a woman's heart works, Mr. Jarvis." Robert replied. "Just let me know when he returns. I wish to speak to him."

"Yes, sir. I'll do that."

Robert found Michael and climbed into the gig. After they drove out into the village proper, he turned to his servant.

"Did you hear any gossip about Polly while you were in the yard?"

"None, sir. No one had seen her, either." Michael shortened the reins. "I asked most specifically."

"Then where is the damned girl?" Robert muttered to himself as they retraced their journey back to Kurland Hall.

If Polly hadn't purchased a ticket to leave on the mail coach, had she persuaded someone to drive her all the way to London? It was possible that some besotted fool might have done so, but in that case, who had dealt with James? Was it possible that the two incidents were entirely unrelated? Past experience told Robert that they must be inextricably entwined.

He set his gaze on the horizon and attempted to order his thoughts as the two men approached the gates of Kurland Hall. Mrs. Jarvis had also mentioned that Polly had received a letter. Had she not needed to buy a ticket because someone had sent her money or driven down to Kurland St. Mary to pick her up? If they had, that might explain why James had been knocked out. Had he witnessed something? Gotten involved in a scuffle with Polly and some unknown man?

Robert was heartily glad when the gig drew up in front of his home. If there was anything he needed right now, it was a conversation with his eminently sensible wife.

Chapter 5

"Sir Robert?"

Lucy looked up as Foley came into the breakfast parlor, his expression anxious. After she had discussed everything with Robert the previous evening, Lucy's sleep had been disturbed by violent dreams that had kept her awake half the night.

"What is it?" Robert lowered his paper.

"Giles Durley is here and wishes to speak to you urgently."

Robert dropped his newspaper onto the table. "I'll come at once."

Lucy rose, too, and Robert looked back at her. "You don't need to disturb yourself, my dear."

She raised her chin. "I am coming with you."

He didn't bother to object again but set off at a fast pace, leaving her rushing along behind him. The Durley family were farmers on the side of the Kurland estate that sloped down toward the river, and had been there for several generations.

"Sir Robert, Lady Kurland." The famer took of his hat and bowed to them both.

"Good morning, Mr. Durley. What do you need to see me about?" Robert asked.

Giles grimaced. "We were working on the new drainage ditches, sir, like you told us to do, and we found a body at the bottom of one of them."

Lucy pressed her fingers to her lips while Robert instinctively stepped in front of her as if to shield her from the horrible news.

"Do you think it might be Polly Carter, our missing nursemaid?"

"Yes, sir. Me and the missus met the lass the last time we were in Kurland St. Mary." Giles cleared his throat. "We covered her up all decent like, and I have her in the back of my cart."

"Thank you." Robert nodded. "Perhaps you might take her body down to Dr. Fletcher's house in the village, where she can be properly laid out."

"If you wish, sir." Giles put his hat back on. "The poor lady. May she rest in peace."

"Amen," Lucy whispered as Giles bowed and left them in the study. She turned to Robert and struggled to clear her throat. "We should go to Dr. Fletcher's."

"*I* will go." He held up his hand. "Please don't argue with me."

"I am not going to argue with you. I am going to fetch my cloak!" Lucy responded and whisked herself away before he could say another word.

Robert didn't say anything as Lucy climbed into the gig with him, her expression resolute. He'd learned over the years that his wife was almost as stubborn as he was, and that he must choose his battles wisely. She might look frail, but she was never one to shirk her responsibilities, and he respected that, even though it sometimes made him worry.

Before he left, he told Foley to keep an eye on James, who was now recuperating in his room, and not to let anyone in to visit with him. As Foley had guessed what had happened to Polly, he was quick to act on Robert's orders and sent Michael upstairs to sit outside James's door.

Robert didn't bother to make conversation as he drove the gig down the drive of Kurland Hall and along the country road to Kurland St. Mary village. There weren't many people out at this time of day, but those who saw the gig raised their hats or curtsied as they progressed past the farm cottages, the small collection of shops, and onward toward the duck pond, where the village school sat opposite Dr. Fletcher's house.

The children were out playing in the schoolyard, watched over by the new teacher and one of her assistants. Robert acknowledged the schoolmistress's wave as he circled the pond and came to a halt outside the doctor's house. Unwilling to encounter Penelope, Patrick's acerbic wife, he assisted Lucy down from the gig and entered the house from the side door where his friend welcomed his patients.

The room Patrick used to concoct his medicines and perform surgical tasks was beyond his study, and Robert headed toward that door.

Patrick glanced up as Robert appeared, looked past him, and raised an eyebrow.

"Lady Kurland? Perhaps you might go and speak to Penelope. She is remarkably upset by this matter and could do with the benefit of your sound advice and calm counsel."

"It seems as if you are both determined to keep me away from the body," Lucy said. "I will go and speak to Penelope, but do not expect me to remain with her for the rest of our visit!"

Robert came in and closed the door; the smell of cleaning fluids and other unpleasant substances weaved around his nose, making him close his mouth tightly. There was a body laid out on the large marble slab Patrick had somehow obtained from a butcher's shop and used for his examinations.

"It's definitely Polly Carter," Patrick said.

"Do you have any idea how she died?" Robert asked.

"She was strangled. That much is obvious already." Patrick lightly touched Polly's waxen cheek. "See the mottled purple of her skin and the bruising around her throat?"

Robert leaned in to observe more closely. In death, Polly looked like a beautiful, sculptured angel.

"She obviously tried to fight off her attacker." Patrick gestured at her hands. "She's even broken some of her nails, and there's blood as if she scratched his face . . ." He paused. "She's even got a handful of the bastard's hair clutched in her fingers."

Robert's gaze traveled down from Polly's damaged throat to the disarray of her clothing. One of her boots was missing, and her dress was muddied and torn at the hem.

"Was she raped?" he asked abruptly.

Patrick didn't flinch at the brutally direct question. They'd worked together during the worst military campaigns in France and Spain. This wasn't the first dead woman they had seen or had to deal with in their official capacities.

"I don't know yet." Patrick straightened up. "I'll need to remove all her clothing and take a closer look at everything."

"Are you quite certain that the injuries couldn't have been caused by her simply losing her way and falling into the drainage ditch?" Robert asked.

"Unless she had her hands around her throat and was attempting to strangle herself when she fell, then no," Patrick said dryly. "I assume she attempted to fight off an attacker who ended her existence."

"I wish this hadn't happened right now," Robert muttered. "Lucy will insist on getting to the bottom of it, and I'd much rather she stayed home, put her feet up, and looked forward in peaceful anticipation to the birth of our second child."

Patrick chuckled. "If that is what you truly wish, then I believe you married the wrong woman. With all due respect, if Lady Kurland chooses to involve herself in this matter, no one is going to stop her."

Robert took a seat at Patrick's desk. "As I suspect you are correct, I intend to stay here and watch you work before I venture forth to issue a full report to my wife."

"Well, I won't say I didn't tell you so." Penelope poured Lucy a cup of tea and then sat back in her chair.

"Tell me what?" Lucy wasn't in the mood to be helpful, while Penelope was oozing smugness.

"That it was a mistake to hire Polly Carter."

"You told me that she would run off with Robert," Lucy pointed out. "As far as I can tell, she didn't run off anywhere and has probably been murdered."

"Lucy, when you employ a girl like that—"

"Like what?" Lucy asked. "Polly was extremely hardworking and well-liked by all the staff up at the hall."

Penelope waved away her reply. "She was far too beautiful, and you know it. Girls like that *always* bring trouble on themselves."

"I hardly think that her being beautiful means that she deserved to be murdered," Lucy said stubbornly. "You are quite beautiful, and no one has murdered you, yet."

Penelope sat bolt upright. "Because I understand that being beautiful is a burden, and that I have to be very careful not to be *over-familiar* with any man."

"Polly was not over-familiar, and even if she was, it doesn't mean that she deserved to be killed." Lucy put her cup down with such force that the saucer rattled.

Penelope tutted. "Please don't get angry, Lucy. It is bad for the baby."

"I am *not* angry, I am simply—"

"Attempting to defend the indefensible," Penelope spoke over her. "Perhaps Polly did something that enraged her attacker? Mayhap she had more than one lover, and was playing the odds, and got caught?"

"And maybe she was just walking down to the village

on her afternoon off and was attacked by a crazed mad-
man for no reason whatsoever!" Lucy realized her voice
was rising with every word, and that she *was* now shouting, and was, in fact, quite angry after all.

She shot to her feet, almost knocking her cup over. "I
am going to speak to Dr. Fletcher. Please excuse me."

Penelope stood, too, her hand outstretched. "Lucy, please
don't do that, Patrick said—"

Lucy marched toward the door, Penelope at her heels,
and went into Dr. Fletcher's empty office. Robert appeared
at the interior door and blocked her view of whatever Dr.
Fletcher was doing to the body on the marble slab.

"Perhaps you might wait until Dr. Fletcher has finished
his examination, my dear."

Lucy glared at him. "I would prefer to see Polly now."

He came toward her, and his fingers closed gently on
her elbow. "And I would prefer it if you waited. You are
obviously upset."

"I am upset because Penelope has been regaling me for
the past quarter of an hour with her *opinions* of how Polly
should've been more careful."

"That's not what I said at all, Lucy!" Penelope exclaimed. "I merely suggested that she might have inadvertently caused what happened."

"Which is what my wife just said." Robert motioned for
Penelope to step back from the doorway. "Will you allow
me to come into the parlor and explain what Dr. Fletcher
has discovered so that he may get on with his work?"

"If you must." Lucy was aware that she sounded grudging, but she wasn't prepared to moderate her tone.

"I will go and see if Francis is enjoying his midday
meal." Penelope excused herself after one last reproachful
glance at Lucy and stomped up the stairs, her head held
high.

Robert drew Lucy into the parlor and closed the door
behind them.

"You were rather rude to Penelope."

"She was being insufferable," Lucy replied. "She immediately assumed that poor Polly had done something to deserve to be murdered!"

Robert leaned up against the door and regarded her carefully. "One cannot completely discount the notion that Polly's death was not a random act of violence, though."

"What are you suggesting?"

"I'm saying that it is unlikely there was a murderer roaming the Kurland lands who luckily came across Polly and killed her."

His calming tone steadied her, but she was still not willing to give up the fight. "Then you do think she caused her own death."

"No!" He frowned at her. "Stop jumping to ridiculous conclusions, and look at the facts. We know that Polly was attracting a lot of attention from men. We also know that she was afraid of one of those men."

Lucy nodded. "Bert Speers."

"Exactly. And James was attacked yesterday, which is another strange coincidence, wouldn't you say?"

"I suppose you do have a point." Lucy moved restlessly around the room. "But Penelope—"

"Often says things that are insensitive and rude." Robert interrupted her. "And thus her opinion, in this case, can be discounted."

Lucy went over to Robert, who immediately wrapped his arms around her.

"I'm sorry."

He kissed the top of her head. "For getting annoyed with Penelope? It's hardly the first time you've done that."

"I'm . . . a little emotional at the moment," Lucy confided, her cheek settled comfortably against the dark blue of Robert's waistcoat.

"I can't say I've noticed," he said dryly.

Lucy placed the palm of her hand on his chest and burrowed even closer. "When my mother was pregnant with the twins, one of our maids was let go because she was with child."

He stilled. "I don't understand what—"

"Anna and I were upset because we'd liked her very much. Cook said she had deserved her fate, and that it wouldn't have been right to have a fallen woman in a good Christian household with innocent girls around." Lucy slowly raised her head to look at Robert. "But how could that be true when it was my father who had sinned with her?"

"Lucy, my dear love . . ." Robert cupped her cheek. "I had no idea." He gently kissed her nose. "Did your father know the child was his?"

"I assume so, seeing as he sent money to her family every year for the child's upkeep." Lucy took a deep, shuddering breath. "I'm sorry. I have no idea why I felt the need tell you that particular family secret."

"Probably because you are with child, and because you are worried about Polly."

"Precisely." She found a smile somewhere, glad for his prosaic answer, and tried to appear reasonable. "Now, what were you going to tell me about Polly?"

Robert's brow creased. "Are you sure you want to know what Patrick told me, or would you prefer not to hear the details?"

"I'd like to know. Polly is—I mean, was—one of our servants."

"She was strangled," Robert said flatly. "She obviously attempted to fight off her attacker, but whoever it was prevailed."

"My goodness," Lucy whispered.

Robert took her hand and led her to sit by the fire. "One thing I learned from my days in the cavalry, investigating such matters, was to look at my men's faces to see if anyone had been scratched or hit." He grimaced. "It narrowed the field of suspects considerably and often proved a good indicator of the culprit or culprits."

Lucy shuddered. "Did James have a scratched face?"

Robert shifted in his seat. "Yes, but he had been fighting with Bert Speers and was left in a bramble patch on his parents' farm."

"Do we know where Bert Speers is?"

"Presumably, still at the Queen's Head. After we leave here, I'll go down and speak to Mr. Jarvis."

"Poor Polly," Lucy murmured. "I need to return to Kurland Hall and let Agnes and the rest of the staff know what has happened."

"We'll go as soon as Dr. Fletcher has finished his examination," Robert promised. "I really would prefer it if you let me deal with this. I promise I will tell you everything he says."

"As you wish." Lucy realized she was far too tired to argue with him. The thought of seeing Polly's dead body made her uncharacteristically nervous.

"Thank you." Robert reached over to squeeze her fingers and gestured at the tea tray. "Do you think Penelope would mind if I helped myself to some tea? It's rather too early to start on the brandy."

When Patrick came to find him, Robert followed him back into his surgery where Polly's body was now decently covered with a sheet.

"As far as I can tell, she wasn't raped," Patrick said. "But she did receive several blows to her body that resulted in bruising and cuts."

"With a weapon?" Robert asked.

Patrick grimaced. "No, just someone's fists." He went to wash his hands. "Poor girl didn't stand a chance."

"I assume you can keep the body here until we find out what Polly's family wants to do with it?"

"Yes, of course. Our cellar is very cold." Patrick gestured at a box on his desk. "Do you wish to take her clothing?"

"I suppose I should." With some reluctance, Robert

picked up the box. "I know that my wife will wish to keep everything for Polly's family."

"Do you have any idea who might have done this, Major?" Patrick asked, instinctively reverting to Robert's old cavalry rank.

"Seeing as every man in Kurland St. Mary thought Polly was the most beautiful woman they'd ever seen, the list of suspects is quite wide," Robert commented. "But I have a few ideas."

Patrick dried his hands and opened the door into his study. "I saw her with James, your footman, a few times in the village."

"Indeed." Robert wasn't going to be drawn on the possibilities quite yet.

"I also heard that James was knocked out the other day."

Robert paused to look back at his friend. "Who told you that?"

Patrick shrugged. "Just the usual village gossip. Remember, I go in and out of people's homes every day. They tell me some very interesting tales."

"I'd appreciate it if you kept your suspicions to yourself."

Patrick had the gall to laugh. "As if that would make a difference in a small place like this, where everyone knows everyone else's business. Something as sensational as a murder will only encourage more gossip."

"Unfortunately, due to our past experiences in this matter, I know that all too well." Robert sighed. "Thank you for your help."

Patrick offered him a mock salute. "You're most welcome, Major."

Robert went across to the parlor and discovered that Penelope had brought her son down from the nursery. He had nothing against the boy, who had the sweet nature of his father. He also had no interest in amusing any child but his own.

Lucy had already risen and was coming toward him, her expression expectant.

"Do we need to leave, my dear?"

"Yes, if we are to speak to Mr. Jarvis at the Queen's Head and alert our staff to this dreadful occurrence." He bowed to Penelope, who was feeding her son a biscuit from her plate. "A pleasure to see you, Mrs. Fletcher. Thank you for the tea."

"You are most welcome, Sir Robert." Penelope's glance slid toward Lucy, and she lowered her voice. "One can only hope that your wife will recover her temper soon."

"My wife is entitled to her own opinions," Robert said. "And she is more than capable of speaking for herself." He offered Lucy his arm. "Shall we go, my lady?"

Lucy was smiling as he handed her into the gig.

"What is so amusing?" Robert asked.

"You are." She patted his cheek. "You might not agree with a word I say in private, but in public you are always on my side and my staunchest defender."

"Which is just as it should be." He walked around and hauled himself up into the gig. "Do you wish to accompany me to the Queen's Head before we go back to the hall? It is on our way."

"That would suit me very well." Lucy settled her skirts around her and drew her cloak closed at the throat. "Did Dr. Fletcher have anything more to add to his conclusion that Polly was strangled?"

"Only that she was beaten," Robert said, his gloved hands curling into fists. "I wish I had the bastard who did that to her in front of me now."

"I am not one to revel in violence, but in this instance, I cannot help but agree with you." Lucy said.

"Dr. Fletcher mentioned that he had seen Polly out walking with James."

"Oh, dear." Lucy sighed. "If Dr. Fletcher noticed them together, then everyone in the village will immediately leap to the obvious conclusion."

"That James murdered Polly?" Robert frowned. "He grew up here with a family who are well known and liked. Do you really think people will believe that about him?"

"Whether they believe it or not is hardly the issue, is it? They will talk about it. James had better stay up at the hall until we have cleared this matter up."

Robert negotiated the turn onto the village high street. "But what if it was James?"

Lucy was quiet for some while before she answered him. "We already know that love can turn ugly—that reasonable people can do unthinkable things when they feel threatened."

"Agreed." Robert slowed the horse down and nodded to one of the local shopkeepers who had stepped out to watch them go past. "Don't forget, we still have to speak to Bert Speers."

He drew the gig up in the enclosed courtyard of the Queen's Head, glad that it wasn't market day and that the mail coach had long since gone. One of the ostlers ran out to hold the horse's head.

"Morning, Sir Robert."

"Good morning, Fred. We'll only be here for a short while, so there's no need to stable the horse."

"As you wish, sir. I'll get one of the lads to hold onto him for you then."

"Thank you." Robert helped Lucy down, and they went through the side door that led directly into the inn.

Mr. Jarvis came to greet them, his expression troubled.

"If you're here for Bert Speers, sir, he didn't come back last night."

"Did he not?" Robert glanced down at Lucy before returning his gaze to the landlord. "Are his possessions still here?"

"Yes, sir. I checked his room." Mr. Jarvis grimaced. "I heard about what happened to Polly Carter. If Bert does turn up, I'll lock him up myself."

"If you would, I'd appreciate it greatly." Robert nodded. "And let me know immediately, because it is imperative that I speak to him."

"Understood, sir." The innkeeper nodded.

Robert escorted Lucy back to the gig, and they rode home in silence along the narrow cow-parsley-lined lane until they turned in through the gates of Kurland Hall.

"I'd best speak to Agnes first." Lucy visibly braced herself.

"We'll speak to her together." Robert briefly clasped her hand. "I assume she has an address for Polly's mother?"

"Yes." Lucy lapsed into silence again as they pulled up in front of the main door.

"Are you feeling quite well?" Robert asked as he walked around to help her down. "Would you prefer it if I spoke to Agnes alone?"

"I'd prefer it if we both talked to her." She flashed him a tired smile. "And then I might take a restorative nap."

He ushered her straight through the hall and into his study, where he asked Foley to make them some tea and to fetch Agnes. While they awaited her arrival, Robert paced in front of the fire.

"You wished to see me, Sir Robert, my lady?" Agnes spoke from the door.

She looked her usual immaculate self, her lace collar ironed to perfection and her petticoats rustling with starch.

"We have some sad news about your cousin, Polly," Robert said. He strongly believed in getting straight to the point when being the bearer of bad news. "Her body was discovered in a drainage ditch on the Durley farm."

Agnes gasped and pressed her hand to her mouth. "Oh, my lord."

"I'm sorry for your loss, Agnes. I can assure you that Lady Kurland and I will do everything in our power to find out what happened to Polly and, if necessary, to bring the wrongdoer to justice."

"What have I done?" Agnes whispered, her eyes wide

and her words barely audible. "Why did I ever allow myself to get caught up in this terrible muddle?"

Robert raised an eyebrow and looked over at Lucy, who approached Agnes.

"I'm not quite sure what you are trying to say, Agnes. No one is blaming you for what happened." Lucy said.

"If I hadn't allowed *that woman* to come here . . . and bring such grief to this family—"

"As I just said, Agnes, no one is blaming you," Lucy said firmly. "I know that you and Polly didn't always see eye to eye, but that's often how it is with one's family. It doesn't mean that you didn't care for her or that you should feel guilty in any way."

"But she *wasn't*." Agnes was openly sobbing now.

"Wasn't what?" It was Lucy's turn to offer Robert a puzzled glance.

"Part of my family." Agnes gulped hard. "I'd never clapped eyes on her in my life before she turned up at Kurland Hall."

Chapter 6

As Agnes continued to cry, Lucy led her to a seat by the fire, offered her a new handkerchief, and waited patiently for the storm to pass. When Agnes appeared to have sufficiently composed herself, Lucy met her gaze.

"I thought Polly was your cousin."

"She *is*, ma'am—well, Polly Carter is, but that wasn't her."

"I don't quite understand. Are you saying you were duped?

"No, my lady."

"If the Polly we met wasn't your cousin, then why didn't you mention it when she arrived bearing a letter from me offering her a position in my nursery?" Lucy asked.

Agnes swallowed and stared down at her apron. "Because when she came upstairs after meeting with you, she handed me a letter from my cousin Polly explaining what had happened, and why she was here instead."

"And yet you didn't think to mention it to me or to Lady Kurland?" Robert intervened, the irritation in his voice quite apparent. "Did it not occur to you that introducing a complete stranger into our household, one who was to care for our *son*, was perhaps something that we should have been made aware of?"

Agnes dissolved into tears again, and Lucy frowned at

Robert. He was far too used to dealing with military sub-
ordinates to have the finesse necessary to coax answers
out of a distraught female.

She curbed her own impatience until Agnes composed
herself.

"You said that your cousin Polly sent you a letter. What
did she say?"

"She asked me to let the Polly you know take up her position."

"Did she explain who she was sending in her place?"

"No, my lady. I don't even know her real name. My
cousin Polly said that the deception was necessary, and
that she would vouch for her friend."

"And that was sufficient for you to allow this fraud to
take place?" Robert asked.

Agnes's worried gaze flicked toward Robert, who had
retreated to the window seat but was still staring at her in-
tently.

"She gave me money," Agnes whispered. "A lot of
money—more than two years' wages."

Lucy attempted to conceal her surprise and disappointment with her son's nurse, but feared she made a bad job
of it as Agnes again began to weep.

"I'm so sorry, my lady, sir. I don't know what I was
thinking. She promised me 'Polly' would be gone in a
month, which didn't seem long enough for her to cause
any mischief." Agnes looked up. "And she was good at
her job, respectful to me for the most part, and Ned liked
her. If that hadn't been the case, I would've told you earlier, I *swear* it."

"But Polly agreed to stay on for another quarter," Lucy
said slowly. "Is that why you were arguing just before she
disappeared?"

"Yes, my lady. I told her I would reveal the truth if she
stayed on."

"And what was her response?"

"She laughed and told me to go ahead and see how long

I kept my own job. She said she liked it here." Agnes dabbed at her eyes. "I knew she was right. I wished with all my heart I had never allowed myself to get caught up in something so wrong."

Robert cleared his throat. "Don't we all?" He walked back over to the fireplace and stared down at Agnes. "Perhaps you might return to the nursery. My instinct is to let you go without a reference, but Ned has had enough disruptions in his life this week without depriving him of his nurse. We will reconsider your employment at the next quarter day."

Agnes stood and bobbed a curtsey. "Thank you, Sir Robert. I am so sorry, my lady."

She rushed out of the room, and Robert turned to Lucy. "Please don't suggest that I was too harsh with her."

"I won't. I have never been so shocked in my life! What on earth possessed her to do such a foolish thing?"

"Money, of course," Robert said grimly. "Two years' wages for what she thought was going to be one month of a different Polly Carter in our house? I can almost understand her reasoning—except this concerns *my* house and *my* son, and I can't help but be enraged by such a deliberate deception."

Lucy let out a slow breath. "If Agnes was desperate enough to conceal what she had done, was she desperate enough to kill Polly?"

"I hadn't thought of that." Robert paused before continuing, his gaze assessing. "But I doubt she would've had the strength to strangle Polly."

"Perhaps she paid someone to do it for her?" Lucy suggested. "She certainly had the money to do so."

"It is still rather unlikely, but I will not discount it," Robert said. "Should we get rid of Agnes immediately, then?"

"My instinct is to agree with you, but if we do suspect her of murder, then it would be better if we knew where she was," Lucy said. "I'll ask Anna to supervise the nursery and pay close attention to everything Agnes does."

"I suppose it will have to suffice." Robert moved restlessly around the room. "But I have to tell you, Lucy, that the mere idea that Agnes and Polly were around our son *appalls* me."

"I'm sorry, too." Lucy met his gaze squarely. "As I was responsible for hiring Agnes in the first place, the blame lies squarely with me."

He waved away her concerns. "She isn't the first person to be corrupted by money, and she won't be the last. You did everything you could."

Lucy rose to her feet. "I'll go and speak to Anna, and then I'll go to Polly's room, and see if I can find any evidence of who she really might be."

"That's an excellent idea. I had Foley take up the box of her possessions Dr. Fletcher gave me to her room as well. Let me know what you discover." Robert went over to the door.

"What are you going to do?" Lucy inquired.

His face settled into grim lines. "I'm going to have another conversation with James."

Robert went up to the top floor of the house, where Michael was sitting patiently outside James's bedchamber. Michael jumped up when he saw Robert and stepped back from the door.

"Morning, Sir Robert."

"Good morning, Michael. You may go down to the kitchen. I'll let you know when you should return."

"Yes, sir."

Robert went into James's small room, bending his head to avoid the blackened beams that formed the structure of the Elizabethan roof. James was sitting up in bed, a Bible at his side.

"Sir Robert, I'm feeling much better today. May I resume my duties?"

"Not quite yet." Robert sat on the only chair and stared

at his footman. The bruises and scratches on his face were less vivid now, but still obvious.

"We found Polly Carter."

The relief on James's face was immediate. "Is she all right?"

"No. Her body was recovered on the Durleys' farm."

James briefly closed his eyes, his hand fumbling to find his Bible. "I . . . don't know what to say."

"Perhaps the truth?"

"I *told* you what happened, sir," James blurted out and then stopped, a look of horror transforming his expression. "Do you think—I *killed* her?"

Having learned the value of silence early on in his military career, Robert continued to study James.

"I *loved* her! Why would I want to do that?"

Robert shrugged. "Love is a very strong emotion, and closely akin to hate."

"I didn't kill her." James's mouth set in a firm line.

"Then who did?"

"Bert Speers? Mr. Fletcher?" James shook his head. "Anyone but me, sir, I *swear* it."

Robert let another long moment elapse before he replied. "I am the local magistrate, and I'm responsible for investigating and prosecuting crime in this vicinity. It is therefore my duty to find out who killed Polly Carter. I will carry out that duty without regard to whether I know the murderer or his family."

"You're saying that if it is me, you'll send me to hang."

"Yes." Robert held James's anguished gaze. "Now, is there anything else you wish to tell me about what happened when you last saw Polly Carter?"

Lucy went into Polly's bedchamber and surveyed the contents of the room. On her instructions, no one had entered or attempted to clean it since Polly's disappearance had first been discovered.

She started by stripping the bed linen and found nothing

but a small, tattered piece of shawl tucked under the pillow that looked as if it might have belonged to a child. Ned had a blanket that he loved to curl his fingers into while he slept. Lucy wondered whether Polly had kept her own keepsake. Not that it had helped to keep her safe from the monsters . . .

Lucy dropped the dirty bed linen outside the door and turned her attention to the trunk in the corner. She sat on the chair and methodically emptied out the contents, checking pockets and the insides of shoes and handkerchiefs as she went. A faint smell of perfume permeated the garments along with another, more oily scent Lucy couldn't identify. At the bottom of the trunk she discovered a set of playbills for a theater in London and took them over to the window to read.

The playbills featured a variety of theatrical experiences, including recitations of Shakespeare, dancing, comedy, and tragedy, which was fairly standard for the more popular theaters in London. Two of the bills were for a theater called the Corinthian, which apparently was located close to Covent Garden, and the third was for the Prince of Wales.

Lucy hadn't visited London very often and couldn't remember attending a performance at either of the establishments. Had Polly kept the playbills because she had enjoyed the shows, or was there a closer connection? At this point, that could be anything. Lucy could only hope that closer inspection would reveal more clues as to Polly's real name and previous occupation.

She laid all the garments on the bed and lined up the shoes on the floor beneath it before turning to the dressing table. She tidied up the hairpins, spare buttons, sewing thread, and needles into their respective containers. Opening the first drawer, she checked and then rolled up the woolen stockings before placing them on the bed along with Polly's spare petticoats and underthings.

The second, smaller drawer held Polly's spare handkerchiefs, neckerchiefs, and mittens. There was also a garish red lip color in a tin that smelled as strongly of oil as the trunk. Lucy reached farther into the drawer and discovered a small velvet box tucked right at the back.

"Goodness me," Lucy murmured as she turned the key to reveal the contents. "I wonder where this jewelry came from. It is rather fine." She carefully lifted out a diamond necklace and two rings and checked beneath the satin lining of the box. There was a single card wedged into the box with distinctive slashing handwriting on it.

"To Flora Rosa, with my continued devotion." Lucy read the words out loud. Unfortunately, the final signature was impossible to decipher.

Lucy kept the playbills and the jewelry box on the dressing table and packed everything else away. She would take her findings to Robert and see what he had to say on the matter.

Before she left, Lucy's gaze lingered on the trunk.

"Is that your real name? Flora Rosa?" Lucy whispered. "It doesn't sound real, but I wish you peace, and I swear that I will do everything I can to get you justice."

She closed the door behind her and went down the stairs to find Robert.

He was sitting in his study, a frown on his face as he massaged his forehead.

"Ah, Lucy, come in."

She shut the door and went over to his desk, placing the items she'd found on the surface.

"What did James have to say for himself?"

"He insists he didn't kill her, but he did admit to catching up with her before she reached the church."

"My goodness." Lucy brought her hand to her mouth.

"He says that they argued, she told him to leave her be, and he let her walk away from him."

"I assume this was before he was hit on the head?" Lucy asked.

"Yes." Robert grimaced. "He's now saying that he thinks he saw her with Bert Speers just in front of the church. I'm not sure I believe him."

"Because now that he knows Polly is dead, James needs to make sure he is seen as innocent?" Lucy suggested. "And implicating Bert Speers is the easiest way to clear his own name?

"Yes, that's exactly what I thought." Robert let out a frustrated breath. "Am I being too cynical? I've known James all his life. He's never struck me as the kind of man to murder someone and then blatantly lie about it. I've known people to kill in a moment of anger, but they are usually so overcome with guilt and remorse after the fact that, when confronted with the evidence, they usually confess."

"I think you are dealing with him in exactly the right way," Lucy hastened to reassure him. "You are attempting to be fair but not allowing your natural tendency to defend someone you have personal knowledge of to override your judgment."

"I can try and find out if anyone in the village saw Polly walking with another man that day," Robert suggested. "That would help to corroborate James's story. But until then, I think he'd do better to stay in his room."

"I agree." Lucy nodded. Have you heard anything from Mr. Jarvis at the Queen's Head?"

"Not yet." Robert shoved a hand through his hair. "Did you get Polly's mother's address from Agnes?"

"Yes. I will write to her immediately and get Michael to take the letter directly down to the mail coach so that it will be received as quickly as possible."

"Good," Robert said and gestured at the items Lucy had placed on his desk. "What have we here?"

Lucy handed him the playbills and opened the jewelry box to reveal the card "I think that Polly's name might be Flora Rosa. Somebody wealthy must have given her these jewels."

"Then why was she working here as a nursery maid for a pittance?" Robert asked.

"She did say that she was glad to get out of London," Lucy said slowly. "Maybe she was running away from something or somebody?"

"And decided to bring her problems into my household?" Robert demanded.

"It didn't make any difference, though, did it?" Lucy reminded him. "She still died."

"And embroiled us in yet another case of murder," Robert grumbled.

"The card is addressed to Flora Rosa." Lucy attempted to regain her husband's attention and draw him away from his personal grievances. "The signature is unreadable."

Robert picked up the card, put on his spectacles, and squinted at the handwriting. "It's a single word. That's all I can make out. Flora Rosa sounds like the name an actress might use."

"I didn't think of that." Lucy pointed to the playbills. "Is she listed in them?"

Robert started reading, discarding the first two bills from the Corinthian and pausing as he ran his gaze over the long list of players at the Prince of Wales.

"Ah. Here she is. It doesn't say what part she plays, but there is definitely a Flora Rosa listed."

"I suppose our Polly could've worked for this actress and stolen the jewelry," Lucy pointed out.

"But our Polly was certainly beautiful enough to have enjoyed some success on the stage and to have gained herself an admirer."

"As I have no knowledge of such things, I will assume that you are correct." Lucy gave him a rather sharp gaze.

Robert shrugged. "As a young man, I did loiter in the green rooms of some theaters."

"I am aware of that—seeing as that's how you met Mrs. Jarvis from the Queen's Head."

Lucy would rather not discuss his youthful appreciation of the ex-actress, who had remembered him rather too well for Lucy's liking when she'd given up the stage and married the landlord of the local inn.

"I wonder if Mrs. Jarvis might still have contacts with the theater in London?" Robert said. "She might even have heard of Flora Rosa."

"I doubt it, but I am quite happy to ask her," Lucy offered. "But if we really want to find out what happened to send Flora Rosa running to Kurland St. Mary, we will have to go to London and investigate the matter for ourselves."

Robert put the jewelry and the playbills in his desk and locked the drawer.

"Before we get ahead of ourselves, my dear, perhaps we should discuss what else we can discover here. Bert Speers is still missing, and James is not telling me the whole truth. The only suitor I can completely clear of murdering Polly is Dermot Fletcher, who spent the last two days at my side catching up on his work."

"We don't know exactly when Flora Rosa was murdered. Dermot could've trapped her somewhere and killed her later." Lucy demurred.

"We did go out and speak to the Durleys, so perhaps you have a point." Robert groaned. "Maybe Dermot saw her wandering around their fields with another man and was overcome with rage."

"I agree that it sounds unlikely." Lucy paused. "I forgot something."

"What?"

"To examine the clothes Flora was wearing when she died."

"I told Foley to leave the box in her bedchamber. Wasn't it there?"

Lucy rose to her feet. "I think I moved it to strip the bedclothes. I'll go and find it right now. I am so forgetful!"

Robert had no desire to poke through his murdered

nursemaid's garments, but he waited patiently for Lucy to return with the box.

When she did, she extracted Flora's gown and wrinkled her nose at the creased fabric before setting it aside.

"Is there anything in a pocket?" Robert asked.

Lucy gave him a patient look. "Her dress doesn't have pockets." She delved in the box and brought out a long strip of narrow fabric with two bags attached to it. "Here they are."

She frowned as she explored the interior of one of the bags. "I haven't found her coin purse yet, or her wages, and they don't appear to be here, either. Perhaps it was just a robbery."

"I doubt that, but please carry on," Robert said.

She undid the string on the other bag, which produced a crackling sound, and withdrew a letter that she held up to Robert.

"Mrs. Jarvis said she'd received a letter. That must be it." He gestured at Lucy to read it.

Lucy unfolded the single sheet and held it up to the light.

"My dear friend, all is not well here. Your flight has been discovered, and your destination is known. Be very careful."

"Well, that isn't very helpful," Robert said.

"It does indicate that Flora was in danger," Lucy pointed out. "And that Polly Carter was trying to protect her."

"We don't know if that letter was from Polly," Robert countered.

"Who else would be writing to her?"

"Her protector?"

"Surely, if she had a powerful or wealthy man 'protecting' her, she wouldn't have felt the need to run away in the first place." Lucy held up a finger. "Unless that was who she was running away from."

Robert took the letter and read it for himself. "The handwriting is quite crude and probably not that of a gentleman, which might indicate that you are correct about the letter being from Polly."

"Thank you." Lucy looked at him expectantly. "Now when do we depart to London to find the real Polly Carter and ask her what on earth is going on?"

Chapter 7

Lucy made her way to the kitchen, the box containing Flora's possessions in her hands. She would ask the house-keeper to launder the clothing and return everything to Flora's bedchamber.

Robert had avoided answering her question about the necessity of a trip to London by claiming he had to meet with Mr. Fletcher and leaving his study before she could stop him. As it was unlike him not to be honest with her, she had a suspicion that his reluctance to engage on the matter was because he didn't want her to come with him.

"Of course, he doesn't want you to come," Lucy murmured to herself. "Why would you even doubt that?"

"Excuse me, my lady?"

Lucy looked up to discover Foley holding the door into the kitchen open for her.

"Good morning, Foley." Lucy stepped past him. "Is Mrs. Bloomfield here?"

"I believe she's out at the Home Farm this morning, my lady," Foley said. "I told her to take one of the footmen with her. We don't want what happened to young Polly happening again, now, do we?"

Lucy nodded and took the box through to the scullery.

"Will you ask her to have these clothes laundered and re-turned to Polly's room?"

"I will, my lady." Foley followed her back into the kitchen. "I was just about to take this message to Sir Robert." He held out a folded piece of paper. "It came from the Queen's Head."

"Thank you." Lucy scanned the letter. "Will you bring the gig around to the front of the house and *then* take this to Sir Robert?"

By the time her husband emerged from the house, she was already sitting in the gig awaiting him. His steps slowed as he approached, and he raised an eyebrow.

"You're coming with me?"

"Indeed." She offered him a challenging smile. "Have you not yet learned that I am not very biddable?"

"I knew that before I married you." He stepped up into the gig and took the reins from her. "I did have hopes that vowing to *obey* me might curb your impulses, but it seems that I was mistaken."

She bristled at his words—and then realized he was smiling, and contented herself with pinching his arm instead.

"You will not stop me coming to London with you, either."

"I'll certainly try." Robert set off. "But perhaps we should call a truce and deal with Mr. Jarvis at the Queen's Head before we commence hostilities?"

The journey down to the inn didn't take long, and they were soon pulling up in the busy stable yard. Robert got out and handed Lucy down, and one of the ostlers moved the gig out of the way.

Mr. Jarvis met them in the hall, his expression grim.

"He arrived back here this morning on the mail coach. He wasn't very cooperative, so I put him in the cellar and locked the door."

"Thank you." Robert touched Lucy's shoulder. "Perhaps you could ask Mrs. Jarvis if you might examine Bert's possessions while I go with Mr. Jarvis and deal with this matter?"

For once, Lucy decided to humor him. She had no desire to be stuck in the cellar with an angry or violent man.

"As you wish." She smiled sweetly at Robert.

"See how easy it is to obey one's husband?" he murmured into her ear before turning back to Mr. Jarvis and following him into the public bar of the tavern.

Lucy sniffed and went to find Mrs. Jarvis, who was more than willing to allow her access to Bert's shared room above the stables.

"I'll come in with you, sir, if you don't mind," Mr. Jarvis said.

"I don't mind at all," Robert replied as Mr. Jarvis picked up a large cudgel propped against the outside of the locked and barred door.

Like a lot of the older buildings in Kurland St. Mary, belowground the inn had remnants of the monastery and church that had once stood in its location. The elegant, curved ceilings of the cellar, with their stone pillars, looked somewhat out of place among the barrels and dusty bottles.

The second they entered the room, Bert Speers sprang up from his cloak-covered bed and came toward them. His hair and clothing were disordered, and his chin was black with stubble.

"What the bloody hell is going on? Why am I being held here and treated like a criminal?"

"I was hoping you could tell me that," Robert said. "Where have you been for the last three days?"

"I don't have to answer to you," Bert sneered.

Robert turned to Mr. Jarvis. "As his employer, I'm fairly certain you have the right to ask the same question."

"Aye, you can't just disappear for days without telling anyone where you've gone, Bert."

Bert rolled his eyes, which did nothing to endear him to Robert. "I had to go home. My mother needed me."

"You didn't think to ask my permission?" Mr. Jarvis asked. "Why not?"

"Because I had to go immediately! I told Jeremiah."

"Strange that Jeremiah didn't mention it to anyone, then."

"That's not my fault, Mr. Jarvis, now, is it?"

"Where exactly did you go?" Robert inquired.

"Back to London," Bert said. "Where else? I bought a ticket and got on the mail coach. If you don't believe me, ask Henry Haines next time he's here."

"I will ask him," Mr. Jarvis said. "Don't you worry about that."

Robert leaned back against one of the upright casks of ale and regarded Bert carefully. "Perhaps you might clarify something else for us. When did you last see Polly Carter?"

Bert frowned. "What's she got to do with anything?"

"Please answer the question," Robert ordered, his tone hardening.

"Why? Has she been telling tales about me again?"

"She hasn't said a word." Robert kept his gaze on Bert's face. "When did you last speak to her?"

"That's none of your business."

"Don't you be disrespectful to Sir Robert." Mr. Jarvis brought the cudgel up toward Bert's face in a menacing manner. "You answer his question or I'll wallop you."

"I spoke to her the day before I left," Bert said grudgingly. "I told her to stop playing silly games and getting me into trouble, or I'd make her pay for it."

"Did you now?" Robert let the silence fall around them.

"Did I what?" Bert frowned.

"Make her pay?" Robert continued to stare until Bert started to shift his feet.

"I might have tried to shake some sense into her, but if she's saying anything different, then she's lying."

"She's dead," Robert said flatly. "Perhaps your attempt

to 'shake some sense into her' turned violent and you *inadvertently* murdered her."

A red flush rose from Bert's throat to suffuse his face. "I didn't bloody kill her!"

Mr. Jarvis glanced at Robert. "I'd lay odds on who the liar is here, sir."

"I didn't kill her!" Bert shouted, the sound echoing off the low stone ceiling. "Why would I do that?"

"Because you are a violent jealous man?" Robert asked. "The kind of scoundrel who would rather beat a woman who chooses not to care for him than find someone else?"

He straightened up and met Bert's furious gaze. "You'll stay here until I can speak to Henry Haines."

"You can't do that!" Bert growled.

"I damn well can." Robert stepped closer. "As I've already told you, I'm the local magistrate, and it's my job to investigate local crime and prosecute offenders."

He nodded to Mr. Jarvis. "Let's leave him to think about his choices, shall we? Perhaps a period of quiet reflection will make him more forthcoming."

As Robert and Mr. Jarvis left, Bert spun away to repeatedly smash his fist against the wall.

"I don't care what he says, Sir Robert. It's as clear as day that he's guilty," Mr. Jarvis observed as they mounted the stairs back to the bar.

"That remains to be seen, but he didn't do himself any favors behaving like that, did he?" Robert agreed. "No wonder Polly was afraid of him."

"Well, as to that, sir . . ." Mr. Jarvis paused to shut and lock the cellar door behind them. "I *did* see her talking to him once or twice without there being any trouble. Which was why when Mrs. Jarvis told me that he'd been following her home, I wondered what was going on."

"I didn't realize that," Robert said. "I received the distinct impression from Polly that she was afraid to go near him."

"Maybe they were in the middle of a lover's tiff, and

Bert lost his temper with her when she didn't want to make up?"

"What time does the mail coach usually arrive?" Robert asked.

"Around eight in the morning, Sir Robert." Mr. Jarvis poured two pints of ale and handed one to Robert. "Do you want to speak to Henry yourself?"

"I think I'd better," Robert said. He took a grateful sip of his beer and then another, more appreciative swallow. "I think I'll sit here, finish my ale, and wait for Lady Kurland to find me."

Mrs. Jarvis cast a disgusted look around the small cramped room and wrinkled her nose.

"It smells like a fox's den in here and looks like one as well. I'm right sorry about that, Lady Kurland."

Lucy remained in the doorway as Mrs. Jarvis stomped through the mess, picking up garments and throwing them randomly onto the two beds.

"Which side belongs to Bert Speers?" Lucy asked.

"This side. The one that looks like he emptied out his entire possessions on the floor before he left us in the lurch for three days."

"Maybe he did empty everything out," Lucy said slowly. "Perhaps he wanted to make sure that there was nothing here to incriminate him if he didn't return."

"Which begs the question of why he came back," Mrs. Jarvis said.

Lucy slowly raised her head from her contemplation of the mess. "I suppose we'd better look through everything and see if we can find that out."

Breathing carefully through her mouth, Lucy delved into the pile of clothing and checked pockets and straightened garments until there was a neat pile on the bed. She picked up one of the discarded boots and gingerly turned it upside down. A small leather purse fell out, and she picked it up.

"That doesn't look like a man's purse, does it, my lady?" Mrs. Jarvis commented.

"No, it doesn't." Lucy released the leather string and counted the coins that fell into her palm. "I wonder where he found this?'

"And why he hid it in his boot." Mrs. Jarvis held out a folded letter to Lucy. "This was folded up, real small-like, in his waistcoat pocket."

Lucy read the letter and frowned. "I can't make much sense of it."

"Give it here." Mrs. Jarvis whisked it out of her hand. "Looks like lots of numbers to me. Maybe bets he intended to place? He did like to gamble, that one."

Lucy reclaimed the grimy piece of paper, put it aside with the purse, and contemplated the pile of clothing. What had brought Bert Speers back to Kurland St. Mary? She would take the things they had found back to Robert and see if he had gained any information from Bert that might help uncover his reasoning.

Mrs. Jarvis set about tidying Jeremiah's side of the room while still muttering about both men and their lack of cleanliness. Lucy waited until she'd finished and then stood up herself.

"I would appreciate it if you kept what we found to yourself, Mrs. Jarvis. I don't want Bert knowing we've been through his possessions."

"I won't tell a soul." Mrs. Jarvis drew a cross over her bosom. "Except for Mr. Jarvis, that is. I can't keep anything from him."

"As he accompanied Sir Robert down to the cellar, I think he will have his own secrets to keep, don't you?" Lucy opened the door, letting in a welcome blast of fresh air. "You have both been very helpful."

"If Bert was the one to murder that poor girl, then he deserves everything he gets," Mrs. Jarvis said fiercely. "I'll be the first one at his hanging if he's guilty." She sighed. "He did seem to be really sweet on her at first, but seeing her with James set him off in a black mood, and he never recovered from it."

Lucy reentered the inn and found her husband ensconced on a stool, enjoying a pint of ale with the innkeeper.

"Are you ready to depart?" she asked.

In reply, Robert drained his tankard, offered Mr. Jarvis some coin, which was declined, and came over to Lucy.

"Bert will be residing in the cellar for at least another night while we investigate his claim to have been in London for the past three days." He nodded to Mrs. Jarvis and led Lucy out to the coach yard. "Did you find anything interesting?"

"Yes, indeed. I'll show you when we get home." Lucy allowed him to assist her into the gig, and they set off.

Robert waited in his study for Lucy to go upstairs, take off her bonnet, and check in on Anna and Ned. Dermot had left some correspondence on his desk for him to sign, so he occupied himself with that until his wife reappeared.

"Is everything all right in the nursery?" Robert asked.

"Ned is rather ill-tempered. Anna says he is missing his Polly and his James." Lucy sighed. "Agnes is not herself, either."

"I'm quite glad to hear she at least has a conscience," Robert replied as he poured them both some coffee. "If she was happy as a lark again, I might reverse my decision about keeping her on."

"It is just so unsettling for Ned," Lucy said. "I promised to take him down to the stables later, but he cried and said he wanted to go with James."

"I'll take him," Robert said abruptly.

His wife studied him for a long moment. "Mayhap we could both go."

"I'm quite capable of dealing with my son for an hour or two."

"I know you are, but he does tend to get rather excited around the horses, and—"

"You wouldn't want me panicking and making things worse." Robert finished the sentence for her.

"I wasn't going to put it quite like that, but—"

"It's all right. I am well aware of my limitations." Robert scowled at her. "Take him yourself."

She reached for his hand, his gaze steady. "Come with me. Ned would be thrilled."

"Perhaps tomorrow after I've spoken to the mail coach driver." He finished his coffee in one gulp and refilled his cup. "Now, would you like to hear what Bert Speers said, or do you want to tell me what you found in his room?"

Lucy brought out a small leather purse and placed it on the desk. "I found this wedged in one of Bert's boots."

Robert opened it and allowed the coins to spill out. "It's hardly a fortune, is it?"

"It's exactly what we paid Polly for her first month of service," Lucy said. "And I just showed the purse to Agnes, who confirmed that Polly had one that was very similar."

Robert counted the coins. "You didn't find Polly's purse with her, did you?"

"No, which makes one suspect that this might well be hers, and that Bert took it from her at some point."

"He claimed he saw her in the village and warned her not to make up stories about him, or she'd be in trouble."

"He *admitted* that?"

"Yes, which I found quite remarkable. When I told him Flora was dead, he lost his temper, insisted he hadn't killed her, and that he'd been in London for the past three days visiting his sick mother."

"How very convenient for him," Lucy sniffed

"Indeed." Robert paused. "He didn't seem particularly surprised, either. But if he did kill her, why on earth did he come back to Kurland St. Mary?"

"Mrs. Jarvis had the same thought." Lucy nodded. "Everything in his bedroom had been turned upside down as if he'd departed in a great hurry. Perhaps he came back because he realized he'd left Flora's purse here and feared it would be discovered."

She offered him a much-folded piece of paper. "He also had this in his pocket. Mrs. Jarvis thought it might have something to do with his betting on the races."

Robert frowned at the list of numbers. "I'm not sure what it is. When one bets on a horse, one usually has the odds *and* the name of the runner, and this is just a jumble of numbers."

He placed the paper on the desk and flattened it out with his palm. "It could be anything at this point."

"The fact that Bert kept it in a safe place, and had obviously been doing so for a while, might indicate that it is important, yes?" Lucy asked.

"I'm not discounting it in the least," Robert assured her. "I'm more interested in seeing what he has to say about having Flora's purse in his possession."

"Perhaps he stole it from her to teach her a lesson." Lucy sipped her coffee and ate one of the biscuits Foley had provided on the tray. "He did admit to speaking to her, didn't he?"

"He said he gave her a good shaking." Robert grimaced. "Perhaps her purse fell out while he was doing so."

"I doubt that if it was in her pocket under her skirts," Lucy objected. "Unless she had it in her hand." She set her cup down and leaned forward. "It almost sounds as if you are trying to find excuses for Bert's behavior."

"Not at all. I'm attempting to think of every possible explanation before I get ahead of myself and start casting blame where it doesn't belong."

"But Bert practically admitted to killing her!"

"No, he didn't. He flatly denied it."

"Then he obviously lied."

"Mr. Jarvis told me that he'd seen Flora and Bert talking perfectly amicably at the inn on several occasions, and he was surprised when I'd asked him to keep Bert away from her."

"That was probably when Bert was attempting to court her."

"I suppose so." Robert crossed his arms and stared out over the parkland. Something was nagging at him, and from his wife's expression, he was conscious that he was failing to adequately address what it was.

"What about James?" he asked abruptly.

"James saw Bert and Flora together, was hit on the head, and was deposited at his father's farm," Lucy said firmly

"So if Bert was with Flora, who hit James?"

Lucy's mouth formed a perfect O as she stared at him. "Maybe Bert saw James watching them, ran back to knock him out, and then took James to the farm."

"Leaving Flora alone?"

Lucy's brow creased. "This is all getting remarkably complicated, isn't it?"

"That is one thing we can agree on completely," Robert said. "If James is telling the truth, who hit him on the head? Is there someone else involved that we do not yet know of?"

"Mr. Fletcher?" Lucy suggested. "Have you spoken to him about any of this yet? He did say he saw Flora walking down to the village that day."

Robert frowned. "As I already mentioned, he was with me the day Flora was killed."

"All of it?" Lucy asked. "Can you absolutely swear that he couldn't have gotten away from you at some point?"

Robert relapsed into silence, his booted foot tapping impatiently against the floor.

"I can't possibly conceive of Dermot being a murderer."

"I agree, but if he saw Flora, perhaps he saw James or Bert or some other person of interest." Lucy suggested.

"I'll talk to him after I've spoken to James again."

"Thank you." Lucy sighed. "I asked Foley to send a message down to Mr. Snape to collect Flora's body from Dr. Fletcher's."

"Mr. Snape does have excellent storage facilities. I'll pay for the coffin and for his time." Robert finished his second cup of coffee. "I'll wager Patrick will be glad to release the body into the care of the undertaker. He says that his wife objects to him storing bodies in her cellar."

"She would," Lucy remarked rising to her feet as she smothered a yawn. "I hope the real Polly Carter's mother replies to my letter soon. I sent her enough money to cover its delivery to us."

"You'll probably never see that again." Robert rose and went to open the door for her. She paused to look up at him.

"Which gives us all the more reason to go to London and speak to her directly!"

Chapter 8

Having made no headway with James, who was stubbornly sticking to his story that he'd only seen Bert Speers with "Polly" and had not spoken to either of them afterward, Robert turned his attention to his land agent. He had invited Dermot to accompany him down to the Queen's Head early the next morning and now sat beside him in the gig. He'd promised Lucy he would return by eleven so that they could take their walk with their son.

"Do you think Bert Speers is the culprit, then, Sir Robert?" Dermot asked as he expertly turned the corner onto the country road.

"He certainly seems to have some grievance with Polly." Robert glanced over at his land agent. "Did you ever see them together?"

Dermot took a while to answer, his gaze fixed on the road in front of them. "I saw them."

"Mr. Jarvis suggested that not all their encounters were acrimonious."

"No, they weren't." Dermot relapsed into silence again.

Robert was just about to prompt him with another question when his companion rushed into speech.

"She seemed quite friendly with him at first. Then, later, she confessed that he was angry because she was spending time with me, and that he thought she was getting above herself."

Robert pondered that interesting information. It mirrored almost exactly what Polly had apparently said to James.

"I have begun to wonder whether Polly was just"—Dermot paused—"playing with all of us."

"What makes you say that?" Robert asked.

"Mayhap she enjoyed us fighting over her."

"It's possible."

"It seemed like it was all a big game to her sometimes. That she didn't take any of us seriously."

"Maybe she didn't."

It occurred to Robert that if Flora had indeed been an actress and a dancer, her ability to play a role might have stood her in good stead in the unfamiliar world of Kurland St. Mary. Being agreeable to all had its advantages.

"Not that she derived any pleasure from seeing us fight over her," Dermot said. "In fact, she found it extremely annoying and told me in no uncertain terms to stop."

"Which perhaps validates your observation that her heart wasn't really involved in any of her interactions."

"Sadly, yes." Dermot grimaced and sighed heavily. "She never really cared for me, did she? She just reflected back my own desire for her."

Remembering how easily Flora had calmed his own fears and made herself amenable to his orders, Robert found some truth in that.

"When you saw her that last morning walking down to the village, did you follow her?" Robert asked.

"As I was intending to visit the Queen's Head to send a letter to my sister in Ireland, I had no *choice* but to follow her."

"Did you see her with anyone?"

"James, who was ahead of me, caught up with her, and they had a somewhat animated discussion before she stormed off toward the High Street."

"What did James do after that?"

"He followed her for a little while, and then I lost sight of him." Dermot fumbled with the reins as he turned into the coaching inn. "I saw Polly meet with Bert, though." His expression darkened. "He grabbed hold of her arm and thrust his face into hers. I yelled at him to stop, but I don't think either of them heard me because I was too far away."

"Did they leave together?"

"Yes. I don't think Polly had much choice in the matter, seeing as Bert had hold of her arm and was dragging her along behind him."

Robert turned to stare fully at Dermot. "Forgive me, but I find it hard to believe that a man who professed to be in love with a particular woman would make no effort to intervene when she was accosted by another man."

A flush of color stole up from Dermot's collar to cover his face. "You . . . ordered me not to get involved with her, sir. I tried to do as you said."

Robert continued to stare at his subordinate until Dermot jumped down from the gig and spoke to one of the ostlers. Perhaps Lucy had been right, after all, and his land agent was not averse to lying about what had happened, either.

Unwilling to let the matter drop, but aware that he needed to speak to the driver of the mail coach before he left the inn, Robert got down from the gig and headed out into the crowded yard. A collection of passengers was boarding the coach, and one of the ostlers was putting up their baggage on the roof.

Robert sidestepped around two chickens in a crate and narrowly avoided standing on a small child almost obscured in his mother's skirts.

"Excuse me, ma'am." He briefly raised his hat and concentrated his attention on the elderly man sitting on the box, who was shouting out instructions as to the loading of the coach.

"Are you Henry Haines?"

"Yes, sir." The man touched the brim of his old-fashioned tricorn hat. "You must be Sir Robert Kurland. Mr. Jarvis said you'd be wanting a word with me." He checked the time on his pocket watch and beckoned to Robert. "Climb up here so I can hear you proper. We don't have much time at this stop."

Robert gave one harried glance at the four horses harnessed to the coach and vaulted himself upward to sit beside the driver.

"One of Mr. Jarvis's ostlers, Bert Speers, claims he rode with you to London three days ago. Is that correct?"

"Aye, he did." Henry nodded. "I brought him back, too."

"Did he stay on the coach until it reached London?"

"I didn't see him leave." Henry turned to bellow something to one of the ostlers about the placement of a bag. "Sorry, sir."

"Whereabouts in London did you drop him off?"

"Whitechapel."

"And you picked him up there three days later?"

"I picked him up in Mayfair, sir, which was something of a surprise, but he paid me the extra fare." Henry checked his watch again. "I didn't see that pretty young nursemaid of yours going back to London, either."

"So I understand." Robert grimaced.

"I do remember her traveling down here, though. She was sitting up top, and she got to talking with Bert, who was just starting his new job as an ostler here."

"They arrived on the same coach?" Robert made sure to clarify the coachman's words.

"Aye. They chatted all the way, merry as larks." Henry shook his head. "God rest her soul."

"Amen to that," Robert said.

Henry put his watch away and reached for his horn. "We'll be leaving in a minute, Sir Robert, so unless you fancy a trip to London, you might want to get yourself off the coach."

"Thank you for your help." Robert contemplated the

jump and decided that dignity be damned. He would sit on his arse and slide down carefully. "I wish you safe passage to London."

"Thank you, sir."

As soon as Robert reached the ground, Henry blew on the horn, and the activity around the coach redoubled, their actions reminding Robert of a frenzied swarm of bees.

"Last call!" Henry shouted as the final passenger scrambled up to the roof and the ostlers slammed the doors and stood back. "Next stop Clavering!"

Robert held his breath as Henry maneuvered the impossibly laden coach beneath the arched entrance to the stable yard and out onto the road. As a child, he'd loved to come down to the inn with his father to see the teams of horses. Back then, he would've been up on their backs, examining every horse and asking a thousand questions. He already suspected Ned would be the same.

So Bert had been to London, which still didn't absolve him of murdering Flora but did, at least, corroborate his account of not being in the vicinity of Kurland St. Mary for three days. Robert paused at the door. But if Bert had been away when Flora's body was discovered, when had he learned that she was dead?

He sought out Mr. Jarvis and found him in the kitchen, eating a hearty breakfast.

"Morning, sir. Fancy something to eat before we go and speak to Bert?"

Robert studied the huge slab of sizzling gammon and four eggs on Mr. Jarvis's plate, and his mouth watered.

"That would be most welcome."

"Then sit yourself down, sir."

Mr. Jarvis pulled out a chair as his wife placed a clean plate in front of Robert and dished him up a succulent piece of ham and two eggs.

"Thank you, Mrs. Jarvis."

She winked at him as she returned to the stove and refilled

the pan. Robert spent the next few minutes indulging his more physical appetites by slowly chewing the home-cured and -smoked gammon, which had been fried to perfection.

Eventually, after downing half his ale, he turned to Mr. Jarvis, who was on his second plateful of food.

"Did you tell Bert that Polly was dead when he arrived back here?"

"No, sir. I left that to you."

"But you said he was in fighting humor when he got off the coach."

"He was, sir, but that might have been because he'd taken three days' leave without telling me and knew I was going to be angry with him."

"Did he ever mention that his mother was sick before?"

"He never mentioned he had a family. Said he grew up in an orphanage and was sent to work in the stables of some London toff before he took up boxing."

"He boxed?"

"He used to, sir. When he applied for the position, he said he'd lost his taste for fighting and wanted a more secure job."

Recalling Bert's broken nose, broad frame, and pugnacious expression, Robert could absolutely imagine him in the ring. If he still followed the sport, the piece of paper Lucy had found in his belongings might be a list of betting odds for fights.

"And he started here about a month ago? Henry Haines said he arrived on the same coach as Polly Carter."

"That's right!" Mrs. Jarvis entered the discussion. "I'd forgotten about that. Bert helped her off the roof of the coach and brought her bags down."

Robert drank his ale and declined Mrs. Jarvis's offer of more food. When the innkeeper finished eating and set his plate to one side, both men descended into the cellar again. This time, Robert halted outside the door.

"I need to speak to Bert alone. Can you wait out here and only come in if I shout for you?"

Mr. Jarvis frowned. "Are you sure about this, sir? He's not afraid of a fight."

"Obviously." Robert took out his pistol. "I do have some protection, Mr. Jarvis. I won't allow him to overcome me."

"As you wish," Mr. Jarvis didn't look happy as he unlocked the door. "But don't hesitate to call out if you need me. There's no shame in needing reinforcements, sir."

Having been in the military, Robert was fully cognizant of that fact. He went into the room to discover Bert sitting against the opposite wall, his cloak around his shoulders and his dark gaze fixed on the door. Robert set his pistol on the top of the nearest beer barrel, within easy reach of his hand.

"Good morning, Bert."

His companion didn't reply.

"How did you know Polly Carter was dead if you were in London when her body was discovered?"

"I didn't know she was dead until you told me."

"Yet you didn't seem shocked by my disclosure."

Bert shrugged. "Some might say she had it coming."

"So you weren't surprised that she had been murdered?"

"I didn't say that, sir." Bert met his gaze. "I told her to be careful. She wouldn't listen, and she ended up dead."

"For a man who professed to be in love with her, you seem remarkably pleased that she died."

"It's not my fault if she wouldn't bloody listen, now, is it? I did my best to warn her."

"To warn her not to talk to any other man but you?"

Bert opened his mouth as if to reply and then closed it again.

"After you accosted Polly on the street, where did she go?" Robert asked after a lengthy silence.

"I didn't notice, sir. I had to get back to work."

"She didn't follow you to the inn?"

"Not to my knowledge."

"And you didn't drag her off with you?"

Bert scowled. "I wish I had. Maybe she'd still be alive if I'd locked her in my room for a few days."

"You were seen by more than one person arguing with Polly and then forcing her to accompany you away from public view. Where did you take her, and what did you do with her?"

"I didn't do anything that she didn't deserve, sir," Bert responded. "You can ask me as many questions as you like, and you'll still get the same answer!"

"Did she deserve to be killed?" Despite his growing frustration, Robert pressed on. "Did she, perhaps, refuse to accept your ultimatums and you accidentally killed her in a fit of rage?"

"I didn't bloody kill her!" Bert snarled.

Robert reached inside his pocket and drew out the blue purse Lucy had found.

"Then how did Polly's purse end up hidden in the toe of your boot?"

Bert shot to his feet, his gaze on Robert's palm. "Where the bloody hell did you get that from? I—" He stopped and breathed out hard through his nose. "That just *proves* it wasn't me."

"How so?" Robert asked.

"Because if I'd murdered the silly cow, I wouldn't have been stupid enough to steal her purse and leave it in my possession!"

It was Robert's turn to shrug. "Most murderers make mistakes. Isn't that why you returned to Kurland St. Mary? To rectify your error?"

"I came *back* because—" Bert closed his mouth and sat down again, his arms crossed over his chest.

"Because what, Bert?"

"Someone is trying to make me look guilty, sir. Someone

wants me to be blamed for this. *That's* the man you should be looking for, not me."

"Does this man have a name?" Robert asked mildly. "Because from what I can see, all the evidence of this crime points to you. You were seen arguing with Polly, you even admit to doing so. You were seen dragging her off, and *you* have her stolen purse in your possession."

"You're wrong, sir. Polly herself told me that she'd seen the man, which was why we were arguing in the first place! If you'd just let me out of here, I could prove it in an instant!"

"Of course, you could." Robert put the purse back in his pocket. "I'm afraid you'll have to stay right where you are for now. If you suddenly remember the name of the man you say we should be looking for, then please let me know."

Bert made a frustrated sound. "If you let me out, I can find him for you."

"If you tell me his name or give me a description, I can find him myself." Robert reclaimed his pistol. "If there is such a man in Kurland St. Mary, he should be easily recovered."

"He's probably gone back to London by now."

"And you foolishly imagine I'll let you go to London to find him?" Robert turned to the door. "You must think I'm a complete flat. Good day, Bert."

"You can't keep me here forever!"

Robert knocked on the door and looked over his shoulder at Bert. "I am aware of that, but as the local magistrate, I can send you to the county town to await trial for murder whenever it suits me."

Bert glowered at him. "If you do that, you'll be condemning an innocent man to death."

"Then you'd better come up with the name of the man you insist is the real murderer before I do so, hadn't you?"

Robert waited until Mr. Jarvis secured the door behind him before heading for the stairs.

"Did he admit it yet, sir?"

"No. He's insisting that someone else is responsible."

Mr. Jarvis's disbelieving snort echoed Robert's thoughts.

"If he doesn't change his tune soon, I will be sending him off to await trial at the county assizes," Robert said as he emerged into the hallway of the inn.

"Aye, sir. But don't you worry in the meantime. I'll keep him safe for you here."

"I appreciate that." Robert shook the landlord's hand. "Are there any letters to take up to the hall?"

"No, sir, are you expecting something in particular?"

"Just a letter from London." In fact, Robert was fairly certain they would never hear from Polly's mother, but he refused to give up hope.

"I'll send one of the boys up if we get anything later, sir." Mr. Jarvis walked through to the yard with him, his keen gaze settling on his ostlers, who were standing around with very little to do.

"Get Sir Robert's gig out, Fred!" Mr. Jarvis bellowed.

As Dermot had walked into the village to speak to some of the tenants, Robert climbed up, took possession of the reins, and left the inn, his mind full of the complicated conversations he'd had that morning. James and Dermot were not being honest, and Bert Speers was intent on denying what would seem to be a clear case against him.

Robert heaved a sigh. There was no way around it. If he wanted to find out exactly what had happened to the real Polly Carter and why his nursemaid had been murdered, he would have to go to London. Probably with his wife, because unless he incarcerated her in the cellar alongside Bert Speers, she would never allow him to leave without her.

Lucy smiled as her son ran ahead of them, his gaze fixed on the distant stables. He had all his father's determination, and she had no doubt that if left to his own devices, he would prefer to spend his days with the grooms and horses. She glanced over at her husband, who was walking alongside her, his expression thoughtful, his blue gaze turned inward.

"Did you manage to convince Bert to confess his crime?"

"No." He grimaced. "*He* tried to persuade *me* that there is another man involved in the matter—a man he conveniently refused to name."

"Yet you still seem troubled."

"You know me too well." His slight smile warmed her. "As I told Bert, he is the one who was seen threatening Flora—something he admits—and he was seen dragging her off somewhere. He then ran off to London to see a 'sick mother' when Mr. Jarvis told me he was raised in an orphanage."

For once, Lucy remained silent as Robert continued to talk.

"And then we have the mystery of what James was up to, and Dermot telling me that he saw Bert with Flora and did nothing to stop him because he didn't wish to disobey my orders."

"That sounds highly unlikely," Lucy conceded.

"I don't like all these loose ends, Lucy. As the local magistrate, I should assess the evidence and immediately send Bert to the assizes, but my instinct tells me I'm missing something important."

"I'm not sure what," Lucy pointed out. "It seems quite clear to me. Bert was obsessed with Flora, disliked her enjoying the company of other men, and strangled her in a fit of jealous rage."

Robert stopped walking and flung his arms wide. "Then why in God's name did he come back to Kurland St. Mary?"

Lucy frowned. "Perhaps he felt guilty and *wanted* to be found out?"

"Then why not confess everything instead of stubbornly insisting that he didn't kill her, and that someone else is making it look like he did it? None of this makes sense."

"And I haven't heard from Polly's mother, either," Lucy reminded him.

Robert resumed walking again. "There's no escaping it, my love. We're going to have to go to London, speak to Polly's mother, and try to find out what happened to the real Polly Carter."

Chapter 9

Confident that, in her absence, Ned would be well looked after by Anna and a very repentant Agnes, Lucy was looking forward to her visit to London. She hadn't been there since her marriage and was eager to explore the shops, visit the theaters, and enjoy the new fashions. Robert gave her a substantial amount of pin money that she rarely spent in the village. She had funds at her disposal and a long list of requests from Anna and Rose to satisfy.

Her only concern about the whole journey was currently sitting opposite her in the carriage . . .

"I am so looking forward to staying with your uncle, the earl of Harrington, Lucy! I'm certain that your family move in the very best circles, and that, as we both know, *is* where I belong."

Lucy caught Dr. Fletcher's attempt to stifle a grin as his wife expounded on her own family connections and her conviction that she would've been greatly missed by the ton.

When Robert had informed her that he intended to bring Dr. Fletcher with him, Lucy had accepted the need for a strong man to accompany her husband into the somewhat dangerous area around Whitechapel, where Polly's mother lived. She had *not* anticipated that Penelope would insist on joining them, leaving her own son in Lucy's nursery "to keep Ned company."

It was, however, quite like Penelope to blatantly ignore Lucy's sensibilities in order to further her own plans. It was also why Penelope had ended up spending six weeks in Bath at the Kurland town house and had given birth to her son there.

Sometimes one just had to accept one's fate, but Lucy was getting somewhat tired of it.

"Where exactly is the Harrington residence, Lucy?" Penelope inquired.

"Portland Square."

Penelope sighed blissfully. "How lovely! And are all your cousins still living at home?"

"Both of them are still there. I believe Julia is engaged now and will be marrying next year. Max is unlikely to be allowed to move out until my uncle decides he is mature enough to do so."

"Do they entertain much?"

"I have no idea." Lucy faked a yawn and settled into her seat. "I do hope you will excuse me, Penelope, but I am rather tired."

Robert, who could sleep anywhere, was already dozing, lulled by the motion of the carriage. It would take them at least two long days and four changes of horses to get to London in a timely manner, with stops at inns along the way. Lucy could only hope that Penelope did not intend to question her about her family for the entire journey.

Eventually, they drew up outside her uncle David's imposing mansion in Portland Square, and Lucy allowed Robert to help her out of the carriage. The front door of the house opened, and a stream of liveried servants came down the steps and immediately started unloading the baggage. Robert surreptitiously stretched out his injured left leg, which never did well on long carriage rides, and started haltingly up the stairs.

He waited for Lucy and the Fletchers to join him in the grand black and white tiled hall where an imposing butler greeted them.

"Sir Robert, would you care to follow me? Lord and Lady Harrington are awaiting you in the drawing room."

The butler turned to ascend yet another flight of stairs, and Robert grimaced. Lucy went to his side and offered him her arm, and they made their laborious way up the steps. Robert shared his muttered opinion that town houses were the very devil, necessitating endless stair climbing, sometimes over seven floors.

"Lady Kurland, Sir Robert Kurland, Dr. Fletcher, and Mrs. Fletcher." The butler announced them and stood aside to allow Lucy to enter the room.

"Lucy, my dear!" Lucy's uncle David came forward and drew her into an embrace. "You are looking very well, my girl, very well indeed."

"As are you," Lucy smiled up at him. He looked quite like her father, but was far more forthright and always full of energy. "Thank you for allowing us to stay with you for a few days."

"It's our pleasure." He turned to Robert and shook his hand. "How are you, sir?"

"Very well, thank you, my lord." Robert turned and gestured toward the Fletchers. "May I introduce you to the earl of Harrington, Mrs. Fletcher, Dr. Fletcher?"

Penelope curtsied low. "A pleasure, my lord."

"Dr. Fletcher and I served together in the Hussars, and he was single-handedly responsible for saving my life," Robert said.

The earl exchanged bows with Dr. Fletcher and offered Penelope an appreciative smile. "You are both most welcome." He looked over at his wife, who was speaking to Lucy. "I believe we have arranged a dinner party for the night after this to celebrate your arrival. Is that not correct, Jane?"

"Indeed we have." Lucy's aunt Jane, who was a formidable society hostess, smiled at them all. "You will have the opportunity to meet Julia's intended, and Max has promised me that he will attend."

"Has he?" The earl raised an eyebrow. "Good, because I've been meaning to speak to him about overspending his allowance."

Aunt Jane slid her hand through Lucy's elbow and turned toward the door. "I am sure that you are all quite exhausted by your journey. I will show you to your rooms and will expect to see you at dinner at promptly six o'clock."

After a sumptuous dinner and some animated conversation, Robert retired with Lucy to their bedchamber. With the help of his valet, Silas, he set about changing his best coat for an older one and put on a sturdy pair of boots.

"There is no need to tell your uncle where Dr. Fletcher and I are going, my dear." Robert slid his pistol into his pocket, along with a small sharp knife. "Let them think that all of us are having an early night after our travels."

"You forget that in a house this size there are always servants on call. My aunt and uncle will be perfectly aware that you went out, but I doubt they will ask *me* about it."

He flashed her a conspiratorial smile. "They'll probably think we're off to a gambling hell or a brothel."

"Which is exactly why they will not inquire!" Lucy sat forward. "Please be careful, Robert."

"We are only going to visit the two theaters that Flora had playbills for and inquire about her there." Robert stood up. "If we're lucky, we might find Polly Carter as well."

"Somehow I doubt that. Tomorrow I intend to call on Polly's mother."

"I will come with you."

"You are more than welcome to accompany me, but if you find out something important at the theater tonight, you might wish to make the best use of our time here and investigate that."

Robert paused as he buttoned his coat. "If I do have to go elsewhere, you will take Silas with you."

"Of course, I will. I'm not unintelligent."

He went over to kiss her cheek. "I know. Now, don't stay up until I return. You need your rest."

"I fear you are right." She sighed and placed a hand over her stomach. "I have no notion why sitting in a carriage is so tiring."

"Perhaps Mrs. Fletcher is the cause of your symptoms rather than the carriage ride."

"And yet you allowed her to come on this journey with us."

"I didn't have a choice." He kissed her cheek again. "I do apologize."

She waved an irritable hand at him, and he retreated to the door. As Silas left, Robert asked him to make sure that Dr. Fletcher was ready to leave, and to send up Betty, Lucy's maid, to help Lucy get ready for bed.

He went down the main staircase into the grand entrance hall and immediately encountered the butler, who had more gravitas than the earl himself.

"Are you going out, Sir Robert?"

"Yes, I am."

The butler inclined his head. "Then I will make sure that someone is up and alert for your return."

"There's no need," Robert said. "We can enter through the kitchen."

"That would hardly be fitting, now, would it, sir?"

"It will be a lot easier." Robert held his gaze. "Thank you for your concern, but I don't wish to cause additional work for any member of the earl's staff."

The butler gave a slight sigh. "As you wish, sir. I will make sure that the kitchen door is left unlocked."

"Thank you."

Patrick came down the stairs just as the butler glided off into the nether regions of the house.

"Is everything all right?"

Robert grimaced. "I forget how restrictive London society is sometimes."

"Which is why we both prefer to live in the countryside." Patrick headed for the door. "Shall we go? I expect it will be easy to pick up a hackney cab if we walk down to the main thoroughfare."

In the rarified air of Portland Square, the lamps were lit, and there were no loiterers in the cobbled street or in the garden center. Robert carried his walking cane, but that was more as a precaution and a potential weapon than because he needed it. Since Patrick had opened up his leg again and he'd enjoyed the spa waters in Bath, he'd been in remarkably good health.

"Where first?" Patrick asked as they approached the much busier main road.

"Covent Garden. The Corinthian is just behind the church."

Patrick hailed a hackney cab, and they were soon delivered to the front of a small theater huddled between a bank and a church. It was an insignificant place and quite unlike the more fashionable theaters where Robert squired Lucy. It was, however, exactly the sort of place he had frequented as a young officer of the Hussars.

"Let's go around to the back." Robert indicated an alley to the right of the building. "But be on your guard."

It had never occurred to him as a young man convinced of his own invincibility to worry about such things. He and his companions had roamed around the city, oblivious to the dangers in a reckless fashion that made him shudder now. The thought of Ned behaving in such a way made him feel quite unwell . . .

A single lantern illuminated the shabby stage door. Robert knocked, and a burly individual who looked remarkably like an English bulldog opened the door.

"What do you want?" he asked, his gaze sweeping over Robert and his companion

"Good evening," Robert said. "I wish speak to the manager of the theater for a few moments."

"Do you now?" The man held out his hand. "I might see about making that happen for a small fee, if you gets my meaning."

"Indeed." Robert placed half a crown in the man's palm and waited until he was invited in over the threshold.

"Come this way, sir."

Despite their giggles and calls, Robert averted his gaze from the skimpily attired females who were changing their garb behind the stage and focused on his destination.

"Gentleman to see you, Mr. Bourne."

"Thank you, Will."

Robert waited until Will left him and Patrick alone with the man in front of them, and then focused his attention on him. Mr. Bourne was a large man with an even larger moustache and very bushy eyebrows.

"What can I do for you?"

"I'm wondering if you currently have a Flora Rosa in your employ?"

Mr. Bourne's welcoming smile died. "Did the little bugger ditch you, too?"

"I'm not quite sure I understand you."

"She was working here, all right, and then suddenly, she says she's gotten a better offer, and off she goes without a word of thanks." Mr. Bourne shook his head. "I was foolish enough to employ her when she was just a child, and that's how she repaid me. With all due respect, sir, did she leave you for that toff?"

"Leave me?" Robert suddenly realized Mr. Bourne's meaning and almost recoiled. "Her family are concerned for her safety, and as one of her cousins works for me, I offered to inquire for her when I was next in London."

Mr. Bourne didn't look particularly convinced by Robert's

hastily contrived explanation but didn't seem inclined to argue about it, either, which suited Robert perfectly.

"Just to make sure that we are talking about the same woman, was Flora Rosa blond-haired and very pretty?" Robert asked.

"Yes, indeed. And she was a passable actress as well." Mr. Bourne nodded. "Much better than I realized after all her bamboozling, promising to stay here forever, to elevate my theater with her talent . . ." He sighed. "I heard she went to the Prince of Wales on the Strand, but I haven't bothered to go and see her perform. What's the point?"

"I will certainly ask for her there," Robert said. "Did you ever employ a woman called Polly Carter?"

Mr. Bourne shook his head. "The name's not familiar to me, but you might care to ask Will on your way out. He knows everyone who has been employed here for the last ten years."

"Thank you for your assistance, sir." Robert handed over his card. "If you do see Flora or Polly Carter, I would appreciate it if you would let me know. I am currently residing at number nine Portland Square if you need to reach me."

"Fancy address, eh?" Mr. Bourne's shrewd gaze re-assessed Robert's worth.

"My wife's family."

"Married up, did you?" The manager gave him an approving nod.

"Not that it is any of your business, but yes," Robert replied. "Thank you again."

He turned and followed Patrick out, down the corridor and through the green room. The dancers were now on-stage, so there was no one to impede their departure or offer unsolicited advice. Patrick paused at the door to ask Will something, and then they were both out in the rapidly cooling night air.

"He doesn't remember Polly Carter," Patrick remarked as they made their way back down the alley to James

Street. "We can walk down to the Strand from here if you like."

"Yes, let's walk."

It wasn't very busy, which was a blessing, and there was no rain, which made the cobbled streets much easier to walk on. Keeping a close eye on his pockets, Robert skirted the delights of Covent Garden proper and headed down Southampton Street. The unpleasant stench of the River Thames wafted up to them, making Robert catch his breath.

"I am not the sort of man to inquire too deeply into your private life, Major, but perhaps you might enlighten me as to why we are searching for two women, one of whom is currently dead and awaiting burial in Kurland St. Mary?"

"Lady Kurland and I believe that the woman we knew as Polly Carter was actually an actress called Flora Rosa."

"Ah." Patrick walked another few steps. "Why was an actress impersonating your nursemaid?"

"That is the question I am attempting to answer. As far as I understand it, Polly Carter sent Flora down to Kurland St. Mary to avoid some trouble in London."

"I doubt Mr. Bourne would've come all that way to find her."

"I agree, but you never know." Robert paused on the corner of the Strand, which was a much busier road and looked both ways. "I hope we will find out more at the Prince of Wales."

"Did someone murder Flora thinking she was Polly, or was Flora murdered for herself?" Patrick asked.

"I hadn't thought of it like that." Robert stopped to look at his friend with grudging admiration. "I assumed Flora failed to escape whatever or whoever was pursuing her in London. If we find no trace of Polly Carter, either, I might have to reconsider."

The Prince of Wales was a better class of establishment than the Corinthian and probably twice the size. Robert noted several private carriages dropping off their occupants, which indicated that the audience was probably of a higher social class.

There was no obvious entrance to the rear of the theater, so Robert stepped inside to ask for directions from one of the footmen.

He was directed down a narrow lane to the left, which, after a right turn, eventually led around and past two other buildings to the rear of the theater. The stage door was brightly lit, and there was a man on guard outside it.

"Good evening. I wish to speak to the manager of the theater," Robert said.

"Then you'll have to call back tomorrow, sir. Mr. Frobisher doesn't allow visitors in while the performance is on. He likes to direct his full attention on the show."

"Which is admirable, but what about during the interval or between acts?" Robert asked. "I need only a few moments of his time."

"He will not see you, sir." The man was respectful but firm. "He will be here tomorrow afternoon, working on the new production, if you wish to speak to him then."

Unwilling to draw too much attention to himself by getting into a pointless argument, Robert nodded. "Thank you. I will come back."

"Is there a message you wish to leave for Mr. Frobisher, sir?"

"No. I'll speak to him tomorrow. Thank you."

Robert retreated, Patrick at his side.

"Why didn't you leave a message?" Patrick asked as they walked away.

"Because I'd rather see his face when I ask my questions than give him the opportunity to think up a story."

Patrick chuckled. "Which is exactly why all the men under your command were so afraid of you." He paused to read the playbill at the front of the theater. "Shakespeare, followed by dancers and a contemporary farce."

"As the theater appears to be prospering, I have to assume he knows his audience," Robert commented.

A hackney cab pulled up behind Robert, and he stepped aside to avoid being knocked down by the gaggle of gentlemen who were descending, intent on rushing into the theater. None of them thanked him for his efforts or excused themselves, which irritated Robert, and then made him realize he was getting old.

One of the men turned to shout back at a companion, his face illuminated in the theater lights before he went into the theater proper.

"Interesting," Robert murmured.

"What is?"

"I just saw Lord Northam, my cousin Henrietta's husband."

Patrick shrugged. "Maybe he enjoys Shakespeare."

"Somehow I doubt it. The man barely knows how to read." Robert stared into the theater. "According to my aunt Rose, who does not like him at all, he does have a fine appreciation of the female form. At her daughter's behest, she once paid off one of his mistresses who was with child. Northam refused to accept any responsibility in the matter."

Patrick snorted. "Typical."

"I wonder if he comes to this place often." Robert turned away from the theater. "It might be worth the attempt to find him at his club and ask him if he has any memory of Flora Rosa."

Robert looked up to find that Patrick's attention had wandered down the street.

"Is there something the matter?"

"Not at all." Patrick grinned at him. "Seeing as our investigations have ended for the night, maybe we might stop for a tankard of ale at the Crown and Anchor?"

"I think that is an excellent notion," Robert agreed and clapped his friend on the shoulder. "Let's go."

Chapter 10

"It is very kind of you to see me, Mrs. Carter."

Lucy smiled reassuringly at the pinched face of Polly Carter's mother, who had only very reluctantly allowed Lucy through her front door. It was almost midday, but very little light filtered through the lace curtains and dirty front window of the terraced house in St. Giles where the Carter family resided. Silas, who had accompanied her when Robert had decided to go and speak to his cousin's husband, remained outside the front door, his billy club prominently displayed and his expression menacing.

"I apologize for not apprising you of my intended visit sooner."

Mrs. Carter's gaze fixed on the unlit fire in the grate, and she ducked her head low. She wore a gray dress with a high neckline and very little ornamentation that made Lucy's choice of a fashionable blue ensemble positively garish by comparison. They were sitting in the cramped parlor at the front of the house on the two chairs that faced each other across the fireplace.

"Did you receive my letter about Polly?" Lucy asked.

"I don't read too well, my lady."

"Ah, was one of your family able to read the letter to you?"

"Mr. Carter did. He told me not to bother my head about one of Polly's friends getting herself into trouble."

"So Polly did know Flora Rosa?"

"Polly works as a seamstress at the theater, my lady. That's probably where she met the woman."

"Which theater?" Lucy asked.

"The Prince of Wales on the Strand."

Lucy nodded. That information certainly established a connection between the two women. "Did you ever meet Flora?"

"Oh, no, my lady." Mrs. Carter pursed her lips. "Mr. Carter doesn't approve of such goings-on. He didn't want Polly working there, either, but she wouldn't listen to him."

"Mr. Carter doesn't approve of the theater?"

"He believes it is ungodly and sinful, ma'am." Mrs. Carter glanced at the table beside Lucy, where a large family Bible was prominently displayed. "And when we received your letter asking whether we knew this Flora, he was rightfully angry with Polly for dragging us into a scandal."

"Did he and Polly argue about it?"

"Yes, my lady." Mrs. Carter sighed. "Polly hasn't been back to see us since."

"She doesn't live here with you?"

"She has her own place near Covent Garden with some friends."

"Could you give me that address?" Lucy asked. "It is imperative that I speak to Polly as soon as possible."

Mrs. Carter reluctantly obliged, and Lucy stored the information in her memory.

"How often do you see Polly, Mrs. Carter?"

"She usually comes during the day when her father is out and helps with the younger ones. She does a lot of her work at night—repairing costumes after the performances, refitting understudies, and generally making sure the props are still usable. So once she's had a sleep, she comes to see me."

"You must be proud to have brought up such a helpful daughter."

Mrs. Carter's expression didn't reflect much pride. "She is not good at obeying her father, and she causes many disruptions to the peace of this household."

"Did Polly read my letter herself?"

"Yes, indeed," Mrs. Carter nodded vigorously. "Mr. Carter *made* her read it before he expressed his disapproval about her immoral friends."

"And that caused an argument and Polly left?"

"Yes, my lady." Mrs. Carter hesitated. "Usually after one of their rows, Polly still comes to see me, but she hasn't been in for over a week."

"Did Polly say anything to you about the letter, or about what happened to Flora Rosa?" Lucy asked.

"She seemed . . . shocked and became tearful, which was when Mr. Carter lost his temper with her for caring about an immoral woman who had probably met her just end."

Lucy rose to her feet. "I don't wish to disturb you for too long, Mrs. Carter, so I will take my leave. Thank you for your help in this matter." She took her aunt's calling card out of her reticule and placed it in Mrs. Carter's lace-mittened hand.

"If Polly does return, I would appreciate it if you could let me know. I'm staying with my aunt and uncle at this address, and I would very much like to speak with her. I had hoped to deliver a letter for her from her cousin, Agnes."

Mrs. Carter glanced down at the card but didn't seem inclined or able to read it. "If you see Polly yourself, my lady, would you tell her to come home?" For the first time, she looked worried. "I would very much like to see her myself."

"Of course, Mrs. Carter." Lucy closed her bag and made sure she had her umbrella with her. "I will certainly do that."

She went back out to the front of the house, where despite his menacing demeanor, Silas had gathered a small crowd of youthful admirers. Compared to a lot of streets in St. Giles, the Carters' road was remarkably clean, with a drain down the center of the cobbles containing only water and no refuse, human or otherwise. Lucy abhorred the poverty in the countryside but found the scale of misery in the capital far more harrowing.

"Are we going back to Portland Square now, my lady?" Silas asked as he followed her to the end of the road.

"No, we have one more visit to make." Lucy looked up and down the street. "Which is the best way to reach Covent Garden?"

Silas frowned. "It isn't far from here, my lady, but I suggest we find a hackney cab." He, too, scanned the street. "We will probably need to walk down to the main road. I doubt many drivers venture in here for fear of being robbed."

"I suspect you are right." Lucy was glad that she'd put on her stout walking boots. It started to rain, and she handed Silas her umbrella to protect them both.

"I don't suppose any of the children you were talking to mentioned Polly or the Carter family?" Lucy asked.

"They said that the old man was a miserable sod—begging your pardon, my lady—and that no one liked him much."

"He didn't sound very likable," Lucy commented, and she increased her pace as the rain came down faster.

"Mr. Carter works as a clerk down at the docks and preaches at one of the local religious halls when he has the time."

Lucy cast Silas an approving glance. He'd gleaned almost as much information from the doorway as she had from inside the house.

"Are you sure that you don't want to return, my lady?" Silas asked again. "Sir Robert told me to make sure you didn't wear yourself out."

"I am feeling quite well, Silas." Lucy spotted a hackney and waved energetically at the driver. "I assure you that after we visit this last address, I will be more than happy to return to my uncle's."

* * *

Robert signed into his cousin's club and was welcomed into the dining room by a waiter who led him directly over to where his cousin's husband was sitting.

"Good afternoon, Northam." Robert bowed.

"Kurland." Lord Northam offered Robert a seat opposite him. "Would you like a brandy before we eat?"

"No, thank you." Robert nodded at the waiter, who disappeared as silently as he had arrived. "How is my cousin?"

"Henrietta is in good health and is currently visiting my mother up in Northamptonshire."

"That is a shame. I was hoping to pay my respects to her in person," Robert said. "I have a letter from her mother."

"Give it to me." Robert passed it over, and Lord Northam made a face as he stowed it in his coat pocket. "I doubt she'll want to read it. She hasn't forgiven Rose for marrying that rector fellow yet."

"That 'rector fellow' is the younger son of an earl and seems very fond of her," Robert commented.

"Well, you would say that, seeing as he's your wife's father, isn't he?"

"I'd say that anyway." Robert held Northam's gaze. "Henrietta should have no fears on her mother's account. Mr. Harrington is a true gentleman."

"Henrietta doesn't care how Mr. Harrington treats her mother." Northam waved a dismissive hand. "She's worried about her inheritance, and quite frankly, so am I."

"Mr. Harrington certainly didn't marry Rose for her money." Robert had never imagined he'd end up defending his father-in-law, but something about Northam's attitude toward Rose had always set his hackles rising.

"But what if she dies first? Will he inherit everything?" Northam complained. "From what I understand, he has three sons and a daughter from his previous marriage left to provide for. Rose's money would certainly help with that."

"I have no idea who she has left her money to. Surely, that is between her and her solicitor?" Robert asked.

"Not according to Henrietta. She's deliberating writing to her mother and demanding a substantial sum up front."

Robert pretended to look puzzled. "Didn't Aunt Rose settle a large sum on Henrietta when she married you?"

"That *pittance* is all gone." Lord Northam looked up as the waiter appeared, ordered himself another brandy, and took the suggestion to have the game pie for his dinner, as did Robert.

Robert had helped his aunt set up the marriage settlement, and he knew that was an outright lie. His cousin and her husband had always treated Rose like their own personal bank, while conveniently looking down on her for being not the "right class."

It was hard to bite his tongue and continue listening to Northam's complaints while he waited for the opportunity to ask some questions of his own. But after Northam's fourth brandy, and well into his dinner, Robert broached the subject of his cousin's theater-going habits.

"I saw you going into the Prince of Wales Theater on the Strand last night," Robert said.

"Did you now?" Northam winked. "Good thing my wife is away then, isn't it?"

"Was it a good show?" Robert asked.

"Didn't see it. I had a more . . . personal quarry in mind in the green room."

"Did you ever meet an actress called Flora Rosa there?"

Northam set down his glass and stared at Robert. "That's a very specific question, Kurland. Has someone been singing her praises, so you thought you'd go and have a gander for yourself?"

"Her cousin works in my house. She asked me to deliver a letter to Flora while I was in London."

"I can't imagine any cousin of Flora's working in a

country house, but I'm not going to argue with you."
Northam leaned in closer and whispered, "Lady Kurland
not with you on this trip, eh?"

"Lady Kurland accompanied me," Robert said as pleasantly as he could. "Our nurse entrusted the letter to her,
and I am merely attempting to deliver it."

"If you say so." Northam winked again, and Robert
barely managed not to plant him a facer.

"Anyway, if you want Flora, you're too late. She's already found a protector, and seeing as he's as rich as Croe-
sus, he's set her up in a nice little house in Maida Vale, and
she's retired from the stage."

"Do you have a name for this man?" Robert asked.

"Viscount Gravely. Do you know him?"

"I can't say that I do."

"He's a widower with two sons. He made his fortune in
India and came back to England about three years ago."

Robert might not know him, but he was fairly certain
Lucy's aunt Jane would. As a society hostess, she knew
every aristocrat in the country, and all their secrets.

"I doubt he'll be open to offers for her, seeing as he only
just persuaded her to accept his protection." Northam
chewed noisily and finished his wine before wiping his
chin.

"I have no intention of 'bidding' on a woman. I am simply attempting to deliver a letter." Robert also finished his
wine and sat back. "Well, this has been delightful, but I
have to be going. Lucy's aunt and uncle are having a dinner party for us tonight, and I need to try on the new coat
from my tailor."

He was, in fact, heading back to meet with the manager
of the Prince of Wales, but that was the last thing he intended to let slip to Northam.

His companion held up his brandy glass to the waiter. "I
know where you're off to, Kurland, you can't fool me. But
rest assured, I'll keep mum if I see Lady Kurland."

Robert pushed in his chair and fought to keep the loathing from his voice.

"Thank you for dinner, and give my best to Henrietta."

"Right, ho, I will."

Robert was still seething when he arrived at the theater and was ushered inside the empty building to meet Mr. Frobisher. The manager sat in the front row of the empty stalls, watching what was obviously a rehearsal for his next production. In the daylight, the theater looked as shabby and threadbare as an actor without his stage paint and costume.

Robert introduced himself and settled into the seat beside Mr. Frobisher, who had the alert face of a terrier and red, bushy whiskers to make the likeness even more applicable. He sent his cast off for a break and gave his full attention to Robert.

"How can I help you, sir?"

"I am inquiring about a woman called Flora Rosa."

"Not another one." Mr. Frobisher sighed. "I regret to tell you that she has decided not to continue her career on the stage and has gone off to be a kept woman. Which in my opinion is a waste of her talent and beauty."

"So she did work for you, then?"

"Indeed. I persuaded her to abandon the abominable Corinthian and offered her a chance to shine here instead." He snorted. "Unfortunately, she shone rather *too* brightly and caught the eye of an aristocrat, and that was that."

"The man who persuaded her to leave was Viscount Gravely?"

"Yes." Mr. Frobisher met Robert's gaze. "Why are you asking all these questions? Is Flora in trouble? Are you a Bow Street Runner?"

"I am merely trying to establish her identity. Did she have any family?"

"Not that I know of. She grew up in an orphanage, was

placed as a kitchen maid, and swiftly decided her beautiful face and figure would provide her a far more lucrative career on the stage. She was correct about that. If she'd stayed, she could've gone on to become one of the greats." Mr. Frobisher paused. "Has something happened to her?"

Robert made a quick decision. "May I ask you one more question? And then if you are willing, I will attempt to explain myself."

"If you wish."

"Do you have a Polly Carter working here?"

"I did until about a week ago. She hasn't come in for a while."

Robert slowly exhaled. "This is going to sound as fantastic as one of your more lurid plays, but I have reason to believe that Flora Rosa, who was masquerading as Polly Carter, is now lying dead in the cellar of the Kurland St. Mary undertaker."

Mr. Frobisher blinked slowly and leaned in. "Please, *do* go on."

Robert returned to the Harringtons'. He had just enough time to try on his new coat and to proclaim that the fit was perfectly adequate before it was time to dress for the dinner party. He met up with his wife in their dressing room. For a while, there was no chance for conversing as Betty and Silas helped them into their best clothes.

"Thank you, Silas. You may go now, and please, don't wait up for me," Robert said.

"Thank you, sir." Silas gave Robert's sleeve a last brush and went out.

Robert studied his new blue coat in the mirror and considered the gray waistcoat his tailor had persuaded him to wear under it. Did he look too flashy?

Lucy glanced over from her dressing table. Betty had just finished arranging her hair and was sliding in some jeweled pins to keep everything secure.

"You look very nice, my dear."

He frowned at his reflection. "Is the color perhaps a little bright?" He fingered the cuffs. "And these silver buttons?"

His wife's quiet chuckle made him turn to face her.

"From a man who used to dress up in a uniform created by the Prince of Wales that included fur, gold buttons, and silver lace."

"I suppose you do have a point," he acknowledged. "Now that I think of it, the colors are rather similar."

"You always choose blue." Lucy rose from her seat and shook out the satin skirts of her green gown. "I think you feel most comfortable wearing it."

"After twelve years in uniform, I suspect you are right." He went over to take her hand. "You look beautiful."

"Hardly that." She made a face. "But I do at least look *presentable*, and considering the caliber of Aunt Jane's guests, that will have to do."

"You are the granddaughter of an earl and the wife of a baronet, and can hold your head high in any company." Robert kissed her nose. "I have no doubt that you will enjoy the evening far more than I shall."

"Did you find out anything interesting from Lord Northam?"

"Only that he is a wastrel and doesn't deserve a penny of my aunt's money."

"I believe we already knew that. What about his connections at the theater?"

"He knew who Flora was. He said that she recently took up with a 'protector' and left the theater."

"Did he know who it was?"

"Yes, a Viscount Gravely. As far as Northam knows, Flora Rosa is living a life of luxury in a house bought for her in Maida Vale."

Lucy grabbed his sleeve. "Perhaps Polly is there!"

"Was she not at home?" Robert asked. "Silas said that you spoke to her mother."

"She doesn't live there anymore, and I can quite see why. Her father is very religious and doesn't approve of her working in a theater, and her mother seems too afraid of her husband to do anything but agree with him."

"Then where *does* Polly live?"

"In a house near Covent Garden." Lucy went over to pick up her gloves, the emerald necklace Robert had given her for Christmas shining in the candlelight. "I went there as well, but no one has seen her for over a week." She looked back at Robert. "Her mother hasn't seen her since she got my letter. Polly and her father had an argument over it."

"This is somewhat of a hindrance to our plans to speak to her." Robert frowned. "One can only hope that she, too, has not been a victim of this murderer."

"Bert Speers came back to London for three days after Flora disappeared," Lucy said slowly. "Perhaps he came back to find Polly and make certain she could never share her story with anyone."

"It does seem all too likely, but I will continue to hope we can find Polly."

"I asked her mother to let us know if she returned home." Lucy arranged a shawl over her elbows and checked her reflection in the mirror.

"And I asked Mr. Frobisher to do the same thing if she returned to her job at the theater." Robert reached for his wife's gloved hand. "Unfortunately, for the moment—until I get the opportunity to speak to Viscount Gravely—all we can do is wait."

Chapter 11

Robert paused in front of the steps leading up to Viscount Gravely's house and briefly considered how much money the man had made in trade to be able to afford such a place. Not that he had any issue with how a man created his wealth, unless it was through the slave trade. His mother's family wealth gained in the industrial north ably propped up his own finances.

He'd asked Lucy's aunt if she could introduce him to Viscount Gravely, and as she had already met the man, she had agreed to write a note suggesting he might allow Robert to meet him on a matter of some urgency. An invitation to visit had arrived promptly, and Robert had immediately set out before his wife had returned from her shopping expedition with Penelope.

Patrick was busy visiting the London hospitals, reconnecting with his peers, and attending lectures about new scientific discoveries, while Penelope was reveling in the social interactions of the very well-connected Harrington family. Robert was rather keen to get back to Kurland St. Mary and could only hope that the viscount would help him reach some conclusions as to the mystery surrounding Flora Rosa.

He went up the steps and knocked on the front door,

which was opened by a butler with a turban wearing a distinctly un-English embroidered coat.

"Welcome, Sir Robert. Lord Gravely will see you in his study. Please follow me."

"Thank you." Robert followed the softly spoken man into the depths of the house until he paused and knocked on a door.

"Your visitor, my lord."

Robert stepped into the room and immediately went still. It was crammed full of souvenirs from a life spent overseas and smelled like the interior of a spice cabinet.

"Sir Robert?" A frail, wizened man with a somewhat yellowish skin gestured at the chair in front of him. "Please."

"Viscount Gravely." Robert bowed and took the seat, his nose twitching at the trail of smoke coming from some burning sticks on the desk.

"I appreciate you seeing me on this somewhat delicate matter." Robert wasn't one to waste time on pleasantries. "I understand that you recently took a young actress under your protection?"

"That is correct, although what it has to do with you is beyond me."

"Was her name Flora Rosa?"

His host simply nodded, his distaste for the nature of the conversation more evident with every second.

"You installed her in a house in Maida Vale."

Again, there was no answer, and Robert sat forward. "I do not ask these questions with any pleasure, my lord, but I do wish to know the answers."

"I am not aware that I am obliged to tell you anything, sir. This is not a court of law."

"I am merely trying to establish that you knew Flora Rosa," Robert persevered. "When did she leave her house in Maida Vale?"

"Whoever told you that she did?"

"You are suggesting that she is still there?" Robert raised an incredulous eyebrow. "Then, if that is the case, perhaps you would furnish me with her address so that I can go and pay my respects to her and clear up the current confusion."

Lord Gravely looked down at his joined hands. "You suggested that you had important information to share with me about this matter. If this is not merely a fishing expedition to see if you can persuade her to become your mistress rather than mine, then I wish you would get to the point!"

Robert gave up all pretense of trying to be reasonable. "I am looking for someone to identify the body of a woman who I suspect is Flora Rosa and who was murdered in my home village of Kurland St. Mary."

Because he was looking carefully at the viscount, Robert clearly saw the man's shock at his deliberately harsh words. He rose to his feet.

"If you wish to discuss the matter or offer me your assistance, please be advised that I am staying with the Harrington family in Portland Square for the next two days before returning to Kurland St. Mary. If you still insist that your mistress is alive and well, and happily residing in Maida Vale, I would ask that I might speak to her, and offer both her and you my apologies."

The viscount looked up. "I have nothing further to say to you."

"As you wish." Robert inclined his head an icy inch. "I appreciate your time and consideration."

He turned on his heel and walked out, keeping a very tight rein on his temper. He should have brought his wife with him. She was far better at extracting information from people than he was.

He looked ahead and saw two men in the hallway. They appeared to be arguing about something. Both of them turned as Robert approached.

"Are you Sir Robert Kurland?" the taller one asked.

"Yes."

"I'm Trevor Gravely, and this is my brother Neville. We understand that you have just been speaking to our father." Trevor glanced at his brother, who frowned at him. "Would you mind very much if we asked you if this was about his mistress?"

Robert studied the two young men, who looked nothing like their father, both being tall and fair. He wondered whether they had stayed in England with their mother while the viscount had been occupied in India.

"Why do you want to know?"

"Because I have information that I think might help you," Trevor Gravely said. "Would you be willing to accompany us to a coffee shop so we can discuss the matter further?"

Robert retrieved his hat and cane from the silent butler and came to a decision.

"Yes, indeed. I would appreciate your thoughts on the matter."

He followed the two men out into the square and down toward the river where there were more people around. The fragrant smell of coffee caught his nose as the brothers turned down a side alley and approached the small shop.

They found a table in the corner and ordered their drinks. Around them, other men discussed business issues and politics, sometimes quite loudly, while smoking clay pipes and eating the meat pies the shop also offered.

"Before we start, you should be aware that your father refused to divulge any information about his mistress to me," Robert volunteered. "In truth, he claimed that all was well, and that she was still living happily in Maida Vale."

Neville grimaced. "She's not there. She ran off over a month ago, taking a substantial sum of cash and all the jewelry my father foolishly bestowed on her."

"You did not approve of the liaison?"

"Why would we?" Trevor answered him. "She is younger than us, and hardly the kind of woman a man of our father's class should be associating with."

"It is not uncommon for elderly men to take young mistresses," Robert pointed out. "Perhaps he was lonely."

Trevor snorted. "Or he was beguiled by a pretty face and an avaricious mind."

"I thought your father was a renowned businessman? I doubt he would allow himself to be 'beguiled,'" Robert continued. "Does your father realize that Flora Rosa is missing?"

"Of course, he does," Trevor said.

"Then why did he deny it?"

Neville sighed. "I think he is feeling ashamed for being bamboozled, and the thought of anyone outside the family knowing what happened is embarrassing for him."

Robert sat back as the waiter placed his pot of coffee in front of him. "Thank you. Where do you believe Flora Rosa is now?"

Neville cleared his throat, his anxious gaze on his brother. "I assumed—we *both* assumed—that she had taken up with another man."

"Why would you assume that?" Robert asked.

"Why would we not?" Neville raised his eyebrows. "Flora is well known as an actress and an ambitious woman. There are many gentlemen who would be happy to become her protector."

Robert considered his options and decided to be blunt. He had an awful sensation that he was running out of time to solve Flora's murder.

"Then I regret to inform you that she is dead."

"God, *no!*" Neville blurted out, his voice shaking with emotion.

"I . . . I beg your pardon?" Trevor croaked. "Did you say *dead*?"

"Murdered, actually," Robert said. "That's what I came

to tell your father today. I need someone to come down to Kurland St. Mary to identify her body."

The brothers glanced at each other.

"We both met her. We could identify her," Trevor said hesitantly. "We had no *idea* . . . we thought she'd just moved on to another man."

"It's certainly complicated," Robert said diplomatically. "But if one of you were willing to come down to Kurland St. Mary and make sure that we have the right woman, we could get on with the business of giving her a proper burial."

Trevor patted his brother's arm as Neville struggled to speak. "It's all right. I can go. I wouldn't ask that of you."

"No, you *can't*—I mean, I must—" Neville shot to his feet, his face pale. "If you will excuse me for a moment, Sir Robert?"

Trevor waited until Neville was out of earshot before turning back to Robert. "I do apologize for my brother's behavior. He's terribly upset. He was the first person to meet Flora Rosa, and he was vastly taken with her. He made the mistake of introducing her to our father, and that was that." He grimaced. "The little bitch changed her allegiance in a flash."

"I'm sorry to hear that, but perhaps, as things stand, your brother was well rid of her."

Trevor sipped his coffee. "I hate to speak ill of the dead, but I think we're all well rid of her. Hopefully, next time, my father will form a liaison with someone more suitable."

"Would you object if I went to visit Flora's house in Maida Vale?" Robert asked.

"Not at all." Trevor produced one of his cards and wrote the address on the back of it. "Just give this to Mrs. Pell, tell her I sent you, and she'll be happy to let you in."

As they traveled away from the center of the city, Lucy glanced out of the carriage window, watching the houses gradually become less grand and the vistas less opulent. When Robert had returned from meeting Viscount Gravely and his two sons, she had been hard pressed to hide her frustration at the way the discussion had gone. She couldn't fault Robert for his direct attempt to alert the Gravelys to the fate of Flora Rosa, but she wished she'd been there to aid him.

"What if Dr. Fletcher is right?" Robert suddenly spoke after sitting in frowning contemplation for the past half an hour.

"Right about what?" Lucy asked.

"That the murderer came to kill Polly Carter and accidentally killed Flora instead?"

"I suppose it is possible," Lucy allowed. "But my inclination is to believe that Flora Rosa was killed for herself. She certainly stirred up something of a hornet's nest in her life, didn't she? I can't imagine what it would be like to have men fighting over *me*."

"I'd fight for you," Robert observed.

"Of course, you would, my dear." She smiled fondly at him. "But we are speaking of Polly Carter, who appears to have been working as a seamstress at the theater while Flora Rosa acted on the stage and acquired a large crowd of admirers."

"But what if Flora saw Polly being killed and fled to Kurland St. Mary to avoid the same fate?" Robert speculated.

"Flora had the protection of a peer of the realm. Do you not think she would've asked him to direct the authorities to investigate Polly's murderer?"

"I suppose that would've been the sensible thing to do." Robert pondered the matter for a moment. "What do you make of the two sons being involved in the matter?"

"It sounds remarkably embarrassing to me." Lucy shuddered. "Why on earth would an older man take his son's mistress away from him?"

"Because he could? And because Flora realized that the

father would be more able to support her financially? We don't know for certain that Flora was Neville's mistress, just that he met her first. Needless to say, neither of the Gravely sons have much love for Flora Rosa any longer."

Lucy held onto the strap as the carriage turned a sharp corner into a tree-lined street of modest terraced houses with small front gardens.

"Were they really shocked to hear that she was dead?"

"I'd say so." Robert paused. "Although neither of them seemed particularly surprised. The only person who showed any real emotion was Neville, the younger son. He was so devastated he could barely speak." Robert sighed. "In truth, the sons seemed relieved that Flora was no longer around to bother their father."

Lucy had no answer for that. The carriage, which they had rented at the local mews, slowed down and eventually stopped opposite one of the identical yellow-bricked houses.

Robert looked out of the window and checked the number on the door. "This must be the place." He got out from the carriage, spoke to the driver, and then came around to help Lucy down. "I told him to come back in two hours. That should give us sufficient time to search the place and interview the remaining staff."

Lucy went ahead of him, opened the cast-iron gate, and went up the central path to the square-set house. It was modest in size, consisting of a bow-fronted window on either side of the front door with two identical stories above it.

Robert knocked on the door, which was opened by a middle-aged woman who didn't look particularly pleased to see them.

"Are you Mrs. Pell?" Robert asked. "I have a note for you from Mr. Trevor Gravely."

Mrs. Pell insisted on inspecting Trevor Gravely's card very carefully before she allowed Lucy and Robert inside the door.

"I'll be in the kitchen if you need me." She stomped off

to the back of the house, leaving Lucy and Robert alone in the narrow hall.

"Charming," Robert murmured.

"Where shall we begin?" Lucy asked.

"How about we start at the top and work our way down on either side of the house?" Robert suggested. "I doubt we will find much to interest us, but we should be as thorough as possible."

"Agreed." Lucy raised the hem of her skirt and went up the stairs. "And when I am finished, I will go and speak to Mrs. Pell in the kitchen."

"You think you will finish more quickly than I will?" Robert asked.

"Naturally." Lucy raised her chin.

"You are probably right. And when I am done, I will question any male staff still in residence."

Neither of them spent much time in the attics because it appeared that most of the staff that had tended Flora Rosa either lived out or had already left. Lucy was more certain of success when she opened a door on the first floor and was engulfed in a wave of stale perfume.

Robert disappeared into the opposite room, which smelled of cigar smoke and which had probably been occupied by Viscount Gravely.

Lucy stood with her back against the door and surveyed the bedchamber. There was a large four-poster bed made up with pink and lace linen, two comfortable chairs by the fire, and a chest of drawers. An ornate dressing table took advantage of the light pouring through the front window of the house. To Lucy's disappointment, it was remarkably devoid of substance or character. Flora's room at Kurland Hall had displayed more of her tastes and personality than this blank space.

It was fairly obvious that someone must have been in and tidied up everything after Flora's departure. Was it Mrs. Pell? Or had Polly Carter come to the house and removed all traces of the woman she was trying to help?

Refusing to be thwarted, Lucy set about opening drawers, peering into cupboards, and checking under the bed. The dressing table held no hairbrushes or cosmetics, and the perfume that still lingered in the sir had long been packed away. From all accounts, Flora had not arrived at Kurland Hall with much luggage, so where had everything gone? Where were her London gowns, hats, and outdoor wear?

Robert said the Gravely sons had suggested that Flora had been given a lot of jewelry, yet Lucy had found only one necklace and a couple of rings among Flora's possessions. The more Lucy thought about it, the more she was convinced that the rest of Flora's things must be somewhere else.

In the back of one of the dresser drawers, Lucy discovered a note that had half-slipped under the back of the drawer, leaving a ripped piece behind. She carefully drew it out and considered the words.

Meet me after the performance, or else I'll tell him—

She didn't recognize the handwriting but did wonder at the implied threat. Was this simply another note from an unwanted admirer that Flora had stuffed in the drawer? Or had she kept it for a reason? Lucy was beginning to believe that the life of a beautiful actress involved far more hazards than she had ever imagined. Perhaps it was better to lack talent and looks, and be loved just for yourself.

There was an interior door leading into a shared dressing room that reached across the front of the house to the room next door. Lucy walked into it and noticed that none of the cupboards had clothes in them. She went to open the door into the other side and found it locked.

"Robert? Are you still in there?" Lucy knocked on the wooden panel.

Her husband opened the door and regarded her keenly. "Did you find anything interesting?"

"Not really. I suspect that someone has cleaned up very

carefully." She looked up at him. "But where are all Flora's things? She certainly didn't take them to Kurland St. Mary."

"Maybe she pawned them to afford her ticket on the mail coach, or perhaps the servants here disposed of everything on Viscount Gravely's orders."

"Was there anything of interest in his room?" Lucy asked in return.

"Nothing—except the man obviously likes cramming his personal rooms with as many artifacts as a museum." He pointed at the far wall. "I wonder if he personally shot all those stuffed animals?"

"I thought you said that he was sickly?"

"He is now." Robert grimaced. "Perhaps he is trying to recapture the glories of his youth—which would also explain his desire to set up a woman young enough to be his granddaughter as his mistress."

She showed him the scrap of note, and he sighed.

"Poor Flora. I am beginning to feel that most of the men in her life were not very kind to her."

"I suspect you are right." Lucy eased a hand onto the small of her back as the baby kicked hard. "Do you think you could deal with the two downstairs rooms while I go and speak to Mrs. Pell?"

Robert's keen gaze searched her face. "Are you overdoing it?"

"I would certainly like to sit down for a while, but other than that, I am feeling quite well," Lucy retorted.

"Then go." He offered her an elaborate bow. "And good luck getting Mrs. Pell to reveal anything at all."

Lucy went down the stairs and made her way to the back of the house, where Mrs. Pell was sitting at the kitchen table with a cup of tea beside her. The housekeeper didn't bother to get up or even offer Lucy a greeting, which didn't really surprise her. Having dealt with the awfulness of Mrs. Fielding, who had been both her father's cook and bed warmer in the rectory for years, Lucy wasn't easily cowed.

Lucy rubbed a hand over her rounded stomach. "Do you have another cup somewhere? I would love some tea."

"Third cupboard on the right of the stove. Help yourself."

"Thank you, I will." Lucy found a cup and took it to the table. She sat directly opposite Mrs. Pell and helped herself to the contents of the teapot and the plate of shortbread that sat beside it.

"What wonderful shortbread, Mrs. Pell. Did you make it?"

"I did."

"Then Flora Rosa was a lucky woman to have you as her cook and housekeeper." Lucy munched determinedly on the dry biscuit. "And the house is kept so well. I wish my housekeeper was as dedicated as you are, Mrs. Pell."

"Thank you, ma'am." Mrs. Pell offered her the plate again. "Have another piece."

"Thank you." Lucy smiled at the woman. "Do you have a family, Mrs. Pell?"

"I have three of my own, and two grandchildren; one boy is three and the other five."

Lucy undid her coat to show her rounded stomach. "I have a two-year-old son and another child due at Christmas. Which is why I am appreciating your shortbread, as I find I get tired and hungry during the day."

"My daughter was the same way," Mrs. Pell said grudgingly. "Like a little rabbit, always nibbling on something."

Lucy chuckled. Mrs. Pell's expression softened fractionally as Lucy asked her a thousand questions about her grandchildren and family. Growing up in a rectory and having to take her mother's place in coping with the parishioners had given Lucy the perfect set of skills to converse with anyone. After a while, she guided the conversation back to her original purpose.

"I suspect you are wondering why Sir Robert and I are invading your house while your mistress is missing." Lucy sipped her strong tea.

"You're not the first to come barging in here, my lady, and I doubt you will be the last."

"Oh? Who else has come?"

Mrs. Pell crossed her arms over her chest.

"Did a woman named Polly Carter ever come here?" Lucy asked. "Her cousin Agnes works in my nursery. I *had* hoped to deliver a letter to Polly from Agnes while I was in London."

Mrs. Pell stared at her for a long time before she reluctantly opened her mouth again. Perhaps it was not going to be as easy as Lucy had anticipated. "Polly *did* mention she had a cousin called Agnes."

Lucy fought to conceal a spurt of triumph as another piece of the puzzle slid into place.

"Agnes is very good at her job. I believe she was attempting to persuade Polly to forgo her work at the theater and come and work for me." Lucy patted her stomach. "As I am expecting again, I am eager to add to my nursery staff."

"Polly was a good girl," Mrs. Pell commented.

"I spoke with her mother recently. She hadn't seen Polly for a while." Lucy ventured into more problematical territory. "Has she been to see you since your mistress left?"

Mrs. Pell made a great show of pouring herself more tea and pursed her lips in thought. "I don't rightly know when I last saw Polly."

"She didn't help Flora Rosa leave here?"

"That dratted girl left in the middle of the night without telling anyone where she was going," Mrs. Pell said. "And the mess she left you wouldn't believe!"

"How horrible for you," Lucy said sympathetically. "Did you have to clean everything yourself, or did you have help?"

"We had a maid back then—Marjory, who also works next door—and she helped me set things to rights." Mrs. Pell shook her head. "I had to send young Paul, the boot boy, to tell Viscount Gravely that she'd gone and to send the stable hands out looking for her." She sighed. "No one could find a trace of the stupid girl."

"Well, leaving in the middle of the night is never very wise," Lucy agreed. "How awfully trying for you and your staff."

"Viscount Gravely didn't come himself, but he sent Mr. Neville and Mr. Trevor, and they did their best to help. Mr. Neville was beside himself."

"Where do you think Flora went?" Lucy asked.

"To another man?" Mrs. Pell sniffed. "We all know that actresses are just better-dressed whores, don't we?"

"Has anyone seen her with another man since she left?"

"Not that I know of. She's probably staying indoors until the fuss dies down and her new protector can come to some kind of financial arrangement with Viscount Gravely."

"Was she hard to work for, then?" Lucy added more tea to Mrs. Pell's cup.

"To be fair, she wasn't much trouble, and she was always very pleasant to me. She didn't hold parties here, and she kept very much to herself, entertaining only the viscount when he turned up, which wasn't often, and going to work at the Prince of Wales."

"When you decided she was unlikely to come back, did you box up her clothes to send them on to her?"

"No need. She stripped the place bare when she left." Mrs. Pell's truculent tone emerged again. "It was my day off. I'd been down to Southend to see my sister. When I returned, she'd up and gone during the night."

"But how did she carry everything?" Lucy wondered.

"I suspect she must have had help, which goes to show that she'd found a new man."

"That would make perfect sense," Lucy agreed. "I do hope Viscount Gravely didn't blame you for anything?"

"He's not been here since she left, my lady, so I haven't seen him. But he's kept me on to keep the place nice while he decides what to do with it."

"He is lucky that you chose to stay on and do your job so competently," Lucy said admiringly.

"It's much easier to look after a house than its occupants." Mrs. Pell shrugged. "I'm the only one who lives here full-time now."

"How many staff did you have before Flora left?"

"Marjory, the kitchen maid, and the boot boy." Mrs. Pell ticked them off on her fingers. "And Mr. Biggins, the man who took care of the horses, but he lives at the livery at the end of the street. I'd send Paul down when she needed the carriage."

"Did you hire your own staff, Mrs. Pell?"

"No, they all came from Viscount Gravely's various establishments."

"And that's where they have probably returned," Lucy guessed. "At least they weren't all out of a job when this unfortunate event happened."

The kitchen door opened, and Robert came in. Mrs. Pell immediately stiffened as Lucy offered him a warm smile.

"Ah, there you are, my dear. You will be pleased to hear that Mrs. Pell remembers Polly Carter but hasn't seen her for a while." She held her husband's gaze. "I told her that we'd originally been seeking Polly to deliver a letter to her from Agnes and only learned about Flora Rosa because of that."

Robert placed two calling cards on the table. "I am glad that you have seen Polly, Mrs. Pell. If she turns up here again, will you please let us know? We would like to speak to her before we leave London."

Chapter 12

They exited the house together, and Lucy waited until Mrs. Pell had shut the door before turning to Robert.

"I didn't mention that Flora Rosa was dead."

"So I gathered." He paused by the carriage. "What do you want to do now?"

"I suggest we go and speak to the parlor maid next door, and then to Mr. Biggins at the mews."

"You have been busy." Robert smiled at her. "What if I go and find Mr. Biggins, and you concentrate on the maid?"

"You had better take me up in the carriage first in case Mrs. Pell is watching us through the curtains," Lucy suggested. "You can drop me off at the alley between the mews and the livery stables. I can walk back to the house next door."

"As you wish." He opened the door for her with a flourish. "And then we will return to the Harringtons, and you will rest until dinnertime."

"I'm not going to argue with you," Lucy said as he handed her up the steps. "I am quite fatigued."

"Then perhaps we should postpone our visits until tomorrow?"

She turned and placed a hand on his shoulder. "I'd much

rather we didn't. I want to go home. The longer we stay in London, the more I miss my dearest Ned."

He met her gaze and nodded. "Although your aunt and uncle have been most hospitable, I am more than happy to leave this place myself."

He walked around the carriage, had a word with the driver, and got in the other side.

"What exactly am I supposed to be asking Mr. Biggins?"

"Ask him about Flora Rosa and whether he remembers Polly, and try to confirm that he is employed by the Gravely family."

Robert snapped a salute. "Yes, my lady."

They moved off and stopped again after the carriage had executed the turn onto the next street

"Everything is arranged, my dear," Robert said. "Shall I wait for you at the livery stables?"

"Yes, please." She offered him an encouraging smile, straightened her bonnet, and descended from the vehicle without waiting for his assistance. He watched her walk off down the cobbled alley, her head high and her step firm. Despite his steady belief in her abilities, he still worried when she set off anywhere by herself. She did have a tendency to end up in trouble, and as she was currently with child, his concerns were higher than usual.

At the livery stables, he asked for Mr. Biggins and was directed into the office at the rear of the building. A wiry, dark-haired man who had the look of a jockey stood up as Robert approached.

"What can I do for you, sir?"

"Are you Mr. Biggins?" Robert asked.

"Indeed I am."

"Did you work for the lady who lived at number seventeen Gloucester Street?"

"I did, sir. A pretty lass and a rising star of the theater." He grimaced. "She's gone now, though. Took my sunshine away with her, didn't she?"

"When did you last see her?" Robert asked.

Mr. Biggins gave him the eye. "Who's asking, and why?"

"I'm Sir Robert Kurland. I've been trying to trace the cousin of our nursery maid, who was supposed to come and work for us, but she seems to have disappeared. She apparently worked with Flora Rosa. I was hoping that the lady might help me discover Polly's whereabouts."

"Polly Carter?"

"Yes." Robert looked searchingly at Mr. Biggins. "Do you know her?"

"I sometimes took her up with Miss Flora to the theater. She was a nice girl. Not a beauty like Miss Flo, but a pleasant and respectable young woman." Mr. Biggins got out his pipe. "I can't say I've seen her recently. Viscount Gravely closed the account with the livery about a month ago, after Miss Flora left."

"Did he come here personally to deal with you?"

"No, his son summoned me to his big house on Grosvenor Square and paid me off. He did offer me my old job back in the stables, but I told him I'd decided to stay here and manage this place."

"Why was that? Were you unhappy at the Gravelys'?" Robert asked.

"The pay is better here, and I can arrange my own time, which I appreciate after getting up at the crack of dawn every day just in case one of the Gravelys wanted to ride or needed a carriage." Mr. Biggins got out his tobacco pouch and filled the bowl of his pipe. "And there's no chance of being promoted there because the bloke who held this job before me went back to work for the Gravelys, and he's been with them since he was a lad."

"Why did he leave this position?" Robert asked.

"Miss Flora didn't like him. I thought the viscount would kick him out on his ear, but apparently he took him back."

"Why didn't Miss Flora like him?"

"She resented him 'spying' on her." Mr. Biggins lit his

clay pipe and sucked on the stem to draw the air through. "Now, I was asked to keep an eye on her myself, but I did it a lot more discreetly than Bert, and she never complained or realized I was reporting back to the Gravelys."

"And Bert went back to work for the Gravelys?" Robert asked slowly.

Mr. Biggins shrugged. "As I said, he was a good worker and never caused any trouble before he met Miss Flora."

"Did you help Miss Flora move her baggage to a new residence?" Robert decided he had nothing to lose in simply asking the question.

Mr. Biggins looked around and then lowered his voice. "I *might* have helped her out with that, sir, but that's only between you and me."

"Where did you take her belongings?"

Mr. Biggins looked Robert up and down expectantly, and with a sigh, Robert produced a gold crown. "Will this help jog your memory?"

"Well, thank you, sir." Mr. Biggins pocketed the coin. "If you'll give me a moment, I'll write the address down for you."

After knocking on the kitchen door of the house next to Flora Rosa's, Lucy was let into the kitchen by the very woman she'd wanted to see. Marjory Wallis was a chatty girl who explained that she was alone in the house because her mistress was shopping in town and Cook had taken the day off.

"She'll return to cook dinner in the evening, if it's wanted, but knowing Miss Eileen, she won't be coming home until the small hours, anyway." Marjory winked at Lucy and patted the bench seat of the kitchen table. "She's an actress, and she goes to grand parties, and all kinds of dinners, and balls . . ."

Marjory paused to breathe. "Now would you like a cuppa? I bet that Mrs. Pell didn't offer you one. She's a mean old biddy. I don't miss working there at all—except for the extra pay, and that Miss Flora was so kind and sweet to everyone."

She filled the kettle and set it on the stove. Lucy resigned herself to drinking more tea, which in her current condition was somewhat burdensome.

"I want to be an actress one day," Marjorie confessed. "Although I'm not beautiful like Miss Flora and Miss Eileen, I do have a good singing voice, and I can dance."

Lucy swallowed back her desire to advise Marjory to stay in her current position and merely smiled.

"Were you surprised when Miss Flora left so suddenly?"

"Well, yes, seeing as she'd only just settled in with Viscount Gravely, and she seemed so happy and grateful to be under his protection." Marjory paused to place a jug of milk on the table. "She told me once that she felt safe for the first time in ages."

"And then she just left?" Lucy waited as Marjory half-filled the teapot that sat next to the kettle and brought it over. "Did she seem upset before that?"

Marjory sat opposite, her expression worried. "She was certainly upset about something. I found her crying in the parlor one day." She grimaced. "I couldn't help but hear there had been an argument going on earlier."

"Between her and Viscount Gravely?"

"It was hard to tell from the kitchen, but it did sound like him." Marjory poured the tea. "He was telling her she was stupid, and that she was imagining things. *Mr.* Gravely came around to see her later, and she said he was very kind to her indeed." Marjory laughed. "In truth, I think she saw more of the Gravely brothers than she did their father."

"Oh dear." Lucy added lots of milk to her tea and sipped politely. "Perhaps things had soured between her and the viscount, and she was thinking of moving on."

"That's what everyone thinks, but . . ." Marjory gripped

her hands together on the table. "Where is she? If she had a new man to flaunt, why isn't she back at work in the theater?"

"Perhaps she feels it is too soon to show she has changed . . . allegiances?" Lucy suggested.

"But for an actress, such notoriety would bring the public to see her in droves," Marjory replied. "She'd be even more in demand and more famous than ever."

"I hadn't thought of that," Lucy admitted.

"I'm worried about her, ma'am." Marjory met Lucy's gaze straight on. "She always said that if she ever did leave Viscount Gravely, she would take me with her, and I haven't heard a word." She paused. "I *did* wonder whether she'd gone back to *Mr.* Gravely, and that's why she'd gone to ground, but I doubt the viscount would've put up with that!"

Lucy considered what to say next. Should she tell Marjory the truth or leave things as they were? As the maid obviously liked to chat, telling her that Flora was dead might spread the news back to Mrs. Pell and complicate matters even further.

"Did you ever meet a woman called Polly Carter at Miss Flora's?" Lucy asked.

Marjory sipped her tea, her gaze sliding past Lucy's toward the kitchen door as if she was imagining someone entering. "Yes, she sometimes came back with Miss Flora from the theater to fit her costumes. Do you know her?"

"In truth, I am looking for her. I have a letter from her cousin Agnes that I am attempting to deliver. I had hoped that Polly was staying with Miss Flora, as she has not been home to see her mother recently." Lucy paused. "I don't suppose you know where Polly might be staying?"

"I don't, ma'am, but if I see her, I'll be sure to tell her that someone is looking for her."

"I would appreciate that." Lucy offered Marjorie her card. "I will be returning home in a day or so and would hate to miss her."

Lucy took her leave of Marjory and walked back down the quiet alleyway in deep thought. Flora had been arguing with someone just before she'd left and had confessed to being worried about something. Apparently, Viscount Gravely had just gone along with the general impression that she'd left him for another man.

Had he really not known that his mistress had disappeared completely? Robert had met the viscount and his family and hadn't been convinced that they were ignorant of Flora's death. But how would they have known about a murder in Kurland St. Mary unless someone from their household had been present when it occurred?

"Ah, there you are, my dear." Robert hailed her from the entrance to the livery. "Are you ready to leave? I have a lot to tell you."

He helped her up into the carriage and shut the door, leaving them in relative privacy. Lucy sank back into the seat, aware that her feet were hurting and that she really did need to sleep . . .

The next thing she knew, a burly footman was carrying her up to her room while Betty drew the curtains and pulled back the bedclothes. Robert appeared briefly at her side.

"I'll see you at dinner, my love."

She grabbed his hand. "But I have so much to share with you!"

He smiled and kissed her fingers. "It will keep. I have a lot to tell you, too."

Dinner at the Harringtons proceeded in its usual fashion, with excellent food and clever conversation—something Robert enjoyed participating in but didn't miss in his own home on a daily basis. He planned to visit the address Mr. Biggins had given to him on the following morning, speak to the Gravelys again, and leave for Kurland St. Mary the day after. Like Lucy, he was missing his son and his home too much to stay away for much longer. He also had a sense that the mystery behind Flora's death was rapidly becoming clearer.

He pictured her beautiful face as he sipped his port. From all appearances, she had done little to deserve her fate, and the person who had ended her life ought to suffer for it. Jealousy was rarely becoming in anyone, and killing the object of your supposed love? Something he could never fathom at all . . .

He looked down the long table toward his wife, who was conversing amiably with her dinner partner. She did look well, and his fears about her current condition receded somewhat. He might admit to being slightly overprotective of Lucy, but she did have a remarkable ability to find herself in dangerous situations.

Penelope Fletcher appeared to be enjoying herself immensely at the dinner party. She had gathered a small circle of respectful admirers around her since renewing her acquaintance with the ton, something his friend Patrick appeared to find amusing rather than worrying. Like Flora, she was a beautiful woman. Robert was glad she'd decided he wasn't good enough to marry her, but he was still rather perplexed as to why Patrick seemed so happy with her.

In fairness, Penelope had chosen to give up her dreams of London society and live in a small village with an Irish doctor who was unlikely to ever make more than a comfortable living. Idly, Robert wondered what would've happened if Flora and Penelope's lives had been reversed. Would Flora have succeeded in marrying a duke, and would Penelope have allowed herself to become a man's mistress or striven to be the best actress in London? He suspected they would both have found a way to succeed on their own terms, as did most resourceful women.

He reminded himself that Flora had reached high and was now dead. Perhaps Penelope's decision to embrace love instead of status had been a wiser choice after all . . .

Robert sipped his wine and helped himself to more fish.

The earl of Harrington had approached him earlier in the evening about a potential opening for a seat he controlled in parliament. He'd offered it to Robert with the assurance that he would not dictate matters of policy on most matters, as he believed their interests were already well aligned. Lucy could have told her uncle that was not the case, as Robert truly wished to address the inequalities in the current voting system and would, if given the chance, probably vote to abolish his own seat.

But it was something to think about and discuss with Lucy when they returned home. At the moment, all he wanted was for Flora's murderer to be brought to justice. And in his opinion, returning to Kurland St. Mary would help greatly with that matter.

At a signal from the countess, the ladies rose from their seats and left the dining room, leaving the men to their port and conversation. Robert extracted a cigarillo from his case and prepared to sit back and listen to the latest political scandal while his wife enjoyed her tea. If he did intend to take up a seat in the House of Commons, he should, perhaps, pay better attention to current affairs.

He got up to find a light for his cigarillo. A commotion in the entrance hall caught his attention, and he walked over to the door to observe what was going on. There was an older man dressed in an ill-fitting coat, tricorn hat, and white stock tie waving a book in the face of the usually unflappable Harrington butler.

"I demand to see that woman now!"

"Lady Kurland is not at home to the likes of you, sir!" the butler raised his voice to match his opponents. "Now, if you won't leave, I will call the Watch."

Robert quietly closed the door into the dining room behind him and advanced into the hall.

"Is something the matter?"

The butler turned to him. "Not at all, sir. This . . . gentleman is just leaving."

Robert regarded the red-faced man. "What do you want with Lady Kurland?"

"She's here, isn't she?" The man shoved a card under Robert's nose. "She gave this to my wife."

Robert raised his gaze to the man's angry face. "Who are you, exactly, sir?"

"I'm Mr. Carter. Polly's father."

"Ah." Robert turned to the butler. "Would you find somewhere for me to speak to Mr. Carter, and ask my wife to join us?"

"Are you quite sure about this, Sir Robert?" the butler asked. "Because—"

"Quite sure," Robert said firmly. "Please lead the way."

He followed the stiff-backed butler down one of the corridors that led toward the servants' stairs until he opened a door into a cramped office that belonged to the earl of Harrington's secretary.

"I will fetch Lady Kurland, sir, and if you permit, I will ask one of my footmen to wait outside this door in case you need anything." The butler bowed.

"As you wish." Robert lit one of the candles from the embers of the fire, banked up the coals, and lit the remaining candles in the candelabra.

"Please make yourself comfortable, Mr. Carter."

"There's no comfort on this earth, Mr. Kurland, that will cover the stench of sin."

"I beg to differ, sir, but please remain standing if you wish."

Mr. Carter glared at him, one hand pressing the leather-clad book to his chest as they waited for Lucy to join them. Robert didn't bother to fill the silence with polite chatter. He had a sense that Mr. Carter would not respond well, and he had no desire to enrage the man further before he knew why he'd turned up at the Harringtons'.

Lucy came in, her gaze moving instantly from Robert to Mr. Carter, who scowled at her.

"You must be Mr. Carter, Agnes's uncle. She is such a

credit to your family." Lucy said pleasantly. "I will make sure to tell her that we saw you while we were in town. Do you have any message you wish me to pass onto her?"

"I didn't come here to talk about Agnes."

"Then why did you come?" Robert asked.

"Because she," Mr. Carter pointed at Lucy, "has been upsetting my wife."

"How so?"

"By coming around, asking questions, stirring things up that don't need to see the light of day." He frowned at Robert. "You, sir, should have your wife under better control."

Robert's lips twitched, but he didn't reply. He was fairly certain Lucy was perfectly capable of defending herself.

"All I did, Mr. Carter, was ask your wife if she had seen her own daughter," Lucy stated.

"Well, she ain't," Mr. Carter still addressed his remarks to Robert. "And she isn't going to be seeing her for a long time."

Lucy stiffened, and Robert leaned forward, took her fisted hand in his, and gently drew her back to stand in front of him.

"Why is that, Mr. Carter?"

"Because Polly came around today to see her and said she's leaving London for good because of you lot."

"Because of us?" Robert frowned. "I hardly see the logic of such a statement when we have never even met her."

"She's leaving because you have been going around town asking after her and making her afraid."

"Afraid of what?" Robert persisted. "We merely wish to deliver a letter to her from her cousin Agnes and ascertain that she is well. What's the harm in that?"

"Because Polly does not need your attention or that of any aristocrat!" Mr. Carter snapped. "I knew allowing her to work with those whores and posturers at the theater would turn out badly. And I was right. Her reputation is ruined."

"Simply because she worked at a theater? How small-minded of you, sir," Robert replied.

"I know my Bible, Sir Robert. She has consorted with sinners and now must pay the price by being separated from her family."

"I thought she already was," Robert said, and continued by asking, "Didn't you make her leave because she was friendly with Flora Rosa?"

Mr. Carter's color grew noticeably redder. "Polly was brought up in a godly home! She only needed to repent of her wickedness, and she would've been allowed back into the fold."

"Then seeing as she obviously hasn't repented and would rather leave London than come back to live at home, I hardly see what this has to do with me or my wife." Robert glared at Mr. Carter. "You are at fault, and you chose to come here merely to vent your spleen on an innocent party, my wife, because you are angry that your daughter disobeyed *you.*"

He stalked over to the door. "We have nothing to apologize for." He opened it wide. "I bid you good night, sir."

For a moment, Mr. Carter locked gazes with Robert, and then, with a last indignant sniff, he turned and walked away, his nose in the air. Robert beckoned to the footman stationed outside door.

"Escort Mr. Carter to the front door, please. And make sure he leaves."

"Yes, Sir Robert."

He turned to see his wife sink down into one of the chairs and regarded her from the doorway.

"Are you all right?"

"Yes, but what on earth was that all about?" Lucy asked.

"I'm not quite sure, but we did learn one important thing." He sauntered back toward her. "Polly Carter isn't dead, and that, my dear, was well worth hearing."

Chapter 13

Lucy plaited her hair into a single braid and climbed into bed to wait for Robert to emerge from the dressing room. After dealing with Mr. Carter, they had parted company again and gone to complete their social duties. It was now almost midnight, and Lucy, who was not used to keeping town hours, was almost ready to fall asleep again.

Robert emerged from the dressing room wrapped in his silk banyan and got into bed beside her.

"Did you know your uncle was going to offer me the opportunity to represent his interests in parliament?"

"He did mention it, but I thought it would be best for him to approach you directly," Lucy said.

"How very diplomatic of you."

She smiled at him. "What did you say?"

"I said I would consider my options." Robert settled back against the headboard. "The thought of having to live in London while the House is in session doesn't appeal to me much."

"It's not a place I would choose to raise our children, either," Lucy said. "Until they are older, I would probably not accompany you."

"Which would make for a very lonely existence." Robert kissed her cheek. "I miss my son more than I anticipated."

Lucy savored his unguarded response. He was not a man who expressed his emotions easily, and the fact that he was even admitting that he missed Ned was worthy of note. She yawned again and hastily covered her mouth.

"Do you want me to blow the candles out?" Robert inquired.

"Not yet. I'd like to tell you what happened today with Marjory, the parlor maid, and review the possibilities about Flora's murderer."

'Please go ahead."

His somewhat smug smile was unexpected, as was the way he leaned back on the pillows and invited her with an extravagant gesture to continue.

"Marjory was the chatty sort and told me quite a lot about the goings-on in Flora Rosa's house. She also raised an interesting question. If Flora had found a new protector, why wasn't she flaunting him at the theater to enhance her reputation?"

"Because someone had murdered her and left her body in a ditch in Kurland St. Mary?"

Lucy ignored her husband's attempt at sarcasm. "Marjory also said that Flora was still close to Viscount Gravely's sons."

For the first time, Robert looked thoughtful. "Which disputes their account of hating her somewhat."

"Exactly." Lucy nodded. "Marjory wondered whether Flora had gone back to Neville, and *that* was why Viscount Gravely was so angry about what had happened."

"I definitely don't think Viscount Gravely would've approved of her taking up with his son again after he'd spent all that money on her."

"Perhaps he didn't approve?" Lucy faced Robert. "Perhaps he decided to teach Flora a lesson?"

"And pop down to Kurland St. Mary and kill her? I think Mr. Jarvis or one of the village gossips might have noticed if a viscount had appeared in their midst." Robert countered.

"But *what* other man?" Lucy frowned. "I agree with Marjory. If there was someone else, I'm fairly sure we would have found him by now. Don't you think he might be wondering where she's gone as well?"

"You're also assuming that Viscount Gravely somehow knew Flora had switched places with Polly Carter and taken her job at Kurland Hall. How do you think he would know that?" Robert asked.

"Seeing as Polly is doing everything she can to stay away from us, maybe she told him." Lucy suggested.

She searched his face, but he seemed remarkably unperturbed by all her suggestions.

"What is it?" she demanded. "What aren't you telling me?"

"These are all very interesting theories, my dear, but I have an even better one." He grinned infuriatingly at her.

Lucy raised her eyebrows and sat back. "Then do, pray, tell."

"Mr. Biggins wasn't the first Gravely employee to drive Flora Rosa around."

"So?"

"The original driver was a man named Bert, who quarreled with Flora and was replaced when she complained about him to Viscount Gravely."

"*Our* Bert?"

"Apparently so." Robert's smile disappeared. "One might begin to come to the conclusion that our journey to London was wasted, and that we had the culprit safely locked up in Mr. Jarvis's cellar all along."

Lucy stared at him. "Are you quite certain it is Bert Speers who worked for Viscount Gravely?"

"I believe so. Mr. Biggins described him to me quite accurately. I'll attempt to confirm it tomorrow when I speak to Viscount Gravely."

"But what if Viscount Gravely sent Bert to murder Flora?"

"I suppose that is possible." To her annoyance, he didn't sound in the least bit convinced. "But surely Bert has already half-convicted himself. He was seen with Flora, and he admits to manhandling her. Maybe, for once, this is far more straightforward than we realized. Bert falls in love with Flora, he oversteps his place, and she complains about him to Viscount Gravely, who removes him from his position. Angry that he has been denied access to his "one true love," Bert decides to follow her down to Kurland St. Mary and kill her."

"But—"

Robert held up a finger. "Will you at least concede that I might be right? You do tend to overcomplicate things."

She regarded him in silence, her arms folded over her chest. "I just like to make sure that I ask all the questions, even the silly ones."

"You certainly do."

"And sometimes I am right to do so." She raised her chin.

"I can't argue with that." Robert agreed, mollifying her slightly, and then ruined it by patting her cheek. "I promise that I will speak to Viscount Gravely tomorrow and make sure that Bert Speers was employed by him. Will that suffice to make you believe the matter is settled?"

"What about Polly?"

He frowned. "What about her?"

"Aren't you worried about what has become of her?"

"I assume that after we leave London and stop attempting to speak to her, she will resume her life as usual."

Lucy sniffed. "I think you are wrong."

"And I think you are making mountains out of molehills." He kissed her nose. "Shall we agree to disagree and go to sleep? We will have a busy day tomorrow. Not only must I speak to Viscount Gravely, but Mr. Biggins gave me the address of a place where he took Flora's possessions when she left."

"What?" Lucy sat bolt upright again. "Why didn't you mention this earlier?"

"Because I didn't want you to get all excited about something that has no bearing on our investigation."

"Only if your scenario is correct," Lucy reminded him.

He started to blow out the candles beside the bed. "I'm not saying we can't go and look, so don't get too cross with me."

Lucy lay down on her side and allowed Robert to put his arm around her. She feared her mind was wrestling with too many possibilities for her to sleep.

"Ouch," Robert murmured against her ear. "The little blighter just kicked me."

"Serves you right," she whispered back. He chuckled, and his arm tightened around her

Her eyes closed despite her worries, and she smiled her way into sleep.

After instructing Betty to let Lucy sleep for as long as she needed, Robert tiptoed out of the bedchamber, ate a hurried breakfast, and walked around the back of the house to the Harrington mews to borrow a horse. He'd willingly take Lucy to Flora's other address, but he saw no reason to inflict Viscount Gravely on her. He also hated riding so much that the mere thought of getting on the back of a horse was making him feel physically sick.

He reminded himself that it was only a short distance to Grosvenor Square, and he needed an excuse to visit the Gravely stables before he confronted the master of the house. The Harrington groom was rather surprised when he asked for the oldest, most docile horse in the stables, but he was far too well trained to ask awkward questions.

After two minutes of contemplating getting up on the back of the horse and failing to execute his plan, Robert decided he was bloody well going to walk his steed the quarter mile to the Gravely House and be damned to anyone who saw him. He could always claim that the horse had gone lame.

When Robert arrived at the Gravely House mews, he waited while his horse was led away and asked to speak to the head coachman.

Five minutes later, he was on his way up to the house. He hadn't sent notice of his arrival and hoped to catch the viscount before he left home. From his quick survey of the stables, none of the carriages or horses had been absent, which he assumed meant that all the Gravely men were present.

He knocked on the front door, and the Indian butler let him into the hall before asking his business.

"Good morning. I'd like to speak to Viscount Gravely."

"He is not available to callers yet, Sir Robert. Would you like to leave your card?"

"I'd prefer to see him immediately. Can you go and tell him I'm here?"

The butler frowned. "Viscount Gravely is not well, sir. He is still in bed."

"And I would still like to speak him." Robert held the butler's gaze. "I'm leaving town tomorrow, so it is imperative that I see him on a matter of great importance."

"What's going on?"

Robert turned as Trevor Gravely came down the staircase dressed for a morning ride, a whip dangling from one of his hands.

"Good morning, Mr. Trevor." The butler bowed. "This gentleman wishes to see your father, sir. I am trying to explain that the viscount is not well enough to receive visitors."

Trevor stared at Robert. "Is this about that woman?"

"Yes, I just need to clarify a couple of points with your father, and then I promise I will leave him in peace."

"I'll take him up," Trevor announced to the butler.

"Don't worry, Ahuja. I'll take complete responsibility for this."

Robert handed over his hat and cane to the reluctant butler, and followed Trevor up the stairs.

"My father is awake and eating his breakfast. I spoke to him just before I came down. I'm not sure why Ahuja didn't want you to see him."

Robert was fairly certain that Viscount Gravely wouldn't want to see him but said nothing as Trevor knocked on the door and went in.

"Father? Sir Robert Kurland is here to see you."

Trevor stepped aside, allowing Robert to see that the viscount was propped up on his pillows in his large bed, reading the paper. His expression when he saw Robert was not encouraging,

"I thought we had agreed to part company on this matter, Sir Robert."

Robert shrugged. "I don't remember agreeing to that. I asked you to let me know if you had any further thoughts about the murder of your mistress."

"I don't." The viscount looked past Robert to his son, who was leaning against the door frame. "Tell Ahuja to escort Sir Robert out."

Trevor sighed. "Father, just let him speak, and then I promise I will escort him out myself. This attempt to pretend that everything is fine is ridiculous."

The viscount slammed his glass down on the tray with such force that the liquid inside spilled over the top. "If I am going to be subjected to Sir Robert's company, then you will leave us in peace!"

Trevor held up his hands. "As you wish."

He left the room, and Robert turned his attention to the man in the bed.

"Do you have a man named Bert Speers currently in your employ?"

There was a flicker of interest in the viscount's eyes. "No."

"Did you ever have such a man?"

"It's possible that he once worked in my stables. He left a while ago."

"Why was that?"

"I don't think that's any of your business, sir."

"It is when he has turned up in my village and is currently incarcerated in the cellars of my local inn. I am the local magistrate, and I can assure you that I take accusations of murder very seriously indeed."

The viscount put down his knife and carefully wiped his thin lips with his napkin.

"What an interesting coincidence that Speers turned up in Kurland St. Mary."

"Indeed." Robert tried to hold the viscount's gaze. "I understand that Bert drove Flora Rosa's carriage for a while."

"Did he?" The viscount raised an eyebrow. "I leave such piddling matters to my head coachman and butler to manage."

"I've already spoken to your coachman. He confirmed that Bert Speers worked for you, and that he drove Flora Rosa for a while before she asked for him to be replaced."

"If you know all this, why are you bothering me with this matter?"

Robert took a moment to gather his rapidly diminishing patience. "Do you not care that your mistress was found murdered?"

"She chose to leave me." The viscount looked up at Robert. "What happened to her after that is hardly my concern, is it?"

"From what I understand, she left because she was afraid of someone."

"Then perhaps she should have stayed and trusted that I would take care of her."

"Perhaps she felt you would not believe her concerns." Robert countered.

"She was an actress, Sir Robert; she often elaborated her misfortunes. Her whole life was based on dramatic notions and silly fantasies."

"I'll wager she *did* tell you she was afraid, and you chose not to believe her. She ran away to save herself and ended up dead in a ditch anyway."

His companion shrugged. "I suppose you might put it that way."

Robert was way past being pleasant now. "Or it might even be simpler. She was afraid of *you*, ran away, and you had her hunted down and killed."

The viscount gave a slow smile. "Now who is dealing in silly fantasies?" He nodded toward the door. "I suggest that as you have asked your impudent questions and heard my answers, then you will leave quietly before I call for assistance."

Robert studied the old man for a long moment before he took a step away from the bed.

"I see it was a mistake to assume you would be concerned about the fate of the woman you bought and paid for."

"Surely objects that allow themselves to be sold are hardly worth your anger or your attention, Sir Robert?" The viscount pushed the breakfast tray away from him. "Are you going to ask me for money to pay for her funeral next? The jewelry I lavished on her should easily pay for the most extravagant of funerals."

Robert inclined his head an icy inch. "I wouldn't think to bother you with such niceties, my lord. Before her death, Flora worked in my house and is, therefore, my responsibility. Good day to you."

"And to you."

Robert had almost reached the door before the viscount spoke once more.

"If you appear on my doorstep again, Sir Robert, I will instruct my butler not to let you in the house."

Robert looked over his shoulder. "I doubt I will ever

have reason to seek you out again, my lord. In truth, if I saw you in the street, I would probably cross it to avoid having to acknowledge your existence."

To his chagrin, the viscount smiled again. "As I am near death, your scorn does not bother me in the slightest. When you reach my age, sir, you too might be willing to close your eyes and do whatever is necessary to avoid such . . . a minor storm in your continued existence."

"As I would never consider the murder of anyone a 'minor inconvenience,' my lord, I'll beg to differ."

Robert yanked open the door with some force, startling Trevor Gravely, who was leaning against the wall in the corridor outside.

"Thank you for allowing me to speak to your father." Robert set off down the stairs, Trevor in pursuit. "You have my address. If you wish to come down to Kurland St. Mary to identify Flora Rosa's body, please let me know. You will be more than welcome to stay at Kurland Hall."

"Thank you, Sir Robert." Trevor managed to get ahead of Robert when he stopped to retrieve his hat and cane, and opened the front door. "Please forgive my father. He is not well."

"He—" Robert paused. There was no point in reviling the man to his own son. "It was good of him to see me when he was still abed."

"He was very worried when Neville became involved with Flora."

"Worried enough to ask her to be his mistress?"

Trevor grimaced. "I know it does sound rather odd, but Neville could be . . . rather intense when he imagined he was in love. I suspect Father thought he would save Neville a lot of unnecessary grief."

"Are you suggesting that Flora might have been afraid of your brother and asked your father to help out by offering her his protection?"

"Good Lord, no!" Trevor gaped at him. "I'd never even

thought of that! I just mean that Neville tends to fall in love easily and can become rather obsessed, leading to . . . misunderstandings. My father might have believed it was his duty to step in and quash all his hopes. Neville was perfectly fine about it, by the way. He even *thanked* Father for stopping him from making a fool of himself."

"And instead allowed your father to be the fool?"

"You don't understand," Trevor said earnestly. "Father showed Neville what Flora was really like—a woman who wanted as much money as she could accumulate before her looks and mediocre talent faded."

"And Neville appreciated that."

Trevor grinned. "It took a while, but, eventually, yes, he did."

Trevor followed Robert all the way to the stables, his expression anxious as he attempted to apologize yet again for his father and brother. Robert didn't interrupt or offer his own opinion of the man. If Viscount Gravely truly were dying, his judgment would soon be in the hands of a far greater power than Robert's.

He finally managed to shake Trevor off as his horse was brought around. He thanked the groom and walked his own patient steed out of the stables and around the corner. As he walked back toward Portland Square, his hand tightly gripping the bridle, he wondered why Viscount Gravely had even bothered to find a mistress when he was so ill? Had he simply done it to spite his youngest son? Or had he tried to teach the lad a lesson, as Trevor thought? It seemed unlikely, but perhaps the viscount had no real relationship with either of his sons after having been abroad for most of their lives, and treated them accordingly.

Had he feared that Flora would extort too much money out of the seemingly gullible Neville, and put a stop to it by offering her more immediate gains? A man knowing he was near death might make such a decision to safeguard his son's inheritance, even if it made his son hate him. And if the viscount truly had nothing to fear except death, maybe he would have stooped low enough to order Flora's demise.

Robert firmly reeled in his imagination and reminded himself of Bert Speer's guilt. When he returned to Kurland St. Mary and sent Bert off to trial at the assizes, the truth would surely emerge.

He arrived back at Portland Square and went up the back stairs to his bedchamber to change into a less damp coat. There was no sign of Lucy, who had probably gone down to breakfast. He was eager to join her, his morning activities having made him hungrier than usual.

He put on his second-best coat, made sure his boots were presentable, and went down again, this time using the main staircase.

"Sir Robert?"

He was hailed from the hall by Penelope Fletcher and walked over to speak to her. She looked as beautiful as ever and, from a cursory glance of her fashionable clothes, was the happy recipient of a lot of Lucy's aunt's castoffs.

"Yes, Mrs. Fletcher?"

"Have you decided when you intend to return to Kurland St. Mary?"

"I intend to leave by the end of the week."

She frowned. "So quickly?"

"I didn't plan to stay this long, ma'am, but needs must."

"Is Lucy worn out with it all? She's never been entirely comfortable with the position she now holds, has she?"

"She seems in good spirits." Robert paused. "Why? Do you think otherwise?"

"Not at all, I was just wondering if that was the reason you wanted to leave so quickly."

"I am quite certain, if you wish to stay another week, ma'am, that the Harrington family would not object."

"Not *me*." She made a face. "Patrick is enjoying himself so much that I hate to tear him away. *I* want to go home and see my son."

Aware that he might have grossly misjudged the depth of her maternal affection, Robert hastened to reassure her.

"If your husband wishes to stay, I'm sure that it could be arranged."

She touched his sleeve. "If you could speak to the earl about the matter, I would *greatly* appreciate it. I do not think it is my place to do so."

"As soon as I have arranged my own travel plans, I will certainly ask the earl if Dr. Fletcher can continue to be his guest for a week."

"Thank you." She smiled at Robert. "I am already looking forward to spending the journey back to Kurland St. Mary in the company of you and Lucy."

Robert walked into the breakfast room. The thought of being cooped up in a carriage with Penelope for several hours a day without the buffer of her husband between them was not something he would ever wish for. His wife would not be very happy about it, either.

"Ah! There you are, Robert." Lucy looked over at him. She was alone in the vast room. "Have you eaten?"

"Not yet." He piled a plate high with victuals and came to sit beside her. Unlike many women she didn't immediately pepper him with questions about where he had been and allowed him to eat his fill before he started talking. "I went to see Viscount Gravely."

She studied him for a moment before she poured him some coffee. "From the expression on your face, I assume it didn't go well?"

"He's an awfully unpleasant man, Lucy." Robert sawed through a piece of gammon. "I cannot understand for the life of me why Flora decided to take him up on his offer."

"Money?"

"So everyone insists, but we both met Flora, and I don't know about you, my dear, but she didn't come across as the grasping sort to me."

"No, she didn't," Lucy said thoughtfully. "But one can't

forget that she was apparently a very good actress. Maybe she fooled us both."

Robert sighed and swallowed a mouthful of ham. "Mayhap she did. She does seem to have meant many different things to different people."

"None of which justifies her murder," Lucy reminded him. "Do you still intend to visit the address Mr. Biggins gave you?"

"Yes, indeed." He ate an egg and another slice of gammon, and immediately started to feel better. "We can go as soon as you are ready."

Chapter 14

The address took them out of the east side of London toward Bethnal Green, which was not an area Lucy was familiar with. Dr. Fletcher had offered to accompany them as he had been there earlier in the week visiting a friend who worked in one of the hospitals established in that region.

"I'm not sure why Flora would have ended up here." Robert frowned as he looked out of the window at the rows of small houses and increasingly narrow streets.

"Perhaps her family came from here," Dr. Fletcher suggested.

"I don't think she ever knew her family," Robert said. "She grew up in an orphanage and was put into service when she reached the age of fourteen."

"There is a large orphanage right next to the hospital, and a workhouse," Dr. Fletcher said. "I have visited them all and struggle to believe that any child emerged from that unhealthy environment alive."

"If she grew up here, perhaps she still has friends whom she trusts?" Lucy asked. "She told *me* that she came from a large family, but she told Mr. Frobisher something completely different. One has to wonder whether she picked up her skills with children helping to tend the smaller ones at the orphanage."

"That sounds logical." Robert nodded. "I expect she was more likely to lie to you about this particular matter because she wanted to be seen as competent with children than she was to lie to Mr. Frobisher at the Prince of Wales."

Lucy peered out of the carriage window as the natural lighting gradually disappeared, displaced by tall rows of houses with slate roofs and large front windows. It was not a pleasant area or somewhere Lucy would ever like to live, and she pitied anyone who was forced to endure it.

Dr. Fletcher noticed where she was looking.

"The Huguenot refugees who built these houses were often weavers and lace makers who needed as much light as possible for their work—hence the large windows."

"Are there still many of these weavers around here?"

"Not that many." Dr. Fetcher grimaced. "The new factories arising in the north can produce a much higher volume of lace than any single person these days. Most of these houses have been divided into smaller living accommodations, with whole families squeezed into two rooms. It is not ideal."

Lucy could only nod in agreement.

"Which street are we going to?" Dr. Fletcher asked.

Robert consulted the piece of paper Mr. Biggins had given him. "Paradise Row. Do you know of it?"

"Only for another reason." Dr. Fletcher chuckled. "Mendoza lived there."

"Good Lord!" Robert stared at his friend. "Is this where he established his academy?"

"Apparently so."

Lucy poked Robert in the side. "Who is Mendoza?"

He looked down at her as if she were witless. "Daniel Mendoza, the boxer."

"I believe I have heard my father mention him," Lucy said cautiously. "He wrote *The Art of Boxing*."

Both men were now staring at her approvingly. She allowed herself a small congratulatory smile.

"My brother Anthony was always quoting the text."

"Well, it appears that Flora once lived on the same street as the great man himself," Dr. Fletcher said. "Perhaps even in the same house."

"We shall see about that," Robert muttered as the carriage finally came to a stop. "From the look of the place, one would need to be handy with one's fists simply to survive."

"As long as we stay together and don't show off any valuables, we should be fine," Dr. Fletcher said encouragingly.

"Unless you wish to stay in the carriage, my dear." Robert turned to Lucy.

She considered her choices. "I think I'd rather come with you than be left out here by myself."

"Then stay close behind me," Robert advised. "We'll let Dr. Fletcher bring up the rear."

Lucy allowed him to help her out of the carriage and stared up at the blackened stone façade of the small terraced cottage. It was at the end of the row, and a dark passageway to the left of the house presumably led to the rear. The street was choked with debris and filth. There was no garden or cast-iron fencing, and the front step touched the pavement.

Lucy had a sense that she was being watched but was unable to work out from where, as it felt as if a hundred pairs of eyes were fixed on her. As they approached the front door, the curtains twitched. Robert knocked loudly, but there was no reply. Dr. Fletcher stepped back, his gaze fixed on the upstairs windows.

"There is definitely someone up there," Dr. Fletcher said. "Perhaps I should go around to the rear of the house while you stay here?"

"I'll go," Robert said firmly. "If anything happens, make sure you get Lady Kurland to safety immediately."

"Robert—" Lucy reached out her hand, but it was too late. He was already moving away from her down the alley.

Robert opened the back gate of the small walled and cobbled yard, and went inside. The back door was ajar, and he went toward it, pausing to open it more widely, and then closed it behind him.

Someone clattered down the stairs toward him. "Is that you, Marj? I'm almost ready to go." There was a bumping sound of a case being dragged behind them. "There's someone at the front door. I don't like the look of this at all!"

As the woman came into the kitchen, Robert opened his mouth to speak and was met with a screeching sound.

"Bloody *hell*!"

A second later, he was engulfed in a load of clothing that temporarily blinded him, and he staggered against the table. By the time he'd unraveled himself from the stockings and petticoats, he was alone, and the back door was wide open again.

"Devil take it!" Robert growled as he stomped through to the front of the house to open the door.

His wife and doctor stared at him apprehensively as he invited them inside the house.

"What happened?" Lucy finally asked.

"Someone threw their clothing at me and escaped out the back."

"So I can see." Lucy stepped forward and removed a gauzy silk stocking that clung to his shoulder. Dr. Fletcher was openly chuckling now. "Did you see who it was?"

"Only for a second. It was a dark-haired woman. She barely entered the kitchen before she screamed and threw everything she was holding in my face." Robert rubbed a hand over his jaw. "She thought I was someone called Marj. When she realized her mistake, she reacted accordingly."

"Marj?" Lucy asked. "I'll wager that's the parlor maid

who used to work for Mrs. Pell. She knew Polly, and she was very fond of Flora."

"She said she was ready to go, and I believe she had her bonnet on, which is why I don't have a particularly strong memory of her face." Robert frowned. "One has to suspect that I finally got to meet Polly Carter, my dear. She certainly looks more like Agnes than Flora did."

"On the assumption that Polly won't be coming back, shall we take the opportunity to look around the house?" Lucy asked. She pointed at the corner of the kitchen, where there was an open trunk. "I assume this was where the clothing thrown at you was supposed to go."

Lucy went over to examine the contents of the trunk. "There is no carrier address, which is a shame, because that might have helped us determine where Polly intended to fly away to next." She looked up at Robert. "Why don't you take Dr. Fletcher and search the rest of the house while I stay here in case Marjory does actually arrive?"

"As you wish," Robert said stiffly, aware that he still had his dignity after the mortification of being downed by an armful of clothes.

While Robert and Dr. Fletcher stomped off to deal with the rest of the house, Lucy took the opportunity to tidy the fallen clothes and place them in the trunk. Despite the seriousness of the occasion, the sight of her husband festooned in women's stockings would stay with her for a long time. She fought a smile as she closed the lid of the trunk and looked around the small kitchen.

The fire was out, and the whole place had a look of emptiness that didn't surprise Lucy. Polly knew that she was being searched for and that eventually someone would end up at the house and had already made plans to move on. But why? Why was she so afraid to meet with them?

"Afternoon, Polly! Sorry I'm a bit late, but—" Marjory came in through the back door and stopped with a gasp when she saw Lucy sitting at the table. "What the bloody hell are you doing here?"

"I might ask the same of you." Lucy rose from the table and went to shut the back door. "You didn't mention that you knew where Polly Carter was living all along."

"What have you done with her?" Marjorie demanded, her hands on her hips.

"Nothing. She left before we could speak to her," Lucy said.

"I don't believe you." Marjory's gaze narrowed. "She said that if you found her, she'd be dead in a minute."

"What a peculiar thing to say." Lucy blinked at her. "I am hardly likely to kill the woman I wanted to take on in my nursery."

"Polly *lied* to you."

"I am well aware of that." Lucy remained with her back to the door, preventing Marjory from escaping. "I'm still not sure why all this subterfuge was necessary."

"Because Miss Flora needed somewhere safe to go, and Polly offered her the chance to take her job." Marjory's lip wobbled. "But Flora wasn't safe there, either, was she? Which means that you and the man she was fleeing were obviously in this together."

"Which man?"

Marjory glared at her. "You *know!*"

Lucy rubbed her temple with her fingers and prayed for patience. "If I knew who had killed Flora, I would immediately inform the authorities and have him apprehended. How do *you* know Flora is dead?"

Marjory opened and closed her mouth and then glared at Lucy. "Polly told me."

"And Polly immediately assumed that my family and the murderer were somehow in cahoots?" Lucy shook her head. "She couldn't be more mistaken. Sir Robert and I are only anxious to speak to Polly to discover who killed Flora so that we can get justice for her."

"Polly said—"

Lucy held up her hand. "Polly is mistaken. When you next see her, please tell her that she has nothing to fear from Sir Robert or me. If she had bothered to speak to us herself, she would've discovered that none of this ridiculousness was necessary."

"But—"

"Please stop arguing with me." It was Lucy's turn to interrupt Marjory. "I am tired. I wish to go home, see my son, and settle down to await the arrival of my new baby. Instead, I am traipsing around London trying to help someone who is convinced I wish to murder her!"

Marjory eased toward the table and pulled out a chair.

"You sound a little overwrought, ma'am. Why don't you sit down and put your feet up?"

Lucy was no longer in the mood to be placated. "I'll sit down when I return to my carriage, thank you. Has Polly been living here all the time?"

"When Flora moved her belongings from Viscount Gravely's house, Polly came here to take care of everything," Marjory said. "She expected Flora to come back to London quite quickly, but then she heard about what happened, and she was afraid."

"Of me, apparently," Lucy said. "Which is ridiculous, when she should have been afraid of whoever made Flora flee London. Who was that, by the way?"

Marjory grimaced. "If Polly knew, she certainly didn't tell me, and with everything that's been going on, I'm beginning to be glad about that."

"You should be," Lucy said severely. "Who owns this place?"

"The Gravely family own the land and the houses." Marjory seemed to have decided that Lucy was no longer a threat and was almost back to her chatty self. "Flora and Polly knew the bloke who rents this place. He let them stay here for as long as they wanted if they helped out with the rent."

"Have you met this man?"

"No, ma'am. Polly did say that Mr. Gravely came down the street once with the rent collector, and she and Flora hid upstairs until he left."

Marjory jumped as male voices echoed in the hall and glanced nervously up the stairs. Lucy hastened to reassure her.

"My husband and our family physician are here with me. You have nothing to fear."

Marjory didn't look convinced, her gaze moving between Lucy, the back door, and the corridor that led straight through to the front.

"If you want to go and find out what has happened to Polly, please do so," Lucy offered, stepping away from the door. "Tell her that we mean her no harm and only wish to help."

"Yes, ma'am." Marjory hurried toward the door as if afraid that Lucy would change her mind. "I'll tell her. I promise."

"Well, I still think you should have made the girl stay until I was able to question her." Robert repeated his point as he took off his coat.

They'd left Bethnal Green and arrived back in Portland Square with time to dress for dinner and very little else. As it was their last evening in London, neither of them had wanted to disappoint their hosts by retiring early. The earl had extended an invitation to the Fletchers to stay on for another week, and Dr. Fletcher had accepted, which meant that Penelope would be traveling back with Robert and Lucy.

His wife was lying on the bed with her feet propped up on a cushion and one hand cradling the small mound of her stomach. Despite her obvious tiredness, she was still managing to be remarkably obstinate.

"Marjory would not have told you anything new. She was quite terrified at the thought of even meeting you."

"I would've done my best to set her at ease!" Robert protested.

"There was nothing more to say. I was more interested

in sending her after Polly to reassure the girl that neither of us had any intention of *murdering* her!"

"Polly sounds like a fool," Robert said. "Although why am I surprised? She is the one who thought up this ridiculous scheme to change places with an actress and foist that woman onto my household." He tore off his cravat and threw it onto the chair.

"We don't know who thought up the idea. It might have been Flora," Lucy objected. "Did you know that the house belongs to the Gravely family?"

"How could I if you didn't allow me to speak to Marjory?"

"Oh, Robert, will you please stop being difficult!" Lucy snapped. "It was far more useful for us to divide our time while we were at the house to gain as much information as possible."

Robert started on his cuff links. "The house was full of Flora's belongings. There were two bedrooms that had obviously been used by women, and one more masculine one. The man's room was still undisturbed."

"Were you able to find out anything about the man?"

"Only that he wasn't a gentleman. He had only one spare coat in the cupboard, and a single pair of good shoes." Robert wrapped his dressing gown around himself and sat on the chair facing Lucy on the bed. "Flora had an extensive wardrobe, but Polly's room was cleared out."

"Thank you." Lucy offered him a conciliatory smile. "One has to assume that Flora and Polly met this man through his connection with the Gravely family."

"I would agree with you, but one also has to ask why Flora fled from one Gravely-owned property to another."

"It doesn't make much sense, does it?" Lucy agreed. "Unless she thought Viscount Gravely would never imagine she'd stay that close."

"A double bluff?" He frowned. "Then I suppose it worked. We found Polly, not Viscount Gravely."

"Polly wasn't hiding from the viscount. She was hiding from *us*."

He registered the irritation in her voice.

"I find that as hard to believe as you do, my love." Getting up, he walked over and sat beside her on the bed. "You might be a little severe at times, but I've never considered you a murderer."

She reached for his hand. "I want to go home. Robert. I am sick and tired of this whole business." There was a catch in her voice that caught at his heart. "If the Gravelys and Polly do not wish to accept our help in solving this murder, we will do the right thing by Flora and bury her with dignity in Kurland St. Mary churchyard, and forget all about them."

"And let a murderer go free?" Robert asked.

She raised an eyebrow. "As you are convinced that we have the murderer locked up in the cellar of the Queen's Head, such matters will be resolved when he comes to trial."

Robert studied his wife's tired face. It was unlike her to admit defeat, and part of him was tempted to play devil's advocate, because the involvement of Viscount Gravelys in the matter had begun to concern him, too. But he wanted to take her back to Kurland Hall, see her reunited with their son and happy in her own home.

"Then we shall leave tomorrow and put all this behind us." Robert kissed her cheek. "Why don't you go to bed while I finish undressing?"

Chapter 15

"Ned!"

Lucy took off her bonnet, knelt on the floor, and opened her arms wide to allow her son to run into them. As soon as the carriage set her down at the front door of Kurland Hall, she'd gone straight up the stairs to the nursery.

"Did you bring me a present?" Ned asked as he kissed her face.

Behind him Anna chuckled. "Are you not pleased to see your mama?"

"Yes." Ned kissed her again, his dark blue gaze fixed on hers. "But I like presents."

Lucy rose to her feet with some difficulty and patted her son on the head. "When Betty has finished unpacking, I'm sure there will be something there for you. Why don't you go down and see if you can find your papa?"

In truth, she'd spent more of her time in London purchasing presents for Ned than looking at the latest fashions, and she could only hope he'd appreciate what she'd chosen.

"I'll take Francis down to Mrs. Fletcher, ma'am." Agnes came into the room, her expression gloomy, holding Penelope's son by the hand. "I've packed his things."

"Thank you, Agnes," Lucy said.

Ned ran off down the stairs, and Agnes followed, leaving Lucy with her sister.

"How has everything been in the nursery?" Lucy asked.

"Ned has been very well behaved." Anna smiled as Lucy took a seat beside the fire. "He missed you quite a lot more than you might imagine from his greeting."

"Did Agnes behave herself?"

"She did her work, and she was never unkind to Ned, but she hasn't exactly been a pleasure to deal with."

"In what way?" Lucy asked.

Anna shrugged. "She's just rather miserable."

"As well she should be after inflicting an actress on us instead of her cousin," Lucy reminded her sister. "An actress who ended up dead in a ditch."

Anna winced. She had always been a more sensitive soul than Lucy. "Did you find out who she was in London?"

"Yes, and a lot more, but Robert is convinced that he's already found the culprit and that our trip was unnecessary."

Anna reached out to take Lucy's hand. "You sound upset. Are you not feeling well?"

Knowing her sister's fear of all things related to pregnancy, Lucy managed to smile.

"I'm just tired after having to put up with Penelope for two days in a closed carriage."

"Dear Lord, that would, as Father might say, try the patience of a saint."

"I forget how Dr. Fletcher manages to defuse the worst of her comments or laugh her out of the sullens." Lucy sighed. "He stayed in London for another week."

"It must be quite vexing when your husband's best friend marries the woman he was first engaged to and you have a duty to be nice to her," Anna remarked.

"It most certainly is," Lucy agreed. "But she does love Dr. Fletcher, and it was her idea that he stay on for another week."

Anna's face registered surprise. "There is no accounting for who one falls in love with, is there?"

"No. And Dr. Fletcher does bring out the best in Penelope." The sisters smiled at each other before Lucy reluctantly eased herself out of the chair. "I have to go back down, say good-bye to Penelope, and supervise the unpacking."

"Then I will come with you. I need to speak to Cook." Anna linked her arm through Lucy's. "I had a long letter from my new husband yesterday. He is already at sea and managed to send his missive from their first port of call in France."

"Is he well?"

"Very well, and happy to be at sea again—although he tries to hide it." Anna's smile was a mixture of fondness and concern. "He does miss me, though."

"How could he not?" Lucy patted her sister's hand. "But he can be assured that you will be well looked after by your family, and by his own, while he is away at sea."

"He knows that. After you have the baby and are settled again, I will go and stay with his family for a while. It will eventually be *my* home, so I am looking forward to becoming better acquainted with his relatives and the people who live in the valley."

"They will love you," Lucy predicted.

"One can only hope."

Below them, the hall was still littered with boxes and trunks. Foley stood in the middle of the mess, directing the two footmen as to where to take each item. For a moment, Lucy wondered why it was taking so long, and then remembered the lack of another pair of hands.

"James is still locked in his room, I presume?" she asked Anna.

"As far as I am aware, he is," Anna confirmed. "And he isn't very happy about it. Mr. Fletcher has been remarkably quiet as well this last week."

"I'm sure Robert will speedily resolve this issue now that we are home again. He cannot like having a member of the staff sitting idle," Lucy commented.

Anna went off toward the kitchen. Lucy continued down the stairs, avoiding the baggage, and went into her husband's study, where she found Ned sitting on his father's lap playing with the buttons of his greatcoat.

She paused in the doorway to appreciate the two dark heads bent close together as Ned told Robert some long story and his father nodded along as if it all made perfect sense.

Robert looked up first and smiled at her.

"I swear Ned has grown an inch in a week!"

"I have!" Ned visibly sat up straighter and puffed out his chest.

"I believe you are right." Lucy smiled at them both. "Has Penelope already left?"

"Yes, did you wish to speak to her? Her son was balking at leaving. I picked him up, threw him into the carriage, handed Mrs. Fletcher back into it, and sent them on their way."

"I had nothing I particularly wished to say to her, so all is well." Lucy gestured at Ned. "Do you want me to take him back to the nursery? I swear it is the only part of the house not currently being disturbed."

"I've got to change out of this coat, but I'm quite happy if he wants to come with me."

Ned nodded and took an even firmer grip on his father's sleeve.

Robert gently set his son on his feet and took his hand. "Then let's go and see how Betty and Silas are faring in our bedchamber."

It was another full day before Robert found the time to go down to the Queen's Head. He'd released James from captivity with the strict instructions that he was to remain at Kurland Hall and not visit the village or his parents. If he disobeyed, Robert had already told him he would be instantly dismissed. Robert was fairly certain there was more to the story of James being knocked out, but on the long carriage ride home, he had come to the conclusion that James wasn't a murderer.

Which left Bert Speers . . .

Robert alighted from his gig at the Queen's Head and went inside to find Mr. Jarvis. The innkeeper accompanied him down to the cellar with the key and agreed to wait outside while Robert spoke to Bert.

When Robert entered the room, Bert didn't bother to get up from his seat on his pallet. His beard had grown in, and he looked even more ferocious than before.

"You're back, are you?" Bert sneered.

"Indeed." Robert leaned against the door, one hand in his coat pocket close to his pistol. "I was in London for a few days. I made the acquaintance of your employer."

"I'm employed here by Mr. Jarvis."

"Perhaps I misspoke. Your former employer, Viscount Gravely."

"What about him?"

"I understand that you used to work in his stables, and that at one point you were responsible for driving an actress named Flora Rosa from her house in Maida Vale to the theater and anywhere else she wished to go."

Bert looked at Robert with grudging respect. "You have been busy, haven't you?"

Robert shrugged. "As I mentioned, I am the local magistrate. I take any murder committed in my jurisdiction very seriously indeed. Why did you deny knowing Flora?"

"You never asked me about any Flora."

"Are you suggesting that you were unaware that Flora, a woman you were acquainted with in London, and Polly Carter, a woman you also knew, had swapped identities?"

Bert said nothing, and the silence lengthened until Robert grew tired of it.

"You arrived on the same coach as Flora. Quite a coincidence, that."

"Whatever you're thinking, Sir Robert, you're wrong," Bert growled. "Flora wasn't afraid of me. She was running from that other man I told you about."

"The mythical man who arrived in Kurland St. Mary, murdered Flora, and disappeared without anyone having seen him but you?"

"Why don't you ask your own bloody staff a few questions, sir?" Bert retaliated. "James and your precious Mr. Fletcher were hanging around Flora that day as well."

"Yes, and they saw Flora fighting in the street with you, not some unknown man."

"Then ask Mr. Jarvis and Mr. Haines about the man who got off the coach! *That's* why she came to find me that last day. She wanted me to make sure he left her alone."

"Then tell me his *name*. You obviously know it."

Bert gave him a disgusted look. "I can't because you'll start meddling again and make things worse. I prefer to fight my own battles. When I find that scoundrel, he won't survive for long, I can tell you that."

"I don't believe you." Robert held Bert's angry stare. "I think it is all much simpler than that. You met Flora in London and wanted her for your own. When she refused to have anything to do with you, you followed her down to Kurland St. Mary and killed her."

"I bloody well did not!" Bert shot to his feet. "That's just stupid!"

"It makes a lot of sense to me," Robert replied. "Which is why I am going to have you sent to the local assizes to await trial for the murder of Flora Rosa." He waited for a moment before adding. "Unless you have any further information you wish to share with me?"

"I've told you the truth."

"Your truth, perhaps, but with no evidence to back it up, how am I supposed to believe you?"

"Did you speak directly to Viscount Gravely?"

"Yes. He confirmed that he had employed you."

"That's all?" Bert turned away and slammed his fist against his open palm. "Maybe you didn't ask him the right questions."

"What would you have liked me to have asked him?" Robert paused, half-turned toward the door, his curiosity aroused.

"Why I bothered to rush up to London to tell him what was going on? Why he chose to ignore my advice?" Bert shook his head. "The stupid besotted, old fool. He never wanted to see what was right in front of his bloody nose."

"Are you suggesting that Viscount Gravely committed this murder?"

Bert went back to his bed and sat down, his hands linked together in front of his spread knees. "He's bloody well responsible, all right."

The absurdity of the claim almost made Robert smile. "Good luck proving that at your trial, Bert. I suggest you think up a more plausible defense before you are laughed out of court for accusing a peer of the realm of murder."

"You're wrong about all of this, Sir Robert. This is all Viscount Gravely's fault."

"If I'm wrong, give me the evidence to prove it," Robert snapped. "So far, nothing you have said is worth attending to." He inclined his head a stiff inch. "Once the body has been identified—"

"I could do that for you," Bert interrupted.

"There is no need. Someone from London will be coming down to do that fairly soon."

"Polly?"

"I have not yet had the pleasure of meeting the real Polly Carter. Apparently, our arrival in the capital made her go into hiding."

"Clever girl." Bert almost smiled. "You'll be accusing her of murdering her friend next."

"Polly could help clear this matter up in seconds," Robert reminded him. "All she has to do is talk to us."

"And risk what happened to Flora?" Bert asked. "Viscount Gravely doesn't like loose ends. If he finds Polly, she'll be in big trouble for making things worse."

"Viscount Gravely is an invalid who rarely leaves his home."

"He has enough money and power to get whatever he wants," Bert argued. "And if he wants Polly dead, like her friend Flora, he will find a way to make it happen."

Robert considered Bert anew. "Is that what you did?"

"I'm not sure I follow you, sir."

"Did you murder Flora for Viscount Gravely?"

Bert had the temerity to laugh. "Now who's making things up out of thin air, Sir Robert? Do you think I'd be sitting in here if I'd killed her? If I'd been responsible, I damn well wouldn't have come back to Kurland St. Mary."

"Then why did you come back?" Robert asked, intrigued despite himself.

"Because I'm a fool, that's why." Bert sighed. "If Viscount Gravely comes down here to identify the body, let me have a word with him, eh? He'll clear my name. I'm certain of it."

"By implicating himself? Somehow I doubt that." Robert banged on the door. "Rest easy, Bert. Viscount Gravely is too ill to bother to save you."

"If it's not Polly coming, then who is going to identify the body?" Bert shouted the question at Robert's back. "Tell me!"

Robert ignored Bert and pulled the door closed behind him.

"Tell me!" Bert carried on yelling, his voice now muffled by the thick oak door.

Mr. Jarvis relocked the door and pocketed the key.

"I do apologize for the inconvenience of having a man locked in your cellar for two weeks," Robert said as they went back up the stairs. "I will soon have him removed to Hatfield for trial."

"It's been no trouble, Sir Robert. We make sure he's fed

and watered just like the other guests and the horses at the inn," Mr. Jarvis replied. "He's calmed down a lot in the last few days."

"I appreciate all your efforts." Robert shook the landlord's hand. "Now I must get back to Kurland Hall. I have a week's worth of farm business to catch up on."

Robert climbed into the gig but made no effort to hurry home. He idled along the county road, his thoughts occupying him until he reached the stables of Kurland Hall and relinquished the reins into the hands of one of his grooms. He had a sense that something was eluding him, that if he could just shake the pieces together again, they would somehow form a more cohesive and understandable picture.

As usual, when he felt undecided, his steps turned toward his wife's favorite sitting room at the back of the house, where the light was better for her needlework. She was sitting in a chair by the window, sewing, her head bent over some minuscule garment he assumed was for their future child. She looked well and happy. Seeing her like that brought him an unexpected sense of peace.

She looked up and smiled at him.

"Did you speak to Bert?"

"I did. I told him I would be sending him for trial."

"And how did he react to that?"

Robert grimaced and sat in the chair opposite hers. "He declared his innocence, suggested that Viscount Gravely was the culprit, and said that Polly would be next."

She set her sewing aside. "Did you believe him?"

"I asked him to produce evidence to support his claims, and he offered me nothing."

"Which indicates that he is still lying to you," Lucy said. "Then why are you hesitating?"

He offered her a sharp glance. "What makes you think I am?"

"I know you, Robert Kurland." She met his gaze. "You are one of the most decisive men I have ever met, and yet I can still hear the uncertainty in your voice."

He sighed. "Perhaps it is because I am trying to over-complicate things and will not believe the evidence of my own eyes."

"Or maybe something Bert said made you think that things aren't so clear-cut?" Lucy suggested.

"Why the devil won't he just admit what he's done?" Robert burst out. "Why continue to deny everything, and even implicate a peer of the realm rather than accept responsibility for his crime?"

"It certainly was a strange thing for Bert to say." Lucy frowned. "From what you have told me about Viscount Gravely, he would barely have the strength to strangle *anyone*."

"I suggested to Bert that maybe he had been paid by Viscount Gravely, his past employer, to do his work for him, and he laughed in my face."

"Your idea has merit." Lucy stared out of the window and worried her lower lip before turning back to Robert. "I could quite see that happening—Viscount Gravely sent Bert down to Kurland St. Mary with Flora and told him to kill her if she refused to return."

"Versus Viscount Gravely descending on our small village, finding our nursemaid, and strangling her himself in a remote field?"

"If the viscount did insist on coming to Kurland St. Mary, maybe Bert took Flora to him," Lucy said. "Bert was seen with Flora in the village by both Mr. Fletcher and James, and we know he went off with her."

"You believe Bert marched Flora an unspecified distance to where the viscount awaited them, killed her, and then dumped her dead body in the field?"

"It's possible." Lucy paused. "If Viscount Gravely did come in his carriage, it might also explain how James was hit on the head."

"How so?"

"Maybe the viscount's coachman knocked James out and then took his body to his parents' farm for discovery."

"How would he know where James lived?" Robert demanded. "The more complicated we make this, the worse things get!"

A sharp knock on the door made them both start as Robert bade the person enter.

Foley came in and bowed low. "Sir Robert, Mr. Jarvis sent a message for you, He said that it is very urgent."

"Thank you." Robert took the note, put on his spectacles, and read it before turning to Lucy.

"Mr. Jarvis is sorry to report that while Bert was being given his midday meal, he overpowered the maid who brought it to him, and escaped from the cellar." Robert screwed up the note and threw it onto the fire.

"Now we really are in the basket."

Chapter 16

"Where do you think Bert will go?" Lucy asked Robert as she followed him up the stairs to their bedchamber. It had begun to rain, and he had decided to change his coat before he returned to the Queen's Head.

"Back to London?" Robert looked absolutely furious.

"The mail coach won't arrive until tomorrow morning," Lucy reminded him. "And I doubt Mr. Jarvis will let him get on it."

"True." Robert strode into their shared dressing room and threw his coat onto a chair. "Which is why I intend to drive up the London Road and see if I can discover our fugitive before he gets too far."

He opened up his cupboard and took out his heavy caped driving coat. "Don't worry. I'll take one of Mr. Jarvis's grooms with me to manage the horses."

"You don't wish me to come with you?"

"It's not necessary." He grimaced as she helped him put on the coat. "I'm afraid that he is going to find Polly and kill her."

"I am worried about the same thing," Lucy agreed. "Is it worth sending a message to Polly's parents or Mrs. Pell, to tell them to watch out for Bert's appearance?"

"We'd do better asking Viscount Gravely, but I suspect he wouldn't be very helpful."

"What about the sons?"

Robert paused as he wrapped a scarf around his throat. "That's a good idea. Both men seem worried by their father's behavior and eager to let the matter of Flora Rosa drop. They might well be willing to intervene if Bert turns up at their place and make sure he is stopped."

"The poor girl," Lucy murmured as she tucked the ends of Robert's scarf securely in place. "If you like, I'll write to them immediately."

"There's no need. "I'll do it when I'm closer to London and can pay someone to deliver the letter faster." He kissed her briskly on the forehead. "I'll try to be back before it gets dark, but it depends on what I find."

"Be careful," Lucy said.

He winked at her. "Always."

After he left, she picked up his discarded coat and held it against her cheek. She felt rather unnecessary, and she wasn't sure if she liked it. Normally, in such cases, she tended to be the one rushing around while her husband sat back and waited for her to slow down and agree with his conclusions. Now she was left behind to worry while he ventured into danger.

She replaced the coat in the cupboard and closed the door. As the worrier, she appreciated his prior concerns for her rather more acutely now.

Lucy and Anna were just finishing their dinner when Robert came into the dining room and asked Foley to fetch him up a bottle of red wine from the cellar. He didn't have the look of a man who had achieved his purpose and was limping badly. Lucy wasn't surprised when he sat down at the table, drank a whole glass of the wine Foley provided, and let out a frustrated breath.

"We couldn't find him anywhere. I went damned near halfway to London, asking every driver on the road if they'd seen him. We also went into every inn, and there was no sign of him."

"Did you manage to send a note to the Gravelys?" Lucy asked.

"Yes. They should've received it by now. I paid for a fast delivery at the last inn we inquired at."

"Oh, dear," Lucy sympathized. "I asked Foley to speak to our staff and tell them to keep an eye out for Bert on Kurland property."

"I doubt he'd come here, but I appreciate the thought." Robert attacked his beefsteak with the savagery of a starving wolf. "I'll wager he'll go straight back to Viscount Gravely, and that's the last we'll ever hear of him."

"Can't the courts in London do anything?" Anna asked.

"Not unless someone files information about the murder with a magistrate, and as it didn't happen in London, that probably won't occur. No magistrate is going to take on a peer of the realm over such a matter as the death of his young mistress." Robert grimaced. "He could've strangled her in plain view, and he'd still probably be exonerated."

"How terrible," Anna said. She wiped her mouth with her napkin and rose to her feet. "Will you both excuse me? I have to write a letter to Harry."

Robert stood and bowed. "Good night, Anna. I do apologize for my bad temper."

"On this occasion, your temper is completely justified." She sighed. "There is a vast amount of inequality in our world, that's for certain. Poor Flora Rosa."

Robert sat back down and continued to eat his dinner, while Lucy finished her dessert.

"If Bert has gone to Viscount Gravely for assistance, there is very little we can do about it, is that right?" Lucy finally asked.

"That is unfortunately true. As a magistrate, I can alert the courts as to Bert's disappearance, but as he wasn't formerly charged, there isn't much else I can do." Robert helped himself to more wine. "Perhaps this is the one occasion when our attempt to find justice for a murdered soul will bear no fruit."

"That seems wrong."

Robert raised an irate eyebrow. "What else would you have me do, my dear? Go back to London, storm into Viscount Gravely's house, and demand to see Bert? The viscount already said he would have me thrown out if I dared to step foot over his threshold again."

It was Lucy's turn to frown. "I didn't say you had to do anything. I merely remarked that it seems unfair that no one will be held accountable for Flora Rosa's death."

Robert slapped the table hard enough to make the porcelain plates tremble and chime. "But you're right! I *should* be doing something. Flora was in my employ when she died, and she is my responsibility."

"Perhaps Polly will come to her senses and contact us," Lucy said hopefully.

"If Polly has any sense, she will already have left London, and she should never return." Robert finished his second glass of wine and pushed his plate away. "Bert himself intimated that if Viscount Gravely gets his hands on her, she won't survive the experience."

"Why is he so vindictive?" Lucy wondered.

"Because he can be? He is old, wealthy, and dying, and he no longer cares about such social niceties as not murdering his own mistress."

"And if Marjorie is right and Flora Rosa was about to leave him for his son again, he might well have taken such a matter very personally indeed," Lucy mused. "We have learned to our cost that jealousy is a very powerful motivator."

"Yes, perhaps looking old and foolish didn't sit well with him." Robert reached over to take her hand. "Are you ready for bed, my dear? I own to being quite exhausted after the day's unexpected activities."

"I think I will sit up for a while. I have a letter to finish to Anthony."

"Give him my best, won't you?" Robert stood and came around to pull out her chair. "I doubt there are many of my old cavalry friends left in the regiment, but be sure to ask him to remember me to them."

"I always do." She smiled up at him. "He seems very settled in India and gives no indication that he intends to return home."

"It's a very long way. He'll probably come back when he's looking for a wife, or if he inadvertently makes his fortune and can sell his commission." He kissed her gently on the lips. "Don't stay up too long, will you, my dear?"

"I won't." She searched his face, saw the lines of tiredness etched there. "Sleep well, my love."

When Robert had gone, Lucy retraced her steps to her sitting room, where one of the maids had banked up the fire and set a branch of lit candles beside her desk. Her desire to write to Anthony had disappeared. She picked up the baby gown she had been smocking and carried on sewing. She found the rhythm soothing, and it allowed her mind to wander at will.

Poor Flora Rosa still hadn't been given a proper burial. If Robert truly believed Bert would be protected by Viscount Gravely and that the viscount was above the reach of the law, then perhaps, for the first time ever, they would have to admit defeat.

It was a lowering thought, and not one she was comfortable with. All she could do was pray about the matter and hope that, for once, her husband's instincts were proven wrong.

Over breakfast the next morning, Lucy was pleased to see that Robert looked much more the thing. She'd spent a restless night, unsettled by dreams of her nursemaid, and was more than willing to hope that this new day would prove uneventful.

"I know that it is early, but do you wish to accompany me to the Queen's Head?" Robert asked. "I want to speak to Mr. Jarvis and watch the mail coach come in."

"I intended to go into the village to visit Penelope this morning. Perhaps you could take me as far as the inn, and I could walk through the village to the Fletchers' house."

"If you wish." Robert finished his coffee. "Are you ready to leave?"

Used to her husband's somewhat peremptory ways, Lucy finished her tea with all speed and nodded. "Yes, of course."

Less than a quarter of an hour later, she was sitting in the gig as Robert guided the horse into the coach yard. Mr. Jarvis came out to greet them, his battered face a picture of misery.

"Morning, Sir Robert. Lady Kurland. There's no sign of the blighter, if that's what you've come down to ask me about." He sighed heavily. "I can't believe I let my guard down like that."

"It's not your fault, Mr. Jarvis," Robert said. "I should have formally charged him and removed him to a proper prison."

"He ran at Janie when she went through the door and then clobbered me with his tray before I could shut him in." Mr. Jarvis turned to Lucy. "I went down like a sack of grain. The next thing I knew, Mrs. Jarvis was sitting on my chest crying and screeching like a barn owl."

"Did he say anything before he escaped?" Lucy asked as Robert gave the reins of the gig over to one of the stable boys.

"He was muttering a lot when Janie went in, and pacing back and forth. I think he was disturbed by Sir Robert's visit. Maybe he knew he was about to be incarcerated and decided to make a break for it before that happened."

"Quite possibly," Lucy agreed. "But did Bert say anything specific?"

"Only that Sir Robert was completely wrong, and that

the last thing any of us would want was the Gravely family, whoever they are, descending on this village."

Lucy didn't enlighten him as Robert came to join them.

"I'll be off then," Lucy smiled up at her husband. "Do you plan to stay here for a while?"

"I'm not sure." Robert frowned. "Do you want me to send the carriage to pick you up from the Fletchers' later, or shall I come and collect you?"

"If you are finished with your business here in an hour or so, please do come. Otherwise, I will wait for the carriage."

"As you wish." Robert nodded. "I think I'll take a moment to look in the cellar and see if Bert left behind anything of interest before his escape."

Robert waited until Lucy had left the inn and went down into the cellar with Mr. Jarvis. There was nothing to indicate that Bert had been incarcerated there for so long.

"Did he take a horse?" Robert asked Mr. Jarvis, who was still apologizing to him.

"I didn't think to ask, what with me being knocked out and all that." Mr. Jarvis groaned. "Good Lord, I have let you down, sir, haven't I?"

"As you say yourself, you could hardly chase after him when you were unconscious, Mr. Jarvis." Robert turned to the door. "May I go and ask your stable hands if Bert stole a mount?"

"Of course, sir. I'll come with you and make sure that you get to speak to every single one of them."

They progressed out to the stables, and Mr. Jarvis called out to his head ostler.

"Did Bert take a horse yesterday?"

Fred scratched his nose. "He took his own horse, yes. He strolled in here as if he owned the place, taking us all by surprise, and off he went before anyone thought to lay a hand on him."

"Did he have any baggage?" Robert asked.

"No, and Douglas says that Bert stole his hat and coat." He nodded at the innkeeper. "I meant to tell you about that this morning, sir, but it slipped my mind."

"Better late than never, I suppose," Robert intervened, as Mr. Jarvis's face grew alarmingly red. "Thank you for your assistance."

"I wonder if he had any money." Robert stared out across the yard as the head ostler walked away from them.

"Not on him in the cellar," Mr. Jarvis said. "I took his purse away."

"Do you still have it?"

"I locked it up in my strongbox. Would you like to see it, Sir Robert?"

"I'd like to make sure it's still there," Robert replied and retraced his steps into the house.

He was rapidly coming to the conclusion that unless something extraordinary happened, he would never prosecute Bert Speers for murdering Flora Rosa and disrupting the peace, not only of the village but also of Kurland Hall and his wife.

Bert's purse was still in the strongbox, and contained rather more money than Robert had anticipated. There were at least three folded five-pound notes and lots of sovereigns.

"I didn't realize you paid your ostlers so well, Mr. Jarvis," Robert commented as he weighed the coins in his hand.

"I don't, sir." Mr. Jarvis studied the money, his eyes wide. "He either stole it or brought it down with him from London."

"I wonder who else was paying him," Robert mused. "I suspect I know, but I wish to God I could confirm it."

Three sharp blasts of a horn penetrated the silence. Mr. Jarvis relocked the strongbox and looked at his pocket watch. "Mail coach is late today."

"I'd like to watch and see who gets on, Mr. Jarvis." Robert followed his host out of the door. "I'll stay out of the way."

"Don't you worry, sir. We'll all be watching," Mr. Jarvis said.

He walked out into the yard, his expression grim, and waited until the coachman brought the team of four horses to a complete standstill before he approached the box.

"Morning, Mr. Haines."

"Morning, Mr. Jarvis. Sorry we're late. There was a herd of sheep all over the road a mile or so back. I had to slow down or kill the lot of them."

Robert, who had positioned himself near the door with a good view of the coach, paused to wonder whether the sheep were his, and how the devil they had got out. A trickle of passengers came from the inn, ready to board the coach. Robert knew all of them, and at least two of them stopped to pass the time of day with him. There was no sign of Bert, unless he'd managed to disguise himself completely.

Robert transferred his attention to the coach, where the passengers who wished to get down to stretch their legs or who were leaving the coach were emerging from the interior or climbing down from the roof.

A young woman alighted and looked around nervously, one hand to her throat, the other clutching a large bag. Something about her hesitation caught Robert's attention, and he started toward her, only to have his passage blocked by the arrival of a farm cart pulled by a dray horse the size of a small barn.

"There he is!" Mr. Jarvis bellowed so loudly that the dray horse took exception to his tone and tried to buck out of his traces, which set off the team of coach horses.

For a moment, Robert's world took on a nightmarish quality as the huge horse reared up on his hind legs, almost upsetting the empty cart. The hooves, which were the size of dinner plates, whistled past Robert's ear as he ran for the safety of the inn wall.

He fought to breathe normally as the entire yard seethed and bubbled like a witches' cauldron.

"I've got him, Simon!" Mr. Jarvis finally managed to bring the dray horse under control. "Get the leader, Fred!"

By the time everything settled down and Robert forced his way through to the mail coach, Mr. Jarvis was holding forth.

"I saw Bert, Sir Robert! He came in off the street and went straight for the coach!"

"What happened to the woman who got off?" Robert asked urgently.

"Which one?" Mr. Jarvis asked.

"The dark-haired one."

"She screamed when she saw, Bert, I can tell you that," Mr. Jarvis said. "But I don't know what became of either of them because I had to attend to the horses. Did you check inside the inn?"

"I doubt Bert went in there," Robert countered.

"Sir Robert?" the coachman shouted down to him. "He took her. Bert took her by the arm and dragged her out onto the street."

Mr. Jarvis looked at Robert. "Your gig is still outside. Shall we see if we can find them? He hasn't had much of a start."

Robert was already in motion, pausing only to check inside the coach before he climbed up onto the box seat and let Mr. Jarvis take the reins.

"Which way?" Mr. Jarvis asked as they exited the yard.

"Not into the village."

Mr. Jarvis clicked to the horse, and they set off at some pace, Robert shading his eyes to look ahead, and for once thanking God that the landscape was so flat.

"Up there, on the side of the road. I think I see them." Robert pointed. "By that open gate."

As they neared the two figures, it became apparent that they were engaged in a struggle.

"Oi!" Mr. Jarvis shouted. "You leave that young woman alone, Bert Speers, and come back here to face justice!"

Robert got one glimpse of Bert's face before he shoved the woman to the ground and made off over the grassy field. He wondered whether Bert had deliberately slowed the mail coach by releasing the sheep so that he had a chance to look inside and see who was arriving at the inn.

"Do you want me to go after him, sir?" Mr. Jarvis asked as he pulled up the gig.

"No, I think he will outrun us both, and he's probably left his horse hereabouts." Robert carefully got down from the gig and went to the woman's side. Her bonnet had been knocked askew in the fight and hid her face. He knelt down by her side and rolled her gently onto her back.

Wide brown eyes stared up at him in terror.

"Are you, by any chance, Polly Carter?" Robert asked politely.

"Bloody hell," she breathed. "Not you again."

She closed her eyes and went as limp as a newborn.

"Yes, Penelope. I will be sure to mention it to Robert when I return home," Lucy said patiently.

She was currently drinking tea in Penelope's front parlor while her hostess repeated a list of grievances about the state of the house, which was owned by the Kurland estate. Apparently, in Penelope's absence, some of the slate tiles had come loose, and there was water coming in through the roof.

"I know that such a matter means little to you, Lucy, but waking up with water dripping onto one's face is not pleasant at all." Penelope offered her a sliver of cake and another cup of weak tea.

"I'm sure it isn't." Lucy accepted the second slice of seed cake and waited for Penelope to remark unfavorably on her appetite, but for once, Penelope's attention appeared to be elsewhere.

"And when my dear Dr. Fletcher is away from home, all these decisions fall on *me*."

"Did you ask Dr. Evans to look up on the roof for you?" Lucy mentioned Dr. Fletcher's new assistant, who currently lived in the attics. "If there is water coming into the house, one might think that he would be aware of it."

"I will ask him to look tomorrow when the light is better, but I doubt he will be able to do anything. He is a quiet, scholarly man who rarely ventures outside."

"Is he settling in well?" Lucy asked. She'd hardly had a chance to become acquainted with the shy young Welshman since his arrival in the winter. "Do Dr. Fletcher's patients accept his ministrations?"

"They obviously prefer my husband's attention, but he appears to be quite satisfactory." Penelope glanced toward the window at the sound of an approaching vehicle. "Someone is driving rather fast. It usually means they are coming to see my husband."

She rose to peer out of the window. "It appears to be Sir Robert and Mr. Jarvis from the Queen's Head."

Lucy went to join her. "What on earth?"

She picked up her skirts and ran to open the front door as Robert and Mr. Jarvis carried a woman up the garden path.

"Is Dr. Evans here?" Robert called out. "We need his assistance."

Penelope turned back. "I'll go and see if he is upstairs. Bring the patient through to the back, please! I don't want blood on my best carpet."

Lucy held the door open as Robert and Mr. Jarvis came through. The woman they carried between them was unfamiliar. Her face was bruised and bloodied, and she appeared to be unconscious.

"I think this is Polly Carter," Robert murmured to Lucy as he went past. "Bert Speers attacked her."

"Bert Speers?" Lucy followed them down the hall into the doctor's study and examination room, where they carefully laid Polly on the bed. "He didn't leave?"

Robert drew Lucy to one side as Mr. Jarvis went back to make sure the gig was secured at the side of the house. "One has to wonder whether this is why he came back to Kurland St. Mary. Mayhap he realized that at some point, Polly would have nowhere else to turn except her cousin Agnes, and he decided to murder her here."

He briefly told Lucy what had occurred at the inn, and then left with Mr. Jarvis when Dr. Evans came in to examine his patient. Lucy remained in the room, as Penelope preferred not to have to deal with her husband's patients.

After a short while, Dr. Evans looked over at Lucy. "Well, she's been hit in the head at least twice and manhandled quite badly, but she's still alive."

"Thank goodness for that!" Lucy exclaimed. "Will it be all right to move her up to Kurland Hall?"

She had no intention of leaving Polly Carter anywhere Bert Speers might gain easy access to.

"I'd prefer it if she could stay here at least for one night, so I can keep an eye on her. Head injuries can be quite deceptive sometimes. A patient might insist that they are well enough to get up and later suddenly drop dead like a stone."

"Well, we certainly don't want that to happen," Lucy replied.

Dr. Evans folded Polly Carter's hands together on her chest. "She should regain consciousness fairly soon."

"Thank you, Doctor," Lucy smiled at the young man. "I will ask Mrs. Fletcher if she has a spare nightgown for our patient to make her rest more comfortably."

Lucy would also have to speak to Robert about guarding the doctor's house until Polly was well enough to be moved up to the hall. Dr. Evans had a very soothing way with him that contrasted strongly with the rather bluntly spoken Dr. Fletcher.

Lucy left the doctor with Polly and went back into the

parlor, where Robert was being accosted by Penelope about the state of her roof, while poor Mr. Jarvis looked as if he wanted to be anywhere but there. Lucy had nothing but sympathy for his plight and hastened to intervene in the somewhat heated discussion.

"My dear, Dr. Evans says we should leave the woman here overnight until she regains consciousness. Perhaps you could take Mr. Jarvis home and then bring our carriage back with Betty and my night things."

Robert frowned. "I don't want you staying up all night in your condition. I will certainly bring Betty back, but she will stay up, and you will return home with me."

Lucy met his gaze and reluctantly gave in. At least she'd distracted him from his argument with Penelope. "As you wish." She turned to her hostess. "If that is acceptable to you?"

Her companion tossed her head, making her blond ringlets bounce. "It seems that as this house belongs to the Kurland family, and I am beholden to them for *everything,* that I can hardly say no."

"I'll be on my way, then." Robert gave Penelope another glare before heading to the door with Mr. Jarvis. "Thank you for your hospitality, ma'am."

Penelope shook her head and tutted as the front door was slammed shut. "Sometimes, Lucy, I am amazed that I almost married Sir Robert. Thank goodness I changed my mind and allowed you the opportunity to deal with his temper."

"Was he not helpful about the roof?" Lucy inquired.

"He suggested it was not at all important at this time, and that as the wife of a doctor, I should perhaps reassess my priorities!"

"He is rather concerned about the young woman," Lucy offered.

"And *why* is he so concerned about her, Lucy?" Penelope turned on her, blue eyes sparking fire. "What is she to him? I warned you about this, didn't I?"

Unwilling to embark on an explanation of the tangled lives of Polly Carter and Flora Rosa, Lucy was forced to hold her tongue, which was proving harder by the second.

"If you'll excuse me, Penelope. I'll go and speak to Dr. Evans about our patient and make sure she is comfortable."

Chapter 17

After two days with no sign of Bert Speers, Dr. Evans allowed Lucy to take Polly up to Kurland Hall. He was somewhat perplexed by her still being unconscious, but he reassured Lucy that Polly occasionally drifted back into some semblance of awareness, and said that she should encourage this when it occurred.

Lucy did wonder whether Polly was deliberately choosing not to remain conscious because she was still convinced that they wished ill on her. But why had she come to Kurland St. Mary if that was still the case? If she'd spoken to Marjory and accepted that the Kurlands were trying to help solve Flora's murder, Lucy had to assume Polly had come to find them.

Lucy ate her breakfast slowly as Robert read the daily newspaper. She considered whether it was worth attempting to speak to Polly even though she appeared to be insensible. Perhaps if she just talked about what had happened, Polly would instantly recover. Agnes had identified her cousin, and Lucy could see the likeness between them. She'd also volunteered to sit with her whenever Ned was napping, which had proved very helpful.

"The post, my lady." Foley deposited a silver tray beside her piled high with correspondence. Lucy set about sorting it, pausing when she noticed a letter marked urgent from Dr. Fletcher.

"Robert?"

As usual, her husband didn't immediately respond from behind the barrier of his newspaper, and Lucy raised her voice.

"Robert! There is a letter here from Dr. Fletcher. May I open it, or do you want to do so?"

"You do it." He didn't even bother to lower his paper.

She broke the wax seal, which bore her uncle's crest. He had also franked the letter.

"Robert." Lucy's voice trembled.

He lowered his paper. "What?"

"Marjory is *dead*."

"Who is Marjory?"

"The parlor maid who used to work for Flora, and who also knew Polly." Lucy passed the letter over to Robert. "Mrs. Pell came to find us at the Harringtons' and luckily met Dr. Fletcher instead. She said Marjory was found in the kitchen next door. She'd been strangled."

"Good Lord, the poor woman." Robert read the letter. "Is it possible that Bert returned to London and killed her?"

"It's certainly possible if he left the day Polly arrived," Lucy confirmed and sighed. "Poor Marjory, she had aspirations to go on the stage, and was a good and loyal friend to Polly and Flora."

"For which she paid with her life." Robert remarked. "The more I think about Bert Speers getting away with all this, the worse I feel about my decision to keep him in Kurland St. Mary and not the county gaol."

"You did what you thought was best at the time with the information you had," Lucy reminded him.

"Don't try and exonerate me." He scowled at her. "I failed Flora and Marjory."

She reached over and took his fisted hand in hers. "You cannot change what happened, can you? Therefore, all you can do is move forward and do your best to bring their murderer to justice."

"*How*?" Robert asked.

"I would start by writing to Viscount Gravely, and making sure that he understands the implications of aiding or abetting Bert Speers."

"I can certainly do that."

"And I will write to my uncle, and see if he can use his influence to persuade the viscount to reveal where Bert is."

"It's a start," Robert said and raised her hand to his mouth to kiss her knuckles. "Thank you, my dear. I know I can always rely on your good sense to set me right."

Lucy smiled. "I appreciate the compliment, but I must admit that usually *I* am the one who relies on *your* common sense, not the other way around."

She pushed back her chair. "I will go and write to my uncle immediately."

"And I will write to Viscount Gravely. He might have denied me access to his house, but he can hardly object to a letter."

Lucy wrote her letter and left it with Robert, who intended to send it off with his as quickly as possible. Leaving him to finish his missive, she went upstairs and paused outside the room where Polly was being cared for. Going in, she found Betty sitting beside the bed, knitting, while she watched over the patient.

"How is she?" Lucy asked.

"She hasn't stirred," Betty replied. "I managed to get a few sips of water down her throat earlier, as Dr. Evans suggested."

"Well done," Lucy said. "Would you mind going up to the nursery and telling Mrs. Akers that I intend to come with her on her walk with Ned? I will watch over Polly while you are away."

"As you wish, my lady."

Betty was one of the few Kurland servants who had been trusted with Polly's true identity.

After Betty left, Lucy took her place beside the bed and looked at Polly's slack, unresponsive face. The left side of her head was still badly bruised, as were her upper arms where Bert had attempted to drag her away with him. Lucy wrapped her fingers around one of Polly's wrists and spoke slowly and clearly.

"Polly, if you can hear me, I want you to know that you are safe and protected at Kurland Hall. There is no need to be afraid. Sir Robert and I only wish to help discover who murdered Flora Rosa and bring them to justice. Perhaps, when you wake up, you can tell us what has been going on. I promise that we will believe you."

Lucy felt slightly foolish speaking to an unconscious person, but she was at her wit's end. And if her words could penetrate Polly's torpor, then she was certainly willing to try.

For a brief second, her hopes flared as Polly blinked and restlessly moved her head from side to side, but she subsided into nothingness again. Lucy let out a breath she had been unaware of holding, and her baby kicked hard against her stomach.

She would repeat her plea to Polly once a day and pray that, at some point, the girl would wake up. Her only concern was that by the time Polly was able and willing to tell her tale, Viscount Gravely would have concocted a story to defend himself and Bert. No one would believe a lowly servant like Polly against a peer of the realm.

Betty came back in, and Lucy rose to her feet. There was no point in worrying about things that she could not control. She would walk with Anna and Ned down to the stables and consult with Dr. Evans when he came to visit his patient at three.

Robert looked up as he finished folding and sealing his letter to Viscount Gravely, and found his land agent had come into his study.

"Ah, there you are, Dermot. Can you arrange to have

both these letters taken down to the Queen's Head and delivered to London with all speed?"

"Yes, Sir Robert." Dermot took the letters but remained pinned to the spot.

"Well, get on with it," Robert suggested.

"I forgot to tell you that I sent a man to fix my brother's roof."

"Good."

Dermot still didn't move.

"I . . . wanted to ask you something, sir." He swallowed hard. "The woman who came with Dr. Evans?"

"What about her?" Robert asked.

"Does she have something to do with the disappearance and death of Polly Carter?"

Robert set down his pen. After attempting to write a letter to Viscount Gravely that wouldn't immediately be thrown on the fire, his patience was already wearing thin. Perhaps this was a good moment to revisit his concerns about Dermot's interactions with Flora. He'd be damned if he would find the truth out otherwise.

"Why would you think that?" Robert asked.

Dermot shrugged. "I just overheard something when I was in the kitchen, and I began to wonder . . ."

"I'm still not certain why you are wondering anything when your own relationship with Polly Carter could be viewed in a very unfavorable light."

"What?" Dermot blinked at him. "I mean, I beg your pardon, sir?"

"You were angry with Polly for not returning your affection," Robert pointed out. "Shortly afterward, she was murdered on a farm that you and I had visited that very week."

"I did *not* murder her, Sir Robert." Despite his pallor, Dermot met Robert's gaze straight on, the outrage in his eyes quite visible. "I would *never* do anything so underhanded. How could you even think such a thing of me?"

"Then why do you continue to lie to me about why you

didn't go after her when you allegedly saw Bert Speers dragging her off down the high street?" Robert demanded. He was tired of all the deception, particularly from members of his own damned staff, who should know better. Dermot was supposed to be his most trusted employee. "If you truly cared for her, you would've intervened, and perhaps she would be alive today!"

The last part wasn't particularly fair, but Robert was beyond that. If he was ever to work out what had happened to Flora Rosa, he had to get to the bottom of all the deceptions and lies that had piled up around her.

"I didn't go after her, because—" Dermot stopped speaking and gazed helplessly at Robert.

"Because what?"

"I . . . became distracted," Dermot said carefully. "I am not proud of what happened, but I at least attempted to do the right thing and make sure he was placed somewhere safe."

"Oh, for God's sake. That's it, isn't it?" Robert stood up, startling Dermot, and marched over to the door. He opened it and bellowed.

"James! Come into my study immediately!"

Robert waited by the door until James appeared, looking remarkably apprehensive. He guided him into his study, where his footman took one look at Dermot and almost bolted. Robert shut the door before either of them decided to make a run for it.

He returned to stand behind his desk. "Now, let's have it. Who hit who first?"

James raised his hand. "I cast the first blow, sir." His cheeks reddened. "He told me to leave Polly alone, and I came back and thumped him."

"Is this true?" Robert looked at Dermot.

"Yes, sir." Dermot admitted. "And then I hit him back, and he went down like a stone."

"I tripped over a branch!" James protested. "You hardly touched me."

"That's not correct, you—"

"Be quiet! Both of you." Robert held up a hand. "I am not interested in your claims to boxing greatness. I am merely concerned with finding out what happened next."

"I tried to rouse James, but without success," Dermot said. "I didn't want to leave him lying by the church, so I decided that the best thing to do was to take him to his parents' farm, which was where he had been heading anyway."

"Then why didn't you take him right up to the front door?" Robert asked.

"Because I didn't want them to know what I'd done," Dermot explained. "As your land agent, I am in a position of authority on this estate. I didn't want James's parents to think badly of me."

"It's a shame you didn't think about that before you acted like a jealous fool over a woman who would never have consented to be your wife," Robert said acidly.

"I agree I acted impulsively," Dermot said. "I am ashamed of that."

Robert looked from James to Dermot. "What I still don't understand is why neither of you owned up to this beforehand."

James cleared his throat. "You thought I'd murdered Polly, sir."

"So why not tell me the truth?" Robert snapped.

"Well, it was like this, sir. I thought that, being as I was knocked out and at my parents' house, that would be enough for you to realize that I couldn't possibly have killed Polly, without me muddying the waters by telling you about a stupid fight and getting Mr. Fletcher into trouble as well."

Robert digested that meandering statement and slowly breathed out through his nose. He'd dealt with a fair number of young soldiers in his military career, and their absurd logic never ceased to amaze him.

"I felt the same way, Sir Robert," Dermot piped up. "I knew that James was in trouble when you had him locked in his room. I thought that bringing up our fight might only make things worse for him."

"Did it not occur to either of you halfwits that telling me everything might have helped me catch Polly's murderer faster?"

Dermot and James exchanged an embarrassed look, and then replied in unison.

"Not really, sir."

James continued. "What could our disagreement have to do with Bert Speers grabbing hold of Polly?"

"For one thing, if the two of you hadn't been so busy fighting each other, one of you might have been able to follow Bert and make him *unhand* Polly. Did you think of that?"

Silence fell, and Robert made no effort to break it as both men suddenly looked wretched.

"Your stupid, cock-of-the-north behavior wasn't exactly that of men who were truly in love with Polly, was it?"

"I'm sorry, sir," Dermot muttered. "I let you and Polly down."

"Aye," James added. "I acted the fool, and she paid the price."

Robert made no effort to console them. He'd observed that for a lesson to hit home, sometimes it needed to settle in and burn a little.

"Now, before I send you both on your way, is there anything either of you would like to tell me about what else happened on that day?" Robert asked.

"I can't think of anything, sir," Dermot said, and James nodded.

"Then you may go about your business, and be grateful that I am not in the humor to give both of you your marching orders," Robert said.

"Thank you, sir." Dermot checked his pocket for the letters. "I promise I will never allow anything like this to happen again."

Robert nodded and watched his land agent depart in something of a hurry. James lingered, a thoughtful look on his face.

"There was one thing, Sir Robert."

"What is that, James?"

"I did speak to Polly that day. She told me she couldn't walk out with me because she was meeting Bert. I insisted she could do better for herself. She laughed and said that I'd got it all wrong, and that she and Bert had grown up together, and that he was her best friend and worst enemy."

James sighed. "She patted my cheek, told me to be a good boy, and that she would be going back to London shortly, and I was not to worry about her."

He met Robert's gaze. "I still can't quite believe it was Bert who strangled her."

"If she truly said that Bert was her best friend *and* her worst enemy, perhaps his worst side won out," Robert suggested quietly.

"I suppose that might be it, sir." James didn't sound convinced. "All I know is that she didn't look like a woman who was afraid of him at all."

"Which might be why he found it so easy to walk away with her and murder her."

James's face crumpled. He rubbed furiously at his cheeks as tears started to fall.

"I let her down, Sir Robert. I loved her, and I let her go without a whimper."

"You did what she asked you to do," Robert reminded him. "Don't blame yourself for that." He paused. "In truth, we all let her down, didn't we?"

Chapter 18

"I cannot believe that Mr. Fletcher and James were so busy fighting each other that they let Bert walk away with Polly right under their noses!" Lucy stared at Robert aghast. "And why didn't James tell you this in the first place?"

Robert, who was pacing the length of her sitting room, turned toward her again. "Because he thought admitting to fighting with Dermot would lead me to disbelieve he was at his parents when Polly was killed, and to assume he was the murderer."

She opened her mouth to speak, and he cut across her.

"I know. His reasoning is completely illogical. I barely stopped myself from leaping across my desk and knocking him out cold again."

Lucy considered what he had told her anew and sighed. "This doesn't really help much, though, does it?"

"Well, it eliminates those two fools from my list of suspects—not that I had come to believe either one of them was capable of murder—and it does clear up some loose ends."

"It certainly does." Lucy frowned. "I wonder what Flora meant about her and Bert being friends for a long time? Do you think she made it up to reassure James that everything was fine, or do you think she meant it?"

"James seems to believe she was telling the truth, but we can't forget that Flora was, by all accounts, a very skillful actress."

"Perhaps she was trying to prevent James from interfering because she knew her meeting with Bert was going to be difficult," Lucy suggested.

"That's certainly possible," Robert agreed as he finally stopped pacing and took the seat opposite her. "What if she did know him well, though?"

"Bert? I suppose she might have known him from the orphanage. I wonder if it is possible to find out such a thing?"

"Mr. Biggins mentioned that Bert was an orphan. He might know which orphanage he came from."

"Would he tell you if he did?"

"I don't see why not." Robert shrugged. "He isn't employed by the Gravely family any longer, so they have no leverage over him." He sighed. "I suppose you want me to write to him as well?"

"It might help," Lucy said.

"I don't see why," Robert grumbled as he moved to sit at her small writing desk and helped himself to her best pen and a sheet of paper. "My expenses this month are triple what they usually are after all these postal fees."

"It's still cheaper and less ruinous to your health than riding all the way to London," Lucy reminded him as he wrote his letter, sanded it, and sealed the outside with her crest.

He swung around to look at her, his face still set in a frown. "I'd still rather hear from Viscount Gravely myself than rely on the post."

"But he won't allow you in his house," Lucy said.

"There's always a way in." Robert propped up the letter against the lamp.

"I'd rather you left that part of the puzzle to my uncle David. He is very good at getting what he wants."

"So I should imagine." Robert rose to his feet. "How is Polly?"

"Much the same." Lucy grimaced. "Dr. Evans doesn't know why she hasn't regained consciousness yet."

"Dr. Fletcher will be back soon. Maybe he'll take a look at her and see if his partner missed anything."

"I did wonder if she is pretending," Lucy confessed.

"Why would she do that?"

"Perhaps she still believes she is in danger."

"From us?" Robert looked impatient. "If I'd wanted her gone, I would've left her with Bert." He picked up the letter. "I'll take this down to the Queen's Head."

Lucy had just finished her letter to Anthony when Anna came to find her, a note in her hand. Despite the unavoidable absence of her new husband, Lucy had never seen her sister look quite so serenely beautiful.

"Aunt Rose wants us to have dinner at the rectory tonight to celebrate Father's birthday. She also asks if you could bring Ned."

"I have no objection to dining at the rectory," Lucy replied. "But if Ned is to accompany us, I don't wish to stay late."

"Rose has anticipated your concerns and suggests we arrive at five and dine well before six." Anna checked the note.

"Then as long as Robert is in agreement, I am happy to attend."

"He is. I just spoke to him in the entrance hall, and he said to ask you." Anna confirmed.

Lucy opened her desk drawer and took out a slim volume with a marbled leather cover. "On the recommendation of Uncle David, I purchased a book for Father when I was in London."

"What is it about?" Anna asked.

"Some obscure history of Greece that our father has apparently always wanted."

"In Greek, I assume?" Anna sighed. "And I just knitted him a new scarf."

"Which he will appreciate when he is out hunting in all weathers." Lucy smiled at her sister. "I do believe Ned has drawn him a picture of a horse, which will please him more than anything either of us could offer."

Anna's laughter rang through the room, and Lucy suddenly felt much better. If they were unable to capture Bert Speers, life would still go on, and moments like these with her sister made her remember that.

"I'll go and write a reply to Aunt Rose, then," Anna said. "And if you wish to come and walk with me and Ned, we will be leaving in an hour."

The rectory was ablaze with lights when Lucy and her family arrived in the carriage after deciding that the walk there and back might be too much for Ned to manage at such a late hour.

"Come on, my boy." Robert lifted Ned down from the carriage and kept a firm grip on his collar as his son attempted to run past him. "No, we don't have time to go to the stables to see your grandfather's horse. If you behave yourself, I'm sure someone will take you to see him after we have eaten."

While this discussion occurred, Lucy got out of the other side of the carriage by herself, as did Anna. She went around to take Ned's other hand.

"I have your picture here, Ned. Don't you want to give it to your grandfather and wish him a happy birthday?"

"Yes!" Ned lunged toward the path. "Come on!"

Lucy was still smiling as they were ushered into the house and discarded their cloaks and hats in the hallway. She could already hear her father holding forth in the drawing room, his loud, jovial tone, which he used to drown out his congregation, was hard to miss.

She let go of Ned's hand as they entered the room, as

did Robert, and watched as her son, who had no fear of his rather fierce grandfather, ran straight over to him.

"Happy Birthday, Grandfather!" Ned grinned up at his relative. "Papa says you are one hundred and two!"

Lucy glanced over at Robert, who shrugged innocently.

"Not quite, young man." The rector didn't take offense. "What have you brought me?"

Ned handed him the rolled-up piece of paper and hopped impatiently from one foot to the other as his grandfather slowly revealed his drawing.

"It's Apollo! Your horse!" Ned said.

"By Jove, so it is!" He looked over at Lucy. "This is remarkably detailed. Did he sneak into my stables and draw my favorite horse by eye, or did he do this by himself?"

"From memory, sir, I believe." Robert came to stand beside Ned and dropped an affectionate hand on his shoulder. "He certainly refused to take any advice from me."

"It is perfect, Ned." The rector looked down at his grandson, delight shining in his eyes. "I will have it framed and put up in my study. Thank you."

Ned's grin was so huge that Lucy couldn't help but smile back at him. She proffered her own parcel.

"Happy Birthday, Father."

"Thank you, my dear." He undid the string and brown paper and considered the slim volume within. "Oh my word! Wherever did you find this?"

"In an antiquarian bookstore, with a little help from Uncle David," Lucy said.

"Well, well." Her father put on his spectacles, opened the book, and started reading the preface.

"Ambrose?" Aunt Rose came by, gently patted his arm, and deftly removed the book from his hand. "Dinner is almost ready. I will send Meg upstairs to hurry along our other guests, and then we will be ready to proceed."

"As you wish, my dear."

Amazed at her father's continued good humor, Lucy could only applaud Rose's way of managing her scholarly and somewhat selfish father. In the past, when her father had received a new book, he would retire to his study, eat his meals in there, and become deaf to the calls of society and his parochial duties.

"Grandfather?" Ned was tugging on the rector's sleeve. "Will you take me to see Apollo so that we can show him his picture?"

"Certainly, but after dinner."

Ned's face fell. "But—"

"Ned?" Lucy stepped forward and took him firmly by the hand. "You heard what your grandfather said. Now come and make your bow to the other guests."

She greeted the Culpeppers, who lived in the village and had two children, one a similar age to Ned whom he often played with. Mr. Culpepper was her father's curate and did most of the work of running the large rural parish. Mrs. Culpepper was Penelope's younger sister and was nothing like her at all.

"Is Penelope coming?" Lucy asked.

"She was invited, but she declined to come because Dr. Fletcher isn't home yet, and she didn't wish to come without him." Dorothea smiled. "Her devotion to Dr. Fletcher is something to admire."

"Indeed." Lucy agreed. "Did my father mention he had other guests?"

"I believe someone arrived this afternoon," Mr. Culpepper said. "An old friend of his from university."

"How pleasant for him." Lucy smiled as she noticed Aunt Rose gathering her guests together by the door to the dining room. "Please excuse me. I must go and find Sir Robert."

With Ned firmly in hand, she turned toward the door, only to see her husband marching toward her, his expression furious.

"You'll never guess who else is coming to dinner, my dear."

Lucy raised her eyebrows as Robert stepped out of her way and pointed toward the doorway.

"Viscount Gravely and his two sons."

Lucy fought a gasp. "Now, that *is* rather unexpected."

"And somehow I doubt it is a coincidence, either. Do you?" Robert murmured. "I can't wait to find out what flimsy excuse Viscount Gravely used in order to invite himself to *my* village."

"Sir Robert." Viscount Gravely, who was seated at the rector's right hand directly across the table from Robert, inclined his head. "What a surprise to see you here."

Robert didn't bother to answer him but looked steadily back through the candlelight until the viscount dropped his gaze.

"I didn't realize that you knew my son-in-law, Gravely," the rector intervened.

"We met in London. Your brother introduced us," Viscount Gravely said. "I suppose I shouldn't be surprised to find him here at your dining table, Ambrose, when I met him in your family house."

"Kurland is married to my oldest daughter, Lucy."

Viscount Gravely looked down the long table to where Lucy was sitting with his two sons. "Ah, how delightful."

"What brings you to Kurland St. Mary, my lord?" Robert asked. "I was led to believe that you were no longer capable of leaving your house."

"When I was in India, I picked up a form of wasting fever that sometimes leaves me in a weakened condition and I have to retire to my bed." Gravely offered Robert a tight smile. "On the occasion of your visit, I was recovering from a bout of sickness."

"But that still doesn't explain your sudden desire to visit my village."

"*Your* village?" Viscount Gravely raised an eyebrow. "I suspect my friend Ambrose might take issue with that."

"Not at all," the rector said jovially. "My son-in-law is correct. All the land hereabouts, apart from that owned by the diocese, is held by the Kurland family, which has been here since the reformation of the monasteries."

"You still haven't answered my question, my lord," Robert said gently. "Why choose to come now?"

"Because meeting the earl of Harrington reminded me that I wished to discuss with my old friend Ambrose some interesting material that I had accrued on my travels through India."

"Indeed." Robert hoped his skepticism showed on his face. "How long do you plan to stay?"

"Surely that is of no interest to you?" Viscount Gravely met his gaze. "I promise not to interfere with your pursuits."

"I was thinking of bringing Gravely up to Kurland Hall tomorrow, Robert. He would enjoy seeing your munitions room and the secret passages under the stairs."

"I'm afraid that won't be possible." Robert smiled at his father-in-law and rose from his seat. "If you will excuse me for a moment?"

He left the rector openmouthed and walked out of the room into the hall, where he paused to gather his composure. The nerve of the man—to sit there opposite him, daring him to expose his wrongdoing . . .

"And what brings you to Kurland St. Mary, Mr. Gravely?" Lucy addressed her question to the younger of the Gravely brothers, who was sitting beside her at the table.

Neville glanced nervously across at his brother. "I . . . was worried about my father's health and decided that it would be better if I accompanied him."

"How very thoughtful of you." Lucy commented. "I had no idea that Viscount Gravely knew my father."

"I understand that they have been friends for a considerable time, my lady, and that visiting the earl of Harrington inspired my father to . . . to reconnect with Mr. Harrington."

Lucy glanced toward the head of the table, where Robert had suddenly risen to his feet and walked out of the room. She considered following him and then realized that would leave Ned unattended. She decided to stay seated and hoped that whatever had happened between her husband and the viscount hadn't resulted in a heated argument across her father's dinner table.

"Please excuse me," Trevor Gravely also rose and placed his napkin carefully beside his plate.

"Trev." Neville grabbed for his brother's sleeve but was shaken off.

"Is your brother unwell, Mr. Gravely?" Lucy inquired.

"No, he's one of those annoyingly healthy people who rarely even catch a cold." Neville attempted a smile.

"Did you return to England for your schooling, Mr. Neville?" Lucy attempted to set him at ease. "Or did you remain in India?"

"No, my lady. My mother couldn't abide the climate, so she came back with us while we both attended school." His anxious gaze shifted back toward the door through which his brother and her husband had gone.

"Did your mother return to India at some point?"

"She much preferred to live here and died a few years ago in our house in London."

"My condolences," Lucy said.

"Thank you." Neville looked as if he might cry. "I still miss her. She meant the world to me."

After making sure that Ned was fully engaged in talking with Anna, Lucy leaned in closer toward Neville.

"Are you feeling quite well, sir?"

"I'm . . . just wondering what has become of my brother."

"I'm sure he will return momentarily," Lucy said soothingly. "If you came to support your father, why did your brother come to Kurland St. Mary?"

"That's a very good question, Lady Kurland, and one that only Trevor can answer. The only thing I would say is that, as my older brother, he has a tendency to think that he should fix everything for me."

"I suspect that is common with older sisters and brothers, Mr. Gravely. I certainly have been accused of meddling in my younger siblings' lives," Lucy agreed.

"Yes, but Trevor"—Neville sighed—"tends to overreact to the slightest misdemeanor on my part. He still tells everyone how I 'accidentally' murdered the kitchen cat as though it is a highly amusing story."

"It certainly doesn't sound amusing," Lucy said.

"It was an accident." Neville shifted in his seat. "A horrible accident, and I wish he would just stop *talking* about it."

There was a rising note in Neville's voice that made Lucy want to reach for his hand and soothe his ruffled feathers. She hastened to change the subject.

"Did your father return home with your mother to set up the household?"

"No, he was too busy. Mother did it all herself." He smiled more normally. "As a charitable woman, when she recruited her staff, I think she offered employment to half the orphans in East London in one fell swoop."

"How wonderful of her." Even as she spoke, Lucy was furiously making connections in her head. "I wonder if she ever employed a boy called Bert Speers?"

Neville almost choked on the sip of wine he'd just been drinking and stared at Lucy in horror.

"He is currently working as an ostler in the Queen's Head. I believe he said he'd been taken straight from an orphanage and employed by a big London house in their stable." Lucy kept up her artless chatter. "Wouldn't it be wonderful if it had been your mother who had employed him?"

Neville was now shaking so badly that his wine threatened to leave the glass entirely.

"I have no recollection of such a name, my lady," he

said stiffly. "It would be something of a remarkable coincidence if my mother had employed him, would it not?"

"Indeed. How silly of me." Lucy smiled at him. "My husband often scolds me for my ridiculous flights of fancy."

Ned tugged at her sleeve, and she returned her attention to him.

"What is it, Ned?"

He pointed at his empty plate. "I've finished my dinner. Can I go and see Apollo now?"

Glancing at her hostess, Lucy saw her give the signal for the ladies to retire.

"Yes, you have been very well behaved indeed. I will ask your aunt Rose if you may visit the stables immediately."

"Sir Robert?"

Robert turned to see Trevor Gravely coming after him, his expression contrite.

"I expect you are wishing all of us to the devil."

"Yes." Robert didn't bother to be pleasant. He was far too angry.

"I'm afraid it's all my fault." Trevor motioned toward the rector's empty study, and Robert followed him inside. "I made the mistake of confiding in Neville as to my intentions to travel down here and identify Flora Rosa's body." He swallowed hard. "He grew very agitated, and the more I tried to calm him, the worse he became. He even tried to hit me. Eventually, I had to enlist the aid of father's butler to restrain him."

Trevor stared out of the window. "I thought we had moved beyond such overwrought displays of emotion, but I was wrong. Neville's feelings for Flora ran far deeper than I think any of us realized."

"Is it true that Flora was thinking of leaving your father and returning to your brother?" Robert asked.

Shock flashed across Trevor's face. "Who in the devil's name told you that?"

Robert didn't attempt an answer and waited as Trevor

took a hasty turn around the room, his hands behind his back.

"I don't know who said that, but yes, Neville did tell me that might happen. I must confess that I didn't believe him because . . . he does tend to daydream about Flora rather obsessively."

It seemed to be a reoccurring theme with Neville's father as well, but Robert didn't point that out. "You still haven't explained why your entire family has descended on Kurland St. Mary."

"As I said, it was my fault. After Ahuja helped me subdue Neville, he must have told Father what I planned to do—or Neville told him he was coming with me. Father decided he couldn't trust either of us and opted to join the party." He paused to study Robert's face. "He really is acquainted with Mr. Harrington. They were at school together, and they have written to each other over the years."

"What does your father hope to achieve here?"

"I'm not really sure." For a moment, Trevor looked worried. "I suspect he is concerned that Neville will insist on seeing Flora's body, and that he will somehow publicly disgrace himself and our family."

"By mourning her?"

"You don't understand, Neville isn't . . . ," Trevor sighed. "I feel disloyal even saying this because he is such a remarkable brother, but like my father, he has his obsessions, and Flora was one of them."

"How exactly does your father intend to stop Neville from seeing Flora's body?"

"I don't know," Trevor said. "This whole matter has become so complicated that I have no idea what will happen next. Is Flora's body being held up at Kurland Hall?"

"No," Robert said.

"Ah, then she's in the village." Trevor nodded. "Which is a shame, because it means that it won't be easy to shake off Neville when I go to see Flora."

"I suppose I could invite him up to the hall," Robert

suggested somewhat reluctantly. "My father-in-law suggested allowing your father to visit me tomorrow. I could make sure that Neville is included in that invitation."

"That might work." Trevor nodded. "If you can stomach dealing with my father. I understand that he banished you from our house."

"Indeed." Robert half-turned to the door. "But once you have done your duty and identified Flora, I expect you to persuade your father and brother to leave this place immediately."

"Don't worry about that, Sir Robert," Trevor said fervently. "I'll have them out of here in a flash."

Robert returned to the dining room, along with Trevor, and retook his seat, only to have to stand again as the ladies left the gentlemen to their port. Lucy made a point of coming past his chair and pausing to speak to him.

"Is everything all right?"

"Not really." He squeezed her hand. "Give me a moment with your father, and then I will come and tell you all."

"As you wish. Ned is going to visit Apollo, and then we shall see how tired he is and whether we need to go home." She went out with Ned and closed the door behind her, shutting Robert in with his father-in-law and a man he was beginning to dislike intensely.

"I do beg your pardon for leaving the table so abruptly," Robert said to the rector. "I suddenly remembered that the thing I was supposed to be doing tomorrow would not be possible until Dr. Fletcher returns home. I just sent a note to his wife to apprise her of the change of date."

"Does that mean I can bring the Gravelys up to the hall?" the rector asked.

"Yes." Robert smiled. "That would be delightful."

Chapter 19

"You invited Viscount Gravely and Neville to Kurland Hall?" Lucy stared at Robert as though he had grown two heads. "*Why?*"

They had just returned from saying good night to Ned in the nursery. Robert had been on the point of ringing for Silas and Betty when his wife had decided to pick a fight with him.

"Trevor needs to identify Flora's body. If Neville sees him setting out to do so, Neville might follow him and cause a scene."

Lucy considered that, her lips pursed in thought. "Neville is rather an emotional young man. I spoke to him at length at the dinner table. He denied all knowledge of Bert Speers, even though we already know that Viscount Gravely acknowledged his employment."

"Why the devil were you talking to Neville Gravely about Bert Speers?" Robert demanded.

"There is no need to shout. I went about it in a very indirect way."

"You shouldn't have mentioned him at *all*. Didn't you just say that he sounded rather unstable?"

"If we are to find out what is going on, Robert, some-

times one has to attempt to ask the difficult questions!"
Lucy squared up to him. "And what were you doing talking to Trevor Gravely, then?"

"I didn't exactly seek him out. He came to apologize for
bringing the whole family down upon us."

"As well he should." Lucy sniffed. "What on earth was
my father thinking, inviting a man he hasn't seen for twenty
years to visit him?"

"Your father was manipulated, much as we have been,"
Robert said. "At least Gravely's weakness and apparent
inability to leave his house have been unmasked. There's
no reason why he couldn't have come down here and
strangled Flora, or done the exact same thing to Marjory."

"Except it would've been much easier for Bert Speers to
do it for him," Lucy reminded him.

"Then, is that what we believe?" Robert asked. "That
Viscount Gravely and Bert Speers conspired together to
murder Flora, and then Marjory, and are still after Polly?"

"It seems the most logical explanation to me." Lucy
studied him. "The problem is proving it."

"Indeed." Robert sighed and flung himself down into a
chair beside the fire. "And now I have committed myself
to hosting Viscount Gravely in my house."

"Perhaps you should use it as an opportunity for some
plain speaking." Lucy came to stand in front of him, her
arms folded over her bosom. "Tell him you intend to prosecute Bert Speers for Flora's murder. Suggest to him that if
he is harboring Bert, he should be aware that you have directed my uncle to lay information against Bert at Bow
Street and set the Runners on him."

Robert smiled at his wife's resolute expression. "Bravo,
my dear."

"Are you making fun of me?"

"Good Lord, no. I wouldn't dare." He caught her hand
and drew her down to sit in his lap. "I am merely admiring

your logic and congratulating myself on marrying a woman of such good sense."

He kissed her cheek. "My only concern with alerting him to the fact that I intend to set the Runners on him is that it will give him the opportunity to send Bert abroad, never to be seen again."

"I suppose you are right." Lucy sighed. "Because even Bow Street would balk at suggesting that a peer was involved in a murder, with no evidence to show except conjecture. Perhaps you should just tell Viscount Gravely that you intend to continue to pursue and prosecute Bert, and that nothing will be allowed to stand in your way."

"I will certainly do that." He kissed her again. "When they are here, I will rely on you to detach your father and Neville from the viscount so that I can have a quiet word with him in private."

She kissed him back. "That, my dear Robert, will be the easy part."

Despite Robert's best efforts to be a good host and Lucy's father's jovial presence, it was obvious that Viscount Gravely and his son were not entirely at their ease as they walked around Kurland Hall. Neville looked as if he expected a ghost to jump out at him from every corner, and Viscount Gravely looked bored. Robert supposed that for a man used to plundering the treasures of India, a small Elizabethan manor house in the southeast of England was rather commonplace.

The only time the viscount did show any interest was when they entered the oldest part of the structure, which had been used as a magistrate's hall for as long as anyone could remember. Lucy maneuvered her father and Neville through, into the picture gallery, and shut the door behind her, leaving Robert and Gravely alone for the first time.

"This was the original hall of the house. I hold a quarterly court for my tenants and local landowners here, and deal with the majority of petty crime." Robert stepped up onto the raised dais at one end of the paneled hall in front of an enormous fireplace. "We set the table here and allow anyone who wishes to express an opinion to offer it."

"How very medieval of you," Viscount Gravely said dryly, his gaze fixed on the stained-glass window to his right.

"It is a system of justice that works very well for the most part." Robert stared at the viscount's averted profile. "If a matter is too serious for me to make a judgment on, I send the accused to the quarterly assizes in the county town of Hertford." Robert paused deliberately. "That's what I should have done with Bert Speers instead of keeping him in the cellar of the Queen's Head while I completed my investigation."

"Bert is still being held at the local inn? Whatever for?" Gravely asked.

"Murdering your mistress. But you already knew that, seeing as Bert has been keeping you informed of his progress all along."

"What a ridiculous notion," Gravely replied. "If Bert is guilty of murder, that is on him."

"Is it, though?" Robert stepped down of the dais. "Then why would he run straight to you?"

"I thought you said he was currently incarcerated?"

"Unfortunately, he escaped a few days ago."

The viscount tutted. "How very irresponsible of you, Sir Robert. One expects better from our local magistrates."

"Then you deny seeing him?"

"Of course, I do." The viscount raised his eyebrows. "Are you suggesting that I would aid or harbor a *criminal*, Sir Robert?"

"Ah, so if he does turn up in London and comes to you at some point, you will immediately turn him over to the authorities?"

"If he is a murderer, of course, I will. But to be perfectly frank, you don't have the evidence to prove even that, or else you would've instantly charged him and sent him to the assizes."

"I'm fairly certain I know exactly where to lay the blame, my lord." Robert held the viscount's mocking gaze. "And if I ever have the opportunity to prove it, you will be hearing from me again."

"Strong words, sir, from a man who has nothing of real substance to say."

"I have the body of a young woman awaiting burial after being strangled," Robert snapped. "Would you care to see her? Or would that offend your sensibilities too deeply?"

For a moment, the viscount looked away, his expression suddenly blank. "Her death was . . . unfortunate."

"*Unfortunate?* A delay in getting to a ball is 'unfortunate.' The deliberate murder of a young woman is something else entirely."

"Then one can only hope that the murderer will soon be brought to justice." Viscount Gravely headed for the door. "I wish you all the best with your endeavors."

"I intend to pursue this matter until I am satisfied; don't you worry about that," Robert said loudly as the viscount opened the door. "I never give up on anything."

He let his guest leave and stayed where he was for a few moments to allow his temper to settle. The peace and antiquity of the venerable room spread over him. He slowly raised his head to study the image of justice depicted in the stained-glass window. One of the scales had been broken by a stray bullet during the Civil War and had been replaced by a clear piece of glass, but it hardly affected the overall sentiment of the piece.

Whatever Viscount Gravely said, Robert truly believed that at some point Flora Rosa's murderer would be held to account. With that belief firmly in mind, he exhaled and went to find his guests.

＊　＊　＊

Lucy paused yet again to see where Neville had gone. He was several paces behind her, staring out of the windows looking over the front of the house. Her father had decided to go up to the nursery to surprise Ned, and Lucy had been more than happy to see him go.

"I do apologize, Lady Kurland," Neville said. "I was just looking to see if Trevor had arrived yet."

"I believe you said he had gone out riding and would join us when he was ready." Lucy offered.

"That's right, but as he doesn't know the area, I'm beginning to wonder if he's gotten lost and if I should go and look for him." Neville walked slowly toward her.

"It is very hard to get lost here, Mr. Gravely, as the fields are so flat, and the steeple of St. Mary's church is easy to navigate back toward. I'm sure your brother will join us soon. Would you like to come down to the drawing room and have some refreshments while we wait for your father?"

Neville finally appeared to remember his manners and meekly followed her back toward the landing, where they could descend the shallow oak stairway into the main entrance hall.

A scream penetrated from one of the upper stories, and Lucy stiffened at the sound of pounding feet on the servants' staircase to her right. The door burst open, and Polly, still wearing her nightgown, ran toward Lucy, swiftly followed by James.

James reached Polly before Lucy, gently locked his arms around her waist, and lifted her off her feet.

"It's all right, my lady. I've got her. Dr. Fletcher is coming to see her very soon."

"Thank you, James," Lucy said.

Lucy held the door open for James to carry the now-struggling Polly back up to her room.

She turned to her companion "I do apologize, Mr. Gravely, I—" She stopped speaking as she registered the look of horror on his face. "What is it?"

He gulped once and then stared at Lucy. "What in God's name is *she* doing here?"

Lucy braced herself. "I'm not sure what you are referring to, sir."

"That woman!" Neville pointed a shaking finger at the door. "This is a *disaster*! She's not supposed to be—"

Lucy stepped right in front of Neville as he lurched toward the door, praying that his good manners would not allow him to knock her down.

"I don't know who you think you saw, Mr. Gravely, but you are quite mistaken. That woman is one of my nursery maids. She has been suffering from a fever for the last week and is still delirious."

"I—must have been wrong." Neville looked away from her. "I beg your pardon, my lady."

Lucy touched his arm. "Will you come down and have some tea? I'm sure your father won't be much longer."

She was more shaken by the incident than she was prepared to acknowledge. What appalling luck for a member of the Gravely family to see Polly Carter, of all people. She would have to tell Robert what had happened as soon as possible.

Just after her father joined them in the drawing room and Anna had been introduced to Neville, Robert appeared with Viscount Gravely at his side. Neither of them looked as if they had come to blows, but the icy disdain between them was blatantly obvious.

On the pretense of making Robert hand out cups of tea, Lucy managed to get him close enough to whisper in his ear.

"Polly escaped her room and Neville saw her."

"*What?*" Robert almost dropped the cup.

"James caught her and took her back to bed. Dr. Fletcher has been sent for."

"Why did she choose to escape now?" Robert muttered.

"Just a ghastly coincidence." Lucy paused. "Unless she somehow knew Viscount Gravely was here and panicked."

"And ran straight down the stairs into his son's arms?" Robert had delivered the tea and returned to her. "I thought she was unconscious."

"And I told you I suspected she was pretending," Lucy reminded him.

"Maybe she thought Neville Gravely might save her from *us*?" Robert retorted.

"I hadn't thought of that." Lucy handed him another cup of tea. "I can only hope that Neville believed my explanation that the woman was my nursery maid."

"I somehow doubt that." Robert nudged her. "Look at his face. He can barely manage to maintain a polite conversation. He knows whom he saw, and he is dying to tell his father."

"Good morning, Lady Kurland, Sir Robert." Robert looked up to see Trevor Gravely entering the drawing room. "I do apologize for my late arrival."

Robert went over to speak to Trevor, leaving Lucy dispensing tea.

"Good morning. I'm afraid that you missed the tour, but you are more than welcome to come back another day, if you so desire." Robert lowered his voice. "Did you have the opportunity to see the body?"

"Indeed, I did." Trevor bowed. "And I can confirm that it is Flora Rosa. May she rest in peace."

Robert slowly exhaled. "Thank you for that. Now at least I can bury her with her proper name on her headstone."

"I doubt that's her real name, but I understand your relief, Sir Robert." Trevor's attention swung to his brother. "What's wrong with Neville? He looks as though he's seen a ghost."

"Perhaps he did," Robert ventured. "This is a very old house, after all." He took Trevor across the room to speak to Lucy and receive a cup of tea, and went over to where Neville was staring into space.

"Did you enjoy your tour, sir?" Robert asked.

"Indeed, it was . . . fascinating." Neville's smile wasn't convincing at all.

"I understand that you met our new nursery maid, who has been quite unwell with a fever." Robert met Neville's gaze. "I'm sure that you and your father would hate to become unwell yourselves, which is why I was just recommending to your brother that you keep your visit to Kurland St. Mary as short as possible."

Neville nodded. "I quite agree with you, Sir Robert. In truth, I cannot wait to get away from this place."

Robert escorted the Gravely family and his father-in-law back out into their gig and waited until they all departed down the drive toward the rectory. He had a strong suspicion they hadn't heard the last from Neville and wanted to speak to his wife immediately.

She was still in the drawing room when he returned, collecting cups and placing them on the tea tray, a thoughtful look on her face.

"Robert—"

He spoke over her. "We have to decide what to do about Polly. Where would be the best place to keep her safe?"

Lucy gave him an odd look. "Here, of course."

"But that idiot Neville is bound to blurt out what he saw to his father and brother!"

"I'm quite sure that he will," Lucy agreed. "Which is why this is the best place to protect Polly and catch anyone who chooses to come after her."

Robert studied his wife. "You mean we should set a trap and see if Viscount Gravely takes the bait?"

"Exactly." Lucy smiled approvingly at him. "You know this house better than anyone. We can make sure that

Polly is placed in a room where we can observe her very closely and prevent anyone from finding her."

"The priest's room," Robert said decisively. "With the false wall and the space behind it to hide someone to watch over Polly." He nodded. "That is an excellent notion. We can have someone guarding the exterior door as well."

"James already knows about this Polly Carter, and I am certain that after his recent failures, he would be delighted to guard her," Lucy said. "We can also get Isaiah and Isaac up from the stables if we need them."

"Have you been up to see Polly yet?" Robert asked,

"I haven't had time," Lucy said. "Do you want to come with me?" She set the last cup on the tray. "I am very interested in hearing what she has to say."

They walked through into the entrance hall just as Dr. Fletcher arrived, and after exchanging pleasantries, they ascended the stairs together. As they went up, Robert explained about the arrival of the real Polly Carter. Patrick expressed his surprise at her surviving what had happened in London and at her journey to Kurland St. Mary.

"Evans says that there is no reason for her not to have regained full consciousness," Patrick remarked. "But I have seen patients who have remained comatose for weeks and then woken up with no knowledge of what happened to them, so don't expect her to be able to tell you anything."

"That's not very helpful," Robert said. "And seeing as she tried to run away earlier, one might assume that she has regained her senses somewhat."

"It depends." Patrick paused by the door where James was sitting. "She might have lapsed into unconsciousness again."

Robert snorted as Patrick unlocked the door. Betty, Lucy's maid, was sitting by the bed beside Polly.

"She's asleep, Dr. Fletcher. Do you want me to wake her?"

"Asleep or unconscious?" Dr. Fletcher came to sit on the

side of the bed and took Polly's hand in his, his fingers on the inside of her wrist. "She doesn't seem very aware to me."

He leaned closer. "Polly? Can you hear me? This is Dr. Fletcher. You are quite safe here."

Polly didn't stir, and Robert watched somewhat impatiently as his friend continued to sit on the bed and observe his patient.

"I don't think she's pretending, Sir Robert," Patrick finally said. He stroked the thin tip of his pen over her skin, and she didn't react at all. "I don't know quite what is going on, but I suggest you leave her in peace."

"James said that when he was halfway up the stairs, she stopped fighting, swooned again, and didn't respond to him after that," Betty added.

"Knowing James, he probably hit her head against the stairwell," Robert grumbled rather unfairly.

"I suspect it's more that she is too afraid to face what is going on in the present," Patrick said slowly. "I've seen such cases before—usually after a person has suffered a traumatic event. They deliberately retreat into unconsciousness."

"Like almost being killed by Bert Speers?" Robert asked as he turned to the door. "Will it be acceptable to you if we move her into a different room?"

"That's perfectly fine, as long as you make sure it is secure, and that someone is watching over her at all times."

"Don't worry about that, my friend," Robert said grimly. "I'll make absolutely certain it is as safe as the Tower of London."

Robert left the room with Lucy, told James to report to him in his study after he'd been relieved by Michael, and set off down the stairs. Polly was the last remaining link to Flora Rosa's death, and Robert intended to make sure that she lived to speak her truth. He needed a plan to thwart any attempt by Neville or Viscount Gravely to contact Polly. His staff was capable and loyal to a fault. He had no doubt that if they obeyed his orders and the fates were kind to him, he might successfully catch a murderer. Who it would be, he wasn't yet quite certain.

"I'm going down to the rectory," Robert announced as he went into his wife's sitting room. He'd spoken to his staff, moved Polly to the priest's room, and made certain that she was well guarded

"For what purpose?" Lucy swiveled around in her chair to look at him.

"To have a few words with Neville Gravely. He and his brother seem keen to take their father home as soon as possible, and I intend to encourage them."

"I thought we had decided to let matters take their course and see if the viscount dared come after Polly himself." Lucy said with a frown.

"I'd rather not risk Polly's life. If we can keep her hidden, get the Gravely family to leave, and receive her evidence when she finally wakes up, I'm happy to wait."

"But what if she has no recollection of anything before she was injured? Dr. Fletcher said that is often the case." Lucy objected.

Robert scowled. "You are being rather difficult this morning, my dear."

"I'm merely wondering at your logic. There is nothing wrong with that. And I cannot agree that Neville is innocent in this affair. His whole demeanor seems guilty to me."

"I suspect he is simply embarrassed by his father."

"You forget that several people, including his own brother, have told us Flora was planning to return to Neville." Lucy paused. "Or what if that is what she told him and she changed her mind again? He would have reason to be angry enough to murder her himself."

"He doesn't have the gumption," Robert said dismissively.

"Yet he has the look of a guilt-ridden, desperate man. Maybe his horror at seeing Polly was more on his own behalf than on his father's."

Robert glared at her. "Why do you have to bring all this up when we have already agreed that Viscount Gravely and Bert Speers conspired to murder Flora?"

"Because that is what you usually do, my dear," Lucy said firmly. "You always temper my emotional instincts with your more rational thoughts. Why do you object to me doing the same to you?"

"Because—" Robert glared helplessly at her and then let out a frustrated breath. "I just want the Gravelys to leave Kurland St. Mary as quickly as possible."

"I understand your desire completely, but I'm still worried about Neville."

Robert hesitated. "Trevor did suggest that his brother was somewhat obsessed with Flora, and that he was more worried about him than his father."

"Then maybe we should be worried about him, too." Lucy suggested. "Perhaps Viscount Gravely came down here to keep an eye on *Neville* rather than the other way around."

"I told our staff to alert me to the presence of any of the Gravely family or Bert Speers in our house, so even it if is Neville, he will not get to Polly."

"Of course, you did." Lucy smiled at him approvingly, and Robert had the familiar sense that his sometimes too clever wife was masterfully managing him. "I would expect nothing less of you."

"I'll just speak to Trevor, then." Robert found himself capitulating.

"What an excellent idea." She paused. "Or you could leave well alone, and wait for one of the Gravelys to expose themselves as the murderer."

Robert cast her one last scathing look and headed for the hall, where his gig awaited him. He was willing to be pushed so far and no more.

As he proceeded down the drive, his ire faded, and he found himself smiling. It was unlike him to be the more passionate one about a murder suspect, but this case felt very personal because it came far too close to his beloved son. He'd never particularly wanted to be a father, but watching Ned grow up was proving remarkably interesting. After almost losing his life at Waterloo and facing the prospect of being an invalid for the rest of his days, his hopes of having a family had evaporated. And when Lucy had struggled to conceive, he'd realized that having her was far more important than a mythical heir.

But the moment Grace Turner had placed Ned in his arms he'd been totally smitten. The boy's unguarded affection and lack of fear made Robert proud to be his father and unexpectedly willing to involve himself in his son's life.

As Robert approached the rectory, he noticed a lone horseman departing from the Harrington stables. It wasn't the rector, who was usually accompanied by several of his dogs, and it definitely wasn't Viscount Gravely. The rider turned at the last moment, giving Robert a perfect view of his face.

"Where are you off to, Neville Gravely?" Robert murmured.

Knowing how easy it was to be seen in the flat, barren countryside, he took off his hat, buttoned his coat, wrapped his scarf over his lower face, and hunkered down in the driving seat in an attempt to look more like one of the local farmers. He also kept well away from Neville, his knowledge of the area standing him in good stead.

He knew immediately where Neville was heading when he took one of the rutted farm tracks to the left. Robert increased his speed, remained on the county road, and looped around to the back of the deserted farm buildings where the Mallard family had once lived. He left the gig secured on the side of the road, scrambled awkwardly through the ancient hedgerow, and continued on foot toward the back of the barn.

It was so quiet that he easily heard Neville call out to someone inside the barn. Staying well concealed behind a bramble bush, Robert saw a familiar man emerge from the barn.

"Bert Speers," Robert murmured to himself. "Now what the devil is Neville doing with him?"

Chapter 20

Hard as it was to swallow, it was possible that his wife might have been right about Neville Gravely all along . . .

Robert retreated back to the road and got into the gig. There was no point in attempting to apprehend Bert because he would simply flee again, and Robert didn't have the ability to chase him over the fields. He reckoned his best chance to find out exactly what was going on was to go back to the rectory and wait for Neville to return.

He drove back as fast as he could, left the gig in the stables, and went through into the main house, where he discovered his father-in-law in his study, writing at his desk. The rector set down his pen and looked at Robert over the top of his spectacles.

"Good morning, Robert. What a pleasant surprise! Did you bring young Ned with you?"

"I did not." Robert closed the door behind him. "Is Viscount Gravely here?"

"I don't believe he's come downstairs, yet. Do you wish to speak to him?"

"I do," Robert said. "And his sons."

"Trevor is in the garden with Rose, enjoying a stroll, and Neville has gone out for a ride." The rector paused. "Is something the matter?"

"Nothing that need concern you, sir." Robert bowed. "But there is a matter I need to clear up with them before they leave."

"You don't seem very enamored of my guests, sir."

"In truth, I wish them gone from our village, and I hope never to meet any of them again."

"Strong words." The rector eyed him curiously. "I pray you don't intend to come to blows in my house over this 'matter' of yours."

"Not if I can help it." Robert bowed again. "I just wanted you to be aware that I was here, and not to worry if you hear shouting."

"I assume you don't wish me to mediate between the parties?"

"No, thank you. What I have to say should remain confidential. I appreciate your offer, though."

Robert went out again and stopped the parlor maid who was walking through to the kitchen.

"Fiona, can you go upstairs and ascertain if Viscount Gravely is dressed?"

"I'll go and ask his valet if you like, sir."

"Don't ask. Just look for me, will you?"

"Yes, sir."

Fiona went up the stairs and came down again quickly. "He is dressed, sir, and sitting by the fire eating his breakfast."

"Thank you." Robert smiled at the girl. "If either of the Mr. Gravelys comes in, will you ask them to meet me in the drawing room?"

"Yes, sir."

Robert went up the stairs and straight into Viscount Gravely's room. There was no sign of the valet, which meant there was no one to prevent Robert from marching up to his prey.

"Good Lord, not you again. Can't a man eat his breakfast in peace?" Viscount Gravely murmured.

Robert sat opposite him and waited until the viscount met his gaze.

"Even though I am unlikely to ever achieve a prosecution in this matter, I think I deserve to hear the truth from you."

"The truth about what?"

"Flora Rosa's murder." Robert sat forward. "If you didn't kill her yourself, did you order Bert Speers to do so?"

"Why would you think I would answer that question now?" The viscount's smile was all teeth. "What possible benefit would that be to me?"

Robert shrugged. "Well, it might prevent me from arresting one of your sons."

"On what grounds?"

"Meeting with a known fugitive. If Neville has been helping a wanted criminal from avoiding arrest, he is complicit." Robert shrugged. "If I can't get Bert, a Gravely will do just as well."

"*Neville?*" The viscount's knife clattered down onto his plate.

"Yes, the man who first met Flora Rosa, and who was supposedly willing to take her back, even though she had been bought by his father."

"Who told you that piece of nonsense?"

The viscount's indolence had disappeared, replaced with obvious annoyance.

"Did Neville bring Bert here to finish off the last remaining witness to his crimes?" Robert asked.

"I don't know what you are trying to suggest," the viscount said. "Didn't you tell me yourself that Flora is dead?"

"And what about Marjory?"

The viscount frowned. "I have no idea who you are talking about."

"Then help me understand this tangle! If you didn't kill Flora, did Neville? Or did you pay your loyal employee

Bert Speers to do the job for you?" Robert waited, but the viscount merely stared at him. "And what about Polly Carter?"

"The woman Flora Rosa impersonated?"

"Ah, you remember *her*?" Robert asked.

"Of course, I do. She and Flora were very good friends." The viscount nodded.

"Did you set Bert to watch the mail coach for her arrival here? If I hadn't been in the inn yard that morning, watching for Bert, I would never have known that she had arrived, or seen Bert try and abscond with her."

Viscount Gravely slowly put a hand to his throat as if he was choking. "Polly Carter is *here*?"

Robert stared at him in consternation. "Of course, she is! Why else are *you* here?"

"I should have known . . ." Viscount Gravely grabbed for the bell and rang it vigorously until his valet appeared. His color was worsening by the second. "Send my sons up to me immediately."

Robert rose to his feet. "Please don't pretend that Neville didn't tell you he saw Polly Carter at our house yesterday."

"Oh, dear God . . ." The viscount raised his face to the heavens and started to gasp for breath. "This is a nightmare. Where are my *sons*?"

The door opened, and Trevor came in.

"What the devil is going on?" He rushed to his father's side. "Father, *please*."

"Where is *Neville*?" The viscount wheezed. "I told him not to leave your side!"

Trevor turned to Robert. "Have you seen him? He said he was going for a ride."

"I saw him briefly. I am surprised he has not returned yet," Robert replied, his worried gaze on the viscount, who was growing more agitated and breathless by the second. "Your father does not look well. I will ask the rector to send for my physician immediately."

He turned to the door.

"Wait!" the viscount wheezed, his hand outstretched toward Robert. "Don't let him get to her, *please.*"

"I'll do my best," Robert said and went down the stairs, stopping only briefly to report to his father-in-law and ask for his assistance.

He had to assume that the lack of Neville's appearance meant that he was already headed up to Kurland Hall. He needed to return home with all speed.

"Sir Robert!" He turned as he reached the stables and saw Trevor running after him. "Let me come with you. If anyone knows how to stop Neville, it is me."

"Come, then, but if your brother is attempting to hurt anyone in my house, be aware that he will first answer to me," Robert said grimly.

Lucy was in the nursery, rearranging her cupboards, when something crashed to the ground in the room next door, followed by a female scream.

"Where is she?"

Lucy stifled a gasp, crept toward the half-open door, and peered through the gap.

Bert Speers stood in the center of her nursery, brandishing a wicked-looking knife at Agnes.

"What on earth are you playing at, Bert?" Agnes demanded. "If Sir Robert catches you here—"

"Where's your cousin?"

"I don't know what you are talking about." Agnes raised her chin. "And keep your voice down, or you'll wake the young master from his nap."

"Where is Polly? I know she's here. Just take me to her, and I won't hurt a hair on your head."

"I don't—" Agnes gasped as Bert grabbed hold of her arm. "Let go of me!"

"Take me to Polly—or else, you stupid cow!"

"I'll take you to her room, Bert, but it won't do you no good. She's guarded night and day."

"Let me worry about that."

Lucy let out a very shaky breath as Bert forced Agnes to walk in front of him and out the door. She ran and checked that Ned was indeed still sleeping and slipped down the back stairs as fast as she could.

"Foley! Bert Speers is here, and he has Agnes." Lucy gasped, her hand pressed to her bosom as she entered the kitchen. "Where is Sir Robert?"

"He hasn't returned from the rectory yet, my lady. Mr. Neville Gravely just presented himself at the front door, and per Sir Robert's orders, I turned him away."

That might explain how Bert had managed to get into the house undetected while Foley was occupied. It also led to Lucy wondering whether Neville and Bert were working together.

"Did he leave?"

"I'm not sure, my lady." Foley paused and, for the first time, looked every one of his years. "What do you wish me to attend to first? Ensuring Agnes's safety, or finding out what has happened to Mr. Neville?"

"Is Isaac here?"

"He's guarding the priest's room, my lady."

"Then where is his brother Isaiah?" Lucy asked.

"Inside the hidden room."

"And James?"

"I'm right here, my lady." James had just come into the kitchen. "What may I assist you with?"

"Bert Speers has Agnes and is demanding to see Polly."

"The blaggard!" James slapped his fist against his thigh. "In broad daylight, too!" He turned toward the door. "I'll make sure he understands he is not welcome here."

Lucy grabbed his sleeve. "Don't fight him if he still has Agnes in his clutches. Just hold him at bay until Sir Robert comes back."

James didn't look particularly happy at her request, but he nodded. "As you wish, my lady."

Michael appeared from the garden, carrying a basket of herbs and followed by Anna.

"What on earth is going on?" she asked and came to Lucy's side. "You look as if you are about to swoon!"

Lucy had noticed that herself and had a firm grip on the edge of the table. "Anna, can you go up to the nursery and stay with Ned?"

"Yes, of course!" Her sister didn't ask any further questions and disappeared up the stairs.

"And Michael? Can you find Sir Robert and make sure he comes home immediately? I believe he went to the rectory in the gig. Tell him that Bert Speers is in the house and that he has a knife."

Lucy paused to breathe as spots appeared in front of her eyes. Cook patted her sleeve.

"You should sit down before you fall down, my lady."

"I . . . can't do that." Lucy forced herself to stay upright. "Bert Speers is in my house, and I cannot allow him to hurt another member of my staff!"

Despite Foley's best efforts to dissuade her, she left the kitchen and returned to the upper floor, straining her ears to hear Bert's rough voice or Agnes's tart replies. Did Agnes know that Polly had been moved to a different room? She had been occupied with Ned all day and hadn't been able to sit with Polly.

Acting on instinct, Lucy headed toward the room where Polly had previously been held. The door was now flung wide open, and within the room, Bert was getting angry.

"Where the bloody hell is she, Agnes?"

"I . . . don't know. She was here last night, I swear it," Agnes replied.

"I don't believe you."

Lucy winced at the sound of a slap, and Agnes screeched.

"You bloody bastard!"

Lucy gripped the handle of a cooking pot she'd taken from the kitchen and deliberated her next move. Should she go in and confront Bert, or wait until she gathered reinforcements?

Even as she took one uncertain step forward, a hand curved around her neck and gently pulled her back. Her weapon slid to the floor with a clang.

"I do apologize, Lady Kurland," Neville said in her ear as he pressed the blade of a knife against her skin. "But it is absolutely imperative that you take me to Polly Carter, or your life will be in danger."

Bert came out of the room with Agnes and stopped short at the sight of Lucy and her captor.

"About bloody time you showed up, Nev," Bert growled. "Take us to Polly, Lady Kurland. Now."

Robert abandoned the gig at the front of the hall and went in through the front door, Trevor at his heels. James was just coming down the stairs and rushed toward him.

"Sir Robert! Bert Speers is here, and he's got Agnes!"

"Damnation!" Robert said. "Is Mr. Neville Gravely here, too?"

"He tried to get in, but Foley wouldn't let him," James reported. "Did you see him on the drive?"

"I doubt he's left if he thinks Polly is here," Trevor entered the conversation. "How about I look around and see if I can find him while you deal with Speers, Sir Robert?"

"Please, go ahead." Robert nodded, and Trevor set off toward the kitchens. "Where is Lady Kurland?"

"I'm not sure, sir." James had already turned back toward the stairs. "Bert came into the nursery and took Agnes. Her ladyship came down to the kitchen to tell us. I'm just going up to see whether I can find Bert."

"I'll come with you," Robert said grimly as he checked that he had his pistol in his coat pocket. "Does Agnes know we moved Polly last night?"

"Probably not, sir. She might have taken Bert to the wrong room, which might buy us some time," James said. "Shall we go there first?"

Robert's gaze had already moved between the two corridors that radiated from the upper landing and alighted on what looked like a mob scene at one end.

"There's no need. I can see them heading toward Isaac." He went down the corridor, almost tripping over Agnes, who was sprawled on the floor. Motioning to James to slow down, he advanced toward the group of figures currently arguing outside the locked and guarded door to Polly's room.

"I don't want to hurt you, lad, but I need to get in there," Bert Speers said.

"I take my orders from Sir Robert, not you," Isaac replied. "And he told me to sit here and guard the door." He folded his arms across his massive chest. He was probably a foot taller and twice as wide as Bert.

"Would you like to give that order, Lady Kurland?"

As Neville joined the conversation, Robert went still as he realized his wife was locked close to Neville's chest and that there was a knife at her throat.

"I cannot," Lucy said, her voice clear and steady. "Isaac is correct. Only Sir Robert can open that door for you."

"Not even if I slit your throat?" Bert asked.

"You wouldn't do that, now, Bert!" Isaac blurted out. "Why hurt Lady Kurland? What's she ever done to you?"

"For God's sake, Bert. Don't make things even worse than they have to be," Neville pleaded with his conspirator. "I have no intention of—"

Robert stepped out into the center of the hall and aimed his pistol straight at Neville's head.

"Then you will kindly let go of my wife."

"Gawd, now his bloody lordship's here," Bert said. "And the cat really is among the pigeons." He held up a hand. "You don't understand nothing, Sir Robert. Let me take Polly, and we'll say no more about it."

"You, be quiet," Robert snapped at Bert and turned to Neville. "And you, unhand my wife, or I will shoot."

"And risk her getting hurt in the process?" Bert asked. "I don't think you want to do that now, do you?"

It was Neville who moved first and released Lucy before he sank down to his knees.

"I can't do this anymore. I'm sorry, Bert. I just *can't*—" He burst into noisy sobs, his head in his hands.

Bert's expression was resigned as he stared at Robert. "I should've known not to trust a toff."

Robert kept his gun on Bert and spoke to Lucy. "Are you unharmed, my dear?"

"Yes, I am." There was a wobble in her voice that someone would pay for later, but his pride in her resilience increased anew.

"Would you do me the kindness of attending to Agnes and taking her up to the nursery?"

"Yes, of course." Lucy went by him, taking a moment to squeeze his shoulder as she passed. "Do you wish me to send for Michael and any of the other male servants in the house to assist you?"

"Yes, send Michael."

Robert waited until he heard Agnes respond to Lucy, and until the two women walked away, before he addressed Bert and a still sobbing Neville.

"I am not going to make the mistake of letting you go again, Bert. You and your companion will face justice at the assizes for the murder of Flora Rosa and the attempted murder of Polly Carter. Surrender your weapons."

Bert sighed dramatically and glanced down at Neville. "It seems that I've been caught well and good, Sir Robert. Now will you hear what I have to say?"

Neville slowly looked up and staggered to his feet, swaying like the wind. "No, don't tell him, don't tell him *anything*! It will kill my father!"

"Your father is already dying," Robert said bluntly. "Perhaps he needs to understand the legacy he has left the world in his youngest son. Isaac, will you escort Mr.

Gravely down to my study, and James, will you accompany Bert? Mr. Harrington has already sent for the local constable. He should be awaiting us downstairs."

Bert took a hasty step forward. "What about Polly?"

"She is none of your concern anymore." Robert stared him down.

"You don't understand!" Bert shouted, and James stepped forward, grabbed hold of Bert, and slapped a hand over his mouth.

"I've got him, sir."

"Good," Robert said. "Then let's get them both down to my study."

Lucy walked Agnes slowly back toward the nursery and settled her in bed before returning to the main room, where Anna was playing with Ned on the rug in front of the fire. Lucy wanted to go to bed herself and forget about the terrible day, but as the mistress of the house, she had to make sure all her staff were content, and that her husband was no longer in any danger.

"Anna, I—"

She stopped talking as the tableau in front of her, which defied sense, slowly registered.

"Lady Kurland, how nice of you to join us," Trevor Gravely said heartily. Her sister lay motionless on the floor. Ned was currently being held tightly in front of Trevor, who had a gun to her son's head.

"Mama—" Ned tried to come to her, and Trevor yanked him back hard.

Lucy somehow found her voice and looked directly into her son's frightened eyes. "Stay still, my love. Don't give this man any excuse to hurt you."

Ned's lip quivered. "I don't like him. He hit Auntie Anna."

"That's because he is not a good man," Lucy replied. "But if we do as he wants, I suspect he won't hurt us and make matters worse."

"How well you understand me, Lady Kurland," Trevor said. "Now, take me to Polly Carter so I can end this ridiculous farrago once and for all."

"If you release my son, I will willingly take you to her," Lucy parried.

"No." Trevor stood up, taking Ned with him. "He comes with us."

"If you insist." Lucy briefly closed her eyes as nausea gripped her, and turned to the door, her limbs shaking so badly that she wasn't certain how she remained upright. She knew she should be asking Trevor to explain himself, but her terror for her son jammed her throat and threatened to overcome her.

Despite her hopes for rescue, the house was surprisingly quiet as she walked ahead of Trevor toward the priest's room where Polly lay. She needed to think of a plan to free Ned, but her mind was too sluggish. To add to her consternation, there was no one sitting outside Polly's room guarding it and no sign of Robert, Bert Speers, or Neville Gravely.

She stopped and looked back at Trevor. "I don't know where the key is."

"I doubt that." He met her gaze, his own eyes cold. "Find it, or I will hurt your son."

Ned whimpered and turned his face away, straining his body against his captor's hold.

"I am not lying. There is usually someone sitting outside this door who holds the key, and they are missing." Lucy paused. "I suspect they are with Sir Robert and your accomplices."

"My *accomplices*?" Trevor chuckled. "I suppose you are talking about my brother and Bert. I consider them more as my jailers, attempting to thwart all my schemes and make things so complicated that here we are, Lady Kurland, with you having to make a choice between sacrificing that baby in your belly and yourself for your son or letting me kill him."

"I—" Lucy glanced desperately at Ned, who had started to quietly cry. "I can go and find the key if you wish."

"Don't be stupid, Lady Kurland. The moment you walk away from me, you will alert the house to my purpose, and hope that *somehow* you will save your son, Polly, and yourself. Please be advised that will not happen. If you want to save your family, you will have to offer up the sacrifice of Polly. And why not do that? What does a stupid serving girl from London owe you?"

"No one deserves to die at your hand," Lucy said shakily.

"They do if they insist on interfering with what is mine," Trevor replied and tightened his grip on Ned. "This is an old house; there must be another way into this room through the servants' stairs. Find it."

Lucy took a deep, steadying breath and pointed to the end of the corridor. "We can access the servants' stairs there and enter the end room, which links through into this one."

"Well done, Lady Kurland." Trevor smiled down at Ned. "Your mother is quite remarkable, isn't she? Lead the way, ma'am."

Lucy walked slowly down the hallway until she reached the door. If Trevor wanted to kill Polly, he would have to let go of Ned. Perhaps in that instant she could shove her son to the side and attempt to stop Trevor in some way. If she died in the attempt, then so be it. At least Robert would have his son.

She opened the door, and it almost hit someone coming the other way. Even as she registered Foley's presence, he held his fingers to his lips, and she stared straight ahead as if he wasn't there.

As Trevor stepped into the small dark landing behind her, squashing Ned between them, she pointed to the left. "We can go through this door, and—"

Even as she spoke, Foley threw the chamber pot he held at Trevor's head, and the gun went off, the explosion loud in the enclosed space. As Trevor cursed and attempted to right himself, Lucy tore Ned from his grip and shoved Trevor hard until he lost his balance and fell down the stairs with a series of loud thumps.

"Mama!" Ned burst into tears as Lucy gathered him to her bosom and held him for dear life.

She was shaking so hard she could scarcely breathe as a growing commotion erupted behind the door, which was suddenly wrenched open.

"Where is he?" Bert demanded.

Lucy wordlessly pointed downward, and Bert clattered down the narrow stairs, cursing as he went. Robert appeared, his expression frantic as he drew Lucy and Ned out of the small space and into his arms.

"God . . . I thought I'd lost you . . . ," he muttered into her hair. "Thank *God*."

"Thank Foley," Lucy managed to reply. "Is he all right?"

"He's . . ." Robert met her gaze. "He's been shot. Dr. Fletcher is on his way."

"He saved us," Lucy whispered. "He hit Trevor with a chamber pot, which threw him off balance and allowed me to get Ned and push Trevor down the stairs."

"You were your usual remarkable and resourceful self," Robert said, his voice still shaking. "And thank the good Lord for that."

Eventually, Robert drew Lucy and Ned to their feet. "I think we should put Ned to bed, make sure that Anna is recovering, and reconvene to the drawing room to hear what Bert and Neville have to say for themselves, don't you?"

Chapter 21

"Trevor's not right," Neville blurted out. "He's never been right. We had to leave India because he was caught torturing animals, and then we went through three different schools because he was so wild."

Robert was sitting beside his wife on the couch in the drawing room. He had his arm around her shoulders and didn't give a damn about what anyone thought of such a public display of affection. His butler had been shot, his wife and son terrorized, and he wanted answers.

Bert, who was standing in front of the fireplace, nodded. "I first met Trev when he tried to kill one of the stable dogs. I beat him up, and he never tried anything again. He was afraid of me." Bert shifted his feet. "That's why when she was alive, the viscountess asked me to keep an eye on him when he was home from school."

"Of course, you worked at the Gravely stables after you left the orphanage," Robert said. "You knew the viscount's sons better than he did."

"Yes, sir. I left for a while to try and become a boxer, but it was a dangerous life. I came back and asked the viscount for a job when I heard he'd returned home for good." Bert paused. "Why isn't he here, by the way? I told you that if you'd just let me talk to him, we could sort this muddle out."

"I offered Viscount Gravely the opportunity to tell me the truth several times, and he declined," Robert replied. "I suspect he was quite happy to allow you to take the blame for any murders committed by his son."

"Of course, he was, the cold-blooded bastard," Bert muttered. "But why isn't he here attempting to clear his son's name?"

Robert grimaced. "He's currently under the care of my physician and had to remain at the rectory."

"What's wrong with him?" Neville asked tremulously.

Robert grimaced. "When I spoke to your father this morning, I didn't have the full facts in my possession. He grew very agitated when he realized that you were my suspect."

"He would," Bert said.

"As I left, he was gasping for air. I've since had a note from Dr. Fletcher to say that he thinks the viscount had some kind of a seizure." Robert paused. "But Trevor spent a few minutes alone with his father before he came after me. It's also possible that he tried to silence your father permanently before his valet came back and prevented him from completing his purpose."

Neville collapsed onto a chair, one hand over his mouth. "Dear God."

"Your father is hardly blameless in all this, sir." Robert glared at Neville. "Perhaps you would care to start at the beginning and explain exactly how Flora Rosa ended up being murdered?"

Neville looked apprehensively over at Bert, who nodded. "Might as well spill everything, Nev, and make sure that your brother is held accountable."

Neville bowed and got to his feet.

"Trevor met Flora first, and he became obsessed with her." He swallowed hard. "I'd seen this play out before, and the women usually ended up being . . . hurt, and I would have to pay them off. But Flora wasn't interested in Trevor and kept him at bay until I became worried that he would lash out at her. I told Father what was happening and asked him if he could help because Flora wasn't some prostitute who would easily be forgotten, but a rising star of the theater with many men vying to be her protector. She'd become afraid of Trevor, and she willingly agreed to accept my father's offer of a house and his protection as long as she could continue her career in the theater."

Neville sat back in his seat and surveyed the room. "We thought that Trevor would back down, that Father asserting his power would make him find another, easier target, but he wouldn't stop pursuing her. I ended up spending a lot of time at her house because she was so afraid Trevor would appear, and he ended up getting jealous of me *and* my father."

Bert started speaking again. "One night, Mr. Trevor followed Flo home and tried to choke her. She was absolutely terrified, and after Viscount Gravely declined to believe her, she knew she would have to get out of the relationship."

"Which is when I assume her friend Polly Carter suggested that Flora take her place as our new nursery maid?" Robert asked.

"Yes, sir," Bert nodded. "As soon as she could, Flo escaped from the house and went to my place, where Polly was waiting for her."

"Your place?" Lucy suddenly sat upright. "*You* own the house in Paradise Row in Bethnal Green?"

"I don't own it, my lady. I rent it from the Gravely estate," Bert replied. "It kept Flo safe for a day or so while Polly sold off some of her stuff to bribe Agnes and to pay Flo's fare down to Kurland St. Mary."

"And you accompanied her," Robert said slowly.

"Yes, sir." Bert looked down at his boots. "Someone

had to keep an eye on her. I pretended to be in love with her so that no one would question me always hanging around and asking impudent questions."

"You were certainly very adept at that," Robert commented dryly. "How did Trevor discover Flora was here?"

Neville raised a hand. "I fear that was my fault. I decided to visit Bert's house to see if Flora was safe, and Trevor must have followed me. Flora had already left for Kurland St. Mary, but Trevor must have gotten the key to the house from our land agent and found out something that led him to your village. He boasted that he knew where Flora was and that he would soon find her, whatever I did."

"I wonder if Polly still had Agnes's letter with our address on it?" Lucy looked up at Robert. "Trevor could have found that."

"Seeing as Polly wrote that note to Flora, telling her that she had been unmasked, one has to suspect she did," Robert said. "So, at some point, your brother Trevor gets away from you, comes down to Kurland St. Mary, and waits for the opportunity to murder Flora."

"Yes, Sir Robert." Neville nodded.

Robert looked over at Bert. "And what were you doing when Mr. Trevor Gravely abducted and killed her? Weren't you supposed to be protecting her?"

A tremor passed over Bert's face. "I met with her in the village on her day off. She showed me Polly's letter and said she thought she'd seen Trevor on the mail coach. I told her to go straight back to Kurland Hall and not leave the grounds until I gave her permission to do so."

He grimaced. "She never liked being told what to do, and we had a bit of a fight. She was thinking about running away again, and I took her purse off her so she couldn't go anywhere." He paused to look over at Robert. "That's why it was hidden in my boot, sir, but I couldn't tell you that because I knew what you'd think. I marched Flo back toward the hall, arguing all the way, and waited until she entered the grounds before I left to get back to work and see if I could find any trace of Trevor.

"He must have grabbed her just after I left." Bert slowly exhaled. "The bastard. I was halfway back to the inn when I heard someone yelling. Thinking it was Flo, I ran back toward the church." He nodded at the door, where James stood guard. "I saw your footman and land agent having a fight over who Flo liked more. I admit, I stopped to watch the mill, which meant I didn't get back to Flo in time. As soon as I couldn't find her, I knew what that evil bugger had done, and I went back to London to confront Viscount Gravely. I was even stupidly hoping that maybe Trev had just taken Flo with him and I could rescue her." He cleared his throat. "Instead, I lost the person I loved most in the world."

Silence fell as Bert's voice cracked, but Robert wasn't in the mood to be conciliatory or sympathetic quite yet.

"If you had just told me the truth, Bert, we could at least have discovered who killed Flora earlier and stopped Trevor from murdering Marjory as well."

"At first, I thought Flo might still be alive." Bert raised his head. "I was working for Viscount Gravely, sir, and I was honor bound to tell him what was going on. I couldn't betray him in case he could find Trevor and make him release Flo. I soon realized that the viscount was more interested in protecting his son than in bringing him to justice, and we parted ways." He shot Robert an angry glare. "Why do you think I came back to Kurland St. Mary the second time?"

"I don't know."

"To make sure Trev didn't come down here again without someone being here to tell him to leave you all in peace. But that didn't work out too well, did it?"

"Yes, why *did* you all end up in Kurland St. Mary again, Mr. Gravely?" Robert turned back to Neville.

"Because you invited Trevor to identify Flora's body. He was delighted by that notion," Neville's mouth twisted. "At that point, Bert and I didn't know where Polly had gotten to, and we were scared to let Trevor out of our sight. I reluctantly decided I had to tell Father what was going on. When he realized that he had a connection in Kurland St. Mary, he decided we would both accompany Trevor and make sure he behaved himself. We thought if he identified Flora, that might be the end of it."

"Did Trevor know that you suspected him of killing Flora?"

"He was far too arrogant for that," Neville said. "He thought it was all an amusing game and that he was in charge of it." He paused. "He'd watch me sometimes with such malicious glee in his eyes that I'd feel like my life was worth nothing to him. He wanted Flora, Father and I had tried to prevent him from having her, and he was going to do his damnedest to make all of us suffer."

"Which brings me to my last point," Robert said. "Why in God's name didn't you identify yourselves when you came up to the hall today and ask for my help rather than scaring my wife and knocking out my child's nurse?"

Neville cast an accusing glance at Bert, who shrugged.

"I can't say you've endeared yourself to me, Sir Robert, what with locking me up in a cellar for weeks and ignoring all the hints I gave you. l must confess I thought a bit of a scare might pay you back a little."

"A little?" It was Robert's turn to glare back. "You *deliberately* kept me in the dark so as not to anger your employer, and even if you didn't actually murder Flora or Marjory, you damn well didn't help them much, either."

"I *thought* that after proving to Viscount Gravely that his son was a murderer, he would deal with Trev once and for all, but he chose not to do that." Bert held Robert's gaze, his throat working. "I was wrong, sir, and I paid dearly for trusting the family that gave me a home after the orphanage. No justice for Flo or for me. All I wanted to do was help Nev stop Trevor getting to Polly, and then I was going to wash my hands of the lot of them."

"Were you in the same orphanage as Flora?" Lucy asked.

"Of course, I was. She's my bloody sister!" Bert looked affronted. "I held her in my arms five minutes after she was born. She was beautiful even then." Bert's voice cracked again. "Our mother died when Flo was five, and we were all taken into the orphanage in Bethnal Green. I kept an eye on her as much as I could, but it wasn't easy."

He met Lucy's gaze, tears glistening in his eyes. "She was beautiful and clever, and didn't deserve to die at the hands of Trevor bloody Gravely."

"That is something we can both agree on, Bert," Robert said. "Would you be willing to testify against Mr. Trevor Gravely at his trial for murder?"

Bert glanced over at Neville. "No offense, Nev, but I think it's time Trevor got what he deserves, don't you?"

"Yes," Neville whispered. "I've spent my whole life trying to stop him, and I still failed. I am exhausted. Poor Flora Rosa, poor Marjory."

Robert rose to his feet. "May I suggest that you both stay here at Kurland Hall until I have arranged for Trevor to be charged and placed in gaol."

It was less of a suggestion and more of an order. Both Bert and Neville looked too drained to argue with him. Robert wasn't certain if he could charge them for lying to him in his capacity as local magistrate. He wasn't about to mention that line of investigation before he carefully studied the law and consulted with his colleagues. The thought that they might get away with inflicting such damage on those in his household didn't sit well with him.

"Will I be able to see my father?" Neville asked unsteadily. "He'll want to know what is happening."

"Your father is in no state to receive you or such news," Robert said firmly. "In truth, it might even make him worse. I will send Dr. Fletcher to speak with you at his earliest convenience, and I suggest you follow his advice to the letter."

Neville subsided into his seat again. If Robert had his way, it would be a very long time before Viscount Gravely was informed about his oldest son's current position. Hopefully, that meant there would be little time for aristocratic meddling with the justice system.

"Is Trevor all right?" Neville asked, causing Robert to reluctantly admire his dogged determination.

"He suffered a few bruises and was knocked out when he fell down the stairs," Robert answered him. "Dr. Fletcher says there are no bones broken. Trevor is currently locked up in my cellar, with Isaac and Isaiah guarding him, and no one will be allowed to see him."

Neville shuddered and looked over at Bert. "I don't want to see him. He's a persuasive devil."

Bert held open the door. "Then come along, Nev. We'll muddle through this together, eh?"

Robert offered Lucy his arm. "Perhaps you might care to take a tour of our various patients. I swear this place feels more like a hospital than a home today."

"I would be delighted to accompany you," Lucy said and looked over at James. "Perhaps you could escort our guests up to their bedchambers and make sure that you and Michael are available to wait on them."

"Yes, my lady."

Bert might have snorted, but he quickly concealed it and obediently followed Neville out of the room, with Michael shadowing him, just in case he changed his mind and decided to make another run for it.

Lucy leaned heavily on Robert's arm as they went up the stairs. "What a tangled mess."

"Indeed. I suspect that we will never have answers to all our questions, but if I have anything to do with it, Trevor, at least, will stand trial."

"If Viscount Gravely allows it," Lucy said.

"From what Dr. Fletcher told me, the viscount was already ill and, after this seizure, might never regain his ability to speak."

Lucy nodded. "Then, perhaps there is some sort of justice in that he will never again be able to defend the indefensible."

They walked in silence toward Anna's bedroom and found Dr. Fletcher making his rounds. He had tended to the small cut on her head and expressed his hope that, apart from a lingering headache, she was on the mend. She was currently sleeping, with her maid watching over her. He also reported that Polly was awake and willing to talk to them, and that Agnes had bruised ribs and was sleeping well after a dose of laudanum.

"Thank you, Dr. Fletcher," Lucy said.

He smiled at her. "I think I'll stay here tonight, if that is all right with you, my lady. I have more patients to tend to here at the hall than in the entire village."

"You are most welcome to stay," Robert answered for both of them. "I hope you'll deduct your bed and victuals from the rather large bill I'm anticipating."

Dr. Fletcher winked at him. "As we are acquaintances of long standing, I will certainly bear that in mind when I do my calculations."

They went on down the corridor to see Foley, who had been settled in great state in one of the guest bedrooms.

The old man was propped up against his pillows with his arm in a sling. Lucy went over to the bed and bent to kiss his wrinkled and bruised cheek.

"Thank you, Foley. You saved our lives."

"It was my pleasure, my lady," Foley said stoutly. "I couldn't allow that blaggard to hurt you or our precious young master."

Robert reached over and carefully shook Foley's undamaged hand. "I suspect you are more than ready to retire now, aren't you? Just say the word, and I'll find you a nice peaceful place on the estate where you hopefully won't ever be shot at again."

"I'll wait until Christmas, Sir Robert, if that's all right with you, and until James has proved satisfactory," Foley replied. "I am a man of my word."

"As you wish," Robert smiled at his oldest retainer. "Now, we'll leave you to your rest, and we'll see if James is capable of managing this household without you."

Foley sniffed. "I doubt that, sir, but I'm sure he will do his best."

Lucy was still smiling as they proceeded down the corridor toward their bedchamber.

"What if it was our son?" Robert suddenly said.

"Who was like Trevor?" Lucy asked.

"Yes." His brow creased. "Would I not do everything in my power to save his life?"

Lucy looked up at him. "You, my dear, have a strong sense of justice running through your veins. I suspect that, even though it would break your heart, you would do the right thing."

"I suspect I would." Robert sighed. "I *hope* I would."

"What did Viscount Gravely protecting and indulging Trevor for all those years actually achieve?" Lucy asked. "Nothing except the unnecessary deaths of two women and the gradual blurring of Viscount Gravely's own morals into accepting and ignoring the inexcusable."

"You are right, as always, my love." Robert gently kissed her nose. "You should take yourself off to bed."

She hesitated. "I have to see Ned before I sleep. There is no one in the nursery except Betty this evening, and he is *quite* unsettled."

Robert gave her a wry look. "Then why don't you take him to sleep with us tonight? I'm sure he'd appreciate it."

His wife frowned at him. "You've always insisted that children and dogs have no place in your bed."

He wrapped his arms around her and drew her close. "Well, just this once, I will relax my rules. Tonight, I will truly appreciate having all my family together in one place."

"Amen," Lucy whispered.

"Unless Ned starts kicking me as much as the babe in your belly, at which point I will either eject Ned or leave myself."

Lucy pressed her forehead to Robert's waistcoat and finally allowed herself to smile. She was safe, her family was secure, and she would never, ever take that for granted again.